ROBERT BIERSTEDT

Head, Department of Sociology and Anthropology
New York University

ADVISORY EDITOR TO DODD, MEAD & COMPANY

Contemporary Sociology

AN INTRODUCTORY TEXTBOOK OF READINGS

Contemporary Sociology

AN INTRODUCTORY TEXTBOOK OF READINGS

/28 - Chpt. 1, 11

EDITED BY

Milton L. Barron

THE CITY COLLEGE OF NEW YORK

DODD, MEAD & COMPANY

New York Toronto 1966

Library of Congress Catalog Card Number: 64-21461

Third Printing

Printed in the United States of America

For George and Sophie

Preface

In the liberal arts and sciences, an introduction to a discipline is far more formidable for the interacting participants—the college instructor and his students—than is generally appreciated. The instructor, a part-time scholar or researcher whose own undergraduate initiation into the broad dimensions of his field has become only a vague although pleasant recollection, can afford to take very little for granted when he confronts a score or more novices in the classroom for the first time. In all likelihood, for example, he cannot even safely assume that his new disciples, admittedly of high intelligence, have any awareness of the essential nature of the subject they are about to explore. It is not unreasonable at this point to draw a parallel between most college students and hospital patients. Unlike the purchasers of other goods and services, both the student and the patient are inclined to submit meekly and somewhat reluctantly to the mysterious ingestions they are informed they need and must take, either to recover or to graduate—hopefully, in each instance, with a minimum of time, expenditure, and discomfort.

In the case of sociology, the instructor's commodity is a pig-in-a-poke of the highest order. Hardly any beginner enters a course in introductory sociology with a clear notion of what is about to happen. Some anticipate a more complex version of the "social studies" to which they were exposed in their primary and secondary school curriculum. Others look forward to a course of training in social amelioration or reform. Still others view it in terms of an analysis of the pathologies of our way of life: slums, delinquency, divorce, and discrimination, to mention only a few. Within a semester lasting usually no longer than fifteen weeks, the instructor's awesome task is to inform his students what sociology is all about, what it is uniquely equipped to do, and what it cannot do. In four months his goal is to motivate and instruct his students toward something they have never done before—to think sociologically, that is, to be scientific in observing the influence of social structures, interrelationships, and interaction on human thinking, feeling, and behavior.

Although in recent years audiovisual aids, field trips, and modest research exercises have become increasingly useful tools to re-enforce his classroom efforts, the textbook is still the principal pedagogical device available to the sociology instructor in achieving his goal. Relying heavily on this central reading, he seems constantly to weigh the merits of competing volumes, the established versus the new, and he not infrequently shifts allegiance to a more promising text. A year or two later, somewhat disillusioned perhaps, he may revert to a revised edition of his original choice.

Ideally, besides being well written, scholarly, and interesting, what should an introductory textbook in sociology be and do? I think it should be designed to fulfill at least six needs and purposes. First, it should delineate *the scope of the discipline*—its field of coverage as distinguished from those of the other social sciences, the underlying and unifying sociological approach toward a vast and complex array of phenomena, and the subdivisions of that approach. If this can be realized without being unduly encyclopedic and superficial, so much the better. Second, an introductory textbook needs to specify *the basic concepts* of sociology, the key verbal instruments in the discipline that describe, analyze, and generalize about human life in groups. Third, it should introduce the student to *methodology,* indicating how scientific method in general and sociological methods and research techniques in particular test and verify "educated guesses" about the nature and impact of social variables on human behavior. Fourth, it should reveal the processes of *theory* construction in sociology. That is, it should not only explore outstanding sociological attempts to build abstractions and generalizations about social relationships, but should also portray something of the different levels of theory-building, from hypothesis to all-inclusive theoretical system. Fifth, it needs to employ the kinds of *empirical data* that sociological research gathers as foundations for abstractions and generalizations about people in society. Last, an ideal introductory textbook should give some illustrations of the *application* of the sociological approach to an understanding and solution of social problems.

The book that follows these prefatory remarks represents an effort to satisfy these needs and purposes through selected readings. Invented many years ago, textbooks of reading in sociology as well as in other disciplines have become especially appropriate and useful ever since World War II. They supplement, and in many instances, even replace the standard texts. The typical and irrefutable justification for the more extensive use of books of readings in recent years is that the postwar influx of undergraduates has made intolerable demands on the resources of all except the most affluent college and university libraries for so-called "outside" reading assignments. A book of readings obviously can alleviate this burden on library facilities considerably. There are, moreover, other highly convincing rationalizations for a book of this kind. True, it can rarely boast of the integration and consistency afforded by the authorship of a standard textbook. But a well-edited book of readings in turn has many intrinsic advantages and can overcome the oft-repeated criticisms leveled at many standard textbooks by instructors and the better students who point to their oversimplification and unduly condensed coverage of important facts and ideas, and their desiccated, unimaginative, and pedestrian style of writing. By relying on carefully selected and edited material extracted intact from periodicals and monographs, a book of readings can be more authoritative, dramatic, and stimulating, and thereby pedagogically superior to its standard precursor. It can, in fact, serve as the central textbook in a course rather than as an aid or supplement. At the very least, it should serve as the second textbook, giving the student the best of two feasible kinds of academic reading experiences.

Three alternative uses are suggested for this book. Many instructors will find it suitable as the central text in their introductory course. Others will prefer the more conservative usage, employing it as a supplement to any one of the two-score and more standard textbooks currently enjoying widespread adoption. Finally, there will be instructors who will find its most efficient exploitation as the text in their advanced courses for upperclassmen on principles of sociology.

The nature and level of the sixty selections incorporated here call for some explanation. There are no excerpts from books or monographs. All readings are derived from journal, periodical, and magazine articles; and in each instance the major substance of the article or its entirety, never a minor fragment, was adopted. The rationale is that an article forms a coherent unit, as its author had intended, whereas it is more difficult to find the same coherence in a book excerpt, no matter how superior its quality. In selecting articles for their cogency, breadth (rather than narrow empirical coverage), readability, information, and interest, no effort was made to choose the easy and discard the difficult reading. Sociology, contrary to the myth prevalent in undergraduate subculture, is inherently no easier than the related social sciences. It is high time that sociologists who eliminate a demanding but articulate and valuable reading because it may be "asking too much" of their students realize that they foolishly risk trading away well-deserved respect for their discipline for the widespread disrepute from which sociology suffers among many undergraduates.

All sixty selections are from recent issues of sixteen different journals, periodicals and magazines; that is, they were written and published during the years following the closing months of World War II, a period which witnessed the greatest development of American sociology into its present form. Fewer than one-fourth of the selections were originally published in the late 1940's; approximately one-half first appeared in print in the decade of the 1950's; the rest were published during the first three years of the 1960's.

In limiting the reading selections to contemporary material, there was no intended inference that the classics, the contributions of the founding fathers and their disciples, are obsolete and therefore unworthy of the student's attention. The classics should be read in the original elsewhere, particularly if the student proceeds to advanced and elective course work. At that point he or she may come to understand and appreciate the influence of the pioneers on contemporary sociology.

I feel that I must indicate that no attempt has been made in this volume to cover or represent all branches and divisions of contemporary sociology. A quick glance at the table of contents will reveal, for example, that pieces on human ecology, collective behavior, and the sociology of education are absent, although the topics are given minor treatment under other headings. In our effort to present the approach of contemporary sociology to the undergraduate student, we have not found it necessary—or even desirable—to be encyclopedic in our coverage.

Aside from making the selections, my major role as editor has been to attempt to provide foci, emphases, and co-ordination throughout the book. Accordingly, each of the six major parts has a lengthy editorial note introducing and commenting on the issues and major points that follow. Interstitial discourses between selections seek to bring about the organization and connective tissue that would otherwise be lacking. At the conclusion of each part, a selected list of supplementary readings is given for those who wish to pursue the major topic beyond the limits of what the text offers. I am deeply grateful and acknowledge in the pages that follow my obligations to the sixteen sources and the fifty-five authors of the sixty articles on whose original labor I built. For whatever misuse I may have made of their efforts, I assume full and exclusive responsibility.

Professor Robert Bierstedt, advisory editor of Dodd, Mead & Company's sociology series, and Mrs. Genia Graves, William Oman, and Edward Webster, of the company's executive staff, were constant sources of encouragement and advice throughout this venture. As always, Mrs. Elizabeth Flannery, secretary of the Department of Sociology and Anthropology at The City College of New York, contributed unstintingly in performing several crucial tasks while I was out of the country on sabbatical leave. Lastly and typically, I took for granted but nevertheless fully appreciate the tolerance and forbearance displayed by my wife and son during my absences from family interaction so that I could complete the project.

M. L. B.

New York, N.Y.
July 1964

Acknowledgments

For their kind permission to reprint the copyrighted materials on which this volume depends, I extend my thanks to the following authors and periodicals. In those cases where my obligation is for more than one article, the figure in brackets indicates the number of contributions.

AUTHORS

Robert F. Bales
Reinhard Bendix
James M. Beshers
Robert Bierstedt [2]
Peter M. Blau
Zena S. Blau
Herbert Blumer
Donald H. Bouma
Ely Chinoy
Marshall B. Clinard
Allison Davis
Joseph S. Davis
Kingsley Davis [2]
David Easton
Milton M. Gordon
Alvin W. Gouldner
Robert J. Havighurst
J. O. Hertzler
George C. Homans
Morton M. Hunt
Herbert Hyman
Morton B. King, Jr.
Dudley Kirk
Russell Kirk
Mirra Komarovsky
Paul F. Lazarsfeld
Alfred McClung Lee [2]
Stanley Lieberson
Seymour M. Lipset [2]
Francis E. Merrill
Robert K. Merton [2]
Wilbert E. Moore [2]
Richard T. Morris
Talcott Parsons
Charles Perrow
Ralph Pieris
Robert Redfield
Arnold M. Rose
James A. Schellenberg
Leo F. Schnore
John Sirjamaki
Neil Smelser
Frederick F. Stephan
Samuel A. Stouffer
Edwin H. Sutherland
G. E. Swanson
Jackson Toby
Melvin M. Tumin [2]
Helmut R. Wagner
Charles K. Warriner
Leslie A. White
William Foote Whyte
Louis Wirth
Dennis H. Wrong [2]
J. Milton Yinger

PERIODICALS

American Anthropologist
American Sociological Review [34]
Behavioral Science
Commentary [2]
Social Problems [2]
The American Journal of Sociology [9]
The Annals of the American Academy of Political and Social Science
The British Journal of Criminology
The British Journal of Sociology
The Delphian Quarterly
The Milbank Memorial Fund Quarterly
The New York Times Magazine [2]
The New Yorker
The Public Opinion Quarterly
The W. E. Upjohn Institute for Employment Research
World Politics

Contents

PART ONE

Sociology and Its Contemporary Issues

INTRODUCTION

The founding fathers of their field of inquiry, according to some contemporary sociologists, were the Greek philosophers in ancient times who contemplated and speculated about the nature of society. Yet one may argue with considerable validity that before as well as after Plato people were and always have been, at the very least, amateur sociologists. For to ask and to answer questions about social life and its impact on human thoughts, feelings, and behavior are, in a very crucial sense, sociological endeavors.

Nevertheless, the real beginnings of professional and systematic sociology as we know it today came in the nineteenth century. At that time in France, England, Germany, and the United States, a handful of scholars sought to observe and collect what they considered to be representative social facts as well as to make armchair speculations about life in society, checking facts and speculations against each other. One of these pioneers, the Frenchman Auguste Comte, has since come to be known as the father of sociology, having coined the name for the new science. He also made a vigorous but far from successful effort to define its relationship to the older and established sciences.

A hundred years of fruitful growth have not completely destroyed all misconceptions about the scope of sociology and its proper place in the scientific world. Some false notions are perpetuated carelessly by professional sociologists themselves even today. For example, the president of the American Sociological Association at its fifty-seventh annual convention in 1962 was pressed by a journalist for a layman's definition of what sociology is all about. He was quoted as equating sociology with all social science. "Wherever you encounter a contact between man and his environment," he said, "you encounter an aspect of sociology." [1] Counterbalancing this erroneously broad definition is the equally erroneous narrow one. An illustration is to be found in Israel's secondary school system, where an established part of the curriculum is "sociology," defined as political thought, or the changing theories of *the state,* such as those found in Plato's *Republic* as contrasted with those discernible in More's *Utopia.*[2]

Sociology today is not a synonym for the social sciences as a whole; it is merely one of them. Nor should it be confused with any other specific social science, such as political science or economics. Sociology is the social science whose task is to acquire knowledge about patterns of social interaction and about the influence of social systems on the mental, emotional, and behavioral responses of human beings. It differs, then, from psychology in at least two respects: unlike psychology, which is concerned with the *individual* behavior patterns of *animals* as well as *humans,* the focus of sociology is exclusively on *human* and *group* behavior patterns. People, according to sociology, tend to behave the way they are socially expected to behave. To put it another way, any study of human beings, regardless of specific subject matter (it could be voting behavior, unemployment, or aging), operating on the premise that "society is something more than the sum of individuals who compose it, is sociological, and this frame of reference can be applied to any area whatever of human life." [3]

In sociology, a social unit is the "independent," or causal, variable; and human thinking, feeling, or behaving is the "dependent," or effect, variable. In actual practice, sociology has taken on other dimensions, too, each of which it may or may not share with such related social sciences as, notably, the other general behavioral sciences of anthropology and psychology. With few exceptions, for instance, sociologists traditionally have studied the nature and influence of social structures on *human behavior in the all-inclusive group, or society, in which the sociologists themselves are members and participants.* American sociologists, in other words, have typically concentrated their attention on American society, developing an American sociology; their counterparts in other societies have tended toward the same societal introspection. Psychology, in the same fashion, has developed with the use of observations and data about individual behavior collected in the psychologists' own societies. There is nothing compulsory about this kind of introspection on the part of sociology and psychology, just as it has not been a requisite of cultural anthropology—but nevertheless a strong tradition—to take the opposite perspective, to go outside the anthropologists' own societies, preferably to nonliterate societies, for anthropological studies and analyses of patterned behavior. There are advantages and disadvantages in each approach.

Nor is it mandatory, although it has become typical, for sociologists, psychologists, and cultural anthropologists (but not historians) to be more concerned about *contemporary life* than about the behavior of earlier generations. It is technically true, of course, that shortly after the sociologist observes, records, and

[1] *The New York Times,* September 2, 1962.
[2] Sraya Shapiro, "Sociology in the Schools," *The Jerusalem Post,* November 7, 1962.
[3] William Petersen (ed.), *American Social Patterns* (Garden City, N.Y.: Doubleday & Co., 1956), pp. 2, 3, 5.

analyzes his subject matter, it has receded into history. However, insofar as he has a choice of social phenomena, the sociologist without demeaning good historical data seems to have more confidence in and prefer, all other things being equal, that which is ongoing or recent over that which took place before his own lifetime.

Again like anthropology and psychology (but unlike history), sociology is a *generalizing* social science. It is not interested in specific and unique persons, dates, and events for their own sake. Rather, it uses these data wherever possible to abstract generalizations about people and their repetitive patterns of social organization and behavior. For example, the characteristics of group leadership and the class system as a basis of social stratification preoccupy sociologists, but the personal traits of the incumbent President of the United States and the idiosyncrasies of the Boston Brahmins do not.

On the other hand, sociology until quite recently has differed from anthropology and psychology in its *reluctance to analyze all blocs of social behavior* that fall into its realm. Confronted by the already firmly established, institutionally specialized social sciences—economics and political science—that were societally introspective and contemporary in focus and emphasis like sociology, the early sociologists timidly avoided most economic and political behavior, concentrating instead on the social institutions of marriage and the family and religion. The development of sociology and the growing realization that there has never been a genuine sociological division of labor with economics and political science—the latter only rarely examined the relationships between social forces and industrial and political behavior—led to the crumbling of sociological inhibitions and the establishment in the last generation of two new thriving disciplinary subdivisions: industrial and political sociology.

In one other respect sociology differs from anthropology and psychology: it is *a social science exclusively* in that its focus is never on anything other than human behavior. The other disciplines, on the other hand, each have one subdivision, animal psychology and physical anthropology, which give them partial affiliation with the biological sciences.

The fact that sociology, anthropology, and psychology have *a share and convergence in social psychology* only serves to lend emphasis to its strategic importance. Socialization, the process by which the human individual's personality is molded and sustained by the groups with which it is affiliated, is clearly a legitimate concern of all three disciplines. Psychological social psychology differs from sociological social psychology only in points of disciplinary departure. Anthropological social psychology examines the socialization process in societies outside the western cultural tradition, thereby contributing valuable cross-cultural perspectives to the western-oriented social psychology of sociology and psychology.

We add a final introductory word on the relationship of sociology and the other social sciences to social work and psychiatry. One category should not be confused with the other. Sociology, anthropology, and psychology are different but related scientific approaches to satisfy man's curiosity about himself and his behavior. Social work and psychiatry are not sciences but rather "helping" disciplines, applying the findings of the social sciences, among others, to the alleviation of man's personal and social problems.

In the article that follows, the reader receives an unusual insight into what sociology is about: a personal and professional portrait of an outstanding, contemporary American sociologist and, incidentally, author of two articles in this volume, Professor Robert K. Merton. Often referred to as "Mr. Sociology" because of his prestige, versatility, and intermediate position in the discipline's controversies, Professor Merton was selected for one of the "profiles" that appear as a regular feature in *The New Yorker* magazine. Here one can begin to learn to appreciate the curiosity that motivates a sociologist to find out "how it comes to be so" and the amazing range of sociological endeavor in American sociology today.

1. HOW DOES IT COME TO BE SO? *

MORTON M. HUNT

As a rule, one of the rewards of a profession is the deference that the public accords its label. Doormen beam upon anyone called Judge, clubwomen flutter about an author like pigeons about stale bread crusts, and practically everybody fawns on a physicist as though he were some kind of thaumaturge. Sociologists, who have a special idiom for expressing such things—and almost everything else—say that the way people react toward a profession reflects its "popular image," and, with something less than total detachment, they appear much concerned about the relative standing of their own image. Robert K. Merton, of Columbia University, one of the most eminent members of the profession, concluded a study of the matter a while back on a note of mingled chagrin and optimism. "The popular images of the social sciences are neither as well-defined nor as prestigeful as those of other relevant professional fields," he wrote. "When men regard their lowly status as unjustified, they come to consider the possible sources of this status. There is now a slowly emerging interest among social scientists in examining their place in society." Meanwhile, most other people don't know what sociologists do, and don't much care. Even those who think they know are often wrong. Intellectuals like Joseph Wood Krutch and V. S. Pritchett have spoken of sociology as though it were only a matter of sampling public opinion by means of polls; obituary columns frequently bestow the title "sociologist" on deceased settlement workers; and the nearest thing to the popular image of a sociologist right now is Vance Packard, who, according to one disgruntled insider, "is as much a sociologist as Scopes was a Darwin."

Actually, Merton, a tall, hollow-chested man of fifty, as thin-lipped, rimless-spectacled, and earnestly talkative as the Hollywood stereotype of a minister, but with a quizzically twisted smile as a giveaway, isn't personally much troubled by the public misconceptions, because his own principal "reference

* *The New Yorker,* January 28, 1961, pp. 39–63.

group"—a sociological label for the people by whose opinion one judges oneself—consists not of doormen, clubwomen, and the like but of his fellow-specialists. By and large, *their* image of him is just dandy. His admirers call him "a formidable role-model" for the younger men in his profession, and if this has a lumpy, pedantic sound, it is perhaps preferable to the plain-English clichés they sometimes apply to him, like "a sociologist's sociologist" and "Mr. Sociology." Merton's articles and books on such disparate subjects as bureaucratic structure, the interrelationship of religion and science, and the effects of radio propaganda have been scattered like dandelion seed throughout the field of sociology and have taken firm root in both the texts and the footnotes of many hundreds of technical writings by others, and in 1957 the American Sociological Society (now Association) acknowledged his status by electing him its president. Even a detractor of his has sourly conceded that Merton is "a prestige symbol," claimed by all factions of modern sociology.

Symbol or not, most of Merton's neighbors in Hastings-on-Hudson, where he lives in a large Tudor house behind a high fence, have little idea of what he does. Most of them are aware that he is a professor of sociology at Columbia, that he has a wife, three children, and fifteen cats, and that he turns on the lights in his upstairs study at four-thirty every morning. Socially, they know him to be an agreeably convivial fellow who, despite his somewhat austere appearance, steadily and tirelessly does away with Scotch, neat, and displays a surprising catholicity of interests and a talent for good conversation, impaired only slightly by the fact that he is alarmingly well informed about everything from baseball to Kant and is unhesitatingly ready to tell anybody about any or all of it. Most of his social acquaintances tend to think of him as some sort of humanist scholar. One neighbor, the sculptor Jacques Lipchitz, tried to pin him down for a visitor by saying, "Merton is interested in everything human. He collects so much information! But I have absolutely no idea what he does with it all, or what he makes out of it. I would say that he *analyzes* it somehow. He's a scientist, I think."

In a way, Lipchitz was not too far off. What Merton does in his study after four-thirty every morning is to evaluate, classify, and abbreviate into notes the masses of material derived from his own reading and from surveys, interviews, and tabulations made under his direction by a dozen graduate students. Picking out some item from the previous day's intake of intelligence, he studies it, pauses to puff on his pipe and stare meditatively at the ceiling, then turns to a battery of ten staggeringly cross-indexed filing cases containing the thousands of figures and millions of words he has compiled over the last twenty-five years and rummages through one of them for a document to compare with the paper before him. Having drawn some conclusion from the comparison, he jots a few notes on a pad, looks up a handful of obscure allusions, computes a quick mean deviation or chi-square analysis, and rattles off his findings on a typewriter, using paper of three different colors for extra-special cross-referencing. The subject matter at hand may be shallow and tedious (the availability of baby-sitters in a Connecticut town), complicated and interminable (the changing attitudes of medical students, year by year, toward clinical work as opposed to research), or abstruse and philosophical (the meaning of the concept of "non-membership" in a group), but in almost every case Merton is trying first to discover small—and then larger and larger—similarities in his raw material, and to develop hypotheses that will sum them up. Thus, his study of the baby-sitter situation led to a hypothesis concerning "social perception," or the way community intimacy breeds confidence and trust; his investigation of trends among medical students yielded the hypothesis that professional "role-acquisition" occurs gradually; and his definition of "non-membership" became part of a theory involving reference groups.

This search for categories and universals is only natural in the case of a science that is still pretty raw and immature, as sociology undeniably is today. Its major objective right now is to formulate a crop of sweeping new analyses of man and society, arrived at by observation and experience and crystallized into technical words and phrases. At their worst, these words and phrases are simply pretentious, and at their best they are indispensable inventions for dealing with fresh subjects, ideas, and techniques. Vague though most people are about sociology, quite a few alert laymen have become avid consumers of the crystalline form of the product. Sociologists have recently supplied the segment of the American public that it terms "image-makers" with such terms as —well, "image-makers"—and with such other terms as "status symbol," "ethnic minority," "organization man," "inner-directed man," "other-directed man," "social mobility," and "cultural lag." Merton himself has added a number of such words to the professional language, at least one of which has made the trip from Morningside Heights down to Madison Avenue and thence into the public ken. Back in 1943, while following up a lead provided by his Columbia colleague Dr. Paul Lazarsfeld, a Viennese mathematician and psychologist turned sociologist, he interviewed scores of people in a middle-sized New Jersey town in an effort to identify the major means by which ideas and opinions are disseminated through a community. As Lazarsfeld had suspected, the principal disseminators proved to be certain persuasive or well-regarded persons at every social level. Merton grew tired of referring to these as "people of strong interpersonal influence" and, in a published paper, labelled them simply "influentials." From there, the word diffused into the sociological writings of others, and presently it was spotted by a couple of advertising men at the *Saturday Evening Post,* who decided that it nicely described *Post* readers —or at least presented a useful popular image of them. When a series of *Post* teaser ads appeared in the *Times* in the spring of 1957 asking "Who is the Influential?," Merton stared at them with the mixed emotions of a man returning to his ancestral home and finding that the lawn he painstakingly landscaped in his youth has been turned into a public playground.

Merton and his associates, of course, are not engaged in playing a mere semantic parlor game with the public. Sociologists are the inheritors of an ancient and serious tradition. The Greek philosophers, the Fathers of the Church, and the various philosophers of the Renaissance and the Enlightenment all speculated upon the nature of society and tried to offer ethical prescriptions for its improvement. In the nineteenth century, however, a few of their successors, perceiving an analogy with other fields of knowledge, began to argue that the study of society should be considered a branch of science rather than of ethics. In 1837, Auguste Comte, the French mathematician and philosopher, invented the word "sociology" and, uninhibited by a lack of detailed supporting facts, manufactured a whole batch of sprawling, all-embracing theories to suit it—or himself. But sciences are not so easily brought into being, and no university in the world had a department of sociology until 1892, when one was set up at the University of Chicago. Harvard loftily ignored the new science until 1930, and as late as 1939 there were still fewer than a thousand practicing sociologists in this country. (No other country had anything like that number.) Since 1939, though, the profession has undergone a remarkable growth, and today the American Sociological Association has forty-five hundred regular and associated members, plus two thousand student fledglings. Few other professions can show a similar rate of expansion.

Why sociology has been growing so rapidly is a complicated question, but obviously the accelerated pace of change in the world and the runaway complexity of modern society have much to do with it. Sociology first showed signs of taking hold when, laying aside Comte's grand theorizing, it borrowed bits and scraps of technique from psychology, anthropology, and census studies, developed some bits and scraps of its own, and began to tackle specific social ailments, such as urban slums, divorce, and criminal gangs. More recently, however, these ailments—though still far from being completely understood, and equally far from being cured—have begun to seem less inviting to many sociologists than the comprehensive study of normal human phenomena, such as social stratification, the effects of communication, the transmission of authority, and the nature of group affiliation. And this has suddenly struck a responsive chord in certain quarters. A wizened tribal elder squatting by his fire, or even a bewigged courtier of the Restoration period, could feel reasonably sure that things would go on pretty much as they always had, and he was fairly well prepared by custom and upbringing to deal with the quirks of his fellow-man and with crises in his world. Leaders of society in our own volatile time have no such comfortable assurance, and consequently, though they may mistrust professors of sociology, they turn to them for explanations—or at least for illuminating background material. Nearly a third of the sociologists in America today are directly employed by business, government, hospitals, or welfare institutions, and an ever-increasing proportion of the research being done by the remaining two-thirds, working in academic institutions, is supported by grants from outside. Merton himself, although he has refused many offers to supervise sociological studies for business, industry, and government, has worked for the past seventeen years with his friend Lazarsfeld at building up the Bureau of Applied Social Research, at Columbia—an outfit in which the governing word is "Applied." The Bureau was created in 1937 by Lazarsfeld as the Office of Radio Research, and its object was to study the place of radio in American society. Since then, it has undergone a metamorphosis, partly through Merton's efforts, from a tiny, two-man operation into a semi-autonomous division of the university, with seventy employees and an annual budget of half a million dollars. Some of the research done by the Bureau is candidly commercial (e.g., "Comparative Effect of Advertising in Radio and in Print"), and some of it is not aimed primarily at practical accomplishment (e.g., "The Logical and Mathematical Foundations of Latent Structure Analysis"), but in either case its projects are valuable sources of research training for graduate students, are greatly expedited by the use of expensive machines, and are delightfully financed by foundations, industry, labor unions, and government.

Sociology has become involved in so many specialized forms of activity that one can scarcely speak of "a typical sociologist." At one extreme is the opinion-sampler, diligently keeping a fever chart of the whims of voter and consumer; at the other extreme is the Olympian systems-theorist, churning out opaque abstractions about values, stability, and change, and hoping to find the $E = mc^2$ of civilization. In between are the social psychologists, totting up the personal characteristics of lovers in the form of mathematical matrices; the business sociologists, hunting with Rorschach blot and multiple-answer test for weak spots in corporation structure; the demographers, charting the ebb and flow of the populations of cities and suburbs with the help of electronic computers; the methodologists, splitting hairs over each other's logic and experimental designs; and many others. But if there is no such thing as a typical sociologist, Merton is at least an all-round one, having done some work in almost the whole range of specialties. At times he has rung hundreds of doorbells, asked thousands of questions, and compiled the resulting facts and figures into reams of charts and tables; at other times he has lived with dusty, forgotten books, like an antiquarian, while trying to relate, say, seventeenth-century military inventions to the social climate of their period; at still other times he has dwelt on the heights, philosophizing about the general sociological theory known as "structural and functional analysis." Whenever he speaks about the aims and limits of his profession, what he has to say is apt to reflect his panoramic background. "At the summit of human thought," he told a seminar at Columbia a short while ago, "some sociologists are seeking a single unified theory—a generalized body of explanations as to what cements societies together, how institutions fit into a social framework, how discrepant values arise and work their changes upon a society, and so on. My friend and occasional colleague Talcott Parsons, of Harvard, is doing just that, and, I think, making useful progress. But for most of our energies to be channelled that way would be decidedly premature. Einstein could not have followed hard on the heels of Kepler, and perhaps we haven't even had our Kepler yet. Just as it would stifle sociology to spend all its time today on practical problems before developing theory sufficiently, so it would to spend all its time on abstract, all-encompassing theories. Our major task today is to develop *special* theories, applicable to limited ranges of data—theories, for example, of deviant behavior, or the flow of power from generation to generation, or the unseen ways in which personal influence is exercised."

Merton's clarity of speech is a welcome phenomenon in modern sociology, yet a few of his more esoteric-minded colleagues appear to feel that their professional utterances should not be so easily understandable. And when Merton indulges in metaphor and other literary devices—so rarely used in sociology as to be called Mertonisms by some of his associates—their uneasiness turns into dark distrust. They brand as heresy such sentences of his as "The purely abstract theorist runs the risk that, as with modern décor, the furniture of his mind will be sparse, bare, and uncomfortable." Worse yet, Merton has a penchant for sneaking an occasional little academic joke into a serious discussion, as when, in addressing the American Sociological Society a couple of years ago, he said with a characteristic self-deprecating smile, "Neither under the laws of logic nor under the laws of any other realm must one become permanently wed to a hypothesis simply because one has tentatively embraced it." Many of Merton's writings, furthermore, are liberally flavored with apposite references to literature and history. An introduction he wrote to an anthology called "Sociology Today" either quotes or alludes to John Aubrey, Charles Darwin, Herbert Spencer, Seneca, Descartes, Hegel, and John Stuart Mill, and another of his books, "Mass Persuasion," is sprinkled with choice morsels from Thomas Hobbes, Plato, Aristotle, de Tocqueville, Julian Huxley, and Kate Smith.

All this has merely confirmed the suspicion of some sociologists that Merton, despite his grave and scholarly demeanor, is not only indecently clear-spoken but inwardly frivolous. Not long ago, a candid young colleague reported this view to him, whereupon Merton peered at him owlishly through his glasses and observed mildly, "You know, of course, what St. Augustine said on the matter: 'A thing is not necessarily true because badly uttered, nor false because spoken magnificently.' " "Great!" said the young colleague, gazing at him in open admiration. On the other hand, an older sociologist has remarked, "There is less to what Merton says than appears on the surface. He casts a spell over the younger men, but I suspect that later on they're going to wonder just what their euphoria was all about." To a detached observer, it would seem that if introducing a semblance of literary grace into modern sociology is casting a spell, then it is a spell worth casting. Humanists have for some time derided sociologists for their tendency to cement abstract words together with a thick mortar of dependent and parenthetical clauses, producing a bulwark of impenetrable prose. Merton's Harvard friend, Talcott Parsons, is often cited as the worst offender of all. In a recent article, for instance, he suggests that one way to classify and differentiate among social systems

can perhaps most usefully be designated as the "instrumental-consummatory" axis. This means that the alternative of consummatory primacy may be divided, according to the external-internal reference, into the case where consummatory interests for the system as such in relation to the situation external to it (goal-attainment) constitute the primary reference, and the case where the consummatory interests of the units in their relations to each other (integration) constitute the primary reference. Instrumental primacy, on the other hand, may refer either to instrumental considerations for the system as a whole relative to the external situation, or to the instrumentally significant resources of the units in their internal functional references.

The layman may well suppose this to be hundred-proof double-talk, and even Merton, though he was once a student of Parsons and greatly admires his work, has admitted that sometimes he cannot easily make out what his former teacher is talking about.

Criticizing the obscuring qualities of most sociological prose, Jacques Barzun, the versatile Columbia historian, has written in his "The House of Intellect" that by repeatedly using a given made-up abstraction the sociologist is gradually "confirmed in the belief that the vague entity to which he gave a generic name does exist as a thing." To this, Merton has an answer of sorts. "There *is* a good deal of empty jargon in our writings," he admitted to a guest the other evening after dinner in Hastings. "But much of what is thought of as jargon is actually the emerging technical language of a developing science—a more precise and condensed means of communication than the vernacular. The test of any specimen is whether it says much in little or little in much." He unbent his lean frame from the sofa, pushed a couple of cats off a side table, and picked up a copy of T. S. Eliot's "Notes Towards the Definition of Culture." "Here," he said. "Listen to this: 'A man should have certain interests and sympathies in common with other men of the same local culture as against those of his own class elsewhere; and interests and sympathies in common with others of his class, irrespective of place. Numerous cross-divisions favor peace within a nation, by dispersing and confusing animosities.' All very well and clearly said, but a sociologist would only have had to write, 'Cross-cutting status-sets reduce the intensity of social conflict in a society,' and he'd have said it all—and more."

Another complaint about modern sociologists is that they labor long and mysteriously to prove the perfectly obvious. Merton concedes that in his day he himself has occasionally been guilty of the charge. In the summer of 1935, while working toward his Ph.D. at Harvard, he spent several tedious months tracking down recent high-school graduates and determining, by means of intricate statistics, the relationship between their school grades and their success in getting jobs. The world was hardly electrified to learn that the superior students got jobs more readily than the dull ones. Hundreds of similar papers are published in sociological journals each year, laboriously testing such self-evident hypotheses as "Engaged people 'date' a lot more today than they did fifty years ago." (Finding: They do.) To sociologists, however, no hypothesis is self-evident without proof, and this is the crux of their dilemma. Folk wisdom and popular knowledge are not necessarily accurate; indeed, for almost any proverb there is an equally cogent one that contradicts it. That being the case, sociologists consider it entirely reasonable to question and examine *any* popular assumption. "No matter what we find, we're in trouble with the Philistines," Merton says, in a faintly amused tone. "If we find that a widespread belief is true, we're called bores for confirming something that everyone already knows, and if we find that it is untrue, we're called heretics. If we test a hypothesis that is not generally believed and find that it *is* false, we're considered fools for wasting time and money on a silly undertaking, but if we find that it's *true,* we're called charlatans for claiming that something false is true." Last summer, addressing the World Congress of Sociology, in Stresa, Italy, Merton amplified his defense. "Perhaps the most pervasive polemic against sociology," he said, "stems from the charge by some sociologists that others are busily engaged in the study of trivia, while all about them the truly significant problems of human society go unexamined. This charge typically assumes that it is the particular objects under study that fix the importance or triviality of the investigation. To some of his contemporaries, Galileo and his successors were obviously engaged in a trivial pastime as they watched balls rolling down inclined planes, rather than attending to such really important topics as means of improving ship construction."

Happily, there are several ways for sociologists to escape their dilemma. One is to explain *how* and *when* a particular truth is true, thus giving it content and precision and raising it above the level of a mere platitude. Nothing could be more obvious, for instance, than the fact that a man makes friends only among the people he happens to meet, and that chance and geography therefore play an important part in human relationships. But Merton, by charting the patterns of friendship in a suburban housing project, has found that so seemingly trifling a factor as the direction in which the front door of a building faces is statistically significant. Tenants whose front doors open on the street are very likely to make friends across the street, while those whose doors open on the side of the buildings make their friends from among their next-door neighbors. His findings do nothing to flatter humanity, but, as he points out, flattery is not the function of the scientist.

Another solution to the sociologists' dilemma is to discern some unsuspected social mechanism in a parcel of familiar facts. At Harvard, Merton chose seventeenth-century science as the subject of his doctoral dissertation, and while he was preparing the paper he began collecting odds and ends of information about the squabbles that great scientists have engaged in over priority of discovery. Descartes charged Hobbes with plagiarism, for example, and Newton got into a fight with Leibnitz about which of them had invented the calculus. The reaction of the public to such wrangles is usually no more than "What a remarkable coincidence!" or "To think that great men should be so petty!," but Merton dug into the matter and for twenty-one years after receiving his degree kept adding intermittently to his file on the subject, waiting for some ray of illumination to explain why such highly intelligent men—all dedicated to the cause of knowledge and most of them shy, self-effacing scholars who were thrust unwilling into the controversy by their friends in the interests of fair play—should have been at one another's throats so bitterly. Four years ago, he came to a conclusion. "As we know from the sociological theory of institutions," he wrote, "the expression of disinterested moral indignation is a signpost announcing the violation of a social norm." In this instance, he went on, the social norm is a man's right to fame, which for a scientist is something more than the mere gratification of his vanity; the concrete rewards of discovery, unlike the marketable ones of technology, can be derived only from fame. Recognition that a scientist has done a thing first and made it known is therefore the major "property right" he can possess, and thus, Merton concluded, the matter of priority becomes a grave social issue, transcending personal vanities and hungers.

This kind of analysis—involving some unsuspected factor and offering an explanation that is at the very least plausible—is what most delights the sociologist's heart, and Merton's abiding concern for the unsuspected factor is often unwittingly reflected in his speech. "Ah, to be sure, but that is only the surface aspect," he frequently says, and "All this still does not ask or answer the *real* question. Now, if we restate the matter . . ." Dr. Kingsley Davis, professor of sociology and demography at the University of California, who has known Merton since they were at Harvard together, says of him, "It is his knack for seeing the ordinary world through extraordinary eyes that is characteristic of him and of good sociology. One tends to feel, after reading an analysis of his, 'I hadn't thought of it that way before, but that is really the way it works.' "

Merton's interest in social structure, it might be argued, stems from his childhood, which he spent almost at the bottom of his own social structure. He was born in 1910 in a South Philadelphia slum, where rows of dingy, decrepit houses sheltered first-generation immigrants from Italy, Ireland, and —Merton's parents among them—Eastern Europe. His father, a small, slight man with a ripe Slavic accent, alternated between carpentry and truck driving. Although Merton, the second of two children, spent his juvenile years in the kind of environment that is nowadays condemned as an incubator of neurosis and delinquency, his recollection of it is that it was nothing of the sort; he remembers it as a friendly, noisy, and continuously interesting place to live. Gang warfare was as much a feature of slum life then as it is now, and he became thoroughly adept at it. "I was a good and loyal gang member," Merton once told Lazarsfeld, who, having grown up in middle-class Vienna, finds Merton's childhood as curious as the folkways of the Kwakiutl, "but things weren't as dangerous as they are today. Our boundaries weren't so rigid, and our membership wasn't ethnically restricted. Of course, I took part in the fights of my gang, but they were always more ceremonial than deadly. Most of the time, we fought at a distance, throwing rocks and bottles." Meanwhile, like many other children born here to impoverished immigrant parents, he felt the stirrings of an almost obsessive hunger for learning; by the time he was eight, he had become a regular visitor to a neighborhood public library, where he read extensively, sampling literature of all kinds and taking particular pleasure in biography. Then, when he was twelve, he began to study magic with his next-door neighbor, a semi-pro conjurer. Merton's fingers were dexterous and his tongue was apt for the patter, and shortly he was earning from five to ten dollars a show at neighborhood social functions. In fact, he might have made magic his career if it had not been for a show that he put on before several hundred children at a Sunday school. As a finale, he performed the Houdini needle trick—seeming to swallow several needles plus a length of black thread, washing them all down with a glassful of water, and then pulling the thread out of his mouth with the needles neatly strung on it. A couple of days later, he began getting agitated messages from mothers, demanding that he return to the Sunday school, tell the children that it was all a trick, and make them quit trying to eat thread and needles. Merton decided to take up something less harrowing, and turned to philosophy. Winning a scholarship at Temple University, he matriculated there in February, 1927, and got top grades from the start. James Dunham, who doubled as dean and professor of philosophy at the university, considered him a lucky find in a field of study where the pickings were growing leaner and leaner, but Merton let him down when, in his sophomore year, he took an introductory course in sociology given by a young instructor named George E. Simpson, and in a matter of weeks underwent something akin to a conversion. "It wasn't so much the substance of what Simpson said that did it," Merton recalls. "It was more the joy of discovering that it was possible to examine human behavior objectively and without using loaded moral preconceptions." Simpson, who was single and lived on the campus, all but adopted Merton, making him not only his research assistant but his principal drinking and talking companion as well.

By 1931, when Merton graduated from Temple and, with the help of a fellowship, became a graduate student at Harvard, he had acquired not only an itch for sociology but a taste for classical music and an ability to fox-trot and to play a respectable game of tennis. In the little world of sociology at Harvard, whose inhabitants tended to be tweedy, baggy of pants, and as argumentative as Talmudic scholars, social and intellectual graces like these marked him as a comer. Lack of ready money didn't seem to cramp his style—after all, he had learned in his youth how to get along on very little—and as he went on to establish a brilliant academic record under men like Pitirim Sorokin, Talcott Parsons, George Sarton, and L. J. Henderson, he managed to survive handily on five hundred dollars a year, a feat he achieved in part by subsisting for long stretches on sandwiches and milkshakes and by making his own whiskey. His agreeable manner won admiration beyond the campus, too. "Bob had a way with him that was inordinately attractive to intellectual women," a former fellow-student says, with only a trace of faded envy. "I doubt that there was any bright girl who met him who didn't fall for him." One girl who was inordinately attractive to him, in turn, was a handsome, auburn-haired social worker named Suzanne Carhart, who had attended Temple with him, and in 1934, when Harvard made him an instructor, he married her.

For all his sociability at Harvard, Merton was, as he has been ever since, an extremely hard worker, keeping long hours and sleeping little. He devoted one of his graduate-school summers to visiting all the Hoovervilles and hobo jungles of Boston, interviewing their homeless tenants to find out who they were and had been and where they came from. He spent four or five months immured in the cellar of Harvard's Widener Library classifying tens of thousands of patents issued in the United States between 1860 and 1930 in order to chart the fluctuations in the rate of invention within each industry and to relate these fluctuations to changing social conditions. And for his doctoral dissertation he doggedly read 6,034 biographies in the fine type of the Dictionary of National Biography—just as a starter. At the urging of his professors, Merton submitted papers on these three studies, as well as on some of his other efforts, to a variety of learned journals, including the *Quarterly Journal of Economics,* the *American Journal of Sociology,* the *American Sociological Review,* the *Isis,* and the *Osiris,* and, phenomenally, none was ever rejected. Clearly, the young man was on his way.

To some extent, these papers were youthful tours de force, but Merton's next effort—in 1936, while still in his middle twenties—was a theory of such striking insight and utility that when word of it got around, it established him once and for all as a major figure in sociology. As a graduate student, he had read the writings of the French sociologist Émile Durkheim, one of the founding fathers of the new science, who, after compiling and studying statistics on the suicide rates in many countries, had expressed the belief that they differed according to the prevalent degree of something he called *anomie;* that is, a breakdown of social standards leading to a lack of cohesion and solidarity within a society. Merton assigned himself the task of discovering what produces *anomie,* and eventually concluded that it is most severe in societies where people do not have access to acceptable means for achieving their cultural goals; if, for instance, a society powerfully impelled its members to accumulate wealth (or to attain power or to become holy), and yet offered inadequate acceptable means of doing so, the resulting strain would make many people violate norms, and so create *anomie.* At this point, it seemed to Merton that perhaps he had hit upon a sociological explanation of all kinds of rule-breaking behavior, and he undertook to formulate it by creating theoretical combinations of human attitudes toward both goals and means, varying one factor at a time until he had what he felt was a complete set of five categories. In the first category (Conformity), he put persons who are satisfied with both the goals of their society and the accepted means for reaching them; in the second (Innovation), those who are sympathetic with the goals but find the means so confining that they turn to new ones (the avant-garde artist, the sharp trader, the scientific radical, the racketeer); in the third (Ritualism), those who lose sight of the goals but cling blindly to the means as an end in themselves (the organization automaton, the religious compulsive, the *petit fonctionnaire*); in the fourth (Retreatism), those who simply abandon both the goal and the means (the vagrant, the bohemian); and, finally, in the fifth (Rebellion), those who vigorously seek to introduce a new pattern of both goals and means (the true rebel, the remaker of society). Reducing his theory to a shorthand form of sociological notation, Merton produced the following chart:

A TYPOLOGY OF MODES OF INDIVIDUAL ADAPTATION

Modes of Adaptation	*Culture Goals*	*Institutionalized Means*
I. Conformity	+	+
II. Innovation	+	−
III. Ritualism	−	+
IV. Retreatism	−	−
V. Rebellion	±	±

Chilly and unprepossessing though the chart may look, it was truly a thing of beauty to Merton and many another sociologist, bringing into one readily comprehensible taxonomy such seemingly unrelated deviant personalities as Cubists and alcoholics, lone-wolf inventors and religious martyrs, executives and beggars, card-carrying Communists and members of the Society of the Cincinnati. Although everything Merton had learned about aberrant behavior from his gang days on seemed to fall into place, he still felt shy about publishing so sweeping a concept at his age, and he did not make it public for nearly two years. Then he outlined it in a brief essay, which appeared in the *American Sociological Review* in 1938. Sociologists everywhere reacted with what they call "resonance"—praising it, attacking it, expanding upon it, or incorporating it bodily into their own studies—and soon almost every new work on any aspect of deviant behavior either adhered to Merton or criticized his discovery and professed to offer an improvement on it. "To be frank," one of these critics has said, "I find his typology too neat and too pat to ring true. But there just isn't any other generalized theory of deviant behavior around. The job he's done is so polished and stimulating that until something better comes along we'll all have to use it."

With the publication of this paper, Merton was firmly established as one of the leading young theorists of his field. Two years later, he advanced in one leap from his instructorship at Harvard to a professorship at Tulane, where he became chairman of the department of sociology. His tenure there was short-lived, though, for in 1941 he accepted an invitation to join Columbia University as an assistant professor in one of the most active sociology departments in the country, where he would work in the company of such men as Robert Lynd, the explorer of Middletown, and the scholarly Robert MacIver. Not until some time after his arrival on Morningside Heights did Merton learn that he had been hired almost as much for his symbolic value as for his ability. The sharpest fight in modern sociology—a field in which there is even more sectarian bickering than there is in psychiatry—is between the mathematically oriented, opinion-sampling empiricists and the pontificating, concept-making theorists. The sociology department at Columbia was so badly split between these factions that for several years it had been impossible to hire a new man, simply because the two sides couldn't agree on one. At last, a compromise was arranged: each side would make one appointment. The empiricists chose Lazarsfeld, who had already created his Office of Radio Research, and the theorists chose Merton, at that time an excellent specimen of a concept-maker.

For a while, the two newcomers had little contact with each other. Then, in November of 1941, Lazarsfeld felt that, as the older man, he ought to do the graceful thing and acknowledge the existence of his opposite number. He invited the Mertons to dinner, but on the afternoon of the engagement he got an urgent call from the Office of Facts and Figures (the predecessor of the O.W.I.), requesting him to conduct an audience-reaction test that evening on a new radio program that had been devised as part of the agency's prewar morale-building effort. When the Mertons arrived, Lazarsfeld met them at the door of his apartment and said, as the guests recall it, "How nice, how nice that you are here at last! But don't take off your coat, my dear Merton. I have a sociological surprise for you. We will have to leave the ladies to dine alone together, and we will return as soon as we can." Then he bustled off with Merton to a radio studio where a score of people were listening to a recorded broadcast of "This Is War" and pushing "Like" or "Dislike" buttons wired to a computing machine. Merton found the whole thing a bore, and thought regretfully of the *gulasch* and *palatschinken* that he was missing. But after the program, when an assistant of Lazarsfeld questioned the audience as to the reasons for its recorded likes and dislikes, Merton perked up; he detected theoretical shortcomings in the way the questions were being put. He started passing scribbled notes to Lazarsfeld bearing such cabalistic phrases as "fluctuation of the polygraph curves" and "inadequate specification of the effective stimulus." Lazarsfeld beamed at his dinnerless guest and scribbled delighted rejoinders. As a second batch of listeners entered the studio, Lazarsfeld asked Merton if he would do the post-program questioning. Merton did, and his errant host said afterward, "Marvellous job! We must talk it all over. Let's phone the ladies and let them know we're still tied up." This they did, and then unchivalrously went down to the Russian Bear, where they ate caviar, drank champagne, and talked sociology until long after midnight.

In the two decades since, Merton and Lazarsfeld have been tireless collaborators at the Bureau of Applied Social Research, and devoted friends. (Characteristically, they have made a scientific issue of their relationship, in a joint study published under the title "Friendship as Social Process.") At intervals during their collaboration, Merton has co-authored two published books with his friend's wife, who in a recent volume (by other hands) was beguilingly indexed as "Kendall, Patricia L., see under Lazarsfeld, Paul, and Merton, Robert K." It is largely because of his collaboration with Lazarsfeld that Merton is now looked upon not as a typical theorist but as a many-sided sociologist who sees some good in each of the science's warring factions and is a champion of unity. Merton's view of himself, however, is not colored quite so brightly. Despite the external impression he creates of effortless brilliance, he alternates between quiet satisfaction with his own efforts and desperation at their shortcomings; his family and close friends can tell which phase he is in merely by the sound of his hello. As time has passed, he has become more and more a perfectionist in his work, fussing endlessly to find the right phrase, the accurate theoretical construct, the precisely appropriate bit of empirical evidence. In consequence, it now takes him nine or ten years to finish off an important project and release it to the printer—extraordinary behavior in a field where most men deluge the editors of scientific journals with almost weekly reports on every complicated little study, every half-completed big study, and any study, big or little, about to be started. Stacked on a shelf of Merton's study, in neat brown leather binders, are the typescripts of enough completed books and finished research to make a respectable bibliography—if he could only be persuaded to release them. Once, when an acquaintance gently taxed him with letting perfectionism unduly restrict his published output, he replied, with uncharacteristic tartness, "On the contrary, I've published too much. As for a lot of other men, I suspect they've published *much* too much." Perfectionism notwithstanding, in the last quarter of a century Merton has written, edited, or collaborated on ninety published articles and books. Since 1954, his major project has been his study of medical students—an attempt to determine how they gradually acquire the values, the attitudes, and the emotional equipment of physicians. The project is being supported by the Commonwealth Fund, and the spadework is being done at the Cornell Medical Center, Western Reserve, and the University of Pennsylvania by half a dozen younger associates of Merton's. Thus far, only one book and a dozen or so brief papers have emerged; the rest—thousands of pages of typescript and notes—is still aging in the bottle. Other Mertonian *crus* laid away to await maturity include a book on the sociology of science, a book on the practical uses of sociology, and a mass of essays, articles, and chapters of an untitled over-all review of structural and functional theory. His friends hope he will soon settle down to the magnum opus they feel he is capable of producing—an integrating work, which will weave the scattered strands of theory into a sturdy fabric. On good days, Merton thinks that some of his unpublished manuscripts are the beginnings of such a work; on bad days he is glumly certain that nothing of the sort can be written by anyone for at least fifty years.

One might say of Merton, using the terms of his trade, that he is a formidable role-model whose image in his peer-group is splendid, whose self-image is markedly ambivalent, and whose public image is nil. One might add that he is a deviant personality, because he writes too well for a sociologist and gets up too early for a bourgeois, and also because he lives by choice in a racially integrated neighborhood. Like most other sociologists, Merton maintains that his attitude toward minority groups derives less from his personal feelings than from the sociological evidence. In any case, when the Mertons arrived in New York from New Orleans nearly twenty years ago, they rented a house in Hastings and went looking for one to buy. The house they eventually chose as best suited to their needs, tastes, and pocketbook was in a section known as Pinecrest, which they knew was almost the only racially integrated, stable, middle-class community in Westchester. Merton, however, denies that this had anything to do with their decision. "Sue and I simply liked the house and the area," he says. "The fact that Negroes lived there was incidental—so did some people of French origin, and a couple of Mayflower descendants, and a lot of others. Your parlor liberal would say that they're all human beings, and all the same. That's well-meaning but absurd. Actually, they're all culturally and socially different, which I find interesting. But I must admit we didn't take even that asset into consideration when we moved there. We just liked the place." The Mertons have liked the place ever since, and when they needed more space some years ago, they simply moved two hundred yards down the road. Pinecrest is still racially integrated and stable, but liberalism alone has not been sufficient to keep it that way; a good many community meetings and arguments have been required to prevent the whites from succumbing to periodic waves of resentment or panic and upsetting the balance of about eight Negro families to forty white ones. In these efforts, Merton has played an active part, speaking to his neighbors on the subject in a reassuringly scientific fashion. As a result, he has done a lot of good for the local popular image of a sociologist. But he still has trouble with outsiders. At a large party a while ago, someone introduced him to a visiting United States congressman as a prominent sociologist, and the congressman said he wondered whether Merton would mind if he asked a perhaps impertinent question. Merton urged him to go right ahead. "Well, then," said the congressman, "considering the present state of the world, all this talk about status-sets, image-makers, social mobility, cultural lag, and so on, strikes me as, frankly, rather pointless. Why don't you sociologists get to work and contribute something useful?"

Merton looked thoughtful for a moment, and then, in a mild and reasonable tone, said, "When someone asks of scientific research 'What is it good for?,' he misses the whole point of the scientific attitude, which must ask, rather, 'How does it come to be so?' And the answer to that precedes the practical applications. It's not the sociologist's fault that society is in bad need of his help today, when his science is still immature. Suppose that three centuries ago Harvey had been told to limit himself to the problem of coronary thrombosis just when he was trying to establish the fact of the circulation of the blood? If sociology in its present state were to address itself only to practical problems, it would never become the science you yourself want it to be—a science whose benefits will be as wonderful as they are unpredictable."

"Very nicely put," said the congressman, "but I still don't get what you fellows are really trying to do."

"That damned popular image again!" Merton mumbled into the depths of his raised whiskey glass.

"I beg your pardon?" said the congressman.

"Oh, nothing," said Merton.

In the preceding profile of Professor Robert Merton, reference was made to two major categories of sociologists: "the mathematically oriented, opinion-sampling empiricists, and the pontificating, concept-making theorists." This is an admittedly exaggerated but nevertheless useful polarization of sociologists as essentially either fact-gatherers and collectors of observable social data on the one hand or abstractors and generalizers about social life on the other. Actually, most sociologists do not fall neatly and exclusively into one or the other category, for by necessity they engage in both processes. They collect social facts not for their own sake but rather to build social theory, and the theory in turn is supported or refuted by the data at hand.

James A. Schellenberg in the article that follows proposes that sociology today, depending on (*a*) the extent of the time and space of the data investigated, and (*b*) the level of abstraction employed in the investigation, actually can be divided into a threefold classification. In historical and cultural sociology, the efforts of the sociologists are directed toward broad description of the trends of society through time or toward the comparison of two or more societies at a given time. In clinical and concrete sociology, a given social situation, restricted by time and space, is the object of analysis. Finally, in the case of the third division, logico-experimental sociology, hypotheses or "educated guesses" about the relationships between two sets of social phenomena in a given society are tested.

2. DIVISIONS OF GENERAL SOCIOLOGY *

JAMES A. SCHELLENBERG
Western Michigan University

Sociology is often criticized as being ambiguously general or too broadly eclectic. It is held that a scientific organization of knowledge is hindered by the variety of content and method grouped together as sociology. On the other hand, a case can also be made against excessive division of the subject matter of sociology into "fields" or "areas" and "sub-areas." There is a danger that basic forms and primary forces of social life will be forgotten in the shuffle of special sociologies. Both under-generalization and over-generalization, it would seem, may be pitfalls for sociologists.

This paper is an attempt to clarify the nature of general sociology by suggesting a division of its subject matter. It is intended that the categories developed should be sufficiently comprehensive to represent the broad scope of sociology without the listing of numerous sub-areas. Furthermore, the categories should correspond more closely to the habitual operations of sociologists than to an ideal scheme of what sociologists should be doing.

A BASIS OF CLASSIFICATION

A division of the subject matter of sociology on the basis of "scope" or "range" has been suggested by C. Wright Mills, James B. Watson, and Florian Znaniecki. Mills distinguishes between the "macroscopic" and "molecular" research-ways in social science: sociologists of the first type "attempt to generalize types of historical phenomena, and in a systematic way, to connect the various institutional spheres of a society, and then relate them to prevailing types of men and women." The molecular type of inquiry, on the other hand, Mills points to as having a smaller range of problems and greater possibilities for objectivity, cumulative development, and quantification. Watson makes a similar characterization of types of study, using "psychological" and "cultural" as polar labels for the differences of scope of theories of cultural change.

Znaniecki hints at a comparable classification by pointing out that American sociologists seem to emphasize specific problems which can presumably be solved by the factual evidence derived from direct observation. As a consequence most sociological research is carried on in such areas as

> a laboratory, a clinic, a hospital, a place where a small number of people regularly congregate, a kindergarten, a school building with or without its neighborhood, a

* *American Sociological Review,* Vol. 22, No. 6, December, 1957, pp. 660–663.

classroom within a college or a whole college campus, a prison, a summer camp, a military center, a section of a factory or an entire factory, sometimes also the area where workers live, a village, a town, the habitat of a tribal or rural community or an ecological part of the city. [Such a focus of study ignores] the enormous multiplicity and complexity of social phenomena developing on the national scale, the continental scale, and the world-wide scale, as well as the historical background of these phenomena.[1]

Another division of sociology may be made on the basis of whether the phenomena studied are viewed, as much as possible, as concrete unities, or whether attention is focused on key variables abstracted out of the situation. The nature of language requires that all concepts represent abstractions from concrete reality, but science often goes many steps further in the refinement of such abstractions in the process of building theoretical systems. The distinction here is between the attempt to study social life in the "reality" of its natural setting—in all its "concrete wholeness" and with a minimum of abstraction—and, on the other hand, the attempt to isolate key variables of social reality within the situation that may be universal in their application. This is essentially the distinction between science in the natural-history sense and science in the hypothetico-deductive sense. An application of this distinction to the analysis of anthropological literature is Watson's polarity of "developmental" and "causal-correlational" theoretical interests.

These two bases of distinction—(1) the extent of the range in time and space of the data to be investigated, and (2) the degree of abstraction in the process of investigation—together offer suggestive divisions for the subject matter of sociology. A formal application of these criteria would lead, by dichotomizing each, to four ideal types of sociology with perhaps such names as "concrete-microcosmic," "concrete-macrocosmic," "abstract-microcosmic," and "abstract-macrocosmic."

However, if interest is less in creating a formal model than in clarification of the observed varieties of sociology, it would seem that the concrete-abstract dichotomy would not be particularly useful in clarifying the "macroscopic" range. In the first place, a considerable amount of abstraction is made necessary by the importance of selection from the wide range of phenomena studied. That is, it is extremely difficult to represent the broader features of cultures and societies in thoroughly concrete terms. In the second place, careful building and precise testing of theoretical models of abstract social science can better be done with studies of limited situations than with broad historical and cultural studies. Thus the broader ranges would also be less readily applicable to the development of a systematic experimental science.

By thus eliminating the abstract-concrete distinction with regard to the broader ranges of subject matter, one could consider sociology as divisible

[1] Florian Znaniecki, "Basic Problems of Contemporary Sociology," *American Sociological Review,* 19 (October, 1954), p. 519.

into the remaining three types. For convenience we shall identify these types as (1) historical and cultural sociology, (2) concrete and clinical sociology, and (3) logico-experimental sociology.

Historical and cultural sociology typically has societies and cultures or some broad phase of a complex society as its area of endeavor. One may deal with trends in a society or civilization (the historical approach) or follow lines of cross-cultural comparison (the anthropological approach), but in either case the unit of study is "society" in a rather broad sense. This range of sociology is devoted to describing main trends or chief features of complex societies. Data are typically a result of second-hand observation, based on a careful evaluation of the reliability and representativeness of sources. Analysis is commonly in terms of either explicit or implicit "ideal types," and the process of analysis demands a great degree of judgment on the part of the sociologist to separate the significant from the irrelevant. The approach thus must be largely qualitative, though quantitative data may have a vital place in the factual underpinnings.

Clinical or concrete sociology deals not with trends of the broad social order, but rather with a total situation within restricted limits of time and space. The limits are usually imposed by the group or organization under consideration, and the aim is to understand the situation in its entirety or the "system" as a functioning unit. The concepts that prove useful for this range of study are those that give the investigator a general sense of reference in approaching concrete situations. Herbert Blumer has aptly labeled these as "sensitizing" concepts, distinguishing them from more "definitive" concepts. A variety of specific methods may be used in concrete sociology, but in any case skilled observation must play the major role. Indeed, the area of concrete sociology can be delineated as the area in which "participant observation" may be used as a key method of research.

Logico-experimental sociology deals with relationships of variables abstracted out of concrete phenomena. The aim is to discover those aspects of social phenomena that may be seen as keys in determining other phenomena, and to describe the kind and measure the degree of the relationships between such "independent" and "dependent" variables. This is the part of sociology that most thoroughly shares the aims and methods of certain physical sciences, for here the emphasis is not on concrete analysis or natural-history description but rather on testing hypotheses and establishing a predictive hypothetico-deductive system. Concepts of a truly experimental sociology must be definitive —that is, the concepts must refer "precisely to what is common to a class of objects, by the aid of a clear definition in terms of attributes or fixed bench-marks." And above this, if a successful hypothetico-deductive system is to be developed, the concepts must bear logical relationship within a theoretical system at the same time that they bear specific relationship to observable facts. Methods of logico-experimental sociology usually reserve a key place for exact measurement; but quantification and measures of significance do not preclude the necessity of a creative imagination for perceiving key variables and forming hypotheses concerning their relationships.

DISCUSSION

The foregoing classification of the subject matter of sociology is based directly upon two criteria: the extent in time and space of the data to be investigated, and the degree of abstraction in the process of investigation. It has also indicated how differences in concepts and methods are relevant for these distinctions.

To prevent any misunderstanding, it may be well to mention in passing some problems that are *not* relevant to this classification. In the first place, each of the divisions could probably be pursued equally well with the same definition of sociology. At least this would be true with such definitions of sociology as "the science of social behavior," "the study of group life," or "the study of social phenomena." In the second place, these distinctions need not renew the battle over the question of value judgments in sociology. Each of the divisions could be formulated in propositions of the "is" form without any "should be" statements; and at the same time the observations of any division may contribute directly to the sociologist's personal convictions or to his recommendations for social policy. In the third place, the distinctions should not be conceived as encouraging a dichotomy between "theory" and raw empiricism. In all divisions both thoughtful generalizations and verified factual data are equally indispensable.

It remains now to point out the positive contributions of this threefold division of the subject matter of sociology. The principal motive behind the distinctions has been the clarification of the needs of sociology as an advancing science. The distinctions can serve to distinguish fundamental needs, uses, and methods of sociological study.

The question of sociology's most urgent need is asked and answered with great frequency. Nearly every sociologist has his convictions about the direction in which sociology should be moving. Not always, however, do the preachments of individual sociologists take into consideration the full range of the subject matter of sociology, and what one sociologist advocates can usually be better understood if interpreted in terms of the range of sociology with which he habitually deals. Thus when Carle C. Zimmerman deplores the "existentialism and sociological sterility" in the crop of contemporary sociologists, what he seems to have in mind is the lack of sociologists who can deal skillfully with broad trends of contemporary history; when Elton Mayo deplores the scholasticism of young sociologists, his attention is focused primarily upon the needs of sociology as an area of clinical science; and when George A. Lundberg calls for more scientific social scientists, he has in mind primarily the growing range of logico-experimental sociology.

It seems to the writer that much is sometimes wasted in prescriptions for the study of sociology that do not consider the wide range of sociological subject matter. The macrocosm of historical and cultural sociology, the topics of clinical and concrete sociology, and the area of logico-experimental sociology are all worthy of attention and development. They are all legitimate areas of study, and one who defines sociology only in terms of one division is usually exhibiting his own bias. Perhaps sometime in the future sociology may develop into a science more sharply delineated by specific problems; but it is this writer's plea that in the meantime we can afford to be tolerant of wide varieties of sociological approaches among us.

This classification of the divisions of sociology may lead to the recognition of the variety of purposes and uses behind the study of sociology. Even when motives are as scientifically pure as simple curiosity, still such "simple" curiosity is apt to take various forms. For some curiosity is widely projected to questions of class, nation, civilization, or humanity; for others curiosity is directed to the total dynamics of the groups and organizations within which they feel they live and move and have their being; and to still others this curiosity may be that of uncovering key principles of social behavior. But motives are not always so pure or non-utilitarian as simple curiosity. There are motives of a desire to "save" our society or at least to enhance the social health of our nation; there are other motives of relieving the tensions of groups and organizations, such as lessening the friction in a production unit of a factory or the reproduction unit of a home; and there are also the motives of hope for a more exact manipulation of men. To admit these motives of sociological study is not to despair of objectivity, but rather to aid toward clarification of the points of departure upon which an objective study may be built. We need not assume only one point of departure with pure enough motives for the foundations of a scientific sociology.

The methods and concepts suitable for one division of the subject matter of sociology may not fit the problems of another. In this respect the social sciences might draw upon other sciences to illustrate the problem. In biological sciences, for example, the broader studies of comparative anatomy or evolution do not require the same technical methods or intellectual habits as do the fields of biochemistry, biophysics or experimental physiology; and somewhere between are studies of general physiology and gross anatomy. It would be extremely out of place for a student of anatomy who is working on a cadaver in order to study the way certain muscles are attached to certain bones (a thoroughly concrete level of study) to feel that he must act as if he were performing an experiment in biophysics.

The moral should be clear. The subject matter of sociology covers a wide range, and different sets of methods are fitting for problems of different areas of sociology. There is room for progress in historical and cultural sociology and in clinical or concrete sociology, as well as there is need for advancement in sociology as a logico-experimental science.

One of the major differences between amateur sociology, which has always existed, and the professional sociology that came into existence in the nineteenth century is that the former relies almost solely on speculation and personal experience or common-sense observations about people in society. The latter, however, distrustful of the limitations of personal experience when confronted with complex and wide-ranging social phenomena, seeks to insure that the phenomena are representative before attempting to make sociological generalizations. From the professional sociological point of view, the following dialogue suggests what happens all too frequently when laymen blissfully proceed from personal experience—no matter how accurate their observation—toward generalizations.

First Citizen: "Do you know that American Indians still walk single file?"

Second Citizen: "Really! How do you know?"

First Citizen: "I saw one walking that way yesterday."

In the brief but interesting account that follows, Jackson Toby describes the technique he discovered and effectively utilizes to disrupt his students' dependence on personal experience in validating principles about social life. He suggests that adequate sampling of social phenomena, among other things, is necessary to compensate for the shortcomings of one's own personal observations.

3. UNDERMINING THE STUDENT'S FAITH IN THE VALIDITY OF PERSONAL EXPERIENCE *

JACKSON TOBY

Rutgers University

After listening to me talk for a half-hour on research in the field of child socialization, a freshman raised his hand to comment, "In all of my eighteen years, I never came across any of those things you were talking about." The class laughed, but I found that other students are also unwilling to believe anything that they cannot confirm by their own experience. It does no good to point out that they get to meet in a lifetime only an insignificant proportion of the human race and that, moreover, a white Protestant New Yorker has little chance of knowing Southern Negroes, European priests, or even American farmers. Personal experience is so convincing that they discourse with assurance on topics about which I dare to make only the most tentative observations. At first I was non-plussed. Then I got an idea. If I could shake their confidence in the validity of personal experience, perhaps they would prefer the cautious, pedestrian conclusions of social science.

My program of subversion includes the following illustration of the limitations of "experience": I ask the class whether anyone has noticed, in traveling

* *American Sociological Review,* Vol. 20, No. 6, December, 1955, pp. 717–718.

by bus or streetcar, that there are more public conveyances going by in the *wrong* direction. A few students agree that this is so. "You mean that, no matter which way you wish to go, more buses come by going in the opposite direction?" The class begins to mumble that you see the same number in both directions, that it only *seems* there are more buses coming the other way. The handful of students who spoke up first feel trapped and hasten to disavow their original position.

"No, it is not an illusion," I assure them, "you actually have observed more buses going in the wrong direction!" No matter which direction you want to go in? How can that be? Disbelief is writ large on their faces. "Suppose you want to travel *east.* A bus comes heading *west.* Do you take it?" Of course not, they snort. "You wait five minutes more, and another bus comes heading *west.* Do you take it?" No. "How many buses do you see heading west that day?" It depends on how long it takes for *my* bus to come. "As many as five?" Possibly. "How many do you see heading east?" They begin to catch on. Only *one* because, as soon as a bus comes going in my direction, I take it!

"Over the years you can accumulate quite a bit of experience testifying that public transportation companies are engaged in a conspiracy to frustrate your travel plans. Of course, it is neither the bus company nor a malevolent deity. You observe the comings and goings of buses while waiting for one, and this biases your conclusions. When buses go by in the wrong direction, you may fume, curse the bus company, or spend your time counting them. But no matter how many there are, you do not board any of them. Let one bus come on your side of the street, and you get on. This is your mistake. If you want to prove to yourself that paranoid conclusions are unjustified, you have to restrain the impulse to get someplace. Station yourself at the bus stop at 6 A.M. and stay there until sunset, counting the buses as they go by in *both* directions. This is the only scientific way to mobilize the testimony of experience on this problem."

So far, none of my students has been scientist enough to accept my challenge.

Common sense and personal observations, as Professor Toby has just indicated, are unfortunately used to refute the findings of sociology when the two are in conflict. Equally unfortunate is the tendency to call on common sense to support sociological findings when the two appear to be in agreement. In such instances, one frequently hears the common-sense observer remark that sociology is merely restating in complicated form what is obvious, or already known, to everyone.

In a book review of the first two volumes of *The American Soldier,* a landmark of sociological and social psychological research findings based on attitudinal surveys during World War II, Paul Lazarsfeld confronted this problem head on as the central task of his role as reviewer. Selecting six of the findings about the American soldier that were published in the volumes, he cleverly and convincingly demolished the argument that sociological generalizations in such cases always tell us nothing we do not already know. While Professor Lazarsfeld, like any other competent sociologist, would insist that what is taken as obvious is frequently found to be wrong, he would concede that it is often necessary for the sociologists' research to confirm the commonplace.

4. SOCIOLOGY vs. COMMON SENSE *

PAUL F. LAZARSFELD
Columbia University

Finding regularities and determining criteria of significance are concerns the social sciences have in common with the natural sciences. But there are crucial differences between the two fields of inquiry. The world of social events is much less "visible" than the realm of nature. That bodies fall to the ground, that things are hot or cold, that iron becomes rusty, are all immediately obvious. It is much more difficult to realize that ideas of right and wrong vary in different cultures; that customs may serve a different function from the one which the people practising them believe they are serving; that the same person may show marked contrasts in his behavior as a member of a family and as a member of an occupational group. The mere description of human behavior, of its variation from group to group and of its changes in different situations, is a vast and difficult undertaking. It is this task of describing, sifting and ferreting out interrelationships which surveys perform for us. And yet this very function often leads to serious misunderstandings. For it is hard to find a form of human behavior that has not already been observed somewhere. Consequently, if a study reports a prevailing regularity, many readers respond to it by thinking "of course that is the way things are." Thus, from time to time, the argument is advanced that surveys only put into complicated form observations which are already obvious to everyone.

Understanding the origin of this point of view is of importance far beyond the limits of the present discussion. The reader may be helped in recognizing this attitude if he looks over a few statements which are typical of many survey findings and carefully observes his own reaction. A short list of these, with brief interpretive comments, will be given here in order to bring into sharper focus probable reactions of many readers.

1. Better educated men showed more psycho-neurotic symptoms than those with less education. (The mental instability of the intellectual as compared to the more impassive psychology of the-man-in-the-street has often been commented on.)

2. Men from rural backgrounds were usually in better spirits during their Army life than soldiers from city backgrounds. (After all, they are more accustomed to hardships.)

* Excerpt of "Review of *The American Soldier,* Vols. I and II," in *The Public Opinion Quarterly*, Vol. 13, No. 3, Fall, 1949, pp. 378–380.

3. Southern soldiers were better able to stand the climate in the hot South Sea Islands than Northern soldiers. (Of course, Southerners are more accustomed to hot weather.)

4. White privates were more eager to become non-coms than Negroes. (The lack of ambition among Negroes is almost proverbial.)

5. Southern Negroes preferred Southern to Northern white officers. (Isn't it well known that Southern whites have a more fatherly attitude toward their "darkies"?)

6. As long as the fighting continued, men were more eager to be returned to the States than they were after the German surrender. (You cannot blame people for not wanting to be killed.)

We have in these examples a sample list of the simplest type of interrelationships which provide the "bricks" from which our empirical social science is being built. But why, since they are so obvious, is so much money and energy given to establish such findings? Would it not be wiser to take them for granted and proceed directly to a more sophisticated type of analysis? This might be so except for one interesting point about the list. *Every one of these statements is the direct opposite of what actually was found.* Poorly educated soldiers were more neurotic than those with high education; Southerners showed no greater ability than Northerners to adjust to a tropical climate; Negroes were more eager for promotion than whites; and so on.

If we had mentioned the actual results of the investigation first, the reader would have labelled these "obvious" also. Obviously something is wrong with the entire argument of "obviousness." It should really be turned on its head. Since every kind of human reaction is conceivable, it is of great importance to know which reactions actually occur most frequently and under what conditions; only then will a more advanced social science develop.

From its earliest days more than a century ago down to the present, sociology has undergone a continuous and at times vehement barrage by outside critics, and sporadically even by members of the profession itself. Besides the allegation that sociology is merely common-sense observation about social behavior, four principal criticisms are directed against it.

According to the first criticism, much of sociology pretends to be science but is in fact only "scientism" or pseudoscience, lacking the objectivity, uniformity, and rigor of "real" science (that is, natural science), and dealing with erratic human beings. A second allegation, consistent with the first, is that sociology in its zeal to appear scientific has become infatuated with unnecessary jargon and meaningless statistics. Many questions are considered under such forbidding titles as "the role of primary groups in the intergenerational transmission of sociopolitical information." In simple terms this means "what children learn about politics from their parents in contrast to what they learn from their playmates." As a consequence of this crude and pretentious language, nonprofessional popularizers in such books as *The Status Seekers, The Organization Man,* and *The Exurbanites* are replacing sociologists in publicizing social phenomena. Third, sociology is attacked for fostering the dangerous idea that its development as a science will make man ultimately predictable and therefore controllable in a new social order. Last, sociology is accused of being fundamentally unable to grasp true knowledge of man and society; this is the legitimate province only of men with wisdom and insight, such as poets, theologians, political theorists, moralists, and jurists.

The following statement of these and other allegations by Russell Kirk was ostensibly directed at the social sciences in general. Actually, as the reader will readily note, it was aimed primarily at sociology. Its publication in the Sunday magazine of *The New York Times* provoked nationwide discussion and controversy.

5. IS SOCIAL SCIENCE SCIENTIFIC? *

RUSSELL KIRK

Long Island University

Sociology has become a power in the land. Since Gunnar Myrdal's "An American Dilemma" was cited as a basis for the Supreme Court's anti-segregation decisions, reforming social scientists have felt themselves approaching, at last, the high estate they have long claimed for themselves.

Certainly their realm has grown mushroomlike in this century. Scarcely any American now eludes its influence: "Social studies" is a required course in nearly every public school. Teacher-training is heavily laden with social-science indoctrination, at the expense of the humanities and the natural sciences. For the past two decades, the big foundations have poured hundreds of millions of dollars into the social sciences. And, recently, the Federal Government began to subsidize social-science research.

Still, the social scientists' standing is insecure. They are split into warring camps, the basis of their authority remains in question, and there lingers a certain public reluctance to grant them the respect they covet. If a professor declares roundly, "I speak as a social scientist," some other professor may mutter, "That stuff isn't science—it's only scientism."

Among themselves, indeed, the social scientists are divided and vague as to any definition of their discipline. It is "the science of society," of course; and Auguste Comte expected sociology to be the master science, all branches of learning merging upward into it. But in America, the disciplines of economics and politics already were established before sociology made its appearance; and so, often, the sociologist is forced either to deal with marginal activities or to indulge in grand generalizations about society. For the typical college student, sociology consists of "introductory sociology"—mostly talk about in-groups and out-groups—"marriage and the family" and "social problems."

The serious sociologist, nevertheless, aspires much higher. He asserts that his discipline is, or ought to be, as truly scientific as are the natural sciences.

* *The New York Times Magazine,* June 25, 1961, pp. 11, 15, 16, 18. Copyright by The New York Times. Reprinted by permission.

He claims that he, like the natural scientist, describes, predicts and controls phenomena; he lays down "laws" of behavior; he is the engineer and the architect of a new, rational social order.

His opinion polls, his analyses of out-groups, his indices of prejudice, his statistical computations of popular choice (and nowadays he is intoxicated with the computing machines), all are intended to convert mankind into a predictable and controllable species.

He may advocate, for instance, with Dr. Stuart C. Dodd, director of the Washington Public Opinion Laboratory, "Project Aimscales"—a plan to ascertain exactly, through a labyrinthine system of preference polls, "America's current inventory of national goals," and to improve those goals.

"Aimscales of the future," Mr. Dodd writes, "will be able to measure with increasing precision the sizes of the itemized target ends, and subtarget means thereto; their costs in terms of man-hours of effort, money, alternatives displaced, or other appropriate terms; their scheduling in regard to any needed regional differentials or adjustments for diverse conditions; and the all-important attitudinal dimensions of the citizens and their leaders. . . ." Such is the language and the objective of the social scientist par excellence.

Philosophically, the representative social scientist is an empiricist of the positivist variety; emotionally, he is often a secular evangelist. Yet despite his increasing influence in many quarters, he is not quite so confident as Comte was that the future belongs to him and his science. Jacques Barzun suggests that the term "behavioral sciences" is supplanting the older term "social sciences" because of the sociologist's "desperate conviction that man does *not* behave and should be made to with the help of science."

About three years ago, a youngish instructor in sociology declared to me, somewhat defiantly, "I really believe that we can teach everybody the scientific approach."

A touch of shrillness in his "really" suggested that even this zealot was experiencing doubts. For today's humanitarian social scientist is discouraged by one hard fact: only in totalitarian states have positivistic doctrines of social reconstruction on "scientific" lines been applied thoroughly. So, he is forced back upon studies in "democratic behavior patterns"; but if "democracy" is his ideal, how can he ever attain the status of priest-scientist that Comte ordained?

Thus, the aims of social science remain in dispute: whether this discipline is meant to give coherence and fresh meaning to older disciplines; whether it is intended to work toward a terrestrial paradise; or whether it ought to rest content with recording group behavior.

Is this branch of study, strictly speaking, a science at all? Pitirim Sorokin, perhaps the best-known of American sociologists, maintains that it is indeed a science—but a science which requires something more than the empirical method for its basis, and which ought to recognize and respect knowledge already possessed by the several intellectual disciplines, including the sociological discipline itself.

Undeniably, much of what has passed for social science has been mere scientism, or pseudo-science. Loosely employed, the word "science" means simply any orderly and reputable study, on systematic principles.

But the social scientists have not been satisfied with so general a claim to the laurels of science: many of them have asserted that their discipline must be, or perhaps already is, as exact and regular a science as physics, or chemistry, or botany, or geology. (Some, indeed, have used the term "social physics.") Envying the natural sciences, they have sought to emulate the methods of their natural-science colleagues, and to assert parallel claims of certitude in prediction and control.

"The nemesis of such simulacra," Sorokin writes, "is sterility and error—and this nemesis is already walking abroad among the contemporary psychosocial sciences. . . . In spite of our narcissistic self-admiration, of the enormous energy and funds spent in pseudomathematical and statistical research, its achievements have been singularly modest, its sterility unexpectedly notable, and its fallacies surprisingly numerous."

One consequence of this common social-scientist passion for imitating the outward forms of natural science is the development of an amazing jargon, incomprehensible even to nineteen-twentieths of the body of university graduates and, one suspects, often unclear to most sociologists themselves.

This "scientific" vocabulary of the sociologist, to which every professor feels free to add at will (by way of establishing his claim to "originality") resembles the deliberate obscurity of the learned Marxist—an opaqueness intended to convert the vulgar through awe of erudition.

The medical word "synergy," for instance, redefined to convey the meaning of the "the sum total of energy which any group can command and expend," obscures rather than enlightens. The word "valence" is borrowed from physics and converted to mean "attraction in society"—which is not at all like its natural-science meaning and is severed from its linguistic root.

Even a popular and comparatively lucid sociological writer like David Riesman twists terms to suit his passing purpose and, perhaps, to impress his general readership—using the word "anomic," for example, to mean being cut off from the tone and temper of a society, which is a borrowing from Durkheim's *anomique,* the masterless man.

In an age which requires the restoration of clarity and of reasonable persuasion, this pedantry in terminology is a sorry tendency. Genuine science does not need to cloak itself in convoluted verbiage.

More serious than this debauching of language is what Sorokin calls "quantophrenia," or infatuation with statistical surveys and nose-counting. Because the natural sciences are non-moral—that is, they have to do only with things and animals less than human—the aspiring "behavioral scientist" endeavors to develop a methodology which will be equally indifferent to moral norms—that is, to standards and models for humanity.

For old normative judgments, the social scientist of this persuasion substitutes opinion surveys and numerical compilations. However, as Carlyle wrote, "Statistics is a science which ought to be honorable, the basis of many most important sciences; but . . . a wise head is requisite for carrying it on. Conclusive facts are inseparable from inconclusive except by a head that already understands and knows."

So there have sprung up the immense behavioral research centers, most notably the Center for Advanced Study in the Behavioral Sciences, at Stanford University, almost a Mecca for this persuasion. The University of Michigan has a whole series of such institutions, supported by very large sums from foundations and government—the Center for Research on Conflict Resolution, the Research Center for Group Dynamics, the Survey Research Center.

C. Wright Mills, a radical gadfly among sociologists, suggests that very often the research assistants in behavioral institutes are chosen from among the second-rate: "I have seldom seen one of these young men," he writes, "once he is well caught up, in a condition of genuine intellectual puzzlement."

Deficient in imagination, they mistake fact accumulation for wisdom. The ancient Greeks had one word, philodoxer, for the lover of opinion, and another word, philosopher, for the lover of wisdom; and they knew that these two are a world apart. Much modern opinion-and-behavior investigation is only philodoxy.

Such behaviorists often ignore theory and history in favor of the currents of the year or the decade: awareness of the drift is all. One young behavioral professor said to me recently, when the name of a distinguished historian of ideas was mentioned, "How does he think he knows all this? Did he make a survey?" Resentment of unusual imagination and obsession with nose-counting are the behaviorist's form of anti-intellectualism.

Absurdities result. One behavioristic study, cited by Barzun and Graff in their "Modern Researcher," came to the solemn conclusion that "if in a given society an aunt resides with or near the mother, and assists in giving care to the child, the latter will regard her as a mother; less so, or not so, if the aunt lives at a distance."

Thus do some sociologists establish, as brilliant new discoveries, on scientific principles, the tiny secrets of the bassinet.

Another expensive survey, financed by the Federal Office of Education, proposed to analyze "succorance and playmirth"—that is, seeking of comfort and companionship in fun—among small children. The researchers came to the enlightening conclusion, after much statistics-juggling, that little boys like to play with little boys, and little girls with little girls.

And the absurdities can grow into serious errors about men and communities. If a behavioral researcher acting from the assumptions of nineteenth-century positivism investigates religious beliefs, he is likely to discover exactly what he expected to find: that religious convictions are unscientific, irrational, absurd and perhaps dangerous. He is against prejudice—but, unaware of his own prejudices; because he has been deliberately cut off from theological, humane and historical disciplines, he may mistake his petty private rationality for self-evident truth.

Or if the behavioral scientist assumes that political conservatives are ignorant bigots, he usually finds by his opinion surveys that the conservative folk he interviewed were just that. Ignorant and bigoted folk give ignorant and bigoted answers; ergo, ignorant and bigoted folks are conservatives.

In reality, one can understand the significance of such a term as "conservative" only by painstaking historical and political studies; but too many behavioral researchers confound their unconscious prejudices with complete objectivity.

As Raymond Aron—the most widely read of living French sociologists—remarked recently, the typical American sociologist tends to be "liberal," in part because "many stem from semi-marginal groups: first-generation Americans, Jews, and natives of central Europe are more common among American sociologists than Back-Bay Bostonians."

And although the complete behaviorist may deny the existence of "value-judgments" and normative understandings, nevertheless he does not escape, in his researches, the influence of his own value-judgments, even though they are unwittingly held as vague sentiments or animosities.

In his introduction to "The Human Meaning of the Social Sciences," one well-known behaviorist, Daniel Lerner, declares that the social sciences have shown modern man that "there are no more eternal mysteries . . . there are no more eternal verities"; man is revealed as "plastic, variable, and amenable to reshaping." And the energetic social scientist intends to set to work promptly at that reshaping, free from authority, prescription and value-judgments.

The trouble with this view of social studies and their purpose is that to act without any norms except vague humanitarian sentiments may bring a nation into grave peril. It may injure the institutions which shelter community and freedom at home, and lead to the gravest of mistakes in foreign policy—in the administration of a foreign-aid program in Afghanistan or Laos, for instance.

For the social scientist is not really dealing with things soulless or inanimate or abstract, as does the natural scientist. The sociologist's subject, embarrassing though it may be to the eager reformer, is man, living and erratic man, in complex humanity.

Human beings are the least controllable, verifiable, law-obeying and predictable of subjects. If man were predictable, indeed, he would cease to be truly human. Andrew Hacker, of Cornell University, therefore writes forebodingly about "the spectre of predictable man"—the man of the future whose coming so many behaviorists view complacently, the man of "Brave New World."

Now, of course, there can be ascertained certain general rules concerning human behavior in community; indeed, a large body of literature on the subject has long been available—though often ignored by the novelty-seeking behavioral scientist. But the more important part of this literature is not "scientific" in the strict modern sense. This knowledge is the work of poets, theologians, political theorists, moralists, jurists and men of imagination generally.

One may learn a great deal about the first principles of human nature from Dante or Samuel Johnson; but this is not the sort of knowledge that fits into the calculations of the astronomer or the engineer. Plato and Cicero, Montesquieu and Burke are the sources of much wisdom concerning the civil social order; but they are not "scientists" in the sense of the natural sciences.

Even when one finds a philosopher like David Hume, severely logical and methodical, the zealot for "social science" must be dismayed by Hume's conclusion that rational accounting for morals and politics is simply impossible.

In fine, I think that the behavioral scientist has been the victim of illusion when he has attempted to solve all the ills to which community is heir by the application of the techniques of physics and chemistry and biology.

"It is this false analogy with mechanics and mathematics," Prof. S. Herbert Frankel of Oxford says, "that accounts for the facile belief that the problem involved in living and working together in a community is similar to the problem of finding, by abstract thought or logical deduction, the 'unknown' factor in an equation. In the realm of organic life there is, and can be, no final solution—other than death itself. . . . Those who arrogantly write solutions upon their political banners . . . offend the very nature of all social evolution, which rests on the slow unfolding of institutions, laws, and habit-patterns of thought and action." Amen to that.

By deliberately cutting himself off from tradition and theory, by ignoring theology and ethics and humane letters, the average social scientist of our generation has deprived himself of the principal instruments for understanding human behavior—or for effecting any enduring improvement of society, let alone the "solution" of human striving which he often seeks.

If a scientist at all, he has become a scientist without reliable means for measuring and weighing. Infatuated with the empirical method, the doctrinaire social scientist omits from his calculations the higher and more enduring elements in human behavior.

As Sorokin argues, modern social science desperately needs reinvigoration of social theory and observation through the employment of reason and the recognition of poets' and philosophers' genius. Only by a return to the true sources of wisdom—which in part are intuitive—can the critic of society find standards by which to measure our present discontents and to propose remedies.

Neither the utopian sociologist of the old positivistic breed nor the survey-taking behaviorist of our time is prepared to confront the Gorgon's head of twentieth-century social disintegration. What social studies need more than anything else, I suspect, is the recovery of norms: a restoration of normative disciplines, a return to the knowledge of standards for human personality and for the just order. Some imaginative sociologists—one may cite as an example

Robert A. Nisbet, in his book "The Quest for Community"—already have turned that way.

Imagination, in the long run, rules the world—not scientific research, and still less scientific sham. It is pointless, and at heart unscientific, to survey the shifting opinions of the hour unless one recognizes standards in opinion—that is, sources of truth. And it is pointless to ape the natural sciences when one has to deal with whimsical and impatient and irrational mankind.

So I venture to suggest that we professors of social disciplines might do well if we talked less about the claims of social science and more about the realities of social art. Modern society, in many ways sick, needs, not the short-sighted manipulations of the research technician, but the artist's touch.

Invited to answer the charges of Professor Kirk three weeks later in the same publication, Robert Merton took up each of the assaults after collectively identifying them as a version of "the curious admixture of illogic and sentiment that makes up the creed and canons of anti-sociology," and as evidence of "the need for the very kind of sociological inquiry they caricature." He contended, for example, in his defense of sociological terminology, that technical and precise nomenclature is essential to any scientific endeavor. It seems stranger in sociology than in, let us say, physics, only because the sociologist is dealing with familiar rather than esoteric materials. Also, it is an interesting comment upon the difference in status between disciplines that we do not criticize physicists for talking about a "neutrino" or "anti-matter." The simple fact is that human group behavior is complex and variegated. Lay language often does not do justice to this quality.

Professor Merton, in his full rebuttal that follows, goes even further. Succinctly, he samples what is going on in sociological research, citing important accomplishments in subjecting popular social beliefs to responsible sociological investigation and in the findings about complex social organizations and the unanticipated consequences of social interaction. He concludes that sociologists like himself are not much disturbed by their anti-sociological critics; instead, they are resolutely moving ahead in their efforts to build a "new science of an ancient subject."

6. THE CANONS OF THE ANTI-SOCIOLOGIST *

ROBERT K. MERTON
Columbia University

Once again the season of the anti-sociologists is upon us. The academic year has ended and professors are ready to turn from talking to writing. A self-selected few will dust off and publish yet again the litany that fiercely imprecates sociology and all its works. This year, the avowed conservative

* *The New York Times Magazine,* July 16, 1961, pp. 14, 19–21.

professor of political science, Russell Kirk, got in first. His version will serve to exhibit the curious admixture of illogic and sentiment that makes up the creed and canons of anti-sociology.

Some sociologists find these assaults tiresome. To me, they have the peculiar charm of testifying to the need for the very kind of sociological inquiry they caricature. For each jaded version reads as though it were written by a sociologist-*manqué*. Each purports to describe the behavior of sociologists, to explain that behavior and, even more ambitiously, to describe and explain the responses to it.

With practiced ease, for example, Mr. Kirk reviews the work of thousands of social scientists and promulgates the first canon that "the representative" specimen is an "empiricist of the positivist variety; emotionally, he is often a secular evangelist." Had Mr. Kirk allowed himself to profit from the introductory course in sociology he so deplores, he might have learned of the danger of creating out of his private impressions a stereotype of the aims and behavior of large numbers of people, all the while pretending to have caught hold of the representative reality. But amateur sociologizing has no place for disciplined inquiry. Rather, it assumes that statements become authoritative simply by being put into the black and white magic of print.

The second canon declares the absurdity and impiety of statistics dealing with the behavior of men in society. For nothing significant about man's behavior can be counted. If it could be counted, it would be immoral to do so. Everyone knows that no good can come of it.

To support his canon, Mr. Kirk cites Carlyle, who knew little about the primitive statistical methods of his own day and nothing, obviously, about the mathematical bases of modern statistics. As further proof, he quotes the attack by the sociologist Pitirim A. Sorokin on "quantophrenia" or in uncritical devotion to faulty statistics. Unlike myself, Mr. Kirk has not had the benefit of having been Professor Sorokin's student, and so does not know, apparently, that Sorokin used vast arrays of social statistics in every one of his major works and, in "Social and Cultural Dynamics," states that "quantitative judgments . . . in verbal form" are inevitable in any substantial work of history.

No doubt it is more inviting to assume statistics of human behavior. The amateur sociologist will explain, for example, why it is that we have such high rates of mental illness in what Mr. Kirk feels free to describe as our age of "twentieth-century social disintegration." But while the amateur sociologist explains *why* this is so, the disciplined sociologist proceeds first to find out whether it really *is* so. Only through painstaking analysis of the statistics of mental illness—as in the work of Herbert Goldhamer and Andrew Marshall—do we find that we had best postpone our ready-to-hand explanations, if only because it now seems probable that the rate of confinement for mental illness is no higher today than it was during the past century.

Turning up like death and taxes, the third canon of the anti-sociologists declares the sociologists to be both perpetrators and victims of jargon. Here, the anti-sociologist knows himself to be on altogether safe ground, for just about everyone can be counted on to be "against jargon" in the same penetrating sense that President Coolidge's minister declared himself against sin.

Perhaps it is time to distinguish between jargon and that essential of all disciplined thought, technical language. Technical language is a more precise and condensed form of thought and communication than colloquial language. It is designed to fix definite meanings in which each word has ideally only one denotation and is deliberately deprived of connotations. Jargon, in contrast, is a muddled and wordy imitation of technical language.

The mere unfamiliarity or unesthetic quality of language is no criterion. Jargon and technical language sound alike to someone untrained in the discipline where the language is employed.

All this is only prologue to the pair of canons central to the anti-sociologists' creed. Briefly put, these hold, first, that sociological truths cannot be discovered, for there are no detectable uniformities in human behavior, since man is incorrigibly unpredictable. And second, that sociologists constitute a danger to society, for they provide the knowledge through which men can be molded to fit a new and obnoxious social order. I need not burlesque the logic of the anti-sociologists, for they have preceded me here. I need only review it.

It would seem clear that, if there are no discoverable uniformities about man in society, there can be no sociological knowledge employed to regiment him. Should anti-sociologists admit that there are such uniformities, they can scarcely argue that these uniformities can be discovered by the defective sociology of today, with its inapplicable statistics, its tattered jargon, and its total misunderstanding of human nature.

Forced to acknowledge that there are discoverable uniformities in social life and that modern sociology, for all its limitations, discovers some of them, would they then propose to exorcise this knowledge for fear that it might be used to violate civilized values? On this last line of retreat, the anti-sociologists would join forces with the anti-intellectuals and totalitarian regimenters of thought they ostensibly combat. They would declare themselves guardians of us all, alone able to distinguish dangerous from undangerous knowledge.

The remaining canons of the anti-sociologists are transparently trivial. Criticism among sociologists, for example, is described by the anti-sociologists in the militant metaphors of "warring camps" and "internecine warfare." Perhaps they should pause before advocating monolithic agreement on intellectual issues. It would be a curious reading of the history of thought to suggest that the absence of disagreement testifies to a developing discipline.

As for the anti-sociologists' canon that gives them alone access to the recorded wisdom of the past—from Plato to Montesquieu and Burke—this need only be stated to refute itself.

Since the anti-sociologists impose their grotesque versions of the methods of sociological inquiry upon a public too busy to look for themselves, a few words should be said about those methods. Social scientists believe it no longer sufficient to describe the behavior, attitudes, values and social relations obtaining in a complex society simply on the basis of a large but scattered array of documents, both public and private, and on educated guesses about what people are thinking and feeling. Studies of the historical past, of course, have no alternative. But in the study of present-day societies, these procedures are giving way to systematic, though far from perfected, methods.

One such method is the "sample survey," which sounds out the practices and attitudes of a group selected as representative of the larger population from which they are drawn. This type of survey is now part of the intellectual landscape. However, the "opinion polls" in the popular press do not begin to reproduce the analytical uses to which such surveys are put by academic sociologists.

Furthermore, it is with this instrument as with the rest: the most devastating criticisms of its misuse have come, not from the anti-sociologists who know about it only through casual inspection, but from the professional sociologists who are prepared to study their sometimes disappointing experience with it. For they, at least the best of them, know that, whatever the worth of one or another tool of inquiry, it is the questions put into the inquiry that determine the significance of the results. If the questions are trivial, then the answers will be trivial.

For sociology as for most other scientific disciplines, the electronic computer has emerged as a new resource. Contrary to the imagery of the anti-sociologists, this machine is not the universal mind of our day. It must be told what to do. But, as with most technical creations, the computer has a capacity for deflecting men from the pursuit of purposes that genuinely matter. It tempts its tenders to cast all manner of raw data into its maw and wait for the thoroughly digested product that will itself be senseless if the thought of its managers is without sense. The potential victims, by their professional training, are best qualified to recognize and to counter this danger.

With or without the computer, today's sociology makes no attempt to substitute science for ethics and esthetics or to displace humanism with scientism. Every responsible sociologist, and there are not a few, knows that his knowledge is no substitute for artistic thought.

The thinking humanist, for his part, recognizes that the social scientist who knows his business seeks only to provide an understanding of certain, not all, aspects of the behavior of men and the organization of human society. The intellectual gulf between humanist and social scientist has begun to be bridged. The late Gilbert Murray, critic and classical scholar, said that sociology is "destined to bear abundant and ever-increasing fruit." The political journalist Richard Rovere, has observed that "those of us who have been educated in the twentieth century habitually think in sociological terms, whether or not we have had any training in sociology."

After all this, it is only natural to ask: what is going on in sociology and what does it all amount to? It would be foolish to answer this question by staking out the boundaries of sociology, as though it were a piece of real estate. That is not the character of intellectual property. But we can, in this short space, at least hint at the answer.

In the large, sociology is engaged in finding out how man's behavior and fate are affected, if not minutely governed, by his place within particular kinds, and changing kinds, of social structure and of culture. This means that sociology moves across a wide, varied and, to the layman, often bewildering range of topics and problems.

In doing so, one of its principal functions is to subject popular beliefs about man and his works to responsible investigation. As I have implied, the sociologist asks about many of these beliefs. "Is it really so?" The popular assumption, for example, that the rate of social mobility in America has recently declined has been put in question by systematically assembled data.

The alleged breakdown of the American family, with obsequies read regularly over the remains by those who should know better, has been found to be specious; thorough analyses of data on divorce and death find American marriages remaining intact more often now than they once did. Or, to tackle one last widespread assumption, people who reject orthodox religious beliefs are not more apt to engage in crime than people who hold fast to such beliefs.

Some of the findings of sociology take a considerable time to enter the public domain. For more than a generation, sociologists have found that complex organizations of widely different kinds—economic, political, military, educational—exhibit the same tendencies. These tendencies make for the "bureaucratic man," who is shaped by organizationally induced pressures to conform to the rules even when this means that conformity gets in the way of doing the job effectively. How far this is inevitable remains to be seen, and inquiries are now under way to find out how these tendencies can be counteracted.

Basic to sociology is the premise that, in the course of social interaction, men create new conditions that were not part of their intent. Short-run rationality often produces long-run irrationality. Public health measures may go awry; financial incentives may lead to a decline rather than an increase in production; intensified punishment may aggravate rather than curb crime. Growing recognition of this has become one of the sources of an enlarged use of sociological research in such fields as medicine and public health, social work, law, education, the ministry, architecture and city planning, business, organized labor and agriculture.

Yet it must be added that sociologists, perhaps better than the anti-sociologists, know they are just beginning to acquire the knowledge needed to cope with the many social ills man has the inveterate capacity to contract.

We sociologists need to be saved from the anti-sociologists only in respect to the exaggerated claims they make for our prowess and accomplishments. It is they, not we, who say that "sociology is a power in the land." It is they.

not we, who make the absurd claim that sociology has the power and the intent to turn men into robots and to construct a new social order. The men and women at work in sociological inquiry have more modest and less sadistic hopes. Like their colleagues in other scholarly and scientific disciplines, they recognize that this "very new science of an ancient subject" has still a long way to go. And undisturbed by the cannonades of the anti-sociologists, they are methodically proceeding on their way.

Not all sociology today is anchored in fact and scientific method, even though Professor Merton stressed in the previous article that the mainstream of sociological activity has developed in that direction. Within the discipline itself there are reputable scholars who ask their profession to retain some of its earlier affiliation with the humanities as a producer of cogent, unverifiable ideas about man in society. One of the most articulate of these humanistic, philosophical sociologists is Robert Bierstedt. In his presidential address before the Eastern Sociological Society, Professor Bierstedt points out that a criticism that may be made of contemporary sociology is that it suffers from too narrow a conception of inquiry. The scientific method, however important it may be, does not exhaust the resources of scholarship in the discipline. In the present state of sociology, a cogent thesis informed by a "theoretic bias" is frequently more enlightening than a true hypothesis, even though the latter qualifies as knowledge and the former does not.

In any event, asserts Professor Bierstedt, sociology owns a proper place not only among the sciences but also among the arts that liberate the human mind.

7. SOCIOLOGY AND HUMANE LEARNING *

ROBERT BIERSTEDT

New York University

Presidential addresses, I take it, are ritualistic in character and, whether the association in question be dedicated to the encouragement of barber-shop quartet-singing, the preservation of Manx cats, or the advancement of sociological knowledge, they correspond to other kinds of ritual that may variously appear in a society. Rituals, unlike rites, carry no connotations of secrecy and, like ceremonies in general, they emphasize the special importance of certain events, for example, the annual meeting of the Eastern Sociological Society. The annual meeting itself is a ritual whose primary purpose is to call public attention to the importance of sociology. The meeting has other functions of course: authors seek publishers, publishers seek authors, old members exchange reminiscences in the bar, new members canvass the academic market-

* Presidential address read at the annual meeting of the Eastern Sociological Society, April, 1959; in *American Sociological Review,* Vol. 25, No. 1, February, 1960, pp. 3–9.

place, and both old and new members occasionally listen to the learned communications of their colleagues.

Now rituals, of course, involve a whole cluster of norms and statuses. The ritual of the presidential address, for example, confers special privileges and immunities upon the person who occupies the status of speaker and requires special dispensations on the part of those who occupy the status of members of the audience. Among the prerogatives of status is the permission granted to the speaker to indulge in criticism and exhortation to a degree that would, in other circumstances, breach the etiquette of scientific communication. This is a norm to which I intend to conform. The audience in its turn is expected to listen with indulgence and even with patience—provided the address lasts no more than thirty minutes—to almost anything the speaker may want to say. In this respect too—I mean about the thirty minutes—I promise to conform to the norm. The audience, in addition, is not required to agree with anything in the spoken editorial, and certainly not to remember any of it.

But it is time to begin. Let us proceed to the criticisms and exhortations.

We are apt to agree, first of all, that criticism of one's own discipline is a commendable thing, exhibiting as it does a virtuous combination of modesty and sophistication. Sociologists, it has often been observed, are humble people, so humble indeed that they are sometimes accused of harboring an inferiority complex. Those of us, doubtless the majority, who express dissatisfaction from time to time about the state of our discipline may be interested to learn that a similar self-questioning can be found elsewhere in the republic of letters. We may even be astonished to read the following in an essay written by Douglas Bush, Professor of English at Harvard: "No one would ever speak of 'the plight of the natural sciences,' or of 'the plight of the social sciences,' but it is always proper to speak of 'the plight of the humanities,' and in the hushed, melancholy tone of one present at a perpetual death bed. For something like twenty-five hundred years the humanities have been in more or less of a plight." In another part of his essay Professor Bush talks, not without irony one may suppose, about the "solid and tangible virtues" of both the natural and the social sciences in contrast to the general lack of esteem accorded the humanities.

Now obviously Professor Bush does not himself believe this about the humanities. Before he finishes his article he restores them to a position of pre-eminence in the academic hierarchy and dwells at length on the importance of the cultivated mind and of those studies that are "worthy of a free man." I am very glad that he has done this, because I wish to contend in what follows, and contend quite seriously too, that whether or not sociology is or ought to be a science it owns a rightful place in the domain of humane letters and belongs, with literature, history, and philosophy, among the arts that liberate the human mind.

Several years ago, in 1948 to be exact, the late and gentle and much admired Robert Redfield addressed himself to this issue in a lecture entitled

"The Art of Social Science," delivered at the University of Chicago. In this lecture he recognized and paid tribute to those aspects of social science that are scientific in character—in the sense, mainly methodological, that the physical sciences are scientific. But he went on to suggest that the social sciences ought to be something more and that, indeed, in the highest reaches of their accomplishment they were a great deal more.

Redfield recounts the time when he was a member of a committee of social scientists commissioned first to select outstanding examples of research and then to appraise them from the point of view of the methods employed. The books nominated by the historians and sociologists as of unusual merit were, respectively, *The Great Plains,* by Walter Prescott Webb, and *The Polish Peasant,* by Thomas and Znaniecki. In the process of appraisal "a curious thing happened":

> Herbert Blumer, who analyzed *The Polish Peasant* for the committee, came to the conclusion that the method in that book was really unsuccessful because the general propositions set forth in the work could not be established by the particular facts adduced. The committee had to agree. Yet it remained with the impression that this was a very distinguished and important work. Webb's history of cultural transformation in the American West fared no better at the hands of the young historian who analyzed that work. He pointed out many undeniable failures of the author of *The Great Plains* to use and to interpret fully some of the evidence. And yet again a majority of the committee persisted in the impression that Webb's book was truly stimulating, original, and praiseworthy.
>
> Of course, one does not conclude from this experience that the failure of facts to support hypotheses, in whole or in part, is a virtue in social science or is to be recommended. No doubt these books would have been more highly praised had these defects been proved to be absent. But does not the experience suggest that there is something in social science which is good, perhaps essential, apart from success with formal method; that these works have virtues not wholly dependent on the degree of success demonstrated in performing specified and formalized operations on restricted and precisely identified data.[1]

Redfield goes on to extol the merits of three other treatises in sociology, treatises that must now be regarded as of classical significance in the history of our discipline—Veblen's *The Theory of the Leisure Class,* Sumner's *Folkways,* and Tocqueville's *Democracy in America.* All three of these works are quite innocent of the paraphernalia of formal method and yet all three managed to say something of lasting importance about man in society. Veblen used no questionnaires, Sumner no coefficients of correlation, and Tocqueville was wholly untrained in the modern techniques of field investigation. One does not imply by these examples—and this it is necessary to reiterate—that either ignorance or neglect of formal method is a virtue. One does imply that something more than method is required to achieve a genuine superiority. The reason these writers were great sociologists is that they were humanists first, and

[1] *American Journal of Sociology,* 54 (November, 1948), pp. 181–182.

if they had not been great humanists they could never have become great sociologists.

It has often been said that the social sciences share their subject matter with the humanities and their methods with the sciences. Although this is a suggestive observation, it errs perhaps in sharpening a little too much the distinction between the humanities and the social sciences. For it must be apparent that in the case of the three books mentioned it is difficult to distinguish the sociological from the humane concern. So clear is this to me that I can only wonder at our reluctance in general to acknowledge it. That reluctance does obtain is, I think, beyond dispute. Certainly we do not encourage our students or our younger colleagues to emulate these authors. We usually agree to call such writers sociologists only long after they are dead and would refuse admittance altogether into our guild of those younger men, humanistically inclined, who might want to follow in their footsteps. Imagine what would happen, for example, if one of these three men—Veblen, Sumner, or Tocqueville—were to present himself as a doctoral candidate at any of our leading departments of sociology today with a couple of sample chapters of his *chef-d'oeuvre* under his arm. He would almost certainly be advised to forget the whole thing and to turn instead—if you will forgive the language—to a study of the goal-structures and opportunity-structures of role-oriented actors.

Redfield tells us finally that each of these three books is an expression of some perception of human nature, that each brings forth significant generalizations, and that each reflects a fresh and independent viewpoint with respect to its subject-matter. These three qualities in turn are functions not of formal method but of the creative imagination of their authors. From these and many more examples of a similar kind we are driven to an unpopular inference. For it seems to be the case that we confront in sociology today the rather odd paradox that the significance of our research varies inversely with the precision of the methods employed. Or, as Redfield put it in another paper on this subject: "The emphasis on formal method sometimes carries the social scientist into exercises in which something not very important is done very well."

Now many of us may accept these consequences with equanimity on the ground that conclusions of modest proportions are the price we pay for precision, and that precision, in turn, is one of the most fundamental requirements of the scientific enterprise. For my own part I have to express what is doubtless a minority view and say that I regard this situation with regret. Is sociology to be a niggling business, doing the easy thing because it is accurate, and avoiding the difficult thing because it is imprecise? We have often been told, and by numerous hostile critics, that sociology is a mean and petty science, pursued by people who take delight in counting the privies in Pittsburgh and discovering, with the most versatile of techniques, that people with high incomes spend more money than people with low incomes. I exaggerate, of course, and it would be invidious in any event to select examples from the literature. But it is distressing to think that sociology can be associated with the solution of problems of a trivial kind and that the more precise our research becomes the more our science resembles the deaf man in Tolstoy, muttering answers to questions that no one has asked him.

As a matter of fact, the versatility and complexity of some of our new techniques may account in part for the public indifference to our discipline. Many of these techniques are so complex, and many of our concepts so opaque, that they have interest and meaning only to other sociologists and have no relevance to the society at large. Nor do they produce results that have any claim to a universal attention or a public appreciation. The situation with respect to both methods and concepts sometimes reminds me of the little old lady at the zoo who inquired of the keeper whether the animal in the cage in front of her was a male or a female hippopotamus. "Lady," he replied with dignity, "that is a question that could conceivably be of interest only to another hippopotamus."

An over-emphasis upon facts, of course, can have the same consequences as an over-emphasis upon methods. I have been inclined to wonder on occasion why it is, in contradiction of all of our rules, that those who have been most factual and utilitarian in the history of thought should be so very much less respected in the long run than those who have been theoretical and even speculative in their principal endeavors. Suppose we compare the two French sociologists Frédéric Le Play and Auguste Comte. Le Play was the careful, patient, and diligent investigator, a man who with ingenuity and persistence collected an enormously useful set of facts about the domestic budgets of workers' families in several European countries. Comte on the other hand was a man who collected no facts of any kind, indulged in outrageously speculative dreams about the possibility of a science of society, was guilty of philological bad taste in coining the word "sociology," and invented a ridiculous religion. And yet the faith of a Comte in the possibility of a science of society is more important to us today than the facts of a Le Play and of the two there is little question which has the larger significance in the history of our discipline.

If we cross the English Channel we find a similar situation in the comparison of Charles Booth and Herbert Spencer. Booth, of course, made an exhaustive statistical study of poverty in London and no fewer than seventeen volumes were required to contain his facts—facts of indubitable utility in their time and place. Spencer on the other hand was an egregiously wrong-headed billiard player and philosopher who imposed upon us all an erroneous theory of society from which it took us several decades to extricate ourselves. Now it is doubtless true, as Crane Brinton once remarked, that no one reads Spencer any more. But no one has even heard of Booth—except, of course, a few antiquarians like ourselves. Once again the philosopher was wrong and the fact-gatherer was right. But what a privilege to be so wrong!

The inference, however unfortunate, is also unmistakable. Books of speculation will be superseded and will remain for us only historical curiosities to be preserved in the museum of the mind. But books of facts succumb even more easily to the lethal challenges of time. Some theories indeed, the "false" as well as the "true," achieve an immortality, whereas the truth that facts possess does not always protect them from an early oblivion.

Our preoccupation with method has still other consequences, not yet mentioned. It frequently dominates our inquiries and determines the kinds of questions we address to society; that is, the method becomes the independent variable, the problem the dependent one. Instead of setting for ourselves tasks of large dimensions and then devising methods appropriate to their solution, we are apt to ask only those questions that are answerable in terms of methods presently available. We have even been invited to forego those larger problems of human society that occupied our ancestors in the history of social thought and to seek instead what T. H. Marshall called, in his inaugural lecture at the University of London, "stepping stones in the middle distance," and other sociologists since, "theories of the middle range." But what an anemic ambition this is! Shall we strive for half a victory? Where are the visions that enticed us into the world of learning in the first place? I had always thought that sociologists too knew how to dream and that they believed with Browning that a man's reach should exceed his grasp.

But enough of criticism. Some of my comparisons, as you no doubt recognize, may be meretricious and all perhaps are exaggerated. They may be meretricious in the sense that it is always easy to compare the brilliant and profound philosopher in sociology with the dull and mediocre statistician, the creative theorist with the unimaginative researcher. Such comparisons are as illicit as the reverse would be—the ingenious and versatile researcher *versus* the confused or unintelligible theorist. Nor do I have any intention of resurrecting the ancient methodological argument, the one that raged in the pages of our books and journals a couple of decades ago, as to whether or not sociology is or ought to be a science. Let me emphasize for the record my own conviction that sociology ought to be as scientific as it possibly can be, that it ought to conform to all the canons of scientific inquiry, and that conclusions ought to be public and publicly verifiable. When I say that sociology ought to be a science, however, I do not imply that it should be *only* a science. I think we ought to take much more seriously and literally the view that sociology can also serve as a bridge between the sciences and the humanities and that in a very important sense it belongs to the realm of humane letters.

Let me try to speak constructively now and invite your attention to the suggestion that the establishment of true propositions—the scientific task—may not be an altogether satisfactory or even desirable goal for some of our sociological endeavors. Let me illustrate what I mean. In my own opinion one of the greatest pieces of sociological research ever conducted by anyone is Max Weber's *The Protestant Ethic and the Spirit of Capitalism*. And yet none of us, I submit, has any idea whether or not Weber's thesis is "true." It has in fact been criticized, as we all know, by Brentano in Germany, Robertson in Scotland, Tawney in England, Beard in the United States, and Fanfani in Italy.

Most of the criticisms are relevant and many are penetrating. We continue, however, in spite of them, to regard Weber's sociology of religion as a distinguished contribution to sociology, one of the most distinguished in the entire literature. Its author's stature as a sociologist is not only not diminished but is positively enhanced by the critical attention his work has received. We admire this work not because it is "true"—indeed its truth escapes all of the ordinary canons of scientific verification—but because of the excellence of its conception, the erudition of its argument, and the general sociological sophistication that informs it. We admire it, in short, not for its "truth," but rather for its cogency.

Now it may be that we shall have to deny the name of knowledge—the accolade of the label, as it were—to theses of this Weberian kind, and I am perfectly prepared to acquiesce in such a decision. Of course I do not presume to know what knowledge is. My own preference as a solution to this epistemological puzzle is simply to recall the jingle Oxford students used to recite about Benjamin Jowett:

> My name is Benjamin Jowett;
> I'm the Master of Balliol College
> Whate'er can be known, I know it,
> And what I don't know is not knowledge.

However difficult an ultimate definition may be, I am sure that all of us would agree that in order to qualify as knowledge a proposition needs to be public in character, the product of shared experience, and verifiable by successive approximations. An item of knowledge then, if not absolutely true, is at least temporarily true in the sense that it has resisted repeated attempts at falsification.

In terms of these criteria, however, it is clear that Weber's observations concerning the relationship between the economic ethic of Protestantism and the development of capitalism do not qualify. The obvious fact, however, that many small researches do qualify for inclusion in the category we call knowledge whereas the massive researches of Max Weber do not must give us pause. In the present condition of our disciplines, and in the foreseeable future, we may be better advised to aim for cogency rather than for truth. It is the cogency of Weber's thesis, and not its truth, that fills us with admiration and that gives it its commanding position in the history of sociological research.

In this connection I should like to introduce another somewhat wayward notion. We have always insisted, with a proper bow to Francis Bacon, upon the elimination of bias in our inquiries and have emphasized the need for as complete an objectivity as it is humanly possible to attain. We have often suggested that in the social sciences, as contrasted with the physical sciences, objectivity is a condition to be achieved and not one initially given in our scientific situation and that this fact creates greater difficulties for the sociologist, for example, than for his colleagues in physics, chemistry, and biology, and requires perhaps a more alert responsibility. We have realistically recognized, of course, that a complete objectivity, though a methodological *desideratum,* is nevertheless for any individual a psychological impossibility and that what we should hope for is not a total absence of bias but rather an overt awareness of it. Finally, we have admitted in our wiser moments that behind every great sociologist there stands a social philosopher and that not even the scientific sociologist can ultimately escape the ethical and political consequences of his own approach to the problems of society.

All of this is to the good. And yet, I want to suggest the alternative possibility that objectivity may not be as desirable a criterion as it is commonly thought to be. For certain purposes, including the kind of sociological research I have been advocating by implication, it might be preferable to utilize what I shall call "the theoretic bias." The theoretic bias would enable us to push a particular interpretation of social phenomena just as far as it is reasonable to go in our effort to shed illumination upon it. It would candidly employ exaggeration as an heuristic device. In examining the problems of social change, for example, an objective approach is apt to be a pallid and unsuccessful one. These problems are not in fact amenable to solution with methods currently available. It would seem to be much better, therefore, to take a single factor and to push it to an extreme as a possible mode of interpretation. Thus, Marx used the theoretic bias to support the role of the economic factor, Buckle the geographic factor, Freud the psychological, Weber the ideological, Durkheim the sociological (in a special sense), and so on. Each one of these thinkers was lured into excess by his enthusiasm for his own bias and each was surely guilty of exaggeration. The greatest thinkers, however, have not been the neutral and objective ones, but those who have turned their biases to good account. And each biased conclusion, of course, is open to refinement, modification, and correction by others of a contrary kind, so that the outcome over the course of time is, if not knowledge in a narrow sense, a much more sophisticated appreciation of the problem than would otherwise be possible. I am inclined to wonder, in short, whether in our assault upon some of the larger problems of sociology biased theses may not serve us better than objective hypotheses.

I hesitate to sound even remotely Hegelian in this connection and hasten to disclaim any metaphysical implications these remarks may seem to contain. All I want to suggest is that successive rebuttal and reaffirmation may be as effective in the treatment of one kind of problem as successive approximation is in another and that in the give and take of argument and counter-argument we have much to gain. In any event, I advocate the theoretic bias on the ground that one of our most imperative needs in contemporary sociology is not more theory, in the sense in which our theory has recently developed, but more theses—that is, positions advanced, taken, defended, lost, and won again in the eternal dialectic that is the life of the mind. The result may not be knowledge, but the reward can nevertheless be great if it helps us to construct a sociology that is responsive to the intellectual challenges of our time.

I have been constrained in these sentences to emphasize that scientific method, as important and indeed as necessary as it is, does not exhaust the resources of scholarship in sociology and that, as we aspire for significance, objectivity and the pursuit of truth may have less to offer us than the theoretic bias and the search for cogency. You may of course reject the criticisms that led to this conclusion and ignore the exhortations. But I should still maintain, in brief conclusion, that sociology has an honorable place in the realm of humane letters and that it belongs with the liberal arts as well as with the sciences. We have seldom been able to escape the public belief that it is the principal business of sociology to solve social problems; and the identification of our discipline with such problems is too well known to require comment. That sociology might also have something to do with culture in the narrower and non-sociological sense of intellectual cultivation seems seldom to have occurred to anyone, including sociologists.

I invite your attention, therefore, to the fact that sociology, like the other arts, is one of the ornaments of the human mind, that its literature extending from Plato to our contemporaries is in a great and humane tradition, that sociology—like all of the liberal arts—liberates us from the provincialisms of time and place and circumstance, that the social order is a study worthy of a free man, and that society itself, like every other thing that has ever agitated the restless and inquisitive mind of man, is a fit and dignified subject of inquiry.

May I say finally that we are easily misled. "It is not the lofty sails but the unseen wind that moves the ship." It is not the methods and the concepts that move our sociology along, but memory and desire—the memory that other men in other times have also asked questions about society and the desire that our answers, in our time, will be better than theirs.

Professor Bierstedt's plea for more humane learning is only one sign of a widespread controversy that has taken shape in American sociology since the end of World War II. Largely because of the prewar influence of Sorokin and Parsons at Harvard, and the Lynds, MacIver, and Lazarsfeld at Columbia, sociologists have moved sharply away from the social philosophy and melioristic social-policy origins of their discipline toward a scientific emphasis on formal theory and precise research methods. They also have subscribed to the functional approach which encompasses the specific components of a society as parts of an interdependent whole.

This change has not occurred without dissent. Some sociologists insist that the discipline now suffers from insufficient attention to the historical approach and a lack of concern for the humanistic and significant social issues of our time. In the following review of contemporary sociology in terms of change and controversy since World War II, Lipset and Smelser, two outstanding members of the new generation of sociologists, see no irreconcilable clash here. They note that the dispute has been inevitable, representing only one instance of a more general secularization that has affected many fields of knowledge.

8. CHANGE AND CONTROVERSY IN RECENT AMERICAN SOCIOLOGY *

SEYMOUR M. LIPSET AND NEIL SMELSER
University of California, Berkeley

The period since the end of World War II has clearly witnessed basic changes in American sociology. The combination of rapid expansion of both university posts and of available research funds facilitated more diverse large-scale efforts to upgrade the intellectual quality of sociological investigation than occurred in any other comparable period of time. These efforts at innovation have led to considerable controversy about the future pattern of the field both in America and in other countries. In this connection we should like to offer a few reflections, based on American developments in the past several decades, on some of the problems that the rapid growth of an intellectual discipline creates.

In fact the growth of an intellectual tradition is not without the ironies and paradoxes that accompany all growth. The radicals and innovators in one period frequently become conservatives in the next. Indeed, the initiators of trends often come to resist the extension and consolidation of those trends which they themselves set in motion. As a result, intellectual developments are commonly plagued by those controversies, revolutions, secessions, and accusations of heresy and subversion which we associate with the dynamics of religion and politics.

The recent history of the discipline of sociology in America has displayed some of these general characteristics. From its beginnings to the present day, sociology has evolved steadily from its policy-oriented roots towards a more strictly scientific emphasis. This evolution, however, has left and is leaving in its trail a number of controversies and disputes which reflect the tensions inherent in growth. Let us sketch this course of development and comment on the related intellectual turbulence which has accompanied it.

Sociology's earliest concern with ways to handle social problems no doubt infused it with an energy that brought it rapidly to the fore as a major subject of research and study in the United States. Perhaps this policy-oriented side of the field accounts in part for its relatively faster development in America than in Europe. At any rate, in its early days sociology was clearly devoted to dealing with the causes and cures of major American problems—the pathologies associated with immigrant slums, such as family disorganization, juvenile delinquency, crime, suicide, bad housing, etc. The immigrant and the city,

* *The British Journal of Sociology*, Vol. XII, No. 1, March, 1961, pp. 41–51.

both of which were disturbing to the traditional values of small-town Protestant Anglo-Saxon America, became the preoccupation of sociology. Like the applied field of social work to which it was linked, American sociology expressed deep concern with the reintegration of the society. The backgrounds of many early sociologists revealed these concerns. Many were ministers of the gospel; others were scientists and engineers who wanted to apply "scientific methods" to the solution of social evils.

Chicago and Columbia, two of the most important departments of sociology, reflected this emphasis. Chicago, which undoubtedly had more influence than any other department until the 1930's, was best known for its extensive studies on the problems of the metropolis. This focus of Chicago sociology is reflected in the titles of many of the books which appeared in the series of monographs sponsored by the department: *The Gang, The Gold Coast and the Slum, The Ghetto, The Hobo, The Jack-Roller, The Unadjusted Girl.* Perhaps the most influential single piece of research was Thomas and Znaniecki's *The Polish Peasant in Europe and America.* Columbia, until the mid-thirties, also laid heavy emphasis on social reform. Its first professor of sociology, Franklin Giddings, who dominated Columbia sociology from the early 1890's to the late twenties, had a religious home environment (his father was a minister) and academic training in the physical sciences. His belief, derived from Spencer, that social engineering must be based on a general social science, was an important factor in his decision to enter the new discipline of sociology. For him the relationship between sociology and social engineering was unambiguous:

> Facing the facts that the physical and biological sciences have made known to us has enabled us to live more comfortably and longer than man once did. Facing the facts that the social sciences are making known to us, and will make better known, should enable us to diminish human misery and to live more wisely than the human race has lived hitherto.[1]

Correspondingly, the early course offerings at Columbia were weighted heavily in the practical direction. In addition to courses in social theory, historical sociology, and observational and statistical methods, students were required to complete work in criminology, penology, pauperism, poor laws, and the family. The graduate course in Family Organization required students to work with underprivileged families.

Gradually in the 1920's an academic field of study, apart from the concerns of social workers and social reformers, began to emerge more definitely. Though research still focused on the deviant and depressed, more refined methods of analysis began to replace the journalistic and problem-focused approach of the earlier work. Important developments began to stir on the

[1] Franklin H. Giddings, *The Scientific Study of Human Society* (Chapel Hill, N.C.: The University of North Carolina Press, 1924), pp. 37–8.

theoretical level as well. Earlier sociologists had written as if the problems of society were inherent in specific institutions. Increasingly sociologists now began to develop—both on their own and under a new European influence—what came to be known as the functional approach, which views specific institutions and problems as part of an interdependent whole.

The specific character of these changes may be seen in the area of social stratification. Many early American sociologists—for example, Giddings, Sumner, and Cooley—had dealt with larger aspects of social structure such as power and class, but these subjects were not treated as foci for research. Rather they were subjects for lectures and general discussion articles. Not until the Lynds' *Middletown* studies were these topics treated in the light of hypotheses to be tested by actual investigation. The *Middletown* studies were the first empirical researches on a large scale which employed the new functional approach. The work of the Lynds helped to demonstrate that specific social evils could not be analyzed apart from their structural context in society. Their rejection of the "specific-problem" approach in favor of the "functional" approach occurred during the actual course of the research. The Middletown project had begun as a study of the church in the small city under the sponsorship of the Institute of Social and Religious Research. The Lynds, however, came to the decision that they could study the church only through an analysis of the larger system of which it is a part. As they put it, "The stubborn resistance which 'social problems' offer may be related in part to the common habit of piecemeal attack on them. . . . The present investigation, accordingly, set out to approach the life of the people in the city selected as a unit complex of interwoven trends of behavior."

During the years that the Lynds were engaged in their pioneer research, Pitirim Sorokin, originally trained in Europe, introduced American sociologists to the myriad of detailed quantitative investigations of social mobility in Europe, and underlined, in his classic volume, *Social Mobility,* the close link between theory and research. In addition, he and Robert MacIver brought alive to many Americans the importance of systematic theory, an intellectual pursuit which had a long history in Europe but which had been ignored in the policy-oriented American approach.

The work of the Lynds and Sorokin and MacIver thus played a major role in changing the outlook of American sociology. This work set the stage for the investigation of relationships in the larger social structure. One index of this change may be seen in the concepts employed to describe the different classes of society. The early Columbia catalogues used the terms "delinquent," "depressed," and "deviant" to describe groups living in slum areas. Increasingly in the thirties and thereafter the sociologist came to define his problem as the analysis of differences in the behavior and values of the various classes. The question of who is the deviant in the total social structure waned correspondingly.

In the thirties, Talcott Parsons and Paul Lazarsfeld, two young men who were to play major roles in furthering the new trends, entered American sociology. Parsons, in his teaching at Harvard and in his famous volume, *The Structure of Social Action,* enlarged American scholars' awareness of the importance of systematic theory and of the work of several major European sociologists, particularly Emile Durkheim, Max Weber, and Vilfredo Pareto. While Parsons has been concerned from the beginning primarily with the specification of that systematic theory which goes under the name of structural-functional analysis and the theory of action, he also insisted on the necessary relationship between theory and empirical research. Thus, for instance, he elaborated the way in which Durkheim used suicide statistics to test many of his hypotheses concerning the social structure, and both translated and analyzed Max Weber's classic historical study, *The Protestant Ethic and the Spirit of Capitalism.* In the 1930's and thereafter, then, Parsons contributed not only to the development of systematic theory but also to furthering Sorokin's concern with bridging the gap between European and American theory and research.

In the late 1920's and early thirties Paul Lazarsfeld and a number of other young Austrian scholars had been engaged in extensive research in Vienna on the determinants of occupational choice, on buying decisions, on the effects of unemployment and insecurity on family interaction and political attitudes, and on problems of research methodology. To support such expensive group research Lazarsfeld initiated patterns of securing funds for sociological research from governments and business concerns to supplement the limited sums available from foundations.

Upon his arrival in America in 1932 as a Rockefeller Fellow, Lazarsfeld attempted to interest American social scientists in the self-conscious application of research methodology and in the use of quantitative techniques, particularly the survey, in their research designs. Among those impressed with the potentialities of these methods was Robert Lynd, who introduced some of these approaches into his second major work, *Middletown in Transition.* Perhaps more important, he sponsored Lazarsfeld's appointment to the Columbia graduate department. This appointment was significant not only because it brought a major European exponent of sophisticated research methods into one of the key centers of graduate training, but also because it was accompanied by the introduction of a sociological research institute (the Office of Radio Research, now known as the Bureau of Applied Social Research) as an adjunct to a university department. This model of a research institute linked to sociology has been adopted at most other major universities.

In a real sense, then, the early trends set in motion by Sorokin and Lynd have culminated in a sociology which is more consciously oriented towards the objective of building a science of society. The pace-setters in this new "scientific sociology" are identified by both admirers and opponents in the names of Parsons (as well as his students, such as Davis, Levy, Merton, and Moore, and his collaborator, Shils) and Lazarsfeld (as well as names like Guttman and Stouffer). Most important sociological works today attempt to locate their concerns in a body of developing theory. Similarly, sociology has become methodologically more self-conscious. Technical courses in theory and methods are being introduced as required areas of study in centers of graduate training. Many of the recognized younger sociologists, who will set the tone in decades to come, have received their training in the traditions which crystallized in the thirties and forties at Columbia and Harvard.

Such lines of evolution in sociology have given rise to a multi-sided polemic in the field, a polemic which has risen to something of an apex in the last few years. On the one side stand those who believe that sociology, in its theoretical and methodological aspects, should move in the direction of greater scientific adequacy, and thus take its place among the more formal social sciences (such as economics and parts of psychology) or even the physical sciences. On the other side stand a variety of critics, including, interestingly enough, Sorokin and Lynd, who were themselves instrumental in furthering the very trends which they now deplore. Joining these now retired scholars are younger men like Barrington Moore, Jr., of Harvard and C. Wright Mills of Columbia. Many sociology departments, in fact, are now divided intellectually between those who are committed to system theory and/or methodological formalization and their critics. These critics share a disaffection with what they view as excessive abstraction and over-preoccupation with esoteric methodology. From this general theme emerge several more specific issues:

(1) Basically the critics of preoccupation with scientific theory and method argue that all complex social systems must be analyzed primarily from a historical point of view. The analysis of the consequences of specific historical situations is a more important "explanation" of the "system" than is the effort to specify the interrelated functions which the system and its parts serve at any given time.

(2) On still another level, the conflict has become a controversy between the exponents of a functionalist and equilibrium concept of society and those who prefer to view society in dialectical terms as ever-changing and in a state of permanent conflict. Sociology, it is maintained, because of its preoccupation with formal theory and precise methods, has moved away from the significant social and political problems, from the analysis of social change, the nature of power, and the extent of conflict and exploitation which exists in class systems. Many important problems are ignored because they do not fit a "static" functionalist approach or because they cannot be measured precisely.

(3) A related wing of this controversy is the assertion that theoretical and methodological preoccupation leads to political sterility or political conservatism. Critics maintain that "functionalism" becomes an endorsement of the *status quo,* an empty body of study whose primary task is to deflect possible sources of intellectual criticism of society.

(While these three criticisms often come from the same source, they are not necessarily interrelated. We would classify ourselves, for instance, as functionalists concerned primarily with historical and comparative work and concerned with the political and moral implications of sociological research.)

The attempt to dichotomize the study of society into the study of the "imperatives" inherent in social systems on the one hand, and the study of historic sources of specific—often politically significant—patterns of behavior on the other, strikes us as erroneous. It is not necessary to consider the issue in either-or terms. As many methodologists of science have observed, the fact that something is socially significant at any given moment does not mean that studying it directly is the best means for social improvement. The cure for a given disease may come sooner by studying the fundamental body processes rather than the specific disease itself. The study of the laws of blood chemistry may, in fact, be more useful in the cure of mental illness than the development of *ad hoc* generalizations from the psychotherapeutic situation. In short, without a guiding body of theory and methods to enable men to relate their findings to society or its various problems, no real accumulation of valid action-relevant findings is possible.

In addition, the criticism that the efforts to formulate generalizations about systems necessarily conflicts with the analysis of historical processes also strikes us as unwarranted. Mills' and others' criticism of sociological theory for ignoring the Marxian "principle of historical specification" has recently been discussed by Lewis Feuer, a student of both scientific methodology and Marxian thought. After pointing out that Marx never used the expression, "the principle of historical specification" which Mills attributes to him, Feuer goes on to state:

> There is, to my mind, a bit of obscurantism in "the principle of historical specification" which, at the present time, obstructs the advance of social science. The principle rightly warns us to specify clearly the variables in our sociological laws; do not, for instance, enunciate as a law for all economic systems what may be true only of a competitive capitalist one. The principle has its obvious counterpart in physics. Kepler's laws, for instance, are laws for the motions of planets, not for masses in general. But Kepler's laws turned out to be special cases of the Newtonian laws which did apply to all masses. And, in a similar sense, the laws of different societies might likewise be special cases of the operation of universal psychological and sociological laws. To specify the historical structure would simply then be to state the social initial conditions which would bound the operation of the universal laws in the specific historical situation. We cannot indeed understand how one social system evolves into another without using some guiding laws of a common human nature; the revolt of men against their society's mores and values would be otherwise unintelligible. For all Marx's presumable adherence to the "principle of historical specification," he had no hesitance about making trans-historical generalizations. He set forth general laws concerning "all ruling classes," "all ideologies," "all modes of exploitation," and "all history." As for the hypothesis that the past itself is less important for American-type societies than others, that too could be formulated in some cross-societal law. We might say, for example: for

all societies composed of immigrants, the influence of the past will vary inversely with the novelty of the social circumstances.[2]

Obviously an important task of sociology is to locate generalizations which take account of the fact that all complex social systems are also historical systems. As Max Weber argued, historical explanations are crucial if we are to understand the rigidities and flexibilities built into any institution. In fact, the "functionalist" emphasis on key values in a social system is an effort to relate the operation of the system to elements rooted in its history. Within these historical "givens," furthermore, a certain body of theoretical propositions states what kind of system is operating, its relation with external systems, its internal relations, its tensions, its contradictions, and so on. Sometimes, if one utilizes a stable equilibrium model, one emphasizes the self-regulating and restorative mechanisms. For other purposes, one may use dynamic (e.g. moving or unstable) equilibrium models to posit conditions under which the system will move to a new state or disintegrate. And finally, no matter what sort of equilibrium model is posited, the propositions concerning the relationships among the parts of the system are verified, modified, or rejected in the light of research into specific historical sequences. As we see it, then, there is no necessary clash between systematic theory and a concern with social change and historical specificity. As Radcliffe-Brown summarized the issue over twenty-five years ago, when sociology was just entering its "modern era":

> One "explanation" of a social system will be its history, where we know it—the detailed account of how it came to be—what it is and where it is. Another "explanation" of the same system is obtained by showing . . . that it is a special exemplification of laws of social psychology or social functioning. *The two kinds of explanation do not conflict but supplement one another.*[3]

Why, we might ask in conclusion, have controversies like those just sketched, appeared and flourished at this particular time? A partial answer lies, we feel, in the stage of development of the discipline itself. As we have noted, sociology, in its brief history, has evolved gradually towards a concern with scientific canons and away from social philosophy and social problems. The two advance guards in this movement have been the development of systematic research *methods* and the exploration for adequate systematic *theory*. While this process of differentiation of the "scientific" aspects of sociology from its ethical and practical background has been gradual and irregular, it has been powerful and unrelenting.

In broader perspective, this process of differentiation is an instance of the

[2] Lewis Feuer, "A Symposium on C. Wright Mills' 'The Sociological Imagination,'" *Berkeley Journal of Sociology* (Berkeley: University of California, Department of Sociology, Fall 1959), Vol. V, No. I, pp. 122–3.

[3] A. R. Radcliffe-Brown, "On the Concept of Function in Social Science," *American Anthropologist,* New Series, Vol. 37 (1935), p. 401.

tendencies towards the secularization of knowledge which have characterized Western civilization for many centuries. During periods of secularization specific spheres of knowledge come to be established more nearly in accordance with an autonomous set of technical standards and a distinctive rationality. The criteria for truth become less mingled with religious, political, and practical concerns. The separation of several of the physical sciences from the religious cosmology of the sixteenth and seventeenth centuries is a classic instance of the secularization of knowledge. The recent emergence of the social sciences from their broader moral and philosophical traditions seems to be a recapitulation of this process of secularization, though the specific historical setting differs radically.

Secularization never occurs, of course, without a great deal of pain and controversy. In particular, the representatives of the older moral and intellectual traditions (*from* which the new form emerges) experience a sense of loss of importance and authority. Their assertions of right and truth are displaced by competing, secularized assertions, and their sphere of control is pared back. In this sense the rise of the scientific cosmology in post-Renaissance Europe marked a "defeat" for the religious cosmology, for religion no longer defined and controlled the physical universe unequivocally. As a result, the complaints are usually loudest from the parent tradition from which the secularized branch of knowledge arises:

> . . . for over two centuries religion has been on the defensive, and on a weak defensive. The period has been one of unprecedented intellectual progress. In this way a series of novel situations have been produced for thought. Each occasion has found the religious thinkers unprepared. Something, which has been proclaimed to be vital, has finally, after struggle, distress, and anathema, been modified and otherwise interpreted. The next generation of religious apologists then congratulates the religious world on the deeper insight which has been gained. The result of the continued repetition of this undignified retreat, during many generations, has at last almost entirely destroyed the intellectual authority of religious thinkers. Consider this contrast: when Darwin or Einstein proclaim theories which modify our ideas, it is a triumph for science. We do not go about saying that there is another defeat for science, because its old ideas have been abandoned. We know that another step of scientific insight has been gained . . . [In the sixteenth and seventeenth centuries theologians] were always attacking and defending. They pictured themselves as the garrison of a fort surrounded by hostile forces.[4]

In the recent public controversies regarding sociology a similar pattern seems to emerge. Most of the vitriol comes from the side of people who incline towards political sensitivity and broad moral concerns, who see sociology becoming less problem-oriented, less vital, less concerned, less committed, less historical, less humanistic, more sterile, and more conservative politically—and the worse for all these things. Those with moral and ideological identifica-

[4] A. N. Whitehead, *Science and the Modern World* (New York: The New American Library, 1948), pp. 187–9.

tions experience a sense of loss as sociological thought strives—with varying degrees of success—for a closer approximation to standards of scientific adequacy. Furthermore, they tend to see, with the partial truth of all such insights, "empty" theory and "barren" research methods as the twin devils leading sociology fastest from its traditional moral, political, and practical concerns. With few exceptions, however, those identified with the more scientific side of sociology have tended more to "go about their business"; they have been (at least in public) much less defensive, aggressive, and vigorous on their side of the controversy.

In the concluding article of this introductory part of the book, Reinhard Bendix, a colleague of Professors Lipset and Smelser at Berkeley, raises essentially the same issue they confronted but in broader perspectives of time and discipline. He begins with the eighteenth-century philosophies of enlightenment and proceeds to contemporary sociology and the related social sciences. Over all, he traces the replacement of the earlier faith in the power of knowledge and reason held by the precursors of the social sciences with the faith in science held by contemporary social scientists, a "neutral social science which will facilitate the manipulation of social forces and of the general population, regardless of who does the manipulating and for what purpose."

Professor Bendix calls eloquently for a revival of intellectual clarity and enlightened citizenship for as many people as possible as a primary goal of social science research and education against the growing tide of scientific empiricism, specialization, and technical proficiency for the few.

9. THE IMAGE OF MAN IN THE SOCIAL SCIENCES *

The Basic Assumptions of Present-Day Research

REINHARD BENDIX

University of California, Berkeley

A paradox rends the social sciences today. Two contradictory views of the nature of man are asserted simultaneously. On the one hand, we are told that it is possible to know and understand more and more about the nature of man and society, for man to use this increasing body of knowledge and theory to improve his condition, to reduce unhappiness and poverty, and to increase the joy and fullness of life. On the other hand, modern social science teaches us

* *Commentary,* Vol. II, No. 2, February, 1951, pp. 187–192.

to regard man as a creature of his drives, habits, and social roles, in whose behavior reason and choice play no decisive part. Accordingly, man's effort to acquire knowledge about himself and society, and to use such knowledge, are beset with insuperable obstacles; men are regarded as unable to achieve objective knowledge or to be guided by it.

Of course, social scientists do not often hold either of these positions in so bold a form. Most of them gravitate to some compromise when they have occasion to reflect on the larger implications of their disciplines. Sometimes the belief in mass education—in which the social sciences are assigned a major role—is stressed; this implies that all men are capable *in some measure* of guiding their actions by the use of their rational faculties. At present, a more popular resolution of the dilemma is the attitude that some men are rational, but most men are not; and that the few can use their knowledge for the benefit of the many.

Despite such practical compromises the paradox remains, and the questions raised still need examination. Can reason direct human behavior? Is only a small elite capable of being guided by reason? Must the great masses of men be manipulated by elites for their own good? How can we expand the role of reason in human affairs? In the absence of answers to these questions we are left uncertain as to the future of the social sciences. Do the social scientists propose to increase the role of reason in Everyman's guidance of his own destiny and human affairs generally? Or do they propose to expand the knowledge possessed by an elite as to the manipulation and control of the mass of the unreasonable? One view of man's nature would logically lead us to take the first course; the other would require us to take the second. No more important task faces the social sciences today than to determine by which "image of man" they are to be led.

Oddly enough, these two opposing views stem from one and the same source: the three-hundred-year-old effort to determine both the limits and the power of reason in the control of nature and human affairs.

During the 17th and 18th centuries men were inspired by a belief in human reason and human perfectibility. Steeped in theological traditions, they assumed that God, in establishing an orderly universe, had endowed man's intellect with the ability to comprehend it. To understand the laws of nature meant the possibility of controlling the forces of nature. And it seemed logical to infer that the same might be true for society.

This view was given classic expression by Francis Bacon. It seemed obvious to him that the knowledge accumulated by the proper use of reason would always be of value to mankind. "Human knowledge and human power meet in one; for where the cause is not known, the effect cannot be produced." Men must guard against "deliberate and factitious despair, which cuts the sinews and spur of industry . . . all for the miserable vainglory of making it believed that whatever has not yet been discovered and comprehended can never be discovered and comprehended hereafter."

Bacon applied his view of knowledge to the study of nature; the philosophers of the Enlightenment, men like Diderot, Holbach, and Helvetius, applied it to the study of society. In applying to social affairs Bacon's faith in man's ability to acquire and use knowledge, these philosophers took for granted something that has since become less certain. Not only scientists or scholars but *all* men were believed capable of using scientific knowledge for a control of nature. Hence, in developing a science of society, the philosophers of the Enlightenment turned their attention to devising ways by which all men could be educated to control the forces of society. They believed that education would dispel prejudice, replace ignorance, and permit men to act rationally in human affairs. Acting within this tradition, for example, Jefferson gave education a central role in his hopes for an American democracy.

Karl Marx challenged the Enlightenment's view on both these points: he denied that knowledge was sufficient to redirect society, and that human minds could be opened to reason simply by education. With this challenge, he became the fount of one of the mainstreams of modern social science.

Marx was, of course, not the first to question the role of knowledge in society, nor was he the first to show the distorting influence that self-interest can have on our attitude towards human affairs. Previous writers had doubted the feasibility of a rational social order, and many had shown how self-interest leads to bias and prejudice in social thought. But in Marx's view the role of ideas in society and the influence of self-interest on ideas become of overriding importance. To him the content of human history consisted in a series of class struggles, and ideas about society provided the contending classes with arsenals of symbols (ideologies) with which to fight each other. In this view, every idea was involved in this struggle and either intentionally obscured or—if analyzed as an ideology—unintentionally revealed certain aspects of society.

Marx's attitude towards human ideas and human rationality was basically skeptical. Yet Marx was not without hope. He made a heroic effort to regard man's reason as a constructive force in human history, and he believed ideas were exempt in two important ways from the distortions created by the class struggle.

First, he believed there was a way by which men could surmount their class-conditioned ideologies and be induced to submit to reason. They would do so when the social conditions (i.e. the class struggle) which had led to these ideologies were radically altered. In a classless society, in the absence of human misery and human exploitation, men would be able to see and understand society as it really was; they would have a perfect insight into the laws of social life, and in obeying these laws they would experience the ultimate freedom of controlling the forces of society deliberately.

Second, Marx believed that even before the advent of this future society, while humanity was still in the period of capitalism, there would be some men (like Marx, for example) who, having attained a "premature" scientific knowledge of their society, would not have their understanding limited by class interest: ". . . In times when the class struggle nears the decisive hour, the process of dissolution . . . within the old society assumes such a violent glaring character, that a small section of the ruling class cuts itself adrift, and joins the revolutionary class, that class that holds the future in its hands. . . . A portion of the bourgeois ideologists (in particular) have raised themselves to the level of comprehending theoretically the historical movement as a whole." (*The Communist Manifesto.*)

Marx's critique of human reason thus aimed ultimately at an enhancement of reason. While exploring the many ways in which class interest turns social thought into an apology for things as they are, he was yet confident in his own ability to see through this deception, and he believed that some "bourgeois ideologists," at first, and the masses of the working people, later, would see through it as well. With all his deep insight into the abuse of "knowledge" in society, he still believed that man could use knowledge to improve his condition.

This belief was shared by another thinker who has had an enormous influence on modern social science, Sigmund Freud. If Marx questioned the meaning of ideas apart from the material interests and actions of men, Freud questioned their meaning apart from individual strivings and emotions. The ideas and actions of an individual make sense in Freudian terms only when we see them in the context of a man's personal history. Every man seeks to increase pleasure and avoid pain; pleasure and pain are conceived as strictly organic, bodily experiences, and the most fundamental instinct around which they revolve is sex. Ideas, scientific research, artistic creations—in a word, all man's intellectual endeavors—can be analyzed as products of the psycho-sexual life history of the thinker involved. And since, by definition, these activities yield less pleasure than the direct gratification of our instinctual drives, men create culture at the price of sexual renunciation and sexual frustration.

This appears an even more skeptical view of the value of man's intellectual efforts, yet Freud by no means called for the abandonment of substitute gratifications (or sublimation). Rather, he hoped that man would be made happier in his renunciation of instinctual pleasure by a further expansion of reason; where the renunciation had been unconscious and led to torment, it was now to be made in the full light of intelligence and rendered harmless or at least manageable. In hoping for the psychological improvement of the individual, Freud assigned to human reason an important role. When a patient is accepted for treatment in psychoanalytic therapy, he is warned that analysis is arduous in terms of time and expense and that the emotional demands to be made upon him will be severe. But once the patient is accepted, then the success of his treatment depends upon his ability to utilize his rational insight into the origin of his present emotional difficulties. Thus psychoanalysis does take its stand on the side of human improvement through reason, however heavy may be its emphasis on the power of organic drives and on the relative weakness of human intelligence. Under favorable circumstances man is judged to be capable of assessing his personal history, and of reshaping his personal life on the basis of that assessment. To be sure, psychoanalytic therapy is by no means a purely rational process on the part of the patient; but the end product is a rational being.

Marx and Freud contributed to the destruction of the 18th-century belief in human reason and perfectibility. Yet, as we have said, they do not argue that reasoning was altogether futile or that improvement was unattainable. Knowledge or reason, they agreed, are greatly hampered by human interests and personal emotions; to the extent that they demonstrated this, "knowledge" is often less "objective" than men believed. Marx and Freud did not fully share the Baconian and Enlightenment belief that "human knowledge and power meet in one." Yet, despite this insight, they were confident that some men could attain an objective knowledge of man and history and that the scientific knowledge of the few would in the long run benefit the many. Their qualified optimism effected a compromise that combined a faith in the intelligence of the many with the conviction that, under present circumstances, there are only a few who are able to free human understanding of the distortion which results from its involvement with group interests and individual emotion.

Social scientists by and large have since, so it seems, departed from this compromise view. They are indebted to Marx and Freud for deep insights into the conditioned nature of man's quest for knowledge. But they have also gone beyond them by discarding the belief that all men have a common capacity for reason and rational action, either now or in the future.

Marx's view that ideas are embedded in self-interest and social action, taken out of the context of his philosophy of history, has come to mean that any idea must be misleading, any statement must be false, when its speaker or writer represents an interest group. And in assuming that the ideas of a man have no meaning apart from his actions and interests, these contemporary interpretations of Marx show little concern with the "abstract" meaning of the ideas a person expresses. They are concerned instead with learning who his friends are and how his ideas undermine the position of his enemies. This might be called the "pigeonhole theory of truth." The content of a statement is examined in terms of whether its source commends or condemns it.

And for every idea discredited by identification with an interest group, there is another that is not taken seriously because it is "emotionally biased." This might be called the "poker-face theory of truth." To find the "true" meaning of an idea, we need to ask, not "What did he say?" but "Why did he say it?" Thus only a man who can keep a straight face while telling an outrageous lie has a chance of escaping this inquisition into his motives. For the motives of a man become immediately suspect when he reveals that his emotions are deeply involved with the ideas he expresses.

But once we judge what a man says according to who his friends are, we need think of him no longer as a person but only as a member of his group. And if a person is judged in terms of his suspected motives, what he says is no longer important, and "verbalization" becomes "only" the surface manifestation of his subconscious. Reason, and efforts at reason, are thereby depreciated.

These vulgarizations have had a profound impact on the contemporary image of man, and particularly on the image of man in the social sciences. To go from Marx and Freud to the positions held in the social sciences today takes only a short step: it involves simply the abandonment of the residual hope for the governance of men by their rational faculties which Marx and Freud permitted themselves.

Yet is it not also true that the belief in science is stronger today than ever before? Would so many research projects be undertaken if those who initiated them did not believe that the findings produced would result in greater human happiness? And, indeed, most social scientists today believe that they are the true heirs of the 18th century, and are still loyal to its belief in reason and human perfectibility.

But I think that they have deceived themselves. I believe that a *faith in science* has superseded the earlier *faith in reason.*

What is the content of this faith in science, and how does it differ from the earlier faith in reason? Modern social scientists believe that economic interests and traditional beliefs, emotions and cultural conditions, distort our understanding. They no longer believe that men can rid their minds of these impediments to lucid thought: *only scientists can.* Social scientists have become persuaded of the ingrained irrationality of the many, and their own work repeatedly demonstrates to them how difficult it is—even for the expert—to attain objectivity. Their more intensive knowledge of the fallibility of human reason, which is itself an outgrowth of modern social science, leads many social scientists to accept as inevitable an unbridgeable gulf between themselves and the public at large. They assert that there is only one escape from the consequences of irrationality: that is by the application of scientific method. And this method can be used effectively only by the expert few. Research has revealed the many obstacles to understanding among the mass of men. Hence social scientists are less concerned today with improving the understanding of the mass of men, and they are more intent on insuring the objectivity of their own practices. This they do by the use of specific techniques: pre-testing of questionnaires, random sampling, calculation of standard errors, and so on.

The danger of this position is that the social scientists, in their concern to be objective or scientific, run the risk of losing perspective with regard to the ends of their knowledge. That danger is present, in one form, wherever social scientists shy away from a discussion of questions (such as those concerning the purpose of social science) to which the answers must remain tentative and unverified. If the only way to achieve understanding is marked out by the scientific method, and if that method is only accessible to the expert few, then the belief in the intelligence of all men is in effect abandoned. Instead of attempting to make people more rational, contemporary social scientists often content themselves with asking of them that they place their trust in social science and accept its findings. If people do this they will presumably put themselves on safe and sure ground and become free from bias, even though they cannot share in the inquiry that leads to knowledge, and will therefore remain ignorant of the premises and facts upon which it is based.

Inevitably, the methods of research in the social sciences are difficult to handle and equally difficult to explain in short order, and this was bound to alienate the social scientist from the public to some extent: so in speaking of the effects of the social scientist's faith in science, we do not refer to his need to use technical tools. However, the social scientists also draw, from their faith in science, the conclusion that the social scientists must serve as instruments of the civil (or other) authorities, whoever they may be. This startling conclusion—expressed clearly in Alexander Leighton's *Human Relations in a Changing World* (Dutton, 1949)—is, as we may see in Leighton's book and elsewhere, the clear result of the belief that the social sciences *as sciences* must play the leading role in solving our social problems. For if we believe they must play this role as science, that is, as tools, rather than as means whereby men in general may be made more rational, as earlier social scientists believed, then we can only conclude that the contemporary social scientist should confine himself to a study of the facts pertinent to an implementation of policies, and not make suggestions of policies themselves; this is his duty as a value-free scientist, and it harms his science to do more. But further, to gain the material support necessary to expand social science as *science*—and this expansion, to the mind of the social scientist, also means an inevitable improvement in the condition of mankind—the social scientist must gain the support of the man of affairs. And how can he do this but by convincing the man of affairs that his work holds out promise of greater success in the conscious manipulation of social forces and of the "mass mind"?

Thus, beginning with the age-old belief in the liberating power of knowledge and reason, social scientists end up by becoming protagonists of a neutral social science which will facilitate the manipulation of social forces and of the general population, regardless of who does the manipulating and for what purpose. In their eagerness to make the social sciences more scientific, social scientists persuade others and themselves that human advancement is identical with the advancement of scientific knowledge—with *their* scientific knowledge.

As a result, social scientists have often become less concerned with the use to which their knowledge is put than with the question whether that use is compatible with the further development of social science. They emphasize that everything must be done to persuade policy makers that they should use the social sciences, and the problems to be investigated are often selected so as to demonstrate the usefulness or the scientific rigor of the social sciences to the political leader or administrator.

The most striking development in this respect is the increased role of the foundations and the diminished importance of university scholars. The external reason for this shift is, of course, financial, but the question is pertinent whether the allocation of large sums by foundation executives will not undermine the independent judgment of the individual social scientist with regard to what *he* regards as significant. Instances are known in which large funds have been allocated to a university department, not because the department but because the foundation wanted to emphasize a certain field of research. Individual social scientists have been more or less permanently diverted from their original research interests, simply because they did not resist the temptation of funds which were available for other projects.

Some thirty years ago Max Weber addressed this question of the meaning of science in his lecture, "Science as a Vocation." Weber stated that social science could serve three ends. It may enable us to control the forces of society, it provides training for future social scientists, and it makes for intellectual clarity.

It is a measure of how rapidly the 18th-century creed has disappeared in recent years that only the first and second of these ends still appear valid. A generation ago Weber had regarded "intellectual clarity" as one of the most important goals of social science. By receiving training in them the individual citizen would learn to judge alternative courses of action in the light of knowledge of their conditions and consequences. Weber believed that this was a worthy goal of the social sciences, even if they were often found to have no other apparent social utility. Yet, the majority of introductory courses in the different social sciences shows little evidence that intellectual clarity is still the goal today. Instead, these courses give the impression that they are designed for future specialists, not for the individual who seeks clarity on social and political issues. As an impartial examination of introductory textbooks will confirm, students are treated as budding experts, which in many instances will make them poorer citizens. Robert K. Merton, in his introduction to a recent text (*Sociological Analysis,* by Logan Wilson and William Kolb, Harcourt, Brace; 1949), points out that in recent years there has been a shift from an emphasis on a general, semi-philosophical "humanities" approach in sociology textbooks, to an emphasis on techniques and empirical studies. He does not, however, point up the educational implications of these changes.

The serious question which we all confront is thereby posed: must we pay for the greater technical resources and the refined research methods of modern social science with the unconscious and uncritical subordination of intellectual endeavor to the dominant social and political forces of our time? Must we renounce reason for all to gain science for the few and the elites? Must we give up our faith that all men can become reasonable and instead hope that some men—the powerful—will learn to make use of the technical tools of science?

Each person who is concerned with this question will answer it in his own way. As I see it, a major desideratum is that each social scientist should be personally conscious of the link between his research and the social and political and moral forces of his society. Such consciousness can only enhance the intellectual integrity of his work. It should enter into his selection of research problems, wherever possible. This is usually interpreted as the need to make one's values explicit as they are involved in the specific problems under discussion. We should, however, recognize that it is less our opinions on day-to-day problems and more our major underlying assumptions that call for explicit acknowledgment: our beliefs concerning the relation of knowledge and human power, the role of science in society, the position of the intellectual in the community—these are among the problems which we must clarify for ourselves.

There is nothing necessarily degrading in such work as opinion analyses for an advertising company, or anthropological field work for a colonial office, or analyses of price trends for a government agency, and when this work is useful we may properly be pleased—if nothing else is involved. But social scientists are placed in a dubious light when they claim that their work for hire is the ultimate goal of all social science research, and when they plead in extenuation for some of their "pure" work that what is not useful now may or will be useful tomorrow or the day after. It would be far more *useful* in the long run—from the point of view both of science and of humanity—to take one's stand on the ground that our human life is enriched by worthwhile research in the social sciences, that such research is a token of high civilization, worth preserving as an integral part of our quest for knowledge, and that this quest manifests our abiding faith in the constructive and enriching possibilities of human reason. I do not claim that this is an "objective" statement. It is rather a declaration of personal belief that in a world torn by wars of nerves, arms, and words, the universities are institutions of detachment whose academic personnel have an important service to render in the community, one for which they may properly claim recognition from the powers that be. Social scientists, to reiterate, should place their abiding faith in reason rather than an exclusive concern with improving the techniques of social manipulations. This is the only position worthy of the great intellectual traditions of which they are the heirs. It is also the only position consistent with the intellectual defense against the threat of totalitarianism, from without and within.

SELECTED SUPPLEMENTARY READINGS FOR PART I

Berger, Bennett M., "Sociology and the Intellectuals: An Analysis of a Stereotype," *Antioch Review,* Vol. 17, 1957, pp. 275–290.

Berger, Peter L., *Invitation to Sociology: A Humanistic Perspective* (Garden City, N.Y.: Anchor Books, Doubleday & Co., 1963).

Bierstedt, Robert, "Toynbee and Sociology," *The British Journal of Sociology,* Vol. X, No. 2, June, 1959, pp. 95–104.

Bowman, Claude C., "Must the Social Sciences Foster Moral Skepticism?" *American Sociological Review,* Vol. 10, No. 6, December, 1945, pp. 709–715.

Davie, Maurice R. (ed.), *William Graham Sumner: An Essay of Commentary and Selections* (New York, Thomas Y. Crowell Co., 1963).

Gerver, Israel (ed.), *Lester Frank Ward: Selections from His Work* (New York: Thomas Y. Crowell Co., 1963).

Gurvitch, Georges, and Moore, Wilbert E., *Twentieth Century Sociology* (New York: Philosophical Library, 1945).

Hinkle, Roscoe C., Jr., and Hinkle, Gisela J., *The Development of Sociology* (Garden City, N.Y.: Doubleday & Co., 1954).

Hopper, Janice Harris, "To Be a Sociologist," in H. Laurence Ross (ed.), *Perspectives on the Social Order* (New York: McGraw-Hill Book Co., 1963), pp. 452–465.

Lipset, Seymour M., and Smelser, Neil (eds.), *Sociology: The Progress of a Decade* (Englewood Cliffs, N.J.: Prentice-Hall, 1961).

Merton, Robert K., Broom, Leonard, and Cottrell, Leonard S., Jr. (eds.), *Sociology Today* (New York: Basic Books, 1959).

Miller, S. M. (ed.), *Max Weber: Selections from His Work* (New York: Thomas Y. Crowell Co., 1963).

Parsons, Talcott, "Some Problems Confronting Sociology as a Profession," *American Sociological Review*, Vol. 24, No. 4, August, 1959, pp. 547–559.

Rosenberg, Bernard (ed.), *Thorstein Veblen: Selections from His Work* (New York: Thomas Y. Crowell Co., 1963).

Shils, Edward, *The Present State of American Sociology* (Chicago: The Free Press, 1948).

Simpson, George, *Emile Durkheim: Selections from His Work* (New York: Thomas Y. Crowell Co., 1963).

PART TWO

Basic Sociological Concepts

INTRODUCTION

A scientific discipline inevitably issues its own set of concepts, a special and technical nomenclature whose purpose is to identify and describe categorically the phenomena under its jurisdiction. Concepts are verbal images formed by abstractions of, and generalizations about, the particulars of the phenomena under observation and analysis. They enable us to grasp symbolically the constant, repetitive facts we perceive.

Just as students of the so-called natural sciences, such as chemistry, physics, and biology, are expected to master certain basic concepts like element and compound, atom and molecule, cell and tissue, so students of the social sciences must comprehend the most useful concepts that have been devised in their disciplines. In economics, for example, the basic concepts include supply and demand, price and wage, capital and labor.

The purpose of this section is to introduce the student to the basic concepts of sociology. These are:

1. Culture
2. Social organization
3. Symbolic communication
4. Socialization
5. Population
6. Social institutions

The following scheme provides the student not only with a point of departure for the analysis of the meaning of each concept, but also with a comprehensive view of the concepts in relationship to each other.

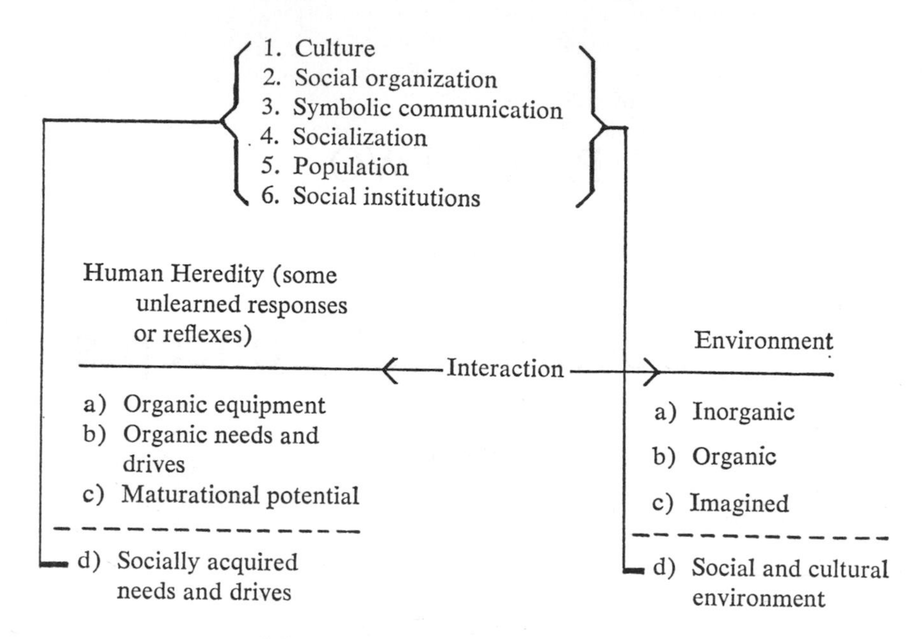

Scheme of Basic Sociological Concepts

Let us begin with the horizontal extremes of this scheme. When systematic sociology began in the nineteenth century, the hereditary make-up of the human animal on the one hand and the raw environment which he faced on the other were considered to be legitimate sociological concepts. That is. the biological and geographical determinism characteristic of nineteenth-century thought led many of the early sociologists to view society as a product molded by the organic-hereditary forces within him or the inorganic and organic resources in the environment that surrounded him. The overwhelming majority of today's sociologists reject both kinds of determinism. Instead, they conceive of heredity and environment as essentially extra-sociological, providing potentials or raw materials and setting limits to the shape of social life. Heredity and environment dictate what may be, what cannot be, but not what must be the case in society.

Consider the earliest species of man, a human animal endowed with organic equipment (prehensile, biped, and the like), motivated by organic needs and drives (such as hunger, thirst, the need for a moderate body temperature), and equipped with a maturational potential (growth in height, weight, and the like). We can safely assume that in order to survive he interacted with the inorganic, organic, and imagined environments in which he found himself. Some of his organic needs and drives were satisfied by a few unlearned responses or reflexes such as swallowing, withdrawal, blinking, and elimination of body waste. But these were insufficient for man. In order to survive, he and other early members of the species had to learn, acquire, and accumulate ways of interacting with their environment.

Culture is what man learns from some other men and in turn transmits to others, the socially acquired and communicated functions of thinking, feeling, and acting. Peculiar to man alone, cultural behavior is man-made, and in turn it makes man what he is. Unlike animal behavior, culture accumulates and changes, but always in a structural or organized context.

Social organization—that is, group patterns formed by two or more interacting humans for the purpose of facilitating the achievement of at least one common purpose—provides the structure within which cultural patterns take shape. A social organization ranges from an association or single-purpose group at one extreme, to society, an inclusive, multipurpose social structure which minimally engages in maintenance and the perpetuation of its members at the other extreme.

Aside from man's unusual intelligence, habit-forming capacity, and tool-making ability, what enabled man to learn, acquire, and accumulate solutions to his problems of survival was his unique skill, *symbolic communication.* Of all animals, man alone is able to form true language, to communicate through symbols and abstractions, thereby enabling the transmission, continuity, and accumulation of what he has learned in satisfying his needs and drives.

The individual human undergoes *socialization,* acquiring a personality by incorporating the culture and finding his place in the social organization. In the process of being socialized, he proceeds in development "from baby to Babbitt," acquiring social positions within each of the groups to which he belongs, and playing roles appropriate to his statuses. Whereas status and role are the overt aspects of socialization, the social self is the subjective aspect. It is the image each human socially acquires or learns about himself.

Affecting communication, socialization, social organization, and the patterning of culture and institutions—and, in turn, influenced by these same social processes—are the underlying vital processes of *population* growth, composition, distribution, and mobility.

Social institutions are those complex and relatively permanent clusters of both structure and function involving specific statuses and roles, and revolving around basic human needs and drives. The major social institutions are marriage and the family, the economy, religion, government, and education.

Finally, returning to the horizontal extremes of the scheme of basic sociological concepts above, we note that in the course of the life cycle, people socially acquire needs and drives to supplement their unlearned, organic motivation. And long before the twentieth century, man's environment was no longer exclusively "raw"; much of it had become man-made, that is, a social and cultural environment.

These basic sociological concepts are taken up in the readings of this section with the exception of social institutions. The latter are sufficiently complex and heterogeneous to warrant separate treatment in Part III.

CULTURE

Of all the concepts in the repertoire of modern sociology and the related general social sciences, notably cultural anthropology, none is more basic and useful than the concept of culture. Sociologists employ it to refer to the way of life shared by members of a specified western and literate society, whereas cultural anthropologists typically use it with reference to the pattern of life characteristic of a nonliterate society or tribe. One of the earliest and probably the most famous of the many definitions of culture was that proposed by the anthropologist E. B. Tylor in 1871: "Culture is that complex whole which includes knowledge, belief, art, morals, law, custom, and any other capabilities and habits acquired by man as a member of society."

In the article that follows, Leslie A. White critically reviews current conceptions of culture in anthropological literature and deplores the extent to which they have gone astray from Tylor's definition. He calls for a return to the tradition established by Tylor in order that cultural anthropology and sociology may properly distinguish between their domains and that of human psychology.

10. THE CONCEPT OF CULTURE *

LESLIE A. WHITE
University of Michigan

Virtually all cultural anthropologists take it for granted, no doubt, that *culture* is the basic and central concept of their science. There is, however, a disturbing lack of agreement as to what they mean by this term. To some, culture is learned behavior. To others, it is not behavior at all, but an abstraction from behavior—whatever that is. Stone axes and pottery bowls are culture to some anthropologists, but no material object can be culture to others. Culture exists only in the mind, according to some; it consists of observable things and events in the external world to others. Some anthropologists think of culture as consisting of ideas, but they are divided upon the question of their locus: some say they are in the minds of the peoples studied, others hold that they are in the minds of ethnologists. We go on to "culture is a psychic defense mechanism," "culture consists of *n* different social signals correlated with *m* different responses," "culture is a Rorschach of a society," and so on, to confusion and bewilderment. One wonders what physics would be like if it had as many and as varied conceptions of energy!

There was a time, however, when there was a high degree of uniformity of comprehension and use of the term culture. During the closing decades of the nineteenth century and the early years of the twentieth, the great majority of cultural anthropologists, we believe, held to the conception expressed by E. B. Tylor, in 1871, in the opening lines of *Primitive Culture:* "Culture . . . is that complex whole which includes knowledge, belief, art, morals, law, custom, and any other capabilities and habits acquired by man as a member of society." Tylor does not make it explicit in this statement that culture is the peculiar possession of man; but it is therein implied, and in other places he makes this point clear and explicit. Culture, to Tylor, was the name of all things and events peculiar to the human species. Specifically, he enumerates

* *American Anthropologist,* Vol. 61, 1959, pp. 227–251.

beliefs, customs, objects—"hatchet, adze, chisel," and so on—and techniques —"wood-chopping, fishing . . . , shooting and spearing game, fire-making," and so on.

The Tylorian conception of culture prevailed in anthropology generally for decades. In 1920, Robert H. Lowie began *Primitive Society* by quoting "Tylor's famous definition." In recent years, however, conceptions and definitions of culture have multiplied and varied to a great degree. One of the most highly favored of these is that *culture is an abstraction*. This is the conclusion reached by A. L. Kroeber and Clyde Kluckhohn in their exhaustive review of the subject: *Culture: a Critical Review of Concepts and History*. It is the definition given by Ralph L. Beals and Harry Hoijer in their textbook, *An Introduction to Anthropology*. In a more recent work, however, *Cultural Anthropology*, Felix M. Keesing defined culture as "the totality of learned, socially transmitted behavior."

Much of the discussion of the concept of culture in recent years has been concerned with a distinction between culture and human behavior. For a long time many anthropologists were quite content to define culture as behavior, peculiar to the human species, acquired by learning, and transmitted from one individual, group, or generation to another by mechanisms of social inheritance. But eventually some began to object to this and to make the point that culture is not itself behavior, but is an abstraction from behavior. Culture, say Kroeber and Kluckhohn, "is an abstraction from concrete human behavior, but it is not itself behavior." Beals and Hoijer and others take the same view.

Those who define culture as an abstraction do not tell us what they mean by this term. They appear to take it for granted (1) that they themselves know what they mean by "abstraction," and (2) that others, also, will understand. We believe that neither of these suppositions is well founded; we shall return to a consideration of this concept later in this essay. But whatever an abstraction in general may be to these anthropologists, when culture becomes an "abstraction" it becomes imperceptible, imponderable, and not wholly real. According to Ralph Linton, "culture itself is intangible and cannot be directly apprehended even by the individuals who participate in it." Melville J. Herskovits also calls culture "intangible." Anthropologists in the imaginary symposium reported by Kluckhohn and W. H. Kelly argue that "one can see" such things as individuals and their actions and interactions, but "has anyone ever seen 'culture'?" Beals and Hoijer say that "the anthropologist cannot observe culture directly; . . ."

If culture as an abstraction is intangible, imperceptible, does it exist, is it real? Ralph Linton raises this question in all seriousness: "If it [culture] can be said to exist at all. . . ." A. R. Radcliffe-Brown declares that the word culture "denotes, not any concrete reality, but an abstraction, and as it is commonly used a vague abstraction." And Melford E. Spiro says that according to the predominant "position of contemporary anthropology . . . culture has no ontological reality. . . ."

Thus when culture becomes an abstraction it not only becomes invisible and imponderable; it virtually ceases to exist. It would be difficult to construct a less adequate conception of culture. Why, then, have prominent and influential anthropologists turned to the "abstraction" conception of culture?

A clue to the reason—if, indeed, it is not an implicit statement of the reason itself—is given by Kroeber and Kluckhohn:

> Since behavior is the first-hand and outright material of the science of psychology, and culture is not—being of concern only secondarily, as an influence on this material—it is natural that psychologists and psychologizing sociologists should see behavior as primary in their field, and then extend this view farther to apply to the field of culture also.[1]

The reasoning is simple and direct: if culture is behavior, then (1) culture becomes the subject matter of psychology, since behavior is the proper subject matter of psychology; culture would then become the property of psychologists and "psychologizing sociologists"; and (2) nonbiological anthropology would be left without a subject matter. The danger was real and imminent; the situation, critical. What was to be done?

The solution proposed by Kroeber and Kluckhohn was neat and simple: let the psychologists have behavior; anthropologists will keep for themselves abstractions from behavior. These abstractions become and constitute *culture*.

But in this rendering unto Caesar, anthropologists have given the psychologists the better part of the bargain, for they have surrendered unto them real things and events, locatable and observable, directly or indirectly, in the real external world, in terrestrial time and space, and have kept for themselves only intangible, imponderable abstractions that "have no ontological reality." But at least, and at last, they have a subject matter—however insubstantial and unobservable—of their own!

Whether or not this has been the principal reason for defining culture as "not behavior, but abstractions from behavior," is perhaps a question; we feel, however, that Kroeber and Kluckhohn have made themselves fairly clear. But whatever the reason, or reasons—for there may have been several—may have been for the distinction, the question whether culture is to be regarded as behavior or as abstractions from it is, we believe, the central issue in recent attempts to hammer out an adequate, usable, fruitful, and enduring conception of culture.

The present writer is no more inclined to surrender culture to the psychologists than are Kroeber and Kluckhohn; indeed, few anthropologists have taken greater pains to distinguish psychological problems from culturological problems than he has. But he does not wish to exchange the hard substance of culture for its wraith, either. No science can have a subject matter that

[1] A. L. Kroeber and Clyde Kluckhohn, *Culture: A Critical Review of Concepts and Definitions.* Papers of the Peabody Museum of American Archaeology and Ethnology, Harvard University, 47(1), 1952:155.

consists of intangible, invisible, imponderable, ontologically unreal "abstractions"; a science must have real stars, real mammals, foxes, crystals, cells, phonemes, gamma rays, and culture traits to work with. We believe that we can offer an analysis of the situation that will distinguish between psychology, the scientific study of behavior on the one hand, and culturology, the scientific study of culture, on the other, and at the same time give a real, substantial subject matter to each.

Science makes a dichotomy between the mind of the observer and the external world—things and events having their locus outside the mind of this observer. The scientist makes contact with the external world with and through his senses, forming percepts. These percepts are translated into concepts which are manipulated in a process called thinking in such a way as to form premises, propositions, generalizations, conclusions, and so on. The validity of these premises, propositions, and conclusions is established by testing them in terms of experience of the external world. This is the way science proceeds and does its work.

The first step in scientific procedure is to observe, or more generally to experience, the external world in a sensory manner. The next step—after percepts have been translated into concepts—is the classification of things and events perceived or experienced. Things and events of the external world are thus divided into classes of various kinds: acids, metals, stones, liquids, mammals, stars, atoms, corpuscles, and so on. Now it turns out that there is a class of phenomena, one of enormous importance in the study of man, for which science has as yet no name: this is the class of things and events consisting of or dependent upon symboling. It is one of the most remarkable facts in the recent history of science that this important class has no name, but the fact remains that it does not. And the reason why it does not is because these things and events have always been considered and designated, not merely and simply as the things and events that they are, in and of themselves, but always as things and events in a particular context.

A thing is what it is; "a rose is a rose is a rose." Acts are not first of all ethical acts or economic acts or erotic acts. An act is an act. An act becomes an ethical datum or an economic datum or an erotic datum when—and only when—it is considered in an ethical, economic, or erotic context. Is a Chinese porcelain vase a scientific specimen, an object of art, an article of commerce, or an exhibit in a lawsuit? The answer is obvious. Actually, of course, to call it a "Chinese porcelain vase" is already to put it into a particular context; it would be better first of all to say "a glazed form of fired clay is a glazed form of fired clay." As a Chinese porcelain vase, it becomes an object of art, a scientific specimen, or an article of merchandise when, and only when, it is considered in an esthetic, scientific, or commercial context.

Let us return now to the class of things and events that consist of or are dependent upon symboling: a spoken word, a stone axe, a fetich, avoiding one's mother-in-law, loathing milk, saying a prayer, sprinkling holy water, a pottery bowl, casting a vote, remembering the sabbath to keep it holy—"and any other capabilities and habits [and things] acquired by man as a member of [human] society." They are what they are: things and acts dependent upon symboling.

We may consider these things-and-events-dependent-upon-symboling in a number of contexts: astronomical, physical, chemical, anatomical, physiological, psychological, and culturological, and, consequently, they become astronomic, physical, chemical, anatomical, physiological, psychological, and culturological phenomena in turn. All things and events dependent upon symboling are dependent also upon solar energy which sustains all life on this planet; this is the astronomic context. These things and events may be considered and interpreted in terms of the anatomical, neurological, and physiological processes of the human beings who exhibit them. They may be considered and interpreted also in terms of their relationship to human organisms, i.e., in a somatic context. And they may be considered in an extrasomatic context, i.e., in terms of their relationship to other like things and events rather than in relationship to human organisms.

When things and events dependent upon symboling are considered and interpreted in terms of their relationship to human organisms, i.e., in a somatic context, they may properly be called *human behavior,* and the science, *psychology*. When things and events dependent upon symboling are considered and interpreted in an extrasomatic context, i.e., in terms of their relationships to one another rather than to human organisms, we may call them *culture,* and the science, *culturology*. This analysis is expressed diagrammatically in Fig. 1.

In the middle of the diagram we have a vertical column of circles, O_1, O_2, O_3, etc., which stand for things (objects) and events (acts) dependent upon symboling. These things and events constitute a distinct class of phenomena in the realm of nature. Since they have had heretofore no name we have ventured to give them one: *symbolates*. We fully appreciate the hazards of coining terms, but this all-important class of phenomena needs a name to distinguish it from other classes. If we were physicists we might call them "Gamma phenomena." But we are not physicists, and we believe a simple word would be better—or at least more acceptable—than a Greek letter. In coining our term we have followed a well-established precedent: if an *isolate* is something that results from the process or action of isolating, then something that results from the action or process of symboling might well be called a symbolate. The particular word with which we designate this class of phenomena is not of paramount importance, and perhaps a better term than symbolate can be found. But it is of paramount importance that this class have a name.

A thing or event dependent upon symboling—a symbolate—is just what it is, but it may become significant in any one of a number of contexts. As we have already seen, it may be significant in an astronomic context: the per-

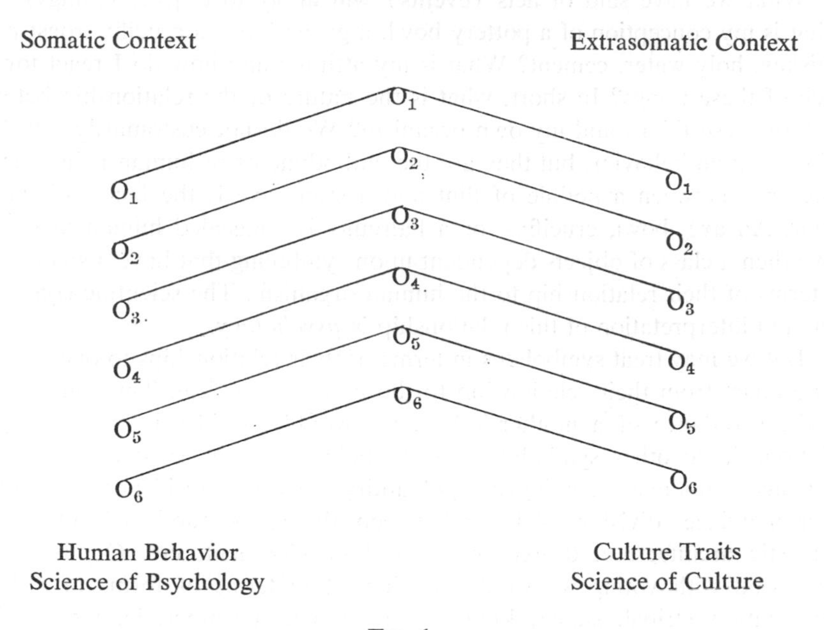

FIG. 1

formance of a ritual requires the expenditure of energy which has come from the sun. But within the sciences of man we may distinguish two significant contexts: the somatic and the extrasomatic. Symbolates may be considered and interpreted in terms of their relationship to the human organism, or they may be considered in terms of their relationships to one another, quite apart from their relationship to the human organism. Let us illustrate with some examples.

I smoke a cigarette, cast a vote, decorate a pottery bowl, avoid my mother-in-law, say a prayer, or chip an arrowhead. Each one of these acts is dependent upon the process of symboling; each therefore is a symbolate. As a scientist, I may consider these acts (events) in terms of their relationships to me, to my organism; or, I may treat them in terms of their relationships to one another, to other symbolates, quite apart from their relationship to my organism.

In the first type of interpretation I consider the symbolate in terms of its relationship to my bodily structure: the structure and functions of my hand, for example; or to my stereoscopic, chromatic vision; or to my needs, desires, hopes, fears, imagination, habit formation, overt reactions, satisfactions, and so forth. How do I feel when I avoid my mother-in-law or cast a ballot? What is my attitude toward the act? What is my conception of it? Is the act accompanied by heightened emotional tone, or do I perform it in a mechanical, perfunctory manner? And so on. We may call these acts *human behavior;* our concern is *psychological.*

What we have said of acts (events) will apply to objects (things) also. What is my conception of a pottery bowl, a ground axe, a crucifix, roast pork, whiskey, holy water, cement? What is my attitude and how do I react toward each of these things? In short, what is the nature of the relationship between each of these things and my own organism? We do not customarily call these things human behavior, but they are the embodiments of human behavior; the difference between a nodule of flint and a stone axe is the factor of human labor. An axe, bowl, crucifix—or a haircut—is congealed human labor. We have then a class of objects dependent upon symboling that have a significance in terms of their relationship to the human organism. The scientific consideration and interpretation of this relationship is *psychology.*

But we may treat symbolates in terms of their relationships to one another, quite apart from their relationship to the human organism. Thus, in the case of the avoidance of a mother-in-law, we would consider it in terms of its relationship to other symbolates, or symbolate clusters, such as customs of marriage—monogamy, polygyny, polyandry—place of residence of a couple after marriage, division of labor between the sexes, mode of subsistence, domestic architecture, degree of cultural development, etc. Or, if we are concerned with voting we would consider it in terms of forms of political organization (tribal, state), kind of government (democratic, monarchical, fascist); age, sex, or property qualifications; political parties and so on. In this context our symbolates become *culture*—culture traits or trait clusters, i.e., institutions, customs, codes, etc., and the scientific concern is *culturology.*

It would be the same with objects as with acts. If we were concerned with a hoe we would regard it in terms of its relationships to other symbolates in an extrasomatic context: to other instruments employed in subsistence, the digging stick and plow in particular; or to customs of division of labor between the sexes; the stage of cultural development, etc. We would be concerned with the relationship between a digital computer and the degree of development of mathematics, the stage of technological development, division of labor, the social organization within which it is used (corporation, military organization, astronomical laboratory), and so on.

Thus we see that we have two quite different kinds of sciencing with regard to things and events—objects and acts—dependent upon symboling. If we treat them in terms of their relationship to the human organism, i.e., in an organismic, or somatic context, these things and events become *human behavior* and we are doing *psychology.* If, however, we treat them in terms of their relationship to one another, quite apart from their relationship to human organisms, i.e., in an extrasomatic, or extraorganismic, context, the things and events become *culture*—cultural elements or culture traits—and we are doing *culturology.* Human psychology and culturology have the same phenomena as their subject matter: things and events dependent upon symboling (symbolates). The difference between the two sciences derives from the difference between the contexts in which their common subject matter is treated.

The analysis and distinction that we have made with regard to things and events dependent upon symboling in general is precisely like the one that linguists have been making for decades with regard to a particular kind of these things and events, namely, words.

A word is a thing (a sound or combination of sounds, or marks made upon some substance) or an act dependent upon symboling. Words are just what they are: words. But they are significant to scientific students of words in two different contexts: somatic or organismic, and extrasomatic or extraorganismic. This distinction has been expressed customarily with the terms *la langue* and *la parole,* or language and speech.

Words in a somatic context constitute a kind of human behavior: speech behavior. The scientific study of words in a somatic context is the psychology (plus physiology, perhaps, and anatomy) of speech. It is concerned with the relationship between words and the human organism: how the words are produced and uttered, the meanings of words, attitudes toward words, perception of and response to words, and so on.

In the extrasomatic context, words are considered in terms of their relationships to one another, quite apart from their relationship to the human organism. The scientific concern here is linguistics, or the science of language. Phonetics, phonemics, syntax, lexicon, grammar, dialectic variation, evolution or historical change, etc., indicate particular focuses, or emphases, within the science of linguistics.

The difference between these two sciences may be illustrated by citing two books: *The Psychology of Language* by Walter B. Pillsbury and Clarence L. Meader (New York, 1928), and *Language* by Leonard Bloomfield (New York, 1933). In the former we find chapter titles such as "The Speech Organs," "The Senses Involved in Speech," "Mental Processes in Speech," etc. In the latter the chapter headings are "The Phoneme," "Phonetic Structure," "Grammatical Forms," "Sentence-Types," etc. We illustrate the distinction between these two sciences in Figure 2.

Figures 1 and 2 are fundamentally alike. In each case we are concerned with a class of things and events dependent upon symboling. In Fig. 1, we are concerned with a general class: symbolates; in Fig. 2 we are dealing with a particular class: words (a subclass of the class symbolates). In each case we refer the things and events to a somatic context on the one hand, and to an extrasomatic context on the other, for purposes of consideration and interpretation. And in each case we have two distinct kinds of science, or sciencing: the psychology of human behavior or of speech; and the science of culture or of language.

Culture, then, is a class of things and events, dependent upon symboling, considered in an extrasomatic context. This definition rescues cultural anthro-

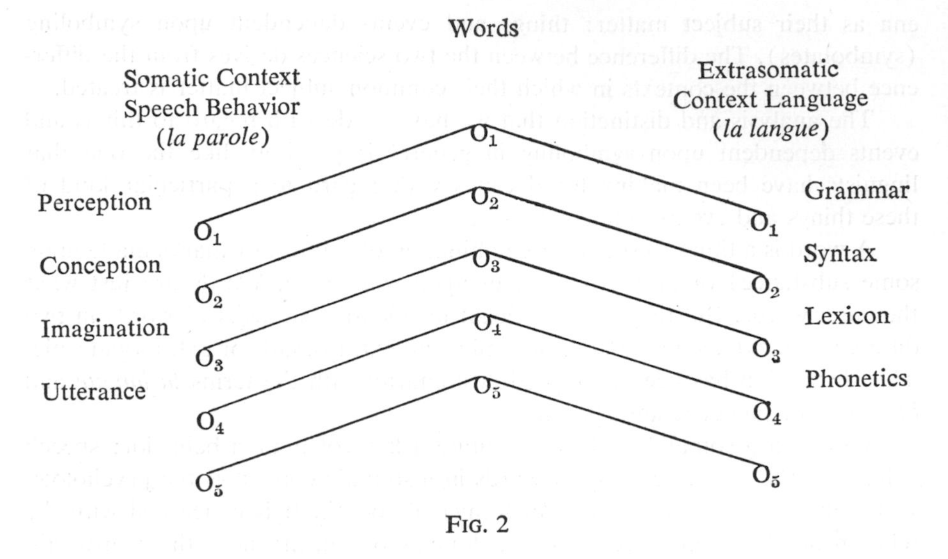

FIG. 2

pology from intangible, imperceptible, and ontologically unreal abstractions and provides it with a real, substantial, observable subject matter. And it distinguishes sharply between behavior—behaving organisms—and culture; between the science of psychology and the science of culture.

It might be objected that every science should have a certain class of things per se as its subject matter, not things-in-a-certain-context. Atoms are atoms and mammals are mammals, it might be argued, and as such are the subject matter of physics and mammalogy, respectively, regardless of context. Why therefore should cultural anthropology have its subject matter defined in terms of things in context rather than in terms of things in themselves? At first glance this argument might appear to be a cogent one, but actually it has but little force. What the scientist wants to do is to make intelligible the phenomena that confront him. And very frequently the significant thing about phenomena is the context in which they are found. Even in the so-called natural sciences we have a science of organisms-in-a-certain-context: parasitology, a science of organisms playing a certain role in the realm of living things. And within the realm of man-and-culture we have dozens of examples of things and events whose significance depends upon context rather than upon the inherent qualities of the phenomena themselves. An adult male of a certain animal species is called a man. But a man is a man, not a slave; a man becomes a slave only when he enters a certain context. So it is with commodities: corn and cotton are articles of use-value, but they were not commodities —articles produced for sale at a profit—in aboriginal Hopi culture; corn and cotton become commodities only when they enter a certain socioeconomic context. A cow is a cow, but she may become a medium of exchange, money (*pecus,* pecuniary) in one context, food in another, mechanical power (Cartwright used a cow as motive power for his first power loom) in another, and a sacred object of worship (India) in still another. We do not have a science of cows, but we do have scientific studies of mediums of exchange, of mechanical power, and of sacred objects in each of which cows may be significant. And so we have a science of symboled things and events in an extrasomatic context.

The locus of culture. If we define culture as consisting of real things and events observable, directly or indirectly, in the external world, where do these things and events exist and have their being? What is the locus of culture? The answer is: the things and events that comprise culture have their existence, in space and time, (1) within human organisms, i.e., concepts, beliefs, emotions, attitudes; (2) within processes of social interaction among human beings; and (3) within material objects (axes, factories, railroads, pottery bowls) lying outside human organisms but within the patterns of social interaction among them. The locus of culture is thus intraorganismal, interorganismal, and extraorganismal (see Fig. 3).

But, someone might object, you have said that culture consists of extrasomatic phenomena and now you tell me that culture exists, in part, within human organisms. Is this not a contradiction? The answer is, No, it is not a contradiction; it is a misunderstanding. We did not say that culture consists of extrasomatic things and events, i.e., phenomena whose locus is outside human organisms. What we said is that culture consists of things and events considered within an extrasomatic context. This is quite a different thing.

Every cultural element has two aspects: subjective and objective. It might appear that stone axes are "objective," and ideas and attitudes are "subjective." But this is a superficial and inadequate view. An axe has a subjective component; it would be meaningless without a concept and an attitude. On the other hand, a concept or an attitude would be meaningless without overt expression, in behavior or speech (which is a form of behavior). Every cultural element, every culture trait, therefore, has a subjective and an objective aspect. But conceptions, attitudes, and sentiments—phenomena that have their locus within the human organism—may be considered for purposes of scientific interpretation in an extrasomatic context, i.e., in terms of their relation to other symboled things and events rather than in terms of their relationship to the human organism. Thus, we may consider the subjective aspect of the mother-in-law taboo, i.e., the conceptions and attitudes involved, in terms of their relationship, not to the human organism, but to other symbolates such as forms of marriage and the family, place of residence after marriage, and so on. On the other hand, we may consider the axe in terms of its relationship to the human organism—its meaning; the person's conception of it; his attitude toward it—rather than to other symboled things and events such as arrows, hoes, and customs regulating the division of labor in society.

We shall now pass in review a number of conceptions of culture, or conceptions with regard to culture, widely current in ethnological literature, and

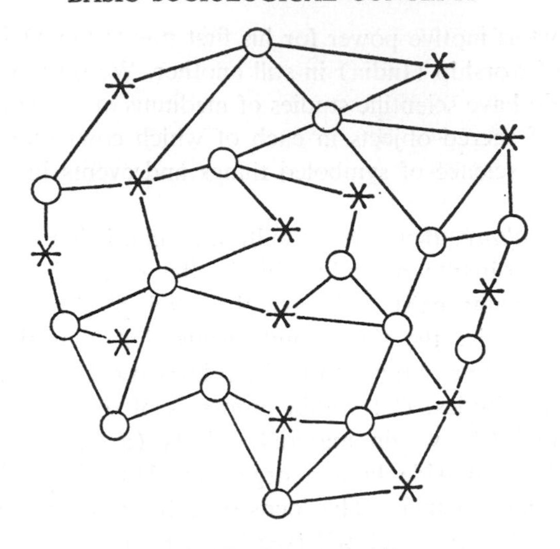

FIG. 3. The locus of culture.

○ = persons
* = objects
—— = lines of interaction, or interrelationship

comment critically upon each one from the standpoint of the conception of culture set forth in this paper.

"Culture consists of ideas." Some anthropologists like to define culture in terms of ideas only. The reason for this, apparently, is the notion that ideas are both basic and primary, that they are prime movers and as such originate behavior which in turn may produce objects such as pottery bowls. "Culture consists of ideas," says Walter W. Taylor, it "is a mental phenomenon . . . not . . . material objects or observable behavior. . . . For example, there is present in an Indian's mind the idea of a dance. This is the trait of culture. This idea influences his body so that he behaves in a certain way," i.e., he dances.

This conception of sociocultural reality is a naive one. It is based upon a primitive, prescientific, and now obsolete metaphysics and psychology. It was Thought-Woman among the Keresan Pueblo Indians who brought about events by thinking and willing them to happen. Ptah created Egyptian culture by objectifying his thoughts. And God said "Let there be light," and there was light. But we no longer explain the origin and development of culture by simply saying that it has resulted from man's ideas. To be sure, an idea was involved in the invention of firearms, but we have explained nothing when we say that firearms are the fruit of thought, because the ideas themselves have not been accounted for. Why did the idea occur when and where it did rather than at some other time and place? And, actually, ideas—matter of fact, realistic ideas—enter the mind from the outside world. It was working with soils that gave man, or woman, the idea of pottery; the calendar is a by-product of intensive agriculture. Culture does indeed consist in part of ideas; but attitudes, overt acts, and objects are culture, also.

"Culture consists of abstractions." We return now to the presently popular definition: "culture is an abstraction, or consists of abstractions." As we observed earlier, those who define culture in these terms do not tell us what they mean by "abstraction," and there is reason to believe that they are not very clear as to what they do mean by it. They make it emphatically clear, however, that an abstraction is not an observable thing or event. The fact that doubts have been raised as to the "reality" of an abstraction indicates that those who use this term are not sure what "it means," i.e., what they mean by it. We do have some clues, however.

Culture is "basically a form or pattern or way," say Kroeber and Kluckhohn, "even a culture trait is an abstraction. A trait is an 'ideal type' because no two pots are identical nor are two marriage ceremonies ever held in precisely the same way." The culture trait "pot" therefore appears to be the ideal form of which each particular pot is an exemplification—a sort of Platonic idea, or ideal. Each and every pot, they reason, is real; but the "ideal" is never realized in any particular pot. It is like the "typical American man": 5′8½″ high, weighs 164.378 pounds, is married, has 2.3 children, and so on. This is, we suppose, what they mean by an abstraction. If so, we know it well: it is a conception in the mind of the observer, the scientist.

There is a slightly different way of looking at an "abstraction." No two marriage ceremonies are ever held in precisely the same way. Well, let us tabulate a large sample of marriage ceremonies. We find that 100 percent contain element *a* (mutual acceptance of spouses). Ninety-nine percent contain element *b*. Elements *c*, *d*, and *e* appear in only 96, 94, and 89 percent, respectively, of the cases. We construct a distribution curve and determine an average or norm about which all particular instances are distributed. This is the typical marriage ceremony. But, like the typical American who has 2.3 children, this ideal is never fully and perfectly realized in any actual instance. It is an "abstraction," that is, a conception, worked out by the scientific observer and which exists in his own mind.

The failure to recognize the fact that abstractions are conceptions has led to confusion both as to their locus and their reality. Recognition of the fact that the so-called abstractions of science (such as a "rigid body" in physical theory; rigid bodies do not exist in actuality) are conceptions in the mind of the scientist clears up both these points: cultural "abstractions" are conceptions ("ideas") in the mind of the anthropologist. And as for their "ontological reality," conceptions are none the less real for being in the minds of men—nothing is more real, for example, than an hallucination.

This point was well made by David Bidney in his review of *Culture, a Critical Review etc.:*

The real crux of the problem centers about what is meant by abstraction and what is its ontological import. Some anthropologists maintain that they are dealing only with logical abstractions and that culture has no reality other than that of an abstraction, but they can hardly expect other social scientists to agree with them, conceding that the objects of their sciences have no ontological, objective reality. *Thus Kroeber and Kluckhohn have confused the concept culture, which is a logical construct, with the actual existential culture . . .* [emphasis ours].[2]

It is interesting to note in this connection that one anthropological theorist, Cornelius Osgood, has defined culture explicitly as consisting of ideas in the minds of anthropologists: "Culture consists of all ideas of the manufactures, behavior, and ideas of the aggregate of human beings which have been directly observed or communicated to one's mind and of which one is conscious." Spiro, also, holds that "culture is a logical construct, abstracted from human behavior, and as such, it exists only in the mind of *the investigator*" (Spiro's emphasis).

"There is no such things as 'material' culture." Those who define culture in terms of ideas, or as an abstraction, or as behavior, find themselves obliged logically to declare that material objects are not, and cannot be, culture. "Strictly speaking," says E. Adamson Hoebel, "material culture is really not culture at all." Taylor goes farther: ". . . the concept of 'material culture' is fallacious" because "culture is a mental phenomenon." Beals and Hoijer: ". . . culture is an abstraction from behavior and not to be confused with acts of behavior or with material artifacts, such as tools. . . ." This denial of material culture is rather awkward in view of the long established tradition among ethnographers, archeologists, and museum curators of calling tools, masks, fetiches, and so on, "material culture."

Our definition extricates us from this dilemma. As we have already seen, it would not be absurd to speak of sandals or pottery bowls as behavior; their significant attribute is not mere deer hide or clay, but human labor; they are congelations of human labor. But in our definition, symboling is the common factor in ideas, attitudes, acts, and objects. There are three kinds of symbolates: (1) ideas and attitudes, (2) overt acts, and (3) material objects. All may be considered in an extrasomatic context; all are to be reckoned as culture. This conception brings us back to long established usage in cultural anthropology: "Culture is that which is described in an ethnographic monograph."

"Reification of culture." There is a kind of conception of culture held by some anthropologists that is much deplored by others who call it "reification." As one who has been especially singled out as a "reifier" of culture, I may say that the term is singularly inappropriate. To reify is to make a thing of that which is not a thing, such as hope, honesty, or freedom. But it is not I who have made culture things. I have merely found real things and events in the

[2] David Bidney, Review of *Culture, a Critical Review etc.*, by A. L. Kroeber and Clyde Kluckhohn. *American Journal of Sociology*, 59, 1954:488–489.

external world which are distinguishable as a class by being dependent upon symboling, and which may be treated in an extrasomatic context, and I have called these things and events culture. This is precisely what E. B. Tylor did. It is what Robert H. Lowie, Clark Wissler, and most early American anthropologists have done. To Émile Durkheim "the proposition which states that social facts [i.e., culture traits] are to be treated as things" lay "at the very basis of our method." It is not we who have reified culture; the elements comprising culture, according to our definition, were things to start with.

To be sure, if culture is defined as consisting of intangible, imponderable, ontologically unreal "abstractions," then to transform these wraiths into real, substantial bodies would indeed be to reify them. But we do not subscribe to such a definition.

"Culture: a process sui generis." "Culture is a thing *sui generis* . . ." said Lowie many years ago. This view has been held also by Kroeber, Durkheim, and others. It has been misunderstood and opposed by many. But what Lowie meant by this statement is made clear in the rest of the passage cited above: "Culture is a thing *sui generis* which can be explained only in terms of itself . . . the ethnologist . . . will account for a given cultural fact by merging it in a group of cultural facts or by demonstrating some other cultural fact out of which it has been developed." For example, the custom of reckoning descent patrilineally may be explained in terms of customs of division of labor between the sexes, customs of residence—patrilocal, matrilocal, or neolocal—of a married couple; mode of subsistence; rules of inheritance, and so on. Or, to express it in terms of our definition of culture: "a symbolate in an extrasomatic context (i.e., a culture trait) is to be explained in terms of its relationship to other symbolates in the same context." [3]

This conception of culture, like "reification" with which it is closely related, has been much misunderstood and opposed. In general, it has been regarded as "mystical." How can culture grow and develop by itself? "It seems hardly necessary," says Franz Boas, "to consider culture a mystic entity that exists outside the society of its individual carriers, and that moves by its own force." Bidney brands this view of culture as a "mystical metaphysics of fate." And it has been opposed by Ruth Benedict, Ernest Hooton, Spiro, and others.

But no one has ever said that culture is an entity that exists and moves by, and of, itself, quite apart from people. Nor has anyone ever said, as far as we know, that the origin, nature, and functions of culture can be understood without taking the human species into consideration. Obviously, if one is to understand culture in these aspects he must consider the biological nature of man. What has been asserted is that, given culture, its variations in time and place, and its processes of change are to be explained in terms of culture itself. This is precisely what Lowie meant when he said that "culture is a thing [process would have been a better term] *sui generis,*" as the above quotation

[3] Robert H. Lowie, *Culture and Ethnology*. New York, Boni and Liveright, 1917:66.

from him makes clear. A consideration of the human organism, individually or collectively, is irrelevant to an explanation of processes of culture change. "This is not mysticism," says Lowie, "but sound scientific method." And, as everyone knows, scholars have been working in accordance with this principle of interpretation for decades. One does not need to take human organisms into account in a scientific explanation of the evolution of currency, writing, or of Gothic art. The steam engine and textile machinery were introduced into Japan during the closing decades of the nineteenth century and certain changes in social structure followed; we add nothing to our explanation of these events by remarking that human beings were involved. Of course they were. And they were not irrelevant to the events which took place, but they are irrelevant to an explanation of these events.

"It is people, not culture, that does things." "Culture does not 'work,' 'move,' change,' but is worked, is moved, is changed. It is people who do things," says Robert S. Lynd. He supports this argument with the bold assertion that "culture does not enamel its fingernails . . . but people do . . ." He might have clinched it by demonstrating that culture has no fingernails.

The view that "it is people, not cultures, that do things" is widely held among anthropologists. Boas tells us that "the forces that bring about the changes are active in the individuals composing the social group, not in the abstract culture." A. Irving Hallowell remarks that "in a literal sense cultures never have met nor will ever meet. What is meant is that peoples meet and that, as a result of the processes of social interaction, acculturation—modifications in the mode of life of one or both peoples—may take place. Individuals are the dynamic centers of this process of interaction." And Radcliffe-Brown pours fine scorn on the notion that cultures, rather than peoples, interact:

> A few years ago, as a result perhaps of re-defining social anthropology as the study, not of society, but of culture, we were asked to abandon this kind of investigation in favor of what is now called the study of "culture contact." In place of the study of the formation of new composite societies, we are supposed to regard what is happening in Africa as a process in which an entity called African culture comes into contact with an entity called European or Western culture, and a third new entity is produced . . . which is to be described as Westernized African culture. To me this seems a fantastic reification of abstractions. European culture is an abstraction and so is the culture of an African tribe. I find it fantastic to imagine these two abstractions coming into contact and by an act of generation producing a third abstraction.[4]

We call this view, that people rather than culture do things, the fallacy of pseudo-realism. Of course culture does not and could not exist independently of people. But, as we have pointed out earlier, cultural processes can be explained without taking human organisms into account; a consideration of

[4] A. R. Radcliffe-Brown, "On Social Structure." *Journal of the Royal Anthropological Institute,* 70, 1940:10–11.

human organisms is irrelevant to the solution of certain problems of culture. Whether the practice of mummification in pre-Columbian Peru was indigenous or the result of Egyptian influence is an example of a kind of problem that does not require a consideration of human organisms. To be sure the practice of mummification, its invention in Peru, or its diffusion from Egypt to the Andean highlands, could not have taken place without the action of real, flesh-and-blood human beings. Neither could Einstein have worked out the theory of relativity without breathing, but we do not need to take his respiration into account when we trace the history, or explain the development, of this theory.

Those who argue that it is people, not culture, that do this or that mistake a description of what they see for an explanation of these events. Seated in the Senate gallery they see men making laws; in the shipyards men are building freighters; in the laboratory human beings are isolating enzymes; in the fields they are planting corn, and so on. And, for them, a description of these events, as they observe them, is a simple explanation of them: it is people who pass laws, build freighters, plant corn, and isolate enzymes. This is a simple and naive form of anthropocentrism.

A scientific explanation is more sophisticated. If a person speaks Chinese, or avoids his mother-in-law, loathes milk, observes matrilocal residence, places the bodies of the dead on scaffolds, writes symphonies, or isolates enzymes, it is because he has been born into, or at least reared within, an extrasomatic tradition that we call culture which contains these elements. A people's behavior is a response to, a function of, their culture. The culture is the independent, the behavior the dependent, variable; as the culture varies so will the behavior. This is, of course, a commonplace that is usually expounded and demonstrated during the first two weeks of an introductory course in anthropology. It is indeed people who treat disease with prayers and charms or with vaccines and antibiotics. But the question, "Why does one people use charms while another uses vaccines?" is not explained by saying that "this people does this, that people does that." It is precisely this proposition that needs to be explained: why do they do what they do? The scientific explanation does not take the people into account at all. And as for the question, Why does one extrasomatic tradition use charms while another uses vaccines, this also is one to which a consideration of people, of human organisms, is irrelevant; it is answered culturologically: culture, as Lowie has observed, is to be explained in terms of culture.

Culture "cannot be realistically disconnected from those organizations of ideas and feelings which constitute the individual," i.e., culture cannot be realistically disconnected from individuals, says Edward Sapir. He is quite right, of course; in actuality culture is inseparable from human beings. But if culture cannot be realistically (in actuality) disconnected from individuals it most certainly can be disconnected in logical (scientific) analysis, and no one has done a better job of "disconnecting" than Edward Sapir: there is not a single Indian—or even a nerve, muscle, or sense organ—in his monograph, *Southern Paiute, a Shoshonean Language* (1930). Nor are there any people roaming about in his *Time Perspective in Aboriginal American Culture* (1916). "Science must abstract some elements and neglect others," says Morris Cohen "because *not all things that exist together are relevant to each other*" (emphasis ours). Comprehension and appreciation of this fact would be an enormous asset to ethnological theory. "Citizenship cannot be realistically disconnected from eye color," i.e., every citizen has eyes and every eye has a color. But, in the United States at least, color of eyes is not relevant to citizenship: "things that exist together are not always relevant to each other."

And so it is perfectly true, as Hallowell, Radcliffe-Brown, and others say, that "it is *peoples* who meet and interact." But this should not keep us from confining our attention, in the solution of certain problems, to symbolates in an extrasomatic context: to tools, utensils, customs, beliefs, and attitudes; in short, to culture. The meeting and mixing of European culture with African culture and the production thereby of a mixture, Euro-African culture, may seem "a fantastic reification of abstractions" to Radcliffe-Brown and others. But anthropologists have been concerned with problems of this sort for decades and will continue to deal with them. The intermingling of customs, technologies, and ideologies is just as valid a scientific problem as the intermingling of human organisms or genes.

We have not asserted, nor do we imply, that anthropologists in general have failed to treat culture as a process sui generis, i.e., without taking human organisms into account; many, if not most, cultural anthropologists have in fact done this. But some of them, when they turn to theory, deny the validity of this kind of interpretation. Radcliffe-Brown himself provides us with examples of purely culturological problems and culturological solutions thereof—in "The Social Organization of Australian Tribes" (1930–31), "The Mother's Brother in South Africa" (1924), etc. But when he dons the philosopher's cap he denies that this procedure is scientifically valid.

However, some anthropologists have recognized, on the theoretical level, that culture can be scientifically studied without taking human organisms into account, that a consideration of human organisms is irrelevant to the solution of problems dealing with extrasomatic traditions. We have cited a number—Tylor, Durkheim, Kroeber, Lowie, et al.—who have done this. But we may add one or two new references here. "The best hope . . . for parsimonious description and 'explanation' of cultural phenomena," say Kroeber and Kluckhohn, "seems to rest in the study of cultural forms and processes as such, largely . . . abstracted from individuals and personalities." And Julian H. Steward remarks that "certain aspects of a modern culture can best be studied quite apart from individual behavior. The structure and function of a system of money, banking, and credit, for example, represent supra-individual aspects of culture." Also, he says: "form of government, legal system, economic institutions, religious organizations, educational systems," and so on, "have aspects which are national . . . in scope and which must be understood apart from the behavior of the individuals connected with them."

There is nothing new about this; anthropologists and other social scientists have been doing this for decades. But it seems to be difficult for some of them to accept this as a matter of theory and principle as well as of actual practice.

"It takes two or more to make a culture." There is a conception, not uncommon in ethnological theory, that whether a phenomenon is an element of culture or not depends upon whether it is expressed by one, two, or "several" individuals. Thus Linton says that "any item of behavior . . . which is peculiar to a single individual in a society is not to be considered as a part of the society's culture. . . . Thus a new technique for weaving baskets would not be classed as a part of culture as long as it was known only to one person." Clark Wissler, Osgood, Bronislaw Malinowski, Durkheim et al., have subscribed to this view.

Two objections may be raised against this conception of culture: (1) if plurality of expression of learned behavior be the significant distinction between culture and not-culture, then the chimpanzees described by Wolfgang Köhler in *The Mentality of Apes* (New York, 1925) had culture, for innovations made by a single individual were often quickly adopted by the whole group. Other subhuman species also would have culture according to this criterion. (2) The second objection is: if expression by one person is not enough to qualify an act as a cultural element, how many persons will be required? Linton says that "as soon as this new thing has been transmitted to and is shared by even one other individual in the society, it must be reckoned as a part of culture." Osgood requires "two or more." Durkheim needs "several individuals, at the very least." Wissler says that an item does not rise to the level of a culture trait until a standardized procedure is established in the group. And Malinowski states that a "cultural fact starts when an individual interest becomes transformed into public, common, and transferable systems of organized endeavor."

Obviously such a conception does not meet the requirements of science. What agreement could one find on the point at which an "individual interest becomes transformed into public, common, and transferable systems of organized endeavor"? Or, suppose an ornithologist said that if there were but one specimen of a kind of bird it could not be a carrier pigeon or a whooping crane, but that if there were an indefinite number then they could be pigeons or cranes. Or, suppose a physicist said that if there were but one atom of a certain element that it could not be copper, but if there were "a lot of such atoms" then it might properly be called copper. One wants a definition that says that item *x* belongs to class *y* or it does not, regardless of how many items of *x* there may be (and a class, in logic, may have only one member, or even none).

Our definition meets the requirements of a scientific definition: an item—a conception or belief, an act, or an object—is to be reckoned an element of culture (1) if it is dependent upon symboling, and (2) when it is considered in an extrasomatic context. To be sure, all cultural elements exist in a social context; but so do such nonhuman (not dependent upon symboling) traits as grooming, suckling, and mating exist in a social matrix. But it is not sociality, duality, or plurality that distinguishes a human, or cultural, phenomenon from a nonhuman or noncultural phenomenon. The distinguishing characteristic is symboling. Secondly, whether a thing or an event can be considered in an extrasomatic context does not depend upon whether there is only one such thing or event, or two, or "several." A thing or event may be properly considered an element of culture even if it is the only member of its class, just as an atom of copper would still be an atom of copper even if it were the only one of its kind in the cosmos.

And, of course, we might have pointed out in the first place that the notion that an act or an idea in human society might be wholly the work of a single individual is an illusion, another one of the sorry pitfalls of anthropocentrism. Every member of human society is of course always subjected to sociocultural stimulation from the members of his group. Whatever a man does as a human being, and much of what he does as a mere animal, is a function of his group as well as of his organism. Any human act, even in its first expression in the person of a single individual, is a group product to begin with.

Culture as "characteristic" traits. "Culture may be defined," says Boas, "as the totality of the mental and physical reactions and activities that *characterize* the behavior of the individuals composing a social group . . ." (emphasis ours). Herskovits tells us that "when culture is closely analyzed, we find but a series of patterned reactions that characterize the behavior of the individuals who constitute a given group." (Just what "close analysis" has to do with this conception is not clear.) Sapir: "The mass of typical reactions called culture. . . ." This view has, of course, been held by others.

Two objections may be raised against this conception of culture: (1) how does one determine which traits characterize a group and which traits do not—how does one draw the line between the two classes, culture and not-culture? And, (2) if we call the traits that characterize a group *culture,* what are we to call those traits that do not characterize it?

It seems probable that anthropologists who hold this view are really thinking of *a* culture, or cultures, plural, rather than of culture in general, culture as a particular kind of phenomena. Thus, "French culture" might be distinguished from "English culture" by those traits which characterize each. But if, on the one hand, the French and the English may be distinguished from each other by differences of traits, they will on the other hand be found to be very similar to each other in their possession of like traits. And the traits that resemble each other are just as much a part of the "way of life" of each people as the traits that differ. Why should only one class be called culture?

These difficulties and uncertainties are done away with by our conception of culture: culture consists of all of the ways of life of each people which are dependent upon symboling and which are considered in an extrasomatic context. If one wished to distinguish the English from the French on the basis of their respective culture traits he could easily specify "those traits which characterize" the people in question. But he would not assert that nontypical traits were not culture.

In this connection we may note a very interesting distinction drawn by Sapir between the behavior of individuals and "culture."

> It is always the individual that really thinks and acts and dreams and revolts. Those of his thoughts, acts, dreams, and rebellions that somehow contribute in sensible degree to the modification or retention of the mass of typical reactions called culture we term social data; *the rest, though they do not, psychologically considered, in the least differ from these, we term individual and pass by as of no historical or social moment* [i.e., they are not culture]. It is highly important to note that the differentiation of these two types of reaction is essentially arbitrary, resting, as it does, entirely on a principle of selection. The selection depends on the adoption of a scale of values. Needless to say, the threshold of the social (or historical) [i.e., cultural] *versus* the individual shifts according to the philosophy of the evaluator or interpreter. I find it utterly inconceivable to draw a sharp and eternally valid dividing line between them [emphases ours].[5]

Sapir finds himself confronted by a plurality, or aggregation, of individuals. (He would have preferred this wording rather than "society," we believe, for he speaks of "a theoretical [fictitious?] community of human beings," adding that "the term 'society' itself is a cultural construct"). These individuals do things: dream, think, act, and revolt. And "it is always the individual," not society or culture, who does these things. What Sapir finds then is: individuals and their behavior; nothing more.

Some of the behavior of individuals is culture, says Sapir. But other elements of their behavior are not-culture, although, as he says, psychologically considered they do not differ in the slightest from those elements which he calls culture. The line thus drawn between "culture" and "not-culture" is purely arbitrary, and depends upon the subjective evaluation of the one who is drawing the line.

A conception of culture could hardly be less satisfactory than this one. It says, in effect: "culture is the name that we give to some of the behavior of some individuals, the selection being arbitrary and made in accordance with subjective criteria."

In the essay from which we have been quoting, "Do We Need a Superorganic?", Sapir is opposing the culturological point of view presented by Kroeber in "The Superorganic." He (Sapir) virtually makes culture disappear; it is dissolved into the totality of the reactions of individuals. Culture becomes, as he has elsewhere called it, a "statistical fiction." If there is no significant

[5] Edward Sapir, "Do We Need a Superorganic?" *American Anthropologist,* 19, 1917:442.

reality that one can call culture, then there can be no science of culture. Sapir's argument was skillful and persuasive. But it was also unsound, or at least misleading.

Sapir's argument was persuasive because he bolstered it with authentic, demonstrable fact. It was unsound or misleading because he makes it appear that the only significant distinction between the behavior of individuals and culture is the one that he had made.

It is perfectly true that the elements which comprise the human behavior of individuals and the elements which comprise culture are identical classes of things and events. All are symbolates—dependent upon man's unique ability to symbol. It is true, also, that "psychologically considered," they are all alike. But Sapir overlooks, and by his argument effectively obscures, the fact that there are two fundamentally different kinds of contexts in which these "thinkings, actings, dreamings, and revolts" can be considered for purposes of scientific interpretation and explanation: the somatic and the extrasomatic. Considered in a somatic context, i.e., in terms of their relationship to the human organism, these acts dependent upon symboling constitute *human behavior*. Considered in an extrasomatic context, i.e., in terms of their relationships to one another, these acts constitute *culture*. Instead, therefore, of arbitrarily putting some in the category of culture and the rest in the category human behavior, we put all acts, thoughts, and things dependent upon symboling in either one context or the other, somatic or extrasomatic, depending upon the nature of our problem.

Summary. Among the many significant classes of things and events distinguishable by science there is one for which science has had no name. This is the class of phenomena dependent upon symboling, a faculty peculiar to the human species. We have proposed that things and events dependent upon symboling be called symbolates. The particular designation of this class is not as important, however, as that it be given a name of some kind in order that its distinction from other classes be made explicit.

Things and events dependent upon symboling comprise ideas, beliefs, attitudes, sentiments, acts, patterns of behavior, customs, codes, institutions, works and forms of art, languages, tools, implements, machines, utensils, ornaments, fetiches, charms, and so on.

Things and events dependent upon symboling may be, and traditionally have been, referred to two fundamentally different contexts for purposes of observation, analysis, and explanation. These two contexts may properly and appropriately be called somatic and extrasomatic. When an act, object, idea or attitude is considered in the somatic context it is the relationship between that thing or event and the human organism that is significant. Things and events dependent upon symboling considered in the somatic context may properly be called human behavior—at least, ideas, attitudes, and acts may; stone axes and pottery bowls are customarily called behavior, but their significance is derived from the fact that they have been produced by human labor; they are, in fact, congelations of human behavior. When things and events are considered in the extrasomatic context they are regarded in terms of the interrelationships among themselves rather than in terms of their relationship to the human organism, individually or collectively. Culture is the name of things and events dependent upon symboling considered in an extrasomatic context.

Our analysis and distinctions have these advantages. The distinctions made are clear cut and fundamental. Culture is clearly distinguished from human behavior. Culture has been defined as all sciences must define their subject matter, namely, in terms of real things and events, observable directly or indirectly in the actual world that we live in. Our conception rescues anthropology from the incubus of intangible, imperceptible, imponderable "abstractions" that have no ontological reality.

Our definition extricates us, also, from the dilemmas in which many other conceptions place us, such as whether culture consists of ideas and whether these ideas have their locus in the minds of peoples studied or in the minds of anthropologists; whether material objects can or cannot be culture; whether a trait must be shared by two, three, or several people in order to count as culture; whether traits have to characterize a people or not in order to be culture; whether culture is a reification or not, and whether a culture can enamel its fingernails.

Our distinction between human behavior and culture, between psychology and culturology, is precisely like the one that has been in use for decades between speech and language, between the psychology of speech and the science of linguistics. If it is valid for the one it is valid for the other.

Finally, our distinction and definition is in very close accord with anthropological tradition. This is what Tylor meant by culture as a reading of *Primitive Culture* will make clear. It is the one that has actually been used by almost all nonbiological anthropologists. What is it that scientific field workers among primitive peoples have studied and described in their monographs? Answer: real observable things and events dependent upon symboling. It can hardly be said that they were studying and describing imperceptible, intangible, imponderable, ontologically unreal abstractions. To be sure, the field worker may be interested in things and events in their somatic context, in which case he would be doing psychology (as he would be if he considered words in their somatic context). And anthropology, as this term is actually used, embraces a number of different kinds of studies: anatomical, physiological, genetic, psychological, psychoanalytic, and culturological. But this does not mean that the distinction between psychology and culturology is not fundamental. It is.

The thesis presented in this paper is no novelty. It is not a radical departure from anthropological tradition. On the contrary, it is in a very real sense and to a great extent, a return to tradition, the tradition esablished by Tylor and followed in practice by countless anthropologists since his day. We have merely given it concise and overt verbal expression.

Early in the course of sociological and anthropological usages of the concept of culture, it became apparent that an analysis of the vast content of culture required the formulation of several refinements of the concept. One highly important subconcept of culture is that of norms, the sanctioned rules concerning proper and improper thinking, feeling, and behavior by members of a society. Norms, in turn, have been subdivided and classified, as in the case of Sumner's distinctions between the folkways (norms, violations of which are not considered a serious social threat), mores (norms, violations of which do threaten the group's welfare), crescive laws (norms which are formalized by the government after having originated in the folkways or mores), and enacted laws (norms imposed on society by the government without any previous foothold in the folkways or mores). However, Sumner took care to point out that his classification offered no hierarchical system of normative restriction and sanction. Laws, for example, are not necessarily more restrictive than are the mores. To illustrate, there is no federal or state law in American society which anyone violates by crossing a picket line set up by a labor union. But the inviolability of a union's picket line is an embedded mos (singular of mores) for members of organized labor that is stronger than most laws.

As was to be expected, contemporary sociology has gone beyond the normative typologies of Sumner and the other pioneers. In the article that follows, Richard T. Morris distinguishes, first of all, between a culture's values and its norms. He proceeds, on the foundation of prior efforts, to offer a classification of norms in terms of their distribution, mode of enforcement, transmission, and conformity.

11. A TYPOLOGY OF NORMS *

RICHARD T. MORRIS

University of California, Los Angeles

Almost fifty years have passed since Professor William Graham Sumner proposed his famous classification of norms into folkways and mores. Since that time there have been few efforts to elaborate or criticize this basic classification, even though there has been a tremendous increase in interest in the empirical investigation of norms during this period. Pitrim A. Sorokin vigorously attacked Sumner's typology, calling it "a kind of grocery basket into which are dumped together [all sorts of norms]," and has replaced it with his classification of law-norms, technical norms, norms of etiquette and fashion, and a final category of norms of "something else," in which the grocery basket is still evident. Ralph A. Linton has contributed the well-known categories: universals, specialties, and alternatives. Most recently, Robin Williams has revised and elaborated Sorokin's classification in his proposal of technical, conventional, aesthetic, and moral norms, and has further suggested a classi-

* *American Sociological Review,* Vol. 21, No. 5, October, 1956, pp. 610–613.

fication in terms of the major dimensions of norms, together with a sketch of the characteristics of a type called "institutional norms."

The typology of norms presented here, while based in part upon these prior efforts, attempts a classification employing additional dimensions (or criteria), directed toward the establishment of the *salience* of particular norms in any given hierarchical, normative system.

It should be pointed out at once that the rather considerable literature on the classification of values is relevant to the problem of typing norms; nevertheless, there is a difference between values and norms, which precludes the direct application of value classifications to the study of norms. To make a very brief distinction between values and norms, it may be said, following Clyde Kluckhohn, that values are individual, or commonly shared conceptions of the desirable, i.e., what I and/or others feel we justifiably want—what it is felt proper to want. On the other hand, norms are generally accepted, sanctioned prescriptions for, or prohibitions against, others' behavior, belief, or feeling, i.e., what others *ought* to do, believe, feel—*or else*. Values can be held by a single individual; norms cannot. Norms must be shared prescriptions and apply to others, by definition. Values have only a subject—the believer—while norms have both subjects and objects—those who set the prescription, and those to whom it applies. Norms always include sanctions; values never do. Although it is true that commonly held values often result in the formation of norms that insure the maintenance of the values, this is not always the case. Nor does it follow that every norm, at the point of its application, involves a presently held value, even though most norms are based upon established values.

As Ralph H. Turner has pointed out, there may be a widely-held value placed upon baseball skills in a society, but no norm which states that baseball *ought* to be played by the individuals in that society, or they will suffer the consequences. On the other hand, there may be a norm that recommends stopping at a red light even when there is no traffic, without a value attached to the instance. A demonstration of the difference between norms and values may be found in attempting to answer the question of when and how children begin to develop values in distinction to norms, i.e. ideas of what is desirable as distinct from shared ideas of what others ought to do, with sanctions attached.

It follows that norms and values must be classified and operationalized in different fashions, using different criteria. Whereas Kluckhohn has suggested a classification of values on the bases of modality, content, intent, generality, intensity, explicitness, extent, and organization, and although this scheme provides valuable insights for the classification of norms, it does not mean that norms can be classified in the same manner, since other criteria are involved, such as degree and kind of sanction, extent and kind of deviation, and the like.

The development of the typology presented here arose partially from the realization that other schemes of classification dealt only with certain aspects of norms. Sumner's classification is based largely upon the degree of conformity required and the kinds of sanction applied. Linton's classification is based upon the mixed criteria of extent of acceptance (universals and alternatives) and extent of application (specialties). Sorokin's classification utilizes the mixed criteria of content, i.e. what areas of behavior or belief the norms regulate, in his distinction between the technical norms and norms of etiquette and fashion, and the criterion of degree of conformity required (obligatory vs. free norms), in his distinction between law norms and moral norms. He also uses the criterion of reciprocity or "two-sidedness" in the latter distinction. Williams uses content criteria, i.e. what areas of behavior are regulated, in his classification of technical, conventional, aesthetic, etc., norms, and suggests the use of such characteristics as extent of agreement, modes of enforcement, explicitness, and specificity as criteria, although he never proceeds to a systematic classification on these bases. He does suggest a single type, institutional norm, which has several of the characteristics.

The various classifications based upon these selected criteria, or characteristics of norms, are useful for the particular problems which these writers had in mind, e.g., the developmental problems of Sumner, the cultural homogeneity problems of Linton, and so on. The present classification is based upon the somewhat different problem of establishing and predicting the salience of norms. It is but a first step, prior to the development of empirical measures of the variables outlined below.

The characteristics of norms selected for the classification are presented as grouped continua. These are arranged so that types or profiles can be constructed by a vertical reading of the characteristics of a given norm on all continua.

I. Distribution of Norm

Extent of knowledge of norm

(1) By subjects (those who set the norm)
very few . . . . almost everyone

(2) By objects (those to whom the norm applies)
very few . . . . almost everyone

Extent of acceptance, agreement with norm

(3) By subjects
very few . . . . almost everyone

(4) By objects
very few . . . . almost everyone

Extent of application of norm to objects

(5) To groups or categories
very few . . . . almost everyone

(6) To conditions
in specified few . . . . in almost all

II. Mode of Enforcement of Norm

(7) Reward—punishment
more reward than punishment .... more punishment than reward

(8) Severity of sanction
light, unimportant .... heavy, important

(9) Enforcing agency
specialized, designated responsibility ... general, universal responsibility

(10) Extent of enforcement
lax, intermittent .... rigorous, uniform

(11) Source of authority
rational, expedient, instrumental .. divine, inherent, absolute, autonomous

(12) Degree of internalization by objects
little, external enforcement, required .. great, self-enforcement, sufficient

III. Transmission of the Norm

(13) Socialization process
late learning, from secondary relations .... early learning, from primary relations

(14) Degree of reinforcement by subjects
very little .... high, persistent

IV. Conformity to the Norm

(15) Amount of conformity attempted by objects
attempted by very few .... attempted by almost everyone

(16) Amount of deviance by objects
very great .... very little

(17) Kind of deviance
formation of sub-norms .. patterned evasion .. idiosyncratic deviation

It should be noted at once that the above selection of characteristics of norms *is* a selection: it does not intend to represent all of the features of norms which may be useful in analysis. For example, the following characteristics were considered as candidates for inclusion in the typology: specificity and explicitness in the statement of the norms, formal vs. informal sanctions, repressive vs. restitutive sanctions, degree and kind of conflict with other norms, locus of conflict (intra-group vs. inter-group), perceived consequences of deviance by subjects and objects. These characteristics were excluded from the typology, either because they seemed not to vary consistently in possible polar types with the other criteria used, or because they were subsumed under the criteria listed in the typology. Probably the most striking omission is the content of the norms.

The classification here is not based upon content criteria, e.g., between technical and aesthetic norms, norms referring to behavior vs. norms referring to beliefs, feelings, or cognition. The position taken here is that these various norms, classified according to content, may all have the characteristics selected for the typology just outlined. In other words, constructed types based upon the characteristics listed above apply equally well to norms in any of the content areas. A further step in the application of the type is to investigate the relations between the types of norms and the content areas to which they apply.

The two types which appear most obviously are the polar ones. Reading down the extreme right-hand end of each of the continua, one may construct a polar type of norm which may be called an *absolute norm:* a norm which is known and supported by everyone, which applies to everybody under all conditions, which is rigorously enforced by heavy sanctions. Reading down the left-hand end of each continuum, the opposite polar type may be constructed which may be designated a *conditional norm,* suggesting its limited application and sporadic enforcement.

The arrangement of the continua above points up at once the similarity between the present typology of norms and the familiar folk-urban, sacred-secular typology of Tönnies, Redfield, Becker, and others. This is not surprising since it has long been hypothesized, sometimes in other terms, that a folk society has a high ratio of absolute norms, and an urban society a high ratio of conditional norms. There is also some resemblance between the absolute norm and Williams' concept of institutional norm.

The placement of existing norms, group, organizational or societal, along the various continua in the typology should result in the formulation of additional mixed types which will be useful in the analysis and prediction of changes in single norms or in the normative structure.

Further theoretical formulation is possible both within the typology as relationships between the continua are discovered, and by means of using established profiles as dependent or independent variables related to outside factors. For example, the investigation of the change in norms regarding communism could proceed within either of the frameworks.

When the various continua have been operationalized, a task now under way, the process of change in norms and the relative salience of norms can be objectively recorded. Eventually predictions can be developed about which characteristics of norms will change, and in what temporal pattern. Research is being carried out at present to investigate in small organizations the relationships between (a) statements of past and intended deviance, (b) perceptions of the characteristics of norms by subject individuals, and (c) perceptions of the characteristics of norms by object individuals.

The complexity and heterogeneity found in multigroup societies call for still other sociological refinements in the concept of culture. Current sociological research and analysis make extensive use of the concept of subculture, such as in studies of delinquency, adolescence, regional and class differences, religious sects, and occupational styles. Here are instances in which our understanding has been enhanced by seeing norms that vary from more general standards as manifestations, in part, of distinctive subsocieties.

Unfortunately, however, the term *subculture* has come to be used in several different ways. In his review of more than one hundred sources in the following article, J. Milton Yinger finds three clearly different meanings, with resultant imprecision in the application of the term. He suggests the adoption of a new term, *contraculture,* in order to distinguish between normative systems of subsocieties and emergent norms that appear in conflict situations. Finally, Professor Yinger explores the usefulness of this distinction with reference to several substantive areas of research.

12. CONTRACULTURE AND SUBCULTURE *

J. MILTON YINGER

Oberlin College

In recent years there has been widespread and fruitful employment of the concept of subculture in sociological and anthropological research. The term has been used to focus attention not only on the wide diversity of norms to be found in many societies but on the normative aspects of deviant behavior. The ease with which the term has been adopted, with little study of its exact meaning or its values and its difficulties, is indicative of its utility in emphasizing a sociological point of view in research that has been strongly influenced by both individualistic and moralistic interpretations. To describe the normative qualities of an occupation, to contrast the value systems of social classes, or to emphasize the controlling power of the code of a delinquent gang is to underline a sociological aspect of these phenomena that is often disregarded.

In the early days of sociology and anthropology, a key task was to document the enormous variability of culture from society to society and to explore the significance of the overly simplified but useful idea that "the mores can make anything right." In recent years that task has been extended to the study of the enormous variability of culture *within* some societies. It is unfortunate that "subculture," a central concept in this process, has seldom been adequately defined. It has been used as an *ad hoc* concept whenever a writer wished to emphasize the normative aspects of behavior that differed from some general standard. The result has been a blurring of the meaning of the term, confusion with other terms, and a failure frequently to distinguish between two levels of social causation.

THREE USAGES OF SUBCULTURE

Few concepts appear so often in current sociological writing. In the course of twelve months, I have noted over 100 books and articles that make some

* *American Sociological Review,* Vol. 25, No. 5, October, 1960, pp. 625–635.

use, from incidental to elaborate, of the idea of "subculture." The usages vary so widely, however, that the value of the term is severely limited. If chemists had only one word to refer to all colorless liquids and this led them to pay attention to only the two characteristics shared in common, their analysis would be exceedingly primitive. Such an analogy overstates the diversity of ideas covered by "subculture," but the range is very wide. Nevertheless three distinct meanings can be described.

In some anthropological work, subculture refers to certain universal tendencies that seem to occur in all societies. They underlie culture, precede it, and set limits to the range of its variation. Thus A. L. Kroeber writes: "Indeed, such more or less recurrent near-regularities of form or process as have to date been formulated for culture are actually subcultural in nature. They are limits set to culture by physical or organic factors." In *The Study of Man,* Ralph Linton uses subculture to refer to various pan-human phenomena that seem to occur everywhere. Thus goodnatured and tyrannical parents may be found in societies that differ widely in their family patterns. This use shades off into other concepts that are similar but not identical: Edward Sapir's "precultural" and Charles H. Cooley's "human nature" refer to biological and social influences that underlie all cultures. Since subculture is only rarely used today to refer to this series of ideas, I shall exclude them from further consideration, with the suggestion that the use of Sapir's term "precultural" might well clarify our thinking.

Two other usages of subculture represent a much more serious confusion. The term is often used to point to the normative systems of groups smaller than a society, to give emphasis to the ways these groups differ in such things as language, values, religion, diet, and style of life from the larger society of which they are a part. Perhaps the most common referent in this usage is an ethnic enclave (French Canadians in Maine) or a region (the subculture of the South), but the distinctive norms of much smaller and more temporary groups (even a particular friendship group) may be described as a subculture. Clyde Kluckhohn, for example, refers to "the subculture of anthropologists" and David Riesman to "subcultures among the faculty."

This second meaning, which itself contains some ambiguities, as we shall see, must be distinguished from a third meaning associated with it when the reference is to norms that arise specifically from a frustrating situation or from conflict between a group and the larger society. Thus the emergent norms of a delinquent gang or the standards of an adolescent peer group have often been designated "subcultural." In addition to a cultural dimension, this third usage introduces a social-psychological dimension, for there is direct reference to the personality factors involved in the development and maintenance of the norm. Specifically, such personality tendencies as frustration, anxiety, feelings of role ambiguity, and resentment are shown to be involved in the creation of the subculture. The mutual influence of personality and culture is not a distinctive characteristic of this type of subculture, of course, for they are everywhere interactive. Thus:

Tendencies for parents to respond harshly to their children's aggressive behavior, for instance, if common to the members of a society, are to be referred equally to the culture and to the modal personality of the parents. But the result in the developing child is not a foregone conclusion: present knowledge suggests that under specifiable conditions outcomes as different as rigid politeness or touchy latent hostility may follow. These consequences in turn may lead to cultural elaborations that seem superficially remote from the cultural starting point, yet are dynamically linked with it. . . .[1]

As this quotation suggests, culture and personality are always empirically tied together. Yet the nature of the relation is not the same in all cases. The term subculture, when used in the third way described here, raises to a position of prominence one particular kind of dynamic linkage between norms and personality: the creation of a series of inverse or counter values (opposed to those of the surrounding society) in face of serious frustration or conflict. To call attention to the special aspects of this kind of normative system, I suggest the term *contraculture*. Before exploring the relationship between subculture and contraculture, however, the range of meanings given subculture even when it is limited to the second usage requires comment.

SUBCULTURE AND ROLE

The variety of referents for the term subculture is very wide because the normative systems of sub-societies can be differentiated on many grounds. The groups involved may range from a large regional subdivision to a religious sect with only one small congregation. The distinctive norms may involve many aspects of life—religion, language, diet, moral values—or, for example, only a few separate practices among the members of an occupational group. Further distinctions among subcultures might be made on the basis of time (has the subculture persisted through a number of generations?), origin (by migration, absorption by a dominant society, social or physical segregation, occupational specialization, and other sources), and by the mode of relationship to the surrounding culture (from indifference to conflict). Such wide variation in the phenomena covered by a term can be handled by careful specification of the several grounds for subclassification. Confusion has arisen not so much from the scope of the term subculture as from its use as a substitute for "role." Only with great effort is some degree of clarity being achieved in the use of the role concept and the related terms "position" and "role behavior." Were this development retarded by confusion of role with subculture it would be unfortunate. All societies have differentiating roles, but

[1] Brewster Smith, "Anthropology and Psychology," in John Gillin, editor, *For a Science of Social Man*, New York: Macmillan, 1954, p. 61.

only heterogeneous societies have subcultures. Role is *that part of* a full culture that is assigned, as the appropriate rights and duties, to those occupying a given position. These rights and duties usually interlock into a system with those of persons who occupy other positions. They are known to and accepted by all those who share the culture. Thus the role of a physician is known, at least in vague outline, by most persons in a society and it is seen as part of the total culture. (This is not to prejudge the question of role consensus, for there may be many non-role aspects of being a physician.) But subculture is not tied in this way into the larger cultural complex: it refers to norms that set a group apart from, not those that integrate a group with, the total society. Subcultural norms, as contrasted with role norms, are unknown to, looked down upon, or thought of as separating forces by the other members of a society. There are doubtless subcultural aspects of being a physician—normative influences affecting his behavior that are not part of his role, not culturally designated rights and duties. But the empirical mixture should not obscure the need for this analytic distinction.

Along with confusion with the role concept, subculture carries many of the ambiguities associated with the parent concept of culture. In much social scientific writing it is not at all clear whether culture refers to norms, that is, to expected or valued behavior, or to behavior that is widely followed and therefore normal in a statistical sense only. This dual referent is particularly likely to be found in the work of anthropologists. Perhaps because their concepts are derived largely from the study of relatively more stable and homogeneous societies, they draw less sharply the distinction between the statistically normal and the normative. Sociologists are more apt to find it necessary to explore the tensions between the social order and culture, to be alert to deviations, and they are therefore more likely to define culture abstractly as a shared normative system. Yet much of the commentary on subculture refers to behavior. In my judgment this identification is unwise. Behavior is the result of the convergence of many forces. One should not assume, when the members of a group behave in similar ways, that cultural norms produce this result. Collective behavior theory and personality theory may also help to account for the similarities.

CONTRACULTURE

Failure to distinguish between role and subculture and vagueness in the concept of culture itself are not the only difficulties in the use of the idea of subculture. Perhaps more serious is the tendency to obscure, under this one term, two levels of explanation, one sociological and the other social-psychological, with a resulting failure to understand the causal forces at work. On few topics can one get wider agreement among sociologists than on the dangers of reductionism. If a psychologist attempts to explain social facts by psychological theories, we throw the book (probably Durkheim) at him; we emphasize the "fallacy of misplaced concreteness." In view of the widespread neglect of sociocultural factors in the explanation of behavior, this is a necessary task. It makes vitally important, however, keen awareness by sociologists that they also deal with an abstract model. Perhaps we can reverse Durkheim's dictum to say: Do not try to explain social psychological facts by sociological theories; or, more adequately, do not try to explain *behavior* (a product of the interaction of sociocultural and personality influences) by a sociological theory alone. Lewis Yablonsky has recently reminded us that an excessively sociological theory of gangs can result in our seeing a definite group structure and a clear pattern of norms where in fact there is a "near-group," with an imprecise definition of boundaries and limited agreement on norms. Carelessly used, our concepts can obscure the facts we seek to understand.

To see the cultural element in delinquency or in the domination of an individual by his adolescent group, phenomena that on the surface are non-cultural or even "anti-cultural," was a long step forward in their explanation. But it is also necessary to see the non-cultural aspects of some "norms"—phenomena that on the surface seem thoroughly cultural. Our vocabulary needs to be rich enough to help us to deal with these differences. The tendency to use the same term to refer to phenomena that share *some* elements in common, disregarding important differences, is to be content with phyla names when we need also to designate genus and species.

To sharpen our analysis, I suggest the use of the term contraculture wherever the normative system of a group contains, as a primary element, a theme of conflict with the values of the total society, where personality variables are directly involved in the development and maintenance of the group's values, and wherever its norms can be understood only by reference to the relationships of the group to a surrounding dominant culture. None of these criteria definitely separates contraculture from subculture because each is a continuum. Sub-societies fall along a range with respect to each criterion. The values of most subcultures probably conflict in some measure with the larger culture. In a contraculture, however, the conflict element is central; many of the values, indeed, are specifically contradictions of the values of the dominant culture. Similarly, personality variables are involved in the development and maintenance of all cultures and subcultures, but usually the influence of personality is by way of variations around a theme that is part of the culture. In a contraculture, on the other hand, the theme itself expresses the tendencies of the persons who compose it. Finally, the norms of all subcultures are doubtless affected in some degree by the nature of the relationship with the larger culture. A subculture, as a pure type, however, does not require, for its understanding, intensive analysis of interaction with the larger culture; that is, its norms are not, to any significant degree, a product of that interaction. But a contraculture can be understood only by giving full attention to the interaction of the group which is its bearer with the larger society. It is one thing to say that the subculture of the rural, lower-class Negro encourages slow, inefficient work. It is another thing to say, with Charles S. Johnson, that such a norm represents "pseudo-ignorant malingering," a contracultural way of describing the same phenomenon. Johnson stressed the conflict element, the extent to which the norm was a product of interaction of white and Negro. There is certainly value in emphasizing the subcultural source of some of the values of southern Negroes. Against racist views or individual explanations, the sociologist opposes the subcultural: If they strive less, have different sexual mores, or otherwise vary from standards of the dominant society, it is in part because they have been socialized in accordance with different norms. But this is not enough, for their similar behavior may be interpreted in part as a shared response to a frustrating environment.

Empirically, subcultural and contracultural influences may be mixed, of course. Delinquency and adolescent behavior almost certainly manifest both influences. The need, however, is to develop a clean analytic distinction between the two in order to interpret the wide variations in their mixture.

ADOLESCENT SUBCULTURE AND CONTRACULTURE

The utility of the distinction between contraculture and subculture can be tested by applying it to several research problems where the concept of subculture has been widely used. There is an extensive literature that interprets the behavior of adolescents substantially in these terms. In the words of R. J. Havighurst and Hilda Taba: "Recent studies of adolescents have emphasized the fact that boys and girls in their teens have a culture of their own with moral standards and with moral pressures behind those standards. This culture has been called the 'adolescent peer culture.' " Or Riesman: "All the morality is the group's. Indeed, even the fact that it is a morality is concealed by the confusing notion that the function of the group is to have fun, to play. . . ." A close reading of the literature on adolescent culture reveals at least four different levels of interpretation, often only partially distinguished:

1. There is a cultural level, in which the roles of adolescent boys and girls are described, or the specialties (in Linton's sense) are designated. There is no reason to introduce concepts other than role or specialty to refer to norms that are generally accepted by elders and youths alike as appropriate to youth.

2. On the subcultural level, there are norms that manifest some separate system of values accepted within the adolescent group. These norms are not part of the role of youth. In part they are unknown to the elders; in part they conflict with standards accepted by the elders. They are learned, not by socialization in the total society, but by interaction within the sub-society of youth. Thus interests, games, speech patterns, and aesthetic tastes may be communicated among an age-group with little reference to the larger culture.

3. There are currents of fashion or of other collective behavior that sweep through an adolescent group, strongly influencing the behavior of its members. Although it is difficult to distinguish fashion from culture—many empirical phenomena have aspects of both—it is wise to keep them apart conceptually.

This is not always done. The terminology of Riesman is closer to that of fashion than of culture, but the net impression of his analysis is that he is thinking of control by the peer group primarily as a cultural phenomenon. And the sentence following the one quoted above from Havighurst and Taba reads: "Boys and girls, desiring the approval of their age mates, follow the fashions of the peer culture in morals, dress, and speech. . . ." If the peer group influence stems from fashion, then strictly speaking it is not culture. The two differ to some degree in their origins, their functions, and their consequences.

4. Many analyses of the control exercised by a youth group over its members employ the *concept* of contraculture, although the terminology and the assumptions are often those of subculture or culture. There is emphasis on the cross-pressures which young people feel: they want to be adults, yet fear to leave the securities of childhood; they experience contradictory adult treatment—a demand for grownup behavior here, the prevention of it there; ambiguity of self-image leads to efforts to prove oneself a full-fledged adult; there is sexual frustration. The peer group may help one to struggle with these cross-pressures, as described by Talcott Parsons: "Perhaps the best single point of reference for characterizing the youth culture lies in its contrast with the dominant pattern of the adult male role. By contrast with emphasis on responsibility in this role, the orientation of the youth culture is more or less specifically irresponsible." This irresponsibility cannot be understood simply as another cultural norm, as part of the "role" of youth, although these are Parsons' terms. It must be studied in the context of strain, of role ambiguity. Some sociologists explain this irresponsibility as merely a manifestation of the youth culture, thus obscuring the personality factors also involved. The description and analysis of an adolescent subculture, to be sure, are an important contribution to the sociology of youth. Many adolescents spend a great deal of time in groups that sustain norms different from those of the adult world; and adults often respond to the behavior that follows these norms in an "ethnocentric" way. To rely on a subcultural explanation alone, however, is to disregard the emergent quality of many of the standards and to minimize the fact that they are often in direct conflict with adult standards (which most adolescents themselves will soon accept).

This sharp conflict of values requires explanation. Parsons states the facts clearly: "Negatively, there is a strong tendency to repudiate interests in adult things, and to feel at least a certain recalcitrance to the pressure of adult expectations and disciplines. . . . Thus the youth culture is not only, as is true of the curricular aspects of formal education, a matter of age status as such but also shows signs of being a product of tensions in the relationship of younger people and adults." At several other points Parsons develops the "reaction" theme and later uses the concept of "reaction-formation." Should these various phenomena be subsumed under the concept of culture? It is one thing for a society to train its youth to certain ways of behaving. It is quite another for a youth group to develop inverse values in an effort to struggle with role ambiguities and strains. The adolescent may experience both as normative sanctions; but that should scarcely lead the social analyst to disregard their differences. I suggest the term contraculture in order to indicate the normative *and* the conflict aspects of this type of situation.

DELINQUENT CONTRACULTURE

The usefulness of separating subcultural and contracultural influences is seen particularly clearly in the analysis of delinquency and of criminality generally. Perhaps in no other field were there more substantial gains in understanding made possible by the introduction of a sociological point of view to supplement and to correct individualistic and moralistic interpretations. There is little need to review the extensive literature, from *Delinquent Gangs* to *Delinquent Boys,* to establish the importance of the normative element in criminal and delinquent behavior. It is a mistake, however, to try to stretch a useful concept into a total theory. A "complex-adequate" analysis may seem less sharp and definitive than one based on one factor, but it is likely to be far more useful. Albert K. Cohen's excellent work, although labelled as a study of the culture of the gang, does not overlook the psychogenic sources of delinquency. In fact, his explanation of the origins of the subculture (contraculture) and its functions for the lower class male makes clear that the norms of the gang are not learned, accepted, and taught in the same way that we learn what foods to eat, what clothes to wear, what language to speak. The very existence of the gang is a sign, in part, of blocked ambition. Because tensions set in motion by this blockage cannot be resolved by achievement of dominant values, such values are repressed, their importance denied, counter-values affirmed. The gang member is often ambivalent. Thwarted in his desire to achieve higher status by the criteria of the dominant society, he accepts criteria he can meet; but the reaction-formation in this response is indicated by the content of the delinquent norms—non-utilitarian, malicious, and negativistic, in Cohen's terms. This negative polarity represents the need to repress his own tendencies to accept the dominant cultural standards. This is not to say that the values of the gang cannot be explained partially by cultural analysis, by some extension of the idea that "the mores can make anything right." But I suggest that Cohen's multiple-factor analysis might have been clearer, and less subject to misinterpretation, had he introduced the concept of contraculture alongside the concept of subculture. One reviewer, for example, completely disregards the "negative polarity" theme:

> In an overall summary, cultural delinquency is a phenomenon of culture, society, and sociocultural experience. It is a positive thing: members of the several social classes are socialized, but there is a differential content in the socialization. Delinquency is not a negative thing; it is not a result of the breakdown of society, nor of the failure to curb criminal instincts, nor of the failure of the family, the church, or the school. The same set of concepts, the same social processes, and the

same set of logical assumptions account for both delinquency and lawfulness. Since delinquency is of this character, it is unnecessary to invent any pathology to account for it.[2]

This statement neither adequately represents Cohen's thesis nor encourages us to explore a number of important questions: Why do only some of those who are exposed to the delinquent "subculture" learn it? Why do those who follow the subculture often manifest ambivalence and guilt feelings? Why do many of the same patterns of behavior occur in areas and among groups where the presence of the subculture is much less clear (middle-class delinquency)? What is the significance of the fact that the delinquent subculture is not only different from but in part at least a reversal of the values of the dominant culture? The use of a purely subcultural model of analysis discourages or even prevents the raising of these questions and thus precludes adequate answers to them.

Cohen and James Short have dealt with several of these issues by suggesting the need for a typology. Specifically for the study of delinquency, they propose five types of subcultures: the parent male (the central pattern described in *Delinquent Boys*), the conflict-oriented, the drug addict, the semiprofessional theft, and the middle-class subcultures. Although the criteria of classification are not entirely clear, these categories are primarily descriptive. The concept of contraculture might be added to this list as a type of subculture, if the one distinctive criterion used to designate a subculture is the presence in a sub-society of a normative system that separates it from the total society. Such a procedure does not seem, however, to produce an adequate taxonomy. If the shift is made from description to analysis, or from an interest in the content of norms to their etiology, an important difference emerges between subculture and contraculture: the one set of norms derives from standard socialization in a sub-society; the other stems from conflict and frustration in the experience of those who share many of the values of the whole society but are thwarted in their efforts to achieve those values.

It should be stressed once more that these are analytic concepts, no one of which is adequate to handle the empirical variations of delinquent behavior. Failure to recognize the abstract quality of our conceptual tools leads to unnecessary disagreements. When Walter B. Miller describes the "Lower Class Culture as a Generating Milieu of Gang Delinquency," for example, he points to an important series of influences that derive from the value system of the lower-class community. In his effort to emphasize this aspect of the etiology of delinquency, however, he tends to overlook the kind of evidence reported by Gresham M. Sykes and David Matza, Cohen, Harold Finestone, Yablonsky, William and Joan McCord, and others concerning collective behavior and personality variables. Surely the evidence is now rich enough for us to state definitely that delinquency is a multi-variable product. The task ahead is not

[2] Frank Hartung, in a review of *Delinquent Boys, American Sociological Review,* 20 (December, 1955), p. 752.

to prove that it stems largely from cultural or subcultural or contracultural influences, but to spell out the conditions under which these and other factors will be found in various empirical mixtures.

CONTRACULTURAL ASPECTS OF CLASS AND OCCUPATION

The same admixture of the concepts of culture, subculture, and contraculture is found in the extensive literature on occupations and classes. Doubtless all three forces are found in many instances, and the research task is to untangle their various influences. It may stretch the meaning of the term too far to speak of the *position* of the "middle-class member," with its culturally designated role specifications, although in relatively stable societies the usage seems appropriate. In such societies, many of the rights and obligations of various status levels are culturally defined. In more mobile class systems, however, subcultural and contracultural norms become important. Our understanding of the American class system has certainly been deepened in the last twenty years by the descriptions of differences, among classes, in value perspectives, time orientations, levels of aspiration, leisure-time styles, and child rearing practices.

The introduction of the concept of subculture has helped to avoid class derived biases in the interpretation of the wide variations in these phenomena. In class analysis as in the study of deviations, however, there may be some over-compensation in the effort to eliminate the distortions of a middle-class and often rural perspective. There is evidence to suggest that differences between classes are based less upon different values and norms than the subcultural approach suggests. The "innovations" of lower-class members, to use Merton's term, are not simply subcultural acts defined as innovative by middle-class persons. They are in part responses to a frustrating situation. They are efforts to deal with the disjunction of means and ends. When the disjunction is reduced, the variations in value and behavior are reduced. Thus Bernard C. Rosen found, "surprisingly," that Negroes in the Northeast made higher scores on an "achievement value" test than his description of Negro "culture" led him to expect. This may indicate that the low achievement response is less the result of a subcultural norm than a protest against a difficult situation. If the situation improves, the achievement value changes. Richard M. Stephenson's discovery that occupational plans of lower-class youth are considerably below those of higher-class youth, but that their aspirations are only slightly lower, bears on this same point. His data suggest that the classes differ not only in norms, but also in opportunity. Differences in behavior, therefore, are only partly a result of subcultural contrasts. The lower educational aspirations of lower-class members are also found to be in part situationally induced, not simply normatively induced. When the situation changes, values and behavior change, as Raymond A. Mulligan found in his study of the response of the sons of blue-collar workers to the educational opportunities of the GI Bill, and as Alan B. Wilson reports in his investigation of the aspirations of lower-class boys attending higher-class schools and upper-class boys attending lower-class schools.

In short, our thinking about differences in behavior among social classes will be sharpened if we distinguish among those differences that derive from role influences, those based on subcultural variations, and those that express contracultural responses to deprivation. The proportions will vary from society to society; the research task is to specify the conditions under which various distributions occur. One would expect, to propose one hypothesis, to find more contracultural norms among lower-class members of an open society than in a similar group in a closed society.

The interpretation of differential behavior among the members of various occupational categories can also be strengthened by the distinctions made above. Here the contrast between role and subculture is especially useful. The role of a teacher consists of the rights and duties that *integrate* him into a system of expected and established relationships with others. The teaching subculture, on the other hand, insofar as it exists, *separates* teachers from the cultural world of others. It is either unknown to others or, if known, a source of disagreement and perhaps of conflict with others. There are also contracultural aspects of some occupational styles of life. In interpreting the differences between the values of jazz musicians and "squares," for example, Howard S. Becker writes: "their rejection of commercialism in music and squares in social life was part of the casting aside of the total American culture by men who could enjoy privileged status but who were unable to achieve a satisfactory personal adjustment within it." Their style of life, in other words, can be understood only by supplementing the cultural and subcultural dimensions with the conflict theme. W. B. Cameron develops the same point. Although he makes no use of the term subculture, he describes the differentiating norms of the dance-band group, presumably a result of the "esoteric" aspects of their art, the differences in their time schedule, and the like. But he also describes the *contra* aspects of some of the norms, and suggests that they derive from the fact that early recruitment ties the jazz musician to the adolescence problem.

CONCLUSION

Poorly defined terms plague research in many areas, particularly in the specification of relationships between sociological and social psychological levels of analysis. Thus "anomie" is still used to refer both to a social structural fact and to a personality fact, although this confusion is gradually being reduced. "Role" may refer, alternately, to rights and duties prescribed for the occupants of a position or to individual performance of that position. And subculture, I have suggested, is used to designate both the traditional norms of a sub-society and the emergent norms of a group caught in a frustrating and conflict-laden situation. This paper indicates that there are differences in the origin, function, and perpetuation of traditional and emergent norms, and suggests that the use of the concept contraculture for the latter might improve sociological analysis.

Hypotheses to guide the study of subculture can most profitably be derived from a general theory of culture. As an illustration, it may be hypothesized that a subculture will appear, in the first instance, as a result of mobility or an extension of communication that brings groups of different cultural background into membership in the same society, followed by physical or social isolation or both that prevents full assimilation.

Hypotheses concerning contracultures, on the other hand, can best be derived from social psychological theory—from the study of collective behavior, the frustration-aggression thesis, or the theory of group formation. One might hypothesize, for example, that under conditions of deprivation and frustration of major values (in a context where the deprivation is obvious because of extensive communication with the dominant group), and where value confusion and weak social controls obtain, contracultural norms will appear. One would expect to find, according to these propositions, many subcultural values among southern rural Negroes. Among first and second generation urban Negroes, however, one would expect an increase in contracultural norms. Both groups are deprived, but in the urban situation there is more "value leakage" from the dominant group, more value confusion, and weakened social controls.

The subculture of the sociologist requires sophistication about the full range of human behavior. This desideratum has led to the proposition that the vast diversity of norms believed in and acted upon by the members of a modern society is not a sign of value confusion and breakdown but rather an indication that urban life brings into one system of interaction persons drawn from many cultural worlds. One unanticipated consequence of the sociological subculture may be that we exaggerate the normative insulation and solidarity of these various worlds. An important empirical question concerns the extent and results of their interaction.

From time to time in the development of sociology, important advances have been made by members of the profession in the clarification of a concept and the integration of its various internal aspects. One such advance was made by Alfred McClung Lee in the following formulation. Professor Lee proposed that culture actually consists of three different levels of social generalization and social compulsion. The first, the least generalized and at the same time the most compulsive of all, is the individual level, defined culturally in terms of a continuum of patterns that range in compulsion from practices to habits. The second, more generalized but less compulsive than the first, is the group level of culture, defined in terms of a continuum that extends from the less compulsive folkways to the more compulsive mores. Last is the societal level of culture, the most generalized and the least compulsive of all, defined in terms of another continuum of compulsion running from conventions to morals.

The inverse relationship between generalization and compulsion at different culture levels suggested by Professor Lee is demonstrated over and over in our society in struggles concerning socialized medicine, freedom of speech, academic freedom, and dominant and minority group tensions, to mention only a few social issues.

13. LEVELS OF CULTURE AS LEVELS OF SOCIAL GENERALIZATION *

ALFRED MCCLUNG LEE

Brooklyn College

In texts in social psychology and sociology, there appears to be unabated confusion in the use of such terms as "mores," "morals," "moral code," "morality," and "moral behavior." At times related to such other terms as "folkways," "customs," "ways," "practices," and "social habits," the description and the use of the terms all too frequently lack as great precision as might be obtainable without doing violence to the facts and generalizations so labeled.

From time to time, writers who have been bothered by this vagueness have either sought to clarify W. G. Sumner's influential folkways-mores theory or have rejected or ignored it and have offered another in its place. As a matter of fact, even Sumner as the sponsor of "folkways" and "mores" as sociological terms raised at least as many questions without attempting to answer them as he did questions for which he provided tentative answers. His definition and usage of the terms, too, left much to be desired in consistency.

The point has frequently been made that "folkways" and "mores" are such vague terms or such general and unusable conceptions that they might well be discarded. Even works by apparent admirers of Sumner's contributions make but general and vague or slight reference to or utilization of the folkways-mores theory of culture. But substantial arguments can be raised in support of the theory's use, albeit in modified and clarified form.

The introduction of the term, mores, as something different from an individual's corresponding habits and still not as tenuous as moral principles, gives a label to recognizable social phenomena for which the English language had not provided an adequate term prior to the publication of Sumner's *Folkways*. The word folkways also has rather appropriate connotations and can be given suitable denotations for sociological purposes. In short, while these terms are not all one might ideally ask, they have achieved wide scientific and popular usage—wider, it is generally agreed, than competing terms. The sociologist, too, can seldom invent new labels of worth for his concepts, but must frequently select words in general usage, especially when possible ones are cur-

* *American Sociological Review,* Vol. 10, No. 4, August, 1945, pp. 485–495.

rent, and give them scientific utility through more precise definition, through more exact relation of labels to objective observations. Examples are race, adaptation, assimilation, conventions, morals, practices, habits, as well as the now popularized folkways and mores.

Popular terminology has the added merit of permitting contributions stated in it to reach non-specialist audiences more readily and more effectively than contributions set forth in esoteric language. It places the sociologist in the perspective of being a clarifier of social thinking about society rather than in that of being merely a creator of verbalizations of possible value to specialists.

Before attempting here something of a reorientation and clarification of a part of Sumner's folkways-mores theory, it will be profitable first to summarize briefly what he apparently conceived that theory to be:

Sumner said that a folkway is "a habit for each [member] and a custom for the [group or] society. . . . It has the power of a habit and custom, and is carried on by tradition." A folkway can be seen, therefore, as a summarizing abstraction, a social construct or patterned typification, derived from the relatively similar behavior (verbal and other) exhibited in the presence of similar stimuli by members of a group or of a number of groups in a society.

Certain folkways become vested with "a moral opinion; namely, an opinion that a usage is favorable to welfare." These folkways Sumner called mores. In other words, as Sumner stated elsewhere, folkways become mores "when they include a judgment that they are conducive to societal welfare, and then they exert a coercion on the individual to conform to them, although they are not co-ordinated by any authority." To emphasize the compulsive nature of mores, Sumner adds that the "mores are social ritual in which we all participate unconsciously. . . . For the great mass of mankind as to all things, and for all of us for a great many things, the rule to do as all do suffices." Or, as Robert E. Park and E. W. Burgess have stated it, "Under the influence of the mores men act typically, and so representatively, not as individuals but as members of a group."

In view of the automatic adherence of individuals to patterns of behavior resembling the types Sumner called folkways and mores, at first glance one would assume that he would work out a differentiation between such conceptions and the more idealized and generalized patterns we call conventions and morals. This anticipation is given some impetus by the appearance of both mores and morals in the subtitle of his book, *Folkways*. But further reading suggests that Sumner merely rejected morals on the whole as a scientific term, even though he made vague use of it from time to time. In *Folkways,* it is said to have been Sumner's purpose "to relieve the conception of custom of . . . indefiniteness and intangibility. . . . It was found necessary to adopt the terms 'folkways' and 'mores' to cover social usages and traditions, in order to evade the set of vague connotations that cling about the more familiar term." Sumner took the position that "philosophy and ethics are products of the folkways. They are taken out of the mores, but are never original and creative; they are secondary and derived. They often interfere in the second stage of the sequence, —act, thought, act."

By not distinguishing between a conception that might well be denominated morals or moral principles and the one that he called mores, Sumner permitted his employment of mores to fall heir to some of the vagaries associated with the other word. About as far as he went in stripping mores of moralistic ideas was in his discussion of "Religion and the Mores." There, in relating religious morals to popular mores, he comments, "No religion of those which we call world-religions, and which have a complete system, is ever put in practice as a whole; the people always take out of it what suits their tastes and ideas, and that means especially their mores. . . . All the elaborate (i.e., civilized) religions impose duties which are irksome, especially if they are interferences with interest or with human passions and appetites. The duties are neglected, and then comes fear of the anger of the deity. At this point ritual enters in as expiation, and atonement, especially in the forms of self-discipline, sacrifice, self-mutilation, scourging, fines, fasting, pilgrimages, church-going, etc." Despite this suggestion of a basis for differentiation, however, the confusion occasioned by lack of distinction is emphasized by the recent identification of mores by Sumner's student, A. G. Keller, with "elementary morals." In more detail, Keller's theory is that the "morals are always secondary, for they are merely the mores which, by their lastingness and real or fancied importance, have become positive and are defined in dogma and rule." This identification of the morals with the mores overlooks their chief characteristic: They are on a different level of generalization from the folkways and mores. As is indicated below, the conventions and morals may well be regarded as societal conceptions, and the folkways and mores as more precise and compulsive group constructs. Consequences to this theory of the fact that groups vary widely in size—from the dyad to something very large—are taken up below.

This outline and critique of certain fundamental aspects of Sumner's folkways-mores theory is naturally too over-brief to be adequate, but it perhaps serves to place certain conceptions before us. As his ideas are developed in greater detail by Sumner in his *Folkways* and elsewhere, however, such questions as the following are neglected: Even in primitive societies with relatively simple structures, are the folkways and mores of the constituent groups of the same order of generalization from individual behavior and of the same order of compulsiveness upon individual behavior as the over-all conventions and morals? Are there not immoral mores and immoretic morals in a great many if not in all societies?

Robert S. Lynd, in his *Knowledge for What?,* speaks of how our culture contains "a wealth of contradictory assumptions," but are these "assumptions" so contradictory when related to group subcultures? Are they not contradictory subcultures—immoral mores, variant mores, and immoretic morals—rather than "assumptions"? Ralph Linton, in his *The Study of Man,* gives considerable emphasis to "cultural alternatives," but to what extent do such differentiations within a culture offer the individual an actual range of choice as to suitable practice patterns? For any given group or class status, is the range not very narrow? What are the consequences of such relationships to individuals as they move temporally through the age groups and as they travel "vertically" or "horizontally" from group to group?

In a brief paper, such questions naturally cannot be answered, even in a tentative sense, but it is proposed to advance here a restatement and an integration of several aspects of a theory of culture that may prove helpful in social and societal analyses, in the study of actual situations such as are suggested by the foregoing questions. This re-orientation and integration resulted from an inability upon the part of the author to verify these aspects of the Sumnerian and certain other theories of culture in terms of actual social observations without the proposed modifications.

In this formulation, it is suggested that culture consists of three levels of social generalization from behavioral phenomena. These are: (1) *the individual level,* which may be defined culturally in terms of a continuum of patterns that ranges from practices to habits; (2) *the group level,* defined in terms of a similar continuum that extends from folkways to mores; and (3) *the societal level,* defined in terms of another continuum that may be thought of as running from conventions to morals or moral principles. If it were not for the aura of absolutism some are now attempting to gather about "values," there would be no objection to that term as a synonym for morals. These continua are the subject of the diagrammatic analogy presented in Figure 1, "Societal, Group, and Individual Aspects of Culture."

These continua, in a given society, are regarded as consisting of elements related to comparable interests and as ranging from patterns accepted automatically and without any marked degree of social compulsion (practices, folkways, and conventions) to patterns concerning adherence to which considerable social compulsion is exerted (habits, mores, and morals).

Before further discussion of Figure 1, it should be noted that the author's conception of "group" is not as categorical or truncated as some might infer from the foregoing. A group is taken to be any aggregation of two or more people who have some similar interest or interests and who thus in this more or less narrowly defined aspect of their lives participate in what amounts to a common area of social interaction on common terms. In general, as the interests served are less immediately physiological (less immediately associated with maintenance and reproduction) or as the groups have fewer opportunities for face-to-face participation, the character of the social interaction becomes more tenuous, and the group folkways and mores are correspondingly more vaguely defined. In tiny groups, the folkways and mores resemble more closely the practices and habits of their members in corresponding areas. In large groups, they resemble more closely conventions and morals.

The significant familial, vocational, religious, and neighborhood groups are types to which "the group level" most obviously applies, types that contrast with "the individual level" and "the societal level." It is recognized, however, that only arbitrary distinctions can be drawn between individual and small group phenomena, as overtly manifested, and between large group and societal phenomena. As in describing other social and societal characteristics, one deals here with phenomena that may be arranged in continua and for which usefully representative types may be selected. Some may regard this sort of analysis as clumsy, despite its close approximation to sense observations, but categorical analyses become obstructive to the determination of significant relationships.

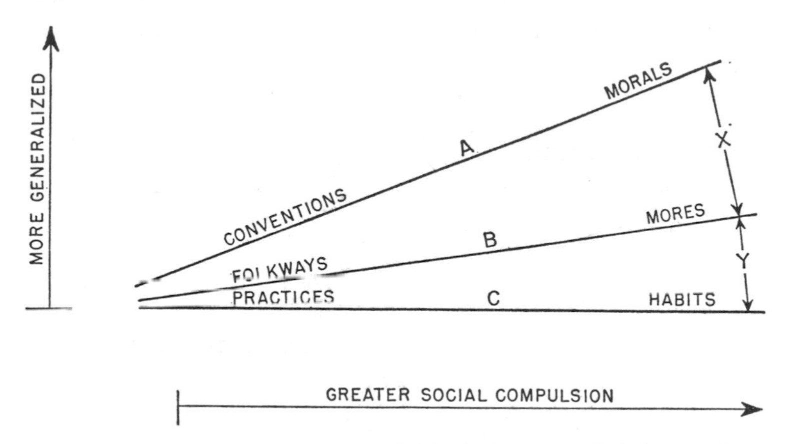

FIGURE 1. Societal, Group, and Individual Aspects of Culture. *A* represents *societal* concepts of behavior patterns arranged in a continuum from conventions to morals; *B* represents corresponding *group* constructs of behavior patterns arranged in a continuum from folkways to mores; and *C* represents corresponding *individual* patterns arranged in a continuum from practices to habits. *X* is a measure of group deviation ("immorality") from societal norms, which may be variously interpreted, justified, or obscured. *Y* is a measure of individual deviation from group norms. The diagram is in terms of one individual in one group in one society, naturally a highly simplified characterization.

For the purposes of the present discussion, it will be assumed that one group continuum is theoretically adequate for purposes of typification, and that the relatively compulsive familial, vocational, religious, and neighborhood groups are sufficiently typical of "the group level" to characterize it, that they are at least sufficiently typical to highlight a workable theory.

To return to the discussion of Figure 1: The patterns of behavior of an individual group-member dealing with some interest are more specific than the typical group construct, the folkway. The individual patterns tend to have unique details, to deviate in various more or less minor ways from group norms. When these deviations are significant and recognized, they are subject to group disapproval or rationalization and to individual justification.

The folkways, in turn, cluster more or less closely about the core of conceptions that have come to be recognized as belonging to the society's conventions-morals continuum. The mores can thus be immoral and group members embody this judgment or a rationalization of it in such statements to novices as, "Let's not be naïve. It's time for you to learn what the score is." The morals of a society can also be regarded as immoretic in terms of a given group's mores. The more or less strained relationship of a given group mos to its corresponding societal moral principle, if significant and recognized, may be subject either to the disapproval of other groups or to socially accepted moral rationalizations. At any rate, such deviations are usually covered with group-satisfying adequacy by the group's own social rationalizations.

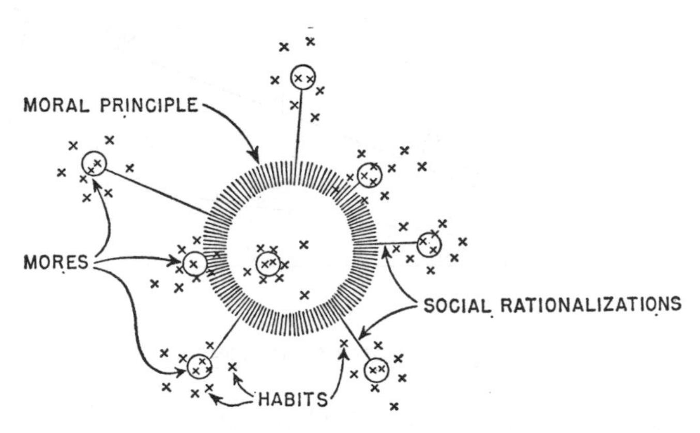

FIGURE 2. A Moral Principle in Relation to Corresponding Mores and Habits. A societal concept, a *moral principle,* is here related graphically to corresponding group constructs, *mores,* of which it is in part a generalization and to which it has a more or less strained relationship, expressed in *social rationalizations*. Each of the corresponding mores is in turn related to the individual patterns, the *habits,* of which it is in part a generalization and to which it has a more or less strained relationship, variously criticized and justified. The habits, in turn, are social generalizations based by the individual and the group upon actual incidents in the behavior of individuals.

For a diagrammatic analogy to typify these theoretical relationships, see Figure 2, "A Moral Principle in Relation to Corresponding Mores and Habits."

These relationships are demonstrated time after time in our society in struggles over so-called socialized medicine, freedom of speech, academic freedom, improved interracial and intercultural relations, and the budgets of civic and religious organizations. Let us discuss each of these three cultural levels in somewhat greater detail:

1. *Individual Level.* The continuum on the individual level from practices to habits was labeled with somewhat more arbitrarily selected terms, it is admitted, than the continua on the other two levels, the group (folkways-mores) and the societal (conventions-morals). By practices, reference is made

to socially exemplified behavior patterns taken on by individuals with little or no social compulsion. They are the individual counterparts of folkways and conventions plus the results of peculiar individual experiences and somewhat unique or variant inferences. Habits are practices the taking on of which has been accompanied by some form of real or fancied, actual or potential, societal and group compulsion; they are the individualized or personalized counterparts of mores and morals plus the results of peculiar individual experiences and somewhat unique or variant inferences. Since these terms are used here in an overt behavioral sense, the problem of whether such patterns are conscious or subconscious may or may not have societal or group significance. The members of the Harvard Psychological Clinic ascribe to a habit system behavior that "has become automatic, that proceeds without much conscious intervention, that recurs repeatedly in the same form." They say that it "is formed by the structuralization (mechanization) of what has frequently recurred, whether determined by the Superego, the Ego or the Id. The habit system accounts for most rigidities, particularly those which the individual himself cannot abandon."

As Leo W. Simmons has concluded, such a person as his Hopi subject is not only a creature, a creator, and a carrier of folkways and mores but also their manipulator. His Hopi "is a *creature* of his culture in the sense that his behavior—his acts, thoughts, and feeling tones or sentiments—are largely molded by it; and it is probably impossible to understand him without recognition of this fundamental fact." To an extent, the person is also "a *creator* of his culture in that he can never quite perfectly match up to the idealized standards, and may occasionally even initiate a variation—by accident, invention, or borrowing—and see it imitated by others until it has become a folkway or *mos*." The individual's role as a slightly imperfect carrier of culture is thus also clear, a transmitter to others of societal and group patterns. As a manipulator, he may have the luck or ingenuity to "utilize the mores to his own advantage," to "marshal them to strengthen his position or to coerce associates into fulfillment of his requirements; or he may even inspire other persons to make sacrifices. If he finds himself in situations of compromise, he may flaunt folkways, ignore mores, and take refuge in 'higher principles,' arguments of expediency, or supernatural indorsements."

The conclusions of Simmons are presented at some length both because of their pertinence to a discussion of the individual level of cultural generalization and also to suggest the consequences of his lack of differentiation between mores and morals. At one point, in discussing his Hopi as a creature of culture, Simmons identifies culture loosely with the mores. At another point, in analyzing in a summary fashion the role of his subject as a manipulator of culture, he assigns a significant role to cultural elements he calls "higher principles" and "supernatural indorsements," phenomena different apparently from the mores and yet societally compulsive and individually useful.

This internalization of the societal and of various groups' cultural patterns gradually turns a physiological phenomenon into a socialized person. Calling the normative aspects of habits, mores, and morals, "values," Gardner and Lois B. Murphy and T. M. Newcomb conclude that, for "better or worse, the child grows up in a world of values; much of his 'continuity,' his 'variability' and most of his 'consistency'—as well as most of his 'inconsistency'—come back ultimately to the pattern of values in terms of which he lives." In this process, to use our terminology, the individual constantly faces mores and morals patterned into roles and institutions; both types of patterning, as is indicated below, have their moretic and their moral aspects.

2. *Group Level.* Mores are practical, expedient, and compulsive; their contrast with society's morals is a measure of what is popularly labeled as group hypocrisy. Mores and other folkways are so inclusive that an adult member of several groups finds himself equipped to handle most problems involving social relationships in terms of the folkways of the groups to which he belongs rather than through reference to more rational procedures. Somewhat of the process of "becoming mature" in a society consists of a person accommodating his moral superego to the requirements of moretic group structures and individual desires and needs. Only in times of critical maladjustment in society do the folkways fail to furnish *folkways*-molded individuals with rather automatic guidance in social relationships, with definitions of the "common sense" things to do. At times of crisis, the resulting bewilderment emphasizes the all-embracing character of such traditional guides, despite inconsistencies between group mores and morals, and the trauma occasioned by being forced to face trying social problems without preconceived and socially tested formulas.

In terms of the institutional and role configurations in which culture predominantly presents itself to individuals, the folkways-mores patterns define the "internal" characteristics of such configurations. Behind the façade provided by morals-defined societal expectations of the proper, right, or "necessary" characteristics of an institution and its associated roles, the folkways-mores patterns define the ways in which an institution and its associated roles "really work." These patterns, which in a professional field conflict sharply with the textbook idealisms dictated by societal expectations (conventions-morals), are the practical and expedient understandings and techniques, the customary ways of exercising power, cutting corners on the morals, handling aggressiveness, exploiting submissiveness, and making the best of public relations and industrial relations situations.

These folkways are largely unwritten, accumulated as a result of "practical experience—not book learning," and fall into role configurations of considerable precision and, for a given time and place, of rather great rigidity. In addition, in their institutional configuration aspect, they also set the relations between functionaries and the "outside world" and between practical procedures and the institution's moral pretensions, as defined for it by society. Such clashes as those between the "practical men of affairs" and the "professors" can be interpreted in terms of the former being chiefly mores-molded and the latter being predominantly morals-shaped men. Only in avowed trades schools under industrial and professional domination, such as those of engineering and business administration, do idealistic societal expectations (morals) give way somewhat to group mores.

In addition to these structural configurations of folkways into roles and institutions, they may also be thought of ideologically as being related to sentiments and interests, even though individuals are rarely able to define their own sentiments with any accuracy and candor. Not only are sentiments not always understood on a verbal plane by individuals but the description of many actual sentiments in such terms is taboo. Such sentiments and deepset interests are psychologically complex emotional biases and canalizations of emotional drive, frequently ambivalent, determined culturally, environmentally, and physiologically. These factors, with a high degree of similarity among individuals in similar settings, help individuals to organize and rationalize their roles and their interpersonal and institutional relationships.

3. *Societal Level.* Conventions are societal generalizations of the folkways of constituent groups over long periods of time, characterized by being sufficiently glittering and general, even though dogmatic, to permit rationalistic avoidances of apparent contradiction. The morals are conventions derived over long periods from the mores of historical and contemporary groups and from traditional human aspirations, frustrations, and ascetic tendencies. Conventions, in other words, are such broadly accepted societal patterns as are included in language and social "mannerisms." Morals, on the other hand, are traditional generalities concerning right, wrong, duties, rights, and taboos handed down in a society and frequently formalized into sets of commandments, codes of ethics, or canons of ethical principles. They contain large elements of asceticism, humanitarianism, and formalism or ritualism. They dominate the teachings of societal surrogates—parents, ministers, teachers—even though they are frequently at odds, as is indicated above, with the group mores of such surrogates and of the groups served by them: "Do as I say, not as I do!"

Morals represent crystallizations of a society's traditional aspirations as vaguely defined somewhat colored by dominant group or class mores. They are chiefly significant in shaping the superegos of the young and in providing the main staples for propagandists—glittering generalities and name-calling symbols, righteous justifications and condemnations, suitably and variously interpreted, for certain social institutions, functionaries, and courses of action. Morals have no necessary congruity with the mores of a society's constituent groups or with the habit patterns of individuals, as Figure 2 suggests by analogy. Such subjects as theology, ethics, and traditional—but not scientific—"social science" concern themselves to a great measure with working out rationalizations between morals and group mores.

As the foregoing discussion of the group level suggested, folkways and conventions can be thought of as falling into role and institution configurations and of presenting themselves largely in those relationships to individuals. They can also be thought of as being organized ideologically—consciously or not—in terms of certain sentiments or major moral premises.

Moral roles and institutional structures are the societal definitions of what roles and institutions ought to be. They are the glittering façades of societal expectations. It is upon the basis of such definitions, by and large, that young people are attracted to professions; if their transition from moral to moretic comprehension is not handled gradually and carefully, disillusionment and even revulsion may result. As Thomas Henry Huxley noted, in his *Science and Morals* (1886), "The foundation of morality is to have done, once and for all, with lying." But men live in all societies more by the mores than by their morals. It sometimes takes a deal of patient and tenuous casuistry, or, more effectively, some obscuring social distances, to give group mores the "proper" social rationalizations, the "proper" relationships morally to societal morals.

With respect to major moral premises, it can be recalled that Abraham Lincoln discerned that public opinion, "on any subject, always has a 'central idea,' from which all its minor thoughts radiate." He referred to "the equality of man" as one such central idea. Morals, the stuff out of which public opinions are chiefly made, also have such central ideas or major moral premises. Such a major moral premise in our society as the Commandment, "Thou shalt not kill," becomes the center of a whole configuration of moral idealizations in peacetime, but in wartime the vagueness of morality and the expedient considerations embedded in the mores permit many professional moralists to sanction the necessity of killing. Similar illustrations are abundant in the fields of race relations, education, democracy, international relations, and elsewhere throughout our society's morals.

In the attempt being made here to reorient a complex sociological theory, adequate illustration would require a vast amount of space. Several examples only will be offered in addition to those given or referred to above; these are offered to emphasize the significance of the changes suggested. John Dollard notes "that the dominant aim of our society seems to be to middle-class-ify all of its members." This is probably due to the prolonged adolescence that is associated with the "strainer" or "get ahead" mores of middle-class people and with their concomitant requirement of longer training periods for their children. Since the social teachings of the children in the home and of students in schools are dominated more by societal morals than by the more expedient and practical mores of any given group, and since middle-class mores are rationalized in a sophisticated manner with societal morals, despite apparent contradictions, the morals-mindedness of middle-class people is thus emphasized. Their leadership in education, religion, and other civic and social affairs gives them an opportunity, especially in the United States, to extend this middle-class characteristic to the children of other classes and groups. In relatively stable societies morally, like England, where highly sophisticated and crystallized rationalizations of morals-mores contrasts are relatively established and unquestioned, the utility to the controlling group of the morals as instruments of social domination is greatly heightened.

A phrase that highlights the characteristics of the three levels of culture is "Honesty is the best policy," a dogma of American morals. Business group mores modify this to "Honesty is the best policy, but business is business." Labor group mores modify the general proposition, in turn, to "Honesty is the best policy, but a worker would be a fool if he didn't look out for Number One." And similar adaptations are available for practically every group in society, whether based upon age, professional, avocational, or other differences and interests. The individual adaptation of such a principle takes somewhat this form, "Honesty is the best policy, and business mores are all very well and should be followed, but in *this* case I've got a higher loyalty to my family and/or myself," a rationalization that leads sometimes to prison and that at least yields fascinating insights into "white collar" and other types of "criminality."

While these theoretical suggestions are presented briefly, it is hoped that they are adequate to propose a practical restatement of culture theory to meet the clinical demands of psychiatrists and students of social structure and dynamics and also to meet in part the need for a more tenable interconnection of psychiatric, social psychological, and societal theories.

SOCIAL ORGANIZATION

Culture, regardless of its level of generalization and degree of compulsion, is never transmitted outside of social structures or groups. Social differentiation, in other words, produces differentiation in thought, feeling, and action. Minimally defined as organizations consisting of two or more interacting individuals, all human groups—large or small, simple or complex, sacred or secular, voluntary or involuntary, formal or informal—share certain common characteristics. First of all, a group is marked by the antagonistic co-operation or bipolar tension of its membership. Whether it is a married couple or the United Nations, an inevitable process in the group is the interplay between the forces of integration and alienation, attraction and repulsion, co-operation and antagonism. Second, to belong to a group is to experience consciousness of like and unlike kind, to become aware of the in-group as distinguished from the out-group. A third characteristic of human groups is ethnocentrism, the tendency to evaluate life from the point of view of the norms and values of one's own group.

However, complete consensus has not developed among sociologists regarding the nature of the group. There are, instead, four major orientations: nominalism, interactionism, neo-nominalism, and realism. In the next article, Charles K. Warriner discusses each of these orientations and notes that neo-nominalism, the common-sense point of view, lacks the validity of realism as a legitimate sociological approach to group analysis.

14. GROUPS ARE REAL: A REAFFIRMATION *

CHARLES K. WARRINER
University of Kansas

The term "group" is an ancient one in the social sciences, but despite its antiquity there is little agreement on the nature of the reality to which it refers —or even if it refers to any reality at all. This problem has been fundamental to many of the arguments of the past. There have been times when we assured ourselves that the issues were resolved only to find that they have arisen again in somewhat different form.

Contemporary writings on the small group —research reports and theoretical statements—exhibit four major orientations to the group and to the question of its reality. Each of these orientations is here presented as a logically consistent point of view. However, it must be remembered that in their concrete representation they are not often so clearly stated or consistent. Any particular author may exhibit elements of several of these orientations.

Nominalism. The oldest, and the most extreme position in the light of contemporary knowledge, is the *nominalist* view that the group is not a real entity, but is merely a term used to refer to "an assemblage of individuals." According to this view, the term is reified if it is used to refer to anything more than the behavior of individuals. Since individuals are the only reality, then the only thing which needs to be or can be explained is their behavior, singly or collectively. This point of view has its most favorable climate in a mechanistic type of psychological theory.

The nominalist orientation is implicit in much of the present work on the small group. A recent issue of the *American Sociological Review,* devoted to small group studies, included several research papers in which the total extra-individual phenomenon was to be found in very brief contact between "subjects" with a minimum of interaction. These papers, no doubt, deal with phenomena which have some bearing upon interpersonal relations, but by no stretch of the imagination can they be called studies of *groups,* as some purported to be.

Interactionism. Pure nominalism as an explicit theoretical doctrine has died out during the past thirty years with the rise of the *interactionist* point of view. The focus upon interaction led to a rejection of the group-individual dichotomy intrinsic to the nominalist-realist argument and to a stress upon the concrete indivisibility of the two. Wirth makes these points explicit:

* *American Sociological Review,* Vol. 21, No. 5, October, 1956, pp. 549–554.

Rather than settling the issue as to whether the individual or the group is the ultimate unit in terms of which social life must be analyzed, the main stream of sociological and social-psychological thought has forgotten this issue and proceeded to analyze social phenomena as complexes of the meaningfully oriented actions of persons reciprocally related to one another.[1]

According to this doctrine, neither the group nor the individual is real except in terms of the other: that is, you-don't-have-persons-without-a-group and you-don't-have-groups-without-persons. In addition to the stress upon the indivisibility of the two, there is an emphasis upon the study of this whole in its concrete entirety and complexity. Finally, the interactionist doctrine has placed emphasis upon the multiplicity of causative factors needed to account for what happens. It combines biological, cultural, personal, and social explanations.

In much of the interactionist literature there are ghosts of the older nominalist thoughtways, most often found as implicit assumptions of and stresses upon the individual as the greater or more basic reality, and of the more fundamental character of biological and psychological explanations of social life. On the other hand, the pure nominalist orientation could not continue unaffected in the face of the evidence on the social origins of personality and the findings on the interconnectedness of social and personal phenomena.

Neo-nominalism. However, the interest in persons and the orientation toward the individual remained and formed the basis for a revised nominalist doctrine. The *neo-nominalist* pattern of thought accepts the proposition that the term "group" refers to an objective reality, but claims that the group is less real than persons for it is, after all, made up of persons and of processes which have their locus and immediate origin in the person.

The exact character of the neo-nominalist view depends to a great extent upon the conception of interaction that is held. The most extreme rejection of the equal reality of the group is possible where the interaction is seen in stimulus-response terms. In this view the interaction itself, though being something different from individuals, is explicable only through individual psychological processes.

The basis for the explanation of group phenomena is perhaps the most clearly distinguishing characteristic of the neo-nominalist view. This is an essentially reductionist philosophy which holds that, since the individual is the more fundamental unit, the final and basic explanations of the group are obtained only when these explanations are couched in terms of individual psychology. Allport, the most persistent exponent of this view, says:

The concept of a causal science on a purely social (non-psychological) plane is untenable, because in all science *explanation* is possible only by drawing upon the

[1] Louis Wirth, "Social Interaction: The Problem of the Individual and the Group," *American Journal of Sociology,* 44 (May, 1939), p. 966.

concepts of sciences at more elementary levels. . . . The true basis for sociology is the social behavior of the socialized individual, in other words, social psychology. The work of sociology is to describe collectivities of social behavior and social change resulting from it in terms of the group, and to explain these phenomena in terms of "the individual." [2]

Realism. The antithesis of these nominalist views has been the realist argument. Realism, like nominalism, has undergone metamorphoses since Durkheim's time, but since the earlier forms of realism are seldom encountered today we shall describe merely what we have called *modern realism.*

This doctrine holds that (1) the group is just as real as the person, but that (2) both are abstract, analytical units, not concrete entities, and that (3) the group is understandable and explicable solely in terms of distinctly social processes and factors, not by reference to individual psychology. In short, modern realism is theoretical, analytical, and anti-reductionist. However, this does not mean that it is non-empirical.

There are relatively few explicit presentations of this orientation. A recent article by two "group psychologists" argues for it and there are occasional incidental papers in the sociological journals. In addition there are occasional research reports which, in an unselfconscious fashion, exhibit this kind of thinking. There are, however, many tendencies in the thoughtways which appear to this author to lead toward the realist orientation.

Of the four doctrines discussed, the neo-nominalist view appears to be in the ascendency today in small group research as well as in other areas of inquiry. Even interactionism has been distorted in this direction. This stress upon the individual, upon explanations in terms of psychology or psychological processes, and upon the lesser reality and importance of the group and other social phenomena have become the sensible, common-sense point of view. Its acceptance does not need to be defended because it is common-sense and because its doctrines are congenial to a period in which there is a general cultural stress upon individualism and the importance of the person.

But progress in a discipline depends upon getting beyond the common-sense orientations of the time. The purpose here is to make this attempt by calling attention to and defending the legitimacy and validity of the realist position, and to propose that this is the most valid and potentially fruitful sociological approach to the study of the group and society. This follows a long sociological tradition: the work of Durkheim, Simmel, and Radcliffe-Brown, among others.

In order to do this within the scope of this paper it will be necessary to be elliptical and to forego the kind of documentation that might be desirable. However, the intention is not so much to prove a position as to call attention

[2] Floyd Allport, "Rule and Custom as Individual Variations of Behavior Distributed upon a Continuum of Conformity," *American Journal of Sociology,* 44 (May, 1939), pp. 897–921; and "The Group Fallacy in Relation to Social Science," *American Journal of Sociology,* 29 (May, 1924), p. 688.

to it and to the bases upon which it can be defended. This effort seems particularly pertinent at this time when sociology, at least as far as its interest in small groups is concerned, is in danger of being displaced by psychologists, some of whom are claiming the field for their own and stressing a psychological orientation as the only valid one:

> We have . . . to establish a branch of psychology concerned with the "personality" of groups . . . in spite of much talk about 'culture patterns,' methods and concepts simply do not exist. The sociologists, recognizing that a group cannot be defined in merely political or economic terms have turned to the psychologist for a science of the living group entity. . . .[3]

Such excesses could be forgiven if it were not for the fact that many sociologists seem to accept the premises and orientations such a statement implies.

THE ARGUMENTS AGAINST REALISM EXAMINED

There are four basic propositions in the thoughtways of contemporary social science that serve as the bases for arguments against the realist position. The propositions are thought to be self-evident and not in need of defense. Such wide-spread uncritical acceptance is itself reason enough for critical scrutiny, but it is our thesis that these propositions are fundamenal fallacies in contemporary sociological thought and are a bar to further progress in the sociology of the group. These propositions are:

1. We can see persons, but we cannot see groups except by observing persons.
2. Groups are composed of persons.
3. Social phenomena have their reality only in persons, this is the only possible location of such phenomena.
4. The purpose for studying groups is to facilitate explanations and predictions of individual behavior.

The first proposition, that we can see persons, but not groups, has recently been criticized by several authors who suggest that the argument involves a confusion between the idea of *individual* and that of *person*. They point out that the individual and the person are different "things" and that it is only the former, the biological structure, which we see directly, while the person is observed only through a series of actions and behaviors.

We can, perhaps, define the problem more clearly by stating it as a situation in which we treat a conceptual entity as a perceptual entity. The only things which we as humans can observe are events within a relatively limited time and space location. Any unity that is microscopic, that extends beyond the scope of our perceptual equipment in space, or whose structural processes

[3] Raymond B. Cattell, David R. Saunders, Glen F. Stice, "The Dimensions of Syntality in Small Groups," *Human Relations*, 6 (November, 1953), pp. 331–356.

are too slow or too fast for our perception must be inferred from partial observations made via instruments or through time series. The fact that we cannot directly perceive their unity does not detract from their essential empirical reality; it merely reflects the human limitation. This appears to be no less true of social phenomena than of physical ones.

Whenever we are dealing with a unity that exceeds our perceptual facility, we postulate that unity from the observation of sequences of events appearing to have a continuity and a degree of causal connection. We create a conceptual unit. When, as a result of the use of this concept, we become fully convinced that it refers to, and essentially coincides with, an empirical, objective unity, we then come to project that conceptual reality upon our limited observations. That is, we call to mind the total thing when we see only a part of it; we come to treat our conception as if it were perception. This appears to be exactly the same kind of process as occurs in the operation of stereotypes except that in the former case we take greater pains, presumably, to make sure that our concept has a sounder basis in empirical fact.

In any case, our argument here is that we cannot "see" persons any more than we can see groups: both are realities which extend beyond the range of human perception. Both are abstractions from and summaries of our observations of more limited aspects of the reality. The proposition that "we can see persons, but cannot see groups" is then a statement about our relative confidence in and acceptance of these concepts, *not a statement about perception or about what exists in external reality.*

We might note here that this argument is often joined with an assumption that the only *realities* are those which have physical substance. The basis for this belief is undermined by contemporary theory in physics, which proposes the interchangeability of matter and motion. As we inquire more carefully into the nature of what we believe is solid substance, we find that the solidity is more often than not the substance of our perceptual limitations.

The second proposition, that "groups are composed of persons," serves as a basic premise for two distinct conclusions about groups: (1) that they are more abstract, less real than persons, and (2) that really basic explanations of groups are in terms of their components, the persons of which they are composed.

This proposition loses its strength once we accept the idea that persons are no more concrete entities than are groups, but it is an idea that is so widely and unquestioningly accepted that it is worth examining independently of our earlier argument.

First, the proposition ignores the fact of interaction and is incompatible with the fact unless interaction is treated purely as a stimulus-response phenomenon, which can be done only through extreme contortion. There is much evidence to show that interaction results in new phenomena which are emergent in the situation and not explicable by reference to the persons as they exist prior to the interaction. The statement thus ignores the fact that in combination here, as in chemistry, the elements cease to be the same thing they were before and that the characteristics of the compound are not the results of a mere blending or mixing of the components.

There is, however, a much more fundamental problem—a problem that raises the issue of what we mean by components, elements, or units and whether there are different orders of components involved in the same concrete phenomenon.

Without going into the lengthy argument necessary we propose that *components*$_1$ (the materials from which a substance is created) have been confused with *components*$_2$ (the structural elements or members unique to and characteristic of the system or unity with which we are dealing). We can clarify the problem by an analogy from common experience. Suppose we ask, "Of what is a chair composed?" We might get this variety of answers: wood and cloth, steel and leather, metal and organic compounds, atoms and molecules, chemical compounds. Each of these is in some senses a correct statement about some chairs, i.e. about certain observable objects. None of these, however, tells us anything about chairs as chairs, as a unique class of phenomena. Rather the answers tell us about the kinds of materials from which chairs may be created or about physical substances in general. The only answer which makes sense when we are investigating chairs, *qua* chairs—rather than chairs as furniture, or as wood products, or as chemical compounds, or as physical substances—is the answer which defines chairs in terms of their common structural parts and arrangements, the parts and arrangements which set chairs off from all other objects. Thus a chair is composed of a seat, legs, back, frame, etc.

In the language of the general semanticists, we have jumped abstraction ladders when we say that chairs are composed of atoms, of metal, or of chemical compounds. These may be characteristics of some or all chairs, but are not the components of chairs.

It would seem then that the proposition that groups are composed of persons tells us nothing about groups as such, but merely says that persons are characteristic of human social life. It describes a characteristic of groups as one kind of social life, but does not indicate the structural components that are involved in groups as a particular kind of unity and reality.

Our third proposition claims that "the only existence of social phenomena is in the individual." The proposition is an ambiguous one and may have several interpretations. It is frequently taken to mean that culture and other social phenomena are distributive only through the individuals in the group. Hence, for example, culture exists only as a sum or average of the beliefs or habits of the members of the group.

This point of view is fostered by such doctrines as Cooley's that the group is one side of the coin of which the individual is the other, and the perhaps misinterpreted statements of ethnographers that one can often find out all about a primitive culture from the study of a few members. These notions suggest that society and culture are mirrored in each individual member of the group.

The fallacy is the assumption that for a social phenomenon to be real it must be internalized by the individual, and results from a failure to make the distinction between knowing and internalization. It is clear that a person may know cultural forms, beliefs, and patterns and know when they are appropriate (much in the way an anthropologist knows a culture which he studies) without these becoming an integral part of his own personality.

When we recognize this distinction, we see that it is possible for social phenomena to exist without being a part of the personalities who are the actors in the situation. Just as an anthropologist may participate in a savage rite in which he does not believe in order not to offend his hosts, so may any actor express cultural beliefs or conform to social actions he does not really believe or are not his personal habits. He may do so for a variety of motivations, but from a sociological point of view the character of the motivations is not the important thing, but the fact that he is motivated and that he knows the belief, ideology, or social act called for in the situation. Internalization or mirroring of social facts in the person is thus not a prerequisite to existence of the phenomenon. Because of this, such phenomena take on a reality independent of persons as persons. This means that we cannot discover social facts through a study of persons except in certain extremely stable and limited societies. As a result, to say that social phenomena have their location in the person is misleading. It would be much more appropriate to say that social phenomena have their reality only through expression by actors, in which case we imply the necessity not only for distinguishing person from individual, but also for distinguishing actor from person.

Support for this argument of the independent reality of social phenomena was found in my own study of a small Kansas village. We learned that there was a public, "official" morality regarding the use of alcoholic beverages that was quite different from the morality observed in other contexts. All the members of the community knew what the official morality was and they expressed it in their public behavior, but many of them did not "believe" it and conformed to other patterns in their homes, in small groups, and away from the village. There was a variety of sentiments (i.e. motivations) which led to the expression of this morality. They ranged from a few who *really believed* that drinking was wrong, to those who felt that it was *good for others* to abstain ("my brother's keeper" attitude), to those who merely felt that it was easiest not to go against the official position. Many other situations, which we now explain in terms of ambivalence of persons, bias, etc., are more easily explained by this formulation and support our conclusion.

The final proposition holds that the only purpose for studying groups is to facilitate knowledge of and prediction for persons. In the final analysis this is a value issue and is therefore not amenable to argument. It is in some ways basic to all the other arguments, however, for a thorough commitment to this value renders the realist approach superfluous. The only reason for realism as defined here is to facilitate the study of groups for their own sake. This author believes that anything which is real and observable is worth studying for itself. I am of the knowledge-for-the-sake-of-knowledge persuasion. But for those who judge knowledge and science in terms of "what good is it?" it might be pointed out that we have seldom perceived the ultimate values or applications of new developments in knowledge at their start.

CONCLUSION

In conclusion we must note that argument against the critics of a position does not prove that position. We have merely suggested that *a priori* rejection of realism is founded upon fallacy and misconception. The proof of the realist doctrine lies not so much in whether its present statement upon ultimate test will prove to be valid, but rather whether the present statement of it leads to fruitful research that would not otherwise be done.

Furthermore, the acceptance of the realist doctrine does not require that other views be rejected as wrong. They, too, reflect some aspects of reality and provide a way of approaching certain problems.

I propose that if we treat groups as real units or systems, if we cease to identify group phenomena with a particular personnel and with personality, if we cease to look for group phenomena in persons, and if we study groups for the sake of learning more about groups, only then will we begin to make real strides in a uniquely sociological problem.

If we accept Professor Warriner's affirmation that the group is not only as real as the individuals who compose it, but that it also possesses distinct processes and traits of its own, our next task is to explore social organization further. What, for instance, are the elements or determinants of groups? And in what system or systems are these determinants found? Seeking to answer these questions some time ago, George C. Homans suggested there are three mutually dependent elements in all groups: operation or activity, sentiment, and interaction. Operation refers to what members of a group do as members; sentiment is the feeling that a group's members have in relation to the group's operation; and interaction is the relationship which the activities of members of the group have to each other. These elements in turn are found in primary (that is, formal and technical) and secondary (that is, informal and social) systems or organizations which are also mutually dependent. The three elements and the two systems affect each other, and each is a resultant of the other, thus providing a dynamic social equilibrium.

Professor Homans subsequently developed and modified this pioneering conceptual scheme in a volume, *The Human Group,* published in 1950. Nevertheless, the following article offers an excellent starting point for the systematic study of social organization.

15. A CONCEPTUAL SCHEME FOR THE STUDY OF SOCIAL ORGANIZATION *

GEORGE C. HOMANS
Harvard University

"It is the office of theoretical investigation," said Willard Gibbs, "to give the form in which the results of experiment may be expressed." If he had put "observation" for "experiment," Gibbs would have stated the purpose of the present paper. It is to provide one form in which may be expressed what we know about social organization. Please note, at the beginning, that more than one form is possible and that, in a limited space, the one suggested here can only be sketched out.

In the field of social organization we now have a great deal of fact. We have descriptions of social groups of many different kinds, from primitive societies to modern factories and communities. Granting that these studies are not everything they may sometime become, many of us feel that they are closely observed and clearly described. We feel also that social groups, no matter how far separated in time or purpose, have certain things in common just because they are examples of organized human effort. We feel that in the necessities of organization itself and not in factors which are often treated as independent of organization: physical environment, racial heredity, the market, infantile experiences, or culture tone, must, in at least one instance, be sought the reasons for the differences and similarities between societies and for changes within societies. Here there are no primitive, industrial, religious, rural, or community sociologies; there is only one sociology—a sociology of organization. For an analytical science, any group is a microcosm.

We have a great deal of fact; we also have a great deal of theory. Some of it has been useful in describing particular kinds of social groups: it needs to be stated with full generality to apply to all groups. Some of it has been stated half-intuitively: it needs to be "spelled out." Some of it has been beautifully clear and explicit, but partial: other elements of theory need to be added to make a satisfactory whole. Yet, whatever the limits of particular statements, there have been signs of convergence, and the present paper tries to present a conceptual scheme toward which some of our theories may be converging. The paper only brings out what has been latent. It puts together things which have been lying around for some time in the literature. It is eclectic rather than original. It takes what it needs where it finds it.

There are signs of convergence. It might be faster if we learned from the

* *American Sociological Review,* Vol. 12, No. 1, February, 1947, pp. 13–26.

experience of the older sciences. Here, stated crudely, are a few of the rules which this experience has shown to be necessary in setting up a conceptual scheme. They have to some extent, perhaps not sufficiently, guided the building of the present one:

1. Look first at the obvious in its full generality. Only then does science economize thought.
2. Do not use high-order abstractions until you have exhausted the possibilities of low-order ones.
3. Talk about one thing at a time. That is, in choosing your words see that they refer not to several classes of fact at the same time but to one and one only. Corollary: once you have chosen your words, always use the same words when referring to the same things.
4. Once you have started to talk, do not stop until you have finished. That is, describe systematically the relationships between the facts designated by your words.
5. Science consists of the "careful and complete description of the mere facts." It drops the "why" and looks at the "how."
6. Cut down as far as you dare the number of factors considered.
7. Recognize that your description must be abstract, since it deals with only a few elements of the concrete thing. Recognize the dangers of abstraction, especially when action is required, but do not be afraid of abstraction.

Perhaps the reason so few of us carry these rules into effect is that they could not be better calculated to make our books and articles dull reading. We still work in the literary tradition, however badly we live up to it, and the rules of writing contradict the rules of theory-building at every point. In writing, the obvious, or what looks like it, is the thing you are most careful to avoid. Since it hurts to talk about one thing at a time, you use words which refer to several things at once. You also use different words for the same thing. If you do not, you lack variety. Systematic discussion, too, is notoriously repetitious, because the same things must be considered in several different connections. Finally writing is always concerned, and must be concerned, with giving a vivid impression of the concrete reality, and its success in doing so is the measure of its charm. The exposition of a conceptual scheme makes hard reading because it breaks all the rules of good literature, but only by breaking these rules and sticking to others will it become science.

The elements of social behavior. The present paper presupposes the direct observation of social behavior. It asks the devastating questions: Looking at the actions of men with eyes innocent of the usual preconceptions what do we see? What simple classification can we start from in this field of fact? Attempting to answer, it sets up, as components of the conceptual scheme, individuals and three elements or determinants of the behavior of individuals in groups, which will be called *operation, sentiment,* and *interaction.*

In ordinary language, *operations* mean the things that men do: operations on the physical environment or on other human beings. The full range of actions included here should be noted. Eating, drinking, plowing a field, tending a machine, putting on a coat, dancing, performing a ritual, and of course talking, though talking gives rise to special problems—all these are labelled operations. What they have in common appears to be some use of the muscles of men. No word is more than a ticket, but the use of the word *operation* here has some drawbacks. It must not be confused with Bridgman's operational theory of concepts, and was chosen because other suitable words had already been taken up. *Work* has a special meaning in the conceptual schemes of physics and may sometimes have an analogous one in sociology. *Behavior* and *action* are perhaps better applied to the whole of which operations are a part.

The definition of *sentiment* is more difficult. If we consider what we mean by the word, all that sentiments have in common seems to be some connection with internal states of the body, not well described except for the grosser sentiments: Cannon's pain, hunger, fear, and rage. In sociology we do not observe sentiments but operations which we take to be manifestations of sentiments, in facial expression, in bodily attitudes, above all, in what people say. Upon the whole, though, throughout human experience, men have successfully acted on the assumption that they could infer the existence of sentiments from what they could see and hear people do and say, and this assumption will have to satisfy us here. Sentiments are a concession to common sense. Note again the full range of things called sentiments here: from fear, hunger, thirst, and lust to such far more complicated matters as liking and disliking for individuals, approval and disapproval of the things they do. The psychologists do not use the word so broadly. The present use applies only to the present circumstances.

The behavior of a man living by himself would exhibit both sentiment and operation. What is it that makes behavior social? This element will be called *interaction*. When we refer to the fact that the operation of one man is followed, or, if you wish, stimulated by the operation of another, and so on in chains, entirely in abstraction from the particular operations performed or sentiments manifested, then we are referring to interaction. It may be especially difficult to think of interaction, consistently, as separate from the other elements of behavior, but it seems to be necessary to keep it separate and in much of our thinking we do in fact keep it separate without admitting as much.

Each of the elements named here has been used as a concept by social scientists. For instance, F. J. Roethlisberger and W. J. Dickson are discussing the Bank Wiring group at the Hawthorne Works of the Western Electric Company. They point out that the group held certain sentiments about such things as the restriction of output and go on to say: "It may be concluded that the individual's position in the group was in large part determined by the extent to which his behavior was in accord with these sentiments." If you will examine what the authors mean by *position*, you may agree that they mean, in part at least, habitual position in the chains of interaction among the members of the group. By *behavior* they refer to the element of operation, and the word *sentiment* with its meaning are the same for them and the present paper. Further, they are describing a state of mutual dependence between the elements of behavior. One element does not vary in independence of the others.

Again, Roethlisberger and Dickson are describing the methods used in analyzing the behavior of the Bank Wiremen: "Each occurrence in which a person entered into association with another person was examined to see whether the relation thus manifested expressed an antagonism, a friendship, or was merely neutral." Here they are talking of the sentiments. They speak further of what they call *participation:* "Two questions were asked: (1) To whom do this person's relations extend? Does he associate with everyone in the group, or are his social activities restricted to a few? (2) Does he enter a great deal or relatively little into social relations with the people with whom he associates?" Here the authors are looking at the extent and frequency of interaction.

By far the best discussion of interaction as a determinant of behavior is that of Eliot Chapple in a brilliant paper which is too little known. The present definition has been taken from him. To him a more general idea can also be traced. It is not enough to discriminate once between the elements of behavior. It is still more important to keep them discriminated and never let the old confusion return. Unless they are kept distinct it is impossible to consider the relations of mutual dependence between them. The only criticism of Chapple which will be made here is that he stopped too soon and did not apply to the elements of operation and sentiment the kind of analysis that he applied to interaction.

Operation, sentiment, and interaction have been called elements rather than variables. For quantitative observation and mathematical treatment, specific variables must represent the elements. It is possible to measure the quantity of the operations of a group (through output records), the extent, frequency, and order of interaction, perhaps even the strength of sentiment. Breaking the elements down in this way is one of the next steps to be taken in studying some kinds of social behavior. But a warning is needed. Sociology will miss a great deal if it tries to be too quantitative too soon. Data are not nobler because they are quantitative nor thinking more logical because it is mathematical. The old-fashioned naturalist, who only used his eyes, was also a scientist. The last emphasis is always on the immediate situation. Nothing which can illuminate it must be ruled out for doctrinal reasons, methodological or political. We shall be blind enough without wilfully narrowing our vision. At the same time, we do not have to learn the hard way. The older sciences have already struggled with the same general problems as sociology. If the solutions have been stated mathematically, they are not to be disregarded just for that reason. No matter where it comes from, we shall need all the help we can get.

There must be a number of possible classifications of the elements of social behavior. The one made here is crude but will be crudely used. It is designed to develop some of the more obvious generalizations of sociology and can be judged only by its usefulness for that purpose. Other men have used such concepts as *status*. There can be no objection, provided the concepts are definitely related to observed behavior. But status, to stick to the example, refers, as commonly employed, to a complicated combination of the elements of behavior. Might it not be wise to establish the first-order abstractions before going on to the second-order ones?

One word about individuals, who are components of the conceptual scheme. It may seem too great an abstraction, but one of the assumptions which must be stated candidly is that physical and mental differences between individuals do not come into the scheme. The fact that a person is a male or a Mongol or an idiot is less important than the fact that he takes a certain part in cooperative activity. In the same way, the fact that he is a father or a president or a pope is less important than his position of leadership. For the purposes of the present conceptual scheme, a proviso which must always be understood, the differentiation made by organization is the only directly significant one.

The primary and secondary systems. In the present scheme, the elements of social behavior are described as mutually dependent in two systems, which will be called the *primary* and *secondary* systems. As usual, these words do not imply that the primary system is earlier or more important than the secondary. They are mere tickets, indicating only that it is sometimes easier to begin the discussion at the primary system. The words, with the insight behind them, come from W. L. Warner. For instance, he writes: "The economic life of a people is essentially concerned with relating the primary technological adaptation to nature and the community's secondary adaptation which is its social organization. . . . The tools and implements are formed into a general order of making and using to exact a supply of food and other creature necessities from nature, and they are then used by the population of a group in a systematized manner through a set of conventions and social usages which are dictated by the social organization. The social organization regulates the technology and helps discipline the distribution and consumption of its productivity." [1] This comes from Warner's description of an Australian black-fellow group, but he applies the same discrimination to a modern American community. In the first volume of the Yankee City series, Warner and P. S. Lunt write: "The type of behavior by which a group adjusts itself to, and partially controls, the natural environment is, as we have said, its technical system; the system of adjustments and controls of the interactions of individuals with each other is the social organization. . . ." Here Warner calls the primary system the technical and the secondary system the social, but the more neutrally-colored terms may be preferable. The distinction appears to be the one Roeth-

[1] W. L. Warner, *A Black Civilization* (1937), p. 138, also p. 10.

lisberger and Dickson make between "formal" and "informal" organization in a factory. Their language is well adapted to industry but is misleading for the study of social organization in its full generality, since in many societies the thing which Roethlisberger and Dickson call "informal" is highly formalized.

In trying to bring out what is latent in Warner's words, this paper makes a further distinction. Put on one hand the environment on which a social group operates, and the plant and tools (including farm animals) with which it operates. Put on the other hand the organized human behavior which makes up the primary and secondary systems. All three items: environment, plant and tools, and systems of human behavior are important and mutually dependent in the concrete phenomena. Here, however, no systematic attention will be given to the first two. They will be taken as given in any particular instance. The picture is of an isolated system whose exchanges with its environment are known. This distinction is like the one C. I. Barnard makes between a "coöperative system" and an "organization," the latter being defined as a "system of consciously coördinated personal activities or forces." Note that the environment is not always the natural environment of the biologist. It is always relative to the group considered, and may include human beings not members of the group. A law court is operating on an environment as surely as a primitive tribe.

Warner discusses social organization in terms of three systems not two. To the technical and social he adds the ideological, the last consisting of the intellectual schemes, the "absolute logics" by which men interpret their world to themselves. The ideological system will not be considered here. In part it is determined by and in part it determines the form of the technical and social systems, but it is different in kind. What we observe of it consists wholly of what men say, write, or depict. Like the environment and the tools, it is of the greatest importance in the concrete phenomena and is left out of systematic consideration only to make the problem more manageable.

The description of the primary and secondary systems must begin somewhere, and it begins here with a group of individuals. A *group* is defined by interaction. The individuals A, B, C, D, E . . . are members, as we say, of group I. Within a given period, A interacts more frequently with B, C, D, E . . . than he does with M, N, L, O, P . . . whom we choose to consider outsiders or members of group II. B also interacts more frequently with A, C, D, E . . . than he does with any one of the outsiders. And so on. It may be true that E interacts about equally with some members of group I and some of group II and so forms a link between groups. In any event, it is possible, merely by counting the interactions, to map out two quantitatively distinct groups. But note again that this definition of a group is entirely relative. It depends on the group you choose to consider. The United States of America is a group in the sense defined, a group of the sort we usually call a society. A society is divided into a complicated hierarchy of sub-groups, and any group with a population larger than two can be divided in this way into sub-groups.

The primary system. The primary system will be considered first and then the secondary. In the primary system, the elements of social behavior are represented as follows. The operations are the ones the group performs on its environment, with the tools at its command, as a result of its initial sentiments. For a primitive group, these are the operations of hunting, fishing, gathering, and the like, the punishment of a crime, the education of the children, and, in the fields where useful operations on the environment are impossible or inconceivable, the performance of rituals. It is useless to go into the whole list. For a group which is not in immediate contact with the natural environment, but is a sub-group of a larger group, the operations performed are those set for it by the larger group. Thus a body of men may be casting engine-blocks in an automobile factory or handing down legal decisions in a court house. In any case, the operations the group performs in the primary system are those it carries out on whatever constitutes its particular environment.

Sentiments are represented in the primary system by the ones which men bring to a group as distinguished from the ones induced in men by the action of the group upon them. For a primitive group, or any other group in immediate contact with its natural environment, these are the sentiments of fear, hunger, thirst, and any other so-called primary drives that we wish to mention. For a working group in a factory, the sentiments in the primary system are much more complex: need for something to do, need to support a family, need for association with others. Such sentiments cannot be called primary in themselves, since they are induced in men by the action of social groups, but they are primary with respect to the group considered. If the sentiments are the ones a member brings to the group, the analysis remains the same whatever their origin.

Finally, the pattern of interaction in the primary system is the one necessary to put into effect the operations required. Here two kinds of interaction can be distinguished, which Barnard calls *lateral* and *scalar*. For a factory group, lateral interaction is illustrated by the man who paints an automobile mudguard and then sends it on to another man who puts it into the final assembly, scalar interaction by the foreman who, to use the conventional phrase, coördinates the work of several men. The organization chart shows the intended pattern of scalar organization in the factory.

Mutual dependence of the elements of social behavior. In neither the primary nor the secondary system are the elements of social behavior independent. They are in a state of mutual dependence with the environment, plant and tools, ideologies, and with one another. Only the last relationship will be considered systematically here: the mutual dependence of operation, sentiment, and interaction.

The three determinants of social behavior are mutually dependent. Only by mathematics can such a situation be described adequately, and mathematics for the moment we cannot use. We do not have the indices which could turn the determinants into variables. Instead we are forced to use ordinary language, which is equipped for handling only one independent factor and one dependent factor at a time. Here, therefore, the mutual dependence of the determinants will be considered by pairs, of which there must necessarily be three: sentiment-operation, operation-interaction, and interaction-sentiment. This method seems inescapable, but its difficulties must be faced. For instance, it is easy to say that the determinants interaction and sentiment are mutually dependent, but when we go on to say just how they are, we are forced to assume something about "other things being equal." L. J. Henderson was fond of saying: "People talk about 'other things being equal' without saying at what point they are equal." In discussing the mutual dependence of interaction and sentiment in the secondary system, we may say: "Other things being equal, persons who interact with one another tend to like one another." This theorem is one of the most important and most often forgotten in sociology. We often act on the assumption that if we can only "get people together" their coöperation will be improved—other things being equal. What are these other things, and where are they equal? If, among them, we consider only the element of operation, we recognize that two persons who interact with one another tend to like one another only if neither of them behaves, that is, performs operations, so as to irritate the other beyond a certain point. If either of them is irritating, the mere fact of bringing them together, increasing their interaction, will increase negative rather than positive sentiments. In short, interaction and sentiment are mutually dependent in a certain way on the assumption, not that the element of operation is out of the concrete phenomenon, for we know it comes in, but that this element is favorable at a particular point. The same problem reappears, of course, with the other pairs. An effort has been made to face it here as soon as it arose. In mathematics the difficulty is handled under the subject of partial differentiation.

Mutual dependence of sentiment and operation. Whether we think of the sentiments we share with the savages: fear, hunger, cold, thirst, and the like, or, in more general terms, of those a man brings to any organized group, in either case we say that sentiment gives rise to operations, or is the motive for operations, and that, the operation completed, the sentiment itself is modified. The connection seems to hold good to some degree whether the operation produces a directly useful result or, like magic, takes the place of such an operation which is unknown or impossible. The character of the connection between sentiment and operation is discussed at length in psychology. We know that it is seldom an unconditioned reflex: the farmer does not plow because he is hungry but because it is time to plow. There is no need to go further, once the place of this body of knowledge in the present scheme has been pointed out.

Mutual dependence of operation and interaction. That the members of this pair are mutually dependent is a matter of experience and a truism of the literature of organization. For any set of operations at least as complicated as two men sawing a log, an accompanying set of interactions is required, without which the successful completion of the operations is impossible. In a modern army or mass-production industry the required pattern of interaction is immensely complex, and the interaction is made possible by specialized techniques of communication. We say that the more elaborate the division of labor the more elaborate must be the process of coördination. Or, as Chapple and Coon write: "The coördination needed in any complex technique is impossible without interaction. As we have seen, most complex techniques involve the activities of more than one person, and, in fact, where people practice a number of complex techniques, extensive interactions must take place to coördinate the work of manufacturing, to secure raw materials, and to exchange the goods produced. In other words, the growth of complexity in technical processes goes hand in hand with an increase in the amount of interaction and in the complexity of the interaction pattern." [2] One more thing should be mentioned. The pattern of interaction is not uniquely determined by the operations. In certain circumstances, there may be several schemes of organization which satisfy equally well the needs of the work to be done. On the other hand, not just any scheme will do. The operations set limits to the pattern of interaction, as indeed the available pattern sets limits to the operations which can be realized. A large amount of learning which it is unnecessary to go into here exists in this field.

Mutual dependence of interaction and sentiment. As far as logic goes, this relationship holds in the primary system, in the sense that if x is a function of y, and y is a function of z, then x must be a function of z. There may even be a direct connection, if interaction with other men, for its own sake, be one of the primary drives of mankind. There is no doubt that the drive exists. Whether we should put it in the same class as hunger and thirst is another question. In any case, this relationship will be considered part of the secondary system, the line between primary and secondary being a matter of convention.

The secondary system. Before any discussion of the ways in which the three elements are represented in the secondary system, some time must be spent looking at this system as a whole. The distinction made by Warner between the primary and the secondary, the technological and the social system has been noted. The former is thought of as the initial means of adjustment of a group to its natural environment; the latter controls and regulates the former. This paper has insisted that the idea must be generalized, that any group whatever has a primary scheme of adjustment to the environment on which it operates, be that environment "natural" or not, and that out of the primary system further social relations arise which, for good or ill, profoundly modify the initial adjustment.

The language used has been Warner's but others have made the same distinction. Some idea of a man's behavior being modified by his membership in a group is fundamental in sociology. We are all trying to bring out its full

[2] E. Chapple and C. F. Coon, *Principles of Anthropology,* p. 250.

implications. For instance, Barnard writes: "When the individual has become associated with a coöperative enterprise he has accepted a position of contact with others similarly associated. From this contact there must arise interactions between these persons individually, and these interactions are social. It may be, and often is, true that these interactions are not a purpose or object either of the coöperative systems or of the individuals participating in them. They nevertheless *cannot be avoided.* Hence, though not sought, such interactions are consequences of coöperation, and constitute one set of social factors involved in coöperation. These factors operate on the individuals affected; and, in conjunction with other factors, become incorporated in their mental and emotional characters. This is an effect which makes them significant. Hence, coöperation compels changes in the motives of individuals which otherwise would not take place. So far as these changes are in a direction favorable to the coöperative system they are resources to it. So far as they are in a direction unfavorable to coöperation, they are detriments to it or limitations of it." [3]

An insight of the same sort comes from the institutional economists. C. E. Ayres writes: "A component part of every culture is a vast system of tools and tool-using activities. Economists are certainly interested in this sort of thing, and their interest is focused not on the engineering aspect of the tools as artifacts but on the pattern of the system of activities so constituted. Furthermore the interest of economists is not limited to these activities. A further component of every culture is another system of activities in which all these tools and all the products of their use are employed to very curious effect. They are employed ceremonially, and their manipulation in this fashion has the effect of establishing claims, exhibiting prestige, dividing the community in terms of 'ceremonial adequacy' along lines which are more or less coincident with those which are objects of interest to anthropologists, sociologists, political scientists, and the rest. These activities also constitute a system which is part of the total system, which is the culture." [4] Ayres, like Barnard, is making the distinction between the primary and the secondary system. He goes on: "These two activities condition each other in both directions." That is, the secondary system and the primary are mutually dependent. One criticism may be made of Ayres. His line between "tool-using" and "ceremonial" activities stems from Veblen, and from Veblen there remains a hint of disapproval of ceremonial. The secondary system is thought of as a drag on the primary: it is wasteful. Sometimes it may be so, but sometimes the social may help sustain the technological. Barnard's statement is much wiser, that the secondary system may be either a resource or a detriment to the primary. At any rate, the institutional economists have made the same kind of distinction as the sociologists and anthropologists.

Warner, Barnard, and Ayres, writing quite simply, as men must write to

[3] C. I. Barnard, *The Functions of the Executive* (1938), p. 40.
[4] C. E. Ayres, *The Theory of Economic Progress* (1944), p. 98.

give a first impression of a complicated phenomenon, speak as if the secondary system could be separated from the primary. When the time comes to refine the theory, a difficulty will have to be faced here. The distinction between the two systems is analytical, conventional if you will, and no more. What we observe are concrete operations, sentiments, interactions. One part of each may be assigned to the primary system and one to the secondary. It would be correct to compare this method with Galileo's description of the path of a projectile in terms of two components: uniform motion in a straight line, and uniformly accelerated motion downward, but for two considerations. In the first place, the physicist who follows Galileo does in fact perform two separate operations. He measures the muzzle velocity of the projectile and the acceleration of gravity. What operations to compare with these do we have in sociology? Only when a new group has been formed to do a particular job have we a chance to watch the secondary system grow out of the primary. In the second place, the two motions the physicist considers are independent of one another. However they be defined, the primary and secondary systems are not independent. Here are the difficulties for someone concerned about the operational definition of concepts, and they are serious. But science proceeds by approximations, and some crude ideas have served well while awaiting refinement. For the purpose of exposition in non-mathematical language, some distinction like that made between the primary and secondary systems seems inescapable.

After these preliminaries, a more detailed discussion of the secondary system can begin. The three determinants of behavior are represented somewhat differently here and in the primary system. Reference to an actual group will illustrate. Roethlisberger and Dickson, in their description of the Western Electric Researches, analyze at length the Bank Wiring Observation Room group. In the room men were at work wiring switchboards for central telephone office equipment, and a large amount of their behavior centered around this chief activity. In the present terms, this was the primary system of the group. But another large field of behavior grew out of and elaborated upon the primary system. The group as a whole had adopted a certain standard of output and kept actual output closely pegged to it. Within the group two cliques had developed, that is to say, a pattern of interaction over and above the one required by the work. The members of each clique felt friendship for other clique members and a certain amount of antagonism, consonant with the unity of the group as a whole, for men who did not belong to their clique. Finally each clique followed its own style of operations. In the games its members played, the food they ate, their topics of conversation, each clique was set apart. Even the degree of restriction of output varied slightly but significantly with clique membership. It is unnecessary to go into further details. The charm of the picture is its familiarity.

In the secondary system, then, sentiment is represented by feelings toward persons and their operations: feelings of liking and disliking for individuals, approval and disapproval of the things they do. "Valuations" might be a good word for the sentiments here, since approval and disapproval are not two things different in kind but two values on a continuous scale. Here also should be included the feelings of constraint which may exist between a person in authority and his subordinates. Operations are represented by the ones which do not directly advance the principal activity of the group but which are, as we say, social: expressions of group membership and differentiation. Finally, the pattern of interaction is more than the one required for the coördination of the operations of the primary system.

Mutual dependence of interaction and sentiment. The aim of this paper is to outline a conceptual scheme and not to elaborate the theorems which may be stated in its terms. On the other hand, there is little point in developing the scheme without showing the uses to which it may be put. In fact the theorems, in the inchoate form, probably suggest the scheme, although any scheme worth its salt, once developed, will suggest further theorems. The elements of social behavior are mutually dependent in the secondary system as in the primary, and the chief theorem of the mutual dependence of interaction and sentiment has already been cited, namely that, speaking relatively, you like persons you interact with frequently and dislike persons you interact with infrequently. Thus, in the Bank Wiring Observation Room, friendships were positively associated with clique membership. The mere fact is the important thing, no matter which determinant you choose to regard as the "cause" and which as the "effect." The theorem seems to be fundamental in sociology and assumed in much of our discussion of the in-group.

The theorem, like all such theorems, does not hold good unless "other things are equal." One of these other things, already mentioned, is the element of operation. Another is authority. If one man is interacting with another and is his superior in authority, experience suggests that new sentiments are often aroused which make the emotional relationship deeply ambivalent, and for perfectly good reasons in that in fact two influences are at work: the interaction and the authority. The latter may cut down the amount of interaction which would otherwise be expected.

Mutual dependence of sentiment and operation. Two kinds of mechanism are represented here, both familiar. The first is similarity and difference. You approve of behavior which is like your own and disapprove of behavior which is different. On the other hand, if you like a certain form of behavior, your own will tend to conform to it. In the Bank Wiring Room, each clique was inclined to ridicule the behavior of the other. One clique even thought that its topics of conversation were more refined. The second mechanism resembles the relationship between sentiment and operation in the primary system in that sentiment is the motive for operations. If you feel liking or disliking for a man you tend to express the sentiment in operations. In primitive societies these exchanges become elaborate, in gift exchanges which may practically take over the distribution of goods, but they are important also in our own society.

Mutual dependence of operation and interaction. You increase interaction with persons who perform the same kind of operations that you do, and decrease interaction with those who do not. Roethlisberger and Dickson point out that in the Bank Wiring Room the output of the members of one of the cliques was distinctly below the standard of the group as a whole: "But, it may be asked, did their low output determine their position in the group, or did their position in the group determine their output? The answer is that the relation worked both ways; position in the group influenced output, and output influenced position in the group. In other words, these two factors were in a relation of mutual dependence." The men in question were members of an excluded clique (interaction) because their output was low (operation), but it was also true that their output was low because they were members of an excluded clique. Here the relationship has been described in terms of interaction and operation alone. In their word "position," Roethlisberger and Dickson seem to include a reference to sentiment as well. Not only was interaction with the clique low but its behavior was given a low value. One purpose of the present conceptual scheme is to break down words like "position" into the simpler elements which we actually observe.

Another example of this relationship is given by the social climber. When he wants to enter a new group, he will model his behavior on the characteristic pattern of the group. He assumes that in the measure that he adopts the pattern, the members will increase interaction with him. Furthermore, since the relationship is always one of mutual dependence, the more he is able to interact with the members, the more likely he will be to copy their behavior faithfully. To pass on to another mechanism, many of the operations men perform merely serve as occasions for social interaction. In the Bank Wiring Room, many of the operations, such as playing certain kinds of games, which were part of clique behavior patterns, led to increased interaction between the members of each clique.

There is no need to labor the point that these types of behavior are so common as to be banal. It may be that the principles of human society, though many enough, are fewer than we have been ready to admit. In many sciences the principles are less complicated than their interweaving in the concrete situation. For each case of mutual dependence among the elements of behavior, enormous complexities are introduced when, instead of considering two individuals or groups, you consider three or more. Thus it is proverbial that increased interaction and positive sentiment between two persons in the in-group implies decreased interaction with and negative sentiment toward third persons who are outsiders. A more general statement is that the relationship between two individuals or groups A and B is not something apart from the relationships between A and C, D, E . . . and those between B and C, D, E. . . . Elaborate systems of relationships arise in this way. Perhaps the best known of these systems (and note that authority is always one of the factors in them) are the family organizations of primitive and civilized societies, but the same principles apply generally.

Dependence of the secondary system on the primary. The primary and secondary systems have been described separately although they are not separate. Not only can the two be divided only for analysis but, even in analysis, they are not independent of one another. The secondary system arises, so to speak, out of the primary and in turn reacts upon it. Barnard's remark is worth repeating: "Coöperation compels changes in the motives of individuals which otherwise would not take place. So far as these changes are in a direction favorable to the coöperative system they are resources to it. So far as they are in a direction unfavorable to coöperation, they are detriments to it or limitations of it." As usual, the important thing is to recognize the mutual dependence of the primary and secondary systems explicitly, systematically, and in its full generality.

Here the dependence of the secondary system on the primary will be considered first, and special emphasis will be given to the element of interaction. Operations in the primary system may, within limits, demand a certain scheme of interaction. In industry a number of men may be working in the same room. Or they may be performing in a certain order different parts of a total operation on an object, so that when one man has done his part he passes the object on to the next man. Or they may have the same foreman. Whatever the reason, geography, flow of work, or supervision, they are, as we say, thrown together. What they do makes it likely or inevitable that they will interact. Furthermore, interaction left to itself increases positive sentiment, which will increase the interaction still more. This last mechanism has been arbitrarily called part of the secondary system, so that, in terms of the present conceptual scheme, the primary system gives rise to the secondary. There is another way of saying the same thing. When men interact in the primary system, it is often observed that they increase their interaction beyond the amount required by the primary system. We call this increment social, and say that any congeries of individuals, brought together in any way, tends to become something more, a social group.

Another mechanism by which the secondary system elaborates on the primary is the following. In the primary system there is usually in every group a man who acts as center of communications, that is, as leader of the group, and in complex organizations these centers are arranged in a hierarchy. The leaders receive information and give orders, and it seems to be a matter of experience that between persons in authority and their subordinates a certain kind of sentiment often exists. It may be called constraint, but under any name the sentiment between two men in this relationship is different from the sentiment between two men who are interacting as equals. Furthermore, between such men, interaction, instead of increasing, tends to be kept near the minimum required by the primary system. This theorem is warranted by the behavior of fathers and sons in many patriarchal families and by the separation between grades in armies. It is subject to the usual limitation of "other things being equal." In particular, if the subordinate is in an insecure position and feels that his advancement depends less on his own work than on his personal relationship with his superior, bootlicking may begin and interaction increase rather than decrease.

Once again, then, the requirements of the primary system give rise to certain sentiments between men, sentiments which have been called part of the secondary system. In this particular case, the sentiments tend to discourage rather than encourage social interaction. The increase of interaction between so-called equals and its relative decrease between superiors and subordinates are the first steps toward the formation of classes in organizations and in society at large.

Dependence of the primary system on the secondary. Barnard argues that once the secondary system is established its influence on the primary may be favorable or unfavorable, and Roethlisberger and Dickson make the same point: "It is well to recognize that informal organizations are not 'bad,' as they are sometimes assumed to be. Informal social organization exists in every plant, and can be said to be a necessary prerequisite for effective collaboration. Much collaboration exists at an informal level, and it sometimes facilitates the functioning of the formal organization. On the other hand, sometimes the informal organization develops in opposition to the formal organization." [5] An example of the latter is the restriction of output adopted through informal organization.

Another example has been made famous by Veblen and referred to in the passage from Ayres cited above. Two parts may be distinguished in any economic activity such as building a house. The form of the house is in part determined by "needs" for such things as warmth and shelter. It is in part, we usually say in its style, determined by other factors, by the social class to which its occupants belong and by more general community custom. Veblen spoke of the effect of these latter factors as "conspicuous expenditure": they brought about a destruction of wealth. In the present terms, the effect of the secondary system is in some way unfavorable to the primary. Conspicuous expenditure is particularly conspicuous at times when the classes are fluid, that is, when people feel a need to make their social position highly visible.

What Veblen and his followers forgot is that if y is a continuous function of x, there is probably a region within which the value of the function is positive not negative. The suggestion has been made that well established social standards of living, which require that families purchase certain goods as a mark of group membership, may help prevent the collapse of the economic system in times of crisis, by sustaining demand. At any rate, the main lesson

[5] F. J. Roethlisberger and W. J. Dickson, *Management and the Worker* (1939), p. 559.

of the industrial research of the last two decades is that effective coöperation is never a matter of the primary system alone, and that developments in the secondary system may either sustain coöperation or break it down.

Finally, the secondary system of a social group may give rise to the primary system of another social group. This happens when the standard of operations in the secondary system becomes a positive program which is to be put into effect and thus requires organization. For example, antagonisms in an industrial plant may lead to the formation of a union. But a union is an organized activity which will have its own primary and secondary systems. In fact the leaders of the union may have the same kind of trouble with their followers that the managers of the factory had originally. The systems are always to be discerned with relation to the particular group in question.

The condition of equilibrium. The elements of social behavior have been described as mutually dependent in two systems, which are themselves mutually dependent in the total social system. Experience in the developed sciences, and, as will be shown, even in our own, suggests that the relationship between the elements is not determinate without some criterion of equilibrium. As L. J. Henderson puts it: "Another characteristic of many ideal systems that is, in general, indispensable in order that conditions shall be determinate is the establishment and use of some definition of equilibrium, whether in the case of statical equilibrium or in the case of dynamical equilibrium. For the abstract conceptual scheme this is as a rule the decisive feature that goes farthest to establish determinate conditions." In a developed science, a general equation of equilibrium will appear which takes its place as one of the equations, equal in number to the number of variables, which describe determinate conditions.

Henderson is writing about an ideal system such as the social system of this paper pretends to be. This kind of system can hardly be set up unless it is provisionally treated as isolated, in the sense that exchanges with whatever constitutes its environment have the value O or some other known value. The criterion of equilibrium applies particularly to such a system. Now nothing is in fact isolated from the rest of the universe, nor are all the exchanges between a system and the rest of the universe known. Nevertheless Newton and Gibbs showed that some systems can without serious difficulty be treated as isolated, even when the influences of the environment are great. As Henderson goes on to say: "With the help of estimates of disturbances introduced from without and of other disturbances that result from actions in the opposite direction, even when such disturbances are very complex, much can often be accomplished when the characteristics of the ideal isolated system are known."

All this is general, a matter of the experience of the older sciences in stating their findings. What is its application to sociology? The crucial question is how far any social system, or, more simply, any group can be treated as isolated without irreparable violence being done to the facts. In the present ideal system, the effects of the environment and of plant and tools are regarded as given in any particular instance. As for concrete systems, primitive tribes, independent national states, and business enterprises in competition with other enterprises may come closest to realizing the conditions for being described as isolated systems. Exchanges with the environment are most nearly determinate. The difficulties are great, yet it is likely that we must, whether or not social systems shall be treated as isolated, adopt some definition of equilibrium. In fact we have done so already. In or out of business, we cannot escape the idea of the "going concern."

An example follows. The emotional constraint between superiors and subordinates is often one of the forces in a social system. Its importance is particularly clear in societies where the family is the unit which performs the essential operations on the environment. Here the father, or, in matrilineal groups, the mother's brother is the supreme authority and the sentiments existing between him and his subordinates, the other family members, help determine many of the other emotional relationships in the family. Similar observations could be made of other kinds of social groups. Now the thing to remember here is that the sentiment between superior and subordinate does not depend on the mere fact that the superior gives orders. Just giving orders has quite different effects. It depends on the giving of orders which will be obeyed —a truism whose implications we neglect at our peril. For the willingness of the members of an organization to obey orders, to accept authority, depends in a complicated way on the working of the organization as a whole. The operations in the primary system must provide a surplus of means of inducing the members to coöperate, and the secondary system must not generate too much antagonism to destroy coöperation in the primary. Of families as of other groups we may say that the organization can maintain itself only if its orders are obeyed, or, alternatively, that only if it maintains itself will its orders be obeyed. In either case, whether we like it or not, we are using a criterion of equilibrium and assuming, like the other sciences, that a particular condition, here an emotional relationship, is determinate only when equilibrium exists. There must be a large number of other conditions in social systems which are determinate only if the systems are going concerns. The greatness of Barnard's book, *The Functions of the Executive,* lies in the fact that, almost alone among sociological treatises, it insists, and keeps insisting, that in the case of equilibrium the amount by which any factor in social organization can be altered without altering all the other factors is strictly limited. The most important things about social groups, the conditions of their life and death, are the ones we study least.

In *An American Dilemma* Myrdal argues that the idea of equilibrium is conservative. Of course some simple-minded notion of statical equilibrium could be used to justify the existing order. The best corrective is not to abandon the idea, which we use whether we like it or not, but to become familiar with its actual employment in the sciences. The fundamental equation of mechanics asserts that for equilibrium the variation of the work done in the system is O. Alternatively, if the system is to pass from an initial configuration to a different final configuration, work will have to be done on the system. In ordinary language, this statement does not claim that change is impossible; it only defines the condition, namely the accomplishment of work, under which change is possible. If the work is done, Myrdal's principle of cumulation may come into play, depending on the conditions and constraints of the system, and the system passes rather rapidly to a new configuration. But these matters of logic have nothing to do with conservative or radical political opinions.

Rate of change may be more significant than change itself. Any conceptual scheme in sociology must be equipped to deal with dynamics, with change in the social system in respect to time. In the broadest sense, the scheme must be historical. If the present one has been described for the statical case, a method which always makes exposition easier, it is not meant to be limited to that. It asks: If one of the elements, or one of the systems, is changing in a certain way, at a certain rate, what kinds of changes may be expected in the others? The idea of equilibrium suggests that it is more illuminating to study even a stable situation in terms of change than change in terms of a stable situation. Social scientists used to talk about the "tyranny of custom." Nothing is more defenseless than a custom, alone. Not single customs but systems of custom survive. For instance, gift exchange in primitive and modern societies have been cited as evidence that we show our sentiments in operations. But any recollection of Christmas proves that we do not give presents to people just because we like them. We also think of what might happen if we did not give the presents. They have ramifications. For the normal situation, both the specific force and the complex of forces are present at the same time. This should be obvious, but apparently is not so to everybody. We can best account for the survival of any system by noticing what happens when a change is introduced in one of the components. At Christmas, at least, our ordinary social thinking follows the method of science.

Of all group typologies constructed by sociologists and anthropologists, probably none is more useful than the distinction between folk society and modern urban society. A folk society is small, isolated, nonliterate, and homogeneous, with a strong sense of solidarity. The way of living is conventionalized into a coherent culture. Behavior in a folk society is traditional, spontaneous, uncritical, and personal; there are no legislation and no experimentation and reflection for intellectual ends. Kinship is the typical category of experience, and the sacred prevails over the secular. The economy in a folk society is one of status rather than of market.

The following article by one of the outstanding students of folk societies, anthropologist Robert Redfield, applies the folk-urban typology to comparative studies of societies and to the study of a given society undergoing change. It raises pertinent questions concerning the necessary and probable interrelations of some of the aspects of one type of society with other aspects. One such relationship is that between disorganization and secularization in urban societies.

16. THE FOLK SOCIETY *

ROBERT REDFIELD

University of Chicago

I

Understanding of society in general and of our own modern urbanized society in particular can be gained through consideration of the societies least like our own: the primitive, or folk, societies. All societies are alike in some respects, and each differs from others in other aspects; the further assumption made here is that folk societies have certain features in common which enable us to think of them as a type—a type which contrasts with the society of the modern city.

This type is ideal, a mental construction. No known society precisely corresponds with it, but the societies which have been the chief interest of the anthropologist most closely approximate it. The construction of the type depends, indeed, upon special knowledge of tribal and peasant groups. The ideal folk society could be defined through assembling, in the imagination, the characters which are logically opposite those which are to be found in the modern city, only if we had first some knowledge of nonurban peoples to permit us to determine what, indeed, are the characteristic features of modern city living. The complete procedure requires us to gain acquaintance with many folk societies in many parts of the world and to set down in words general enough to describe most of them those characteristics which they have in common with each other and which the modern city does not have.

In short, we move from folk society to folk society, asking ourselves what it is about them that makes them like each other and different from the modern city. So we assemble the elements of the ideal type. The more elements we add, the less will any one real society correspond to it. As the type is constructed, real societies may be arranged in an order of degree of resemblance to it. The conception develops that any one real society is more or less "folk." But the more elements we add, the less possible it becomes to arrange real societies in a single order of degree of resemblance to the type, because one of two societies will be found to resemble the ideal type strongly in one character and weakly in another, while in the next society strong resemblance will lie in the latter character and not in the former. This situation, however, is an advantage, for it enables us to ask and perhaps answer questions, first, as to whether certain characters tend to be found together in most societies, and then, if certain of them do, why.

* *The American Journal of Sociology,* Vol. LII, No. 4, January, 1947, pp. 293–308.

Anyone attempting to describe the ideal folk society must take account of and in large degree include certain characterizations which have been made of many students, each of whom has been attentive to some but not to all aspects of the contrast between folk and modern urban society. Certain students have derived the characterization from examination of a number of folk societies and have generalized upon them in the light of contrast provided by modern urban society; the procedure defined above and followed by the writer. This is illustrated by A. A. Goldenweiser's characterization of five primitive societies. He says that they are small, isolated, nonliterate; that they exhibit local cultures; that they are relatively homogeneous with regard to the distribution of knowledge, attitudes, and functions among the population; that the individual does not figure as a conspicuous unit; and that knowledge is not explicitly systematized.

In other cases the students have compared the state of certain societies at an early time with the same, or historical descendant of the same, society at a later time. In this way Henry Maine arrived at his influential contrasts between society based on kinship and society based on territory, and between a society of status and one of contract. In the case of this procedure, as in the case of the next, broad and illuminating conceptions are offered us to apply to folk societies as we contrast them with modern urban society. We are to find out if one of the contrasting terms is properly applicable to folk society and the other term to modern urban society.

In the work of still other students there is apparent no detailed comparison of folk with urbanized societies or of early society with later; rather, by inspection of our own society or of society in general, contrasting aspects of all society are recognized and named. This procedure is perhaps never followed in the unqualified manner just described, for in the instances about to be mentioned there is evidence that folk or ancient society has been compared with modern urbanized society. Nevertheless, the emphasis placed by men of this group is upon characteristics which, contrasting logically, in real fact coexist in every society and help to make it up. Here belongs Ferdinand Tönnies' contrast between *Gemeinschaft* and *Gesellschaft,* or that aspect of society which appears in the relations that develop without the deliberate intention of anyone out of the mere fact that men live together, as contrasted with that aspect of society which appears in the relations entered into deliberately by independent individuals through agreement to achieve certain recognized ends. Comparable is Émile Durkheim's distinction between that social solidarity which results from the sharing of common attitudes and sentiments and that which results from the complementary functional usefulnesses of the members of the group. In the "social segment"—the form of society existing in terms of "mechanical solidarity"—the law is "repressive"; in the "social organ"—the form of society existing in terms of "organic solidarity"—the law is "restitutive."

It may be asked how closely the constructed type arrived at by any one investigator who follows the procedure sketched above will resemble that reached by another doing the same. It may be supposed that to the extent to which the real societies examined by the one investigator constitute a sample of the range and variety of societies similar to the sample constituted by the societies examined by the other, and to the extent that the general conceptions tentatively held by the one are similar to those held by the other, the results will be (except as modified by other factors) the same. For the purposes of understanding which are served by the method of the constructed type, however, it is not necessary to consider the question. The type is an imagined entity, created only because through it we may hope to understand reality. Its function is to suggest aspects of real societies which deserve study, and especially to suggest hypotheses as to what, under certain defined conditions, may be generally true about society. Any ideal type will do, although it is safe to assert that that ideal construction has most heuristic value which depends on close and considered knowledge of real folk societies and which is guided by an effective scientific imagination—whatever that may be.

II

"The concepton of a 'primitive society' which we ought to form," wrote W. G. Sumner, "is that of small groups scattered over a territory." The folk society is a small society. There are no more people in it than can come to know each other well, and they remain in long association with each other. Among the Western Shoshone the individual parental family was the group which went about, apart from other families, collecting food; a group of families would assemble and so remain for a few weeks, from time to time, to hunt together; during the winter months such a group of families would form a single camp. Such a temporary village included perhaps a hundred people. The hunting or food-collecting bands considered by Julian Steward, representing many parts of the world, contained, in most cases, only a few score people. A Southwestern Pueblo contained no more than a few thousand persons.

The folk society is an isolated society. Probably there is no real society whose members are in complete ignorance of the existence of people other than themselves; the Andamanese, although their islands were avoided by navigators for centuries, knew of outsiders and occasionally came in contact with Malay or Chinese visitors. Nevertheless, the folk societies we know are made up of people who have little communication with outsiders, and we may conceive of the ideal folk society as composed of persons having communication with no outsider.

This isolation is one half of a whole of which the other half is intimate communication among the members of the society. A group of recent castaways is a small isolated society, but it is not a folk society; and if the castaways have come from different shops and different societies, there will have been no previous intimate communication among them, and the society will not be composed of people who are much alike.

May the isolation of the folk society be identified with the physical immobility of its members? In building this ideal type, we may conceive of the members of the society as remaining always within the small territory they occupy. There are some primitive peoples who have dwelt from time immemorial in the same small valley, and who rarely leave it. Certain of the pueblos of the American Southwest have been occupied by the same people or their descendants for many generations. On the other hand, some of the food-collecting peoples, such as the Shoshone Indians and certain aborigines of Australia, move about within a territory of very considerable extent; and there are Asiatic folk groups that make regular seasonal migrations hundreds of miles in extent.

It is possible to conceive of the members of such a society as moving about physically without communicating with members of other groups than their own. Each of the Indian villages of the midwest highlands of Guatemala is a folk society distinguishable by its customs and even by the physical type of its members from neighboring villages, yet the people are great travelers, and in the case of one of the most distinct communities, Chichicastenango, most of the men travel far and spend much of their time away from home. This does not result, however, in much intimate communication between those traveling villagers and other peoples. The gipsies have moved about among the various peoples of the earth for generations, and yet they retain many of the characteristics of a folk society.

Through books the civilized people communicate with the minds of other people and other times, and an aspect of the isolation of the folk society is the absence of books. The folk communicate only by word of mouth; therefore the communication upon which understanding is built is only that which takes place among neighbors, within the little society itself. The folk has no access to the thought and experience of the past, whether of other peoples or of their own ancestors, such as books provide. Therefore, oral tradition has no check or competitor. Knowledge of what has gone before reaches no further back than memory and speech between old and young can make it go; behind "the time of our grandfathers" all is legendary and vague. With no form of belief established by written record, there can be no historical sense, such as civilized people have, no theology, and no basis for science in recorded experiment. The only form of accumulation of experience, except the tools and other enduring articles of manufacture, is the increase of wisdom which comes as the individual lives longer; therefore the old, knowing more than the young can know until they too have lived that long, have prestige and authority.

The people who make up a folk society are much alike. Having lived in long intimacy with one another, and with no others, they have come to form a single biological type. The somatic homogeneity of local, inbred populations has been noted and studied. Since the people communicate with one another and with no others, one man's learned ways of doing and thinking are the same as another's. Another way of putting this is to say that in the ideal folk society, what one man knows and believes is the same as what all men know and believe. Habits are the same as customs. In real fact, of course, the differences among individuals in a primitive group and the different chances of experience prevent this ideal state of things from coming about. Nevertheless, it is near enough to the truth for the student of a real folk society to report it fairly well by learning what goes on in the minds of a few of its members, and a primitive group has been presented, although sketchily, as learned about from a single member. The similarity among the members is found also as one generation is compared with its successor. Old people find young people doing, as they grow up, what the old people did at the same age, and what they have come to think right and proper. This is another way of saying that in such a society there is little change.

The members of the folk society have a strong sense of belonging together. The group which an outsider might recognize as composed of similar persons different from members of other groups is also the group of people who see their own resemblances and feel correspondingly united. Communicating intimately with each other, each has a strong claim on the sympathies of the others. Moreover, against such knowledge as they have of societies other than their own, they emphasize their own mutual likeness and value themselves as compared with others. They say of themselves "we" as against all others, who are "they."

Thus we may characterize the folk society as small, isolated, nonliterate, and homogeneous, with a strong sense of group solidarity. Are we not soon to acknowledge the simplicity of the technology of the ideal folk society? Something should certainly be said about the tools and tool-making of this generalized primitive group, but it is not easy to assign a meaning to "simple," in connection with technology which will do justice to the facts as known from the real folk societies. The preciseness with which each tool, in a large number of such tools, meets its needs in the case of the Eskimo, for example, makes one hesitate to use the word "simple." Some negative statements appear to be safe: secondary and tertiary tools—tools to make tools—are relatively few as compared with primary tools; there is no making of artifacts by multiple, rapid, machine manufacture; there is little or no use of natural power.

There is not much division of labor in the folk society: what one person does is what another does. In the ideal folk society all the tools and ways of production are shared by everybody. The "everybody" must mean "every adult man" or "every adult woman," for the obvious exception to the homogeneity of the folk society lies in the differences between what men do and know and what women do and know. These differences are clear and unexceptional (as compared with our modern urban society where they are less so). "Within the local group there is no such thing as a division of labor save as between the sexes," writes A. R. Radcliffe-Brown about the Andaman Islanders. ". . . Every man is expected to be able to hunt pig, to harpoon turtle and to catch fish, and also to cut a canoe, to make bows and arrows and all the other objects that are made by men." So all men share the same interests and have, in general, the same experience of life.

We may conceive, also, of the ideal folk society as a group economically independent of all others: the people produce what they consume and consume what they produce. Few, if any, real societies are completely in this situation; some Eskimo groups perhaps most closely approach it. Although each little Andamanese band could get along without getting anything from any other, exchange of goods occurred between bands by a sort of periodic gift-giving.

The foregoing characterizations amount, roughly, to saying that the folk society is a little world off by itself, a world in which the recurrent problems of life are met by all its members in much the same way. This statement, while correct enough, fails to emphasize an important, perhaps the important, aspect of the folk society. The ways in which the members of the society meet the recurrent problems of life are conventionalized ways; they are the results of long intercommunication within the group in the face of these problems; and these conventionalized ways have become interrelated within one another so that they constitute a coherent and self-consistent system. Such a system is what we mean in saying that the folk society is characterized by "a culture." A culture is an organization or integration of conventional understandings. It is, as well, the acts and the objects, in so far as they represent the type characteristic of that society, which express and maintain these understandings. In the folk society this integrated whole, this system, provides for all the recurrent needs of the individual from birth to death and of the society through the seasons and the years. The society is to be described, and distinguished from others, largely by presenting this system.

This is not the same as saying, as we said early in this paper, that in the folk society what one man does is the same as what another man does. What one man does in a mob is the same as what another man does, but a mob is not a folk society. It is, so far as culture is concerned, its very antithesis. The members of a mob (which is a kind of "mass") each do the same thing, it is true, but it is a very immediate and particular thing, and it is done without much reference to tradition. It does not depend upon and express a great many conventional understandings related to one another. A mob has no culture. The folk society exhibits culture to the greatest conceivable degree. A mob is an aggregation of people doing the same simple thing simultaneously. A folk society is an organization of people doing many different things successively as well as simultaneously. The members of a mob act with reference to the same object of attention. The members of a folk society are guided in acting by previously established comprehensive and interdependent conventional understandings; at any one time they do many different things, which are complexly related to one another to express collective sentiments and conceptions. When the turn comes for a boy to do what a man does, he does what a man does; thus, though in the end the experiences of all individuals of the same sex are alike, the activities of the society, seen at a moment of time, are diverse, while interdependent and consistent.

The Papago Indians, a few hundred of them, constituted a folk society in southern Arizona. Among these Indians a war party was not so simple a thing as a number of men going out together to kill the enemy. It was a complex activity involving everybody in the society both before, during, and after the expedition and dramatizing the religious and moral ideas fundamental to Papago life. Preparation for the expedition involved many practical or ritual acts on the part of the immediate participants, their wives and children, previously successful warriors, and many others. While the party was away, the various relatives of the warriors had many things to do or not to do—prayer, fasting, preparation of ritual paraphernalia, etc. These were specialized activities, each appropriate to just that kind of relative or other category of person. So the war was waged by everybody. These activities, different and special as they were, interlocked, so to speak, with each other to make a large whole, the society-during-a-war-expedition. And all these specialized activities obeyed fundamental principles, understood by all and expressed and reaffirmed in the very forms of the acts—the gestures of the rituals, the words of songs, the implied or expressed explanations and admonitions of the elders to the younger people. All understood that the end in view was the acquisition by the group of the supernatural power of the slain enemy. This power, potentially of great positive value, was dangerous, and the practices and rituals had as their purposes first the success of the war party and then the draining-off of the supernatural power acquired by the slaying into a safe and "usable" form.

We may say, then, that in the folk society conventional behavior is strongly patterned: it tends to conform to a type or a norm. These patterns are interrelated in thought and in action with one another, so that one tends to evoke others and to be consistent with the others. Every customary act among the Papago when the successful warriors return is consistent with and is a special form of the general conceptions held as to supernatural power. We may still further say that the patterns of what people think should be done are closely consistent with what they believe is done, and that there is one way, or a very few conventional ways, in which everybody has some understanding and some share, of meeting each need that arises. The culture of a folk society is, therefore, one of those wholes which is greater than its parts. Gaining a livelihood takes support from religion, and the relations of men to men are justified in the conceptions held of the supernatural world or in some other aspect of the culture. Life, for the member of the folk society, is not one activity and then another and different one; it is one large activity out of which one part may not be separated without affecting the rest.

A related characteristic of the folk society was implied when it was declared that the specialized activities incident to the Papago war party obeyed fundamental principles understood by all. These "principles" had to do with the ends of living, as conceived by the Papago. A near-ultimate good for the Papago was the acquisition of supernatural power. This end was not questioned; it was a sort of axiom in terms of which many lesser activities were understood. This suggests that we may say of the folk society that its ends are taken as given. The activities incident to the war party may be regarded as merely complementarily useful acts, aspects of the division of labor. They may also, and more significantly, be seen as expressions of unquestioned common ends. The folk society exists not so much in the exchange of useful functions as in common understandings as to the ends given. The ends are not stated as matters of doctrine, but are implied by the many acts which make up the living that goes on in the society. Therefore, the morale of a folk society—its power to act consistently over periods of time and to meet crises effectively is not dependent upon discipline exerted by force or upon devotion to some single principle of action but to the concurrence and consistency of many or all of the actions and conceptions which make up the whole round of life. In the trite phrase, the folk society is a "design for living."

What is done in the ideal folk society is not done because somebody or some people decided, at once, that it should be done, but because it seems "necessarily" to flow from the very nature of things. There is, moreover, no disposition to reflect upon traditional acts and consider them objectively and critically. In short, behavior in the folk society is traditional, spontaneous, and uncritical. In any real folk society, of course, many things are done as a result of decision as to that particular action, but as to that class of actions tradition is the sufficient authority. The Indians decide now to go on a hunt; but it is not a matter of debate whether or not one should, from time to time, hunt.

The folkways are the ways that grow up out of long and intimate association of men with each other; in the society of our conception all the ways are folkways. Men act with reference to each other by understandings which are tacit and traditional. There are no formal contracts or other agreements. The rights and obligations of the individual come about not by special arrangement; they are, chiefly, aspects of the position of the individual as a person of one sex or the other, one age-group or another, one occupational group or another, and as one occupying just that position in a system of relationships which are traditional in the society. The individual's status is thus in large part fixed at birth; it changes as he lives, but it changes in ways which were "foreordained" by the nature of his particular society. The institutions of the folk society are of the sort which has been called "crescive"; they are not of the sort that is created deliberately for special purposes, as was the juvenile court. So, too, law is made up of the traditional conceptions of rights and obligations and the customary procedures whereby these rights and obligations are assured; legislation has no part in it.

If legislation has no part in the law of the ideal folk society, neither has codification, still less jurisprudence. Paul Radin has collected material suggesting the limited extent to which real primitive people do question custom and do systematize their knowledge. In the known folk societies they do these things only to a limited extent. In the ideal folk society there is no objectivity and no systematization of knowledge as guided by what seems to be its "internal" order. The member of this mentally constructed society does not stand off from his customary conduct and subject it to scrutiny apart from its meaning for him as that meaning is defined in culture. Nor is there any habitual exercise of classification, experiment, and abstraction for its own sake, least of all for the sake of intellectual ends. There is common practical knowledge, but there is no science.

Behavior in the folk society is highly conventional, custom fixes the rights and duties of individuals, and knowledge is not critically examined or objectively and systematically formulated; but it must not be supposed that primitive man is a sort of automaton in which custom is the mainspring. It would be as mistaken to think of primitive man as strongly aware that he is constrained by custom. Within the limits set by custom there is invitation to excel in performance. There is lively competition, a sense of opportunity, and a feeling that what the culture moves one to do is well worth doing. "There is no drabness in such a life. It has about it all the allurements of personal experience, very much one's own, of competitive skill, of things well done." The interrelations and high degree of consistency among the elements of custom which are presented to the individual declare to him the importance of making his endeavors in the directions indicated by tradition. The culture sets goals which stimulate action by giving great meaning to it.

It has been said that the folk society is small and that its members have lived in long and intimate association with one another. It has also been said that in such societies there is little critical or abstract thinking. These characteristics are related to yet another characteristic of the folk society: behavior is personal, not impersonal. A "person" may be defined as that social object which I feel to respond to situations as I do, with all the sentiments and interests which I feel to be my own; a person is myself in another form, his qualities and values are inherent within him, and his significance for me is not merely one of utility. A "thing," on the other hand, is a social object which has no claim upon my sympathies, which responds to me, as I conceive it, mechanically; its value for me exists in so far as it serves my end. In the folk society all human beings admitted to the society are treated as persons; one does not deal impersonally ("thing-fashion") with any other participant in the little world of that society. Moreover, in the folk society much besides human beings is treated personally. The pattern of behavior which is first suggested by the inner experience of the individual—his wishes, fears, sensitivenesses, and interests of all sorts—is projected into all objects with which he comes into contact. Thus nature, too, is treated personally: the elements, the features of the landscape, the animals, and especially anything in the environment which by its appearance or behavior suggests that it has the attributes of mankind—to all these are attributed qualities of the human person.

In short, the personal and intimate life of the child in the family is extended, in the folk society, into the social world of the adult and even into inanimate objects. It is not merely that relations in such a society are personal; it is also that they are familial. The first contacts made as the infant becomes a person are with other persons; moreover, each of these first persons, he comes to learn, has a particular kind of relation to him which is associated with that one's genealogical position. The individual finds himself fixed within a constellation of familial relationships. The kinship connections provide a pattern in terms of which, in the ideal folk society, all personal relations are conventionalized and categorized. All relations are personal. But relations are not, in content of specific behavior, the same for everyone. As a mother is different from a father, and a grandson from a nephew, so are these classes of personal relationship, originating in genealogical connection, extended outward into all relationships whatever. In this sense, the folk society is a familial society. Robert H. Lowie has demonstrated the qualification that is to be introduced into the statement of Maine that the primitive society is organized in terms of kinship rather than territory. It is true that the fact that men are neighbors contributes to their sense of belonging together. But the point to be emphasized in understanding the folk society is that whether mere contiguity or relationship as brother or as son is the circumstance uniting men into the society, the result is a group of people among whom prevail the personal and categorized relationships that characterize families as we know them, and in which the patterns of kinship tend to be extended outward from the group of genealogically connected individuals into the whole society. The kin are the type persons for all experience.

This general conception may be resolved into component or related conceptions. In the folk society family relationships are clearly distinguished from one another. Very special sorts of behavior may be expected by a mother's brother of his sister's son, and this behavior will be different from that expected by a father's brother of his brother's son. Among certain Australian tribes animals killed by a hunter must be divided so that nine or ten certain parts must be given to nine or ten corresponding relatives of the successful hunter—the right ribs to the father's brother, a piece of the flank to the mother's brother, and so on. The tendency to extend kinship outward takes many special forms. In many primitive societies kinship terms and kinship behavior (in reduced degree) are extended to persons not known to be genealogically related at all, but who are nevertheless regarded as kin. Among the central Australians, terms of relationship are extended "so as to embrace all persons who come into social contact with one another. . . . In this way the whole society forms a body of relatives." In the folk society groupings which do not arise out of genealogical connection are few, and those that do exist tend to take on the attributes of kinship. Ritual kinship is common in primitive and peasant societies in the forms of blood brotherhood, godparental relationships, and other ceremonial sponsorships. These multiply kinship connections; in these cases the particular individuals to be united depend upon choice. Furthermore, there is frequently a recognizedly fictitious or metaphorical use of kinship terms to designate more casual relationships, as between host and guest or between worshipper and deity.

The real primitive and peasant societies differ very greatly as to the forms assumed by kinship. Nevertheless, it is possible to recognize two main types. In one of these the connection between husband and wife is emphasized, while neither one of the lineages, matrilineal or patrilineal, is singled out as contrasted with the other. In such a folk society the individual parental family is the social unit, and connections with relatives outside this family are of secondary importance. Such family organization is common where the population is small, the means of livelihood are by precarious collection of wild food, and larger units cannot permanently remain together because the natural resources will not allow it. But where a somewhat larger population remains together, either in a village or in a migratory band, there often, although by no means always, is found an emphasis upon one line of consanguine connection rather than the other with subordination of the conjugal connection. There results a segmentation of the society into equivalent kinship units. These may take the form of extended domestic groups or joint families (as in China) or may include many households of persons related in part through recognized genealogical connection and in part through the sharing of the same name or other symbolic designation; in the latter case we speak of the groups as clans. Even in societies where the individual parental family is an independent economic unit, as in the case of the eastern Eskimo, husband and wife never become a new social and economic unit with the completeness that is characteristic of our own society. When a marriage in primitive society comes to an end, the kinsmen of the dead spouse assert upon his property a claim they have never given up. On the whole, we may think of the family among folk peoples as made up of persons consanguinely connected. Marriage is, in comparison with what we in our society directly experience, an incident in the life of the individual who is born, brought up, and dies with his blood kinsmen. In such a society romantic love can hardly be elevated to a major principle.

In so far as the consanguine lines are well defined (and in some cases both lines may be of importance to the individual) the folk society may be thought of as composed of families rather than of individuals. It is the familial groups that act and are acted upon. There is strong solidarity within the kinship group, and the individual is responsible to all his kin as they are responsible to him. "The clan is a natural mutual aid society. . . . A member belongs to the clan, he is not his own; if he is wrong, they will right him; if he does wrong, the responsibility is shared by them." Thus, in folk societies wherein the tendency to maintain consanguine connection has resulted in joint families or clans, it is usual to find that injuries done by an individual are regarded as injuries against his kinship group, and the group takes the steps to right the wrong. The step may be revenge regulated by custom or a property settlement. A considerable part of primitive law exists in the regulation of claims by one body of kin against another. The fact that the folk society is an organization of families rather than an aggregation of individuals is further expressed in many of those forms of marriage in which a certain kind of relative is the approved spouse. The customs by which in many primitive societies a man is expected to marry his deceased brother's widow or a woman to marry her deceased sister's husband express the view of marriage as an undertaking between kinship groups. One of the spouses having failed by death, the undertaking is to be carried on by some other representative of the family group. Indeed, in the arrangements for marriage—the selection of spouses by their relatives, in bride-price, dowry, and in many forms of familial negotiations leading to a marriage—the nature of marriage as a connubial form of social relations between kindreds finds expression.

It has been said in foregoing paragraphs that behavior in the folk society is traditional, spontaneous, and uncritical, that what one man does is much the same as what another man does, and that the patterns of conduct are clear and remain constant throughout the generations. It has also been suggested that the congruence of all parts of conventional behavior and social institutions with each other contributes to the sense of rightness which the member of the folk society feels to inhere in his traditional ways of action. In the well-known language of Sumner, the ways of life are folkways; furthermore, the folkways tend to be also mores—ways of doing or thinking to which attach notions of moral worth. The value of every traditional act or object or institution is, thus, something which the members of the society are not disposed to call into question; and should the value be called into question, the doing so is resented. This characteristic of the folk society may be briefly referred to by saying that it is a sacred society. In the folk society one may not, without calling into effect negative social sanctions, challenge as valueless what has come to be traditional in that society.

Presumably, the sacredness of social objects has its source, in part, at least, in the mere fact of habituation; probably the individual organism becomes early adjusted to certain habits, motor and mental, and to certain associations between one activity and another or between certain sense experiences and certain activities, and it is almost physiologically uncomfortable to change or even to entertain the idea of change. There arises "a feeling of impropriety of certain forms, of a particular social or religious value, or a superstitious fear of change." Probably the sacredness of social objects in the folk society is related also to the fact that in such well-organized cultures acts and objects suggest the traditions, beliefs, and conceptions which all share. There is reason to suppose that when what is traditionally done becomes less meaningful because people no longer know what the acts stand for, life becomes more secular. In the repetitious character of conventional action (aside from technical action) we have ritual; in its expressive character we have ceremony; in the folk society ritual tends also to be ceremonious, and ritual-ceremony tends to be sacred, not secular.

The sacredness of social objects is apparent in the ways in which, in the folk society, such an object is hedged around with restraints and protections that keep it away from the commonplace and the matter-of-fact. In the sacred there is alternatively, or in combination, holiness and dangerousness. When the Papago Indian returned from a successful war expedition, bringing the scalp of a slain Apache, the head-hairs of the enemy were treated as loaded with a tremendous "charge" of supernatural power; only old men, already successful warriors and purified through religious ritual, could touch the object and make it safe for incorporation into the home of the slayer. Made into the doll-like form of an Apache Indian, it was, at last, after much ceremonial preparation, held for an instant by the members of the slayer's family, addressed in respect and awe by kinship terms, and placed in the house, there to give off protective power. The Indians of San Pedro de la Laguna, Guatemala, recognize an officer, serving for life, whose function it is to keep custody of ten or a dozen Latin breviaries printed in the eighteenth century and to read prayers from one or another of these books on certain occasions. No one but this custodian may handle the books, save his assistants on ceremonial occasions, with his permission. Should anyone else touch a book he would go mad or be stricken with blindness. Incense and candles are burnt before the chest containing the books, yet the books are not gods—they are objects of sacredness.

In the folk society this disposition to regard objects as sacred extends, characteristically, even into the subsistence activities and into the foodstuffs of the people. Often the foodstuffs are personified as well as sacred. " 'My granduncle used to say to me,' explained a Navajo Indian, ' "If you are walking along a trail and see a kernel of corn, pick it up. It is like a child lost and starving." According to the legends corn is just the same as a human being, only it is holier. . . . When a man goes into a cornfield he feels that he is in a holy place, that he is walking among Holy People. . . . Agriculture is a holy occupation. Even before you plant you sing songs. You continue this during the whole time your crops are growing. You cannot help but feel that you are in a holy place when you go through your fields and they are doing well.' " [1] In the folk society, ideally conceived, nothing is solely a means to an immediate practical end. All activities, even the means of production, are ends in themselves, activities expressive of the ultimate values of the society.

III

This characterization of the ideal folk society could be greatly extended. Various of the elements that make up the conception could be differently com-

[1] W. W. Hill, *The Agricultural and Hunting Methods of the Navaho Indians* ("Yale University Publications in Anthropology," No. 18 [New Haven: Yale University Press, 1938]), p. 53.

bined with one another, and this point or that could be developed or further emphasized and its relations shown to other aspects of the conception. For example, it might be pointed out that where there is little or no systematic and reflective thinking the customary solutions to problems of practical action only imperfectly take the form of really effective and understood control of the means appropriate to accomplish the desired end, and that, instead, they tend to express the states of mind of the individuals who want the end brought about and fear that it may not be. We say this briefly in declaring that the folk society is characterized by much magic, for we may understand "magic" to refer to action with regard to an end—to instrumental action—but only to such instrumental action as does not effectively bring about that end, or is not really understood in so far as it does, and which is expressive of the way the doer thinks and feels rather than adapted to accomplishing the end. "Magic is based on specific experience of emotional states. . . . in which the truth is revealed not by reason but by the play of emotions upon the human organism. . . . magic is founded on the belief that hope cannot fail nor desire deceive." In the folk society effective technical action is much mixed with magical activity. What is done tends to take the form of a little drama; it is a picture of what is desired.

The nature of the folk society could, indeed, be restated in the form of a description of the folk mind. This description would be largely a repetition of what has been written in foregoing pages, except that now the emphasis would be upon the characteristic mental activity of members of the folk society, rather than upon customs and institutions. The man of the folk society tends to make mental associations which are personal and emotional, rather than abstractly categoric or defined in terms of cause and effect. ". . . Primitive man views every action not only as adapted to its main object, every thought related to its main end, as we should perceive them, but. . . . he associates them with other ideas, often of a religious or at least a symbolic nature. Thus he gives to them a higher significance than they seem to us to deserve." A very similar statement of this kind of thinking has been expressed in connection with the thinking of medieval man; the description would apply as well to man in the folk society:

> From the causal point of view, symbolism appears as a sort of short-cut of thought. Instead of looking for the relation between two things by following the hidden detours of their causal connections, thought makes a leap and discovers their relation, not in a connection of cause or effects, but in a connection of signification or finality. Such a connection will at once appear convincing, provided only that the two things have an essential quality in common which can be referred to a general value. . . . Symbolic assimilation founded on common properties presupposes the idea that these properties are essential to things. The vision of white and red roses blooming among thorns at once calls up a symbolic association in the medieval mind: for example, that of virgins and martyrs, shining with glory, in the midst of their persecutors. The assimilation is produced because the attributes

are the same: the beauty, the tenderness, the purity, the colours of the roses are also those of the virgins, their red color that of the blood of the martyrs. But this similarity will only have a mystic meaning if the middle-term connecting the two terms of the symbolic concept expresses an essentiality common to both; in other words, if redness and whiteness are something more than names for physical differences based on quantity, if they are conceived of as essences, as realities. The mind of the savage, of the child, and of the poet never sees them otherwise.[2]

The tendency to treat nature personally has recognition in the literature as the "animistic" or "anthropomorphic" quality of primitive thinking, and the contrast between the means-ends pattern of thought more characteristic of modern urban man and the personal thought of primitive man has been specially investigated.

In the foregoing account no mention has been made of the absence of economic behavior characteristic of the market in the folk society. Within the ideal folk society members are bound by religious and kinship ties, and there is no place for the motive of commercial gain. There is no money and nothing is measured by any such common denominator of value. The distribution of goods and services tends to be an aspect of the conventional and personal relationships of status which make up the structure of the society: goods are exchanged as expressions of good will and, in large part, as incidents of ceremonial and ritual activities. "On the whole, then, the compulsion to work, to save, and to expend is given not so much by a rational appreciation of the [material] benefits to be received as by the desire for social recognition, through such behavior."

The conception sketched here takes on meaning if the folk society is seen in contrast to the modern city. The vast, complicated, and rapidly changing world in which the urbanite and even the urbanized country-dweller live today is enormously different from the small, inward-facing folk society, with its well-integrated and little-changing moral and religious conceptions. At one time all men lived in these little folk societies. For many thousands of years men must have lived so; urbanized life began only very recently, as the long history of man on earth is considered, and the extreme development of a secularized and swift-changing world society is only a few generations old.

The tribal groups that still remain around the edges of expanding civilization are the small remainders of this primary state of living. Considering them one by one, and in comparison with the literate or semiliterate societies, the industrialized and the semiindustrialized societies, we may discover how each has developed forms of social life in accordance with its own special circumstances. Among the polar Eskimos, where each small family had to shift for itself in the rigors of the arctic environment, although the ties of kinship were of great importance, no clans or other large unilateral kinship groups came into existence. The sedentary Haida of the Queen Charlotte Islands were

[2] J. Huizinga, *The Waning of the Middle Ages* (London: Arnold & Co., 1924), pp. 184–85.

divided into two exogamous kinship groups, each composed of clans, with intense pride of decent and healthy rivalry between them. Among the warring and nomadic Comanche initiative and resourcefulness of the individual were looked on more favorably than among the sedentary and closely interdependent Zuni. In West Africa great native states arose, with chiefs and courts and markets, yet the kinship organization remained strong; and in China we have an example of slow growth of a great society, with a literate élite, inclosing within it a multitude of village communities of the folk type. Where cities have arisen, the country people dependent on those cities have developed economic and political relationships, as well as relationships of status, with the city people, and so have become that special kind of rural folk we call peasantry. And even in the newer parts of the world, as in the United States, many a village or small town has, perhaps, as many points of resemblance with the folk society as with urban life.

Thus the societies of the world do not range themselves in the same order with regard to the degree to which they realize all of the characteristics of the ideal folk society. On the other hand, there is so marked a tendency for some of these characteristics to occur together with others that the interrelations among them must be in no small part that of interdependent variables. Indeed, some of the interrelations are so obvious that we feel no sense of problem. The smallness of the folk society and the long association together of the same individuals certainly is related to the prevailingly personal character of relationships. The fewness of secondary and tertiary tools and the absence of machine manufacture are circumstances obviously unfavorable to a very complex division of labor. Many problems present themselves, however, as to the conditions in which certain of these characteristics do not occur in association, and as to the circumstances under which certain of them may be expected to change in the direction of their opposites, with or without influencing others to change also.

A study of the local differences in the festival of the patron village saint in certain communities of Yucatan indicates that some interrelationship exists in that case. In all four communities, differing as to their degrees of isolation from urban centers of modifying influence, the festival expresses a relationship between the village and its patron saint (or cross) which is annually renewed. In it a ritual and worship are combined with a considerable amount of play. The chief activities of the festival are a novena, a folk dance, and a rustic bullfight. In all four communities there is an organization of men and women who for that year undertake the leadership of the festival, handing over the responsibility to a corresponding group of successors at its culmination. So far the institution is the same in all the communities studied. The differences appear when the details of the ritual and play and of the festal organization are compared, and when the essential meanings of these acts and organizations are inquired into. Then it appears that from being an intensely sacred act, made by the village as a collectivity composed of familially defined component groups, with close relationship to the system of religious and moral understandings of the people, the festival becomes, in the more urbanized communities, chiefly an opportunity for recreation for some and of financial profit for others, with little reference to moral and religious conceptions.

In the most isolated and otherwise most folklike of the communities studied the organization of the festival is closely integrated with the whole social structure of the community. The hierarchy of leaders of the community, whose duties are both civil and religious, carry on the festival: It is the chiefs, the men who decide disputes and lead in warfare, who also take principal places in the religious processions and in the conduct of the ceremonies. The community, including several neighboring settlements, is divided into five groups, membership in which descends in the male line. The responsibility for leading the prayers and preparing the festal foods rests in turn on four men chosen from each of the five groups. The festival is held at the head village, at the shrine housing the cross patron of the entire community. The festival consists chiefly of solemnly religious acts: masses, rosaries, procession of images, kneeling of worshipers. The ritual offerings are presented by a special officer, in all solemnity, to the patron cross; certain symbols of divinity are brought from the temple and exposed to the kneeling people as the offerings are made. The transfer of the responsibility to lead the festival is attended by ceremony in an atmosphere of sanctity: certain ritual paraphernalia are first placed on the altar and then, after recitation of prayers and performance of a religious dance, are handed over, in view of all, from the custodians of the sacred charge for that year to their successors.

In the villages that are less isolated the festival is similar in form, but it is less well integrated with the social organization of the community, is less sacred, and allows for more individual enterprise and responsibility. These changes continue in the other communities studied, as one gets nearer to the city of Merida. In certain seacoast villages the festival of the patron saint is a money-getting enterprise of a few secular-minded townspeople. The novena is in the hands of a few women who receive no help from the municipal authorities; the bullfight is a commercial entertainment, professional bullfighters being hired for the occasion and admission charged; the folk dance is little attended. The festival is enjoyed by young people who come to dance modern dances and to witness the bullfight, and it is an opportunity to the merchants to make a profit. What was an institution of folk culture has become a business enterprise in which individuals, as such, take part for secular ends.

The principal conclusion is that the less isolated and more heterogeneous communities of the peninsula of Yucatan are the more secular and individualistic and the more characterized by disorganization of culture. It further appeared probable that there was, in the changes taking place in Yucatan, a relation of interdependence among these changing characteristics, especially between the disorganization of culture and secularization. "People cease to believe because they cease to understand, and they cease to understand because they cease to do the things that express the understandings." New jobs and other changes in the division of labor bring it about that people cannot participate in the old rituals; and, ceasing to participate, they cease to share the values for which the rituals stood. This is, admittedly, however, only a part of the explanation.

The conception of the folk society has stimulated one small group of field workers to consider the interdependence or independence of these characteristics of society. In Yucatan isolation, homogeneity, a personal and "symbolic" view of nature, importance of familial relationships, a high degree of organization of culture, and sacredness of sanctions and institutions were all found in regular association with each other. It was then reported that in certain Indian communities on or near Lake Atitlan in Guatemala this association of characteristics is not repeated. As it appeared that these Guatemalan communities were not in rapid change, but were persisting in their essential nature, the conclusion was reached that "a stable society can be small, unsophisticated, homogeneous in beliefs and practices," have a local, well-organized culture, and still be one "with relationships impersonal, with formal institutions dictating the acts of individuals, and with family organization weak, with life secularized, and with individuals acting more from economic or other personal advantage than from any deep conviction or thought of the social good." It was further pointed out that in these Guatemalan societies a "primitive world view," that is, a disposition to treat nature personally, to regard attributes as entities, and to make "symbolic" rather than causal connections, coexists with a tendency for relations between man and man to be impersonal, commercial, and secular, as they tend to be in the urban society.

These observations lead, in turn, to reconsideration of the circumstances tending to bring about one kind of society or one aspect of society rather than another. The breakdown of familial institutions in recent times in Western society is often ascribed to the development of the city and of modern industry. If, as has been reported, familial institutions are also weak in these Guatemalan villages, there must be alternative causes for the breakdown of the family to the rise of industry and the growth of the city, for these Guatemalan Indians live on or near their farms, practice a domestic handicraft manufacture, and have little or nothing to do with cities. It has been suggested that in the case of the Guatemalan societies the development, partly before the Conquest and partly afterward, of a pecuniary economy with a peddler's commerce, based on great regional division of labor, together with a system of regulations imposed by an élite with the use of force, may be the circumstances that have brought about reduction in the importance of familial institutions and individual independence, especially in matters of livelihood.

The secular character of life in these highland villages of the Lake Atitlan region is not so well established as in the individuated character of life, but if life is indeed secular there, it is a secularity that has developed without the influence of high personal mobility, of the machine, and of science. In a well-known essay Max Weber showed how capitalistic commercialism could and did get along with piety in the case of the Puritans. So it may appear that under certain conditions a literate and, indeed, at least partly urbanized society may be both highly commercial and sacred—as witness, also, the Jews—while under certain other conditions an otherwise folklike people may become individualistic, commercial, and perhaps secular. It is, of course, the determination of the limiting conditions that is important.

Shortly after World War II, new group typologies came under analysis by sociologists, supplementing traditional typologies such as the distinction between folk and urban societies. One of the most important new developments along these lines has been the sociological distinction between small- and large-scale groups, that is, between the face-to-face microscopic social systems ranging in size from two to twenty members at one extreme, and the macroscopic, full-scale or complete societies at the other end of the scale. On the basis of this typology, a new subdivision of contemporary sociology, small-group analysis, has become a well-established and flourishing specialization in the past generation.

A pioneer in small-group sociology was Robert F. Bales. His rationalization was that the systematic analysis of small-group interaction would expand the scope of available empirical data about social organizations, and that this in turn would strengthen our understanding of social systems in the direction of more comprehensive and abstract levels. In the next article, he presents a set of twelve categories of behavior and six interlocking functional problems applicable to any concrete type of small group. He relates them to each other in a method that has come to be called "interaction process analysis."

17. A SET OF CATEGORIES FOR THE ANALYSIS OF SMALL GROUP INTERACTION *

ROBERT F. BALES

Harvard University

In a recent review of the state of research in the field of small groups, Edward Shils makes some remarks which aptly point up the problem to which this paper is addressed:

"Because problems are dimly 'felt,' because they are neither related to a general theory of behavior on the one side, nor rigorously connected with the categories and indices to be chosen for observation on the other, the results of the research can very seldom become part of the cumulative movement of truth which constitutes the growth of scientific knowledge. When concrete indices (and classifications) are not clearly related to the variables of a general theory of human behavior in so-

* *American Sociological Review,* Vol. 15, No. 2, April, 1950, pp. 257–263.

ciety, they tend to be *ad hoc*. Under these conditions they are only with difficulty, applicable, i.e., translatable into another concrete situation by an investigator who seeks to confirm, revise, or disconfirm the previously 'established' proposition." [1]

Probably most of us have some difficulty in thinking of a session between a psychiatrist and patient, a corner boy's gang in a political huddle, and a staff conference of business executives as comparable within a single frame of reference. It is probably more difficult, for example, than thinking of the social systems of China, of Bali, and the United States as legitimate objects for comparative analysis. At least the latter three constitute full scale, and in some sense, complete social systems.

What do the former three groups have in common? They are small face-to-face groups. If we call them social systems, we shall have to say that they are partial, as well as microscopic social systems. To place a slightly different emphasis, it can be said that they are systems of human interaction. At this degree of abstraction there is no necessary incongruity in comparing them with each other, or with full-scale social systems. Both small groups and complete societies can be viewed as types of interaction systems, even though one is tremendously more inclusive than the other. If this point of view turns out to be excessively formal or abstract, we may have to retreat to less generalized frames of reference.

To take the more hopeful view, it may very well be that one of the main contributions of the study of small groups will be an expanding of the range of available empirical data in such a way as to force our theory of social systems to a more general and powerful level of abstraction. If the theory of social systems has been generalized and strengthened by the necessity of making it applicable to a range of full-scale social systems, non-literate as well as literate, Eastern as well as Western, then there is at least the possibility that it will be further strengthened by the necessity of making it applicable up and down the scale from large to small.

However this may be, the present set of categories was developed with this hope, and took its initial point of departure from a body of theory about the structure and dynamics of full-scale social systems. This will not be immediately apparent in viewing the set of categories, nor can it be spelled out to any satisfactory degree in this article. A manual dealing with both the theoretical and practical aspects of the method for those who may wish to apply it in their own research has recently been published. The present paper will give only a simplified introductory description of the method and some of its possible uses.

DESCRIPTION OF THE METHOD

The method is called interaction process analysis. It is a type of content analysis in the basic sense, but the type of content which it attempts to abstract

[1] Edward Shils, *The Present State of American Sociology*, Glencoe, Illinois: The Free Press, 1948, p. 45.

from the raw material of observation is the type of problem-solving relevance of each act for the total on-going process. Hence it has seemed less confusing to refer to what we are doing as "process analysis" rather than as "content analysis."

The heart of the method is a way of classifying behavior act by act, as it occurs in small face-to-face groups, and a series of ways of analyzing the data to obtain indices descriptive of group process, and derivatively, of factors influencing that process. The set of categories as it actually appears on the observation form is shown under the twelve numbers in Chart 1. The outer brackets and labels do not appear on the observation form, but constitute a part of the mental set of the observer. The twelve observation categories are numbered from the top down, but are arranged in a series of complementary

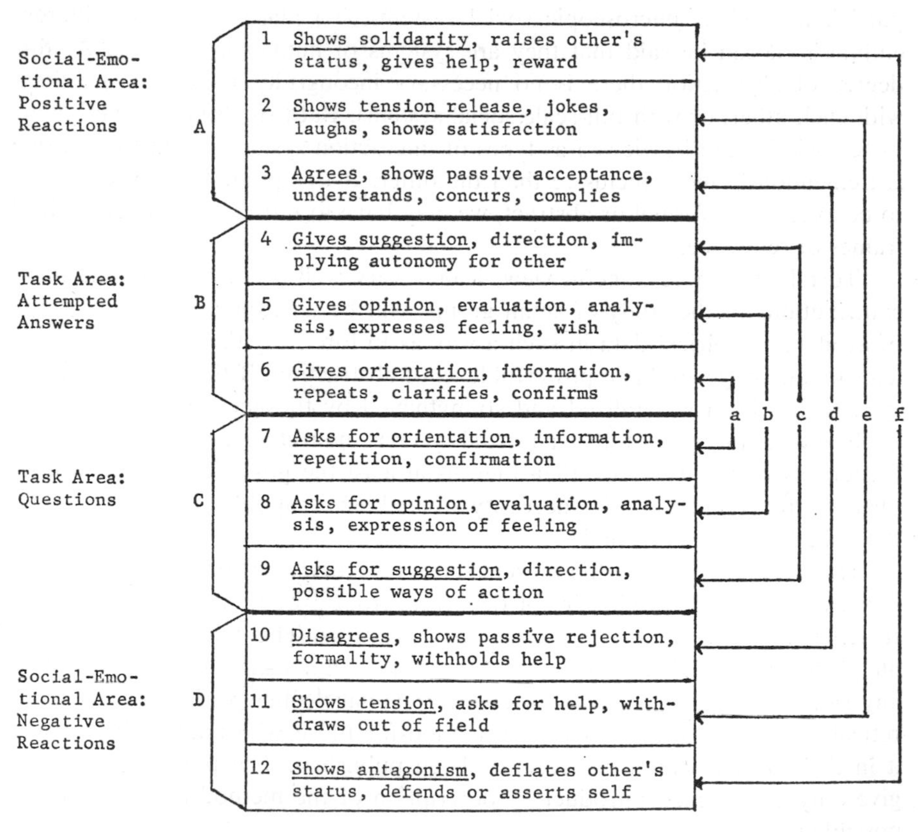

CHART 1. The System of Categories Used in Observation and Their Relation to Major Frames of Reference.

Key:

a. Problems of orientation
b. Problems of evaluation
c. Problems of control
d. Problems of decision
e. Problems of tension-managment
f. Problems of integration

pairs proceeding from the center pair, 6 and 7, outward. The phrases and terms within the numbered categories are only catch-phrases designed to be concretely descriptive of the implied theoretical content of the categories in their usual forms. Actually there are extended definitions of each of the categories, and the central meaning of each is given by its position in the frames of reference to which they are all related as indicated by the labeled brackets on the Chart.

The set of twelve categories (and the actual behavior which is classified under them) are brought into working relation to other bodies of theory in terms of the frame of reference. The key assumption which provides this articulation is the notion that all organized and at least partially cooperative systems of human interaction, from the smallest to the most inclusive, and of whatever concrete variety, may be approached for scientific analysis by abstracting from the events which go on within them in such a way as to relate the consequences of these events to a set of concepts formulating what are hypothetically called "functional problems of interaction systems."

For purposes of the present set of categories we postulate six interlocking functional problems which are logically applicable to any concrete type of interaction system. As indicated in Chart 1, these are in one-word terms: problems of orientation, evaluation, control, decision, tension-management, and integration. These terms are all related to a hypothetical conception of an overarching problem-solving sequence of interaction between two or more persons. As a concrete first approximation we may find it helpful to think of the functional problems as related to an order of "stages" or "steps" in a problem-solving sequence, as their order suggests. Actually this is an over-simplified view. However, in order to illustrate the notion of stages as they may appear under certain conditions, let us take a short description of a fictional group meeting. The same example will serve to illustrate the method of scoring with the categories.

HOW THE SCORING IS DONE

Let us imagine we are observing a group of five persons who are meeting together to come to a decision about a point of policy in a project they are doing together. Three or four of the members have arrived, and while they wait they are laughing and joking together, exchanging pleasantries and "small talk" before getting down to business. The missing members arrive, and after a little more scattered conversation the chairman calls the meeting to order. Usually, though not necessarily, this is where the observer begins his scoring.

Stage 1. Emphasis on problems of orientation: (deciding what the situation is like). The chairman brings the meeting up to date with a few informal remarks. He says, "At the end of our last meeting we decided that we would have to consider our budget before laying out plans in greater detail." The observer, sitting with the observation form in front of him, looks over the list of twelve categories and decides that this remark is most relevant to the problem of orientation, and specifically that it takes the form of an "attempted answer" to this problem, and so he classifies it in Category 6, "Gives orientation, information, repeats, clarifies, confirms." The observer has already decided that he will designate the chairman by the number 1, and each person around the table in turn by the numbers 2, 3, 4, and 5. The group as a whole will be designated by the symbol 0. This remark was made by the chairman and was apparently addressed to the group as a whole, so the observer writes down the symbols 1-0 in one of the spaces following Category 6 on the observation form.

In this one operation, the observer has thus isolated a unit of speech or process which he considers a proper unit for classification, has classified it, identified the member who performed the act, and the person or persons to whom it was directed. If he were writing on a moving tape instead of a paper form, as we do for some purposes, he would also have identified the exact position of the act in sequence with all others. In practice we find that we obtain from 10 to 20 scores per minute in keeping up with most interaction, and that this speed is not excessive for a trained observer.

As the chairman finishes his remark, Member 2 asks the chairman, "Has anybody gone over our expenditures to date?" The observer decides a problem of orientation exists, and so should be classified in Category 7, "Asks for orientation, information, repetition, confirmation." He so records it by placing the symbols 2-1 in a box following this category. The chairman replies, "I have here a report prepared by Miss Smith on the expenditures to date." The observer marks down the symbols 1-2 under Category 6, as an "attempted answer" to the indicated problem of orientation. As the chairman goes over the report the observer continues to score, getting a good many scores in Categories 6 and 7, but also occasional scores in other categories.

Stage 2. Emphasis on problems of evaluation: (deciding what attitudes should be taken toward the situation). As the chairman finishes reviewing the items on the report he may ask, "Have we been within bounds on our expenditures so far?" The observer puts down a score under Category 8, "Asks for opinion, evaluation, analysis, expression of feeling." Member 3 says, "It seems to me that we have gone in pretty heavily for secretarial help." The observer puts down a score in Category 5, "Gives opinion, evaluation, analysis, expresses feeling." Member 4 comes in with the remark, "Well I don't know. It seems to me . . ." The observer puts down the symbols 4-3 in Category 10, "Disagrees, shows passive rejection, formality, withholds help," and continues with scores in Category 5 as Member 4 makes his argument. The discussion continues to revolve around the analysis of expenditures, with a good many scores falling in Category 5, but also in others, particularly Categories 10 and 3, and interspersed with a number in Categories 6 and 7 as opinions are explained and supported.

Stage 3. Emphasis on problems of control: (deciding what to do about it). Finally the chairman says, "Well a little more than half our time is gone."

The observer scores 1-0 in Category 6. "Do you want to go ahead and decide whether we should buy that piece of equipment or . . ." The observer scores 1-0 in Category 9, "Asks for suggestion, direction, possible ways of action." Member 2 says, "I think we should get it." The observer scores 2-0 in Category 4, "Gives suggestion, direction, implying autonomy for other." As Member 2 begins to support his suggestion, Member 3 breaks in with a counter argument, and the discussion begins to grow more heated.

The observer begins to have trouble in keeping up as the members are talking more rapidly and some remarks are left unfinished. He does not forget to keep scanning the group, however, and presently he notices that Member 5, who has said little up to this point, sighs heavily and begins to examine his fingernails. The observer puts down a score under Category 11, "Shows tension, asks for help, withdraws out of field." He enters this score as 5-y, since he has decided ahead of time to use the symbol y to stand for "self," and to use it when activity is directed toward the self, or is expressive and non-focal, that is, not directed toward other members.

Meantime, Member 3, the chronic objector, comes through with a remark directed at Member 2, "Well, I never did agree about hiring that deadhead secretary. All she's got is looks, but I guess that's enough for Joe." The others laugh at this. The observer scores the first and second remarks under Category 12, "Shows antagonism, deflates other's status, defends or asserts self." The laugh which follows is scored in Category 2, "Shows tension release, jokes, laughs, shows satisfaction." In this case the score is written 0-3, all to Member 3.

At this point Member 5 comes in quietly to sum up the argument, and by the time he finishes several heads are nodding. The observer scores both the nods and the audible agreements in Category 3, "Agrees, shows passive acceptance, understands, concurs, complies." The chairman says, "Then it looks like we are in agreement." The observer scores in Category 6, and scores the answering nods in Category 3. Member 3, the chronic objector, who is also the chronic joker, comes in with a joke at this point, and the joking and laughing continue for a minute or two, each member extending the joke a little. The observer continues to score in Category 2 as long as this activity continues. As the members pick up their things one of them says, "Well, I think we got through that in good shape. Old Bill certainly puts in the right word at the right time, doesn't he." The observer marks down two scores under Category 1, "Shows solidarity, raises other's status, gives help, reward," and after a few more similar remarks the meeting breaks up.

THE POSSIBILITY OF EMPIRICAL NORMS

The foregoing is a fictional example, designed to illustrate the nature of the scoring operation, as well as a kind of hypothetical sequence of stages which may occur under certain conditions. To summarize, we might say that during the course of this meeting there were a series of "phases" portrayed, during which one or more of the functional problems included in our conceptual framework received more than its usual share of attention. The temporal order of these phases in this fictional example follows in a rough way the logical order in which we arrange the categories on the observation form in pairs from the center line outward, that is, as dealing with problems of orientation, evaluation, control, and then in rapid order, a special emphasis on final decision, tension reduction, and reintegration. Each of the major functional problems has been made into an implicit "agenda topic."

The categories of activity as classified by the present system are assumed to bear a functional relation to each other similar to the relation of the phases in the meeting just portrayed. The example has been constructed so that in its phases the relations of the categories to each other are "written large," to borrow an idea from Plato. Hence it is relevant to ask what degree the notion of phases on the larger scale is actually to be taken as an empirical description rather than as a logical model. It is important to emphasize in answer to this question that we do not assume nor believe that all group meetings actually proceed in just this way. One of the thorniest problems in the history of thinking about the process of small groups is whether or not, or in what sense there may be a series of "steps" or "stages" in group problem solving. Data will later be published which indicate that under *certain conditions,* which must be carefully specified, a group problem-solving process essentially like that sketched above, does tend to appear. The data indicate that the sequence described is a kind of average sequence for problem-solving groups, that is, an empirical norm. It further appears that departures from the average picture can be used as diagnostic indicators of the nature of the conditions under which interaction takes place.

Similarly, it appears that there are empirical uniformities in the way activities are distributed between persons. We have some data which indicate that, on the average, if we rank order participants according to the total number of acts they originate, they will then also stand in rank order as to (1) the number of acts they originate to the group as a whole (to 0), (2) the number of acts they originate to specific other members of the group, and (3) the number of acts they receive from all other members of the group. In addition, (4) each person in the rank order series addresses a slightly larger amount of activity to the person just above him in the series than the person above addresses to him, with the top person addressing the group as a whole to a disproportionate degree. It seems likely that these uniformities can be tied together in a more comprehensive theory, and that departures from this average picture can be used as a diagnostic indicator of the nature of the conditions under which interaction takes place. Data on this problem will be published later.

Similarly, ignoring time sequence and the specific persons who initiate or receive acts, empirical uniformities appear in the gross frequency with each category of activity tends to occur. Preliminary data on these uniformities are given below.

FREQUENCY OF OCCURRENCE OF EACH TYPE OF ACTIVITY

We have available for this tabulation some 23,000 scores in terms of the present twelve categories, from observations of groups of different sizes and kinds, ranging through nursery school children, high school and college student, married couples, college faculty discussions, etc., on tasks of widely different kinds. We do not know how badly biased this collection of scores may be as a sample of something larger. They are simply all of the raw scores we have to date on all of the groups and tasks we happen to have observed for a variety of reasons. The scorings were made by the present author. The general problems of reliability are treated in the manual mentioned above. Very briefly it may be said that satisfactory reliability has been obtained between observers, but requires intensive training which should be regarded as an integral part of the method.

Table 1 shows the raw scores and their percentage distribution (or rates) in the twelve categories. In order to have certain conventional limits for in-

TABLE I.

TABLE 1. Raw Scores Obtained on All Interaction Observed to Date, Percentage Rates, and Suggested Limits, by Categories

Category	*Raw Scores*	*Percentage*	*Suggested Limits for Inspection of Profiles* *	
			Lower	*Upper*
1	246	1.0	0.0	5.0
2	1675	7.3	3.0	14.0
3	2798	12.2	6.0	20.0
4	1187	5.2	2.0	11.0
5	6897	30.0	21.0	40.0
6	4881	21.2	14.0	30.0
7	1229	5.4	2.0	11.0
8	809	3.5	1.0	9.0
9	172	.8	0.0	5.0
10	1509	6.6	3.0	13.0
11	1009	4.4	1.0	10.0
12	558	2.4	0.0	7.0
	22970	100.0		

* Suggested limits shown have been established for each category by use of binomial confidence limits given in Snedecor, *Statistical Methods,* 1946, p. 4, with p equal "Percentage of total" and n equal 100. This provides relatively wider ranges for the smaller values and although such conventions do not properly reflect the multinomial character of the variation, they provide a first approximation for present purposes.

spection of the variability of particular profiles we have employed an external criterion rather than utilize the variance of our samples, which are known to be quite heterogeneous. Our experience indicates that when the rate for a given category on a particular profile is outside the range suggested in Table 1, we are usually able to connect the deviation with some more or less obvious source of variation in the conditions under which the interaction took place. For example, we find that a profile of nursery school children at free play is over the suggested limits on showing solidarity and showing antagonism, on giving direct suggestions and on disagreement, and is under the limits on asking for opinion, giving orientation, and giving opinion. A group of high school boys in group discussion is over the limits on laughing and joking, and under the limits on giving orientation. A group of faculty members planning a thesis problem with a graduate student is within the limits on all categories. Pending the development of a satisfactory typology of groups, tasks, and other sources of variation, and the accumulation of more experience, this arbitrary procedure for detecting "significant variations" may serve a useful purpose.

APPLICABILITY OF THE METHOD

Verbal interaction accounts for the largest part of the scores, but the categories apply to non-verbal interaction as well. Groups of manageable size for the method fall in the range between two and perhaps twenty, but there is no definitely established top limit—the top manageable size depends upon the character of the interaction. The method is most easily applied in groups where the attention of the members tends to focus in turn on single speakers or members, as in most discussion groups. Hence it might be said to apply to groups small enough so that each member potentially takes into account the reactions of each of the others.

In concrete terms, the groups which one might be able to study with the method are very diverse. They would include a series of groups concerned primarily with substantive problems external to their own process, such as discussion groups, planning groups, policy forming and executive committees, boards and panels, diagnostic councils in clinical work, seminars and classroom groups, teams and work groups, certain kinds of problem-solving groups in experimental social psychology and sociology, etc. In addition, there are certain groups with a primary focus on their own procedure in an impersonal way, for training purposes, such as those formed for training in basic human relations skills, now an important branch of small group research. In a less impersonal way, there are large numbers of small groups which have the interaction or interpersonal relations of the members as a primary focus, whatever their concern with substantive external problems. These would include family and household groups, children's play groups, adolescent gangs, adult cliques, social and recreational clubs, and small associations of a great many kinds. Finally there are groups which might be said to have a primary focus on problems of personal content or experience of members, such as therapy or confessional groups of various kinds, and groups of two, such as therapist and patient, counselor and client, interviewer and interviewee, and a number of others in the general class of professional specialist and client.

Some of these types of groups have been studied with the present method or others similar to it. Some of them are unexplored as yet. Taken together, however, the total range of possible types of groups constitutes a challenging array. If interaction in groups of the diverse sorts mentioned can be brought within the range of a single frame of reference, and can be made to yield data by the same method of analysis, we should be some distance along toward meeting the difficulties which Shils indicates in the comments at the beginning of this paper.

While small-group analysis has developed as a consequence of the work of Professor Bales and his associates, sociologists have not ignored the internal operations of large-scale and complex organizations at the other end of the spectrum. They have explored the important formal as well as informal structures of such groups, and the problems of communication, turnover, morale, and supervision.

But what about the goals of large-scale organizations? In order to understand organizational personnel and their behavior, can one assume that an analysis of the official goals of organizations is sufficient? In the article that follows, Charles Perrow emphasizes that official statements of goals in organizations must not be taken at face value. More relevant to a grasp of organizational structure and function are the operative goals found in policies and daily decisions of the personnel. The analytical sequence begins with four major tasks that must be accomplished in every large-scale organization: the securing of capital, legitimization, skills, and co-ordination. These tasks in turn determine the characteristics of those in authority and power in the organization. Authority, finally, will shape the range and limits of operative goals.

To illustrate the utility of his scheme, Professor Perrow refers to three kinds of complex organizations: voluntary service, nonvoluntary service, and profit-making organizations.

18. THE ANALYSIS OF GOALS IN COMPLEX ORGANIZATIONS *

CHARLES PERROW

University of Michigan

Social scientists have produced a rich body of knowledge about many aspects of large-scale organizations, yet there are comparatively few studies of the goals of these organizations. For a full understanding of organizations and

* *American Sociological Review,* Vol. 26, No. 6, December, 1961, pp. 854–866.

the behavior of their personnel, analysis of organizational goals would seem to be critical. Two things have impeded such analysis. Studies of morale, turnover, informal organization, communication, supervisory practices, etc., have been guided by an over-rationalistic point of view wherein goals are taken for granted, and the most effective ordering of resources and personnel is seen as the only problematical issue. Fostering this view is the lack of an adequate distinction between types of goals. Without such clarification it is difficult to determine what the goals are and what would be acceptable evidence for the existence of a particular goal and for a change in goals.

It will be argued here, first, that the type of goals most relevant to understanding organizational behavior are not the official goals, but those that are embedded in major operating policies and the daily decisions of the personnel. Second, these goals will be shaped by the particular problems or tasks an organization must emphasize, since these tasks determine the characteristics of those who will dominate the organization. In illustrating the latter argument, we will not be concerned with the specific goals of organizations, but only with the range within which goals are likely to vary. Though general hospitals will be used as the main illustration, three types of organizations will be discussed: voluntary service organizations, non-voluntary service organizations and profit-making organizations.

THE OVER-RATIONALISTIC VIEW

Most studies of the internal operation of complex organizations, if they mention goals at all, have taken official statements of goals at face value. This may be justified if only a limited problem is being investigated, but even then it contributes to the view that goals are not problematical. In this view, goals have no effect upon activities other than in the grossest terms; or it can be taken for granted that the only problem is to adjust means to given and stable ends. This reflects a distinctive "model" of organizational behavior, which Alvin Gouldner has characterized as the rational model. Its proponents see the managerial elite as using rational and logical means to pursue clear and discrete ends set forth in official statements of goals, while the worker is seen as governed by nonrationalistic, traditionalistic orientations. If goals are unambiguous and achievement evaluated by cost-accounting procedures, the only turmoil of organizational life lies below the surface with workers or, at best, with middle management maneuvering for status and power. Actually, however, nonrational orientations exist at all levels, including the elite who are responsible for setting goals and assessing the degree to which they are achieved.

One reason for treating goals as static fixtures of organizational life is that goals have not been given adequate conceptualization, though the elements of this are in easy reach. If making a profit or serving customers is to be taken as a sufficient statement of goals, then all means to this end might appear to be based on rational decisions because the analyst is not alerted to the countless policy decisions involved. If goals are given a more elaborate conceptualization, we are forced to see many more things as problematic.

OFFICIAL AND OPERATIVE GOALS

Two major categories of goals will be discussed here, official and "operative" goals. Official goals are the general purposes of the organization as put forth in the charter, annual reports, public statements by key executives and other authoritative pronouncements. For example, the goal of an employment agency may be to place job seekers in contact with firms seeking workers. The official goal of a hospital may be to promote the health of the community through curing the ill, and sometimes through preventing illness, teaching, and conducting research. Similar organizations may emphasize different publicly acceptable goals. A business corporation, for example, may state that its goal is to make a profit or adequate return on investment, or provide a customer service, or produce goods.

This level of analysis is inadequate in itself for a full understanding of organizational behavior. Official goals are purposely vague and general and do not indicate two major factors which influence organizational behavior: the host of decisions that must be made among alternative ways of achieving official goals and the priority of multiple goals, and the many unofficial goals pursued by groups within the organization. The concept of "operative goals" will be used to cover these aspects. Operative goals designate the ends sought through the actual operating policies of the organization; they tell us what the organization actually is trying to do, regardless of what the official goals say are the aims.

Where operative goals provide the specific content of official goals they reflect choices among competing values. They may be justified on the basis of an official goal, even though they may subvert another official goal. In one sense they are means to official goals, but since the latter are vague or of high abstraction, the "means" become ends in themselves when the organization is the object of analysis. For example, where profit-making is the announced goal, operative goals will specify whether quality or quantity is to be emphasized, whether profits are to be short run and risky or long run and stable, and will indicate the relative priority of diverse and somewhat conflicting ends of customer service, employee morale, competitive pricing, diversification, or liquidity. Decisions on all these factors influence the nature of the organization, and distinguish it from another with an identical official goal. An employment agency must decide whom to serve, what characteristics they favor among clients, and whether a high turnover of clients or a long run relationship is desired. In the voluntary general hospital, where the official goals are patient care, teaching, and research, the relative priority of these must be decided, as well as which group in the community is to be given priority in service, and are these services to emphasize, say, technical excellence or warmth and "hand-holding."

Unofficial operative goals, on the other hand, are tied more directly to group interests and while they may support, be irrelevant to, or subvert official goals, they bear no necessary connection with them. An interest in a major supplier may dictate the policies of a corporation executive. The prestige that attaches to utilizing elaborate high speed computers may dictate the reorganization of inventory and accounting departments. Racial prejudice may influence the selection procedures of an employment agency. The personal ambition of a hospital administrator may lead to community alliances and activities which bind the organization without enhancing its goal achievement. On the other hand, while the use of interns and residents as "cheap labor" may subvert the official goal of medical education, it may substantially further the official goal of providing a high quality of patient care.

The discernment of operative goals is, of course, difficult and subject to error. The researcher may have to determine from analysis of a series of apparently minor decisions regarding the lack of competitive bidding and quality control that an unofficial goal of a group of key executives is to maximize their individual investments in a major supplier. This unofficial goal may affect profits, quality, market position, and morale of key skill groups. The executive of a correctional institution may argue that the goal of the organization is treatment, and only the lack of resources creates an apparent emphasis upon custody or deprivation. The researcher may find, however, that decisions in many areas establish the priority of custody or punishment as a goal. For example, few efforts may be made to obtain more treatment personnel; those hired are misused and mistrusted; and clients are viewed as responding only to deprivations. The president of a junior college may deny the function of the institution is to deal with the latent terminal student, but careful analysis such as Burton Clark has made of operating policies, personnel practices, recruitment procedures, organizational alliances and personal characteristics of elites will demonstrate this to be the operative goal.

THE TASK—AUTHORITY—GOAL SEQUENCE

While operative goals will only be established through intensive analysis of decisions, personnel practices, alliance and elite characteristics in each organization, it is possible to indicate the range within which they will vary and the occasion for general shifts in goals. We will argue that if we know something about the major tasks of an organization and the characteristics of its controlling elite, we can predict its goals in general terms. The theory presented and illustrated in the rest of this paper is a first approximation and very general, but it may guide and stimulate research on this problem.

Every organization must accomplish four tasks: (1) secure inputs in the form of capital sufficient to establish itself, operate, and expand as the need arises; (2) secure acceptance in the form of basic legitimization of activity; (3) marshal the necessary skills; and (4) coordinate the activities of its members, and the relations of the organization with other organizations and with clients or consumers. All four are not likely to be equally important at any point in time. Each of these task areas provides a presumptive basis for control or domination by the group equipped to meet the problems involved. (The use of the terms control or dominance signifies a more pervasive, thorough and all-embracing phenomenon than authority or power.) The operative goals will be shaped by the dominant group, reflecting the imperatives of the particular task area that is most critical, their own background characteristics (distinctive perspectives based upon their training, career lines, and areas of competence) and the unofficial uses to which they put the organization for their own ends.

The relative emphasis upon one or another of the four tasks will vary with the nature of the work the organization does and the technology appropriate to it, and with the stage of development within the organization. An organization engaged in manufacturing in an industry where skills are routinized and the market position secure, may emphasize coordination, giving control to the experienced administrator. An extractive industry, with a low skill level in its basic tasks and a simple product, will probably emphasize the importance of capital tied up in land, specialized and expensive machinery, and transportation facilities. The chairman of the board of directors or a group within the board will probably dominate such an organization. An organization engaged in research and development, or the production of goods or services which cannot be carried out in a routinized fashion, will probably be most concerned with skills. Thus engineers or other relevant professionals will dominate. It is also possible that all three groups—trustees, representatives of critical skills, and administrators—may share power equally. This "multiple leadership" will be discussed in detail later. Of course, trustees are likely to dominate in the early history of any organization, particularly those requiring elaborate capital and facilities, or unusual legitimization. But once these requisites are secured, the nature of the tasks will determine whether trustees or others dominate. The transfer of authority, especially from trustees to another group, may be protracted, constituting a lag in adaptation.

Where major task areas do not change over time, the utility of the scheme presented here is limited to suggesting possible relations between task areas, authority structure, and operative goals. The more interesting problems, which we deal with in our illustrations below, involve organizations which experience changes in major task areas over time. If the technology or type of work changes, or if new requirements for capital or legitimization arise, control will shift from one group to another. One sequence is believed to be typical.

VOLUNTARY GENERAL HOSPITALS

We will discuss four types of hospitals, those dominated by trustees, by the medical staff (an organized group of those doctors who bring in private patients plus the few doctors who receive salaries or commissions from the hospital), by the administration, and by some form of multiple leadership.

There has been a general development among hospitals from trustee domination, based on capital and legitimization, to domination by the medical staff, based upon the increasing importance of their technical skills, and, at present, a tendency towards administrative dominance based on internal and external coordination. (The administrator may or may not be a doctor himself.) Not all hospitals go through these stages, or go through them in this sequence. Each type of authority structure shapes, or sets limits to, the type of operative goals that are likely to prevail, though there will be much variation within each type.

Trustee Domination. Voluntary general hospitals depend upon community funds for an important part of their capital and operating budget. Lacking precise indicators of efficiency or goal achievement, yet using donated funds, they must involve community representatives—trustees—in their authority structure. Trustees legitimate the non-profit status of the organization, assure that funds are not misused, and see that community needs are being met. Officially, they are the ultimate authority in voluntary hospitals. They do not necessarily exercise the legal powers they have, but where they do, there is no question that they are in control.

The functional basis for this control is primarily financial. They have access to those who make donations, are expected to contribute heavily themselves, and control the machinery and sanctions for fund raising drives. Financial control allows them to withhold resources from recalcitrant groups in the organization, medical or non-medical. They also, of course, control all appointments and promotions, medical and non-medical.

Where these extensive powers are exercised, operative goals are likely to reflect the role of trustees as community representatives and contributors to community health. Because of their responsibility to the sponsoring community, trustees may favor conservative financial policies, opposing large financial outlays for equipment, research, and education so necessary for high medical standards. High standards also require more delegation of authority to the medical staff than trustee domination can easily allow. As representatives drawn from distinctive social groups in the community, they may be oriented towards service for a religious, ethnic, economic, or age group in the community. Such an orientation may conflict with selection procedures favored by the medical staff or administration. Trustees may also promote policies which demonstrate a contribution to community welfare on the part of an elite group, perhaps seeking to maintain a position of prominence and power within the community. The hospital may be used as a vehicle for furthering a social philosophy of philanthropy and good works; social class values regarding personal worth, economic independence and responsibility; the assimilation of a minority group; or even to further resistance to government control and socialized medicine.

Such orientations will shape operative goals in many respects, affecting standards and techniques of care, priority of services, access to care, relations with other organizations, and directions and rate of development. The administrator in such a hospital—usually called a "superintendent" under the circumstances—will have little power, prestige or responsibility. For example, trustees have been known to question the brand of grape juice the dietician orders, or insist that they approve the color of paint the administrator selects for a room. Physicians may disapprove of patient selection criteria, chafe under financial restrictions which limit the resources they have to work with, and resent active control over appointments and promotions in the medical staff.

Medical Domination. Trustee domination was probably most common in the late nineteenth and early twentieth century. Medical technology made extraordinary advances in the twentieth century, and doctors possessed the skills capable of utilizing the advances. They demanded new resources and were potentially in a position to control their allocation and use. Increasingly, major decisions had to be based upon a technical competence trustees did not possess. Trustees had a continuing basis for control because of the costs of new equipment and personnel, but in many hospitals the skill factor became decisive. Some trustees felt that the technology required increased control by doctors; others lost a struggle for power with the medical staff; in some cases trustees were forced to bring in and give power to an outstanding doctor in order to increase the reputation of the hospital. Under such conditions trustees are likely to find that their legal power becomes nominal and they can only intervene in crisis situations; even financial requirements come to be set by conditions outside their control. They continue to provide the mantle of community representation and non-profit status, and become "staff" members whose major task is to secure funds.

It is sometimes hard to see why all hospitals are not controlled by the medical staff, in view of the increasing complexity and specialization of the doctors' skills, their common professional background, the power of organized medicine, and the prestige accorded the doctor in society. Furthermore, they are organized for dominance, despite their nominal status as "guests" in the house. The medical staff constitutes a "shadow" organization in hospitals, providing a ready potential for control. It is organized on bureaucratic principles with admission requirements, rewards and sanctions, and a committee structure which often duplicates the key committees of the board of directors and administrative staff. Nor are doctors in an advisory position as are "staff" groups in other organizations. Doctors perform both staff and line functions, and their presumptive right to control rests on both. Doctors also have a basic economic interest in the hospital, since it is essential to most private medical practice and career advancement. They seek extensive facilities, low hospital charges, a high quality of coordinated services, and elaborate time and energy-conserving conveniences.

Thus there is sufficient means for control by doctors, elaborated far beyond the mere provision of essential skills, and sufficient interest in control. Where doctors fully exercise their potential power the administrator functions as a superintendent or, as his co-professionals are wont to put it, as a "housekeeper." The importance of administrative skills is likely to be minimized, the administrative viewpoint on operative goals neglected, and the quality of personnel may suffer. A former nurse often serves as superintendent in this type of hospital. Policy matters are defined as medical in nature by the doctors, and neither trustees nor administrators, by definition, are qualified to have an equal voice in policy formation.

The operative goals of such a hospital are likely to be defined in strictly medical terms and the organization may achieve high technical standards of care, promote exemplary research, and provide sound training. However, there is a danger that resources will be used primarily for private (paying) patients with little attention to other community needs such as caring for the medically indigent (unless they happen to be good teaching cases), developing preventive medicine, or pioneering new organizational forms of care. Furthermore, high technical standards increasingly require efficient coordination of services and doctors may be unwilling to delegate authority to qualified administrators.

Various unofficial goals may be achieved at the expense of medical ones, or, in some cases, in conjunction with them. There are many cases of personal aggrandizement on the part of departmental chiefs and the chief of staff. The informal referral and consultation system in conjunction with promotions, bed quotas, and "privileges" to operate or treat certain types of cases, affords many occasions for the misuse of power. Interns and residents are particularly vulnerable to exploitation at the expense of teaching goals. Furthermore, as a professional, the doctor has undergone intensive socialization in his training and is called upon to exercise extraordinary judgment and skill with drastic consequences for good or ill. Thus he demands unusual deference and obedience and is invested with "charismatic" authority. He may extend this authority to the entrepreneurial aspects of his role, with the result that his "service" orientation, so taken for granted in much of the literature, sometimes means service to the doctor at the expense of personnel, other patients, or even his own patient.

Administrative Dominance. Administrative dominance is based first on the need for coordinating the increasingly complex, non-routinizable functions hospitals have undertaken. There is an increasing number of personnel that the doctor can no longer direct. The mounting concern of trustees, doctors themselves, patients and pre-payment groups with more efficient and economical operation also gives the administrator more power. A second, related basis for control stems from the fact that health services in general have become increasingly interdependent and specialized. The hospital must cooperate more with other hospitals and community agencies. It must also take on more services itself, and in doing so its contacts with other agencies and professional groups outside the hospital multiply. The administrator is equipped to handle these matters because of his specialized training, often received in a professional school of hospital administration, accumulated experience and available time. These services impinge upon the doctor at many points, providing a further basis for administrative control over doctors, and they lead to commitments in which trustees find they have to acquiesce.

The administrator is also in a position to control matters which affect the doctor's demands for status, deference, and time-saving conveniences. By maintaining close supervision over employees or promoting their own independent basis for competence, and by supporting them in conflicts with doctors, the administrator can, to some degree, overcome the high functional authority that doctors command. In addition, by carefully controlling communication between trustees and key medical staff officials, he can prevent an alliance of these two groups against him.

If administrative dominance is based primarily on the complexity of basic hospital activities, rather than the organization's medical-social role in the community, the operative orientation may be toward financial solvency, careful budget controls, efficiency, and minimal development of services. For example, preventive medicine, research, and training may be minimized; a cautious approach may prevail towards new forms of care such as intensive therapy units or home care programs. Such orientations could be especially true of hospitals dominated by administrators whose background and training were as bookkeepers, comptrollers, business managers, purchasing agents, and the like. This is probably the most common form of administrative dominance.

However, increasing professionalization of hospital administrators has, on the one hand, equipped them to handle narrower administrative matters easily, and, on the other hand, alerted them to the broader medical-social role of hospitals involving organizational and financial innovations in the forms of care. Even medical standards can come under administrative control. For example, the informal system among doctors of sponsorship, referral, and consultation serves to protect informal work norms, shield members from criticism and exclude non-cooperative members. The administrator is in a position to insist that medical policing be performed by a salaried doctor who stands outside the informal system.

There is, of course, a possibility of less "progressive" consequences. Interference with medical practices in the name of either high standards or treating the "whole" person may be misguided or have latent consequences which impair therapy. Publicity-seeking innovations may be at the expense of more humdrum but crucial services such as the out-patient department, or may alienate doctors or other personnel, or may deflect administrative efforts from essential but unglamorous administrative tasks. Using the organization for career advancement, they may seek to expand and publicize their hospital regardless of community needs and ability to pay. Like trustees they may favor a distinctive and medically irrelevant community relations policy, perhaps with a view towards moving upward in the community power structure. Regardless of these dangers, the number of administration dominated hospitals oriented towards broad medical-social goals will probably grow.

Multiple Leadership. So far we have been considering situations where one group clearly dominates. It is possible, however, for power to be shared by two or three groups to the extent that no one is able to control all or most of the actions of the others. This we call multiple leadership: a division of labor regarding the determination of goals and the power to achieve them. This is not the same as fractionated power where several groups have small amounts of power in an unstable situation. With multiple leadership, there are two or three stable, known centers of power. Nor is it the same as decentralized power, where specialized units of the organization have considerable autonomy. In the latter case, units are free to operate as they choose only up to a point, when it becomes quite clear that there is a centralized authority. In multiple leadership there is no single ultimate power.

Multiple leadership is most likely to appear in organizations where there are multiple goals which lack precise criteria of achievement and admit of considerable tolerance with regard to achievement. Multiple goals focus interests, and achievement tolerance provides the necessary leeway for accommodation of interests and vitiation of responsibility. Many service organizations fit these criteria, but so might large, public relations-conscious business or industrial organizations where a variety of goals can be elevated to such importance that power must be shared by the representatives of each.

In one hospital where this was studied it was found that multiple leadership insured that crucial group interests could be met and protected, and encouraged a high level of creative (though selective) involvement by trustees, doctors, and the administration. However, the problems of goal setting, assessment of achievement, and assignment of responsibility seemed abnormally high. While the three groups pursued separate and unconflicting operative goals in some cases, and were in agreement on still other goals, in areas where interests conflicted the goal conflicts were submerged in the interests of harmony. In the absence of a single authority, repetitive conflicts threatened to erode morale and waste energies. A showdown and clear solution of a conflict, furthermore, might signal defeat for one party, forcing them to abandon their interests. Thus a premium was placed on the ability of some elites to smooth over conflicts and exercise interpersonal skills. Intentions were sometimes masked and ends achieved through covert manipulation. Assessment of achievement in some areas was prevented either by the submergence of conflict or the preoccupation with segmental interests. Opportunism was encouraged: events in the environment or within the hospital were exploited without attention to the interests of the other groups or the long range development of the hospital. This left the organization open to vagrant pressures and to the operation of unintended consequences. Indeed, with conflict submerged and groups pursuing independent goals, long range planning was difficult.

This summary statement exaggerates the impact of multiple leadership in this hospital and neglects the areas of convergence on goals. Actually, the hospital prospered and led its region in progressive innovations and responsible medical-social policies despite some subversion of the official goals of patient care, teaching, research, and preventive medicine. The organization could tolerate considerable ambiguity of goals and achievements as long as standards remained high in most areas, occupancy was sufficient to operate with a minimum deficit, and a favorable public image was maintained. It remains to be seen if the costs and consequences are similar for other organizations where multiple leadership exists.

APPLICATION TO OTHER ORGANIZATIONS

Voluntary Service Organizations. Other voluntary service organizations, such as private universities, social service agencies, privately sponsored correctional institutions for juveniles, and fund raising agencies resemble hospitals in many respects. They have trustees representing the community, may have professionals playing prominent roles, and with increasing size and complexity of operation, require skilled coordination of activities. Initially at least, trustees are likely to provide a character defining function which emphasizes community goals and goals filtered through their own social position. Examples are religious schools, or those emphasizing one field of knowledge or training; agencies caring for specialized groups such as ethnic or religious minorities, unwed mothers, and dependent and neglected children; and groups raising money for special causes. Funds of skill and knowledge accumulate around these activities, and the activities increasingly grow in complexity, requiring still more skill on the part of those performing the tasks. As the professional staff expands and professional identification grows, they may challenge the narrower orientations of trustees on the basis of their own special competence and professional ideology and seek to broaden the scope of services and the clientele. They may be supported in this by changing values in the community. Coordination of activities usually rests with professionals promoted from the staff during this second character defining phase, and these administrators retain, for a while at least, their professional identity. Trustees gradually lose the competence to interfere.

However, professionals have interests of their own which shape the organization. They may develop an identity and ethic which cuts them off from the needs of the community and favors specialized, narrow and—to critics—self-serving goals. Current criticisms of the emphasis upon research and over-specialization in graduate training at the expense of the basic task of educating undergraduates is a case in point in the universities. There is also criticism of the tendency of professionals in correctional institutions to focus upon case work techniques applicable to middle-class "neurotic" delinquents at the expense of techniques for resocializing the so-called "socialized" delinquent from culturally deprived areas. The latter account for most of the delinquents, but professional identity and techniques favor methods applicable to the former. Something similar may be found in social agencies. Social workers, especially the "elite" doing therapy in psychiatric and child guidance clinics and private family agencies, may become preoccupied with securing recognition, equitable financial remuneration, and status that would approach that of psychiatrists. Their attitudes may become more conservative; the social order more readily accepted and the deviant adapted to it; "worthy" clients and "interesting cases" receive priority.

It is possible that with increasing complexity and growth in many of these voluntary service organizations, administrators will lose their professional identity or be recruited from outside the organization on the basis of organizational skills. In either case they will be in a position to alter the direction fostered by selective professional interests. Of course, the problem of coordinating both internal and external activities need not generate leadership seeking broadly social rather than narrowly professional goals, any more than it necessarily does in the hospital. Administrative dominance may stunt professional services and neglect social policy in the interest of economy, efficiency, or conservative policies.

Non-Voluntary Service Organizations. A different picture is presented by non-voluntary service organizations—those sponsored by governmental agencies such as county or military hospitals, city or county welfare agencies, juvenile and adult correctional agencies. Authority for goal setting, regulation, and provision of capital and operating expenses does not rest with voluntary trustees, but with governmental officials appointed to commissions. In contrast to volunteers on the board of a private service organization, commissioners are not likely to be highly identified with the organization, nor do they derive much social status from it. The organizations themselves often are tolerated only as holding operations or as "necessary evils." Commission dominance is sporadic and brief, associated with public clamor or political expediency. On the other hand, the large size of these organizations and the complex procedures for reporting to the parent body gives considerable importance to the administrative function from the outset, which is enhanced by the tenuous relationship with the commissioners. Consistent with this and reinforcing it is the low level of professionalization found in many of these agencies. The key skills are often non-professional custodial skills or their equivalent in the case of public welfare agencies (and schools). Administrators are often at the mercy of the custodial staff if, indeed, they have not themselves risen to their administrative position because of their ability to maintain order and custody.

Nevertheless, professional influence is mounting in these organizations, and professional groups outside of them have exercised considerable influence. Professionals may assume control of the organization, or administrators may be brought in whose commitment is to the positive purposes of the organization, such as rehabilitation of the clients, rather than the negative custodial functions. This appears to have happened in the case of a few federal penal institutions, a few state juvenile correctional institutions, and several Veterans Administration mental hospitals. Even where this happens, one must be alert to the influence of unofficial goals. The organizations are particularly vulnerable to exploitation by the political career interests of administrators or to irresponsible fads or cure-alls of marginal professionals. In summary, the sequence of tasks, power structure, and goals may be different in non-voluntary service organizations. The importance of administrative skills with system maintenance as the overriding operative goal does not encourage a shift in power structure; but where new technologies are introduced we are alerted to such shifts along with changes in goals.

Profit-Making Organizations. Our analysis may appear less applicable to profit-making organizations for two reasons. First, it could be argued, they are not characterized by multiple goals, but relate all operations to profit-making. Second, skill groups are not likely to dominate these organizations; owners control the smaller firms, and professional executives the larger ones. Thus power structure and possibly goals may merely be a function of size. We will discuss each of these points in turn.

If profit-making is an overriding goal of an organization, many operative decisions must still be made which will shape its character. Even where technology remains constant, organizations will vary with regard to personnel practices, customer services, growth, liquidity, an emphasis upon quality or quantity, or long- or short-run gains. An adequate understanding of the organization will require attention to alternatives in these and other areas.

Furthermore, it has often been asserted that the importance of profits, *per se,* has declined with the increased power of professional management, especially in large organizations. The argument runs that since management does not have a personal stake in profits, they consider them less important than stability, growth, solvency, and liquidity. The impressionistic evidence of those who assert this is not supported by a study of James Dent. When asked, "What are the aims of top management in your company?", the response of executives of 145 business firms showed no greater mention of "to make profits, money or a living" among large than small firms, nor among those with professional managers than owner-managers. Because goals stated in this form may not reflect actual policies and because of other limitations, one is somewhat reluctant to take this as a fair test of the hypothesis.

Even though his sample was not representative, and the question asked does not get at what we have called operative goals, his study provides good evidence of variations of stated goals in profit-making organizations. Responses coded under the category "to make money, profits, or a living" were mentioned as the first aim by 36 per cent of the executives; "to provide a good product; public service" by 21 per cent, and "to grow" was third with 12 per cent. When the first three aims spontaneously mentioned were added together, profits led; employee welfare tied with "good products or public service" for second place. Dent found that the variables most associated with goals were size of company and "proportion of employees who are white-collar, professional or supervisory." While goals no doubt are influenced by size, this accounted for only some of the variance. Holding size constant, one might discover the effects of major task areas. The association of goals with the "proportion of employees who are white-collar . . ." supports this argument.

R. A. Gordon and others have asserted that in large corporations it is the executive group, rather than stockholders or the board of trustees, that generally dominates. A study of the role of trustees, frankly in favor of their exercising leadership and control, actually shows through its many case studies that trustees exercise leadership mainly in times of crisis. The generalization of Gordon, almost a commonplace today, appears to be sound: he asserts that the common pattern of evolution is for active leadership by owners in the early years of the firm, then it is passed on to new generations of the families concerned, and gradually responsibility for decision-making passes to professional executives who frequently have been trained by the original leaders. Goals likewise shift from rapid development and a concern with profits to more conservative policies emphasizing coordination, stability and security of employment.

But does this mean that for large, old, and stable firms that operative goals are substantially similar, reflecting professional administration? Does it also mean that for profit-making organizations in general there are only two alternative sources of domination, trustees (including owners) and professional administrators? Our theoretical scheme suggests that neither may be true, but the evidence is scanty. Certainly within the organizations dominated by professional managers there is ample opportunity for a variety of operational goals less general than, say, stability and security of employment. Even these are likely to vary and to shape the nature of the firm. (We exclude, of course, the failure to achieve these broad goals because of poor management or environmental factors over which the organization has no control; we are dealing with operating policies which may not be achieved.) Gordon notes that the "historical background" of a company (he does not elaborate this phrase) and especially the training received by its leading executives may be a powerful factor in shaping management decisions. "It is the 'Rockefeller tradition' rather than the present Rockefeller holdings which actively conditions the management decisions in the Standard Oil companies. This tradition is large responsible for present methods of management organization and internal control, use of the committee system and the domination of boards of directors by [company executives]." Historical factors will certainly shape decisions, but the nature of technology in the oil industry and the trustees' awareness of the prime importance of coordination may have been decisive in that historical experience.

Domination by skill groups is possible in two ways. On the one hand, a department—for example, sales, engineering, research and development, or finance—may, because of the technology and stage of growth, effectively exercise a veto on the executive's decisions and substantially shape decisions in other departments. Second, lines of promotion may be such that top executives are drawn from one powerful department, and retain their identification with the parochial goals of that department. Gordon asserts that chief executives with a legal background are conservative in making price changes and find 'order in the industry' more appealing than aggressive price competition. It is possible that engineers, sales executives, and financial executives all have distinctive views on what the operating policies should be.

Thus, goals may vary widely in profit-making organizations, and power may rest not only with trustees or professional administrators, but with skill groups or administrators influenced by their skill background. Of course, one task area may so dominate a firm that there will be no shifts in power, and operative goals will remain fairly stable within the limits of the changing values of society. But where basic tasks shift, either because of growth or changing technology, the scheme presented here at least alerts us to potential goal changes and their consequences. An ideal-typical sequence would be as follows: trustee domination in initial stages of financing, setting direction for development and recruitment of technical or professional skills; then dominance by the skill group during product or service development and research, only to have subsequent control pass to coordination of fairly routinized activities. As the market and technology change, this cycle could be repeated. During the course of this sequence, operative goals may shift from quantity production and short-run profits as emphasized by trustees, to the engineer's preoccupation with quality at the expense of quantity or styling, with this succeeded by a priority upon styling and unessential innovations demanded by the sales force, and finally with an emphasis upon the long-run market position, conservative attitude towards innovation, and considerable investment in employee-centered policies and programs by management. It is important to note that the formal authority structure may not vary during this sequence, but recruitment into managerial positions and the actual power of management, trustees or skill groups would shift with each new problem focus. Multiple leadership is also possible, as noted in an earlier section.

There are many critical variables influencing the selection of key problem areas and thus the characteristics of the controlling elite and operative goals. They will be applicable to the analysis of any complex organization, whether business, governmental, or voluntary. Among those that should be considered are capital needs and legitimization, the amount of routinization possible, adaptability of technology to market shifts and consumer behavior, possible or required professionalization, and the nature of the work force. Our analysis of profit-making organizations suggests that we should be alert to the possibility of a natural history of changes in task areas, authority, and goals which parallels that of hospitals and other voluntary service organizations. Nonvoluntary service organizations may systematically deviate from this sequence because of the source of capital (government) which influences the commitments of appointive trustees (commissioners), and the character of the administrative tasks. The scheme presented here, when used in conjunction with the concept of operative goals, may provide a tool for analyzing the dynamics of goal setting and goal changing in all complex organizations.

Formal organizations have been studied by contemporary sociologists along the lines of guidance offered by the great German sociologist of an earlier generation, Max Weber. In recent years, there has been renewed interest in bureaucracies and other formal organizations. Defined as planned systems of co-operative effort in which each participant has a recognized role to play and duties or tasks to perform in order to achieve the organizational goals, formal organizations are marked by impersonal mechanisms of control. These mechanisms, whether they be conveyor belts or quantitative records of performance, have similar effects upon the interaction between subordinate and superior, reversing the flow of demand from a downward to an upward direction.

There is a continual process of change in formal organizations. Some of their aspects that contribute to operations frequently precipitate conflicts as well. The unanticipated consequences of the adjustments made to cope with them may, in turn, create further problems. These dialectical processes and three internal dimensions in the analysis of formal organization—structural, organizational, and developmental—are considered in the following article by Peter Blau, one of the outstanding experts in this field of sociological concentration.

19. FORMAL ORGANIZATION: DIMENSIONS OF ANALYSIS *

PETER M. BLAU
University of Chicago

It has been only within the last decade or two that the precise methods of social research developed in interviewing surveys and in observation laboratories have been applied to the study of military services, factories, government agencies, and other formal organizations. Often, however, the research techniques have been adopted without first having been adapted to a new field of inquiry. Quantification, so important for providing evidence in support of generalizations, has often produced an artificial atomization of the organized social structures under investigation. Not that the members of the organization are conceived as Robinson Crusoes on isolated islands. Quite the contrary, the emphasis is all on human relations, but as atoms somehow suspended in free space. Specifically, human relations are treated in the analysis as though they were attributes of individuals, and the group structures of which they are component parts as well as the larger organization of which these groups are parts are neglected.

These tendencies are the result of a fundamental methodological problem.

* *The American Journal of Sociology*, Vol. LXIII, No. 1, July, 1957, pp. 58–69.

Since an empirical study is usually confined to one or two organizations and the investigation of a large sample of organizations is hardly feasible, quantitative evidence for generalizations must be based on the observation of regularities among individual members or subgroups. But, by treating individuals, or even subgroups, as independent units of analysis that can be classified and reclassified according to any one of their characteristics, this procedure necessarily ignores the unique constellation of relationships between groups and individuals in the organization—its *Gestalt*. If, on the other hand, the analysis is focused on the organized whole of interdependent elements, it deals only with a single case and provides no empirical evidence for generalization, no matter how many individuals are observed.

This paper is an attempt to explore this dilemma in the study of formal organizations. For this purpose a secondary analysis of some research findings will be presented first, which is largely concerned with the effect of impersonal mechanisms of control upon the structure of work groups and the flow of communication in the hierarchy. Four dimensions in the analysis of formal organization are suggested.

WORK GROUPS ON THE ASSEMBLY LINE

The distinct difference between having established personal relations with several co-workers and being a member of a work group is clearly illustrated in Charles R. Walker and Robert H. Guest's study of assembly-line workers in an automobile plant. Despite the noise and the fact that hardly any jobs on the assembly line require co-operation between workers, most workers have regular social contacts with a few others stationed near by. Indeed, over three-quarters of them consider friendly contacts with fellow workers one of the things they like best about their job.

Since the workers are strung out along the line, however, the set of interpersonal relations of each differs somewhat from those of everyone else. Tom and Dick are friends, and both have frequent contacts with Harry, who stands between them; but Tom also often talks to three fellows on his right, who are out of Dick's earshot, and Dick has friendly ties with two men on his left, whom Tom hardly knows. There is no common network of social relationships that unites a number of workers and distinguishes them from others by furnishing a socially agreed-upon definition of the boundaries of the in-group. Notwithstanding regular patterns of informal interaction, therefore, work groups do not seem to exist on the assembly line.

This is not merely a matter of arbitrary definition. In the absence of a *shared* set of social relations and a common boundary, there is no single group with which a number of individuals can identify themselves and which, in turn, provides them social support. Perhaps this lack of group support is one of the reasons why assembly-line workers become so quickly and strongly identified with their union. It may also play a major role in the prevalent dislike of work and the high rates of turnover and of absenteeism on the assembly line. Indeed, when the same research team in a second study discovered that work groups sometimes do become established on the assembly line, they also found that absenteeism declined in them.

The men on the assembly line are divided into sections under different foremen. Merely having the same foreman does not give rise to a group structure in the section: the foreman must help to create it. Most important, the foreman must identify himself with his men as a group and "think of himself as also a member of the group"; he sticks up for his men, treats them as equals, and delegates responsibility to them. These things make a foreman a symbol of identification uniting the members of his section. Some foremen, moreover, institute periodic meetings of the entire section. Of particular significance is the establishment of "informal systems of job rotation," which not only reduce monotony and make men more satisfied with work but also help to create group boundaries. If the men in a section intermittently change their positions on the line, their social situation is no longer very different from that of other work groups: each, sooner or later, finds himself close enough to every one of the others for informal contacts. Opportunities for recurrent interaction among all members of the section promote a common network of social relationships and a cohesive group.

But how could foremen become identified with the workers in their section and still discharge their managerial responsibilities? Walker, Guest, and Arthur N. Turner argue that a successful foreman must play a dual role, representing both his men and the management. It may also be, however, that assembly-line production itself has a bearing on the problem. The unrelenting movement of the conveyor constrains workers to a certain output, relieving the foreman of responsibility for their productivity. But, of all his duties, it is only the exercise of control over subordinates that benefits from social distance. Thus, the fact that the conveyor system substitutes in part for the foreman as a mechanism of control makes it possible for him to identify himself with the workers without impeding operations.

To be sure, most of the foremen questioned did not think that assembly-line production facilitates their job. The foreman still has to supervise quality, keep the line manned, and tackle problems of adjustment and morale inevitable in repetitive work.

There is quite a difference, however, between the problems the assembly line creates and those the foreman would have to face in its absence. High rates of turnover and absenteeism make the training of new workers and temporary replacements one of his major responsibilities. To ease the extra burden the absence of a worker places on the rest of the section, the foreman must be skillful in redistributing the work load and in negotiating with management for a quick replacement. The foreman must try to reduce turnover and absenteeism by making the work itself less arduous and the situation as satisfactory as possible. In discharging his responsibility for maintaining quality, he sees to it that the workers' tools are kept in good repair and that the materials they need are delivered to them at the proper time. All these tasks involve helping subordinates rather than making demands on them. The major exception is checking on the quality of performance, but even the significance of such checks is altered by the powerful constraint of the moving line.

IMPERSONAL CONSTRAINTS AND THE FLOW OF DEMAND

The impersonal constraints exerted by production-line methods change the flow of demand in the organization. The concept of flow of demand is derived from the concepts of origination of action and flow of work developed by Conrad M. Arensberg, William F. Whyte, and E. D. Chapple in their studies of patterns of interaction among the members of an organization. Whyte shows, for example, that demands in the restaurant flow not only from management through supervisors down to waitresses and cooks but also from customers via waitresses and pantry personnel to the cooks. The fact that demands are made from two different sources often precipitates problems and conflicts, particularly when the person asked to do something considers himself superior to the one making the request.

Usually, demands flow primarily down the hierarchy from management through supervisors or foremen to workers, although staff experts provide an alternative route. The superior directs operations by giving subordinates instructions and checking their work. Studies reveal, however, that frequent and detailed instructions and close checking of the subordinates' work is not the best method of supervision; on the contrary, such close supervision actually reduces productivity. In other words, the flow of demand down the hierarchy, even if there are no conflicting streams, seems to impede effective operations.

Assembly-line production reverses the direction of the flow of demand. It is the conveyor that assures co-ordination and a certain level of productivity, not the directives of foremen. And, where an impersonal mechanism makes most necessary demands on workers, the major task of the foreman is no longer to issue directives but to be a trouble-shooter—to come to his subordinates' aid when they have difficulties. Hence, the typical interaction is initiated by a worker's demand for the foreman's help rather than by a demand by the foreman on the worker. This reversal is also manifest on the next level in the hierarchy. It has been pointed out that staff experts not merely advise management but, in effect, give orders to foremen and operators. Foremen often feel that staff officials interfere with their work by making unreasonable demands, but the majority of the foremen in the assembly plant studied considered staff and service personnel helpful and felt free to call on them. When management and experts exercise control by planning assembly-line production, there is no need for issuing many directives to the foreman, and so most of the contacts between the foreman and superiors or staff officials come in consequence of his requests for help.

The fact that the foreman is cast in the role of adviser and assistant to his subordinates affects interaction even on the occasions when he makes demands on them. He could not maintain this role if, upon discovering imperfections, he would curtly order a worker to improve the quality of his work. Moreover, since the foreman knows that the standardized quality requirements are generally accepted by workers—he thinks they want to do a good job—he is likely to lay the blame for failures upon the changing speed of the line or the worker's inexperience and not on lack of effort. Thus demands for improvement are likely to take the form of guidance and training rather than commands. Workers, finally, are not so prone to blame the foreman if they have difficulty meeting standards as they might otherwise be, because the speeding line absorbs the brunt of their aggression.

The change in flow of demand engendered by the constraints of the assembly line distributes discretion more equitably between superior and subordinates. Although the demands of superiors are often worded as requests, it is difficult to refuse them—much more difficult than it is to refuse requests of subordinates. Demands that flow downward, no matter how polite, control the conduct of subordinates and restrict their freedom of action. To be sure, the foreman exercises control over workers even if demands flow upward; his counsel and guidance, in effect, influence the conduct of workers. Yet when the flow is upward, workers decide when to call upon the superior; not so when the flow is downward. The superior continues to exercise considerable discretion over granting requests for assistance and over what guidance to furnish, but instead of monopolizing discretion he shares it with subordinates.

There is a fair amount of evidence that the exercise of discretion and responsibility increases satisfaction at work. Thus, Robert Hoppock finds that, the higher the level of skill and responsibility, the greater is job satisfaction. Daniel Katz and Robert L. Kahn confirm this finding, and they also show that on a given occupational level individuals whose superiors permit them to exercise discretion are more satisfied and less often absent from work than others. Feeling free to bring problems to the supervisor, for one thing, is inversely related to absenteeism. Lester Coch and John R. P. French discovered that factory workers who participate in deciding on a change in production accept the change more readily than those without a voice in making it, perform much better once the change is made, and are less likely to quit. These data support the conclusion that the reversal in the flow of demand, since it increases the workers' discretion, contributes to their satisfaction.

The impersonal constraints of the assembly line decrease the worker's discretion on the job, but the upward flow of demand encouraged by these very constraints increases his discretion in his relationship with his foreman. Hence, assembly-line operations reduce work satisfaction at one point while enhancing it at another. This illustrates that a correlation between two "terminal" variables—a formal condition and its ultimate effect in the organization—can be misleading unless the intervening social processes are considered. Moreover, since it is unlikely that demand flows upward in all sections on the assembly line, it is essential to determine the other conditions in the organization on which the reversal of flow depends. In short, to analyze complex configurations, relationships between two variables must be elaborated externally by inquiring into additional necessary conditions as well as internally by examining intervening variables.

MULTIPLE CONSEQUENCES AND CHANGE IN ORGANIZATION

Assembly-line production is not the only impersonal constraint. Evaluation on the basis of published statistical records of performance is another: precise knowledge of how his work compares with others' constrains every employee to try to improve and so exercises control over operations without any direct intervention by superiors. Indeed, the statistical method of evaluation is a more adaptable mechanism of control than the assembly line. It lends itself to being used not only for manual but also for clerical and even professional work, and it can serve to control qualitative as well as quantitative standards of performance, since a variety of errors and successes can be counted and recorded.

A study of two government agencies reveals that statistical records of performance, too, reverse the flow of demand between supervisor and operating officials. The direct influence the records exert on the performance of officials and the exact knowledge of accomplishments they furnish make it unnecessary for the supervisor to check on subordinates frequently and permit him to let them come to him for advice when needed. In fact, the more a supervisor relied on statistical records in his evaluation, the larger the proportion of interactions between him and them that they rather than he initiated. Even when a supervisor talks to a subordinate about improving his performance, statistical evidence transforms the significance of their conference; what might have been a much-resented critical opinion becomes an offer of help to make a better record. Evaluation on the basis of a record also makes it possible to give officials considerable discretion in the discharge of their duties. A quantitative record of performance and a conveyor belt are each impersonal mechanisms of control which, be the setting the semiprofessional work in the two government offices or the semiskilled work in the automobile plant, appear to have similar effects upon interaction between superior and subordinates.

Quantitative evaluation has a series of consequences in an organization. Its introduction in one government agency, for example, raised productivity, improved the relations between interviewers and their supervisors, and promoted a detached, impartial attitude toward clients. But it also fostered competitive tendencies which interfered with operations, and, in response to the new operating problems, new practices and patterns of interaction were developed.

The same aspects of the organization that make essential contributions to operations frequently also create conflicts and problems, and the unanticipated consequences of the adjustments instituted to cope with them may, in turn, produce further problems. Hence, there is a continual process of change in the organization.

DIMENSIONS OF ANALYSIS

The methodological problems posed here may be dealt with by distinguishing a structural, an organizational, and a developmental dimension in the analysis of formal organizations. There is at least one other dimension, which can be called "environmental": the analysis of the relationships between formal organizations and other social institutions, for example, of the connections between the economic or political system and formal organizations; of the relations between the organization of unions and that of companies in an industry; or of the role of the culture in personal conduct in the organization. Obviously, restricting the discussion here to the three intraorganizational dimensions does not mean that the environmental one is any less important.

Structural dimension.—The fact that it makes a difference whether workers on the assembly line merely have friendly relations with several fellow workers or whether a group structure has developed among them raises the question of how the distinct significance of social structure can be taken into account in systematic research. Ever since the early writings of Durkheim, and even though he modified his own position later, it has been recommended that the study of social structure confine itself to indexes that are independent of the behavior of individuals, such as the laws in a society, or the group's resistance to disruption. This procedure, however, entails the danger of reifying the concept of group structure and ignoring the fact that it refers to a network of social relations between individuals which finds expression in their interaction. In any case, it is possible to investigate the effects of social structure by an alternative method.

This method consists of three steps. First, empirical measures are obtained that pertain to those characteristics of the individual members of the groups that have direct or indirect bearing on their relations to each other, such as group identification, sociometric choices, initiation of interacton, or promotions. Second, the measures that describe individuals in one respect are combined into one index for each group, and this index no longer refers to any characteristic of individuals but to a characteristic of the group. Examples of such group attributes are the proportion of members identified with the group, the average number of in-group sociometric choices, the degree of variation in rates of interaction, and homogeneity of interests. Third, to isolate a structural effect, the relationship between a group attribute and some effect is determined while the corresponding characteristic of individuals is held constant. An illustration will make this clear.

To test the hypothesis that the free flow of communication within a work group improves the performance of its members, two kinds of data have been collected in fifty work groups of about ten members each: measures of performance for every individual and the frequency with which he discusses his problems with another member of his own work group. We could investigate whether frequency of discussion and quality of performance are correlated in the entire sample of five hundred. But, if they were, it would show only that individuals who readily discuss their problems with others perform better, not that the network of communication in a group influences performance. A second test would be to divide the fifty groups into those with many and those with few members who readily discuss their problems and to determine whether average performance in the first category of groups is superior. A positive finding in this case, however, might merely be a reflection of a high correlation between the individual's readiness to discuss and his performance and thus still would not supply unequivocal evidence of the significance of the network of communication for performance. If, on the other hand, individuals are first divided on the basis of their frequency of discussion, and it turns out that within each category of individuals about equally ready to talk about their problems those who belong to groups where frequent discussion is prevalent perform better than those in other groups, then it is demonstrated that the network of communication itself influences performance (see Table 1, where the differences between columns indicate the structural effect of the network of communication on performance). This finding would show that, even when the effect of the individual's discussion rate of his problems on his performance is eliminated, just to be in a group where communication flows freely improves performance—other things being equal.

TABLE 1. Performance Scores by Rate and Frequency of Discussion (Hypothetical Example)

Individuals Who Discuss Their Problems	*Groups Most of Whose Members Discuss Their Problems*	
	Often	*Rarely*
Often	.85	.65
Rarely	.70	.40

What would account for such a finding, were it obtained? The fact that an individual discusses his problems with others has consequences for them as well as for himself. He may get specific advice, and, even when he does not, the discussion may clarify his thinking. At the same time the others may learn something from his discussion which they can use in their own work, or their self-confidence may be raised by his often coming to them for advice. Moreover, the observation that others have problems, too, and that they feel free to consult one another probably reduces an individual's anxiety over his own problems even before he starts discussing them. It is, therefore, hypothesized that ego's discussions of his problems contribute to the performance of alters as well as to that of ego. (Of course, every member might alternate between playing the role of ego and that of alter, which means that reciprocity prevails in discussions.) If this is correct, and only if it is, one would actually obtain the finding described, that is, a relationship between the frequency of discussion in the group and performance when the individual's rate of discussion is controlled.

The general principle is that if ego's X affects not only ego's Y but also alters' Y, a structural effect will be observed, which means that the distribution of X in a group is related to Y even though the individual's X is held constant. Such a finding indicates that the network of relations in the group with respect to X influences Y. It isolates the effects of X on Y that are entirely due to or transmitted by the processes of social interaction.

A somewhat different structural effect is reported in a study by Samuel A. Stouffer and his colleagues. Soldiers who have been promoted have more favorable attitudes toward chances of promotion in the army than those who have remained privates. However, soldiers in outfits a large proportion of whose members have been promoted have *less* favorable attitudes toward chances of promotion than others of equal rank in outfits with fewer promoted members. Thus, the frequency of promotions in a group has an unfavorable effect on these attitudes, while the individual's own promotion has the opposite effect. Being promoted raises the individual's status, but the promotion of many other members of his group depresses his status relative to theirs. In short, the promotion of a number of egos decreases the relative status of alters and increases the relative status of egos. Since ego's X has the opposite implications for alters' Y and for ego's Y in this case, the structural effect and that of the corresponding characteristic of individuals are in opposite directions.

Social norms also have structural effects. Workers who firmly believe that it is wrong to be a "rate-buster" are probably less likely than others to exceed informal standards of output. Even workers who see nothing wrong with rate-busting, however, may work slower than they otherwise would if most members of the group believe rate-busting wrong. The reason is, of course, that prevailing social standards are enforced throughout the group and, therefore, influence the conduct of those who do not fully accept them as well as of those who do. Again, ego's X influences both alter's Y and ego's Y. If the pressure of the group is successful, however, one-time deviants will not only conform to the expectations of the majority but sooner or later incorporate them in their own thinking. Once this happens and virtually all members of some groups condemn rate-busting while hardly any of others do, it is no longer possible to use the proposed method of determining structural effects, for it requires a sufficient number of individuals who reject the norm in groups which, on the whole, accept it and of individuals who accept the norm in groups which, on the whole, reject it. This indicates an important limitation of the method. It reveals only the present, not the past, effects of the normative structure of groups. The prevalence of a normative orientation in a group may have three effects upon deviants: intensify their deviant conduct as a reaction to being alienated from the majority, constrain them to conform against their own convictions, or convert their very thinking. Although all three are effects of the social structure, the last would not find expression in what has here been called a structural effect.

A different structural effect is illustrated by a finding of Seymour M. Lipset, Martin Trow, and James Coleman. If the members of a small printing shop are in substantial agreement on political issues, they are more prone to be active in union politics than if there are considerable political differences among them. Not whether the members of a shop are liberal or conservative but their consensus is significant, whatever their political opinion. Wide divergences in political viewpoint among the members of a work group incline them to avoid political topics of conversation to avoid arguments. Sufficient political consensus to provide a basis for cordial discourse, on the other hand, encourages political talk at work, and this stimulates interest in the political activities of the union. In formal terms, if the joint occurrence of X, or of non-X, in ego and alter affects Y, the variance of X in the group will have an effect on Y which is independent of any possible relationship between the individual's X and his Y.

Organizational dimension.—The structure of work groups is, of course, profoundly influenced by the formal organization of which they are parts. Although the analysis of formally established organizations is generally concerned with larger social units than work groups, the distinction between the structural and the organizational dimension is analytical, not one of size. To speak of the interrelations within a social system may refer either to the *social* relations between individuals or groups or to the interdependence of abstract elements in the organization, say, the relationships between personnel policies, supervisory practices, and interaction among workers. The term "organizational dimension" is used to denote the latter type of analysis, whose focus is the configuration of interdependent elements in the organization.

As has been pointed out, the establishment of a relationship between two characteristics of organizations is merely a starting point for elaborating it internally as well as externally. Internal elaboration involves a search for intervening variables, without which the finding that an antecedent condition has a certain ultimate consequence cannot be interpreted and may even be misleading. For example, when it was found that the impersonal control exerted by statistical records of performance gave rise to more impersonal and impartial treatment of clients in an employment agency, one might, on first impression, conclude that impersonality is simply transmitted from the exercise of control down to the contact with clients. Actually, complex intervening processes were responsible for the relationship. Performance records stimulated employment interviewers to concentrate on making many placements and induced them to eliminate all considerations that had no bearing on making placements—in short, all personal considerations—in their treatment of clients. This disinterested approach often created conflicts with clients, which made it difficult for interviewers to remain detached and neither become angry at clients nor modify decisions in order to pacify them. However, the practice developed of relieving the tensions generated by these conflicts by complaining or joking about clients in informal discussions with colleagues. These friendly, *not* impersonal, interactions among interviewers rendered conflicts with clients less disturbing, so that it was easier to maintain an impersonal attitude toward them even at the risk of conflict.

In analyzing an organization, the major independent variables are the formal institutions in terms of which social conduct is organized: the division of labor, the hierarchy of offices, control and sanctioning mechanisms, production methods, official rules and regulations, and personnel policies, and so on. The major dependent variables are the results accomplished by operations and the attachment of its members to the organization, as indicated by productive efficiency, changes effected in the community (say, a decline in crime rates), turnover, satisfaction with work, and various other effect criteria. To explain the relationships between these two sets of abstract variables, it is necessary to investigate the processes of social interaction and the interpersonal relations and group structures. In dealing with these patterns of conduct, psychological processes cannot be entirely ignored. To be sure, the student of organization is not concerned with the effects of psychological characteristics but with those of conditions in the organization on social conduct. However, psychological processes are the *intervening* variables drawn on to explain why social conditions give rise to certain patterns of conduct. Statistical records brought about more impartial treatment of clients, for example, because they motivated interviewers to exclude all irrelevant personal considerations from their decisions in making placements. In sum, intervening psychological variables explain why the conditions in the organization lead to given processes of social interaction, and these social processes, in turn, must be examined to account for the relationships between conditions in the organization and the results they accomplish.

The external elaboration of a proposition that one factor influences another involves a search for the other conditions necessary for the observed effect. Granted that impersonal mechanisms of control tend to reverse the flow of demand, on what other conditions does the reversal depend? Concern with the significance of a combination of conditions introduces the conception of organization as a configuration of interdependent elements. It is often assumed that the concept of *Gestalt* defies quantitative analysis, but this assumption seems unwarranted. If the concept of *Gestalt* means that the organized arrangement of elements in a larger whole has a significance of its own, not attributable to the specific character of the elements, then analysis of variance furnishes a method for its systematic investigation. Thus it is possible to test the hypothesis implied by Max Weber that administrative efficiency is the result of a combination of various characteristics in a bureaucracy, provided that empirical data on these characteristics and on efficiency can be obtained for a large sample of bureaucratic organizations. Although the empirical measures describe only the elements and not their configuration, the significance of the latter would become apparent in the analysis of variance, for this statistical method would supply information not only on the contribution of each characteristic to efficiency but also on the additional contribution made by their combination. The so-called interaction effects would furnish quantitative measures of the significance of the *Gestalt* by abstracting the effects due to the configuration itself from the sum of the effects of its components. While the cost in time and money of such a project is virtually prohibitive, it is nevertheless important to realize that there are no inherent obstacles to the systematic investigation of the complex configurations in formal organizations.

Practical problems, however, cannot be brushed aside. Since it is rarely possible to establish generalizations on the basis of evidence from a representative sample of formal organizations, substitute methods have to be developed, one of which might be internal comparison. The great variations existing in large organizations have not been sufficiently exploited for systematic research. Guided, apparently, by a mistaken notion of *Gestalt,* many investigators are concerned with the "typical" foreman or the over-all pattern of "human relations" in a company instead of deriving limited generalizations from the differences in the organization of the various divisions or departments. In any case, generalizations about the total configuration cannot be supported by evidence collected in only one organization. A second substitute method, which permits making tentative generalizations about total organizations, might be the secondary analysis of a number of empirical studies of formal organizations.

Developmental dimension.—Change in the organization is the result of the very interdependence between elements that is often assumed to imply a stable equilibrium. Even if there were a perfect organization with no problems, changes in its environment would soon create some. But internal as well as external conditions generate change in the organization, since innovations instituted to solve one problem, as already mentioned, have a variety of repercussions, some of which are likely to produce other problems.

> A mistake we often tend to make is that the world stands still while we are going through the process of a given adjustment. And it doesn't. Facts change, we must keep up with the facts; keeping up with the facts changes the facts. . . . When we think that we have *solved* a problem, well, by the very process of solving, new elements or forces come into the situation and you have a new problem on your hands to be solved.[1]

Interdependence entails dilemmas: efficient operation in a large organization depends on many different conditions, and the practices instituted to

[1] Mary Parker Follett, "The Process of Control," in Luther Gulick and L. Urwick (eds.) *Papers on the Science of Administration* (New York: Institute of Public Administration, 1937) p. 166.

establish one of these conditions do not remain solely means for this end but have implications for others; and, since the conditions required for optimum operations are diverse, the measures to improve them are often incompatible. Thus, effective administration is contingent on uniform adherence to regulations as well as on adaptability to a variety of specific situations, but bureaucratic pressures compelling strict conformity to rules also give rise to rigidities that interfere with the adaptability needed to handle special cases. Although evaluation on the basis of accomplished results encourages the responsible performance of complex tasks, it simultaneously engenders anxieties which impede decision-making. Assembly-line methods, while increasing productivity, lead to absenteeism and make operations particularly dependent on regular attendance, to boot. Incompatibility of means, not simply lack of administrative foresight, is responsible for recurrent problems requiring adjustment in the organization and thus for its continual development.

The pattern of change in formal organizations can be described as a dialectical development. The process of solving some problems while frequently creating others is also a learning process in which experience is gained. On the one hand, efforts at adjustment shift from one problem to another as new difficulties arise when old ones are resolved. After assembly-line production has been instituted, reduction of absenteeism and turnover replaces technical questions of coordination as the major area of concern. On the other hand, as one type of problem recurs, it does not remain the same type of problem, since cumulative experience changes the orientation of the members of the organization toward it. This is so of problems confronting work groups as well as of those confronting management. Work groups experienced in maintaining solidarity against excessive demands of superiors will be less threatened by a new and unreasonably demanding foreman than groups that never had to cope with the problem, just as management will find it easier to combat absenteeism if it has successfully done so on previous occasions.

These processes of development are further complicated by changes in personnel which result in the loss of accumulated experience despite the profusion of written records typical of bureaucratic organizations. Of particular importance is the fact that knowledge of the networks of informal relations can be acquired only through direct experience. Alvin W. Gouldner shows that a new manager's inevitable ignorance of informal relations constrains him to resort to formal procedures in discharging his responsibilities even if he is convinced that informal procedures are more effective. Similarly, turnover of personnel on lower levels in the hierarchy undermines the cohesiveness of work groups and threatens informally established co-operative practices.

Conflicts of interests between management and non-managerial personnel, and between other groups, are an additional source of dialectical change. What constitutes adjustment for one group may be quite the opposite for the other, since different interests serve as criteria for defining adjustment, and, when issues between workers and management have been resolved on one level, new ones on a different level often arise. After satisfactory working arrangements have been agreed upon, management introduces new machines, which then create new problems of adjustment for workers. After the union has achieved the right of collective bargaining, it uses it to raise the issue of pensions. Indeed, independent of conflicts between union and management, the successful attainment of an objective stimulates efforts to make further improvements and seek new fields to conquer, and this succession of goals as they are achieved by more ultimate ones is still another force that produces change in the organization.

In sum, dialectical organizational developments are generated by different patterns of change superimposed upon one another. The process of adjustment in the organization changes the kind of difficulties that demand foremost attention, since new ones arise as old ones are resolved, and, simultaneously, experience alters the orientation with which problems are approached. Hence, as efforts at adjustment are turned from one problem to another, their effectiveness tends to increase. There are, however, several different spirals of adjustment of this sort rather than a single one, because conflicts of interests between various groupings in the organization produce diverse conceptions of adjustment. When issues created by these conflicts are settled, the conflicting developments continue and new issues emerge. Thus, the existence of divergent dialectical processes gives rise to yet another dialectical process of adjustment—a spiral linking the other spirals, as it were. The complexity of these developments is further increased by two conditions. Changes in personnel, which are disruptive, notwithstanding attempts to preserve continuity through written records and formalized procedures, reduce the level of adjustment. And the additional demands made on the organization as the result of striving for new objectives once old ones have been successfully attained create new problems of adjustment.

The systematic study of these processes of development requires that the time dimension be taken into account in the investigation of formal organizations. To be sure, there are a number of empirical studies of change in organizations; for example, F. L. W. Richardson and Walker trace the repercussions of a change in production methods in a factory; Gouldner examines the consequences of a change in management for an industrial organization; Philip Selznick analyzes modifications in an organization resulting from its adaptation to a hostile environment; and Robert Michels deals with the changes generated by the very establishment of a formal organization. But the empirical data for most of these studies were collected at one time, and the patterns of change had to be inferred subsequently either from written records or from other evidence. Although preferable to ignoring change completely, the procedure is far from ideal.

The adaptation of the panel technique to the study of formal organizations would yield reliable evidence on developmental processes. It would involve systematic observation as well as interviewing in an organization at repeated intervals, perhaps a year or more apart. Precise indications of both informal and formal changes would be supplied by this method, and intensive interviewing about the changes discovered and analysis of pertinent records would provide information on the social and psychological processes leading to them. Although continuous observation for several years, permitting the investigation of changes as they occur, is preferable to collecting data at periodic intervals, it is rarely feasible. Studies based on repeated interviews with the same respondents have greatly contributed to accurate knowledge about change in opinions and attitudes. This panel design, properly adapted to research on formal organizations, may well prove equally fruitful in the systematic study of organizational developments and, specifically, in testing the hypothesis advanced here that such developments are dialectical.

No analysis of social organization could be considered complete without some consideration of the social positions that structure the individual's relationships with others and specify his rights, duties, power, and prestige. This refers to social status. Role, on the other hand, refers to the behavior that is most likely to be performed by persons occupying given statuses. It calls for the functioning of the individual appropriate to his status for it reduces the ideal culture pattern of the group to individual behavioral terms.

Status and role, in turn, may be either ascribed or achieved. That is, they may be either assigned to the person (ascription) regardless of his choice or effort, or they may be subject to his effort and volition (achievement).

In the next and last article on social organization, Leo Schnore spells out in detail the meanings of ascribed and achieved statuses. At the same time, he corrects several erroneous impressions concerning status change.

20. ASCRIBED AND ACHIEVED STATUSES *

LEO F. SCHNORE

University of Wisconsin

Our initial distinction derives from the literature of anthropology and sociology. It is the widely recognized distinction between *"ascribed"* and *"achieved"* statuses usually credited to Ralph Linton.

Ascribed statuses. Commonly cited examples of universally "ascribed" statuses are age, sex, and certain kinship statuses; these share a non-volitional quality, in that no amount of effort on the part of the individual can alter

* Excerpt of "Social Mobility in Demographic Perspective," *American Sociological Review,* Vol. 26, No. 3, June, 1961, pp. 411–414.

them. An equally apt example is one's place of birth; although one may lie about it, one's birthplace cannot be changed. By contrast, "achieved" statuses are more clearly subject to change, and as the term itself suggests, effort and volition frequently have a role. In addition, one's educational or marital status, his occupation, and his place of residence are not immutably fixed. Even if they cannot be changed at will (since the norms of many societies treat them in ways as fully deterministic as those governing age and sex) they have the common quality of *potential* for change. The basis of the distinction, however, does not turn upon the presence or absence of a capacity for change *per se;* we shall see that at least one ascribed status changes automatically, and that the forms of change taken by various achieved statuses do not reduce to a single type. Nor does the distinction rest, at bottom, upon the capacity for volition to be exercised. As it turns out, this dimension of status—ascription versus achievement—hinges upon whether or not the status can be determined at birth.

As concrete examples, let us consider the universally "ascribed" statuses first. These include age, sex, place of birth, and kinship within the family of orientation. Among these, age stands out distinctly as a changeable status; while all of the others are immutable, one's age is constantly changing from the instant of birth, for aging is a biological fact to be reckoned with continuously. Equally vital for our purposes is the fact that this change has the quality of irreversibility. Trivial as it may seem at first blush, the fact that one's age changes in only one direction turns out to be of critical significance, conceptually and in terms of measurement.

Achieved statuses. Upon superficial examination, it may seem that "achieved" statuses are simply those that are changeable, since it is difficult to conceive of any that are absolutely resistant to change. Why then utilize the ascribed-achieved dichotomy at all? We shall deal with this issue below; it is more profitable, for the moment, to consider some concrete instances of changeable statuses that fall under the "achieved" rubric. Among the important achieved statuses that are commonly recognized are the following: education, occupation, income, religion, marital status, and kinship in the family of procreation. Each of these could serve as the subject for detailed discussion, but two or three of them merit special attention.

First of all, when educational status is defined in terms of school years completed (as in our census system), it has a more or less unique quality. One may add to, but never subtract from, the number of years of attendance. Another interesting case illustrates the importance of the definitions of the categories employed. If one is concerned with marital status, one is likely to work with a set of categories similar to those used in the United States census, viz., single, married, separated, divorced, and widowed. If so, some of the statuses are clearly reversible, in the sense that a person can be divorced or widowed and he may subsequently remarry, at which time he reassumes a status previously held. For some purposes, however, demographers find it profitable to work with only a crude dichotomy: "never-married" (single) and "ever-married" (including the currently married, separated, divorced, and widowed). In this case, the only possible status change is irreversible.

The other achieved statuses are chiefly marked by the fact of reversibility. Adherents of a particular religion may enter and leave, they may join another church or sect, rejoin their original faith, or forswear allegiance to any religious group. Similarly, an individual may move through a whole series of occupations, from time to time reassuming a position that had been previously abandoned. Finally, one can alter his place of residence, with the obvious option of

	Type of status change			
	CHANGEABLE		*UNCHANGEABLE*	
Type of status	*REVERSIBLE*	*IRREVERSIBLE*	*REVERSIBLE*	*IRREVERSIBLE*
ASCRIBED	Automatic "Citizen"	Age	Empty by definition since	Sex Place of birth Kinship in family of orientation "Race"
ACHIEVED	Naturalized Citizen Occupation Income Religion Marital status Place of residence Kinship in family of procreation	Education	reversal is a form of change	"Veteran"

FIGURE 1. Types of Status Change, with Examples

returning to a place previously occupied. Although we prefer to discuss changes in place of residence as "migration," it is important to recognize the fundamental parallel between such changes and those that may ensue between other statuses; they are cognate processes, and offer a number of interesting problems when they are jointly considered.

Status changes. It remains only to identify the traditional interest of sociologists in "social mobility" in these terms. This task will be facilitated, however, if we summarize the foregoing discussion in graphic form. Figure 1 encompasses all of the concrete cases discussed above; note that the "unchangeable-reversible" cells are empty by definition, since reversal is a form of change. It is undoubtedly the irreversible and unchangeable quality of most ascribed statuses, together with the changeable and reversible character of most achieved statuses, that have tempted most writers to emphasize the matter of volition. Our analysis, however, has demonstrated that this is not the crucial basis of distinction; rather, it is the extent to which a status is amenable to assignment at birth.

Sociological interest in statuses has taken a number of directions. Perhaps the most popular approach starts from the image of the individual as simultaneously occupying a number of statuses, each of which constitutes a membership in some group or social category. This line of thought leads naturally to a statistical consideration of the co-occupancy of statuses, as in the work of Gerhard Lenski, Jack P. Gibbs and Walter T. Martin, or (more frequently) into a non-statistical analysis of the compatibility of statuses. Concern with "role conflicts" and "marginality" are typical problems here. Both of these approaches may derive from a simple cross-sectional consideration of statuses held at a given point in time. But still another direction of sociological effort begins with the observation that individuals pass through a series of statuses in sequence during the course of a lifetime. Thus some writers are concerned with modal sequences and with the appropriateness of one status for its probable *sequelae* (e.g., youth for adulthood). Allied concepts that have grown out of this area of discussion include "anticipatory socialization" and "resocialization," and the general interest is longitudinal or developmental, with the individual career at issue.

SYMBOLIC COMMUNICATION

Granted its central position among sociological concepts, social organization or group life is not peculiarly human. We know that many animal species live in groups (although none has the kind of complex, large-scale, and formal organizations of which man is capable) and that some show considerable intelligence and an amazing habit-forming capacity. What accounts for the fact that man alone of all social animals is cultural is his ability to communicate abstractly or symbolically. Only man forms a true language.

Anatole France once said: "That which distinguishes man from animals is lying and literature." This aphorism expressed what is now a widely acknowledged sociological and anthropological truth—that both the transmission and diffusion of culture are established upon some means of communication. Underlying the importance of oral language is that along with writing, its derivative, it provides the only means of communication for the transmission, continuity, and accumulation of culture. As the anthropologist George P. Murdock stressed many years ago, in a society without language each individual would have to begin exactly where his parents did. He would possess only individual habits, and his behavior would be confined virtually to the organic level.

In the next article, Ralph Pieris discusses the role of language in socializing individuals and in creating social solidarity and social differentiation. He demonstrates how sensitive language is to culture patterns and social change in society.

21. SPEECH AND SOCIETY: A SOCIOLOGICAL APPROACH TO LANGUAGE *

RALPH PIERIS
University of Ceylon

SPEECH-COMMUNITIES

The sociologist's interest in language is due primarily to its social effects, its role in sociation or dis-sociation. A common language is an important symbol of social solidarity. The original meaning of the Latin term *barbaros* was probably stammering, stuttering, babbling unintelligibly, and other peoples had similar derogatory epithets, such as the Slav word for German which means mute, dumb. But if a language can unify a group vis-à-vis foreigners or out-groups, it can equally reflect differentiation and divisions of interest within a society. A complex official or formal group like the state or nation contains innumerable informal sub-groups which cultivate minute linguistic differences. Runyon has familiarized us with the slang of the American racketeer or "spiv." The scientific fraternity has its own distinctive speechways; a cynical diarist has left an account of a meeting of the Entomological Society, addressed by a man of "very considerable scientific attainments," in a jargon which his fellow-scientists had come to regard "as symbols of a ritual which they think it pious to accept without question." Similarly, local dialects arise in different parts of a country—the broad accents of the Yorkshireman differ from the Londoner's quaint "cockney."

Speechways are also indices of social distance between different classes of a complex society. In *Great Expectations* the sensitive and impressionable Pip was humiliated by Estella's slighting remarks: "He calls the knaves, Jacks, this boy! . . . And what coarse hands he has! And what thick boots!" Speech and dress distinguished this "common laboring-boy," and with incomparable artistry Dickens traces Pip's reaction to a harrowing experience when he is later made to confide, "I want to be a gentleman. . . . I am not at all happy as I am. I am disgusted with my calling and with my life." In Western Europe today the dress of different social strata varies but little. The hallmark of the London "cockney" is his distinctive mode of speech. The "old school tie" may well be a hackneyed music-hall joke, but a misplaced "h" is sufficient to betray a man's breeding, his education, his social class. A social class is not demarcated by legal decree, although even in Englind the law does on occasion take cognizance of gentility, and "what are called high spirits in university students on Boat Race nights becomes serious misconduct as we move east of Temple

* *American Sociological Review,* Vol. 16, No. 4, August, 1951, pp. 499–505.

Bar." Intra-social *rapport* is the pullulation of behavior-patterns cultivated by persons having common interests or approximately equal statuses. In other words, certain behavior-patterns give rise to classes having a kind of *esprit de corps*. If there is what Sombart calls a "specifically proletarian psyche," it is the creature of social vehicles such as language. Words like "comrade" have a type of linguistic use which B. Malinowski labels *phatic communion* whereby "ties of union are created by a mere exchange of words."

LANGUAGE, ETHOS, AND PERSONALITY STRUCTURE

In view of the importance of language as a socializing vehicle, speech has rightly been regarded as a personality trait. Of the dominant conditioned responses which give rise to relative permanence in the structure of an individual's personality, the symbolic, especially the verbal, is of vital importance. A society dominated by scientific thoughtways demands a language capable of a high degree of precision and abstraction. Malinowski has pointed out that the Trobriand Islanders' practical interest in nature and society extends to their speechways. They refer to all plants for which they have no economic use by the single collective word "bush." In contrast, European botanical classification includes all known flora, irrespective of economic utility. Such an attitude is the product of a scientific ethos. For, as Max Weber has pointed out, even the choice of objects for scientific investigation and the extent of penetration into the infinite causal web are determined by the values dominating the mental climate of the investigator. Speechways reflect thoughtways; there is a reciprocal interaction between the two. Hence the language of a pre-scientific society does not permit the ready expression of causal sequences. Ignorance of physiological paternity makes it almost impossible for Christian missionaries to convey to the tribesmen of New Guinea the Christian dogmas of God the Father and God the Son, the sacrifice of the only Son, the filial love felt by man for his Maker, and so on. Malinowski's contention is that "all this falls somewhat flat in a matrilineal society, where the relation between father and son is decreed by tribal law to be that of two strangers, where all personal unity between them is denied." The language of the Trobrianders expresses subsequence rather than consequence or cause. This lack of cause-and-effect modes of thought conditions their speechways. There are no clearcut temporal categories in Trobriand speechways, and the tenses are ambiguously symbolized. Hence their lack of a sense of history.

Words therefore are instruments for the expression of life-experiences, vehicles for the communication of ideas and for the transmission of adult cultural traditions to children. Speech itself grows out of human interaction, a verbal utterance being meaningless except in its *context of situation*. Speechways then are symbolic of the mores of a society. In other words, the language of a society mirrors the situational imperatives of that society. Thus E. E. Evans-Pritchard contended that any argument which would utterly demolish the validity of Zande claims for the power of the Oracle, when translated into

Zande modes of thought via Zande language, reappears as a complete justification for their entire system of oracular beliefs. Likewise M. West has shown how the process of translation of the English sentence, "You must know that I am thinking of his marrying one of them," into Bengali by Indian students invariably reflected the difference between English and Indian marriage customs. The given sentence was rendered in translation as "I am thinking of marrying one of my girls to him," the underlying idea being the Bengali custom for parents to arrange suitable marriages for their children on caste lines, the ideal of "falling in love" and romantic love being alien to their thoughtways. Similarly the polite euphemism "going to bed with so-and-so" can be current only in a society in which sexual intercourse is performed in a reclining posture. But many people are bedless, and the practices of certain Oriental societies are evidence of different modes of approach. And different expressions, less inhibited, are current.

The stage in the linguistic development of the child is usually parallel to the gradual maturation of his personality. For a few months after birth an infant cannot even recognize another person. "The child's self develops as his communication takes on an objective reference to others." The differentiation of the infantile ego from "the generalized other" is only partly the product of rational thought, largely the consequence of friction, antagonism, and pain involved in the individual's relations with the social and physical world. And the formation of the "I" is accelerated, the independence of the ego-structure fortified, as the child acquires a more effective mastery of language.

"The 'I' is the individuality in the psychical-social sense." But the development of individuality differs from society to society. In a static community in which sociality and mutuality govern the relations between man and man, individuality is imperfectly developed. Linguistic forms mirror the relatively undeveloped ego in the ambiguous first person singular pronoun. In some American Indian languages the collective form of "I" is ordinarily used ("I-amongst-others" or "We"), and the corresponding selective form, "I-for-one," is employed only exceptionally. There is reason to believe that the collective "we" precedes the "I" in linguistic evolution. In feudal societies the plural pronominal forms are frequently used in this way, and a vestige of this is seen in the Royal "we." "Here we seem to have group-consciousness holding its own against individual self-consciousness, as being for primitive folk on the whole the more normal attitude of mind," concludes R. R. Marrett.

SOCIAL STRUCTURE, SPEECHWAYS, AND THOUGHTWAYS

Relative freedom from instinctual determination of behavior is the prerogative of man alone; it is the cultural imperatives that condition the behavior of Homo sapiens. The extent of this cultural determination of thought and action differs, however, from society to society. Let us first consider the role of language in static societies which are highly stratified.

In traditional Ceylon, for example, speechways vividly reflected the rigid status-roles of a feudal society. Caste was the keystone of the social structure. The king chose his provincial governors from the nobility (the *goiwanse,* or farmer caste), although people of low castes may have surpassed them in riches. "But it is the Birth and Parentage that innobleth," commented Robert Knox long ago. Thus women had at least twelve titles, used according to rank; men had parallel designations. There were several words for Thou or You, and they were applied to people according to gentility—Knox lists "To, Topi, Umba, Umbela, Tomnai, Tomsi, Tomsela, Tomanxi," one being higher than the preceding. It is interesting to note here the use of the plural forms Topi, Umbela, Thamusela (Knox's Tomsela), for the singular "you" to indicate heightened respect as compared to the singular forms To, Umba, Thamusé. Every verb could also be rendered according to the respect to be accorded to the person addressed, e.g., "go" could be politely expressed "yanda," a request, or "pala," a command, equivalent perhaps to the English "get away," or, if accented appropriately, "scram!" These forms were provided in the language of the masses, Sinhalese, which is still spoken by over 90% of the Sinhalese population. But linguistic differentiation went further. As Ribeiro put it, "They have a language different from the one in common use, just as Latin among us; only their chief men learn it, and they are of subtle intellect." It was "a learned and dead language—the Pali, derived from and said to be similar to Sanskrit." There are parallel cases of linguistic bifurcation elsewhere. In Italy, the thirteenth century "curiale" was employed by the courts and the poets, while the masses had their diverse local dialects. In England, the "courtly" Latin and French was the language of the literati at different periods; Newton's *Principia* and several works of Milton and Hobbes appeared in Latin, and previous to that, in 1298, Robert of Gloucester said, "For unless a man knows French, he is held of little account." Again, in Java, *Noko* is the language of the nobles, while the commoners speak *kromo,* but the two classes understand each other's language and each uses the other's tongue in conversation. Not so in feudal Ceylon; "the language is too high for me" was a frequent apology of a commoner interpreting a conversation of a priest or chief.

In such a society, as we would expect, "their language is Copious, Smooth, Elegant, Courtly: according as the People that speak it are. Who are full of Words, Titles, and Compliments" (Knox). Some 150 years ago later Dr. Davy commented on the Sinhalese fondness for intricacies of style, the more artificial, the more admired: "I have heard a poem spoken of with delight as an extraordinary effort of genius, the particular merit of which was, that it admitted a great variety of readings, from the left to the right, up and down, and in many other ways, each making sense." Style here was cultivated for the sake of style. But grandiloquence and elaborate literary stylization masks decay; it is symptomatic of artistic stasis. For to stylize is to derealize, to dehumanize, and artistic stylization of this type is symbolic of an ethos which loathes living forms and attempts to elaborate abstract and dehumanized media of artistic expression. In Ceylon this stylization was the outcome of

Buddhism, its intense asceticism being emphasized in the twelfth century when the Church was "purged of heresy" by the expurgation of ritualistic and mystical Hindu corruptions, and the country reverted to the pure form of Buddhism known as the Little Vehicle (Hinyana), which it retains even today. Characteristically, this phase marks the end of the Heroic Age. "Decadence is always archaistic," says A. M. Hocart; "The revolt wears itself out: the energy departs; the monstrous ceases to be vigorous and is merely tame, and nothing is left but that standardized and uninspired art which is the only Indian art known to Europeans."

It is interesting to compare the modern European reaction to living forms. Its keynote is the avoidance of the naturalistic literary and artistic forms of the last century. Stylization in Asia was confined within bounds by a mental climate steeped in archaism. European art-forms are not hemmed in by convention. In their dehumanization of living beings they are unhampered by archaism. The speechways inaugurated by James Joyce are typical of the literary aspect of the modern movement in art. Such literature employs a verbal symbolism private to the author; it revels in neologisms and word-play; and, above all, it is anti-popular, and can be appreciated only by a literary elite.

SPEECHWAYS AND SOCIAL CHANGE

We have seen that social differentiation in an immobile society finds expression in its speechways, particularly in its elaborately gradated terms of deference. Convention and purism marred the freshness and vigor of many an able writer in Italy at the time of the Renaissance, said Burckhardt; others were tempted to rely on harmony and flow rather than on content. But soon there was a struggle to establish an universal language capable of clarity and simplicity of expression. In Europe, the transition from a feudal to an individualistic order, from status to contract, from *gemeinschaft* to *gesellschaft,* had its parallel in linguistic changes.

Now individualism as it exists in contemporary Europe and America is a comparatively recent phenomenon. Mediaeval European society lacked this extensive individual freedom. In fact, the individual was practically chained to his social role. The social order was conceived of as a natural universe to which the individual was by duty bound: "Man was conscious of himself only as a member of a race, people, party, family, or corporation—only through some general category," said J. C. Burckhardt. This mediaeval veil, woven of faith and religion, melted in the Renaissance, and "man became a spiritual *individual.*" This individualization and democratization was reflected in changing speechways.

Forms of address which symbolized manorial overlordship and feudal status-roles were depreciated in an individualistic society which substituted the cash-nexus for feudal status. Thus "master" (Fr. maitre, Ger. Meister), deriving from a designation expressing lordship, in its modern form "mister" is applied to all persons superior to manual laborers. "Your obedient servant" and "yours faithfully" were feudal realities; "yours" literally meant ownership of slaves by their "masters." Today these expressions are conventionalized. Lordship further connoted superhuman attributes. The Anglo-Saxon origin of Lord is *Balder,* the name of a favorite son of Odin, a God. In Germany *Mein Herr* was a phrase applied by a serf to his lord, a symbol of his servility (serfility). Today it is familiarly applied to all and sundry. *Sire* was apparently originally applied only to the highest; *Sir,* a derivation of *Sire,* originally meant King. The female counterpart of *Sir* and *Monsieur* were likewise originally terms of adoration. *Dame* originally meant high born. *Ma Dame,* was contracted to *madam,* or the slipshod *ma'am.* "We find that 'Yes'm' of Sally to her mistress is originally equivalent to 'Yes, my exalted,' or 'Yes, your highness,' " writes Herbert Spencer.

Vulgarization of titles and forms of address is symbolic of a dissolution of the social bonds and status-relations they represented. Such titular devaluation indicates that former status-roles are no longer accorded deference or honor. Bestowal of honor and respectful titles signifies a stratified society, but plurality of honorable titles depreciates their worth. Thus *Lord,* when applied to the descendants of a charismatic leader is devalued by virtue of its traditional or routinized application to a numerous posterity, many of whom are devoid of the original ancestor's "gift of grace." It finally degenerated into an epithet applied to all powerful feudal barons. In the same way, individualized or personal honor was a polemic concept which served the middle classes in their struggle to overthrow the feudal conception of honor and status. These middle classes, struggling for recognition in the social scheme, succeeded in making the soul and the mind rather than mere "empty" titles and manners the sources of honor. "The conspicuously honourable behaviour of the nobility was devaluated to mere gestures, irrelevant politeness, symbols of an insignificant order, against which was set up a realm of 'natural' inner quality accessible to everyone alike." This struggle had its expression in linguistic transformations. To take one more example, the expression *escuyer* originally denoted mediaeval knightly orders, feudal military chivalry. Ultimately it degenerated to the modern *esquire* which describes every one below the status of a knight.

It is evident from the foregoing discussion that language in general, and forms of address in particular, change vis-à-vis social changes. As Max Muller put it, "A struggle for life is constantly going on amongst the words and grammatical forms in each language. The better, the shorter, the easier forms are constantly gaining the upper hand, and they owe their success to their inherent value." In a static society the impetus for linguistic innovation is slight. Hence the "classical" fossil-languages like Latin and Sanskrit are unadapted for modern use. In societies in process of substantial change, ever new speechways add to the richness and range of expression of a language. We have seen that vulgarization of titles was symbolic of a democratic transformation. It was the linguistic counterpart of a widespread erosion of status-relations of mediaeval society. There was less punctiliousness displayed in the removal of the hat as a mark of respect—it was merely touched, not raised. Prostration at the feet of a superior gave way to a low bow which was successfully replaced by a slight inclination of the body, and finally by a mere offhand nod. The scant attention paid in England to details of etiquette, such as raising the hat, has been coupled by Herbert Spencer with the fact that the English are the freest (i.e. the most individualistic, democratic) nation in Europe. This freedom is also manifest in the devaluation of feudal forms of address. W. G. Sumner has shrewdly commented on the advent of slang in America: "A people who are prosperous and happy, optimistic and progressive, will produce much slang. It is a case of play. They amuse themselves with the language." Unsullied by tradition they evolve what is in effect a new language—the American language. It is in this way that hybrid languages arise. French was the corruption of Latin; Creole spoken in Mauritius is in turn a corrupt French. In a society acutely conscious of its cultural traditions, on the other hand, emphasis by purists on standard or "correct" English makes the language more rigid and formal than in a society without these inhibitions.

For any society to act in co-ordination under common norms toward shared objectives or goals, its membership must have the ability to understand and communicate with each other. But this consensus is not easily achieved in modern society, and for that reason it has become the focus of much sociological concern.

What are the obstacles that confront social consensus? Besides the organized groups in modern society that range from informal and intimate to formal and complex organizations, there is the growing detached mass, widely dispersed and varied, anonymous and unattached, devoid of organization, institutions, and rules.

Holding the mass together, in the light of its lack of structure and interaction, are the mass media of communication. They consist of radio, television, motion pictures, and the press. It can be argued, in fact, as Louis Wirth does in the following article, that in a society rapidly taking on the characteristics of a mass society the mass media are becoming the main framework of social consensus.

22. CONSENSUS AND MASS COMMUNICATION *

LOUIS WIRTH

University of Chicago

I have chosen to discuss the topic of consensus because I believe it provides both an approach to the central problem of sociology and to the problems of the contemporary world. I regard the study of consensus as the central

* Presidential address read before the annual meeting of the American Sociological Society, December, 1947; in *American Sociological Review,* Vol. 13, No. 1, February, 1948, pp. 2–15.

task of sociology, which is to understand the behavior of men in so far as that behavior is influenced by group life. Because the mark of any society is the capacity of its members to understand one another and to act in concert toward common objectives and under common norms, the analysis of consensus rightly constitutes the focus of sociological investigation. But to discuss the nature of consensus in all kinds of human groups in different cultural settings would be a formidable task. Similarly, an analysis of the conditions conducive to consensus under varying circumstances would be a vast undertaking. My observations will therefore be directed to the conditions under which consensus functions in mass societies as distinguished from more compact, intimate groups, such as the family and other primary associations.

Before exploring the nature and conditions of consensus, it seems appropriate to indicate the salient characteristics of mass societies. As we look back upon previous social aggregations, such as those of the ancient kingdoms, or at their greatest extent the Roman Empire, we wonder how, given the primitive communications that obtained, such impressive numbers and territories could be held together under a common regime over any considerable span of time. If we discover, however, that these aggregations were not truly societies but were little more than administrative areas, creatures of military domination along the main arteries of communication from some center of power, and that the economic base of their cohesion rested on exploitation of the outlying territories and peoples by the power holders at a center through their representatives who were scattered thinly over the territory, the magnitude of these aggregations does not seem too impressive. Mass societies as we find them today, however, show greater marks of integration. They are aggregations of people who participate to a much greater degree in the common life and, at least in democratic parts of the world, comprise people whose attitudes, sentiments and opinions have some bearing upon the policies pursued by their governments. In this sense mass societies are a creation of the modern age and are the product of the division of labor, of mass communication and a more or less democratically achieved consensus.

II

Since we shall speak of our society as a mass society and of the communication that it involves as mass communication, it behooves us to depict the characteristics of the mass. Its most obvious trait is that it involves great numbers, in contradistinction to the smaller aggregates with which we have become familiar through the study of primitive life and earlier historical forms of human association. Second, and again, almost by definition, it consists of aggregates of men widely dispersed over the face of the earth, as distinguished from the compact local groups of former periods. Third, the mass is composed of heterogeneous members, in that it includes people living under widely different conditions, under widely varying cultures, coming from diverse strata of society, occupying different positions, engaging in different occupations, and hence having different interests, standards of life and degrees of prestige, power and influence. Fourth, the mass is an aggregate of anonymous individuals, as may be indicated by the fact that though millions of individuals listening to a radio program, reading a newspaper, or seeing a movie, are exposed to the same images, they are not aware of who the fellow members of the audience are, nor are those who transmit these images certain of the composition of their audience. These anonymous persons who constitute the mass may be, and usually are, of course, aware that they are part of a mass and they make some assumptions as to who their fellow members are and how many of them there are. They are likewise capable of identifying themselves with their anonymous fellows who are exposed to the same images and may even gain some support from the knowledge of their existence. They may even act as if they had their unanimous support as is illustrated by the slogan "Fifty million Frenchmen can't be wrong," or by the much disputed bandwagon effect resulting from the publication of the results of public opinion polls. Fifth, the mass does not constitute an organized group. It is without recognized leadership and a well-defined program of action. If it acts collectively at all it does so only as a crowd or as a mob, but since it is dispersed in space it cannot even move as these elementary social bodies are capable of action, although it may be far from constituting, as Carlyle thought, "an inert lump." Sixth, the mass has no common customs or traditions, no institutions and no rules governing the action of the individuals. Hence, it is open to suggestions, and its behavior, to a greater degree than that of organized bodies, is capricious and unpredictable. And, finally, the mass consists of unattached individuals, or, at best, individuals who, for the time being, behave not as members of a group, playing specific roles representative of their position in that group, but rather as discrete entities. In modern urban industrial society, our membership in each of the multiple organizations to which we belong represents our interests only in some limited aspect of our total personal life. There is no group which even remotely professes to speak for us in our total capacity as men or in all of the roles that we play. Although through our membership in these organized groups we become articulate, contribute to the moulding of public opinion, and participate more or less actively in the determination of social policies, there remains for all of us a quite considerable range of ideas and ideals which are subject to manipulation from the outside and in reference to which there is no appreciable reciprocal interaction between ourselves and others similarly situated. It is this area of life which furnishes the opportunity for others to entrap us or to lead us toward goals with the formulation of which we have had little or nothing whatever to do. Hence, all of us are in some respects characterized in our conduct by mass behavior.

The fragmentation of human interests in heterogeneous, complex modern societies is so far advanced that as Robert E. Park put it, "What a man belongs to constitutes most of his life career and all of his obituary." The trend in group organization is not merely toward the multiplication and diversification of organizations, but also toward bodies of enormously increased size. We have witnessed in recent decades the development of numerous giant organizations in business and industry, in labor, in the professions, in religion, in government and in social life which seem to dominate our existence and to characterize our civilization.

Many of these organizations have become so colossal that they themselves come to approximate masses. The sense of belonging and of participation which smaller and more compactly organized groups are able to generate is hence largely frustrated by the very size of the typical organizations of our time. This is perhaps a price we must be willing to pay for living in an interdependent and technologically highly advanced world. But it should also constitute a major challenge to the analytical skill and the inventive imagination of social scientists, especially sociologists, for it is to a large extent upon the ability to maintain effective contact between the members and two-way communication between the leaders and the membership of these giant structures that the future of democracy rests.

The problem is complicated by the fact that not only is mass democratic society enormous in scope and intricate in structure, but it presents a dynamic equilibrium in which one of the principal conditions of effective collective action is the accuracy and speed with which the shifting interests and attitudes of great masses of men, whether organized or unorganized, can be ascertained and brought to bear upon the determination of policy.

Another significant feature of modern mass society, and especially of mass democracies, is the instability of the interests and the motives of the members, and the correspondingly frequent changes in leadership and the consequent uncertainty as to the locus of decisive power at any one juncture of events. If the spokesmen in any group are to know whom they are speaking for they must be able to assess how strong or enduring the interests are that they profess to represent, and whether, indeed, the groups for which they speak are at all interested in the issue.

Mass societies, furthermore, involve vast concentrations of power and authority and complicated machinery of administration. Perhaps the most urgent need that goes unmet in such a society is the capacity for prompt decisions in the face of recurrent crises. The fact that concerted action in such societies, if they are to remain democratic, must take into consideration the shifting constellation of public opinion imposes upon those who guide its destinies a responsibility which can only be met by the utilization of all the relevant sources of knowledge and the perfecton of very much more advanced techniques than we now seem to possess.

III

When a social philosopher of the previous generation, Herbert Spencer, undertook to compare human society with the biological organism, he thought he had found that the one thing which human society lacked to make it truly comparable to a biological organism, was a social sensorium which would serve as the equivalent of the central nervous system and "the mind" in the individual organism. Whatever we may think about such analogies, this alleged lack of a social mind to go with the social body is the deficiency that we must supply if organized social life, on the scale on which we must now live it, is to endure. The only reasonable equivalent of "mind" in the individual organism that we can think of as an essential in the social organism can be supplied through consensus.

A thoughtful student has described society as "a highly intricate network of partial or complete understandings between the members of organizational units." Consensus is the sign that such partial or complete understanding has been reached on a number of issues confronting the members of a group sufficient to entitle it to be called a society. It implies that a measure of agreement has been reached. The agreement, however, is neither imposed by coercion nor fixed by custom so as no longer to be subject to discussion. It is always partial and developing and has constantly to be won. It results from the interpenetration of views based upon mutual consent and upon feeling as well as thinking together.

If men of diverse experiences and interests are to have ideas and ideals in common they must have the ability to communicate. It is precisely here, however, that we encounter a paradox. In order to communicate effectively with one another, we must have common knowledge, but in a mass society it is through communication that we must obtain this common body of knowledge. The resolution of this paradox seems to lie in the possibility that though men of diverse backgrounds, experiences and interests, when they first come in contact, are incapable of communicating with and understanding one another, much less arriving at agreement, they must initially be content to grope haltingly for such elementary understandings as can be supplied on the basis of the scanty and superficial common experiences that even the most casual and superficial contact supplies. They must and do live in the hope that as that experience is widened and deepened there will take place a parallel improvement in effective communication.

We live on the assumption that human beings the world over are sufficiently alike in their basic nature and their life careers that even the most alien groups in contact with one another, no matter how indirectly and remotely, will have some elementary capacity to put themselves in the place of the other, that the common understanding that comes through communication will have a cumulative effect, and that every step toward understanding becomes the basis for a still broader and deeper basis of understanding.

Modern society exhibits two major aspects. On the one hand, it consists of organized groups, ranging from informally constituted intimate groups to highly formalized organizations, such as the modern corporation, the union, the church and the state. On the other hand, there are the detached masses that are held together, if at all, by the mass media of communication. The analysis of consensus must necessarily take account of these phases.

On every level of social life calling for concerted action whether it be that of organized groups or the mass, we need a degree of consensus capable of mobilizing the energies of the members or at least of neutralizing their opposition or apathy. Wherever and whenever we seek to enlist the uncoerced co-operation and participation of numbers of diverse men in the pursuit of a common cause, "We need," as John Dewey has said, "one world of intelligence and understanding, if we are to obtain one world in other forms of human activity."

IV

There are many ways that society has developed of inducing consent. We may first point to the kind of acquiescence induced by superior force. Power is not equally distributed among the members of most societies and there probably is no society where it is so equally distributed that all the members are equally capable of exerting their will upon the others. In its extreme form, this inequality of power and influence is exemplified by dictatorship. But even in a dictatorship, while the ultimate monopoly of violence rests with the dictator, the members of the society count for something, and the dictator does not enjoy unlimited opportunity to coerce his subjects. Although, for instance, in the case of the present Soviet regime we are convinced of the actuality of its dictatorial character, we recognize nevertheless that there are certain limits beyond which the dictators cannot go, and that if the conditions of life which they can provide for their people and the hopes that they can hold out to them fall below a certain minimum, there will be rebellion and counter-revolution. Similarly, we act, at least with reference to the Voice of America broadcasts to the Soviet people, as if even their public opinion were of some importance.

Though social cohesion in a dictatorship rests ultimately upon force and violence, it need not at all times exercise this force and violence brutally and arbitrarily. It can be held in reserve for occasions when it is absolutely necessary, and indeed the wise dictator knows this principle of prudence in the exercise of his unquestioned power. Suppression may be the first or last stage in the life cycle. It can, for instance, be translated into law, however authoritarian and arbitrary its character, and into a religious control which may rest upon fear. This attenuated form of the exercise of force has been the practice at least of modern dictators ever since Machiavelli offered his counsel to the dictators of his day. It should be noted, of course, that people may never know that they are exploited and oppressed until they see their own humble status juxtaposed to an actual condition of relative freedom and opportunity that exists in some other society with which they are in contact, or unless they can recall some previous condition of existence in which these forms of oppression did not prevail, or unless, finally, there is held out to them some ideal condition which is possible of achievement and to which they consider themselves entitled. The idea of natural rights is an example of injecting into the minds of men an ideology which serves as an ideal against which they can measure their actual condition, and the experience with this ideology in recent times shows that it has made dictatorship of any kind untenable in the long run. The notion of the inalienable rights of man and of the dignity of the human personality is at work in increasing measure over all the world to challenge autocratic rule in every realm of human life.

Closely related to the type of basis of consensus provided by force and authority is the consensus that rests upon a common identification with great heroes or leaders, of which the charismatic leader depicted by Max Weber is perhaps the fittest example. There are many roads that lead to leadership, although they are not the same roads in all societies. Force and ruthlessness, law and authority, the sacred sanctions of religion or of tradition, or the wisdom or personality of the leader himself, or even the belief in his wisdom or personal qualities, separately or in combination, may establish a man or a group in a position of leadership which can evoke consensus on the part of the followers. Whatever these original sources are, they may be reinforced by propaganda and education and thus come to have a symbolic significance far out of proportion to the original sources.

Just as leaders can serve as instruments for building consensus, so ideas and ideals and the symbols with which they become identified can create cohesion in the group. The Cross and the Crescent, the Stars and Stripes, and the Hammer and Sickle, the Magna Charta, the Declaration of Independence, and the Four Freedoms, not to speak of the popular stereotypes and the slogans which are the stock-in-trade of so much of our present-day propaganda and public relations, are and will continue to be potential forces for creating and maintaining consensus. The instrumentalities of mass communication lend themselves particularly well to the dissemination of these symbols on a scale hitherto thought impossible. We happen to live in a world in which, despite barriers of technology and of politics, the whole human race becomes potentially exposed to the same symbols. They are weapons of offense and of defense, and they are bonds of union or of discord, depending upon the purposes which those who use them have in mind.

Sociologists have long been accustomed to analyze in particular one of the bases of consensus, namely, the consensus that derives from the social heritage of a people, from a common culture, a common history and set of traditions, from the mores, which can make anything seem right, true, good, beautiful and possible. It is this basis of common social life as patterned by these traditions that makes it possible in the last analysis for any group to think of itself and to act as a society, to regard itself as a "we" group and to counterpose this "we" experience to all that is alien. The extent to which force and authority, law, religious sanction and leadership, propaganda and education, and the apparatus of symbols can be used effectively depends in large part upon this substratum of a common basis of knowledge, belief and standards molded by tradition and reinforced by the ongoing social life which embodies that tradition.

The fact that the instrumentalities of mass communication operate in situations already prepared for them may lead to the mistaken impression that they or the content and symbols which they disseminate do the trick. It is rather the consensual basis that already exists in society which lends to mass communication its effectiveness. A number of changes have, however, occurred since the days of the primitive local and isolated group life of our ancestors which have profoundly affected the force of tradition. The movements of population and the contact between people from the ends of the earth, the opening of world markets, and the spread of modern technology, the growth of cities, the operation of mass media of communication, the increasing literacy of the masses of people over all the world, have combined to disintegrate local cohesion and to bring hitherto disparate and parochial cultures into contact with each other. Out of this ferment has come the disenchantment of absolute faiths which expresses itself in the secular outlook of modern man.

One characteristic of this secularism is the increasing skepticism toward all dogmas and ideologies. With this goes the reluctance to accept things on faith or on authority, and the substitution of more or less rational grounds for believing, and where reason fails, to seek legitimation for a belief in personal tastes, preferences and the right to choose.

Another feature of this secularism is the change from naïveté to sophistication. One of the prime virtues on which the modern man prides himself is that he will not be taken in by anybody; that he offers sales resistance to those who offer him a pig-in-a-poke; that he suspects the motives of the salesman of goods or of ideas; that he wishes to see the evidence upon which the appeal rests; and that he claims the right to exercise independent judgment on the validity of that evidence. This has in turn led to a perfection of the means of persuasion through the invention of ways of making the irrational appear rational and of subtle means for making people interested in things that may not be to their interest. It has led to an enormous interest in discovering through scientific means what the interests, prejudices and predilections of men are and how they can be manipulated by appropriate appeals.

This secularism carries with it the disintegration of unitary faiths and doctrines, on the one hand, and their blending into new syncretisms which seek to combine a variety of hitherto incongruous elements in such a way as to attract the greatest number of followers. The symbols and slogans that formerly were characteristic of one party become mingled with those of others in order to woo more effectively the greatest number of adherents. Ideas and ideals that formerly stood for one set of objectives come to be perverted and diluted until they can comprise objectives which formerly seemed incongruous and until it seems that the unambiguous labels under which men formerly united not only no longer differentiate parties but actually can come to have the most contradictory content in order to appeal to all parties.

In addition to force and authority, leadership and personal prestige, ideas, ideals and the symbols into which they are incorporated, and social traditions, we must consider an aspect of the basis of consensus which, though it overlaps with others, is nevertheless so distinctive of our society as to require separate treatment. I refer to public opinion. This, of course, is not an independent force but is an aspect of every ongoing society.

Public opinion is formed in the course of living, acting and making decisions on issues. It is precipitated through the clash of representative ideas reflecting more or less faithfully the positions confronting the respective groups that compose the society. Our society, and others comparable to it, are composed of varieties of constituent groups, occupational and economic, racial and ethnic and religious. Each of these groups articulates its own interests, has its own powers, leadership, creed, political and corporate organization.

Not all members of each group have an equal share of influence nor is the strength of each group determined solely by the size of its membership. These groups are not loose aggregations of men, and it is not necessary for all members of each group to share the official view of the group to which they give their adherence. There will be some who are indifferent or even hostile to what the group stands for without rebelling, as can clearly be seen by looking at our present day political parties or major economic or religious organizations. The role which the individuals play is not determined alone by their age, sex, race, occupation, economic or educational status, although these may significantly influence the character and policies of the groups to which the individuals belong. What counts, rather, is their power, prestige, strategic position, their resources, their articulateness, the effectiveness of their organization and leadership. Within the group those who make the decisions and who exercise the dominant influence are subjected to pressures from all sides and radiate influence upon their group. The old saying: "I am your leader, therefore I must follow you," suggests the extent to which independent judgment is limited even among the leadership. The decisive part of public opinion, then, is the organization of views on issues that exercise an impact upon those who are in a position to make decisions.

The characteristic feature of public opinion in our society lies both in the fact that so many human beings are affiliated with a variety of organized groups, each of which represents only a segment of their interest, and that another large proportion of our fellowmen are unattached to any stable group and in that sense constitute unorganized masses and thereby leave the decision-making to those who are organized and can exercise their corporate power.

In modern democracies, and to some extent in all inclusive societies on the scale of modern states, men exercise their influence and voice their aspirations through delegated powers operating through functionaries and leaders, through lobbies, party organizations, religious denominations and a variety of other organized groups having a complex internal organization of their own. This seems to be the characteristic way of representative democratic government. In the course of the flow of communication the interests and grievances, the sentiments, attitudes and opinions of the people at the bottom may become grossly distorted, and the people at the top may find themselves so remote from their constituents that they may either be ignorant of their actual feelings or may seriously misinterpret the fragmentary knowledge that they do have. It is at this point that public opinion studies may prove significant. We have already witnessed in the United States the rise of what might be called government by Western Union, which is instanced by the story of the lady who went to the telegraph office and said, "I should like to send a telegram to my Congressman to use his own judgment."

V

The various bases upon which consensus rests are, of course, not unrelated to the ways in which consensus is reached. Of these only some of the principal channels may be alluded to here: persuasion, discussion, debate, education, negotiation, parliamentary procedure, diplomacy, bargaining, adjudication, contractual relations and compromise are all means for arriving at a sufficient degree of agreement to make the ongoing life of society, despite differences in interests, possible. Ultimately, consent in the face of differences comes down to a contrast between force and fraud on the one hand, and persuasion and rational agreement on the other hand. In some cases, however, the march of events may bring agreement where previously none was possible. If consent does not precede action there is still a chance to obtain consent in the course of action itself. The submission that comes with coercion, it should be noted, however, does not truly give us consensus. It results rather in what the Nazis called *Gleichschaltung*.

As over against the use of violence and fraud to obtain the pseudoconsensus, which even in authoritarian regimes is a precarious basis of power and social solidarity, democracies must resort to the art of compromise which results in agreements more or less rationally arrived at—agreements, the terms of which neither party wants, but at the same time cannot refuse to accept. Whereas authoritarianism gives us a seeming unanimity, which has been described as the unanimity of the graveyard, democracies rest upon the ultimate agreement to disagree, which is the tolerance of a divergent view. Even democracies, when they are in a hurry or when they are threatened by imminent danger, may sometimes have to resort to the shortcut of coercion, as is typical of the military interludes in democratic history, whereas autocracies may be able to afford at times to allow freedom in considerable areas of living which do not threaten the basis of autocratic power. In general, however, we may say that where consensus exists, coercion is unnecessary and where continuous coercion must be resorted to it is a sign that the regime is either in its initial stages or nearing its end. If might is not right, then might has at any rate to cloak itself in the mantle of rightness to persist, for no authoritarian government can ultimately determine the thinking of people, including what the people think of those who govern them.

The more intelligent and earnest people are, the less likely it is that they will agree on all subjects. Coercion can achieve spurious agreement on all issues, but consent can be obtained only provisionally and perhaps only on those issues which do not threaten too deeply the interests, the ideas and ideals of the heterodox. We seem to have worked out quite pragmatically in our democratic society the limits beyond which we are reluctant to push the struggle for agreement. We have agreed that uniformity is undesirable. We have, for instance, through the Bill of Rights, exempted religion from the sphere of necessary agreement, and we have enlarged the area of political freedom up to a "clear and present danger" line.

We have recognized moreover that it is not necessary to obtain agreement on everything in order to operate as an effectively functioning society. There is embodied in our sense of good taste a sensitiveness to our differences, some of which it is not correct to translate into issues for public debate and discussion. We are willing, frequently, to let our silence count as consent on a good many issues which we think are either too trivial or too delicate to push the point. And above all, we have developed patience to endure heresies and sufferance to endure transitory annoyance in the hope that minorities can, under freedom, develop themselves into majorities, and we have come to believe that for most purposes of life it is more economical, though perhaps less interesting, to count noses than to break heads.

But modern societies, whether they are autocratic or democratic, have learned that in the face of their size and complexity and their internal heterogeneity, the engineering of public consent is one of the great arts to be cultivated. Democracies, as distinguished from autocracies, seem to have taken the longer view by recognizing, as did Machiavelli, that the pseudoconsensus that is achieved by force cannot long endure and weather crisis, when he said: "It cannot be called talent to slay fellow citizens, to deceive friends, to be without faith, without mercy, without religion; such methods may gain empire but not glory." Democracies proceed on the assumption that even if the contending parties fight it out violently there is no assurance that the problem over which they fought won't remain after the stronger has suppressed the weaker. Even military conquest uses the technique of undermining the will to fight of the enemy, and nowadays, even after the enemy has surrendered, we send public opinion pollers among them to learn how best to govern them. The believers in the democratic principle have learned not to be impatient in the process of reaching agreement and that society can go on as long as we agree not to settle our disagreements by resort to force. They have had to learn that society can remain democratic only as long as we recognize and respect that essential residue, the freedom and dignity of every personality, which is no less important than it was before merely because it seems to have become a cliché. They have come to know also, as a contemporary philosopher has put it, that "lacking the consensus a legal crime may be a social virtue and religious heresy a moral duty."

Consensus in mass democracies, therefore, is not so much agreement on all issues, or even on the most essential substantive issues, among all the members of society, as it is the established habit of intercommunication, of discussion, debate, negotiation and compromise, and the toleration of heresies, or even of indifference, up to the point of "clear and present danger" which threatens the life of the society itself. Rather than resting upon unanimity, it rests upon a sense of group identification and participation in the life of a society, upon the willingness to allow our representatives to speak for us even though they do not always faithfully represent our views, if indeed we have any views at all on many of the issues under discussion, and upon our disposition to fit ourselves into a program that our group has adopted and to acquiesce in group decisions unless the matter is fundamentally incompatible with our interests and integrity.

Consensus is supported and maintained not merely by the ties of interdependence and by a common cultural base, by a set of institutions embodying the settled traditions of the people, and the norms and standards that they imply and impose, not merely by the living together and dealing with one another, but also, and not least important, by the continuing currents of mass communication, which in turn rest for their meaningfulness and effectiveness upon the pre-existence of some sort of a society, which hold that society together and mobilize it for continuous concerted action.

VI

To the traditional ways of communication, rumor, gossip and personal contact, to the pulpit, the school and the forum, we have added in our generation the mass media of communication, consisting of radio, television, the motion picture and the press. These new media represent giant enterprises, dependent upon and designed to reach a mass audience. By virtue of the fact that they are dependent upon mass patronage, these media transcend both in their content and in their mode of presentation the peculiar interests and preoccupations of the special and segmental organized groups and direct their appeal to the mass. To reach their mass audiences they are constantly tempted to reduce their content, whether it be that of entertainment, enlightenment or appeal to action, to the lowest common denominator, to what is believed will interest the greatest number, if not everybody. Since these mass media are so often tied to a mass market for their sustenance, they tend furthermore to be as near everything to everybody and hence nothing to anybody as it is possible to be.

Those who manage the mass communication enterprises have, of course, also some incentives to counteract this levelling influence of the mass audience by appeals to the tastes and interests of special groups. The third program of the British Broadcasting Corporation is an experiment in bringing high cultural values to a selected audience and in the effort to enlarge the demand for programs of high quality.

It is upon these mass media, however, that to an ever increasing degree the human race depends to hold it together. Mass communication is rapidly becoming, if it is not already, the main framework of the web of social life. In retrospect we can see how shrewd Hitler and his cohorts were in recognizing that in these instrumentalities they controlled the principal means for moving great masses of men into at least temporary adherence to their objectives and in using them for their own purpose. That they almost succeeded and that the rest of the world had to pay a terrible price in blood and treasure at the last moment to avert their domination over the world might serve as a warning to those who minimize the importance of mass communication and to remind them that we live in an era when the control over these media constitutes perhaps the most important source of power in the social universe. It is interesting to note that modern dictators who espouse the doctrine of the elite and who profess to hold the masses in great contempt, have shown themselves frequently to be more sensitive to the whims of the mass which they profess to despise than have some leaders of democratic societies. They have recognized also that the mass media can be used to manipulate and exploit existing situations and opportunities.

Recent investigations by polling and interview techniques have revealed that despite the dense blanketing of our country with informal educational and propaganda appeals, despite the enormous ramification of organized groups which discuss and disseminate knowledge on issues of current importance, there are vast areas of ignorance on some of the most important issues confronting our society.

The National Opinion Research Center recently found that less than half of the people polled had any reasonably clear meaning of what a tariff was. Other investigations have shown that on even the most central public issues of our time only a small fraction of our people have sufficient understanding to act intelligently. This suggests that the state of public opinion as an aspect of consensus in a society such as ours calls for an unrelenting effort for popular education and for access to reliable sources of information. This does not mean that everybody must be equally well informed on such questions as the tariff, but it does suggest the need for general education to enable the citizen to participate more intelligently and critically in general public discussion as well as to equip him to act with greater knowledge and responsibility in the special interest groups with which he is identified.

If we consider in addition to the vast areas of ignorance, the astonishing degree of apathy and indifference that prevails concerning even the issues of transcendent importance, it becomes clear why mass democracies so often appear incapable of competing effectually with authoritarian societies. Here, again, the price we must pay for the survival of a way of life that we cherish calls for the expenditure of an immensely greater share of our resources than thus far we have been willing to devote to information and education. This calls not merely for continual effort to dispel areas of ignorance, but also areas of indifference which may in part be based upon ignorance. The content of what is to be communicated must therefore be adapted to the audience to which it is addressed, and there must be awareness that we may be speaking over the heads of people or that the symbols that we use may mean entirely different things to others than they do to ourselves. The predominance of the entertainment feature particularly in such media as radio and motion picture does not preclude the appeal to intelligence. It suggests rather that information and education services to be effective must also be interesting.

Communication, as it is carried on largely through verbal intercourse, can be fortified by a body of common experiences shared by the many, and can be dramatized through art and literature and other means for vivifying ideas and ideals, in order to achieve a sounder basis of common understanding. In the world of science we come about as near to a world society as in any phase of human life, and this world-wide scope of communication which science exemplifies might well serve as a model to be approximated in other realms of human experience, for science, including perhaps even social science and philosophic scholarship, has proved its power to surmount local, national, sectarian and class barriers, and even to infiltrate through the obstacles of official censorship. The same appears to be true of music and art.

There has been much discussion recently, more with reference to the radio and motion picture than the older medium of the press, concerning the concentration of control over these mass media of communication. The fact that the media of communication tend toward monopolistic control, as is evidenced by the building up of industrial empires in this field of enterprise has serious implications for mass democracy. The concentration of such power in a few hands—whether through press associations, newspaper columns syndicates, radio networks or motion picture combines may create great imbalance in the presentation of divergent, especially minority views. It may result in the danger of censorship no less real for being unofficial, and may threaten the free and universal access to the factual knowledge and balanced interpretation which underlie intelligent decision.

In a society dominated by centers of unquestioned power and authority, reinforced by sacred traditions and rituals and capable of eliciting unquestioning loyalty to its norms and purposes, such mass communication devices would not constitute a serious problem. They would reinforce, but would not greatly alter the social structure. But in a society where all men irrespective of race, creed, origin and status claim and are to be granted an increasing share of participation in the common life and in the making of common decisions, the control of these media of mass communication constitutes a central problem. If it is consensus that makes an aggregate of men into a society, and if consensus is increasingly at the mercy of the functioning of the mass communication agencies as it is in a democratic world, then the control over these instrumentalities becomes one of the principal sources of political, economic and social power. The harnessing of this power is an infinitely more complex and vital problem than any previous challenge that the human race has had to meet.

In mass communication we have unlocked a new social force of as yet incalculable magnitude. In comparison with all previous social means for building or destroying the world this new force looms as a gigantic instrument of infinite possibilities for good or evil. It has the power to build loyalties and to undermine them, and thus by furthering or hindering consensus to affect all other sources of power. By giving people access to alternative views mass communication does of course open the door to the disintegration of all existing social solidarities, while it creates new ones. It is of the first importance, therefore, that we understand its nature, its possibilities and its limits and the means of harnessing it to human purposes.

VII

Before closing, I should like to allude to the problems of consensus as they arise in some of the more crucial spheres of human interaction in contemporary society. The first of these is the sphere of racial and cultural relations, the second is the field of industrial relations, and the third is the area of international relations. I do not mean to suggest that these are the only areas where we face the problems of consensus. I use them merely for illustrative purposes, recognizing that the same problems are also found in family relations, in informal associations, in local community life, and in the operations of government. These three, however, seem to reflect the most characteristic features of mass communication as it impinges upon consensus in modern mass democracies such as our own.

The spread of industrialism and of capitalism with its world markets and its free workers has given rise among other institutions to giant corporations and giant unions, involving great concentrations of power. The competition and conflicting interests within and between these organizations affects every aspect of social life and determines the level of living and the utilization of the resources of all society. Management and unions, aware of the crucial influence of public opinion upon their relative positions, have not been slow to utilize the instruments of mass communication, both internally and in relation to one another, and in the effort to mold the attitudes and to affect the decisions of society. In so far as these decisions involve national policies, the effort of each side has been directed to rallying support for itself by molding the attitudes and opinions of the larger public.

The relationship between conflicting groups, such as these, illustrates the significance of consensus within the group for the capacity of each to deal with its opponent. From the standpoint of the larger society the need for a more inclusive consensus involving both of these constellations is indispensable for the maintenance of industrial peace. Propaganda appeals directed toward the larger public, the pressure of government and organized bodies in society, such as the churches and the political parties, are among the indispensable elements in the strategy of collective bargaining, arbitration, labor legislation, and the conduct of strikes. The means of mass communication play no less significant a role in the maintenance of mass production and mass markets.

The rise of self-conscious racial and cultural minorities which has proceeded parallel to the spread of the ideal of equality and the institutions of mass democracy through ever larger areas of the world, has accentuated the problems of racial and cultural relations. The contrast between contemporary society and primitive and earlier historical societies with respect to the contact between diverse racial and cultural groups is startling. Whereas everyone in a primitive, ancient and medieval society had a more or less fixed place in the social structure, depending to a large extent upon the character and position of his ancestor, today all of us are men on the move and on the make, and all of us by transcending the cultural bounds of our narrower society become to some extent marginal men. More and more the relations of life that were formerly settled by sacred tradition and custom become subjects of discussion, debate, negotiation and overt conflict. Many of the problems affecting our national solidarity through our loyalties, rest for their orderly adjustment upon the achievement of consensus across the lines of the diverse races and cultures of which America is comprised. The great obstacles encountered by those who attempted to achieve in the face of prejudice and discrimination a national solidarity sufficient to see our nation through the recent war, should recall to all of us the reality of the existence of minorities in our midst. If the experiment of America shows anything, it shows that, despite the many setbacks which the democratic ideal and practice has suffered, we are determined to achieve consensus and have found the road toward it without too much coercion through the idea of cultural pluralism, which is another expression for the toleration of differences.

Nowhere do the problems of racial and cultural relations present themselves more dramatically than they do in our great cities, where the people of varying stocks and cultures live in dense physical concentration. Whereas in an earlier society it was unusual to meet a stranger, under the conditions of life in great cities it is an equal rarity to meet someone who is familiar. Although our face may still light up when, in the crowds of the great cities, we see a friend, we have nevertheless learned to live with people of diverse background and character to a degree sufficient at least to achieve the requirements of a fairly orderly, productive and peaceful society.

What is true of self-conscious minorities impelled by the ideal of the equality of man in our own communities and in our own nation, is increasingly true of the world at large. The so-called backward peoples are increasingly being brought within the orbit of a world society resting upon a world consensus. In this the numerous organized groups and movements, among dominant and minority groups alike, using the instruments of mass communication to bring their ideas before a world public, are increasingly evident.

And finally the question must have occurred to people who are not versed in the language of sociologists and in the serious subjects with which they are preoccupied, why it is that sociologists who claim as their vocation the study of social interaction have paid so little attention to interaction on the grandest scale of all, namely, the interaction between national states and what we call international relations, for in this sphere is exemplified the operation of consensus upon which the future of mankind depends.

We have been making some progress in the building of world consensus. We do have a fairly general recognition of economic interdependence on a world scale. We have a great deal more of traffic across the bounds of nations and of continents than the world has ever seen before. We have even some incipient international institutions whose strength is being tested by the increasing tensions brought about by thc very fact that we live in an emerging single world in which we have contacts and conflicts of interest and of ideas with people of whom we were formerly oblivious. We even can see some semblance of emerging world loyalties which makes the expression "world citizenship" sound less utopian than it did before. The instruments of mass communication, particularly the radio, and, it seems soon, television, combining the faithful transmission of the voice with that of the visual image of the human face and gesture, are particularly well suited to supply the means for the furtherance of understanding across the borders of sovereign states.

As long as we do not have a monopoly of power to coerce all of the other nations and people of the earth into our way of life, the only road we can travel is that of continued negotiation, persuasion and compromise. We should probably, even if we had the power of coercion, not be able to use it on others without destroying the very values which might tempt us to use it.

If our ways of thought and conception of freedom and democracy, our system of economy and our political and social ideals seem to be, as I am sure they seem to many, irreconcilable with those of the only other remaining power constellation in the world, it is well to recall that there was a time when Catholics and Protestants felt very passionately that they could not live in peace in the same state. Time has fortunately proved them wrong. There have been other conflicts in the hisitory of man which seemed at the time equally irresolvable. The uncomfortable but at the same time reassuring fact, however, is that today in this shrunken world there are more effective ways of interfering with the internal life of any society by those without through the instrumentalities of mass communication, which are no respecters of boundaries and which find ways of surmounting all barriers. What is more, these products of mass communication have a way of reaching the great inert masses of the world, for making them restless and mobilizing them for action, or at least for making the dominant groups in their respective societies more responsive to their pressure.

Mass communication will not, of course, by itself produce the minimum of world consensus requisite for world peace and world society. But it does not operate by itself. It operates through and in conjunction with existing and emerging institutions in a climate of opinion and ultimately through and upon human beings. There are other things in the world besides mass communication, but these other things, some of which I have indicated, are tied increasingly to mass communication and through this tie give it its strategic significance.

The media of mass communication, like all the technological instruments that man has invented, are themselves neutral. They can be used to instil a fighting faith or the will to reconciliation. At any rate, the relationship between nations and people that will allow the fullest use of the world's resources to meet human needs under freedom and order and in peace, calls today for nothing less than the building of a world consensus, for a social psychological integration of the human race commensurate with the interdependent far-flung and rich material resources and human energies of the world.

In mobilizing the instrumentalities of mass communication for the building of that consensus, we cannot fail to remind ourselves that along with the perfection of these means of human intercourse science has also perfected unprecedented means of mass destruction. But in the case of neither the instruments of mass communication nor of atomic energy do the inventors of the instrument dictate the uses to which thay shall be put. As a contemporary historian has recently put it: "If our characteristic Western gift [by which he refers to technology] proves to have been a blessing for mankind, it will be a great blessing; and, if a curse, a great curse. If things go well, the epitaph of history on the Franks [by which he means us] may run: 'Here lie the technicians, who united mankind'; and if things go badly: 'Here lie the technicians, who exterminated the human race.' " Except that in the latter case, Professor Arnold Toynbee, the author of these remarks, fails to point out that there may not be anybody left to carve that epitaph.

If we are uneasy today it is not because of these products of science but because of what men may do with these products of human ingenuity. There is a frightful peril in delay, and the realization of this peril is rapidly leading to intellectual paralysis instead of greater intellectual exertion. The atomic bomb will not, we are told, yield to a physical defense or a counter-weapon which will neutralize its destructive potential. The only defense we have is social—the creation of world consensus. Since the mass media of communication are capable of providing the picture of social reality and the symbolic framework of thought and fantasy and the incentives for human action on an enormous scale, the knowledge of their effective use should become the most important quest of social science, and particularly of sociology. The circumstances under which we live do not any longer allow the saints to sit in their ivory tower while burly sinners rule the world.

I hereby extend a cordial invitation to my fellow sociologists, and such other social scientists, including the statisticians, who care to join us, to return to the subject matter for the cultivation of which society sustains us, though let it be admitted, on a none too luxurious level. That subject matter is the life of man in society and the heart of that subject matter today is the understanding of the processes through which consensus on a world scale is created. Unless we solve that problem, and solve it in a reasonably satisfactory way soon, there will be no opportunity to work on any of the others on which our minds or our hearts are set.

SOCIALIZATION

Now that we have examined culture, social organization, and symbolic communication as basic sociological concepts, it is proper to turn to the socialization of the individual. This is the social psychological set of processes whereby the human develops a personality, incorporating the culture and his positions in society into an organized, individual pattern of thoughts, feelings, and actions. In socialization, the individual builds up a way of dealing with others and himself, beginning with his interactions as an infant in his family of orientation.

The socal self refers to the pattern of attitudes and values each personality has socially acquired concerning itself. After the infant has perceived that others respond to his acts, and then has perceived how they respond, the child becomes an object to himself. Placing himself imaginatively in other people's status and role by the process called empathy, the child conceives of himself as he imagines others think of him. The child is now able to base his behavior on this socially reflected self, the self-image. This social self is the internalization of social values, the internalized others, especially the significant others in the person's social environment. Conceptions of oneself, therefore, are largely introjected through the responses to one from others, and for this reason it can truthfully be said that man carries his society around in his head.

In the article that follows, Francis E. Merrill reviews the concept of social self as it emerged from the work of social psychologists like Cooley, Mead, and Sullivan. He is particularly concerned about "the self and the other" as a framework for a special set of social problems.

23. THE SELF AND THE OTHER: AN EMERGING FIELD OF SOCIAL PROBLEMS *

FRANCIS E. MERRILL
Dartmouth College

This paper will explore some of the further implications of a shift in social problems resulting from recent changes in the social climate. An earlier paper examined some of the general relationships between social character and social problems and suggested that many traditional problems are on the way

* *Social Problems,* Vol. 4, No. 3, January, 1957, pp. 200–207.

to amelioration and eventual solution. Among these problems are illiteracy, poverty, child labor, unemployment, undernourishment, old-age insecurity, infant mortality, endemic disease, and similar difficulties which have recently come within the purview of democratic government. These situations are by no means completely eliminated in the United States, much less in the underdeveloped parts of the world. But the technical knowledge and productive capacity to deal constructively with them are part of the heritage of modern democratic societies.

In place of these former concerns, a new type of problem situation has emerged, which likewise reflects a particular sociocultural climate with its own values and norms. This is the growing preoccupation with what might be called "self-other" problems, in which individuals and groups are concerned with interpersonal relationships in general and those involving the self and the other(s) in particular. Central to this preoccupation is the social self, as the product of the perceived and imagined appraisals of others. The investigation of the social self was pioneered by Baldwin, Cooley, and Dewey and given a systematic theoretical structure by Mead. Harry Stack Sullivan further developed this approach and made it the center of his conceptual system and therapeutic technique. In the present context, however, the self-other approach is applied to social problems, rather than to psychotherapy.

A social problem involves a situation, a value, and social action. The action is intended to alleviate or eliminate the situation and thereby enhance the value. Problems of the self and the other(s) are as crucial as they are intangible. Status is as important as material comfort and the deprivation of status as devastating as hunger. Technological and industrial development may eventually solve such problems as unemployment, but, for example, self-other problems of prejudice remain. Basic anxiety is the heritage of the new social climate, and the attempt to minimize this anxiety motivates social action. The latter ranges from informal efforts to win friends and influence people to formal attempts to understand small-group interaction.

THE SOCIAL SELF

The social self has been called "a subject which is its own object." Each person loves himself, hates himself, praises himself, blames himself, and punishes himself. Both the subject and the object of these verbs are the self. Motivation for this action is in large part derived from others, as each projects himself into the minds of others and takes their role toward himself. The social self thus arises in interaction with others, as the individual looks at himself through others' eyes. He feels happy or sad as he evokes praise or blame from those whose roles he takes in his imagination. In so doing, he develops self-attitudes, which range from blissful self-love to extreme self-denigration. The sources of these attitudes are the "significant others" in his environment, whose opinions about him matter very much.

The social self has been viewed in terms of the pronouns "I" and "me." The former is the subject of the self-attitudes, the latter their object. The "I" is the active part of the self, whereas the "me" reflects the attitudes of others. These elements are in constant interaction and give rise to what Sullivan has termed the "good-me" and the "bad-me." The former is the part of the self which reflects affection, tenderness, and generally pleasant treatment from others. The latter reflects dissatisfaction and anxiety arising from lack of affection and approval by the "significant others." People try to avoid thinking and talking about the "bad-me," because it makes them anxious and unhappy to do so. They prefer to think about the "good-me," because this gives them pleasure and generally enhances their self-feeling.

Both the "good-me" and the "bad-me" reflect the actual or imputed judgments of others. The nature of the social self therefore predisposes the person to a concern with these "reflected appraisals." In Mead's words: "The individual . . . enters his own experience as a self or individual . . . only insofar as he first becomes an object to himself . . . and he becomes an object to himself only by taking the attitudes of other individuals toward himself within a social environment . . . in which both he and they are involved." [1]

Under these conditions, the individual tries to maximize the "good-me" and minimize the "bad-me." Comparative inability to reach this goal, together with anxiety concerning the judgments of others, generates social problems of the self-other type. The individual does not receive as much love, affection, understanding, acceptance, or status as he has learned to expect. He desires more of these intangible but vital values so that he may incorporate them into his social self. He is somewhat like Arnold W. Green's unhappy middle-class male child, who has been reared in an atmosphere of comforting security and (sometimes) suffocating affection and is thenceforth unable to recapture this infantile paradise. Self-other problems are thus literally *social* problems, rather than economic, political, or moral problems. As people "take each other into account" and view themselves through the eyes of others, they are acting in a specifically social fashion.

SOCIAL STRUCTURE AND SELF-OTHER PROBLEMS

Social problems reflect social structure. As the patterned behavior of society has changed, the problems have changed accordingly, albeit with a time lag. Some of the traditional social problems reflected an economy of scarcity, in which technological knowledge, productive capacity, and distributive organization were inadequate. As suggested elsewhere, many of those problems are giving way before expanding industrial facilities. Other traditional social problems involved conflicts in social values. The way of life of the Old South incorporates values which are not the same as those of the American creed. Similarly, value conflicts are at the heart of such problems as child labor, slum clearance, sexual laxity, and divorce.

[1] Mead, George Herbert, *Mind, Self, and Society* (Chicago: University of Chicago Press, 1943), p. 138.

Each society has its own structure and its own accompanying problems. The present article suggests that social problems of the self-other type are emerging as increasingly important in American society. Among the structural factors responsible for this trend are the following:

Achieved status. The emphasis in our society upon achieved, as contrasted to ascribed, status needs no documentation. In an earlier day, achievement was gained by physical activity, whether clearing a wilderness, building a factory, or constructing a railroad. Although these activities actually required cooperation with others, the individual could entertain the illusion that he was acting as an independent and self-sufficient individual. Under present conditions, this illusion is no longer possible. In the bureaucratic structure of the large corporation, each man is at the mercy of his fellows, a fact of which he is acutely aware. From the moment he enters the bank, the railroad, or the plant, the aspiring young man is constantly taking the roles of others and viewing himself through their eyes.

Social mobility. In his movements up (or down) the status ladder, the individual is continually conscious of the attitudes of others toward himself. The "empathic responses" are at a premium, and the person who is deficient in the ability to take the role of the other is at a disadvantage. Both those going up and those going down derive their self-attitudes from the reflected appraisals of others. These self-attitudes tend to determine their attitudes toward the world in general. In their study of intolerance among veterans of World War II, Bruno Bettelheim and Morris Janowitz discovered that men who were losing status were much more prejudiced than those who were either gaining status or staying in the same place.

Competition. In societies which emphasize peaceful cooperation, the individual is presumably not so aware of other selves in opposition to himself. But the pervasive emphasis in our society upon competition for scarce goals means that self-appraisal is dependent upon competitive success, which in turn directly affects the attitudes of others. Money is the most important of these goals, and the status of the breadwinner is dependent upon his skill and acumen in this respect. Individuals also compete for status, love, and prestige, which can be gained only from others. Attitudes of others toward the self thus enter into many relationships which are arranged by custom in other societies. Manipulation of others is another element in competitive interaction, and here again each person is made aware of other selves and his own in relation to them. He must take others consciously into account, which increases his awareness of self-other relationships. The more bitter the competition, the more aware he is.

Class differentials. In their study of communication differences between classes, Leonard Schatzman and Anselm Strauss found that the lower class showed a deficiency in the ability to take the role of the other. Persons on this social level communicated with others in terms interesting and significant only to themselves, rather than to their listeners, who were middle-class. In another study, class differences appeared in the tendency to blame, censure, and otherwise act aggressively toward the self. Middle-class persons indicated a strong degree of self-aggression, which appeared as self-discipline, self-blame, and even self-hatred. In contrast, lower-class persons directed their aggressions against others. A society with middle-class values would thus presumably be more concerned with self-other relationships than one where either lower-class or upper-class values predominated.

Mass media. In their depiction of "personalities" and celebrities, the mass media make private emotions and self-conceptions a matter of public interest. The movies, radio, television, and the mass-circulation magazines are concerned, in one way or another, with the glorification of the self as seen through the eyes of others. In this case, the "others" comprise the bulk of the reading, listening, and viewing population. The love-life of a prominent movie actress becomes a matter of national importance, and millions of persons rapturously identify themselves with her. Interpersonal relations become vitally important and adolescents of both sexes and all ages view their own self-other problems as crucial. The mass media depict interpersonal situations because of the informal taboo against "controversial" topics, such as politics, religion, prejudice, or power. The least common denominator is the problem theme which stresses the self and the other.

TYPES OF SELF-OTHER PROBLEMS

Problems of the self and the other are thus intensified by the nature of the culture and the social structure. In one sense, these relationships are basic in *any* social setting, in that the social self is necessarily the product of the reflected appraisals of others. Under present conditions, however, this situation has been intensified by the emphasis upon these relationships and the corresponding individual self-consciousness. Examples of these emerging social problems have been anticipated in the foregoing discussion; they may now be discussed in more detail.

Role-playing. A generic problem of a self-conscious society is the inability of the individual to play the roles expected of him. Social roles are an integral part of the social self, and self-feeling reflects the ability to fulfill the expectations of one's roles. The more complex the society, the more difficult this feat becomes. The person who is chronically anxious about his role-*playing* ability (as distinguished from his role-*taking* ability) is often inadequate in the performance of a role, which further increases his anxiety. He thus becomes prey, in Sullivan's words, to an "anticipated unfavorable appraisal of one's current activity by someone whose opinion is significant." This is an interpersonal, rather than an individual, situation, inasmuch as both the conception of the role and the sense of adequacy (or inadequacy) in playing it come from other persons. Failure in role-playing may cause the individual to distrust his status, his motives, his fellows, and hence, himself. Many of the most pressing problems of the present society derive from role-failure. These roles include those of parent and child, peer-group member, adolescent, lover, mistress, husband, wife, group member, and "100 percent American."

Parent-child relationships. In an earlier generation, parents were primarily concerned with the physical safety, material comfort, and intellectual development of their children. For all practical purposes, these matters are no longer of immediate concern, because they are substantially under control; infant mortality, childhood disease, and material deprivation have been alleviated or virtually eliminated. In this self-conscious generation, however, parents are increasingly aware of the impact of their own personalities upon those of their children. Permissive or nonpermissive training, methods of discipline, relations with other children, and demonstrations of affection are still vital questions.

Peer-group acceptance. In his relations with the peer-group, the child is first introduced to self-other problems in all their stark reality. In the peer-group, from an early age through high school and college, the interactionist conception of the self is perhaps more clearly demonstrated than in any other context. The child is soon made aware of the attitudes of his peers toward himself, and these attitudes are often brutally expressed with no effort to soften the blow. Parents and siblings are ordinarily restrained by affection, custom, and in-group loyalty from expressing their true feelings toward the child. Not so his peer-group. Acceptance by this body is vital to self-respect, and status is made very clear. The child is provided with a virtual running market report on his status. The peer-group reaches its greatest influence during adolescence, when the child is trying to break away from his parents and has not yet attained adult status. In his marginal world, the adolescent looks largely to his peers for guidance, moral support, and self-realization.

Dating. Dating is a competitive game, in which the winner is "loved" because he is successful and successful because he is "loved." Boys and girls who are in demand as dates have prima facie evidence of their acceptance. High self-appraisal follows such acceptance and low self-feelings accompany a failure in this respect. Nothing succeeds like success, and an initial convergence of favorable self-judgments is prolonged into subsequent relationships with the opposite sex. The practice of "going steady" at an early age is a cautious attempt (which has become increasingly structured) to insure the adolescent of at least a modicum of success in dating. Boys and girls who are going steady are always assured of a date and need not run the risk of rejection.

Love and marriage. Closely related to self-other problems of dating are those of love and marriage. In both cases, the self is bolstered by the affectionate responses of another. When one is loved, he feels that he is a better person than before and is correspondingly grateful to the other for thus bolstering his self-attitudes. Lovers enhance each other's self-feelings, a process which may continue throughout their lives. Conversely, those who are unilaterally in love suffer an impairment in self-attitudes and self-respect. Romantic love as a prelude to marriage is one form of this desire for self-approval. Lost or frustrated love after marriage is a major self-other problem.

Conformity and nonconformity. In a stable society, adaptation to group demands is comparatively spontaneous and unreflecting. The members have the same general cultural patterns and are not *consciously* concerned with conformity. In a heterogeneous society, conceptions of the self require a more deliberate and self-conscious adjustment to the group. The mobile population is so large that, in many urban neighborhoods, a large proportion of the residents are and will continue to be "strangers" to each other. This is as true in middle-class suburbs as in lower-class slums. Acceptance requires (or is believed to require) a strong conformity to the superficial patterns of the mass culture. Those who conform will presumably be accepted, and those who do not, will not. This emphasis upon conformity has a stifling effect upon the society and increases intolerance on the part of those who are uneducated and provincial. The most pressing future social problems will involve acceptance of the individual by the group.

Minority-group status. The problem of minority-group status has ramifications ranging from the marginal status of some third-generation Americans to overt ethnic and racial discrimination. In each case, a self-constituted in-group rejects a designated out-group, with resultant impairment of self-feelings. Members of minority groups view themselves through the eyes of the majority, inasmuch as the latter, by definition, dominate the society and impose their definitions upon it. The Negro in America has for generations viewed his social self in terms of the white man's appraisal. The practice of segregation—whether formal or informal, legal or illegal, overt or covert—reacts negatively upon the self-attitudes of the segregated individual. The member of the majority group who holds a violent prejudice is himself marked by insecurity and self-hatred. His own self-feelings form the basis for his hatred of the minority group. In the resulting deprivation of status, the self-feeling of the minority group suffers accordingly. This situation constitutes perhaps the most widespread and corrosive social problem of our society.

SOCIAL ACTION AND SELF-OTHER PROBLEMS

Social problems are believed capable of solution by human action, whether or not any solution has demonstrably been reached. Many of the problems of an earlier day are in a fair way to ultimate elimination in the United States, although not yet in the rest of the world. Problems of the self and the other, however, are infinitely more difficult, if indeed they can ever be "solved" in any meaningful sense. Love, happiness, acceptance, and the rest are "infinite" values, which cannot be gained once and for all, as many of the "old-fashioned" material values can. The quest for self-other values is a never-ending one, and the related problems can perhaps never be completely "solved."

But this does not keep people from trying. A basic goal of the individual, in this or any other society, is to gain status from his fellows and, through reflected self-appraisals, enhance his own self-feelings. In our society, as noted, this process is more self-conscious and contrived. From play-group to the board of directors, the individual spends much of his energy in the sedulous cultivation of his social self.

Each individual works in a number of ways to solve this problem to his own satisfaction. The methods may be classified into two general types: common-sense action and scientific action. This distinction is clearly not absolute and considerable overlapping is apparent. But approaches to problems of the self and the other take two basic forms—the one spontaneous and empirical, the other derived from the sciences of human behavior.

Common-sense action. In his efforts to solve problems of the self and the other, the individual engages in a variety of activities, some deliberate and conscious and others spontaneous and haphazard. The reflected nature of the self provides the rationale behind efforts to "win friends and influence people," to sell oneself, to make oneself the center of group attention, to call the attention of the boss (or the boss' daughter) to one's qualifications, to be "popular" with the boys (or the girls), to be a charming and knowledgeable hostess, and to excel in the leisure arts of an increasingly leisure-conscious society. The individual is no longer judged by his ability as a producer but by his knowledge and skill as a consumer. Leisure is an important consumption commodity, and this consumption requires considerable *savoir faire* and *savoir vivre.*

Problems of the self and the other are at the heart of much of modern advertising copy. The unhappy person who is afflicted with halitosis, dandruff, body odor, or dishpan hands is continually exhorted (a) to beware of his self-image, and (b) to do something about it. Men are reminded that they must dress for other men as well as for women, if they are to retain their male self-image. Women need little urging to accept their obligation to look attractive, seductive, or smart, depending upon the time and circumstance. The buyer of a Cadillac is happily secure in the knowledge that he owns a prominent status-symbol, and prospective owners are lured in the same way. Other automobiles are made to look as much like a Cadillac as possible, so that their owners may bask in this reflected glory.

In the field of industrial relations, much "personnel" work is devoted to individual adjustment to the group and hence to bolstering the worker's self-feeling. In this endeavor, the personnel director makes use of some of the insights of applied psychology, but his efforts are still largely common-sense. The satisfied worker is presumably the efficient worker, and one way to bring about satisfaction is to make him happy about his role in the production process. Although recent research has questioned this all-out self-identification with the job, most programs still act as if a strong self-involvement were a vital prerequisite to industrial efficiency.

Scientific action. Much of the work in the behavorial sciences involves, directly or indirectly, social action toward the amelioration of self-other problems. To be sure, most scientific work is geared to the *understanding* of interpersonal relations rather than to the application of this knowledge to self-other problems. At some point, however, the ordered knowledge will presumably be applied to the basic values of society. Science has a reason for being that is more than idle curiosity, however remote this reason may be from the day-to-day processes of scientific investigation. In their efforts to appear "scientific," the behavioral sciences have protested too much their indifference to human values and goals. The older sciences have no such compulsion to declare themselves remote from all consideration, proximate or remote, of human welfare.

Whether they like it or not, therefore, the researches of the "pure" scientists in the behavioral area will be applied to the enhancement of social values. One of these values is the social self. Among the specific subject matters related to ordered knowledge of self-other relationships are the following: (a) the study of social interaction in the small group; (b) investigations subsumed under the general title of sociometry; (c) empirical work on dating among high-school and college students; (d) the study of the personality needs, both conscious and unconscious, that determine marital choice; (e) the extensive research in child psychology; (f) the investigation of interpersonal relations in marriage and the family; (g) the study of the relationships between culture and personality; (h) the study of social stratification; (i) the analysis of minority-group relationships; and (j) the study of ethnic, religious, and racial prejudice.

These fields of scientific investigation are by no means concerned exclusively with problems of the self and the other. But they all bear upon this field in one way or another. The most direct use of this information is made by psychiatrists and case workers, who are concerned directly with strengthening and rehabilitating individual self-feelings in an increasingly self-conscious society. Marriage counselors, clinical psychologists, clergymen, teachers, doctors, and lawyers are likewise called upon to deal with self-other problems with or without the knowledge derived from the above scientific disciplines.

In final analysis, however, therapeutic activities involve skills and insights which are related only indirectly to applied science. Those who deal with the social self require temperamental qualities which cannot be transferred. Compassion, insight, empathy, and the ability to take the role of the other are at least partially genetic, although they may be enhanced by scientific training. These practitioners will need all the help they can get. Ordered scientific knowledge will be increasingly in demand in the decades to come. In his search for self-fulfillment, man is faced with new and baffling social problems of the self and the other.

Personality is often defined as the totality of biogenic, psychogenic, and sociogenic reaction patterns that develop in human beings. And social psychologists always maintain that the human debt to sociogenic factors (social and cultural influences) in personality development is largest of all. Man, they insist, has relatively little that is fixed genetically; he is extremely flexible, having been born only with random, unco-ordinated vocal and muscular movements. Unlike animals, he remains dependent on others for a relatively long time, and this dependence provides a greater range of personality development.

For years, social psychologists have referred to human cases of extreme isolation in childhood to demonstrate how the lack of socialization and language makes personality development impossible. The cases have typically been "feral" children allegedly reared by wolves in India and subsequently recovered by people, thus making feasible concrete separation and evaluation of the biogenic and sociogenic factors which had heretofore only been analytically separable.

Ramu the Wolf Boy of India, the most recent case, had been recovered in 1954 at which time he walked like a quadruped, lapped food and water like an animal, and made incoherent vocalisms like a wild beast. Unable to sit, he cowered before humans. After seven years of human care in a hospital in Lucknow and at an estimated fifteen years of age, Ramu acquired many human personality traits. But because the years between two and nine are considered vital to personality development, there was virtually no hope that he would ever become completely human.

The difficulty in using such cases of feral children to illustrate scientifically the effect of extreme social isolation on personality development is that there has never been anything more than circumstantial evidence for the claim they were reared by animals and lacked human contact and socialization during the formative years of infancy and early childhood.

Since 1940, however, two other cases of extremely isolated children, both directly traceable from earliest infancy, have overcome the scientific inadequacies of the feral cases. In the article that follows, Kingsley Davis presents the evidence about Anna and Isabelle which reveals that extreme isolation is deleterious to personality. However, if it does not continue beyond age six it need not permanently impair socialization and personality development.

24. FINAL NOTE ON A CASE OF EXTREME ISOLATION *

KINGSLEY DAVIS

University of California, Berkeley

Early in 1940 there appeared in this *Journal* an account of a girl called Anna. She had been deprived of normal contact and had received a minimum of human care for almost the whole of her first six years of life. At that time observations were not complete and the report had a tentative character. Now, however, the girl is dead, and, with more information available, it is possible to give a fuller and more definitive description of the case from a sociological point of view.

Anna's death, caused by hemorrhagic jaundice, occurred on August 6,

* *The American Journal of Sociology,* Vol. LII, No. 5, March, 1947, pp. 432–437.

1942. Having been born on March 1 or 6, 1932, she was approximately ten and a half years of age when she died. The previous report covered her development up to the age of almost eight years; the present one recapitulates the earlier period on the basis of new evidence and then covers the last two and a half years of her life.

EARLY HISTORY

The first few days and weeks of Anna's life were complicated by frequent changes of domicile. It will be recalled that she was an illegitimate child, the second such child born to her mother, and that her grandfather, a widowed farmer in whose house her mother lived, strongly disapproved of this new evidence of the mother's indiscretion. This fact led to the baby's being shifted about.

Two weeks after being born in a nurse's private home, Anna was brought to the family farm, but the grandfather's antagonism was so great that she was shortly taken to the house of one of her mother's friends. At this time a local minister became interested in her and took her to his house with an idea of possible adoption. He decided against adoption, however, when he discovered that she had vaginitis. The infant was then taken to a children's home in the nearest large city. This agency found that at the age of only three weeks she was already in a miserable condition, being "terribly galled and otherwise in very bad shape." It did not regard her as a likely subject for adoption but took her in for a while anyway, hoping to benefit her. After Anna had spent nearly eight weeks in this place, the agency notified her mother to come to get her. The mother responded by sending a man and his wife to the children's home with a view to their adopting Anna, but they made such a poor impression on the agency that permission was refused. Later the mother came herself and took the child out of the home and then gave her to this couple. It was in the home of this pair that a social worker found the girl a short time thereafter. The social worker went to the mother's home and pleaded with Anna's grandfather to allow the mother to bring the child home. In spite of threats, he refused. The child, by then more than four months old, was next taken to another children's home in a near-by town. A medical examination at this time revealed that she had impetigo, vaginitis, umbilical hernia, and a skin rash.

Anna remained in this second children's home for nearly three weeks, at the end of which time she was transferred to a private foster-home. Since, however, the grandfather would not, and the mother could not, pay for the child's care, she was finally taken back as a last resort to the grandfather's house (at the age of five and a half months). There she remained, kept on the second floor in an attic-like room because her mother hesitated to incur the grandfather's wrath by bringing her downstairs.

The mother, a sturdy woman weighing about 180 pounds, did a man's work on the farm. She engaged in heavy work such as milking cows and tending hogs and had little time for her children. Sometimes she went out at night, in which case Anna was left entirely without attention. Ordinarily, it seems, Anna received only enough care to keep her barely alive. She appears to have been seldom moved from one position to another. Her clothing and bedding were filthy. She apparently had no instruction, no friendly attention.

It is little wonder that, when finally found and removed from the room in the grandfather's house at the age of nearly six years, the child could not talk, walk, or do anything that showed intelligence. She was in an extremely emaciated and undernourished condition, with skeleton-like legs and a bloated abdomen. She had been fed on virtually nothing except cow's milk during the years under her mother's care.

Anna's condition when found, and her subsequent improvement, have been described in the previous report. It now remains to say what happened to her after that.

LATER HISTORY

In 1939, nearly two years after being discovered, Anna had progressed, as previously reported, to the point where she could walk, understand simple commands, feed herself, achieve some neatness, remember people, etc. But she still did not speak, and, though she was much more like a normal infant of something over one year of age in mentality, she was far from normal for her age.

On August 30, 1939, she was taken to a private home for retarded children, leaving the county home where she had been for more than a year and a half. In her new setting she made some further progress, but not a great deal. In a report of an examination made November 6 of the same year, the head of the institution pictured the child as follows:

> Anna walks about aimlessly, makes periodic rhythmic motions of her hands, and, at intervals, makes guttural and sucking noises. She regards her hands as if she had seen them for the first time. It was impossible to hold her attention for more than a few seconds at a time—not because of distraction due to external stimuli but because of her inability to concentrate. She ignored the task in hand to gaze vacantly about the room. Speech is entirely lacking. Numerous unsuccessful attempts have been made with her in the hope of developing initial sounds. I do not believe that this failure is due to negativism or deafness but that she is not sufficiently developed to accept speech at this time. . . . The prognosis is not favorable. . . .

More than five months later, on April 25, 1940, a clinical psychologist, the late Professor Francis N. Maxfield, examined Anna and reported the following: large for her age; hearing "entirely normal"; vision apparently normal; able to climb stairs; speech in the "babbling stage" and "promise for developing intelligible speech later seems to be good." He said further that "on the Merrill-Palmer scale she made a mental score of 19 months. On the Vineland social maturity scale she made a score of 23 months."

Professor Maxfield very sensibly pointed out that prognosis is difficult in such cases of isolation. "It is very difficult to take scores on tests standardized under average conditions of environment and experience," he wrote, "and interpret them in a case where environment and experience have been so unusual." With this warning he gave it as his opinion at that time that Anna would eventually "attain an adult mental level of six or seven years."

The school for retarded children, on July 1, 1941, reported that Anna had reached 46 inches in height and weighed 60 pounds. She could bounce and catch a ball and was said to conform to group socialization, though as a follower rather than a leader. Toilet habits were firmly established. Food habits were normal, except that she still used a spoon as her sole implement. She could dress herself except for fastening her clothes. Most remarkable of all, she had finally begun to develop speech. She was characterized as being at about the two-year level in this regard. She could call attendants by name and bring in one when she was asked to. She had a few complete sentences to express her wants. The report concluded that there was nothing peculiar about her, except that she was feeble-minded—"probably congenital in type."

A final report from the school, made on June 22, 1942, and evidently the last report before the girl's death, pictured only a slight advance over that given above. It said that Anna could follow directions, string beads, identify a few colors, build with blocks, and differentiate between attractive and unattractive pictures. She had a good sense of rhythm and loved a doll. She talked mainly in phrases but would repeat words and try to carry on a conversation. She was clean about clothing. She habitually washed her hands and brushed her teeth. She would try to help other children. She walked well and could run fairly well, though clumsily. Although easily excited, she had a pleasant disposition.

INTERPRETATION

Such was Anna's condition just before her death. It may seem as if she had not made much progress, but one must remember the condition in which she had been found. One must recall that she had no glimmering of speech, absolutely no ability to walk, no sense of gesture, not the least capacity to feed herself even when the food was put in front of her, and no comprehension of cleanliness. She was so apathetic that it was hard to tell whether or not she could hear. And all this at the age of nearly six years. Compared with this condition, her capacities at the time of her death seem striking indeed, though they do not amount to much more than a two-and-a-half-year mental level. One conclusion therefore seems safe, namely, that her isolation prevented a considerable amount of mental development that was undoubtedly part of her capacity. Just what her original capacity was, of course, is hard to say; but her development after her period of confinement (including the ability to walk and run, to play, dress, fit into a social situation, and, above all, to speak) shows that she had at least this much capacity—capacity that never could have been realized in her original condition of isolation.

A further question is this: What would she have been like if she had received a normal upbringing from the moment of birth? A definitive answer would have been impossible in any case, but even an approximate answer is made difficult by her early death. If one assumes, as was tentatively surmised in the previous report, that it is "almost impossible for any child to learn to speak, think, and act like a normal person after a long period of early isolation," it seems likely that Anna might have had a normal or near-normal capacity, genetically speaking. On the other hand, it was pointed out that Anna represented "a marginal case, [because] she was discovered before she had reached six years of age," an age "young enough to allow for some plasticity." While admitting, then, that Anna's isolation *may* have been the major cause (and was certainly a minor cause) of her lack of rapid mental process during the four and a half years following her rescue from neglect, it is necessary to entertain the hypothesis that she was congenitally deficient.

In connection with this hypothesis, one suggestive though by no means conclusive circumstance needs consideration, namely, the mentality of Anna's forebears. Information on this subject is easier to obtain, as one might guess, on the mother's than on the father's side. Anna's maternal grandmother, for example, is said to have been college educated and wished to have her children receive a good education, but her husband, Anna's stern grandfather, apparently a shrewd, hard-driving, calculating farmowner, was so penurious that her ambitions in this direction were thwarted. Under the circumstances her daughter (Anna's mother) managed, despite having to do hard work on the farm, to complete the eighth grade in a country school. Even so, however, the daughter was evidently not very smart. "A schoolmate of [Anna's mother] stated that she was retarded in school work; was very gullible at this age; and that her morals even at this time were discussed by other students." Two tests administered to her on March 4, 1938, when she was thirty-two years of age, showed that she was mentally deficient. On the Stanford Revision of the Binet-Simon Scale her performance was equivalent to that of a child of eight years, giving her an I.Q. of 50 and indicating mental deficiency of "middle-grade moron type."

As to the identity of Anna's father, the most persistent theory holds that he was an old man about seventy-four years of age at the time of the girl's birth. If he was the one, there is no indication of mental or other biological deficiency, whatever one may think of his morals. However, someone else may actually have been the father.

To sum up: Anna's heredity is the kind that *might* have given rise to innate mental deficiency, though not necessarily.

COMPARISON WITH ANOTHER CASE

Perhaps more to the point than speculations about Anna's ancestry would be a case for comparison. If a child could be discovered who had been isolated about the same length of time as Anna but had achieved a much quicker recovery and a greater mental development, it would be a stronger indication that Anna was deficient to start with.

Such a case does exist. It is the case of a girl found at about the same time as Anna and under strikingly similar circumstances. A full description of the details of this case has not been published, but, in addition to newspaper reports, an excellent preliminary account by a speech specialist, Dr. Marie K. Mason, who played an important role in the handling of the child, has appeared. Also the late Dr. Francis N. Maxfield, clinical psychologist at Ohio State University, as was Dr. Mason, has written an as yet unpublished but penetrating analysis of the case. Some of his observations have been included in Professor Robert M. Zingg's book on feral man. The following discussion is drawn mainly from these enlightening materials. The writer, through the kindness of Professors Mason and Maxfield, did have a chance to observe the girl in April, 1940, and to discuss the features of her case with them.

Born apparently one month later than Anna, the girl in question, who has been given the pseudonym Isabelle, was discovered in November, 1938, nine months after the discovery of Anna. At the time she was found she was approximately six and a half years of age. Like Anna, she was an illegitimate child and had been kept in seclusion for that reason. Her mother was a deaf-mute, having become so at the age of two, and it appears that she and Isabelle had spent most of their time together in a dark room shut off from the rest of the mother's family. As a result Isabelle had no chance to develop speech; when she communicated with her mother, it was by means of gestures. Lack of sunshine and inadequacy of diet had caused Isabelle to become rachitic. Her legs in particular were affected; they "were so bowed that as she stood erect the soles of her shoes came nearly flat together, and she got about with a skittering gait." Her behavior toward strangers, especially men, was almost that of a wild animal, manifesting much fear and hostility. In lieu of speech she made only a strange croaking sound. In many ways she acted like an infant. "She was apparently utterly unaware of relationships of any kind. When presented with a ball for the first time, she held it in the palm of her hand, then reached out and stroked my face with it. Such behavior is comparable to that of a child of six months." At first it was even hard to tell whether or not she could hear, so unused were her senses. Many of her actions resembled those of deaf children.

It is small wonder that, once it was established that she could hear, specialists working with her believed her to be feeble-minded. Even on nonverbal tests her performance was so low as to promise little for the future. Her first score on the Stanford-Binet was 19 months, practically at the zero point of the scale. On the Vineland social maturity scale her first score was 39, representing an age level of two and a half years. "The general impression was that she was wholly uneducable and that any attempt to teach her to speak, after so long a period of silence, would meet with failure."

In spite of this interpretation, the individuals in charge of Isabelle launched a systematic and skillful program of training. It seemed hopeless at first. The approach had to be through pantomime and dramatization, suitable to an infant. It required one week of intensive effort before she even made her first attempt at vocalization. Gradually she began to respond, however, and, after the first hurdles had at least been overcome, a curious thing happened. She went through the usual stages of learning characteristic of the years from one to six not only in proper succession but far more rapidly than normal. In a little over two months after her first vocalization she was putting sentences together. Nine months after that she could identify words and sentences on the printed page, could write well, could add to ten, and could retell a story after hearing it. Seven months beyond this point she had a vocabulary of 1,500–2,000 words and was asking complicated questions. Starting from an educational level of between one and three years (depending on what aspect one considers), she had reached a normal level by the time she was eight and a half years old. In short, she covered in two years the stages of learning that ordinarily require six. Or, to put it another way, her I.Q. trebled in a year and a half. The speed with which she reached the normal level of mental development seems analogous to the recovery of body weight in a growing child after an illness, the recovery being achieved by an extra fast rate of growth for a period after the illness until normal weight for the given age is again attained.

When the writer saw Isabelle a year and a half after her discovery, she gave him the impression of being a very bright, cheerful, energetic little girl. She spoke well, walked and ran without trouble, and sang with gusto and accuracy. Today she is over fourteen years old and has passed the sixth grade in a public school. Her teachers say that she participates in all school activities as normally as other children. Though older than her classmates, she has fortunately not physically matured too far beyond their level.

Clearly the history of Isabelle's development is different from that of Anna's. In both cases there was an exceedingly low, or rather blank, intellectual level to begin with. In both cases it seemed that the girl might be congenitally feeble-minded. In both a considerably higher level was reached later on. But the Ohio girl achieved a normal mentality within two years, whereas Anna was still marked inadequate at the end of four and a half years. This difference in achievement may suggest that Anna had less initial capacity. But an alternative hypothesis is possible.

One should remember that Anna never received the prolonged and expert attention that Isabelle received. The result of such attention, in the case of the Ohio girl, was to give her speech at an early stage, and her subsequent rapid development seems to have been a consequence of that. "Until Isabelle's speech and language development, she had all the characteristics of a feeble-minded child." Had Anna, who, from the standpoint of psychometric tests and early history, closely resembled this girl at the start, been given a mastery of speech at an earlier point by intensive training, her subsequent development might have been much more rapid.

The hypothesis that Anna began with a sharply inferior mental capacity is therefore not established. Even if she were deficient to start with, we have no way of knowing how much so. Under ordinary conditions she might have been a dull normal or, like her mother, a moron. Even after the blight of her isolation, if she had lived to maturity, she might have finally reached virtually the full level of her capacity, whatever it may have been. That her isolation did have a profound effect upon her mentality, there can be no doubt. This is proved by the substantial degree of change during the four and a half years following her rescue.

Consideration of Isabelle's case serves to show, as Anna's case does not clearly show, that isolation up to the age of six, with failure to acquire any form of speech and hence failure to grasp nearly the whole world of cultural meaning, does not preclude the subsequent acquisition of these. Indeed, there seems to be a process of accelerated recovery in which the child goes through the mental stages at a more rapid rate than would be the case in normal development. Just what would be the maximum age at which a person could remain isolated and still retain the capacity for full cultural acquisition is hard to say. Almost certainly it would not be as high as age fifteen; it might possibly be as low as age ten. Undoubtedly various individuals would differ considerably as to the exact age.

Anna's is not an ideal case for showing the effects of extreme isolation, partly because she was possibly deficient to begin with, partly because she did not receive the best training available, and partly because she did not live long enough. Nevertheless, her case is instructive when placed in the record with numerous other cases of extreme isolation. This and the previous article about her are meant to place her in the record. It is to be hoped that other cases will be described in the scientific literature as they are discovered (as unfortunately they will be), for only in these rare cases of extreme isolation is it possible "to observe *concretely separated* two factors in the development of human personality which are always otherwise only analytically separated, the biogenic and the sociogenic factors."

If "life is with people" in the sense that socialization molds personality more than any other process, it can be deduced theoretically that differences in the patterns of social and cultural training produce different patterns of personality in children. Social class and color differences have long been supected of carrying considerable weight in defining and systematizing different learning environments for children.

Two researchable questions along these lines are immediately suggested. The first is: What are the different training demands exerted on white and Negro children and on lower- as distinguished from middle-class children in both races?

The second question is: What is the extent of difference in the time of beginning, the length of, and other conditions surrounding the training in each instance?

In 1946, Allison Davis and Robert J. Havighurst reported the methodology and findings of one of the pioneer research projects exploring these questions. Conducted in Chicago, the study investigated differences in child-rearing practices according to social class and color, and then it attempted to relate these practices to socialization in general. The major finding was that there are, in fact, considerable class differences in child-rearing practices, but differences between Negroes and whites of the same class are considerably smaller.

One strategic device in sociological research for validating the findings of a specific empirical study is to replicate the study elsewhere. Professors Davis and Havighurst's exploration of social class and color differences in child rearing in Chicago created such a stir in the world of social science that it was almost inevitable that sooner or later a comparable study would be made by other social psychologists.

In the article that follows, the Harvard replication in Boston and the original Chicago study are compared. They show agreements principally in five respects: greater severity of punishment by the lower class in toilet training, higher educational expectations by the middle class, more freedom by the middle class in daytime mobility, and no class difference in care given by the father and in display of aggression by children at home.

Yet there were substantial disagreements between the two studies in other respects. Professors Havighurst and Davis suggest that one reason for this may be the fact that the two studies were not strictly comparable in methodology, such as the sampling, and that changes in child rearing between 1943 and 1952, the years in which the first and second studies were conducted, may account for other disagreements.

25. A COMPARISON OF THE CHICAGO AND HARVARD STUDIES OF SOCIAL CLASS DIFFERENCES IN CHILD REARING *

ROBERT J. HAVIGHURST AND ALLISON DAVIS
University of Chicago

In 1951–52 Robert R. Sears and his colleagues made a study of social class and child-rearing practices which is to some extent comparable with a study made in 1943 by Davis and Havighurst. The results of the two studies agree in some respects and disagree in others. Consequently, it seems useful to present such results of the two studies as are comparable, so as to permit readers to make their own comparisons and draw their own conclusions.

The Samples. The Harvard interviews were held with mothers of kinder-

* *American Sociological Review,* Vol. 20, No. 4, August, 1955, pp. 438–442.

garten children and dealt with the training of the kindergarten child only. The Chicago interviews were held with mothers of pre-school age children but dealt with every child of the mother. The Chicago study dealt with the 107 middle- and 167 lower-class white children of 48 middle- and 52 lower-class white mothers. The Harvard study, on the other hand, dealt with 201 middle-class and 178 lower-class white mothers, and with the same numbers of children. The interviewers were college-educated women who were specifically trained to conduct interviews with the particular instrument used in each study.

In order to make the data more nearly comparable, the Chicago data which involved all the children of a mother have been restudied by taking the one child nearest the age of 5. This makes the Chicago medians somewhat different, but not greatly so, from those that appear in the original article. Also, to make the data more comparable the Harvard data on the age of beginning and completing weaning and toilet training have been reworked to show medians rather than means.

TABLE 1. Nationality * of Mothers, in Percentages

	Chicago		*Boston*	
Nationality Group	*M*	*L*	*M*	*L*
American	...	...	56	43
British, or Canadian	...	...	7	17
American, British, or Canadian	56	11	...	...
Irish	4	19	6	6
Italian, Spanish, Greek	0	8	2	17
Russian, Bulgarian, Yugoslavian, Hungarian, Polish, Lithuanian	27	30	23	11
German, Dutch or Scandinavian	15	15	4	3
Mexican	0	17	0	0
Not ascertained	0	0	2	3
Jewish	27 †	2 †	32 †	9 †
Number of mothers	48	52	198	174

* Nationality means birthplace of mother's parents.
† Included in nationality groups listed above.

As would be expected, the nationality backgrounds of the two samples are different. Nationality was defined as the country of birth of the mother's parents. If one parent was foreign-born, the mother was assigned to a foreign nationality. Table 1 shows the ethnic composition of the two samples. The occupational status of the fathers in the two samples is shown in Table 2, based on the Warner scale of occupations. The Boston sample of lower status parents averages somewhat higher in status than the Chicago sample, due to the inclusion in the Boston lower status sample of a number of lower-middle people.

Only 27 percent of the Boston lower status sample are in the bottom two occupational rankings, while 47 percent of the Chicago sample are at these two lowest levels. Therefore, the two lower status samples are not easily comparable. However, the report of the Boston study indicates that there was little difference between the upper and lower halves of the lower status sample in child-rearing behavior, and the same kinds of differences between the Chicago and Boston studies would have been found if the Boston lower status sample had been restricted to the lowest occupational levels.

TABLE 2. Occupational Status * of Fathers, in Percentages

Occupational Rank	*Total Group*	*Chicago*		*Total Group*	*Boston*	
		M	*L*		*M*	*L*
1	21	44	0	23	44	...
2	17	35	0	17	31	...
3	4	8	0	21	24	17
4	19	13	24	9	1	20
5	15	0	29	17	...	36
6	21	0	41	8	...	17
7	3	0	6	5	...	10
Number of fathers	100	48	52	372	198	174

* Based on Warner's Occupational Rating Scale.

The Boston sample was made up of families having a child in kindergarten in the public schools of two sections of the Greater Boston metropolitan area. Interviews were actually obtained with 80 percent of the mothers of kindergarten children in these particular schools. The Chicago sample of middle-class mothers came from two nursery schools on the South Side of Chicago and from a middle-class apartment area on the North Side. The Chicago lower-class mothers came from three areas on the South Side of Chicago, and most of them did not have children in nursery schools. Interviews were secured with them by passing from one family to another in areas of poor housing. Clearly the Chicago sample is far from a random sample. The Chicago study was aimed primarily at studying individual differences in personality among children in a family and relating them to the children's experience in the family; and for this purpose it did not seem necessary to have representative social class samples. The social class comparisons were initially thought of as a by-product of the study. The Boston sample would seem in some respects to be more representative, although its being limited to mothers of children in public schools caused the exclusion of Catholic mothers who send their children to parochial schools. The Chicago sample had a number of such Catholic mothers, as well as a few upper-middle-class mothers whose children were in a private school.

Feeding and Weaning. Table 3 summarizes the comparisons on feeding and weaning, which appear to indicate the following: (1) a regional difference in the amount of breast feeding; (2) a tendency for more breast feeding by lower-class Chicago mothers than by either group of Boston mothers; (3) middle-class Chicago mothers completed weaning their children earlier than middle-class Boston mothers; (4) a strong tendency for lower-class Chicago mothers to use more of a self-demand schedule in feeding than was used by either Boston group. It is in the area of feeding and weaning that the two studies differ most.

TABLE 3. Feeding and Weaning of Children

	Chicago		*Boston*	
	M	*L*	*M*	*L*
Percent of children ever breast-fed	83	83	43	37
Percent of children breast-fed only	6 *	17 *	...	...
Median duration of breast-feeding (for those ever breast-fed)	3.4 mo.	3.5 mo.	2.4 mo.	2.1 mo.
Median age at beginning weaning	...	...	9.1 mo.	8.2 mo.
Median age at completion of weaning	10.3 mo.*	12.3 mo.*	12.0 mo.	12.6 mo.
Percent of children weaned sharply	20	15	...	...
Mean score, severity of weaning (1:mild; 9:severe)	...	...	4.9	4.9
Percent of children fed "when hungry"	4 *	44 *	...	...
Mean score, scheduling of feeding (1:complete self-demand; 9:rigid schedule)	...	...	5.1	4.6

* Difference significant at the 5 percent level or lower.

Toilet Training. Table 4 compares the data on bowel training. Chicago middle-class mothers began bowel training earlier than lower-class mothers, while there was no class difference among Boston mothers in this respect. On the other hand, Boston lower-class mothers reported completion of bowel training at an earlier age than middle-class mothers, while there was no class difference among Chicago mothers. In both studies lower-class mothers were reported to be more severe in punishment in relation to toilet training.

Restrictions on Movements of Children Outside of Home. The Chicago mothers reported as follows:

Age at which boys and girls might go to the movies alone—lower class reliably earlier.

Time at which boys and girls are expected in at night—middle class reliably earlier.

Age at which boys and girls go downtown alone—middle class reliably earlier.

The only Harvard data which are comparable indicate a tendency (not quite significant) for middle-class children to be allowed to go farther away from the house during the day. This is probably in agreement with the Chicago finding of age at which children were allowed to go downtown alone.

TABLE 4. Toilet Training

	Chicago		*Boston*	
	M	*L*	*M*	*L*
Median age of beginning of bowel training	7.5 mo.*	9.1 mo.*	9.6 mo.	9.9 mo.
Median age of completion of bowel training	17.8 mo.	18.2 mo.	18.6 mo.*	16.4 mo.*
Methods of training children when they soil after training was begun; percent of mothers				
Slap or spank or whip	13 *	40 *		
Mother shows disgust	2 *	21 *		
Scold	11	14		
Talk with or reason with	22	14		
Do nothing, ignore it	51 *	11 *		
Number of mothers	48	52		
Mean score, severity of toilet training (1:mild, 9:severe)	. . .	. . .	3.8 *	4.6 *

* Significant at 5 percent level or lower.

Expectations for Child to Help in Home. Table 5 summarizes the comparative data on what is expected of children in helping at home. None of the Boston class differences is reliable, while the Chicago data indicate a tendency for middle-class mothers to expect children to be helpful earlier than lower-class mothers do.

Parent-child Relations. There were a number of possible comparisons of parent-child relations, which will be summarized briefly. The amount of caretaking of children by fathers shows no class difference in either study. But when the nature of affectional relationships between father and children is evaluated, the lower-class father is found to be reliably less affectionate in the Boston study, while in the Chicago study the lower-class father "plays with" his children more, but the middle-class father teaches and reads to his children more. The studies are somewhat comparable on the matter of the display of aggression in the home (excluding aggression toward siblings). There are no reliable class differences in either study in this respect.

TABLE 5. Requirements for Children to Help in Home

	Chicago	
	M	*L*
	Percent of Mothers	
Age child expected to begin helping at home		
2-5 years	58 *	35 *
6-8	32	45
9 years or more	10	20
Number of mothers reporting	41	51
	Chicago	
Age child expected to help with younger children	Younger *	Older *
Age girls expected to begin to cook	Younger *	Older *
Age child expected to dress self	No class difference	
Average age at which girls expected to help with dishwashing	No class difference	
	Boston	
	M	*L*
Percent of mothers who have given child at least one regular job to do around the house	38	40
Mean score, requirements for child to be neat and orderly in house, e.g., hang up own clothes, etc. (1:no requirements, 9:strict requirements)	5.7	5.6

* Class differences reliable at 5 percent level or lower.

Summary of Agreements between the Studies. It will be seen that there are both agreements and disagreements between the results of the Chicago and Boston studies. The principal agreements between the two studies are the following:

Lower class are more severe in punishment in toilet-training.

Middle class have higher educational expectations of their children.

No class difference in amount of care given children by father.

No class difference in display of aggression by children in the home (excluding aggression toward siblings) (data not shown here, but available to the authors).

Middle-class children allowed more freedom of movement away from home during the day.

Discussion of Disagreements between the Studies. In discussing the disagreements between the two studies it seems important to determine to what extent the Boston study is a replication of the Chicago study. The interviewing methods used were rather similar, and some nearly identical questions were asked. However, the two samples are not strictly comparable. As we learn more about social structure in the United States, it becomes clear that one should not attempt to generalize concerning child-rearing to an entire social class from a sample in one part of the country, even if it is a representative sample. There may be cultural differences between two samples of apparently similar occupational status, due to regional differences, religious differences, and differences of nationality background, all of which may have been operating in the studies being considered here. Furthermore, there may be differences between different occupational groups within the same social class.

Of considerable importance is the limitation imposed by the method of securing data. To an unknown extent, mothers give what they regard as the "expected" or "appropriate" answers when telling how they raise their children. For instance, in Table 6 it will be seen that the Boston lower-class

TABLE 6. Aggression Control

	Chicago	
	M	*L*
Percent of families where mothers let children "fight each other so long as they do not hurt each other badly"	82 *	42 *
	Boston	
	M	*L*
Mean score, permissiveness for aggression (1:not at all permissive, 9:entirely permissive)		
Toward siblings	4.7	4.5
Toward other children in the neighborhood	5.1 *	4.6 *
Toward parents	3.6 *	2.8 *

* Difference significant at 5 percent level.

mothers report themselves as less permissive of aggression by their children toward other children in the neighborhood. But this is difficult to fit with the fact that lower-class children fight more than middle-class children do—a fact on which observers of the social behavior of children agree. Perhaps the fact that mothers were talking about young children (5-year-olds) was significant here; or perhaps the greater frequency of fighting by lower-class children actually brings out more of a feeling on the part of their mothers that they should restrain their children's aggression.

It is conceivable, for instance, that middle-class mothers are defensive about their *severity* and therefore claim to be less punitive or threatening than in practice they are observed to be; whereas lower-class mothers are defensive about their children being *dirty* and *violent* and therefore claim to be more

TABLE 7. Techniques of Discipline

	Chicago	
	M	*L*
Percent of mothers mentioning various procedures as "most successful ways of getting children to obey"		
Reward or praise	78 *	53 *
Reason	53	57
Threaten or scold	53	55
Deprive of meal	0	6
Isolate	13	17
Stand in corner, sit in chair	13	19
Spank or whip	53	51
Number of mothers	45	47
	Boston	
	M	*L*
Mean score, extent of use of each technique (1:no use, 9: extensive use)		
Reward	4.6	4.9
Praise	4.8	4.8
Reason	5.0	4.8
Scolding statements involving withdrawal of love	6.4 *	6.0 *
Deprivation of privileges	4.6 *	5.1 *
Isolation	5.7	5.5
Physical punishment	3.9 *	4.8 *

* Difference significant at 5 percent level.

TABLE 8. Agents of Discipline, in Percentages of Families

	Chicago	
	M	*L*
Who punishes children most?		
Father	2	8
Mother	81	85
Both the same	17	8
	Boston	
	M	*L*
When both parents are present, which one disciplines the child?		
Father	29	32
Mother	39	42
Both or either	32	26

punitive with regard to their children's soiling and fighting than such parents are observed to be. At any rate, this re-enforces the conviction of the present writers that the interview is not nearly so good as participant observation for securing data both on the behavior and the attitudes of parents toward their children.

TABLE 9. Educational Expectations for Children

	Chicago		*Boston*	
	M	*L*	*M*	*L*
Percent of mothers desiring for child				
Grammar school only	0	0	0	0
High school only	7 *	35 *	3 *	23 *
High school, reservations (unless child very anxious for college, earns own way)			6 *	25 *
College, with reservations (unless child doesn't want to go, or financial reverses)			28	32
College	93 *	65 *	52 *	17 *
Graduate school (including medicine, law)			10	1

* Class differences highly significant.

The disagreements between the findings of the two studies are substantial and important. The interviewing seems to have been competent in both studies. Inadequacies of sampling in both studies may be a source of at least some of the differences. Changes in child-rearing ideology between 1943 and 1952 may be in some measure responsible for the differences. The problem of interpreting the statements of mothers answering identical questions about their children who are exposed to quite different environmental stimulation is a major one.

Modern society's complexity, heterogeneity, and dynamism are bound to be reflected, in the long run, in blatant contradictions and conflicts in the statuses and roles of the individual personality. There is no clearer manifestation of the dilemma confronting people in their personal lives as a consequence of social and cultural cross-pressures than that of young adult women of college age in American society.

College girls commonly face mutually exclusive expectations in their sex roles. The families and male friends of these girls are especially effective agents through which they meet these inconsistencies. On the one hand, they are expected to play the "modern" role; this calls for an orientation toward a professional career, competitiveness, intellectuality, and sexless equality of opportunity and expression. But there is an equally strong social and cultural compulsion for college girls to play the traditional "feminine" role, displaying inferiority and submissiveness to the male, emotionality, and a goal of marriage and housekeeping.

Some girls play vacillating roles, corresponding to the pressures of the moment. All suffer from the insecurity that is the personal manifestation of cultural conflict. In the following article, Mirra Komarovsky discusses these points in the context of her study of college seniors. She concludes that the dilemma will endure until such time that the "adult sex roles of women are redefined in greater harmony with the socioeconomic and ideological character of modern society."

26. CULTURAL CONTRADICTIONS AND SEX ROLES *

MIRRA KOMAROVSKY
Barnard College

Profound changes in the roles of women during the past century have been accompanied by innumerable contradictions and inconsistencies. With our rapidly changing and highly differentiated culture, with migrations and multiplied social contacts, the stage is set for myriads of combinations of incongruous elements. Cultural norms are often functionally unsuited to the social situations to which they apply. Thus they may deter an individual from a course of action which would serve his own, and society's, interests best. Or, if behavior contrary to the norm is engaged in, the individual may suffer from guilt over violating mores which no longer serve any socially useful end. Sometimes culturally defined roles are adhered to in the face of new conditions without a conscious realization of the discrepancies involved. The reciprocal actions dictated by the roles may be at variance with those demanded by the actual situation. This may result in an imbalance of privileges and obligations or in some frustration of basic interests.

Again, problems arise because changes in the mode of life have created new situations which have not as yet been defined by culture. Individuals left thus without social guidance tend to act in terms of egotistic or "short-run hedonistic" motives which at times defeat their own long-term interests or create conflict with others. The precise obligation of a gainfully employed wife toward the support of the family is one such undefined situation.

Finally, a third mode of discrepancy arises in the existence of incompatible cultural definitions of the same social situation, such as the clash of "old-fashioned" and "radical" mores, of religion and law, of norms of economic and familial institutions.

The problems raised by these discrepancies are social problems in the sense that they engender mental conflict or social conflict or otherwise frustrate some basic interest of large segments of the population.

* *The American Journal of Sociology,* Vol. LII, No. 3, November, 1946, pp. 184–189.

This article sets forth in detail the nature of certain incompatible sex roles imposed by our society upon the college woman. It is based on data collected in 1942 and 1943. Members of an undergraduate course on the family were asked for two successive years to submit autobiographical documents focused on the topic; 73 were collected. In addition, 80 interviews, lasting about an hour each, were conducted with every member of a course in social psychology of the same institution—making a total of 153 documents ranging from a minimum of five to a maximum of thirty typewritten pages.

The generalization emerging from these documents is the existence of serious contradictions between two roles present in the social environment of the college woman. The goals set by each role are mutually exclusive, and the fundamental personality traits each evokes are at points diametrically opposed, so that what are assets for one become liabilities for the other, and the full realization of one role threatens defeat in the other.

One of these roles may be termed the "feminine" role. While there are a number of permissive variants of the feminine role for women of college age (the "good sport," the "glamour girl," the "young lady," the domestic "home girl," etc.), they have a common core of attributes defining the proper attitudes to men, family, work, love, etc., and a set of personality traits often described with reference to the male sex role as "not as dominant, or aggressive as men" or "more emotional, sympathetic."

The other and more recent role is, in a sense, no *sex* role at all, because it partly obliterates the differentiation in sex. It demands of the woman much the same virtues, patterns of behavior, and attitude that it does of the men of a corresponding age. We shall refer to this as the "modern" role.

Both roles are present in the social environment of these women throughout their lives, though, as the precise content of each sex role varies with age, so does the nature of their clashes change from one stage to another. In the period under discussion the conflict between the two roles apparently centers about academic work, social life, vocational plans, excellence in specific fields of endeavor, and a number of personality traits.

One manifestation of the problem is in the inconsistency of the goals set for the girl by her family.

Forty, or 26 percent, of the respondents expressed some grievance against their families for failure to confront them with clear-cut and consistent goals. The majority, 74 percent, denied having had such experiences. One student writes:

> How am I to pursue any course singlemindedly when some way along the line a person I respect is sure to say, "You are on the wrong track and are wasting your time." Uncle John telephones every Sunday morning. His first question is: "Did you go out last night?" He would think me a "grind" if I were to stay home Saturday night to finish a term paper. My father expects me to get an "A" in every subject and is disappointed by a "B." He says I have plenty of time for social life.

Mother says, "That 'A' in Philosophy is very nice dear. But please don't become so deep that no man will be good enough for you." And, finally, Aunt Mary's line is careers for women. "Prepare yourself for some profession. This is the only way to insure yourself independence and an interesting life. You have plenty of time to marry."

A Senior writes:

I get a letter from my mother at least three times a week. One week her letters will say, "Remember that this is your last year at college. Subordinate everything to your studies. You must have a good record to secure a job." The next week her letters are full of wedding news. This friend of mine got married; that one is engaged; my young cousin's wedding is only a week off. When, my mother wonders, will I make up my mind? Surely, I wouldn't want to be the only unmarried one in my group. It is high time, she feels, that I give some thought to it.

A student reminisces:

All through high school my family urged me to work hard because they wished me to enter a first-rate college. At the same time they were always raving about a girl schoolmate who lived next door to us. How pretty and sweet she was, how popular, and what taste in clothes! Couldn't I also pay more attention to my appearance and to social life? They were overlooking the fact that this carefree friend of mine had little time left for school work and had failed several subjects. It seemed that my family had expected me to become Eve Curie and Hedy Lamarr wrapped up in one.

Another comments:

My mother thinks that it is very nice to be smart in college but only if it doesn't take too much effort. She always tells me not to be too intellectual on dates, to be clever in a light sort of way. My father, on the other hand, wants me to study law. He thinks that if I applied myself I could make an excellent lawyer and keeps telling me that I am better fitted for this profession than my brother.

Another writes:

One of my two brothers writes: "Cover up that high forehead and act a little dumb once in a while"; while the other always urges upon me the importance of rigorous scholarship.

The students testified to a certain bewilderment and confusion caused by the failure on the part of the family to smooth the passage from one role to another, especially when the roles involved were contradictory. It seemed to some of them that they had awakened one morning to find their world upside down: what had hitherto evoked praise and rewards from relatives, now suddenly aroused censure. A student recollects:

I could match my older brother in skating, sledding, riflery, ball, and many of the other games we played. He enjoyed teaching me and took great pride in my accomplishments. Then one day it all changed. He must have suddenly become conscious of the fact that girls ought to be feminine. I was walking with him, proud to be able to make long strides and keep up with his long-legged steps when he turned to me in annoyance, "Can't you walk like a lady?" I still remember feeling hurt and bewildered by his scorn, when I had been led to expect approval.

Once during her freshman year in college, after a delightful date, a student wrote her brother with great elation:

"What a wonderful evening at ——— fraternity house! You would be proud of me, Johnny! I won all ping-pong games but one!"

"For heaven's sake," came the reply, "when will you grow up? Don't you know that a boy likes to think he is better than a girl? Give him a little competition, sure, but miss a few serves in the end. Should you join the Debate Club? By all means, but don't practice too much on the boys." Believe me I was stunned by this letter, but then I saw that he was right. To be a success in the dorms one must date, to date one must not win too many ping-pong games. At first I resented this bitterly. But now I am more or less used to it and live in hope of one day meeting a man who is my superior so that I may be my natural self.

It is the parents and not the older sibling who reversed their expectations in the following excerpt:

All through grammar school and high school my parents led me to feel that to do well in school was my chief responsibility. A good report card, an election to student office, these were the news Mother bragged about in telephone conversations with her friends. But recently they suddenly got worried about me: I don't pay enough attention to social life, a woman needs *some* education but not that much. They are disturbed by my determination to go to the School of Social Work. Why my ambitions should surprise them after they have exposed me for four years to some of the most inspired and stimulating social scientists in the country, I can't imagine. They have some mighty strong arguments on their side. What is the use, they say, of investing years in training for a profession, only to drop it in a few years? Chances of meeting men are slim in this profession. Besides, I may become so preoccupied with it as to sacrifice social life. The next few years are, after all, the proper time to find a mate. But the urge to apply what I have learned, and the challenge of this profession is so strong that I shall go on despite the family opposition.

The final excerpt illustrates both the sudden transition of roles and the ambiguity of standards:

I major in English composition. This is not a completely "approved" field for girls so I usually just say "English." An English Literature major is quite liked and approved by boys. Somehow it is lumped with all the other arts and even has a little glamour. But a composition major is a girl to beware of because she supposedly will notice all your grammar mistakes, look at your letters too critically, and consider your ordinary speech and conversation as too crude.

I also work for a big metropolitan daily as a correspondent in the city room. I am well liked there and may possibly stay as a reporter after graduation in February. I have had several spreads [stories running to more than eight or ten inches of space], and this is considered pretty good for a college correspondent. Naturally, I was elated and pleased at such breaks, and as far as the city room is concerned I'm off to a very good start on a career that is hard for a man to achieve and even harder for a woman. General reporting is still a man's work in the opinion of most people. I have a lot of acclaim but also criticism, and I find it confusing and difficult to be praised for being clever and working hard and then, when my efforts promise to be successful, to be condemned and criticized for being unfeminine and ambitious.

Here are a few of these reactions:

My father: "I don't like this newspaper setup at all. The people you meet are making you less interested in marriage than ever. You're getting too educated and intellectual to be attractive to men."

My mother: "I don't like your attitude toward people. The paper is making you too analytical and calculating. Above all, you shouldn't sacrifice your education and career for marriage."

A lieutenant with two years of college: "It pleased me greatly to hear about your news assignment—good girl."

A Navy pilot with one year of college: "Undoubtedly, I'm old-fashioned, but I could never expect or feel right about a girl giving up a very promising or interesting future to hang around waiting for me to finish college. Nevertheless, congratulations on your job on the paper. Where in the world do you get that wonderful energy? Anyway I know you were thrilled at getting it and feel very glad for you. I've an idea that it means the same to you as that letter saying 'report for active duty' meant to me."

A graduate metallurgist now a private in the Army: "It was good to hear that you got that break with the paper. I am sure that talent will prove itself and that you will go far. But not too far, as I don't think you should become a career woman. You'll get repressed and not be interested enough in having fun if you keep after that career."

A lieutenant with a year and a half of college: "All this career business is nonsense. A woman belongs in the home and absolutely no place else. My wife will have to stay home. That should keep her happy. Men are just superior in everything, and women have no right to expect to compete with them. They should do just what will keep their husbands happy."

A graduate engineer—my fiancé: "Go right ahead and get as far as you can in your field. I am glad you are ambitious and clever, and I'm as anxious to see you happily successful as I am myself. It is a shame to let all those brains go to waste over just dusting and washing dishes. I think the usual home life and children are small sacrifices to make if a career will keep you happy. But I'd rather see you in radio because I am a bit wary of the effect upon our marriage of the way of life you will have around the newspaper."

Sixty-one, or 40 percent, of the students indicated that they have occasionally "played dumb" on dates, that is, concealed some academic honor, pretended ignorance of some subject, or allowed the man the last word in an intellectual discussion. Among these were women who "threw games" and in general played down certain skills in obedience to the unwritten law that men must possess these skills to a superior degree. At the same time, in other areas of life, social pressures were being exerted upon these women to "play to win," to compete to the utmost of their abilities for intellectual distinction and academic honors. One student writes:

I was glad to transfer to a women's college. The two years at the co-ed university produced a constant strain. I am a good student; my family expects me to get good marks. At the same time I am normal enough to want to be invited to the Saturday night dance. Well, everyone knew that on that campus a reputation of a "brain" killed a girl socially. I was always fearful lest I say too much in class or answer a question which the boys I dated couldn't answer.

Here are some significant remarks from the interviews:

When a girl asks me what marks I got last semester I answer, "Not so good—only one 'A,' " When a boy asks the same question, I say very brightly with a note of surprise, "Imagine, I got an 'A'!"

I am engaged to a southern boy who doesn't think too much of the woman's intellect. In spite of myself, I play up to his theories because the less one knows and does, the more he does for you and thinks you "cute" into the bargain. . . . I allow him to explain things to me in great detail and to treat me as a child in financial matters.

One of the nicest techniques is to spell long words incorrectly once in a while. My boyfriend seems to get a great kick out of it and writes back, "Honey, you certainly don't know how to spell."

When my date said that he considers Ravel's *Bolero* the greatest piece of music ever written, I changed the subject because I knew I would talk down to him.

A boy advised me not to tell of my proficiency in math and not to talk of my plans to study medicine unless I knew my date well.

My fiancé didn't go to college. I intend to finish college and work hard at it, but in talking to him I make college appear a kind of a game.

Once I went sailing with a man who so obviously enjoyed the role of a protector that I told him I didn't know how to sail. As it turned out he didn't either. We got into a tough spot, and I was torn between a desire to get a hold of the boat and a fear to reveal that I had lied to him.

It embarrassed me that my "steady" in high school got worse marks than I. A boy should naturally do better in school. I would never tell him my marks and would often ask him to help me with my homework.

I am better in math than my fiancé. But while I let him explain politics to me, we never talk about math even though, being a math major, I could tell him some interesting things.

Mother used to tell me to lay off the brains on dates because glasses make me look too intellectual anyhow.

I was once at a work camp. The girls did the same work as the boys. If some girls worked better, the boys resented it fiercely. The director told one capable girl to slow down to keep peace in the group.

How to do the job and remain popular was a tough task. If you worked your best, the boys resented the competition; if you acted feminine, they complained that you were clumsy.

On dates I always go through the "I-don't-care-anything-you-want-to-do" routine. It gets monotonous but boys fear girls who make decisions. They think such girls would make nagging wives.

I am a natural leader and, when in the company of girls, usually take the lead. That is why I am so active in college activities. But I know that men fear bossy women, and I always have to watch myself on dates not to assume the "executive" role. Once a boy walking to the theater with me took the wrong street. I knew a short cut but kept quiet.

I let my fiancé make most of the decisions when we are out. It annoys me, but he prefers it.

I sometimes "play dumb" on dates, but it leaves a bad taste. The emotions are complicated. Part of me enjoys "putting something over" on the unsuspecting male. But this sense of superiority over him is mixed with feelings of guilt for my hypocrisy. Toward the "date" I feel some contempt because he is "taken in" by my technique, or if I like the boy, a kind of a maternal condescension. At times I resent him! Why isn't he my superior in all ways in which a man should excel so that I could be my natural self? What am I doing here with him, anyhow? Slumming?

And the funny part of it is that the man, I think, is not always so unsuspecting. He may sense the truth and become uneasy in the relation. "Where do I stand? Is she laughing up her sleeve or did she mean this praise? Was she really impressed with that little speech of mine or did she only pretend to know nothing about politics?" And once or twice I felt that the joke was on me: the boy saw through my wiles and felt contempt for me for stooping to such tricks.

Another aspect of the problem is the conflict between the psychogenetic personality of the girl and the cultural role foisted upon her by the milieu. At times it is the girl with "masculine" interests and personality traits who chafes under the pressure to conform to the "feminine" pattern. At other times it is the family and the college who thrusts upon the reluctant girl the "modern" role.

While, historically, the "modern" role is the most recent one, ontogenetically it is the one emphasized earlier in the education of the college girl, if these 153 documents are representative. Society confronts the girl with powerful challenges and strong pressure to excel in certain competitive lines of endeavor and to develop certain techniques of adaptation very similar to those expected of her brothers. But, then, quite suddenly as it appears to these girls, the very success in meeting these challenges begins to cause anxiety. It is precisely those most successful in the earlier role who are now penalized.

It is not only the passage from age to age but the moving to another region or type of campus which may create for the girl similar problems. The precise content of sex roles, or, to put it in another way, the degree of their differentiation, varies with regional class, nativity, and other subcultures.

Whenever individuals show differences in response to some social situation, as have our 153 respondents, the question naturally arises as to the causes. It will be remembered that 40 percent admitted some difficulties in personal relations with men due to conflicting sex roles but that 60 percent said that they had no such problems. Inconsistency of parental expectations troubled 26 percent of the students.

To account for individual differences would require another study, involving a classification of personalities in relation to the peculiar social environments of each. Generally speaking, it would seem that it is the girl with a "middle-of-the-road personality" who is most happily adjusted to the present historical moment. She is not a perfect incarnation of either role but is flexible enough to play both. She is a girl who is intelligent enough to do well in school but not so brilliant as to "get all 'A' 's"; informed and alert but not consumed by an intellectual passion; capable but not talented in areas relatively new to women; able to stand on her own feet and to earn a living but not so good a living as to compete with men; capable of doing some job well (in case she does not marry or, otherwise, has to work) but not so identified with a profession as to need it for her happiness.

A search for less immediate causes of individual reactions would lead us further back to the study of genesis of the personality differences found relevant to the problem. One of the clues will certainly be provided by the relation of the child to the parent of the same and of the opposite sex. This relation affects the conception of self and the inclination for a particular sex role.

The problems set forth in this article will persist, in the opinion of the writer, until the adult sex roles of women are redefined in greater harmony with the socioeconomic and ideological character of modern society. Until then neither the formal education nor the unverbalized sex roles of the adolescent woman can be cleared of intrinsic contradictions.

The changing distribution of chronological age in modern society in the direction of higher proportions of people sixty years of age and over has provoked many new and fascinating social psychological questions concerning personality as it is affected by age. What, for example, are the influences of chronological age as distinguished from those of age identification on other aspects of the self-image of older persons? And what social factors accelerate or retard changes in age identification among older people?

In the following discussion of the research findings on aging in an upstate New York community, Zena Blau shows the extent to which social psychological aging and chronological aging are analytically separable processes. It is age identification, and not chronological age, that conditions older people to see changes in themselves and to recognize that other people have changed in their attitudes toward them. Finally, Dr. Blau reports that of the two major changes in social status common to older people, retirement supersedes widowhood in hastening the onset of old age. This is because the former has greater social implications than the latter.

27. CHANGES IN STATUS AND AGE IDENTIFICATION *

ZENA S. BLAU
University of Illinois

The conceptions individuals have of themselves as young, middle-aged, or old are, of course, related to their actual age. People in their sixties are certainly more likely than people in their thirties to think of themselves as old. But the variations in age identification between persons in the same age group and the similarities between those whose actual age differs indicate that chronological age is only a limiting condition and does not fully explain the changes in age identification that occur in the course of the individual's life span.

In this paper two topics will be discussed: first, the relative influence of chronological age and age identification on other aspects of the self-image of older persons, and second, some of the social factors that hasten or forestall changes in age identification among older people.

A representative sample of 468 people 60 years old and over in Elmira, New York, were asked: "How do you think of yourself as far as age goes—middle-aged, elderly, old, or what?" Fully 60 percent of the respondents considered themselves middle-aged, 38 percent described themselves as old, elderly, or used an equivalent euphemism, and 2 percent gave no answer to the question.

Of course, the likelihood that people consider themselves old rather than middle-aged steadily increases as they grow older. Under 65, only 18 percent define themselves as old, between 65 and 70, 37 percent do so, but in the age group of 70 and over this proportion rises to 59 percent. Old age is, after all, something more than a state of mind, since the aging process is marked by objective physical and behavioral changes. Although these changes usually occur gradually and, therefore, do not immediately intrude upon the consciousness of the individual, one might expect that they become increasingly apparent to him and his associates as the years pass and thus finally bring about identification with old people. Indeed, when asked "How much have you changed in the past 10 or 15 years—would you say hardly at all, somewhat or a good deal?" less than a fifth of those under 70, compared to a third of those who are 70 and over, feel that they have changed "a good deal." (See Table 1.)

However, if age identification is held constant, this relationship between chronological age and perceived change in oneself tends to disappear. These findings suggest that while objective changes mark the aging process, a shift

* *American Sociological Review,* Vol. 21, No. 2, April, 1956, pp. 198–203.

in age identification is a crucial intervening variable for perceiving them. Not all older people, but only those who have shifted their age identification, are likely to perceive these changes in themselves. It seems that neither the knowledge of their years, nor even their white hair and wrinkles, induce older people to perceive that they have changed. As Proust writes:

It does us no good to know that the years go by, that youth gives way to old age, that the most stable thrones and fortunes crumble, that fame is ephemeral—our way of forming a conception—and so to speak, taking a photograph of this moving universe, hurried along by time, seeks on the contrary to make it stand still.[1]

And so, to borrow Proust's metaphor, it is the conception of himself as old, and not the weight of his years as such, that constrains the older person to relinquish the photograph and reluctantly to substitute the mirror.

TABLE 1. Percent Who Perceive "A Good Deal" of Change in Self by Age Identification and Age

	Age Identification		
Age	*Middle-aged*	*Old*	*Total*
Under 70	15 (206)	42 (31)	18 * (273)
70 and over	22 (73)	40 (88)	33 * (175)

* This difference is significant on the .01 level. Numbers in parentheses in all tables are the numbers of cases on which percentages are based.

A similar phenomenon can be observed in respect to the older person's beliefs about the image his significant others have of him. The older people are, the more frequently do they answer affirmatively when asked, "Do you think that the people you see and care most about think of you as an old man (woman)?"

TABLE 2. Percent Saying That Significant Others Consider Them Old by Age Identification and Age

	Age Identification		
Age	*Middle-aged*	*Old*	*Total*
Under 70	7 (206)	45 (31)	13 * (276)
70 and over	14 (73)	50 (88)	32 * (187)

* This difference is significant on the .01 level.

Only about one-eighth of those under 70, but a third of those who are 70 and over feel that their close associates consider them old. (See Table 2.) This

[1] Marcel Proust, *Remembrance of Things Past,* New York: Random House, 1927, Vol. 2, p. 1063.

relationship, however, also tends to disappear if the age identification of respondents is controlled. In other words, regardless of their actual age, people come to believe that *others* consider them old only if they consider *themselves* old.

In sum, various mental states that characterize older people, and distinguish them from others are actually precipitated by shifts in age identification from middle-aged to old. The important question consequently becomes: What are the social conditions that hasten or forestall such shifts in age identification? The rest of the discussion will be devoted to an examination of this question.

In youth and middle-age, the loss of one social status is generally accompanied by entry into another. For example, the status of student is relinquished for a position in the occupational structure, or the young woman may give up her career to become a wife and mother. In contrast, retirement and widowhood, the two major status changes that typically occur in old age, designate the permanent loss of two crucially important social roles and the activities and relationships that define them. It could be expected that these changes in social status of older persons are responsible for shifts in age identification among them, but the data only partly confirm this expectation.

TABLE 3. Percent Identified as Old by Age and Employment Status

Employment Status	*Age* Under 70	70 and Over	*Total*
Employed	18 (136)	41 (37)	24 (170)
Retired	37 (41)	67 (57)	57 (93)

All differences are significant on the .05 level.

Retirants, at each age level, do indeed consider themselves old more frequently than those who are still employed, but the widowed are not signficantly different from the married in this respect. Under 70, less than a fifth of the employed, but more than a third of the retirants identify themselves as old. Among those who are 70 and over, 41 percent of the employed, but fully two-thirds of the retired, regard themselves as old. (See Table 3.) In contrast, at each age level, widowed people consider themselves old hardly more often than those who are still married. (See Table 4.)

TABLE 4. Percent Identified as Old by Age and Marital Status

Marital Status	*Age* Under 70	70 and Over	*Total*
Married	22 (160)	55 (65)	33 (218)
Widowed	26 (81)	60 (99)	46 (173)

The remark of a retirant suggests one of the reasons why retirement predisposes the older person to define himself as old.

When did I start to feel old? Why when I stopped working. I was always real proud that I'd come to Chicago and got a job and supported myself. Then when I couldn't work anymore, why I wasn't good for anything.

Retirement is a *social* pattern which implies an invidious judgment on the part of others in the society about the lack of fitness of *old* people to perform a culturally significant role, whereas the death of the marital partner, being a natural event, and not a socially induced one, does not have such implications in our culture. Thus, the retired individual, but not the widowed one has reason to believe that he is socially defined as old.

Furthermore, retirement removes the individual from a social peer group and thereby disrupts the informal relations developed on the job. The death of the marital partner, on the other hand, disrupts a single, albeit a very significant, social relationship. In other words, the hypothesis is suggested that loss of membership in a peer *group* has more pronounced effects on the self-image of older people than the loss of an intimate interpersonal relationship, and that this helps to explain the differential effect of retirement and widowhood on age identification.

This hypothesis can be tested by determining whether membership in a friendship clique is, indeed, more significant for age identification than relationships with individual friends.

Respondents were asked three questions about their social participation: "How many really close friends do you have here in town that you occasionally talk over confidential matters with?" "Now think of the friend that you know best here in town—how often do you get to see that friend?" and "Would you say you go around with a certain bunch of close friends who visit back and forth in each other's homes?"

Neither the number of friendships nor the frequency of contact with the closest friend is significantly related to age identification. But older people who belong to a friendship clique consider themselves old significantly less often than those who do not participate in such a group. Only 29 percent of the members, in contrast to 41 percent of the non-members regard themselves as old. (See Table 5.) However, this relationship may be a spurious one, since, as they grow older, people tend to participate less in friendship groups, and they also are more likely to think of themselves as old.

Indeed, when age is controlled, the relationship between clique membership and age identification disappears among those who are under 70. The vast majority under 70 still define themselves as middle-aged whether or not they belong to a friendship group. But among people who are 70 and over clique membership makes a considerable difference for age identification. Only half of those who participate in a friendship group, but nearly two-thirds of the others consider themselves old.

TABLE 5. Percent Identified as Old by Age and Membership in a Friendship Group

Friendship Group	*Under 70*	*Age* *70 and Over*	*Total*
Member	20 (115)	49 (53)	29 * (168)
Non-member	24 (164)	63 (136)	41 * (300)

* This difference is significant on the .05 level.

The fact that participation in a friendship clique makes no difference for age identification in the younger group only *appears* to refute the hypothesis that group memberships are more effective in forestalling old age than single relationships. Actually, this hypothesis helps to explain why participation in a friendship clique is less important in the younger than in the older age group. People under 70 are likely to have alternative group memberships. For example, since a majority of the men in this age group are still employed, they participate in work groups and other occupational groups. Younger women, as well, participate more in clubs and organizations than those who are older. Thus, it makes little difference whether or not they also participate in a friendship group as such. But after 70, when participation in these other social groups is the exception rather than the rule, the person's position in a friendship group becomes more important in forestalling a shift in age identification.

Similarly, the belief that his close associates consider him old is influenced by the individual's participation in a social peer group, but not by the number of friends he has. Regardless of their age, those who belong to such a group less often hold this belief than those who do not. (See Table 6.) Indeed, among people 70 and over, two-thirds of the clique members, compared to less than half of the others, deny that their associates consider them old.

TABLE 6. Percent Denying That Significant Others Consider Them Old by Age and Membership in a Friendship Group

Friendship Group	*Under 70*	*Age* *70 and Over*	*Total*
Member	87 (115)	64 * (53)	80 † (168)
Non-member	73 (164)	45 * (135)	60 † (300)

* This difference is significant on the .05 level.
† This difference is significant on the .01 level.

These indications that participation in a social group more effectively forestalls the psychological changes that mark old age than participation in a number of dyadic relationships can be explained by the emergent properties that characterize social groups. Studies of various types of small groups by F. J. Roethlisberger and William J. Dickson, William F. Whyte, George C. Homans and Robert F. Bales, show that recurrent interaction between individuals tends to fix the role of each member relative to the others in the group. The images and expectations that arise among the group members tend to persist and to influence their subsequent behavior toward one another. This stability of the network of relationships within a group of friends or co-workers prevents mutual awareness of gradual alterations that take place in each of the participants, particularly if these changes in the person do not interfere with his ability to share in the activities of the group. Consequently, the recurrent gatherings of the same people lend a sense of continuity to the life of each participant. An incongruous but revealing manifestation of this feeling of immutability provided by the groups is the practice of people who have grown old together to continue to refer to themselves as "the boys" or "the girls."

Participation in a friendship group does, indeed, serve to postpone shifts in age identification, and this provides support for the hypothesis that loss of the work group is one of the reasons why retirement influences the age identification of older persons more than widowhood. Further clarification of these relationships can be achieved by simultaneously comparing the relative impact of widowhood and retirement on age identification among those who do and do not participate in a friendship group.

Table 7 shows the relationship between friendship group, marital status, and age identification. Among those who are part of a friendship group, widowed people consider themselves old, hardly more often than married ones—34 percent as against 29 percent, a difference of only 5 percent. However, among those who are not clique members, the widowed define themselves as old considerably more often than the married—51 percent as against 35 percent, a difference of 16 percent. The death of the marital partner, even though it is a natural event, is more likely to precipitate "old age," if the elderly person does not participate in a friendship group.

TABLE 7. Percent Identified as Old by Membership in a Friendship Group and Marital Status

Marital Status	*Friendship Group*		
	Member	*Non-member*	*Total*
Married	29 (85)	35 * (133)	33 (218)
Widowed	34 (53)	51 * (121)	46 (173)
Difference	5	16	

* This difference, as well as that between proportions among totals, is significant on the .05 level.

Membership in a friendship clique has similar implications for age identification following retirement. (See Table 8.) Among those who do not belong to a friendship group, nearly two-thirds of the retired, compared to only a quarter of the employed consider themselves old, a difference of 37 percent. Loss of employment status makes less difference if people are members of a friendship group: 42 percent of the retired and 21 percent of the employed feel that they are old—a difference of 21 percent. Thus, either change in social status is less likely to produce identification with the "old" if the older person maintains his position in a group of peers. However, the friendship group is less effective in preventing the consequences of retirement than those of widowhood. Among those who have a group of friends, twice as many of the retired as of the employed consider themselves old, but hardly any more of the widowed than of the married do so.

TABLE 8. Percent Identified as Old by Membership in a Friendship Group and Employment Status

Employment Status	*Friendship Group*		
	Member	*Non-member*	*Total*
Employed	21 (66)	25 * (104)	24 (170)
Retired	42 (24)	62 * (69)	57 (93)
Difference	21	37	

* This difference, as well as that between proportions among totals, is significant on the .01 level.

Thus, the data that support one of the two explanatory hypotheses advanced to account for the finding that retirement influences the age identification of older people more than widowhood, furnish indirect evidence for the other one as well. Group memberships are indeed more effective than even intimate dyadic relations in postponing identification with the old, but this factor alone does not account for the differential effects of retirement and widowhood on age identification. Loss of employment status, as a socially induced event, implies a judgment on the part of others that an individual is old, and this is an additional reason why it influences his age identification more than does widowhood, which, as a natural event, is devoid of such a social judgment in our culture.

To summarize: The socio-psychological and physical aging processes can be analytically distinguished. Age identification rather than actual age constrains older people to recognize changes in themselves and to perceive that the attitudes of others toward them have changed. Analysis revealed that of the two major changes in social status that commonly occur in old age—retirement and widowhood—only retirement appears to hasten the onset of old age. Two hypotheses were advanced to explain this difference: one, retirement implies a social judgment that the person has become old, whereas widowhood, because it comes about through a natural event, does not have this implication for the older person; two, retirement has more serious consequences for age identification because it removes the individual from a significant peer group, whereas death of the spouse directly disrupts only a single, albeit a highly significant, relationship. The finding that participation in a friendship group serves to forestall a shift in age identification, but that the number of close friends and the frequency of contact with one's closest friend do not, provides support for the second hypothesis. However, the fact that participation in a friendship group appears to be less effective in retarding shifts in age identification among the retired than among the widowed indicates that the loss of the work group only partially explains the greater influence that retirement exerts on age identification. It, therefore, furnishes inferential evidence for the first hypothesis that the cultural evaluation implied by retirement, but not by widowhood, tends to force the person to recognize that he is socially defined as old.

POPULATION

Before 1800, a time when birth and death rates were high everywhere and natural increase (the difference between births and deaths) was slight, the estimated size of world population was less than a billion. In 1960, it reached almost three billion. The principal reason for the fact that the world's population in 160 years practically tripled in size was the "vital revolution," a complex of cultural inventions affecting births and deaths that was parallel to the industrial revolution.

Beginning in western Europe and its derivatives, the vital revolution controlled deaths and then births in the hub of world power. The first phase was during the nineteenth century at which time death control was implemented while the birth rate remained high, providing a large natural increase in population in western Europe. During the first half of the twentieth century, the death rate leveled off at a low rate, and the introduction of birth control once again brought about a small rate of natural increase in population.

While this slowing down of population growth occurred during the second phase of western Europe's vital revolution, the culture complex of death and birth control was diffused toward the east. As a consequence, and not without some relation to the shifting center of world power in recent years eastward, societies demographically are stratified as follows:

1. Nearly all of western Europe and its derivatives (the United States, Canada, Australia, and New Zealand) have relatively low birth and death rates and a small rate of natural increase.

2. Italy, Spain, Japan, and the Slavic societies of Central Europe have declining birth and death rates, but deaths have fallen more rapidly than births, providing these societies with high rates of natural increase.

3. Asia, Africa, and South America (except for the immigrant descendants of west Europeans) have the so-called underdeveloped countries in which birth

and death rates are still high because of virtually no impact from the vital revolution as yet.

Dudley Kirk, in the following article, discusses the demographic changes after World War II throughout the world, notes the eastward diffusion of the vital revolution, and shows the relationship between these population trends and the shifting of power toward the emerging nations to the east. Although the article was originally published in 1944 and is chronologically the oldest selection in this volume, the student should note that the essence of Dr. Kirk's analysis is as pertinent today as it was a generation ago.

28. POPULATION CHANGES AND THE POSTWAR WORLD *

DUDLEY KIRK

Population Council, New York City

Great changes have occurred and are occurring in the size and distribution of the world's population. These changes are among the more fundamental and predictable determinants of the future. In their larger aspects population trends have shown a great deal of stability in the past and it seems reasonable to suppose that they will continue to do so in the future. They are one of the more certain elements in a most uncertain world. It is the purpose of this paper, first, to make some generalizations about population changes occurring in modern times and, second, to indicate some directions in which they, in association with other social trends, may affect the postwar world.

A generation ago, behind every discussion of population problems there loomed the gloomy figure of Malthus. The writings of demography were filled with the dangers of overpopulation. These dangers have not disappeared; in most of the world there is still a heavy pressure of population on developed resources, and the Malthusian controls of famine, disease, and war are still the major checks to population growth. But a different interpretation of population phenomena has become more popular, partly owing to obvious changes in population trends, partly because of a re-evaluation of the relationship between population growth and economic development in the modern world.

POPULATION TRENDS AS A FUNCTION OF "PROGRESS"

The dismal outlook of never-ending pressure of population on the food supply was dispelled in Western civilization by the achievements of the agricultural and industrial revolutions, and to a lesser extent by the exploitation of new lands and of old peoples. These have combined to provide the eco-

* *American Socological Review*, Vol. 9, No. 1, February, 1944, pp. 28–35. (*Note:* The population figures in this article are out of date; they refer to the situation as of 1944.)

nomic basis for both rising levels of living and extraordinarily rapid population growth. In the past three centuries the population of European races has increased sevenfold: from 100 millions in 1650 to 700 millions at the present time. In the same period it has increased from less than a fifth of the world's total to more than a third. But accompanying the achievement of higher levels of living, both as cause and consequence, has been the spread of the empirical outlook on life conducive to the restriction of family size and the termination of population growth. As is well known, the indefinite continuation of interwar trends would ultimately lead to the depopulation of Western Europe and of Europe overseas.

Rapid population growth and the subsequent slowing of growth arising from control of family size are intrinsic elements in the nexus of cultural traits that are valued as "progress." Their development has not been haphazard. Within Europe, for instance, there has been a clear pattern of cultural diffusion from the initial locus of development in Northwestern and Central Europe. Modern education, improved health conditions, and economic advance are parts of the same cultural complex, indigenous to the West and for many decades past in the process of spreading across the continent. Progress flows along the lines of communication, is assisted by the presence of natural resources appropriate to industrialization, and is checked by natural and cultural barriers, but in general the level of material achievement of any given area in Europe is a function of its distance from the centers of diffusion in the West. Generally speaking, to go eastward in Europe is to go backward in time. The mode of life in some of the remote corners of Europe, as in the mountain districts of Yugoslavia, in Bessarabia, or in the Caucasus, has many points of resemblance to that existing in Western Europe several generations ago. Intermediate areas tend to blend towards one extreme or the other depending upon their geographical location and cultural associations. In these terms Europe is a cultural unit, all in the same stream of development, but with differences in the level of attainment growing from differences in the time at which the transition began from a peasant, self-sufficient society to an urban, industrial society.

Outside of Europe technological civilization has made progress likewise in relation to the accessibility, both cultural and geographical, to the centers of its development. It has now gained a solid foothold even among non-European peoples, and the time has long since passed when our arrogance will permit us to assert that Orientals, for instance, are racially or culturally incapable of establishing a modern industrial civilization. The spread of industry and the growth of cities have been well nigh universal phenomena of recent times. Though in many countries these exist now only in embryonic form, it is questionable if there is a single country in the world that has not experienced some increase in industrial output and in modern urban influences during the twentieth century.

Demographic trends have shown an almost equal, and closely related, consistency in the direction of their development. Every country in the world with sufficiently good vital statistics to permit a judgment of trends displayed declining mortality rates in the interwar period. With few exceptions in the world, and none in the sphere of Western civilization, the birth rates likewise were lower at the end than at the beginning of the period.

THE CONTINUUM OF DEMOGRAPHIC DEVELOPMENT

In regard to demographic matters the different countries of the world may be considered as on a single continuum of development, a continuum having both spatial and temporal significance. It is spatial in that the degree of development is related to the cultural and geographical accessibility to the most advanced countries. It is temporal in that each country in its development is following a great historical pattern common to all. In areas relatively untouched by Western influences, the typical demographic situation today is one of high birth rates and high death rates, with a low value placed on human life both in its inception and in its destruction. Of course this was also the demographic position of Europe at an earlier period. In normal years such areas have a substantial margin of natural increase, which is periodically checked by disasters of one sort or another. As modern influences increase, the beginnings of police control, better transportation, and the application of elementary public health measures all ameliorate the effects of these disasters. Before the war, the British in India, the Dutch in Java, the Japanese in Korea, we ourselves in the Philippines and Puerto Rico, had softened the impact of calamity, and had made effective the normally high rate of natural increase. This is the typical "colonial" situation today, characteristic of most of the Far East, the Mohammedan world, and much of Africa and Latin America. It was the condition of roughly half the population of the globe before the war.

In more developed countries further application of relatively elementary principles in the saving of lives had brought about further declines in the death rates. Later, the advance of modern influences, in the form of urban ways of life and the values which have accompanied this way of life in Western civilization, has resulted in the spread of the small family pattern, first among the upper classes and then among all the urban elements of the population. Such developments have yielded the beginnings of the decline of the birth rate, with clear indication that it would continue if unimpeded by a return to earlier values or by the inauguration of repressive population policies. In Southern and Eastern Europe, in the more progressive countries of Latin America, and in Japan, the decline of the death rate in the interwar period was accompanied by a declining birth rate. In these countries the pattern of fertility decline was established. However, the momentum of past growth, as reflected in the youth of their populations, and the inevitable lag in the decline of fertility from its present levels posit substantial future growth of population in these areas for some years to come.

The countries nearer the centers of Western civilization have progressed further in the transition than those less fully caught up in the rising tide of material values. In the core of Western civilization in Northwestern Europe demographic evolution before the war had proceeded to the point where the birth rate was overtaking the death rate in its decline. The list of countries facing the likelihood of future population decline is a roster of the nations that have led the world in material progress.

The continuum of population development may be divided into three significant segments, each with its peculiar problems in the postwar world. About half the population of the world is in the first stage, the stage of great potential growth. Western influences have made possible a reduction in the death rate without compensating declines in the birth rate. In a relatively stable postwar world these areas will experience tremendous population growth, comparable in amount, though probably not in rate, to that experienced by the Western world at an earlier period of its history. A second, and transitional, stage has been achieved by those nations now caught up in the tide of industrialization and urbanization, but formerly, at least, on the peripheries of Western civilization. In these countries birth and death rates have both been declining, but the birth rates are still sufficiently high to support population growth for some time to come. Finally, there are those countries that face the prospect of depopulation if the net fertility declines of the interwar period are continued.

It would be tempting to consider a multitude of problems that may be encountered at each stage of economic and demographic evolution, but it would be impossible even to list them in the space allotted, and much less to analyze all the permutations and combinations represented in the various parts of the world. Perhaps what is most significant to us now, with the problems of planning a peace a public issue, is the political implications of the differing demographic trends, first, within Europe, and, second, in the relationships between the Western peoples and the rest of the world.

POWER IMPLICATIONS OF POPULATION TRENDS: WITHIN EUROPE

It has been suggested that European peoples, and in fact almost all the nations of the earth, are moving on a continuum of economic and demographic development, representing greater or lesser change in the direction of an urban society. Within Europe, economic development and population change have gone hand in hand. Both have undoubtedly been elements in the changing distribution of political power.

The predominant position of France on the continent of Europe two or three centuries ago was partly a function of the fact that she was the wealthiest and in many respects the most advanced country in Europe. It is also undoubtedly associated with the fact that she was probably at the same time the most populous nation of the continent, not even excluding Russia, which now has four times her population. The economic and political position of France in relation to the remainder of Europe has changed enormously since 1800, and this change is probably not entirely unrelated to the fact that she now stands fifth rather than first among European nations in regard to population size.

The rise of Germany likewise has demographic foundations. In the Napoleonic period, Germans lived in a Europe dominated not only politically, but also numerically by the French. As the result of the economic development of Germany and the population increase made possible by this development, since the middle of the last century Germans have become much the most numerous of the European peoples aside from the Russians. As the largest single group, occupying a central position in Europe, it is natural that the Germans should have sought to bring the balance of political power into line with their growing numerical and industrial importance. That this could have been achieved more effectively through peaceful rather than through warlike means is now unfortunately beside the point.

By virtue of its more rapid natural increase and the Nazi annexation of German-speaking areas, Germany in 1939 had twice the population of France and a considerably larger population that that of Britain. However, from the demographic point of view, Germany had already passed the crest of the wave. The last war had serious consequences. But these were overshadowed by the effects of fertility declines. The population of the old Reich in 1939 was perhaps 6 million less because of World War I. It was 13 million less as the result of the decline of the birth rate since 1910. Prior to Hitler's accession to power the net reproduction rate had fallen to a lower level than that of France, the classic country of depopulation. The Nazi population policies, though moderately successful in their objective of increasing the number of births, nevertheless fell very far short of re-establishing 1910 fertility. The eastward wave of population increase has come and gone in Germany, and she is on the receding side of the tide in company with her Western neighbors. Demographically, Germany is in substantially the same position as England, France, and Scandinavia, all of which face the prospect of stationary or declining populations. War may speed the approach of population decline; postwar population policies may retard it. But the underlying demographic situation will probably not be altered. Aside from an unforeseen volume of immigration the era of rapid population growth in these countries is past.

The populations of Eastern Europe grew much faster than those of Western European countries in the interwar period despite political disorder and the more severe effects of World War I in the East. At an earlier period the large population growth of this region was made possible by the fact that large areas were then in the process of initial agricultural settlement, or, put in other terms, in transition from a pastoral to a settled farm economy. In Russia there was new settlement not unlike that of our own frontier. This agricultural settlement represented a superior form of land utilization, and made possible the support of a far denser population than had formerly existed. More recently the wave of material progress represented by industrialization and an urban way of life has reached Eastern Europe from its centers of origin in the West.

In Russia the contrast of the old and the new resulted in such severe stress on the old social order that it was swept away and the new technical civilization was ushered in with an impetus previously unexampled in history. These developments have made possible rapid population increase such as existed in Western Europe at an earlier period. Despite war and revolution, which apparently cost Russia a total population deficit of 26 millions, including both deaths and loss of births, since 1900 the population of the territory of the Soviet Union has grown more rapidly than that of Western Europe. Its present age structure and fertility levels suggest that the present war will not have a serious retarding influence on her future rapid growth. The youth of the Russian population is suggested by the fact that the median age is under 23 years, as contrasted with 32 in Northwestern and Central Europe now and with a median age of 40 in that region by 1970 on a projection of interwar vital trends. The reported birth rate in the U.S.S.R. for 1938 was 38.3 per thousand population or over twice that of the United States in the same year.

Ignoring the war and assuming fertility declines comparable to those experienced in Western Europe at the same level of fertility, the population of the Soviet Union in 1970 would exceed 250 millions. The war will reduce the growth potential, but barring a demographic catastrophe greatly exceeding that of World War I and the Russian revolution, the U.S.S.R. gives every promise of growing more rapidly than the remainder of Europe. In 1939 the U.S.S.R. had twice the 80 millions living in the area of Greater Germany. In 1970 it will probably have three times as large a population, and there will probably be no Greater Germany. What these differences can mean in terms of military potential may be indicated from the trends of manpower. On the assumptions of growth suggested the U.S.S.R. by 1970 would have more men of prime military age, 20–34, that its six closest rivals in Europe combined. The increase in the number of men of this military age by 1970 would alone be as large as the total German military manpower of that age today, or that to be expected from any reasonable demographic trends to 1970.

As long as the Russians were poor, illiterate, and thinly scattered over an enormous area, their numbers were not very effective against the industrialized nations of the West except in terms of resistance through sheer inertia of size. Even in the present war, distance and weight of numbers have been an important element in the Russian successes. But the Soviet Union is moving into a position in which it will be able to make its people as effective economically, person for person, as those of Western Europe in general and Germany in particular. Since the Russian manpower of a generation hence will almost certainly be greater proportionately than it is today, a future German challenge to Russia and the world along the lines of 1914 and 1939 seems improbable. Demographic trends alone suggest that this conflict is Germany's last chance for European and world domination.

To say that Russia will be powerful is, of course, not equivalent to saying that she will be a threat. Large population growth in Russia does not involve the serious difficulties that it would, for instance, in Germany. In the Soviet Union rapid growth for some time to come is probably necessary for the maximum development of large available resources in relation to existing population. It should present no greater problem than it did in the United States after the Civil War. Russia has ample resources, ample territory, and a great need for labor to develop unexploited areas in Asia and in the Arctic. The problem is not one of resources or of territory. It is rather that of converting a population only two or three generations from serfdom into a literate, physically healthy, technically competent, urban people. At least that is the job as seen by the Russians themselves according to many reports, and it is a job certainly appropriate to the predominant values of our own world.

POWER IMPLICATIONS OF POPULATION TRENDS: EUROPE AND ASIA

A less certain, but ultimately equally significant development is the eastward movement of power, not only in Europe, but in the world. As long as Western European civilization was able to maintain an effective monopoly on the industrial techniques that give power in the modern world, numbers were relatively unimportant in the relations between Western countries and the densely populated Orient. Numbers are an element of power in any social group. But to be effective they must be implemented with resources and skills, and cemented by social cohesion and unity of purpose. Clearly numbers are of little importance when two civilizations of very different values meet. The domination of India by a handful of Englishmen is an obvious case in point. The British had at their command a great technical superiority of weapons and a social organization directed at the achievement of material ends. The British and the Indians simply were not interested in the same things: the goals and values of their respective societies were almost diametrically opposed. To most Indians the assumption of political control by the British was a matter of complete indifference.

This is no longer the case. Whether through the success of our own efforts at indoctrination, or through frank admiration for our achievements, Oriental and other colored peoples are absorbing important elements of our civilization. Thus the Japanese have clearly demonstrated, first, that a non-European people can establish an astonishingly strong industrial civilization almost entirely on its own initiative, and, further, that a poor but industrious folk can accomplish this with a poverty of natural resources that would seem hopeless by Western standards. But in terms of a reasonable evaluation of its economic and political potential Japan seems no more formidable in relation to Asia as a whole than would England, shorn of its empire, in relation to a united Europe. And China, at least, seems on the way to achieving a unity that Europe was never able to accomplish.

It is commonly assumed that overpopulation in China, as indicated by the prevailing poverty of the people, will prove a great barrier to the economic progress of the country and hence to its rise as a world power. However, it needs to be pointed out that China is not so hopelessly overpopulated as is commonly supposed and that this condition does not represent an insuperable obstacle to industrialization. It is perhaps surprising to note that the over-all density of population in China is only half that of Europe west of Russia though her total population is roughly comparable in size. Even in China proper population density is much less than in Western Europe. Overpopulation in China, as elsewhere, is indicated by a high ratio of population to developed resources. It has reality only in relation to a given stage of technological development. In other areas technical changes have obviously brought about enormous changes in the carrying capacity of the land. Four hundred years ago the present area of continental United States supported only 200 or 300 thousand Indians living on the margin of subsistence. With our present technological development, the same area readily supports 130 million or several hundred times as many people, and at a much higher standard of living. In existing circumstances the level of living in a country is much more closely related to its degree of technological development than it is to the absolute numbers of its population. Overpopulation is not a matter of too many people any more than it is a matter of too little economic production.

Considered in this light the problems of the densely populated countries of the Far East take on a much more hopeful aspect than has commonly been attributed to them. Given its present economic structure, it is undeniable that China is overcrowded. But it does not appear fanciful to suppose that at the level of technical efficiency now prevailing in Europe the present population of China could be maintained at something approximating Europe's levels of living. This would assume a potential resource base somewhat comparable to that of Europe west of Russia in an area more than twice as large.

It is obvious that the Chinese population does not now have either the capital or the trained personnel to achieve the present per capita production of Europe in the near future. However, there are compelling precedents in recent history demonstrating that neither of these are insuperable obstacles. In Russia a backward and illiterate peasantry is being converted almost in a single generation into a literate, forward-looking proletariat, rapidly acquiring the skills necessary for efficient industrial production. And on the other side of China is the convincing example of Japan, which has constructed an industrial economy with a paucity of natural resources that would be appalling to any Western people.

In China herself something of the possibilities both for industrialization and for higher per capita output in agriculture has been demonstrated in these war years. In this period China has built up an army of some 10 million men, chiefly taken from the peasantry and consequently withdrawn from agricultural production. At the same time agricultural production in Western China has apparently remained at least as high as before the war, partly because the men withdrawn from agriculture were inefficiently used in agriculture anyway, and partly because even in the space of five years some progress has been made, especially in the use of better seed. These factors combined are sufficient to free 10 million men as industrial workers in this area after the war. Furthermore, the army was provided with small arms, i.e., rifles and light machine guns, and the appropriate ammunition, almost entirely from domestic production. When it is considered that most of China's prewar industries were located in the coastal cities now occupied by the Japanese, such an accomplishment must be considered a remarkable one. The capital for this achievement was naturally obtained at great sacrifice. But the means of industrialization can be wrung from a people living as close to the margin of subsistence as the Chinese if there is a central government with the necessary will and unity.

In these war years China herself has given ample evidence that with a stable government she is capable of great economic progress, even without effective assistance from outside. However, it is certainly true that unless some check is placed on population growth, her growing masses will ultimately consume the margin of production created by technical progress. Past experience has demonstrated, as in Japan, that even in very poor countries technical progress can outstrip population growth for a time and bring about a rising level of living in the face of large increments of population. Yet this can be no ultimate solution. Population growth, if unchecked, must ultimately destroy the gains of more efficient production, and through that destruction hinder and perhaps eliminate further gains. China's problem, then, is a combination of the economic and the demographic. Her material progress will depend on how quickly she is able to make technical advances in production. It also depends upon how quickly she absorbs the pattern of birth control.

Whether Asia will follow the course set by Western Europe in the decline of the birth rate is obviously a crucial question. Where birth control runs counter to the prevailing values, as in India, its diffusion may be slow. However, the influences operating against the acceptance of birth control probably also operate against economic development and against further declines in the death rates. The only Asiatic country to have undergone sufficient industrialization and urbanization to offer a test case is Japan. In that country birth control had apparently established itself before the war. In Japanese cities, where birth control would most likely first achieve general use, the prewar fertility seems to have been only about five-eighths that in the rural areas. In the country as a whole the age distribution and vital trends in the interwar period was similar to those of England between 1880 and 1900, and indicate a stage of demographic evolution comparable to that of England in that period (Figure 1). The Japanese case is not conclusive, but it is illuminating; it suggests that the barriers between the Western and Eastern worlds are not too great to prevent the diffusion of the birth control pattern.

The decline of the birth rate in Asia is eminently desirable as long as the continent faces elementary difficulties in feeding its huge population. Emigration is no real solution for the future. There are no longer empty countries either willing or able to welcome the surplus populations on a scale sufficient to afford relief. The economic problems are serious. And yet it seems probable that given a modicum of political stability, the Oriental countries will be enabled to experience both a rising level of living and rapid population increase for a time. It is true that they have less of a margin above subsistence than the Western countries had at a comparable stage of economic development. But it is also true that they have the experience of the West to draw upon in the solution of their difficulties.

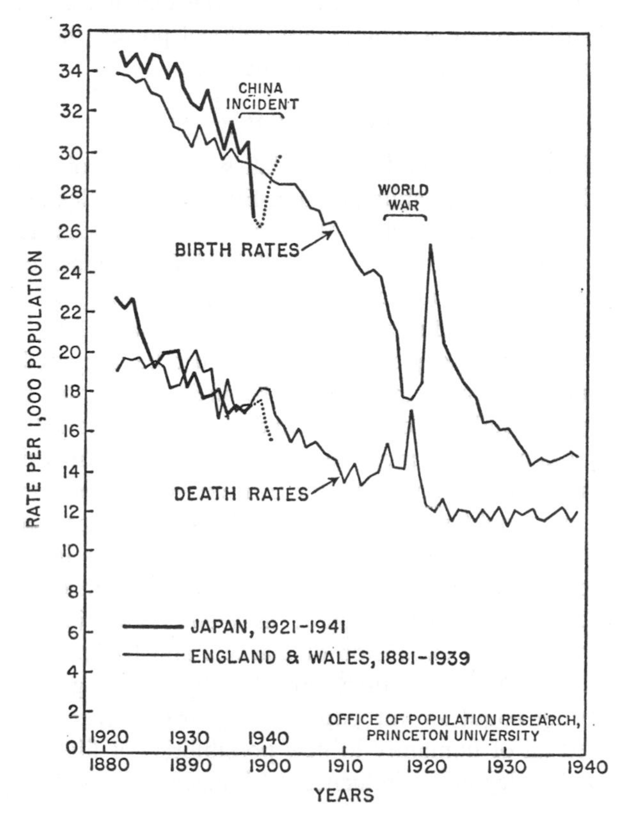

FIGURE 1. Birth and Death Rates in Japan, 1921–1924, and England and Wales, 1881–1939.

Asia as a whole appears to be on the verge of a great awakening. This awakening may take many generations and undoubtedly will not occur evenly throughout the continent. But the tempo of change has been so increased that it seems possible that this awakening will occur with tremendous explosive force, and much sooner than is commonly supposed. If the modernization of Asia follows the course that it took in Europe it will be accompanied by large population increase. Increase of population, and the very mass of the Asiatic population itself, could be ignored in the past as unimportant in the balance of world power. But with the prospect that the Asiatic masses will ultimately learn to forge the tools that will give them power, the differential population trends may become of very great importance. Population increase has been part and parcel of the spread of European populations over much of the globe. In the past European populations have been growing very rapidly in a relatively slowly growing world. The present outlook is for relatively stationary or declining populations among Western European peoples in a rapidly growing world. Western European peoples will almost certainly become a smaller part of the total population of the world. To the extent that numbers are a factor in the distribution of economic and political power, there will be some redistribution of power from old to new centers.

CONCLUSION

What all this means for the future is that we are not going to see again a world in which huge areas inhabited by non-European peoples may be casually regarded as the political playthings of Western European and American powers. The day is rapidly passing when a handful of Europeans, equipped with superior weapons and a complacent and somehow contagious faith in white supremacy, can expect indefinitely to dominate the half of the world that is occupied by the colored peoples. Either we must be prepared to meet the emerging nations halfway, helping them willingly along the road we have travelled to higher standards of living, and the more efficient creation of a better human product, or we must be prepared to maintain white supremacy by force of arms, and in defiance of our own conception of human rights. In the latter case, we would probably be faced with the prospect of an intercontinental conflict that might well dwarf the present war in ferocity and in its threat to the values that are considered the foundation of our society. If we choose to take the path of friendly assistance we will enjoy economic benefits through the rapid expansion of markets and trade. We will probably be serving our own ultimate political interests by speeding the social evolution that will bring about slower population growth. Most important of all, we shall have led all of humanity to new possibilities of life for the common man, freed from the degrading influences of hunger and grinding poverty.

Apart from its impact on international relations and the struggle for power between societies, population growth has profound, underlying significance for the internal structure of societies themselves. The dynamics of births and deaths, age and sex composition, and distribution and mobility of population not only offer the "human resources" that go into the shaping of social structure; these vital processes, in turn, are conditioned by the social and cultural forces of the society in which they occur.

In the article that follows, Joseph S. Davis begins with the comparatively low birth and death rates that characterized American society in the early 1940's. Then he traces the wholly unexpected population upsurge that developed in the ensuing two decades. But most interesting of all are the societal implications and prospects that he draws for the future from this recent pattern of American population growth.

29. IMPLICATIONS OF PROSPECTIVE UNITED STATES POPULATION GROWTH IN THE 1960s *

JOSEPH S. DAVIS
Stanford University

I. DEMOGRAPHIC BACKGROUND AND PROSPECTS SUMMARIZED

The United States is entering the third decade of a demographic revolution of profound significance, which has already contributed much to transform our national position, outlook, and problems.

The 1940s witnessed an unprecedented rise in the prevalence of the married state, a decline in the median age at first marriage, a marked rise in the "general fertility rate" (number of live births per 1,000 women aged 15–44), and first one and then another so-called "baby boom." These were proximately responsible for our wholly unexpected population upsurge.

These developments surprisingly continued in the 1950s, though at a slower pace. Births, instead of declining, flooded to a new high average of 4¼ million a year in 1956–1959. Hence our vigorous population increase was remarkably sustained through the past decade. It is hard to exaggerate the transformation of our population position and outlook between 1940 and 1960.

In the 1960s our population growth is likely to continue vigorous—not rapid, as it was in 1790–1860—if only we escape catastrophic destruction of human and natural resources and severe damage to plant, animal, and human fertility. The numerical gain will probably at least exceed the record-large 28 million increase in the 1950s, by a margin that may be small or considerable. The prospective rate of gain is also unpredictable. It may be slightly below that of the past decade—about 18.5 percent—the highest since 1900–1910; but it will vary from year to year and will probably be slower in the first half of the 1960s than in the second.

A quick cartographic summary of selected data and projections is given in Figures 1–5. Figure 1 is an updated version of Chart 15 in the present writer's pamphlet, THE POPULATION UPSURGE IN THE UNITED STATES (Food Research Institute, December 1949). Plotted on a semi-logarithmic or ratio scale, it shows our population growth in long perspective. One can observe the virtual stability of the growth rate in 1800–1860, its persistent tapering

* *The Milbank Memorial Fund Quarterly,* Vol. XXXIX, No. 2, April, 1961, pp. 329–349.

off in 1860–1930, the severe slump in the 1930s, and the subsequent sustained upsurge.

A few representative projections or "forecasts" published in 1920–1946 serve to bring out the unexpectedness of the reversal in 1940–1960. The highest curves, extending only to 1980, show two of the four latest official projections, published by the Bureau of the Census November 10, 1958. Currently, Series II and III look the more credible, but neither can be wholly trusted.

The inset chart shows the Pearl and Reed 1920 logistic curve, plotted on an arithmetic scale. The fit with decennial census data was fairly close in 1920–1950, but the 1960 census figure will be far above the curve. Its future course is wholly unbelievable, since its most basic assumption has become untenable (see POPULATION UPSURGE, pp. 72–73).

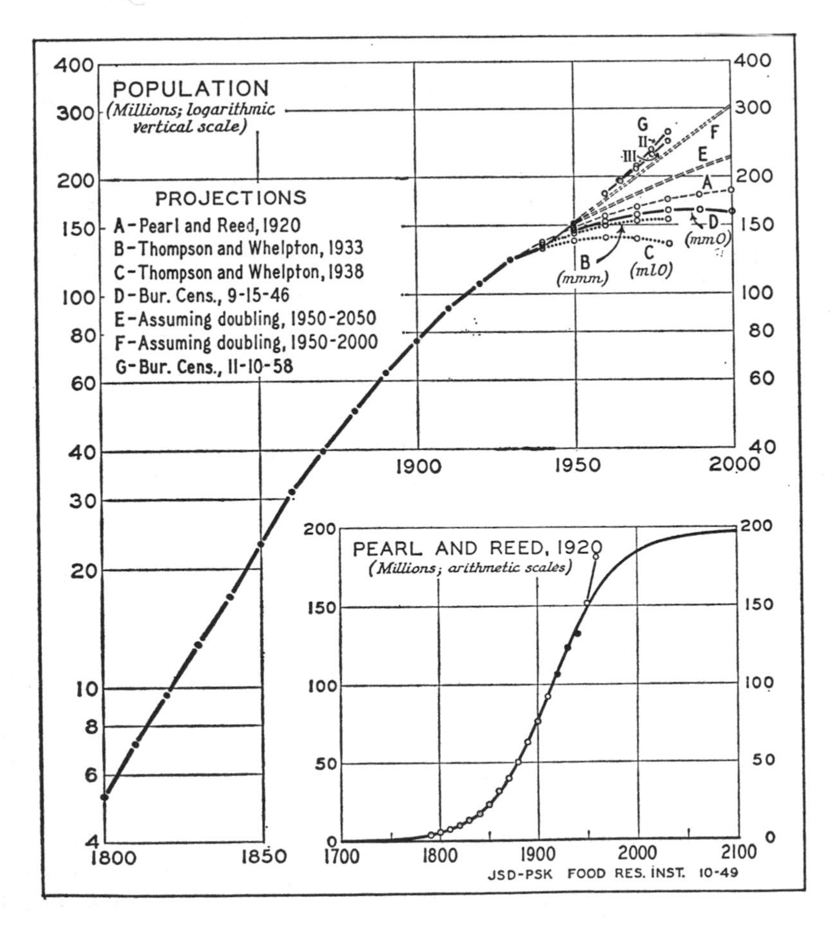

FIG. 1. United States population by decades, 1800–1960, with selected projections.

Figures 2 and 3 together contain eight subcharts of population data and vital statistics for 1910–60, with some projections to 1970 of which no endorsement is implied. Special attention is called to the separate curves for whites and nonwhites in Figure 2, subchart 3 and Figure 3, subcharts 2 and 4. Attention is also called to increases in marriage and fertility rates after 1940 reflected in Figure 3, subcharts 1 and 2.

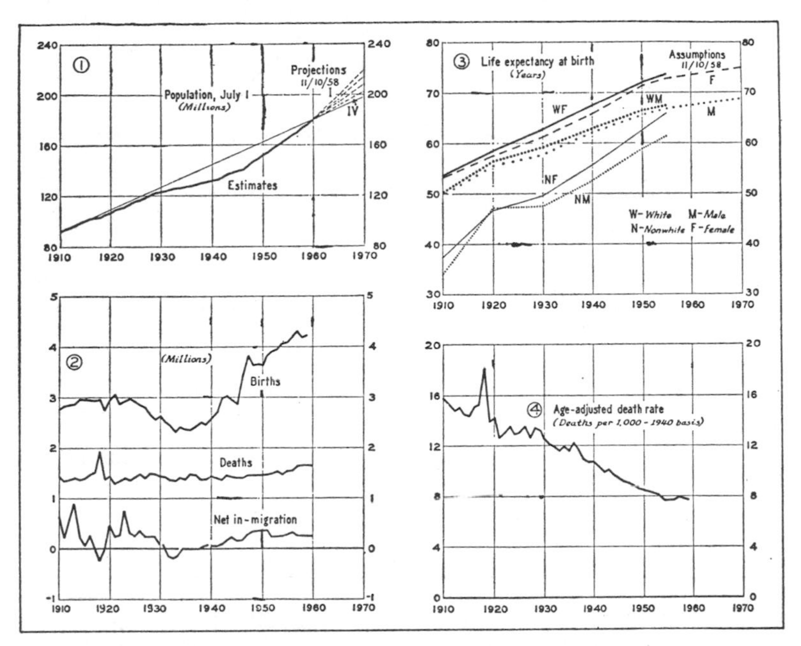

FIG. 2. Population, births, deaths, net in-migration, life expectancy, and age-adjusted death rates, United States 1910–1960, and selected projections.

Figures 4 and 5 together contain nine subcharts, for different time periods, illustrating a number of points made in the first two sections of the paper. Special attention is called to Figure 4, subcharts 1, with its startling projections of births, and 2, showing the notable "echo effects"; Figure 5, subcharts 1 and 2, showing the prospective growth of highly significant age groups under 35; and 4, showing the relative size of age groups 18–64 and the sum of younger and older groups.

We cannot safely forecast the course of the fertility rate or the number of births. Yet we can reasonably expect that births in the 1960s will at least exceed the 40.5 million in 1950–1959, for three reasons: (1) there is no sign that our strong preferences for the married state, and for early marriage, will weaken soon; (2) the number of women reaching age 20, and the numbers in the most fertile age groups, will grow impressively, especially in the second half of the decade; and (3) the prospects are good for avoiding a

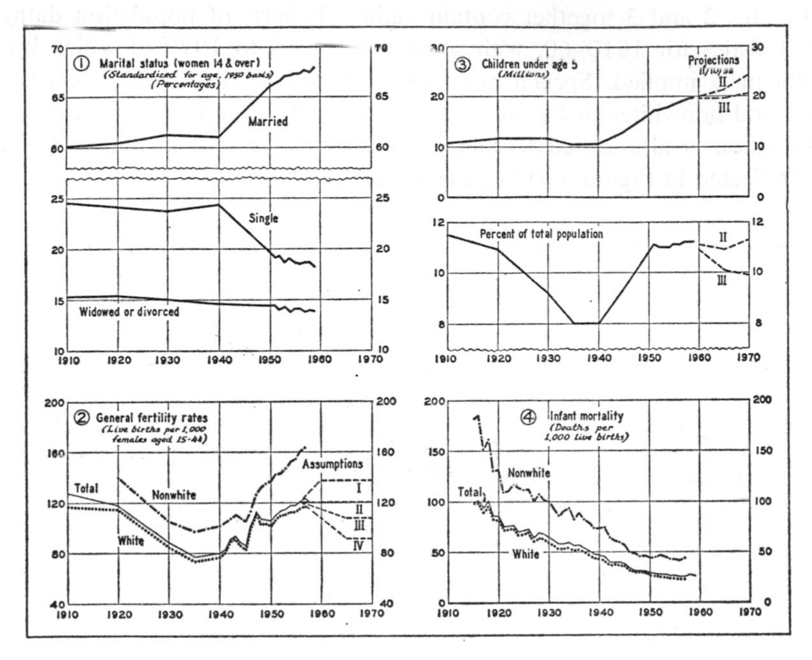

FIG. 3. Marital status, fertility rates, children under 5, and infant mortality rates, United States 1910–1960, and selected projections.

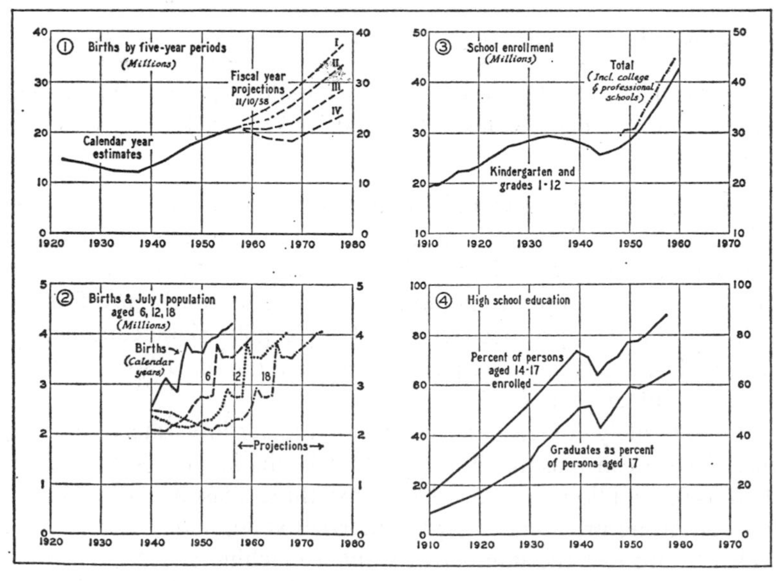

FIG. 4. Births, school enrollment, and high school education, United States 1910–1960, and selected projections.

severe and protracted depression that might seriously curtail marriages and fertility for a time. Conceivably, births may prove even more numerous than 52.7 million in fiscal years 1961–1970—the figure implied in the highest of the four 1958 official projections; but, considering the recent height of the fertility rate, the Series I assumption that it will average 10 percent above the 1955–1957 level (120.5) now seems too liberal.

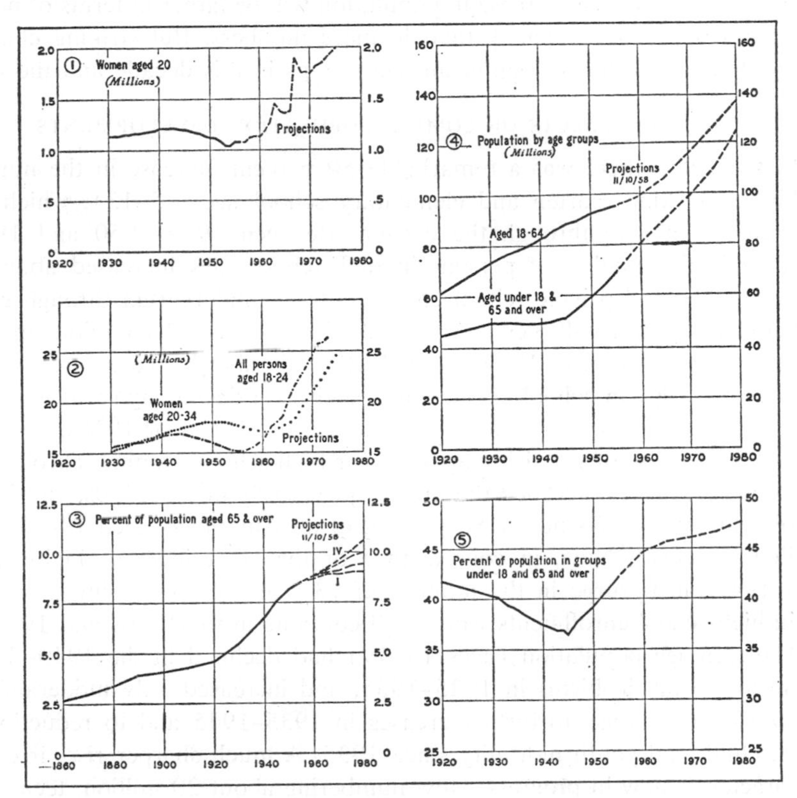

FIG. 5. Trends in the growth of significant age groups in the United States 1860–1960, and projections.

These are the areas of greatest demographic uncertainty as we look a decade ahead—the limit of my assignment. Those in which projections have a solid basis are relatively much more important.

Though much in the unfolding future is obscure, we can have confidence in the statistics of past births—by far the most significant demographic series. We can expect the birth curve to continue to be echoed in curves for one-year age groups, since infant, child, and youth mortality rates have fallen very low and net in-migration is a small element in our population growth. We can put substantial trust in 10-year projections of most age groups over age 10, and expect their total in mid-1970 to be within 2–5 percent of 167.5 million. The numbers aged 14 and over will increase by some 24 million in the 1960s, more than in the two decades 1940–60. Such facts are of high significance for business, economic, and social policy and planning.

The most important population development in this momentous decade will be the growing older of persons now living who were born after 1939. Because of this, and continuing noteworthy gains in health and educational attainment, the effective increase in population will be larger in terms of needs, wants, and productive capacity than in mere numbers. But striking changes will surely occur in highly significant age groups in this decade and the next.

II. SPECIAL ASPECTS OF COMING POPULATION DEVELOPMENTS

In the 1950s there was a remarkable 50 percent increase in the number of children in kindergarten and elementary school ages (5–13), which unexpectedly continued through the decade. Between 1949–1950 and 1959–1960, while the number of persons in high-school ages increased about 33 percent, public and private school enrollments in kindergarten through grade 12 increased by nearly 49 percent, from 28.7 million to 42.7 million. In view of the course of births in 1945–1960, further sizeable increases are in clear prospect. No peak in school enrollments, such as a decade ago was expected to come in the 1950s, can now be expected in the 1960s or 1970s.

Chiefly because of the rising appetite for high-school training, enrollments in secondary schools exceeded the prewar peak early in the 1950s, and in the school year 1957–1958 nearly 88 percent of all Americans aged 14–17 were enrolled in school. Now, in consequence of the great increase in births in 1946–1947, an upsurge in the number of 13-year-olds is causing a marked rise in high-school enrollments which will continue in the 1960s and 1970s.

The teen-age population (ages 13–19) had declined in the 1940s in response to the fall in births in 1925–1935, and increased only moderately in the 1950s, in response to birth increases in 1935–1945 and to reduction in infant, child, and youth mortality since 1935. A much sharper rise, irregular in character, is now in progress. Now numbering about 20 million, teen-agers will increase by about one-third in this decade, to about 70 percent above the low of mid-1950.

The number reaching age 18 declined to a postwar low of 2.1 million in fiscal 1952. It will jump sharply in 1964–1965, reflecting the first post-war peak of births in 1946–1947, and will average nearly as large in the rest of the 1960s. The college age group proper (18–21) will grow relatively fast in this decade, from about 9.6 million to 16.3 million, and will nearly double in 1955–1975.

The age group 18–24 is especially significant, since it includes the great majority of those enrolled in colleges and universities, provides most of the newly married couples, and furnishes most of the first-born children. In the early 1960s this age group will increase by an average of about one-half million a year, and in the second half of the decade by about a million a year. In 1970 it will number about 25 million, 10 million more than in 1957.

The number of women aged 18–24 or 20–24, age groups of special significance for first marriages and first births, declined in the 1950s but will increase by over 50 percent in the 1960s, the more rapidly in the second half of the decade. The number of women in the most fertile age groups, 20–34, declined slightly in 1950–1955 and further in 1955–1960, but will increase nearly 5 percent in 1960–1965 and about 17½ percent in 1965–1970.

The population aged 25–44 will increase by only about 3 percent in the 1960s, as compared with a total population increase probably ranging from 16.3 percent (Series III) to 19.0 percent (Series II). The latest projections for this age group in 1960 and 1970 are 46.8 and 48.2 million respectively.

The percentage of the population in the most productive age groups, 20–64, rose from 51.7 in 1900 to a peak of 59.5 in 1945, then declined to about 52.5 in 1960, in consequence of the post-1940 flood of births and the swelling of the numbers of older people. The decline will continue at a slower pace, probably to about 50.5 in 1970. It is remarkable that American levels of consumption, education, and living have notably risen while a significant "dependency ratio" (the sum of percentages under 20 and over 64) has risen in 1945–1960 from 40.5 to about 47.5.

Projections of the labor force have mostly proved too conservative. The chief economist of the National Planning Association late in 1952, however, quite closely forecast the actual figure for 1960 at 72.5 million. The NPA staff "judgment projection" in October 1959 for 1970 (85.9 million) must therefore command respect, though slightly higher figures are given by the Bureau of Labor Statistics (87.1 million) and the two higher projections of the Census Bureau (87.3) published earlier in 1959.

The big uncertainties still concern labor participation rates, especially for women. The NPA and BLS figures imply a total increase of 13.4–13.5 million during the 1960s comparing with one of 7.8 million in the 1950s. Some such striking increase will doubtless occur, but various uncertainties (e.g., regarding the extent of shortening the workweek, changes in the relative importance of part-time work, and employment of older men) cast doubt on precise forecasts. The most marked increases will almost surely be in workers under age 25 (perhaps 46 percent) and in workers aged 45–64 (perhaps 20 percent), while "the number of women workers will increase at nearly twice the rate for men." The median age of the labor force, which has risen strikingly in the past two decades, will begin an impressive fall in the 1960s.

Completion of childbearing at earlier ages (many of them under age 30) tends to release more mothers from pressing family duties in middle age, permitting them to enter the labor force. It is striking that the number of married women over 35 in the labor force rose from 2.1 million in 1940 to 4.9 million in 1950 and 8.1 million in 1959, implying about a four-fold increase in two decades. The unexpectedly large net increase in the total labor force in 1940–1960 was due mainly to this; and its prospective continuation is largely responsible for the official projection that by 1970 there will be about 30 million women workers, 25 percent more than in 1960.

The persistent tendency to prolong one's schooling, reinforced by evidence that more education tends to increase individual earnings, is raising the median age of entrance into the full-time labor force. Of this we have no precise measure. The numbers reaching age 18 will be much higher in 1961–1964, and sharply higher in 1964–1970, than in most of the 1950s. This will be followed, with some lag, by a heavy flow of young entrants into the full-time labor force, and its effect will be increasingly felt through the decade 1965–1975. The United States Department of Labor estimates that 46 percent of the increase in the total labor force in 1960–1970 will be workers under age 25, and that the increase in this group will be about 10-fold that in 1950–1960. The biggest increases in opportunities for employment will be in professional and technical jobs, and there will be little change in the number of jobs for the unskilled, who have been most subject to extensive unemployment in the 1950s.

The younger persons who will enter the labor force in increasing numbers in the late 1960s and 1970s will have had much more schooling than those who will be leaving the labor force in these years, and illiteracy will be low even among nonwhite entrants. Most of those retiring will have completed well under 8 years of schooling, while something like two-thirds of those entering will have completed high school, and a sizeable fraction of these will have completed four years of college. Granting that exposure to schooling does not ensure educational achievement, and that there are quality deficiencies in schooling, there is no doubt that the educational level of the labor force is rising significantly.

The number of persons in age groups 65 and over (commonly miscalled "the aged") has been and is continuing to increase faster than the total population, but the percentage in these age groups has risen only from 8.1 in 1950 to about 8.8 in 1960 and is likely to be 9.1–9.4 in 1970 and under 10 in 1980. The 1958 official projections indicate that in 1950–1980 the total number will double, but that those aged 65–69 will increase by 75 percent while those aged 85 and over will increase by over 200 percent.

So great has been the increase in the number of young people since 1940 that the median age of the population, which had risen persistently for 150 years, reached a peak in the early 1950s (30.2 years) and will decline for at least another decade or two. In this significant sense, our Nation is now growing *younger*, not older. Moreover, increasing recognition is rightly given to the progressive "youthening of the elderly," which leaves growing fractions of those in age groups 65–74 competent physically and mentally. Though the contributions made by older people are not readily measured—many of them important though nonmaterial—they are surely far below potentials. Here is a significant "new frontier" on which pioneering is under way.

The number of deaths per year, which had risen very slightly in 1910–1950, trended moderately upward in the 1950s, rising from 1.45 million in 1950 to about 1.65 million in 1959. Some such uptrend can be expected to continue through the 1960s and beyond. Yet it is confidently expected that the age-adjusted death rate will resume its long-term downtrend (the recent interruption, in 1954–1959, had a precedent in the 1920s). Life expectancy at birth is expected to continue to rise, at a slowing pace because the levels for various age groups are now so high. Estimates underlying the 1958 official population projections suggest a rise for females from 72.9 years in 1955 to 76.0 in 1975–1980 and to 77.1 in the year 2000. These may prove conservative, especially if widely anticipated "breakthroughs" are made in coping with cancers and heart diseases, which have greatly increased in prevalence as life expectancy has risen.

It is important also to note the rising proportion of nonwhites. In 1900 they made up about 12.1 percent of the population. By 1920 the percentage had fallen to 10.3, and it remained at about this level through 1949. In the 1950s it rose to 11.0 in 1957 and 1958. This rise, largely the result of the much higher fertility of nonwhite women and the more marked improvement in life expectancy of nonwhites, will almost certainly continue in the 1960s.

Finally, a substantial redistribution of our population has accompanied the vigorous growth of the postwar period. Three types deserve emphasis. (1) Important state and regional shifts have taken place. The largest absolute increases in state populations in 1950–1960 were in California (over 5 million), Florida, New York, Texas, and Ohio (1.8 million), in this order, and the largest relative increases in Florida, Nevada, Alaska, Arizona, and California, in this order, while West Virginia, Arkansas, and Mississippi appear to have lost population. (2) Most of the recent growth has been concentrated in the "standard metropolitan statistical areas," reflecting the notable suburbanization of our people, while central cities and truly rural areas have tended to lose population relatively, and in some instances absolutely. (3) Employment in agriculture, like the farm population, has continued to decline, while government, trade, and service occupations have continued to make large gains in employment. Though the 1960s will not faithfully follow the pattern of the 1950s in these respects, further redistribution of population of all three types bids fair to be substantial in this decade.

The prospective population developments in the 1960s have many significant implications and evoke many pertinent observations. I have time to present briefly only a few of each.

III. LEADING IMPLICATIONS

1. The aggregate demand for consumption goods and services in the 1960s —on the reasonable assumption that earnings and total purchasing power will insure conversion of wants into effective demand—will rise significantly more than in the 1950s, because those born since World War II will be a decade

older, their educational level will be higher, and disposable family income will be generally larger.

2. Especially pronounced will be the demands for more educational facilities and qualified personnel. Our ability to meet these demands will be under continuing strain, even though we count as our most vital investment, that in "human resources," what we spend on the schooling of our children, youth, and young adults. (a) The sustained flood of births in the 1950s insures continuing expansion, if at a slowing pace, in needs for elementary education. (b) The expansion will be much sharper in requirements for secondary education, primarily because the numbers aged 14–17 are increasing strikingly, but also because economic incentives keep sharpening appetites for more schooling. (c) For similar reasons, perhaps after a moderate time lag, the demands for facilities and personnel for junior college, 4-year college, and university education will rise even more sharply.

3. The marked increase in the number of teen-agers in the 1960s (probably by about one-third) will not only expand their aggregate demands for all sorts of nondurable goods, cars, schooling, recreational facilities, and part-time jobs, but will also intensify baffling problems of traffic congestion, automobile accidents, and juvenile crime.

4. For lack of education and experience, adverse discrimination, and other reasons, the capacities of nonwhites are not being adequately developed and used to the advantage of the Nation, and rates of unemployment, illegitimacy, and crime are much higher among them. The relatively rapid increase in the nonwhite population, it is necessary to add, must tend to retard their economic and social progress. Disparities between whites and nonwhites are still wide, though they have been very significantly narrowed. Faster progress in this direction will be more urgent in the 1960s, when there will be a marked enlargement of the group of Negro youth.

5. Among the major tasks of the near future will be the smooth absorption of a much enlarged flow of young entrants into the full-time labor force, and appraising and coping with its repercussions on other components of the labor force, on hours of labor, and on part-time employment.

6. Our continuing population upsurge, coupled with the rise in per capita investment required to support our high and rising level of living, virtually assures increasing demands for investment capital in the United States, while the pressure for American investments to supplement limited supplies of domestic capital in the developing nations is increasing because of their population increase and rising "aspirations." Odell recently concluded:

> The demand for investment capital in and from the United States through the next twenty years will be so strong that the greatest economic problem will be to limit the amount of capital investment to a level which can be met primarily from real savings.[1]

[1] Odell, William R. (vice president and director, International Harvester Company): A World Wide Shortage of Investment Capital. In *Problems of Economic Development* (CED, New York, May, 1958), II, 89–93.

Some such emphasis is justified, even if one cannot wholly endorse this assertion.

7. In the second half of the 1960s we can confidently expect a major upswing in family and household formations, though our ability to forecast their timing and extent is still weak. In consequence, a "housing boom" of large proportions will presumably start before the end of the decade and continue in the 1970s. The prospective expansion will exert pressures to enlarge the building industry's labor force, materials, supply, and financing, when other construction requirements will also be making heavy demands. These pressures will also aggravate the already difficult problem of providing and financing investment in local public facilities.

8. Expansion of suburban residential and light industrial areas, together with the decentralization of heavier industry and modern industrial architecture, tend to force land values upward. This process not only yields taxable capital gains to individual landowners, including farmers who own a large proportion of the available land. It also raises basic costs to new users. Here is a pervasive, persistent factor making for price increases, to which the rise in our standards of living also contributes.

9. Water and some other natural resources in limited supply also tend to become scarcer in an economic sense, particularly as changing techniques and higher consumption standards make for increased per capita requirements. These operate to raise capital and product costs, though the aggregate effect on the price level may well be less than through rising land values. The resulting problems should not be minimized, but I can see no cause for alarm over the exhaustion of exhaustible resources in the near future.

10. Expansion of demands for food, fiber, and tobacco at rates assured by growth in adult-male equivalents threatens no shortages and is surely favorable to farmers. But it by no means assures a solution of the farm surplus problem, which continues to be aggravated by technological progress in farming and obsolete political programs of price support. The persistent decline in the farm population, and increasing proportions of their income derived from nonfarm sources, contribute only moderately to raise their per capita income.

IV. PERTINENT OBSERVATIONS

1. Our vigorous population increase since 1940 has certainly contributed to our economic growth and freedom from severe postwar depressions. Similarly, the population prospects for the 1960s are favorable for both economic stability and more rapid economic growth, as well as for meeting the Communist threat, though they insure neither continuous prosperity nor "a 20-year boom." Keynes, Alvin H. Hansen, and others in the 1930s stressed the adverse effects on investment and national income from the retardation of population growth and the threatened decline in Western populations, and also their important influence in intensifying and prolonging business depressions. Their reasoning was broadly sound, though their view of the population outlook soon proved wrong. Among other things Keynes well said:

An increasing population has a very important influence on the demand for capital. Not only does the demand for capital—apart from technical changes and an improved standard of life—increase more or less in proportion to population. But, business expectations being based much more on present than on prospective demand, an era of increasing population tends to promote optimism, since demand will in general tend to exceed, rather than fall short of, what was hoped for. Moreover a mistake, resulting in a particular type of capital being in temporary over-supply, is in such conditions rapidly corrected. . . .[2]

2. The Gross National Product reached a $500 billion rate in the first quarter of 1960, and the 1970 figure is now commonly forecast at $750–800 billion in 1959 dollars. Of the anticipated 50–60 percent increase, a substantial fraction will be attributable to factors associated with our growth in population, families, and the labor force. If we succeed in better realizing our potentials, such forecasts will prove conservative.

3. The decade ahead is surely rich in opportunities but it bristles with challenging problems, many of which grow out of population developments. These developments threaten increases in such evils as air and water pollution, noise, and congestion in various forms, and increased social costs to mitigate or eliminate these. For this decade at least, however, I cannot endorse J. J. Spengler's arguments that "population threatens prosperity" and that "undue population growth [*sic*] is currently tending to debase aesthetic values and to be fostered by such debasement."

4. The need and opportunity for adult education, in the middle and older years of life, are rapidly growing as older knowledge becomes increasingly obsolete, as increased longevity and leisure permit more individuals to enlarge and modernize theirs, as married women take jobs after release from major household responsibilities, and as older persons seek employment after being retired from jobs or positions they have long held. The prospective shortages in the teaching and medical professions, among others, call for increasingly effective development and utilization of human potentials for supplementing the skills of the great body of these professionals, and for evolving new types of jobs and new techniques to meet the swelling demands.

5. The prospective enlargement of the older population (projected at 24 percent in the 1960s) deservedly attracts attention. Yet the notion that our "senior citizens" necessarily impose an increasingly heavy burden on the Nation's economy is ill-founded. To an extent seldom realized, older people are increasingly self-supporting despite low money incomes, if old age insurance benefits, pensions, self-service, mutual service, use of an owned home, and drafts on savings are all taken into account. Most of their needs and wants are simple and small. Increasingly, they are provided with prepaid medical, surgical, and hospital coverage at a cost within their own means or those of their children or interested relatives. There are of course gaps to be filled, as

[2] Keynes, J. M.: Some Economic Consequences of a Declining Population. *Eugenics Review,* Apr. 1937, XXXIX, 13–17.

the current drive for expansion in such coverage at public expense testifies. Fuller utilization of talents and experience of oldsters, not only in unpaid activities but also in remunerative work if they want it, looms large among nationally justified objectives. Whatever net burden the elderly and aged really entail on the economy, moreover, will be the more easily borne as the Nation as a whole grows younger and increasingly productive.

6. The resumption of vigorous population growth since 1940, and its maintenance for two decades, reflect the vitality of the American people, the strength of non-material wants, strong preferences for marriage and family life, and renewed faith in America's future, as well as the generally high level of economic activity. The unexpected upsurge cannot be attributed to policies deliberately designed to promote population growth, though certain public measures incidentally contributed to it. Children have a higher place in American standards of living proper (i.e., levels desired with sufficient urgency to lead to sustained efforts to attain, maintain, or regain them) than before World War II; and in the competition among more goods, more leisure, earlier marriage, and more children, gains in leisure have been least.

7. The sorry experience of the ablest demographic, economic, and educational specialists in looking a decade ahead to the 1940s and 1950s should warn us not to be too sure of our ground as we look to the 1960s. Papers in this area are peculiarly subject to obsolescence, and one must reserve the right to change his views, without undue delay, as new evidence comes to light.

8. I have had to resist the temptation to examine our population prospects in the 1970s and beyond. Both tasks should be seriously undertaken, but no simple extrapolation can be trusted. If our postwar average rate of increase (over 1.7 percent per year) cannot continue indefinitely, the timing and course of its eventual decline are not safely predictable. Whether the demographic developments in progress are wholesome or ominous for the longer future, I have not discussed. Let me merely add that Americans are accustomed to rise to challenges, and that our economic and social history has typically confounded both superoptimists and pessimists of all degrees.

SELECTED SUPPLEMENTARY READINGS FOR PART II

Constas, Helen, "Max Weber's Two Conceptions of Bureaucracy," *The American Journal of Sociology,* Vol. LXIII, No. 4, January, 1958, pp. 400–409.

Goffman, Erving, *The Presentation of Self in Everyday Life* (Garden City, N.Y., Anchor Books, Doubleday & Co., 1959).

Haring, Douglas G., "Is Culture Definable?" *American Sociological Review,* Vol. XIV, No. 1, February, 1949, pp. 26–32.

Hauser, Philip M., and Duncan, Otis D. (eds.), *The Study of Population* (Chicago: University of Chicago Press, 1959).

Hoijer, Harry (ed.), *Language in Culture* (Chicago: University of Chicago Press, 1954).

Jameson, Samuel Haig, "Principles of Social Interaction," *American Sociological Review,* Vol. 10, No. 1, February, 1945, pp. 6–12.

Selznick, Philip, "Foundations of the Theory of Organization," *American Sociological Review,* Vol. 13, No. 1, February, 1948, pp. 25–35.

Strauss, Anselm (ed.), *The Social Psychology of George Herbert Mead* (Chicago: University of Chicago Press, 1956).

Timasheff, N. S., "Definitions in the Social Sciences," *The American Journal of Sociology,* Vol. LIII, No. 3, November, 1947, pp. 201–209.

Tumin, Melvin, "Culture, Genuine and Spurious: A Re-evaluation," *American Sociological Review,* Vol. 10, No. 2, April, 1945, pp. 199–207.

PART THREE

Social Institutions

INTRODUCTION

Social institutions, the central concern of Part III of this book, are partly structural and partly functional in their components. They are of crucial analytical importance to sociology.

Institutions have been defined concisely as the established forms of procedure by which group behavior is carried on. In more detail, a social institution is a complex cluster of cultural meanings, norms, values, and behavior, characterized by a high degree of organization and permanence, and revolving about at least one major human need or drive. Every major institution—whether it is marriage and the family, the economy, religion, or government—has specialized statuses and roles, utilitarian artifacts, ritual and symbols, an organizational pattern, and a code of either oral or written norms and specifications. The anthropologist Bronislaw Malinowski once stated that "the real component units of culture which have a considerable degree of permanence, universality, and independence are the organized systems of human activities called institutions. Every institution centers around a fundamental need, permanently unites a group of people in a co-operative task, and has its particular body of doctrine and its technique or craft. . . . One need does not receive one satisfaction in one institution. But institutions show a pronounced amalgamation of functions and have a synthetic character."

What Malinowski meant was that a given social institution has other functions besides its central and peculiar purpose. This multiplicity of functions leads to sharing and interchanges with those of other institutions. The family in modern society, for example, has as its primary concerns the gratification of sexual, reproductional, affectional, and child-rearing needs. However, it still furnishes one of the accepted institutional structures for economic maintenance, religious observance, and education, despite the transfer of many of these functions to other institutions. Schools have no institutional monopoly on the functions of education in our society, for certain types of knowledge (such as sex lore, techniques of gambling, and even religion) persist and flourish even when they are virtually excluded from the academic curricula.

The functions of any social institution are both manifest and latent. In the case of the former, they are acknowledged publicly and are made explicit, as when the president of a university declares that the functions of higher education are the search for truth, the preservation of knowledge, and the devotion of knowledge to the service of mankind. Equally significant, nevertheless, are the latent functions of higher education which the president may not acknowledge or even recognize, but which are implicit even in the operations of his own university. These include the provision of opportunities for courtship, mate selection, and social climbing; entertainment of the public at athletic events; the training of recruits for professional sports; supplying military officers; and subsidization of the noncommercial talents of artists and writers.

Ever since its modern beginnings in the nineteenth century, sociology has recognized the functional interdependence and strain toward consistency between different institutions. No institution, however classified, can be understood in isolation. Although it was fashionable in early sociology to view this interdependence in patterns of economic determinism as proposed by both Sumner and Marx, studies such as Max Weber's *The Protestant Ethic and the Spirit of Capitalism* modified this in the direction of reciprocal interaction between institutions. The church, for instance, is ostensibly a religious institution; but its existence depends on other institutions and vice versa, and its functions are understandable only by analyzing them in the context of the total social system of which the church is merely a part. To be specific, a celibate priesthood and an order of religious nuns are impossible unless there is such piety in the family system that parents encourage some of their sons and daughters to follow the divine call. Reciprocally, the avoidance of birth control in many marriages is understandable in terms of the religious norms promulgated by the priesthood.

MARRIAGE AND THE FAMILY

Of all the social institutions, the most intensive sociological preoccupation has been on the family. Its high priority in the order of sociological interests can be accounted for by its universality, its versatility in function throughout history, its importance in personality development and cultural transmission, and the fact that in the pioneering days of sociology it was not a vested interest of any other social science.

In the first article on the family that follows, John Sirjamaki points out that cultural configurations are the approved rules and sentiments, existing at a covert level, which motivate the overt behavior of individuals and integrate it into meaningful patterns. Such configurations, when applied to the family, express its value system. He suggests that there are eight configurations that give the American family its present character. Sirjamaki's article, originally published in 1948, is still another illustration of the essentially timeless character of good sociological analysis. It is just as relevant to our understanding of the contemporary American family as it was when it first appeared in print.

30. CULTURE CONFIGURATIONS IN THE AMERICAN FAMILY *

JOHN SIRJAMAKI
University of Buffalo

Most sociological studies of the family deal with it either as a social system or as a social institution. An important supplement to these approaches is the cultural analysis of the family in terms of its dominant configurations. When these can be specified for the family, it is possible to interpret the basic moral ideas which give the family its distinctive and identifying characteristics.

Culture configurations are the moral principles which comprise the social philosophy of a society. They are patterns of covert behavior; as such, they are the culturally approved rules or sentiments which motivate overt behavior and which integrate it into consistent patterns; and they can be deduced only from behavior. Such configurations exist on the level of the culture and arise in the context of everyday living. Members of a society comprehend the meaning of such precepts in the process of socialization, even when they are expressed tenuously or obscurely; and, indeed, configurations are difficult to state abstractly inasmuch as they generally operate below the level of awareness. Taken together, the configurations delineate the ethos of a culture.

Configurations are thus the basic units of the value system of a society. They differ from the absolute ethics of religious or philosophical systems in that they are mundane, practical, this-worldly; having developed within the culture, they express the dominant values which are thought to be necessary for the continued functioning of the society. Ordinarily configurational values are stigmatized by philosophers as base and inferior; Erich Fromm has called them "socially immanent ethics" as contrasted to universal ethics. For the social scientist, however, it is necessary to understand the configurations of a culture, since they motivate behavior much more continuously than do absolute ethical systems. The configurations will tend to support the total culture and to achieve an interrelatedness among themselves. As William Graham Sumner indicated, there is a strain for consistency in the mores.

The concept of the configurations of the culture, and a knowledge of the manner in which these are expressed within an institution, illuminates the study of the family. Configurations reach into the most intimate areas of individual and family behavior; they furnish the meanings and determine right and wrong behavior in courting, in husband-wife and parent-child relationships, in heterosexual social activity, and in ideas about sex. Thus they supply

* *The American Journal of Sociology,* Vol. LIII, No. 6, May, 1948, pp. 464–470.

the moral sentiments by which family members are influenced and make explicable the vagaries of their behavior.

At least four qualifications may be raised concerning the validity of applying culture configurations to the study of the American family. First, since such configurations are inferred by the investigator from the overt behavior of people, he must have available a considerable amount of observational data which, however, is currently lacking. Second, the use of such configurations should await an analysis of the total culture, and this has been attempted thus far in the most tentative manner. The analysis of parts of the culture, however, will assist in the determination of the total culture ethos. Third, generalizations about American culture must be stated in the most broad terms and can attempt only to strike an average, since regional and ethnic subcultures obviously differ from the main pattern. To whom, it may be asked, do configurations apply? The answer is that configurations are generally valid, or will tend to become so, for the entire American society, in the sense that they represent the moral standards by which all behavior is evaluated, and which exert a social pressure to secure some degree of conformance. Families of ethnic minorities thus quite apparently have patterns dissimilar to those of native-born families, but in time the American culture configurations come to influence the actions of at least the immigrant children and to bring their behavior into conformity with the general requirements of society. Finally, configurations are not easily amenable to quantification; they may seem to be accurately stated, but they are difficult to measure. There is no real answer to this objection other than to predicate the statement of configurations upon as careful objective analysis as is possible. A value system patently exists in every culture, and its appraisal should be sought by the social scientist.

The following configurations, among others, appear in the American family:

1. *Marriage is a dominating life-goal, for men as well as for women.*—It is felt that married life is the normal, desired condition for all adults, that it brings the greatest personal happiness and fulfilment, and that it permits the proper exercise of sex for the procreation of children and for individual satisfaction. The single adult life by contrast, according to this attitude, is empty and barren. That there is a considerable societal concern that women marry is generally recognized, but the greater courting and sexual initiative assumed by men has obscured the comparable pressure on them to marry, and adult men who postpone marriage into their thirties become objects of distress and conspiracy among friends and relatives. Most Americans marry in their twenties, and, for a considerable share of them, marriage at that age means a happy union of individual volition and social pressure.

Long ago Professor E. A. Ross pointed out that Americans are the most marrying nation in Western Christendom. United States census figures have shown that since 1890 they have married in steadily increasing proportions and at earlier ages. About 92 per cent of adults will have been married at some time in their lives by the age of sixty-five, and this is a sufficiently high number to suggest that nearly all persons marry who are physically and mentally capable of contracting marriage.

2. *The giving and taking in marriage should be based on personal affection and choice.*—Marriage is thought to be preeminently the linking of the lives of two young people drawn to each other by personal attraction. Arranged marriages, or those based on fraud or calculation, receive considerable disapprobation.

Dating is thought by many sociologists to precede serious courting and to be an educational process leading to it. Willard Waller first analyzed it in terms of its distinctive cultural patterns. In dating, the young woman undoubtedly receives the greatest cultural estimation of her personal qualities: merely to be a young, nubile female of attractive phenotype means that she is the object of considerable masculine attention and chivalry. But, despite this high evaluation of young women, most men grow up in American society with the assumption, culturally derived, that the decision to marry rests with them; they expect in the fulness of time to lead some dear girl to the altar. Women, on the other hand, regardless of their personal qualities, can never be completely sure that they will receive a marriage proposal which they can consider seriously, or, more to the point, be asked to marry by the man upon whom they have fastened their desire. The culture does not permit them to undertake active courting by themselves; to be a man-chaser is to suffer an ostracism which is enforced by the women themselves. Women are obviously not completely helpless in these sentimental matters, but they must use guile and finesse to bring the male to their side.

Since the biological fact of bisexuality predisposes women for the having and rearing of children, and therefore for the maintenance of a home, they are compelled to drive as good a bargain in the marriage market as they can. This they can manage only by a careful exploitation of the rules which specify correct maidenly deportment. Men, on the other hand, have greater volition in their marriage choices and are much more disposed as a result to manage their marital ventures in the bathos of culturally approved romance.

3. *The criterion of successful marriage is the personal happiness of husband and wife.*—Mutual compatibility is made the basis of marriage, and marital bliss becomes dependent upon the emotional sentiments, fluctuating and volatile as they may be, with which a couple regard their relationship. Ultimately their fullest felicity is believed to be achieved by having children, whose arrival and subsequent nurture are viewed as bringing satisfaction to basic biological and social needs. Childless couples are sometimes regarded as possessed of a selfishness which blights their union. Happiness in marriage is thus predicated upon a personal equation, the individual satisfaction and the opportunity for development of the couple.

The cultural accent upon happiness in marriage is of relatively recent origin. Marriages are ordinarily contracted and their success gauged by their contribution in the struggles of life. These may be the partnership co-operation of man and wife, the production of children, the social recognition of adult status, or the stability of marital status. Many such marriages may be buttressed by institutional supports, the most important of which is generally the exchange of property. The spouses may be selected for each other by the parents or other adults, after a careful scrutiny of their relative merits and upon some property agreement, in the belief that normal young people, once married, can fashion for themselves a successful marital life.

A corollary of the American patterns of courtship and marriage which is not always recognized is the logical necessity of a relatively easy system of divorce. From a cultural viewpoint, if marriages are made on the basis of personal and inevitably shifting emotions, without the added support of other institutional devices, then they should be equally easy to dissolve. Persons marry to find happiness and, finding it not, turn to divorce as a way out. The present high divorce rate, therefore, is in this sense made explicable and partially condoned by the cultural rules of marriage.

4. *The best years of life are those of youth, and its qualities are the most desirable.*—A high evaluation is placed upon youth and early middle age in American society, while the old are sometimes treated with indifference and even callousness. Youth is regarded as a period of innocence, energy, and enthusiasm; it is inventive and pragmatic when faced with new experiences and is glad of change—qualities fondly believed to be typical of Americans in general.

Among the young, the unmarried girl, aged perhaps twenty, attractive of face and limb, is the center of attraction in thought and deed. In other societies young men, or old men, or mothers are variously regarded as ideal symbols; in the United States it is the young, pretty girl. She therefore receives at this age the greatest gratification of her ego drives which will probably ever come to her. With men the ideal age is somewhere in the thirties; they need time in which to win occupational and social placement and need not depend so much upon chronological age for their acceptance.

From this high esteem on youth there derive important social consequences. Wherever the young are involved, whether it be in the conduct of schools, or juvenile delinquency, or maltreatment of children, or provision for their play opportunities, there is likely to be at least a quick emotional response to their needs.

Such sentiments as these do not, of course, arise in a social vacuum. They exist, rather, and become understandable in terms of American social history. Youth has received a high evaluation, precisely because its resourcefulness and resilience were valued qualities in the exploitation and development of the American continent. There have been, in addition, as compared to the age groups in European societies, relatively high proportions in the younger age categories in the American population; Americans have in this sense been a young people and correspondingly eager to admire the virtues of youth. The aged, on the other hand, have emerged as a significant social group only recently, and they are not yet favorably regarded.

Related to this cultural theme of youth is the existence of a considerable rift, not to say antagonism, between the generations. The conflict between the old and the young is common enough in human groups; what is significant is its intensity in American society. This is due, in large part, to the rapidity of social change in the United States and to the differing rates with which the generations have adjusted to those changes. Albert G. Keller speaks somewhat nostalgically of the aged in primitive society as revered "repositories of wisdom"; in American society they are unlikely to be regarded as possessors of a truth that has any relationship to their age.

5. *Children should be reared in a child's world and shielded from too early participation in adult woes and tribulations.*—This configuration is obviously closely related to the high cultural esteem of youth. It is modified by social class: the sentiment is held most strongly by the upper levels of society, much less so by the lower, but even among the poor the social conditions of the American community prevent a too considerable precocity among the children.

The cultural ideal is that children shall mature slowly in terms of their nature and age-sex grades in a prolonged child's world, which is characterized by a segregated class of children's activities. In this juvenile social world they are allowed to grow, develop their abilities, indulge in play, and occasionally to perform such small and often artificial tasks as may be assigned them. Generally they are protected from the responsibilities of adults, and laws and custom prevent their too early gainful employment. In many American homes, particularly in the cities, there is actually not much useful work that children can perform even if they wish. Especially in middle-class families is the configuration most completely observed. The child is accepted as an individual, and his relationships with parents are often warm and affectionate.

Joseph K. Folsom has contrasted this pattern with that which prevails in certain western European families, in which the child is incorporated into the family of adults and in which he lives in their world rather than in a segregated youth society. Moreover, unlike the American middle-class child who may become somewhat exhibitionist in his behavior because of the attention shown him, the European youth is often hastened along in the process of maturation and trained to deference and respect toward parents and elders in general.

Such training as the American child receives may start him off with a psychologically secure character structure, but in other respects it prepares him inadequately for later life. Sometimes he has not broken the emotional ties with his parents or developed definite heterosexual interests; hence his fondness for "Mom." During World War II the British thought the American soldier adolescent. James Graham Leyburn has pointed out that the American family is itself often at fault because of its inadequate integration with the larger community. It may be unable, as a result, to prepare and to place its members into job, school, clique and class, association, and other social relationships in the society. Thus it delays the processes of maturation.

6. *The exercise of sex should be contained within wedlock.*—Prior to marriage premarital intercourse is strongly condemned, and sex knowledge is kept hidden from children lest it be damaging to their moral character. After marriage, adultery is similarly proscribed. Sex may thus be legitimately expressed only within marriage, and the speaking of marriage vows makes highly moral sexual behavior which before then had been grossly immoral. The couple, previously prohibited from intercourse, may now embark upon an active, and socially approved, sex life. Sex, to speak figuratively, explodes upon marriage.

About sex there is considerable tension, preoccupation, frustration, shame, and deceit in American society. Judeo-Christian influences, and more immediately Puritanism, have given a sinful cast to sex and have condoned its expression in marriage only because of the grossly physical method of human reproduction. The tradition has particularly valued virginity, more especially in women, before marriage. But the strong interdictions upon sex have tended to heighten rather than to lessen the fascination with sex which exists among Americans. The furtiveness with which it is often approached and the numerous colloquialisms which refer to it indicate the uneasiness with which it is treated. Alfred C. Kinsey's exploration of the sex histories of American males has documented their actual performances. These data indicate that the sex configuration is held with varying intensity at the several levels of society, apparently least so in the lower class. Even here, however, the materials reemphasize the manner in which restrictive cultural attitudes condition and limit sexual outlets.

7. *Family roles of husband and wife should be based on a sexual division of labor, but with the male status being superior.*—According to this configuration, the husband is head of his family, its main economic support, and its representative in the larger community. Women, consigned to domesticity, are mothers and homemakers. These roles, biologically and culturally conditioned, provide for the structuring of all types of heterosexual relationships, in which the presumption of dominance generally rests with the males. Men are trained to develop the qualities necessary to fulfil their roles in economic, social, sexual, and other activities and to view themselves with self-respect when they have secured a competence in their performances. Women, too, are trained to their respective feminine roles, and these generally involve some degree of catering to men, somewhat as a complement to the expectation of greater male initiative. Lewis M. Terman's analysis of the desired pattern of sex typing in husband and in wife indicated how the cultural conception of the manly man and the womanly woman fall into the cultural mold.

Women's behavior is governed by a double standard of morality which expects greater masculine enterprise not only in the sexual spheres but in many other areas of life. Women live, in male estimation, under a blanket of oppressive mores which restrains their ordinary, everyday movements. Where men have a relative freedom of action, women must cater to a public opinion of what is womanly behavior. In social life women are under greater disapproval than men when they smoke or indulge in narcotics. On the job they may encounter much male prejudice which affects their pay and possibilities of promotion. They are more protected by social legislation which governs their hours and conditions of employment.

These cultural attitudes persist despite the social and economic events of modern times which have released women from the control of husbands and fathers. Before the law women have achieved a near-equality with men; they may seek gainful employment and retain their earnings; they have equal rights with men to education; they have all the freedoms necessary to live their own lives as they wish. Democratic sentiments further foster the desire that women develop as persons to enjoy the manifold blessings of American life and to have many of the privileges given men.

Women are thus caught in a process of social change, in which the cultural configuration restrains them to traditional roles, while new ones are proffered by economic and social forces. There is much confusion among them as a result. The young college girl, for example, may have difficulty in knowing to which force to respond: should she be content with the domestic role and look to the main chance of marriage, or should she seek outlets which include both marriage and other roles? Apparently some urban upper-level women find the puzzle extremely hard to resolve and respond to it neurotically.

Men, too, it must be pointed out, suffer in the realignment of roles, since they as much as women are conditioned to the status quo and may find it hard to accommodate themselves to change.

8. *Individual, not familial, values are to be sought in family living.*—The family is obviously affected by the considerable cultural affirmation of individualism, and the lack of a tradition of familism in American culture has further aided in the development of a configuration in which the family exists for the benefit of its members. The emphasis has been upon the individualization of all members of the family, the children as well as the parents, the wife as much as the husband. Obviously, the husband's prerogatives, nurtured in the bosom of the patriarchal family have had to be parceled out to the other members.

There are many important social consequences from the stress on individualism in the family. On the one hand, its promise is for the richer, fuller development of personality. On the other hand, it weakens the unity of the family. The stresses of American life, including industrialization, urbanization, internal migration, and social class, press hard against the frail shell of the family, attenuated as it is by the thinning of larger kin groups and often limited to its own resources in times of crisis. Further, since the family is not primarily important in placing its members into positions in the larger community, its members feel the strain of loyalties divided between the family and the outside affiliations.

If some of the configurations of the American family have been correctly stated, they indicate a social philosophy in which the values of individualism are paramount, or, more specifically, those which support the development of individual personality in the context of family and community relationships. A primary stress is placed on the family as a social group rather than on the functions which it performs for society. The family exists for its members rather than the members for the family. In this respect the family is in relatively close adjustment to the total culture, in which the democratic realization of the potentialities of all its members is an ideal.

But the family is pre-eminently an association based on antagonistic co-operation, and in times of hardship the antagonisms may predominate. The straining of family members for individualistic goals may blunt their sense of obligation to each other and to the larger society. When achievement of the desired values for which they grope seems far off and difficult, individualism may decay into gross egotism and selfishness. The family based on the chimera of personal values seems then faced with a dolorous future.

The American family, however, is not without resources. Contributing to its strength is the immense popularity of marriage, and through marriage the possibility of parenthood, both of them regarded as major life-goals. Staying power is also given the family by the affection and compatibility which draws two people into marriage, the warmth of relationships between parents and children, and the individualization of all members of the family. The structure of the family is such as to permit the desired nurturing of stable and democratic personalities.

In view of the ethos of the culture the direction of evolutionary change in the family, and of desirable efforts at rational adjustments, is in the continued emphasis upon the social relationships within the family and upon the family as a social system through which fundamental life-purposes can be achieved.

The stress on individualism as a value to be sought in American family life is an observation which many family sociologists have shared with Professor Sirjamaki. However, two divergent views have developed concerning the implications of individualism for the durability of the family as an institution. According to one view, the American family is in danger of disintegration, for it reveals the same symptoms as were true of the Greek and Roman family systems prior to their dissolution and the decline of their contextual civilizations. These symptoms were the attitude that marriage is a personal affair, the increased number of divorces for minor reasons, the decreasing number of children per family, the revolt of youth against the older generation and its values, the rise of juvenile delinquency, and the growing pattern of sexual promiscuity.

To counteract this alarmist point of view, a new note among many sociologists since World War II is that the American family, like other western family systems that have become conjugal instead of consanguineal in their structure, is simply changing functions as well as structure to comply with the changing society of which it is an integral part. In the article that follows, Dennis H. Wrong expands on this thesis that the American family is not dying. Rather, it is an evolving institution in which independence, economically and morally, and interdependence, for companionship and love, are sociologically to be expected, given the demands of institutional functionalism.

31. THE "BREAK-UP" OF THE AMERICAN FAMILY *

DENNIS H. WRONG
New York University

The "break-up" of the family has become a perennial theme of American sociologists. It is one with which they are sure to enlist the interest of laymen, harried as everyone is by the problems of relations with the opposite sex, marriage and divorce, and having and raising children. For the last two decades at least, they have warned us that the family is "losing its functions," and that the home is becoming little more than a hotel for its members. They have accumulated the statistics on divorce, bastardy, marital misery, and juvenile delinquency, and they habitually use such drastic terms as "disappearance," "disintegration," and "degeneration" to characterize the condition of the family today. Projects for restoring and "revitalizing" family life are legion among sociologists.

The family whose break-up is thus heralded is the traditional monogamous and patriarchal family of Western civilization. Sociologists point out that this family, developed for the most part in a rural environment, had economic, educational, and recreational functions which it has now relinquished to large business enterprises, schools, and the mass entertainment industries. In just about all the historical civilizations and primitive societies with which we are acquainted, the family has been both the basic economic unit and the major educational agency for its youth. Having lost these functions, what will hold it together?

The modern urban family, the standard sociological critique continues, is held together only by the individual needs of its members. Our socio-economic order does not depend to the extent it once did on the stability and solidarity of the family, and consequently exercises less control over people's domestic lives. The pressures of economic necessity and communal censure no longer play much role in binding the individual to the family group. Sex, marriage,

* *Commentary,* Vol. 9, No. 4, April, 1950, pp. 374–380.

and bearing and raising children are becoming private affairs to be settled by individual decisions at individual convenience rather than by the institutional regulations of law and religion or by the "unwritten law" of accepted codes and mores.

This critique is now to be found in the discussions of marriage and the family in most of the better textbooks, as well as in the sociological works written specifically on the subject. In such texts we will generally find a historical account of the family in pre-industrial Western society and ethnological data on the kinship systems of primitive peoples—and there may be an effort to classify the modern family according to its formal institutional attributes as monogamous, conjugal, patronymic, multilineal, patrilocal, etc. We will also find typologies constructed to indicate the main distinctions between the modern family and earlier forms. Thus, Carle Zimmerman (*The Family of Tomorrow,* Harper, 1949) discerns three basic family types and contrasts the "atomistic" modern family with the "trustee" and "domestic" families of the past. It is clear what *he* thinks of the modern family. Ernest Burgess and H. J. Locke, the authors of one of the most widely used texts on marriage and the family (*The Family,* American Book, 1945), use a more neutral terminology, and distinguish between the "institutional" family of the past, "with family behavior controlled by the mores, public opinion, and law," and the "companionship" family of the present, in which "behavior is determined by the affection and consensus of its members."

This analysis has led rather naturally to an emphasis on empirical studies of "success and failure" in marriage—undertaken with the explicit and implicit hope that they would give guidance to efforts to help stem the tide of disintegration. These studies have involved elaborate statistical investigations of given samples of married couples to find out which type gets divorced ("failure") and which type stays married ("success"), and they reach such conclusions as: marriages have a better chance of success when the bride is virgin and fifteen pounds underweight, when the groom lives in the suburbs, when both are devoutly religious, and when neither is particularly interested in politics. The results of these studies generally lend themselves easily to use by textbook writers and advice-to-the-lovelorn columnists as authoritative scientific evidence to back up their warnings against violating traditional precepts.

Of late, however, this main line of sociological writing and thinking on the American family has been under attack by sociologists who have taken to heart the more recent developments in anthropology and psychiatry. For one thing, these critics object that to use such terms as "disintegration" and "disappearance" in speaking of the modern family only indicates a nostalgic and unscientific preference for one type of family—the family of our rural past, which in any case cannot be restored in modern industrial society. More radical critics have also suggested that it is equally nostalgic and unscientific to consider divorce a sign of "social pathology" and the continuance of marriage a sign of "social health": we must consider the functions and meanings of marriage and divorce in different social contexts. Because the family pattern of today is different from that of an earlier day is no evidence, *per se,* that it is worse; it may be better, if it works better for its members and society in terms of present needs and considerations. Conceivably a society can be perfectly happy and adjusted with a very high rate of divorce.

These critics are also unimpressed by the typologies constructed by the sociologists of the family: these, they suggest, too often give the illusion of analytic depth to what is merely low-grade description blended with inadequate conceptions of causal relationship; their evaluative overtones give away the fact that it is prejudgments that are operating, rather than an objective effort to trace basic connections. For example, Burgess and Locke list just about every conceivable influence on sexual behavior in the last twenty years, from the automobile and avant-garde literature to urbanization, and assert that the decline of Puritan taboos is the result of the "combination of all these converging factors." But what was responsible for this miraculous "convergence"? How can one blithely mix causes on all levels of abstraction? Does such a proliferation of causes indicate real grasp or lead to better understanding?

In short, the critics of the classic American sociology of the family object to the failure to face the fundamental relation between developments in the family and developments in the rest of the society, a failure covered up by the manufacture of terminologies and the accumulation of hosts of "factors" and "causes."

This is the position of the "functional sociologists": the school of sociological thinking led by Talcott Parsons of Harvard and Robert Merton of Columbia. Their ideological orientation derives from the leading ideas of the fathers of sociology—Durkheim, Pareto, Weber—modified somewhat by an interest in contemporary anthropology and psychoanalytic psychiatry. The "functional" in the name of their school refers to their emphasis on the *function* of any social institution—the role it plays in the larger society, rather than its conformity to some earlier pattern or traditional social or moral value. Thus, they would be very chary of speaking of divorce as a sign of social pathology; rather, they would point out that divorce locks in with these social and these emotional problems in our present-day society, permits the release of these tensions, and so on: leaving us with the unstated conclusion that if we reduce divorce, something else (which moralists may find equally unpleasant) will take its place.

From anthropology—particularly from the "functional" anthropology of Malinowski, pursued in this country by such well-known writers as Ruth Benedict and Margaret Mead—they take the point of view of seeing any problem against the background of possible behaviors in all societies, including primitive societies; and a strong awareness of what is possible supports their effort to free themselves from value judgments. (So, for example, knowing that some societies allow premarital sexual freedom, some post-marital sexual freedom, some both, and some neither, G. P. Murdock, an anthropologist from Yale, finds it easy to suggest an active effort to eliminate our sexual taboos.) From psychoanalytic psychiatry and psychology the functional sociologists take the emphasis on the subtle interrelationship of a variety of life-history factors in producing some psychological result, and this, too, supports their opposition to the listing of unintegrated causes.

Functional sociology does not yet have the impressive list of works—texts, studies, and popular writings—on marriage and the family that the older approach to the sociology of the family has piled up. But when we look at such a volume as *The Family: Its Function and Destiny* (edited by Ruth Nanda Anshen, Harper, 1949) we see that the functional sociologists, with their anthropological and psychiatric allies, have almost completely crowded out the older writers on the sociology of the family, and are given sizable scope in which to develop their distinctive point of view.

Let us look first at the lengthy and impressive article in which Professor Parsons tries to show how the family is integrated with the larger social structures of American society. Professor Parsons takes certain formal features of the American family, particularly the fact that one is allowed a free choice of a marriage partner and that there are no kinship regulations closely tying members of the immediate conjugal family with relatives outside it, and shows how they conform to the requirements of our occupational system and class structure. For example, the absence of large and cohesive kin groups like the primitive clan or the Chinese ancestral line permits individuals to be highly mobile occupationally; their background and their family loyalty do not hold them back. And our loose kinship ties also check the possibility of nepotism, which would violate the impersonal evaluation of individual merit on which the more efficient and more democratic occupational system of the United States rests.

Professor Parsons thus ingeniously demonstrates the "functional interdependence" of the family and the other major institutions of American society. However, in order to present his picture of a highly articulated and systematically inter-related network of institutions, he is forced to assume that the units he is relating to one another are fairly stable. For example, he makes much of the difference between the male role as jobholder and economic provider and the female role as housewife and mother, taking her status from her husband. But he must concede that "there are strong tendencies in the United States towards identical treatment of the sexes." However, ignoring the broad implications of this admission, he then says that the difference in roles is *necessary* in order to preserve the solidarity of the family, because if husband and wife both worked, their job statuses might differ and this would impose serious competitive strains on the marriage relationship. This argument rather neatly links sex roles to the occupational system, but, even if its far-fetched character is ignored, it completely overlooks the fact that married women *do* work, and in increasing numbers. Married women, in all classes, now make up a considerable percentage of the total labor force, and there is clearly other evidence as well that sex roles in America are changing. How then can it be "necessary," if the whole system is to keep on working, that women should *not* work?

Professor Parsons' failure to stress present-day changes in sex roles leads to the main point that can be made against the newer, anthropologically influenced efforts to understand the American family: their concentration on efforts to detect in Americans' behavior the patterns and norms of an "American" culture, parallel to the culture of a primitive tribe, is misplaced. It seems to me that the urbanization and mechanization of American life, now in the process of steamrolling traditional values and modes of conduct out of existence, make it impossible to speak with real precision any more of static "culture patterns" or "social norms" governing the sphere of family life. There is no question that the older patterns and norms are severely shaken; but I doubt whether many new ones have emerged in any crystallized fashion, and certainly no total overall system, worthy of being called a culture, is as yet apparent.

If we look at a few of the subjects sociologists regularly deal with in their discussions of the family, we will see that the difficulties involved in pinning down present-day norms and patterns of family behavior are, by comparison with primitive societies, enormous.

COURTSHIP: The term itself evokes anachronistic images of the chaperons, horsehair sofas, stammering proposals, and chaste first kisses after betrothal that were at one time required by a clearly formulated code. We do not need Kinsey to tell us that it is no longer followed by most people, although, with minor modifications, it remains the "official morality" promulgated by the organs of mass communication, upheld by Dorothy Dix, and transmitted by most middle-class parents to their children. Here the voice of Puritanism, the Victorian era, and the rural farm family—not to mention Catholic and Jewish education—still speaks. Its growing irrelevance to actual behavior gives it the status of an "ideal pattern" rather than a "real pattern," to use the language of the anthropologists.

The relaxed censorship standards of Hollywood and the publishing industry, the popularity of such books as the Kinsey report, and the spread of popular psychiatry with its promotion of "sexual adjustment" as an ideal plus the idea that "sexual frustration" is unhealthy, indicate that values are changing. The most marked trend in sexual behavior within the last generation unearthed by the Kinsey statistics is the growing sexual independence of unmarried women. At the very least, there seems to be an increasing acceptance of pre-marital sex relations and a more general awareness of almost universal participation in the erotic life.

Looking at the middle class alone, we see that the majority still probably adhere to a secularized Puritanism which uneasily co-exists with the "having-a-good-time" attitude nurtured by the entertainment industries. Some groups countenance pre-marital sex relations, but only after betrothal; to others the "affair" is an accepted type of pre-marital relationship (and often extra-marital as well); and there are still those who regard a "Bohemian revolt" demanding virtual promiscuity as the essence of modernity. Everything from sheer "having fun" to the orgiastic philosophy of Wilhelm Reich is invoked to justify this variety of behavior. Only in the educated, "liberal" sector of the metropolitan middle class do we find that new values are systematized to any degree. It is here that psychiatry becomes the basis for a new ethic governing sexual conduct (and not infrequently *all* conduct).

The individual often is caught in this confusion and profusion of values, and must fall back upon himself for canons of personal conduct. Who is so lonely as the adolescent girl wondering if she has become a "loose" woman by submitting to her lover, and finding no unanimous community opinion to answer her either negatively or affirmatively? Or the boy responding to the value placed by his male companions on "having an affair" while remaining deeply unconvinced of his right to make sexual demands on girls of his own social status? No wonder attempts to establish an ethic based solely on analysis of the biological and psychological nature of the individual are so popular. A great deal of the intense interest which Americans have in psychoanalysis is due simply to its revelation of what Lionel Trilling has called "a community of sexuality."

The sociologists are hardly consistent with one another in their efforts to extract generalizations from this chaos of shifting standards. Carle Zimmerman, a belligerent traditionalist, thunderously denounces America's "Voice of the Turtle sexual ethics," while those influenced by psychoanalysis continue to speak as if they were engaged in storming the last bastion of Puritanism in the modern world. And these conflicting positions are supported by empirical studies of different segments of American social reality. These writers may accurately characterize certain groups; but they fail to stress the significance of the existence side by side of so many *different* norms for sexual conduct. The demonstration that widely different norms do exist is certainly one of the most significant findings of the Kinsey report. For it is this bewildering diversity of values which is primary to the situation confronted by middle-class Americans growing up in the larger cities today. Not only do they face a variety of possible patterns in their own world, but in social mobility and migration they become aware of new ranges of patterns characteristic of different classes. Surely it is an instance of what Durkheim called "anomie," of the breakdown of norms, that condition which under the more familiar label of "alienation" is recognized as oppressing all of us.

The sociologists would seem to have overworked the concept of "culture." Modern life cannot be fitted into the frames of uniform "culture patterns," and the attempt to force a fit often results in neglect of basic features of *social structure*—the objective realities, such as the need to make a living in a certain social system, which enforce a certain type of behavior regardless of pre-existing norms, values, and social rituals. One of the outstanding characteristics of the modern world is, in fact, the destruction of culture by sweeping changes in social structure. The adjustment to modern industry and modern cities wrecks the complicated and varied cultural patterns built up in the American rural hinterland, or in European villages. Edward Sapir, the late Yale anthropologist, suggested this a long time ago when he distinguished between the "genuine" culture of older societies and the "spurious" culture of an industrialized world.

MARRIAGE: We have already pointed out that a major focus of empirical study has been the "causes" of marital unhappiness. I believe that an inquiry into *why people get married at all* might prove far more revealing than these usually banal undertakings, but since all writers on the family assume the desirability, or at least the permanence, of the institution of monogamous marriage, no one has posed this question for systematic investigation. It is taken for granted that romantic love, and the desire for emotional security or for sanctioned sexual gratification, induce most people to marry.

These motives seem so self-evident that the radical change in the meaning of marriage which they imply is easily overlooked. For marriage was formerly both an economic necessity and a moral obligation, rather than simply a means of satisfying individual psychological needs. Today marriage no longer confers of itself added standing in the community. It no longer symbolizes the achievement of full status as adult and citizen as it did in rural society. While a vague stigma still clings to the middle-aged bachelor, it does not affect his occupational career and perhaps is based on suspicion of homesexuality rather than on an echo of the conviction that failure to marry constitutes unnatural and immoral shirking of responsibility. The spinster, of course, remains an object of contempt and pity, but this attitude will presumably disappear as differences in sex roles continue to diminish. Indeed, no one takes this attitude even today towards an unmarried woman who has achieved some type of distinction. Again, a variety of possible roles is offered to people where one stood before.

It is asserted by both laymen and sociologists that romantic love is the prime basis for marriage in America. To many it is as uniquely American as baseball or hot dogs. Now romance is linked with youth; it is, as a matter of fact, a primary feature of the American "youth culture." However, the boundaries of this youth culture are being steadily expanded downward to a youthful age level where marriage is quite impossible economically. Originally centered on the college campus, it has diffused, with the creation of high school Greek-letter fraternities modeled on those of the colleges, to late and middle adolescents. And now twelve- and thirteen-year-old "bobby-soxers" are also being brought within its orbit.

If, as Denis de Rougemont asserts in another essay in the Anshen volume, "it is the very essence of romance to thrive on obstacles, delays, separations, and dreams," it may be that the romantic dramas of the future will be mainly enacted by youngsters in their early teens facing the economic impossibility of marriage, the jeers of older adolescents who have become confirmed sexual realists, and the indifference of adults who have "settled down" to marriage in a matter-of-fact, utilitarian way. Marriage is already looked on by many as "settling down" rather than as full achievement of adult status or as the blissful climax of romance. Perhaps marriage is becoming an escape from romance—from the emotional wear-and-tear of a succession of bouts with love followed by disillusionment, although the high divorce rate would seem to indicate that it is not a very successful escape.

In any case, the reasons why people marry are problematical and may become even more so. Their problematical character is ignored by the sociologists, who concentrate on the reasons why marriages break up. "To marry or not to marry?" is a real question for many people. Or, more accurately, it becomes "whether to marry now or later?" John Levy and Ruth Monroe, in their book *The Happy Family,* point out that people frequently rationalize a deep-seated reluctance to marry by finding fault with all prospective partners who present themselves. Freely expressed concern over *whom* to marry conceals the more fundamental doubts about *when* to marry. This would have applied to very few Americans of fifty years ago; indeed, there have been few periods in world history in which the desirability of marriage has been as widely questioned as it is today—though the questioning is as yet indirectly revealed in people's behavior and emotions, rather than in thought and speech.

Recent censuses show that about 10 percent of each sex remain unmarried at the age of 45. This figure undoubtedly represents an increase in the number of unmarried people over earlier years; yet it is perhaps equally significant to note that 90 percent of the population still gets married before early middle age.

CHILDREN: The wish for an heir to perpetuate one's name and status was the strongest male incentive to marriage in aristocratic society; later, children were needed as workers on the farm and in the small business when these were predominantly family enterprises; and motherhood has always been considered woman's crowning achievement in her traditional feminine role. Today it is obvious that emphasis on success as a major life goal, the perils of child-raising stressed by popular psychiatry, the uncertainty of the future, and, finally, the availability of birth-control methods, lessen the meaning and value once associated with the creation of one's own image in the person of an offspring. The ambivalence which middle-class parents, both male and female, have towards raising a family has been fully and ably described by Arnold Green in his article "The Middle Class Male Child and Neurosis" (*American Sociological Review,* February 1946). Having children, like sexual conduct and marriage, is increasingly taken out of the realm of "mores" and "culture patterns" and becomes a matter of individual option.

Child-rearing must inevitably become a focal point for the tensions of social change, for parents can scarcely fail to recognize that the world faced by their children differs considerably from that in which they themselves grew up. Margaret Mead and Geoffrey Gorer both attribute the absence of stable patterns for raising children in the United States to historical causes: the influx into the country of immigrants who were of necessity forced to reject much of their Old World culture in adjusting to life in alien America. They contend that the anxiety felt by immigrant parents bringing up children in a strange country, and the inevitable rejection by the young of their parents' way of life, have somehow been universalized and now characterize even families whose forefathers have lived in America for generations.

But large-scale immigration has ended and a third and a fourth generation of descendants of the immigrants are now growing up. Are we to infer that the attitudes of the immigrant population have "diffused" through the rest of society and mysteriously become part of a unitary American "ethos"? The almost exclusive concern with cultural concepts—in this case the "acculturation" of the foreign-born—leads Mead and Gorer to ignore contemporary socio-economic changes which obliterate traditional values and drive as wide a gap between the second and third generations as that created by immigration between the first and second. Everyone, old American and third-generation immigrant alike, is victimized by this process. There is no need to refer to immigration to explain it. Surely suburban living, commuters' trains, and unglamorous office jobs, leading to the father's absence from home most of the day, have as much to do with the decline of paternal authority as a "pattern" of rejecting fathers ostensibly inherited from the children of the foreign-born. Perhaps second-generation immigrants did originate the pattern, but it has not simply persisted just so: it must have been strengthened by these social trends unrelated to immigration. And in the long run it is more valuable to understand the significance of such trends than the particular historical situation of the immigrant family.

Big city urbanism provides the setting in which child-rearing is viewed as an enterprise fraught with danger, and recourse to the "expert" becomes an almost compulsive response. But science, and particularly a new and undeveloped branch of it, is an unstable authority on which to depend, and it has produced a rapid succession of verdicts on child-rearing over the last two decades. John B. Watson told the mother to sterilize herself emotionally before approaching her child in order to "condition its reflexes" as impersonally as possible. Or better still she shouldn't approach the child at all, but should surrender this archaic privilege to the behaviorist psychologist. Today Watson is a back number, and the Freudians tell us that the child must have the demonstrative love of the mother. Approved methods of feeding and toilet training have changed even more rapidly. You pick your pediatrician and you get your technique for rearing children.

These trends in sexual behavior, marriage, and child-bearing and rearing all move in the direction of greater freedom of individual choice. Modern life has broken through the rigidity of traditionally prescribed patterns of conduct. Man's emancipation from the last of the trinity of institutions, Church, State, and Family, which dominated him before the Industrial Revolution, is now well under way.

Bourgeois society had guaranteed religious freedom and created the limited, *laissez-faire* state, but as Max Horkheimer, another contributor to the Anshen volume, points out, *families* rather than individuals were liberated from authoritarian institutions. In fact, the Victorian era, the peak of bourgeois liberalism, has come to symbolize familial control and oppression—the domination of woman by man, of children by parents, and of all by a Puritanical moral code. Professor Horkheimer writes: "Man, liberated from serfdom in alien households, became the master in his own. Children, however, for whom the world had been a penitentiary throughout the Middle Ages, continued to be slaves well into the 19th century. When the separation of state and society, of political and private life, was completed, direct personal dependence survived in the home."

Despite the emphasis on democratic living to be found in contemporary sociology, hardly any American student of the family views it as Professor Horkheimer does, from the perspective of the history of human freedom. Seen in this perspective, most of the current negative evaluations become positive. We can, if we wish, see the variety and uncertainty of behavior in "courtship," marriage, and child-raising as indications of the breakdown and disintegration of the family, as in a sense they are. But we can also see these trends as inevitable *expansions of the area of the personal freedom of the individual.* Of course increased freedom means more uncertainty concerning desirable sexual conduct and more divorce, certainly at first and probably forever: but then we must stop hedging and decide what we really mean by individual freedom and how much of it we want.

And even our failure to discover "patterns," "norms," and "rules," equivalent to those described for primitive societies, and earlier stages of Western culture, can be seen positively: it means that the individual is not faced with one or a few fixed courses of development, but has to create a life for himself that combines the old patterns and desires with new possibilities. This is more difficult, emotionally, and creates a confused situation, socially and morally: but what else can freedom mean?

The study of the family can lead us directly to the consideration of the most important questions of freedom and individuality: perhaps the functional sociologists will yet arrive at the discussion of those questions on a high level.

Meanwhile, it should be clear that none of the trends we have described points in any way to the disappearance of the family, nor even to changes in its formal structure. Although by 1945 roughly one in every three marriages ended in divorce, it is estimated that as high as 70 or 80 percent of the divorcees remarry, which, to say the least, does not indicate a loss of faith in marriage. People continue to have children and raise them in the time-honored and traditional place for such functions, the family. In our mass society the ties of marriage and kinship are almost the only stable framework for close personal relationships.

Indeed, the family we have today, with its freedom from extended kinship bonds and from excessive ceremonial, may be considered as better meeting the needs and more appropriately reflecting the spirit of a free, mobile, and individualistic society; Professor Parsons in his essay is well aware of this.

By one of those ironies of history, this accelerating freedom from the authoritarian family comes at a time when totalitarianism menaces freedom in all areas of life. And as Professor Horkheimer shows, this threat is not unrelated to the family: for on the one hand, totalitarianism restores the authority of the family as a means of raising the birth rate and enhancing national power; but on the other, this is a false restoration, for in reality the totalitarian state demands loyalty only to itself, and it destroys all other loyalties, including those that develop within the family. This would seem to be one more piece of evidence that the freer society and the freer family are closely interrelated and interdependent.

INDUSTRY

The drastic reduction in the structure and functions of the American family portrayed by both Professors Sirjamaki and Wrong in the previous two articles has been largely, although not entirely, connected with a shift during the last century from a family-centered economy to an industrial economy and concomitantly from a predominantly rural to what is now an urban society. Traditionally, the first sociologists, as we have already noted, did not consider the economy as a social institution within the realm of their primary concerns. Economics was already established as a special social science, and the pioneers in the nineteenth century did not dare intrude too boldly on a firmly established discipline.

More recently, however, their own achievement of reputable status in the world of social science, and their realization that economists, concerned mostly with prices and wages, supply and demand, labor and management, and production and the business cycle, were overlooking the sociological aspects of economic behavior, led sociologists to the development of industrial sociology. In the next article, William Foote Whyte, a prominent industrial sociologist, traces the establishment of the new sociological subdivision from its very beginning. He shows that the testing of the "social relations" hypothesis in the Hawthorne Experiment, in order to explain increased and restrained productivity, qualifies as the real starting point for economic institutional analysis by the sociological approach.

32. HUMAN RELATIONS IN INDUSTRY *

WILLIAM FOOTE WHYTE
Cornell University

What are the causes of conflict in industry? How may more harmonious relations be achieved? What are the satisfactions and dissatisfactions men find in industrial work? What factors lead men to increase their productive efforts? What factors lead them to hold back production?

These are some of the questions that students of human relations in industry have been investigating. The questions are not new. Men in industry and social philosophers outside of industry have discussed them for decades and even centuries. But the effort to examine these questions scientifically is new.

THE WESTERN ELECTRIC RESEARCH PROGRAM

Human Relations in Industry as a field of scientific inquiry is little more than twenty years old. The selection of any date for its beginning would be arbitrary, but we may call upon the twelfth experimental period in the Western Electric Research Program as a convenient starting point.

Harvard University's Graduate School of Business Administration under the leadership of Elton Mayo and F. J. R. Roethlisberger had been collaborating with executives of Western Electric's Hawthorne plant in Cicero, Illinois. They were investigating the factors that led workers to produce more or less. First attention was given to some of the physical conditions of work. The first experiment showed that there was no correlation between variations in lighting and productivity.

This led the researchers on to a new experiment designed to measure the effects of rest periods and refreshments upon productivity. Six girls of average previous performance were selected for the test room experiment. The purpose of the experiment was explained to them. They were asked to work at a normal pace and not to speed up or hold back. They were then segregated from the rest of the work force in a room especially provided for them. During the months they worked in the test room, they were under constant observation by a member of the research staff with whom they became quite friendly. Their task was to assemble telephone relays. Each completed relay was dropped into a box where it was automatically recorded so that the experimenters had a record of production day by day, hour by hour.

After providing for a period in which the girls were to get used to their new surroundings without the introduction of any changes in the way of

* *The Delphian Quarterly*, Vol. 39, No. 2, Spring, 1956, pp. 1–5, 40.

rest periods, refreshments or working hours, the experimental changes were begun. Each change was discussed with the girls first before it was put into effect. Each change remained in effect for enough weeks so that its effects could presumably be measured.

In a summary article of this nature, there is no need to detail the exact sequence of these experimental changes. It is enough to report that rest periods were introduced, that refreshments were provided at certain periods of the day, and that the length of the working day was also shortened at one point. Various combinations of changes in these three areas were also tried out.

Through the first eleven periods of this experimental program, the productivity of the test room girls rose steadily. A student less cautious and scientifically minded than the Harvard researchers might have concluded from this experience simply that the introduction of rest periods and refreshments leads to higher productivity, even though the results gave no clue as to which combination of rest periods and refreshments seemed to be most effective. It was precisely at this point that Elton Mayo introduced the crucial test of the effect of rest periods and refreshments. The twelfth experimental period marked a return to working conditions prevailing at the beginning of the experiment —no rest periods, no refreshments and the customary eight hour working day. Productivity in this twelfth period surpassed all pre-existing records.

Some might have been inclined to toss aside the results of the twelfth period as an irrelevant fluke and conclude that after all in general these improvements in working conditions did increase productivity. But Mayo and his co-workers insisted that the results of the twelfth period demanded a revolution in thinking regarding the factors influencing productivity. If productivity rose to a new high upon withdrawal of these worker benefits (rest periods and refreshments), then it could no longer be seriously argued that that remarkable rise in productivity of the test room girls was due to these working conditions.

In abandoning the working conditions theory, the researchers were forced to cast about for new explanations. It was in that search that they took the decisive steps in founding this field of human relations in industry.

The experiment had been set up in the best scientific tradition so that certain working conditions would be varied while every other important factor was held constant. Now the twelfth period proved that the changes in rest periods and refreshments did not explain the changes in productivity. It therefore followed that there must be other factors in the experiment which had not been held constant. The researchers asked themselves what other significant changes had entered into the world of the test room girls.

As they came to look upon the test room as a social situation, some of the answers became evident.

Let us contrast the situation faced by the six test room girls with that faced by other girls on similar jobs in the regular factory departments. Obviously these six girls were singled out for special attention. They were not selected because they were outstanding workers, but nevertheless they were selected. They were not asked to produce an extraordinary amount, but they were informed that they were playing a part in an important experimental program. The evidence of the test room observer shows that they took considerable pride in their part in the experiment.

Furthermore, the girls were removed from the regular channels of factory supervision. In the factory departments, their work had been laid out for them, they had been told what to do and had been closely supervised. No one had consulted them about the conditions of their work. Now, while they were under the constant observation of one of the research team, they were almost completely cut off from the regular channels of supervision. They were consulted about each stage of the experiment. The consultation was more than an empty form as evidenced by the fact that at one point the girls vetoed a research proposal and did not have it imposed upon them. Finally, they were working in the company of an observer who took a friendly personal interest in them.

This picture suggested that while the experiment had focused upon changes in certain working conditions, actually the most important changes introduced were in the field of human relations. The test room girls experienced a marked change in their relations with management and with each other. They built up a tightly knit social group with very considerable pride in their membership in it.

This conclusion applies to the field of productivity but seems to have a much more general relevance. It can be stated in this way. In order to change the activities and attitudes of people, change the relations among them.

This aspect of the Western Electric program has been attacked by some scholars as simply being a discovery of the obvious. The researchers discovered that industry is a society in itself, that individuals are not solely concerned with money or with the physical conditions of work. They are also strongly influenced by the relations that grow up among them. In a sense, the criticism has weight but it fails to recognize the state of knowledge regarding human behavior in industry that existed at the time of the experimental program. At that time, the sociologists and social anthropologists who were busily studying primitive and modern industrial communities had not ventured inside the gates of the factory. A few psychologists were active in industry, but most of them were engaged in developing aptitude and other psychological tests regarding the relation between a man's abilities and the physical and mental work required in different jobs. While it might have occurred to the sociologist if you had asked him that a factory could be looked upon as a social system or community, he did nothing about such an idea until the way had been laid open for him by the Hawthorne experimental program.

Furthermore, at the time of the Western Electric program, popular thinking about human behavior in industry was dominated by certain ideas developed by economists and engineers. The prevailing notion was that man—at least in the factory setting—was an economically motivated individual. He responded as an individual to the financial rewards offered him or to the threats of the withdrawal of such rewards. In such thinking, groups did not exist. Each man responded rationally to his calculations of profit and loss.

The Hawthorne experiments exploded these ideas. The studies of the test room and other studies growing out of it demonstrated that it is futile to think and act in terms of these individualistic economic assumptions. Men live in a society when they are in the plant just as when they are in their communities. If we are to understand their behavior in industry, we must therefore study the relations among the men and women who work together in this industrial society. It was that conclusion that opened up for study the field of human relations in industry and led to a rapidly expanding popular interest in it.

THE HARWOOD EXPERIMENTS

If the Hawthorne experiment showed that changes in human relations were accompanied by changes in productivity, the next logical step would be to set up an experiment in which there were introduced changes in human relations with the deliberately planned objective of affecting productivity by this means. In the sense that the productivity changes were accidentally introduced in the Hawthorne program, it remained now to determine whether social scientists could affect productivity through the deliberate planning and execution of human relations changes. This next step was taken by researchers in the Harwood Manufacturing Company under the leadership of Kurt Lewin, a social psychologist.

The Western Electric study of the Bank Wiring Room had revealed and documented in detail a phenomenon well known to experienced factory management people: restriction of output. It was found that workers did not ordinarily produce up to the limits of their physical and mental capacities even when they were paid on incentive rates, which meant more money for more production. Instead of going all out individually to produce as much as they can, workers seem to get together in informal groups to decide how much constitutes a "fair day's work." They then produce up to that level and not beyond it. When asked why they do not go beyond the agreed-upon point even when they acknowledge that in many cases it would be readily possible, they explain the restriction in terms of fears that management would cut the rates, paying less per unit produced if they stepped up productivity or that they would work themselves out of a job.

This rate cutting argument is used even when no one can cite a specific example of a time when this particular management cut an incentive rate. Of course, there have been cases in which certain managements have cut rates and stories of what has happened in other plants may reach the workers in the plant in question.

Why do workers restrict output? The reasons would vary from case to case, but certain general answers can be given. Workers on the bottom of the chain of command are subject traditionally to the orders and to the changes introduced by supervisors, engineers, time and motion study men and other management officials. Traditional operating procedures of industry call for treating men as isolated individuals and make no provision for the groupings among them that inevitably arise. It is in reaction to this subordinate position, to this constant necessity of responding to changes introduced from above, that men band together informally to establish their own standards of approved and disapproved conduct. Like people in communities everywhere, they build up a culture or way of life. A good part of this culture arises either in opposition to management or else to interpose a cushioning effect upon management's activities. Where conflict between workers and management exists, these standards of what constitutes a "fair day's work" are likely to be most rigidly adhered to and informally enforced by the workers upon each other.

If this explanation of restriction of output is correct, it would then follow that a change in the relations between workers and management would result in changes in worker attitudes toward productivity and would also result in changes in the productive activity itself.

The experiments to be reported here were carried out by Alex Bavelas, John R. P. French Jr. and Lester Coch with groups of sewing machines operators in the Harwood Manufacturing Company plant. These women operated individual machines and were paid on a piece-rate basis. That is, there was a guaranteed minimum hourly wage, but the employees were paid so much per piece and regularly made more per hour than the guaranteed minimum. However, in this case, as in others, there seemed to be a group standard that they would not produce beyond a certain amount, in spite of all management guarantees that piece rates would not be changed.

The first experiment carried out by Bavelas was designed to test the effect of group discussion methods upon productivity. Bavelas met with several groups of workers to discuss with them the problems they found in their jobs, their attitudes toward productivity, and the possibilities that they might want to produce more. The discussions were designed to provide a maximum opportunity for the women to express their feelings about the job and come to their own conclusions. Under Bavelas' discussion leadership, several of the groups did decide to raise their level of productivity, and determine upon new goals. Other groups decided against such an increase, and no effort was made to push them toward a decision to produce more. After the discussions, it was found that the groups that reached a decision to produce more did achieve substantially higher productivity whereas the groups where no such decision was reached remained at approximately the pre-existing levels. Thus the group process had very marked effects upon the activities of these people even though each one operated a machine separate from all the others.

Unfortunately for this experiment, we have only the barest outline of what was done and results achieved. We know very little of the process of discussion carried on under Bavelas' leadership, nor do we know why certain groups decided to increase productivity whereas others made the contrary decision. Despite these limitations, it is evident that changes in human relations led directly to these changes in work activity.

Another Harwood experiment involved the study of the effects of worker participation upon adjustment to changes in work methods. French and Coch had found that when changes in methods of work were introduced by management in the customary manner, one could expect a sharp drop in worker productivity and a concomitant increase in expressions of worker dissatisfaction. In some cases, the workers in time reached higher levels of productivity, but in other cases even when the new methods appeared to be more efficient from an engineering standpoint the workers did not even attain their previous levels of output. Since American industry is highly dynamic both in technology and in work processes, it is important to study the reaction of workers to such changes.

French and Coch began their study with three matched groups of employees who were introduced to similar changes in job method in three different ways. The first or "non-participating," was merely ordered to make the change and given instructions as to the new method. The second group participated through election of representatives who met with management officials to discuss the new methods and to help plan their introduction with management. The third group participated on a total basis with all members of the group meeting with the management people to discuss and plan the changes.

Results of these three different methods of introducing work changes were sharply contrasting. The group which had had changes imposed on it in the customary manner, dropped off sharply in its productivity at the time of the introduction of the change and its productivity remained at least fifteen percent below its pre-existing records for thirty days following the change. The group which had chosen representatives to participate in planning the change showed the sharpest drop of all at the time of the occurrence of the job change. Productivity dropped off about 35 percent on the first day but rose almost steadily each day thereafter. It reached pre-existing levels on approximately the twelfth day following the change and reached the level of approximately 10 percent higher than pre-existing averages by the end of the thirtieth day following the change. The group that had participated on a total basis experienced only a slight drop in productivity on the day of the job change and rose above the pre-existing average on the day immediately after the change. From then on, its productivity fluctuated considerably but showed a steady upward trend so that the workers in this group were more than 15 percent higher than previous averages well before the end of the experimental period.

The change in job methods had other marked effects. Expressions of dissatisfaction with management and with the job change were greatest in the non-participating group of workers, and non-existent in the group which was involved in total participation. The level of morale, then, seemed to be markedly affected by the social process whereby changes were introduced.

RELIGION

We have already stressed in our introductory remarks on social institutions that it is impossible to separate all the functions and purposes of one institution from those of another. Yet it is clear that the economic institution of a society—whether it be pastoral, agricultural, or industrial—is primarily concerned with the satisfaction of the mundane needs for food, clothing, and shelter. Religion, on the other hand, is that social institution which functions to satisfy the needs for certainty, security, and completion beyond the mundane and observable in the universe. Emile Durkheim, in his classic work, *The Elementary Forms of Religious Life,* observed that "the real characteristic of religious phenomena is that they always suppose a bipartite division of the whole universe into two classes which embrace all that exists, but which radically exclude each other. *Sacred* things are those which the interdictions protect and isolate; *profane* things, those to which these interdictions are applied and which must remain at a distance from the first. Religious beliefs are the representations which express the nature of sacred things. . . . Rites are the rules of conduct which prescribe how a man should comport himself in the presence of these sacred objects."

In the next article, J. O. Hertzler, an expert in institutional analysis and the sociology of religion, describes the typical structural features of religion as a social institution and discusses seven major functions that religious institutions perform. He concludes by noting the series of changes undergone by religion in western societies that have diminished its "institutional sway."

33. RELIGIOUS INSTITUTIONS *

J. O. HERTZLER

University of Nebraska

Due to the varied, complex, and protean nature of religion, no interpretation of it in either its individual or its social aspects will meet with universal acceptance. The particular cultist or religious professional can be very explicit about what religion is, or about what passes for religion with him, but many others will not accept his definition, and will disagree with him as to what must be included as essential or rejected as contrary or unimportant. "Religion" for one person or group may be irreligion for others. Yet everywhere religion is a great human reality—a fact both of the individual consciousness and of the institutional order.

* *The Annals of the American Academy of Political and Social Science,* Vol. 256, March, 1948, pp. 1–13.

THE NATURE OF RELIGION

Religion is a spontaneously appearing, perennial, and universal attribute of man. Its beginning is unknown. Among almost all peoples and in all times and places there are aspects of individual consciousness and poignant human experiences on the one hand, and social quests and dominant expressional and regulatory features of the institutional system on the other, which are denominated as specifically religious. From earliest times, as a French writer has said, man has been "incurably religious."

A popular book on religion some years back opened with the dramatic statement: "In the beginning there was fear; and fear was in the heart of man; and fear controlled man." Religion seemingly grows out of the fact that man lives in an atmosphere of uncertaintly, insecurity, and incompletion. He is concerned about the unknowns and inexplicables about him. The element of chance, here and hereafter, everlastingly must be contended with. Man is awed and dismayed by the enormity, the stupendous forces and inexorable processes, the timelessness, of the universe. He feels himself in the presence of something which in its complexity, its power, and its mystery passes comprehension. As he faces the more or less recurrent crises of life—the holocausts of nature, war and revolt, accident, pestilence, and sickness, personal defeat and humiliation, the nature of life, the mystery of death, the enigma of the hereafter—he wonders about the security of himself and his group, about the continuity of himself. There are the disillusionments and tribulations as he associates with his fellow men, as well as the urgent social "needs" that seem to be beyond his satisfaction, or control. There is often a feeling of not living a sufficiently full and good life.

Man has the conception of a supernatural, extrahuman Something, which is the cause and manipulator of forces or powers at work in the universe. He feels that he is dependent upon this power or powers, and that they mightily affect his present well-being; often, also, his ultimate destiny.

Religion is one phase of man's cultural system—a body of attitudes, ideas, and techniques—whereby he explains and adjusts himself to the unknown, the mysterious, and the mighty. By means of the various elements of religion he reaches out beyond the mundane—the material, the social, the readily knowable and observable, the relative, the temporary, the things and affairs more or less within his natural means of control—and tries to achieve a harmonious relationship with this power.

Religion and magic. This effort raises the distinction between religion and its universal and seemingly inseparable complement, magic. Both relate to the mysterious power. Strictly, magic looks upon the universe as mechanistic and passive. There is in the universe mystical force or mana which is independent of human limitations. By the use of proper procedures one can exert power over this mysterious force and thwart it if circumstances so indicate; or, one can appropriate the mana and compel it to serve one's own human ends. Magic is a technique for controlling the unknown cause to produce a desired effect. The process is of a manipulative nature and is practically automatic. Magic is, in a sense, the predecessor and ancestor of science.

Religion, on the other hand, personalizes the supernatural power or powers, and regards them as voluntary agents. It is a technique for communicating with them and establishing friendly relations with them. Religion involves worship and prayer; it implies devotion and allegiance; it is a matter of emotion and moral attitude.

In spite of the distinction just drawn, the difference is one of degree rather than of kind; the occult and personalized aspects of the supernatural cannot be separated. Religion has never entirely displaced magic. Magical practices still persist even in the so-called "higher" religions to this day.

Belief and faith. Basically, religion consists of a set of mighty hypotheses and postulates which we know as beliefs. These are the products of the consciousness of individuals and groups. Most men believe in these unseen forces in the universe, which they usually personify, since they cannot communicate with an abstraction. They believe that these beings pertinently affect the present individual and social welfare and the eternal destiny of mankind. They believe that various individual and social practices and other cultural vehicles will effect communication with and adaptation to these powers. Occasionally a body of ideas which avoids the supernatural passes as religious and is a matter of belief; e.g., the sacredness of man's relationship to his fellow men.

A given group's strongly held beliefs are invariably intertwined with value judgments regarding the supernatural or the sacred. These value judgments combined with the basic beliefs constitute a faith. Faith involves ideals and objectives and aspirations. It is "the substance of things hoped for, the evidence of things not seen" (Heb. 11:1). It has dynamic quality; it gives men strength "to move mountains." To have faith is to be faithful; that is, to hold fast to the values and their implications, to cherish the object or objects of valuation as something good, to translate the values and ideals into thought and action, and often to propagate them. Obviously, religion in its very nature is a matter of many and diverse beliefs and faiths.

INSTITUTIONALIZATION

From earliest times, the basic, engrossing, and more or less continuous human wants and social needs and interests of mankind have been socially satisfied by means of rather complex and durable cultural devices which we speak of as social institutions. These are standardized, accepted, and usually enforced systems of social behavior. They order, regulate, and correlate the activities and relationships of all individuals and subgroups of the culture area as they carry on the operations necessary to satisfy the wants and needs. By means of them human beings, in the different segments of human life, live in a co-operative, disciplined, and predictable manner.

Institutions reflect the physical backgrounds and the general culture of the area of which they are a part; they serve as important carriers of culture elements. They are the products both of long, spontaneous development and of deliberate contrivance. They invariably function as social conservators. The problem with most of them is to keep them flexible and abreast of the times in both their functioning and their structure.

From earliest known times, religion has assumed institutionalized forms. Apparently it must do certain things for individuals and communities, and it cannot exist without social expression and social organization. Even in the most highly personalized religion, in the fleeting cults, and in the modern secularized forms, there is noticeable, however veiled, the influence of institutionalization. Newly originated religions cannot outlast a single generation without taking on institutional forms. Religious systems the world over, though varying greatly as to specific factors, functions, and features, all conform to the general pattern of institutions.

Religious institutions, especially those of the higher cultures, will be briefly discussed with respect to (1) their typical structural features and (2) the main individual and social functions they perform.

STRUCTURAL FEATURES

Most institutions, regardless of the pivotal social systems of which they are functioning parts, are made up of an array of constituent elements or "type parts." These elements are both of an abstract and a tangible nature. Significant are the conceptual and the ideological features, the fairly uniform attitudes and their overt expressions, the habits which cause the individuals and groups to *act* institutionally, the codes and other normative rules, the personnel elements (members and functionaries), and the sentiment-charged symbols, the physical structures, and the utilitarian paraphernalia. Counterparts of these are found in religious institutions.

Theologies and creeds. Most religions have their bodies of ideas, beliefs, doctrines, dogmas, articles of faith, ideals, and ideologies rationalized and systematized in the form of theologies and creeds; occasionally also in mythologies. These are the reasoned interpretations of the religious experience of the particular group; they give the religious views stability, consistency, and order; invariably they are authoritatively established. Some are much more elaborate, systematic, and well-rationalized than others.

The theologies of different religious groups differ and conflict because of the variant interpretations of their religious experiences and their world views. For the individual of the particular religious group, however, the theology brings clarity, order, and durability into his religious experience; for the group, it makes possible unity of belief and the social transmission of the religious conceptions.

Codes. The conduct supposedly required by the supernatural power both among men and toward him, if rapport with him and his followers is to be had, is stated rather specifically in commandments, lists of taboos, bodies of law, moral codes, books of "discipline," and so on. These define religiously satisfactory or essential behavior, or they prohibit undesirable or dangerous behavior. These formalizations of conduct are closely related to the next element.

Practices and techniques. Most religions have their complexes of standardized practices and techniques which function as a means of communicating with the Supernatural, of expressing awe and obedience, reverence and homage, of appeal, of appeasing and propitiating, of securing emotional unity among their own members, of increasing the intensity of their religious feeling, and frequently of propagating their faith. As J. Wach points out, these are the *practical* expressions of religious experience, as distinct from the intellectual; they are religiously inspired acts. Almost universal forms are sacrifices, sacred music, drama, dances or other rhythmic or united responses or performances, hymns and chants, invocations and benedictions, rituals, liturgies, ceremonials, and above all prayer, both private and group.

Among almost all religious groups, whether large or small, whether hierarchically organized or taking the form of a "local congregation," the greater proportion of these techniques, in one form or degree of formalization or another, constitute a set of established patterns of worship. The widespread practices of instructing, indoctrinating, and proselyting may also be placed in this general category of institutional elements.

Organized groups. Among the most obvious features of religious institutions are the associations or organizations of human beings. These consist of persons with similar religious attitudes and interests and holding to a common body of beliefs, values, and objectives. As a group they feel that their massed agreement regarding their beliefs and practices makes these not only the most efficacious but often the sole means of salvation. Religious bodies are face to face only in their local manifestations; mainly they consist of persons and groups scattered over wide areas, even globally, and bound together by an effective system of intercommunication.

The personnel of most religious associations can be divided into laity and priesthood or clergy. The laity are the great mass of co-operating, rank-and-file devotees of a common faith—the element for which all aspects of religion exist in the last analysis. The priesthood or clergy are the specialized functionaries, usually with some degree of hierarchical organization. They are presumed to have exceptional insight into and influence with the unseen Power because of their charismata, and hence serve as special intermediaries between the laity and this Power. They are the expert class that is specially versed and certificated in doctrine and that provides and teaches the special knowledge and interpretation; they perform special acts of intercession and worship; they are empowered to receive confession, arrange forgiveness, and fix penance; they usually advise on numerous matters and provide various social and spiritual services; and in most religious organizations they perform a host of administrative functions relating to the mere mundane operation of the institutional machinery.

Symbols and physical equipment. Almost all religions have their emotion-charged and emotion-eliciting symbols such as the cross or crescent, statuary, images, and other sacred art objects. All have their special material equipment and paraphernalia for conducting their worship and for carrying on their multiple organizational activities. Notable are extensive properties such as shrines, temples, tabernacles, church buildings, abbeys, cathedrals, and so on, equipped with altars, baptismal fonts, organs, pulpits, parish halls, office equipment, not to mention such special and occasional additions nowadays in the United States as steam tables, gymnasia, and bowling alleys.

The churches are the particular though varied form which religious institutionalization takes among the Christian peoples of Western civilization. The church, however, has its counterpart in some degree in all religious systems. A particular church consists of a body of believers with the same faith. It has its special body of doctrine and appropriate organizational form; it canalizes religious behavior, and does much educating and some disciplining.

SOME MAJOR FUNCTIONS

The real justification of a social institution or anything else that *is* is its functioning—the satisfying experiences it offers, the services it renders for human fulfillment and social well-being. This applies also to religious institutions; otherwise religion could not be regarded as a good thing. Religion has significance in both the individual or inner and the collectivist, community, or social aspects of human life. Without attempting even the barest inventory, several of the most significant historical functions of the religions of the higher cultures will be briefly set forth.

Facilitate religious experience. In the last analysis, religions are the means of inducing, formulating, expressing, enhancing, implementing, and perpetuating man's deepest experience, the religious. This is religion's primary raison d'être. Man is first religious; the instrumentalities follow. Religion is a condition within.

There is nothing mysterious about religious experience; it is as normal, natural, and inevitable, with man the special kind of creature he is, as experience of satisfaction with respect to nutrition and reproduction. In common with other types of human experience, it seeks the satisfaction of *needs* of great pertinence. The significant things in it, at the higher religious levels, are the inner emotional, mental, and spiritual occurrences which fill the pressing human needs of self-preservation, self-pacification, and self-completion. What are some of the more important experiences in the so-called higher religions? These will be found to be mutually exclusive.

The chief experience is the sensing of communion with the supernatural power. In the higher religions this involves also a harmonious relationship. As John Fiske put it, man refuses to be psychologically alone in the universe. He wants the feeling that he has something outside and beyond himself and his kind to go to. Prayer in its higher forms is a reverential and usually serene conversation with the Divine, whatever its form is conceived to be. Worship is the various ways in which man expresses awe, respect, gratitude, and allegiance. Prayer and worship epitomize *sacred* experience.

Related to this is the feeling of men that they are relatively secure in an ordered, dependable universe. Man has the experience of being helpfully allied with what he cannot fully understand; he is a co-ordinate part of all energy and being and movement. The universe is a safe and permanent home.

Many of the religions also satisfy for many the need of being linked up with the ultimate and eternal. Death is not permanent defeat and disappearance; man has a "second chance." He is not lost in the abyss of endless time; he has endless being. He experiences a commanding release from materiality, temporalness, finiteness; he believes that he will achieve infinite and eternal completion.

Religion at its best also offers the experience of spirital fulfillment by inviting man into the highest realm of the spirit. As John Burroughs put it in *Accepting the Universe,* "Religion is a spiritual flowering, and the man who has it not is like a plant that never blooms." It summates, epitomizes, relates, and conserves all the highest ideals and values—ethical, aesthetic, and religious—of man found in his culture.

There is also the possibility among higher religions of experiencing consistent meaning in life and enjoying guidance and expansiveness. The kind of religious experience that most moderns seek not only provides, clarifies, and relates human yearnings, values, ideals, and purposes; it also provides facilities and incitements for the development of personality, sociality and creativeness. Under the religious impulse, whether theistic or humanistic, men have joy in living; life leads somewhere. Religion at its best is out in front, ever beckoning and leading on, and, as W. Lippmann put it, "mobilizing all man's scattered energies in one triumphant sense of his own infinite importance."

In addition to these functions within man, there have always been the outer, social functions. The two have never been separable.

Promote social solidarity. Religion and social life have a peculiarly intimate connection. Religion integrates. Some of the oldest, most persistent, and most cohesive forms of social grouping have grown out of religion. A common faith or set of ultimate value judgments, common sentiments, a common worship as well as other common experiences, and an inclusive organization have been potent factors in knitting together in one solidary and co-operating body a number—often a very large number—of believers. These groups have varied widely from mere families, primitive totemic groups, and small modern cults and sects to the memberships of great, widely dispersed world religions.

Durkheim's famous viewpoint is pertinent here, namely, that every "society" is characterized to a certain degree by the possession of a common "religion," for religion is essentially a system of common values, and without these there can be no society. In fact, Durkheim defines religion as ". . . a unified system of beliefs and practices relative to sacred things . . . beliefs and practices which unite into one single moral community . . . all those who adhere to them." His view is that every religion pertains to a community, and, conversely, every community is in one aspect a religious unit.

At any given time most of mankind is divided into vast, more or less integrated groups based upon somewhat unique but uniform religious beliefs. Within these groups there is considerable unity; between them there is, with occasional highly advertised exceptions, competition, even sharp antagonism.

Most of the religious groups function as rallying points. Since religion is a matter of belief and faith, there is latent a lurking doubt among many of the members as to whether the beliefs are right. But if many thousands or millions believe so, the individual is sustained and assured. This same situation, in part at least, leads to proselyting, in that this augments the group, as well as being a means of sharing "a pearl of rare price" with an ever larger fellowship.

The integrating function of religion, for good or ill, has often supported or been identified with other groupings—political, nationality, class, racial, sociability, even economic.

At the same time, religious institutions have aided in amplifying social structure, in creating diversity of social groups, and in the specialization of functions and classes.

Elevate social standards. Most of the advanced religions tend to incorporate the major social values and ideals of the group—the great goals of social conduct which have grown out of group experience. Such magnificent and beneficent conceptions as the Golden Ages, past or future, with the attendant principles of attainment, the Golden or Silver Rules, love as a universal social agent, service of fellow men as an obligation, the high aesthetic and ethical principles related to beauty, goodness, and justice, the "superior man," the "noble path," the brotherhood of man, and the Good Community, here or elsewhere, have invariably stemmed from or been incorporated with religions. Religion has thus functioned as a great social lighthouse.

Through its peculiar sanctions religion has been able to give these values and ideals an emotional drive that has made them socializing *agents* as well. The socially approved values have been impressed upon individuals and groups through creeds and codes and rituals; behavior consistent with them has been greatly stimulated, energized, and more readily enforced. Much maladjustment has been avoided, and much constructive social behavior has been facilitated. As part of religious systems, these great survival values have also been conserved and a continuity has been given to them.

Agent of social control. Religion not only integrates and socializes; it also carries on a related function in most social systems, namely, that of social control. It is a form of social control used by the group to constrain the individual through supernatural power to conform his beliefs and actions to those of his group. Religion aids custom and law in making anything right or wrong.

It is especially significant to note the widespread use of religious sanctions to support the ethical codes and moral practices among many peoples. Strictly speaking, ethical systems consist of the systematized and more or less permanent ideas of right and wrong, or good and bad, in conduct among a people, along with the accompanying principles, customs, and codes. They set up the required, approved, and forbidden areas of behavior. They exist because men *must* behave in certain ways among their fellows; their objectives are purely temporal, social, and utilitarian; they grow out of long-time, everyday experience. Every new ethical rule springs from the necessity of providing for some new social situation.

Almost everywhere, however, these purely temporal social requirements, as prescribed by custom or stated in commandments and legal codes, have been placed under the irrefutable and inexorable jurisdiction of the omnipresent, omniscient, and omnipotent gods. The scheme of supernatural rewards and punishments has been marshaled to support the mundane codes, the codes thus having an efficacy that no mere social imagination or desire for group welfare could provide.

Influence other institutions. Religion has also functioned as a tremendous engine of vindication, enforcement, and sanction of various other institutions. In some instances religious organizations have actually inaugurated social activities in fields not strictly religious.

For thousands of years of man's career, religion has exerted a vast influence over economic and political life. The gods had to be placated if man was to be successful in his economic activities; government and law were based on or allied with divine dictates. Both the economic and the political systems received their validity from on high. Today religion is still called upon to support rulers, contracts, forms of property, oaths, and other legal procedures. Divine blessing is still invoked in behalf of governmental agents and enterprises.

Until a century or so ago most education was under religious auspices and much of it was primarily for the transmission of beliefs and religious usages. Some religious organizations still provide much education, secular and sacred, and try to manipulate public education. Religion has set its stamp on sex practices, marriage, and the family.

Much of the recreation of the past related to religious festivals, assemblies, and holidays; today religious organizations try to provide recreation of a certain moral quality. Until recently much art was used to glorify the gods, illuminate religious experience, and teach religious lessons; religion still seeks to safeguard the aesthetic productions from immoral influences. Through most of history, charitable, or what we now deem social work, activities have been carried on under religious auspices.

Other influences might be mentioned. Religion has been the actual mother of some, now secular, institutions; the foster mother of many.

A therapeutic agent. This is a much emphasized function to which only the barest attention can be given. The various religious experiences and practices have tended to secure extrahuman or superhuman aid in the ills of life; they have had, and for many do still have, much therapeutic value. One of the primary objectives of religion is to answer questions; it never raises them. Individual weaknesses, feelings of insecurity, disbelief and doubt, are lost in the common strength and unity of the religious fellowship. The sense of cosmic peace frees many a person from a host of harassing and distracting fears, frustrations, and anxieties.

The belief in immortality, where held, functions as a redress for the ills and disappointments here and now. The tensions accompanying a repressive consciousness of wrongdoing or "sinning" or some tormenting secret are relieved for the less self-contained and self-sufficient by confession, repentance, and penance. The feeling of individual inferiority growing out of various social situations or individual deficiencies of failures is compensated for by communion in worship or prayer with a friendly but all-victorious Father-God, as well as by sympathetic fellowship with others who share this faith, and by opportunities in religious acts for giving vent to emotions and energy.

Religion is especially important in times of travail, tragedy, and crisis. When natural holocausts—flood, drought, pestilence, earthquake—rage; when men are suffering from man-made catastrophe—war, revolution, economic depression—religion gives them, individually and in groups, great solace. When life on earth appears chaotic, and when great harm and suffering must be endured, men have not infrequently found a refuge in "the everlasting arms." The gods have alleviated much fear and saved men from much more. The great crisic transitions of life—birth, puberty, marriage, death—are also sacramentalized by religion, thus relieving all concerned from much strain in adjusting themselves to the stupendous changes.

A recent study as to why Americans are religious is replete with such phrases as: "provides help in times of stress"; "gives sense of security"; "furnishes moral support"; "gives me courage"; "brings comfort"; "gives strength"; "gives peace"; "brings contentment"; "makes me unafraid to die"; "gives assurance"; "makes me self-confident"; and so on.

SOME SOCIOLOGICAL ASPECTS

There are certain features of religion in its recurrent manifestations in human societies which have considerable sociological pertinence. No effort will be made to give an exhaustive array, but only to present concisely certain social scientific observations regarding the institutional character of religion which have a bearing upon matters treated elsewhere.

Reflect cultural level. The various elements of religious institutions throughout history, like those of other institutions, have been essentially earthy, man-made, and humanly administered. Of course, man did not devise the universe or produce whatever unseen powers there be, but all the interpretations of these modes of adjustment to them are man's.

Everywhere religion is the product of mental and social processes, along with science, philosophy, art, and ethics; everywhere it is a product of group collaboration, a complex engendered by members of a given society under given circumstances. Diversities are explained by all of the influences—physical, intellectual, cultural, historical, and social—which affect individual and group life. From its very nature, religion has been a great variable taking many particular forms both as between and within different peoples, regions, and eras.

It is in such an examination as this that the sociology of religion and the sociology of knowledge meet. As Toy has so well pointed out, the external history of religion is the history of the processes by which religious sentiments, ideas, activities, and organizations have attached themselves to the various conceptions formed by man's observation, reflection, and experience. When intellectual reactions are bottomed in a low or rudimentary culture, religion is crude; when culture is chaotic, the religion will be also; the more substantial the cultural background and the more extensive the cultural horizons, the higher the plane of thought, the more expansive the religious ideas and viewpoints.

The very nature of the gods is a case in point. They reflect and embody man's concepts of both the mundane and the extrahuman powers that are operative. They are rationalizations of man's conceptions of himself; they have rational human qualities and human modes of procedure, and are human beings in all except power. At a low intellectual and cultural level and in a circumscribed environment, they are crude, local, and often malevolent ghosts or spirits. As conceptions of human personality, the dignity of man, and man's other ethical views have been elevated, the gods have improved in moral qualities.

The jurisdiction and sphere of the gods has reflected man's grasp of community and his systems of physical science. A "universal" religion rests on a conception of universal cultural diffusion. When, finally, the conception is reached that all nature is governed by natural law, the theistic view assumes that the deity works through scientifically established natural means.

Similarly, ritual has quite consistently been the religious application of the code of social manners; the abode of the soul has changed with the knowledge of the universe. The methods of establishing friendly relations with supernatural powers have been the same as those employed to approach human rulers, namely, by gifts, petitions, messengers or intermediaries, and tributes.

In general, the religion reflects the whole background and make-up of a people. For example, in the United States, religion in its various "Christian" manifestations reflects different secular groups, interests, and needs; philosophic currents; economic and political conditions; class structure; the multiplicity of the cultures developed by the stocks and varieties of people who make up the population; historical situations such as frontier life, the Civil War, immigration, industrialization, urbanization, and technology.

Reflect social structure. Similarly, religion in its areal and group scope has ranged from the clan or tribal area, through the city-state, the state, the nation, the race, and finally in some instances has affected a fusion of all mankind.

depending upon the prevailing concept of human interrelationships. In its organization it has reflected the general social, including specifically the political, organization. Religion has always, of necessity, organized itself in accord with the general structure of social systems.

Religion has always been dependent upon changing human experience, and it has always been appropriating useful ideas and methods from other departments of life. It is not something apart.

Relation to change. As a strategy for self-preservation and spiritual security and as a medium of social adjustment, religion shifts as all else does—though belatedly, as we will note below. Even during those periods when religious institutions dominated all others, they changed. When religious organization loses its supremacy among institutions, this accommodative tendency is much more readily observed. For example, as physical and biological science has advanced in the last century, man's conception and grasp of the "natural" have greatly modified his interpretation of and dependence upon the "supernatural"; and as social science and his social consciousness have developed, the relative emphasis upon "God" and "man" has been modified. As men have gained confidence in their accumulating knowledge and their demonstrated ability to manipulate nature and themselves, they have felt more secure; they have worried less both about this world *and about the next.* Both naturalism and humanism have affected religion mightily. It has become less God-centered, more man-centered; less passive, more creative; but also less sacred, more secular.

While religion does accommodate itself to intellectual and social change, this adjustment is tardy and subject to much resistance. All institutions, as products of the past, as bulwarks against chaotic social relationships, and as highly organized social instrumentalities, tend to develop inflexibility in their functioning and fail to keep abreast of the needs of the times. However, these tendencies seem to be greater in organized religion than in most other institutional fields. There is so much of the "dead hand" in theology, ritual, and the forms of organization. Why?

Because the major preoccupation of religious institutions is with the unknown and mysterious, and they rest upon belief and faith, they cannot be checked so readily by normal procedures of perception, understanding, and investigation. The doctrine is derived from revelation and authority, hence is strongly authoritarian, even infallible, in character. After the doctrine has been systematized, the rules of faith established, and the forms of worship fixed, then any deviations and opinions at variance with the officially accepted teachings are classed as heresy. Not only is experimentalism not encouraged; it is looked upon with suspicion. Religious organizations, as organizations, are at least as likely as others to develop precedents, to routinize activities, and to acquire a momentum which gives them a holdover power in many of their operations after these have ceased to have pertinence and timeliness. Finally, more than in any other institutional system, religious institutions have a protected position and claim to have a unique finality. The matter is summarized in a phrase by R. M. MacIver: "Revelation stands in the way of revaluation."

In concluding the last three sections, it may be pointed out that the solution is not deinstitutionalization, for the essential contributions of institutionalization outweigh its evils. To conceive of a noninstitutionalized religion is sociologically infantile. The big task is institutional reconstruction. Since religious agencies of all kinds are made by man, they must be and can be continually remade. If men are to meet their spiritual needs in an ever more rapidly changing world, religion must be redefined, clarified, reorganized, and subjected to much thoughtful experimentation.

Religious institutions as determiners. The significance of continual reconstruction of religious institutions is underscored when we examine ever so briefly their influence as determiners of individual belief and behavior. The forces of organized religion are for most men really the determiners of the kind and quality of their religious life. Even in an age of widespread education and of freedom of thought, most people feel incompetent to think out seriously for themselves a satisfying religious philosophy. They lack the philosophic capacity, the intellectual training, and the spiritual audacity. They accept the ready-made beliefs and routines of some organized religious group, frequently that of their parents or their immediate culture group. Even if they break away from their particular group they are very likely to accept, again at second hand, the views of some other group. Relatively few persons "go it alone" with a more or less effective set of beliefs of their own devising.

This means also, of course, that the peculiar religious needs of many individuals are not satisfactorily met. Many people object to accepting faith like the multiplication table. Hence, most faiths are accepted today with considerable mental reservation by at least a portion of the population.

Overinstitutionalization. Organized religions tend to become overorganized, from the very fact of their organization as "going concerns" and the resulting emphasis on their structural aspects, the fact that they are used for control purposes, that they are established and autonomous. They become ends in themselves rather than means. The real end is lost sight of. There is an overemphasis on machinery, fixed and standardized forms and creeds and theologies, and even souls that fit into a special pattern. The personnel, both professional and lay, drift into a more or less perfunctory and mechanical way of acting. Religious experience and expression are then easily confused with theology and ritual, "sacred" aesthetics, ceremonies, minor and very temporary details—even check-writing and attending church-promoted clubs. The organization is likely to pose and exaggerate. This also makes for intolerance and artificiality.

The most sinister fact, though, is that it is easier to administer the affairs of an organization than it is to keep creeds flexible, codes of conduct clear and uncompromised, and the life of the spirit immanent. Historically this has meant either the eventual disappearance of the particular religious organization or, more commonly, reform or schism, especially in the form of new sects and cults.

DECLINE OF INSTITUTIONALIZED RELIGION IN THE UNITED STATES

Among primitive peoples, in most ancient civilizations, in medieval Europe, and in certain portions of the modern world, the prevailing religion has exercised quite uniform control over the entire population of a political, ethnic, or culture area. It was a uniform, universal, and unavoidable social compulsive. But in the Western world increasingly, and especially in the United States, religion has undergone a series of changes which have mightily diminished its institutional sway.

Lack of space prevents more than mention of these changes. Frequently emphasized are: the voluntary nature of participation as against automatic or compulsory membership in other eras and areas, with the attendant loss of enforcement power, especially the enforcement which the state gives various institutions; the encroachment of science upon the realm of the unknown and supernatural, and less preoccupation with the mysteries of life; the divided loyalties and divided organizational support due to the multiplication of diverse and even competitive denominations, sects, and cults, and the consequent confusion of beliefs; the fact that in the United States no more than half the total population admit membership in these various organized groups; the loss of an array of social services to or a losing competition with a host of nonreligious agencies, especially semipublic organizations and the modern "service" state, and the pressure to support these latter, for example, as community chest contributors and taxpayers; the secularization of thought generally as against the theocentric thinking of medieval society, for example, and the accommodation of both laity and clergy to these secular currents; and the loss of much of the prophetic, proselyting, and reformist power of religion.

Organized religion has become a purely voluntary, semiprivate affair; its jurisdiction, for better or worse, is divided, and its power to standardize behavior and exercise social control, either for individuals or for groups, has diminished as that of various other institutions has been augmented; its influence has evaporated from one department of life after another. On the basis of the more common criteria of an institution, some social scientists are inclined to raise the issue as to whether it can properly be designated today as an institution. At any rate, religious institutions have lost their centrality; they "speak with a divided voice."

WHAT NEXT?

The solution of this situation is not a state church with automatic membership and nation-wide hegemony, not an abandonment of freedom of thought and freedom of worship, not any relaxation of tolerance and catholicity of religious thinking and acting. Walking backward is not a way out. However, one of the most luminous texts in the book of life is: "Above all religions is religion." What *is* the next phase of organized religion in the United States?

GOVERNMENT

Unlike the other major social institutions—the family, economy, and religion—political and governmental systems have had limited visibility and crude development as social institutions in the simple, nonliterate societies. Political and governmental functions such as the maintenance of social order, the resolution of conflict, the distribution of power and scarce goods and services, and the formulation of societal policy were largely vested in other institutions, especially the family and religion. There they were adequately supported by the folkways and mores, and informally enforced by sanctions in the hands of such authorities as the patriarchs and religious elders.

When complex, multigroup societies emerged, the inadequacy of these mechanisms and personnel encouraged the rise of a lawmaking process exercised by new and specialized personnel in governmental and political roles. In this manner a new major social institution was established in society.

In the following article, David Easton proposes a broad, theoretical scheme for the analysis of political-governmental systems in the form of an input-output exchange between a system and its social setting. Postulating that political systems develop in a society where there is a scarcity and a demand for that scarcity that cannot be satisfied elsewhere, Professor Easton's political scheme strikes one as being almost analogous to models once proposed by classical economists for the analysis of economic behavior.

34. AN APPROACH TO THE ANALYSIS OF POLITICAL SYSTEMS *

DAVID EASTON
University of Chicago

I. SOME ATTRIBUTES OF POLITICAL SYSTEMS

In an earlier work I have argued for the need to develop general, empirically oriented theory as the most economical way in the long run to understand political life. Here I propose to indicate a point of view that, at the least, might serve as a springboard for discussion of alternative approaches and, at most, as a small step in the direction of a general political theory. I wish to

* *World Politics,* Vol. 9 (1957), pp. 383–400.

stress that what I have to say is a mere orientation to the problem of theory; outside of economics and perhaps psychology, it would be presumptuous to call very much in social science "theory," in the strict sense of the term.

Furthermore, I shall offer only a Gestalt of my point of view, so that it will be possible to evaluate, in the light of the whole, those parts that I do stress. In doing this, I know I run the definite risk that the meaning and implications of this point of view may be only superficially communicated; but it is a risk I shall have to undertake since I do not know how to avoid it sensibly.

The study of politics is concerned with understanding how authoritative decisions are made and executed for a society. We can try to understand political life by viewing each of its aspects piecemeal. We can examine the operation of such institutions as political parties, interest groups, government, and voting; we can study the nature and consequences of such political practices as manipulation, propaganda, and violence; we can seek to reveal the structure within which these practices occur. By combining the results we can obtain a rough picture of what happens in any self-contained political unit.

In combining these results, however, there is already implicit the notion that each part of the larger political canvas does not stand alone but is related to each other part; or, to put it positively, that the operation of no one part can be fully understood without reference to the way in which the whole itself operates. I have suggested in my book, *The Political System,* that it is valuable to adopt this implicit assumption as an articulate premise for research and to view political life as a system of interrelated activities. These activities derive their relatedness or systemic ties from the fact that they all more or less influence the way in which authoritative decisions are formulated and executed for a society.

Once we begin to speak of political life as a system of activity, certain consequences follow for the way in which we can undertake to analyze the working of a system. The very idea of a system suggests that we can separate political life from the rest of social activity, at least for analytical purposes, and examine it as though for the moment it were a self-contained entity surrounded by, but clearly distinguishable from, the environment or setting in which it operates. In much the same way, astronomers consider the solar system a complex of events isolated for certain purposes from the rest of the universe.

Furthermore, if we hold the system of political actions as a unit before our mind's eye, as it were, we can see that what keeps the system going are inputs of various kinds. These inputs are converted by the processes of the system into outputs and these, in turn, have consequences both for the system and for the environment in which the system exists. The formula here is very simple but, as I hope to show, also very illuminating: inputs—political system or processes—outputs. These relationships are shown diagrammatically in Figure 1. This diagram represents a very primitive "model"—to dignify it with a fashionable name—for approaching the study of political life.

Political systems have certain properties because they are systems. To present an over-all view of the whole approach, let me identify the major attributes, say a little about each, and then treat one of these properties at somewhat greater length, even though still inadequately.

(1) Properties of identification. To distinguish a political system from other social systems, we must be able to identify it by describing its fundamental units and establishing the boundaries that demarcate it from units outside the system.

(a) Units of a political system. The units are the elements of which we say a system is composed. In the case of a political system, they are political actions. Normally it is useful to look at these as they structure themselves in political roles and political groups.

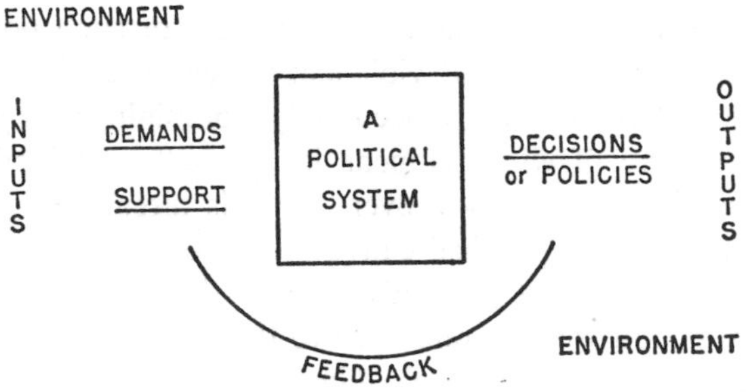

FIGURE 1

(b) Boundaries. Some of the most significant questions with regard to the operation of political systems can be answered only if we bear in mind the obvious fact that a system does not exist in a vacuum. It is always immersed in a specific setting or environment. The way in which a system works will be in part a function of its response to the total social, biological, and physical environment.

The special problem with which we are confronted is how to distinguish systematically between a political system and its setting. Does it even make sense to say that a political system has a boundary dividing it from its setting? If so, how are we to identify the line of demarcation?

Without pausing to argue the matter, I would suggest that it is useful to conceive of a political system as having a boundary in the same sense as a physical system. The boundary of a political system is defined by all those actions more or less directly related to the making of binding decisions for a society; every social action that does not partake of this characteristic will be excluded from the system and thereby will automatically be viewed as an external variable in the environment.

(2) Inputs and outputs. Presumably, if we select political systems for special study, we do so because we believe that they have characteristically important consequences for society, namely, authoritative decisions. These

consequences I shall call the outputs. If we judged that political systems did not have important outputs for society, we would probably not be interested in them.

Unless a system is approaching a state of entropy—and we can assume that this is not true of most political systems—it must have continuing inputs to keep it going. Without inputs the system can do no work; without outputs we cannot identify the work done by the system. The specific research tasks in this connection would be to identify the inputs and the forces that shape and change them, to trace the processes through which they are transformed into outputs, to describe the general conditions under which such processes can be maintained, and to establish the relationship between outputs and succeeding inputs of the system.

From this point of view, much light can be shed on the working of a political system if we take into account the fact that much of what happens within a system has its birth in the efforts of the members of the system to cope with the changing environment. We can appreciate this point if we consider a familiar biological system such as the human organism. It is subject to constant stress from its surroundings to which it must adapt in one way or another if it is not to be completely destroyed. In part, of course, the way in which the body works represents responses to needs that are generated by the very organization of its anatomy and functions; but in large part, in order to understand both the structure and the working of the body, we must also be very sensitive to the inputs from the environment.

In the same way, the behavior of every political system is to some degree imposed upon it by the kind of system it is, that is, by its own structure and internal needs. But its behavior also reflects the strains occasioned by the specific setting within which the system operates. It may be argued that most of the significant changes within a political system have their origin in shifts among the external variables. Since I shall be devoting the bulk of this article to examining some of the problems related to the exchange between political systems and their environments, I shall move on to a rapid description of other properties of political systems.

(3) Differentiation within a system. As we shall see in a moment, from the environment come both energy to activate a system and information with regard to which the system uses this energy. In this way a system is able to do work. It has some sort of output that is different from the input that enters from the environment. We can take it as a useful hypothesis that if a political system is to perform some work for anything but a limited interval of time, a minimal amount of differentiation in its structure must occur. In fact, empirically it is impossible to find a significant political system in which the same units all perform the same activities at the same time. The members of a system engage in at least some minimal division of labor that provides a structure within which action takes place.

(4) Integration of a system. This fact of differentiation opens up a major

area of inquiry with regard to political systems. Structural differentiation sets in motion forces that are potentially disintegrative in their results for the system. If two or more units are performing different kinds of activity at the same time, how are these activities to be brought into the minimal degree of articulation necessary if the members of the system are not to end up in utter disorganization with regard to the production of the outputs of interest to us? We can hypothesize that if a structured system is to maintain itself, it must provide mechanisms whereby its members are integrated or induced to cooperate in some minimal degree so that they can make authoritative decisions.

II. INPUTS: DEMANDS

Now that I have mentioned some major attributes of political systems that I suggest require special attention if we are to develop a generalized approach, I want to consider in greater detail the way in which an examination of inputs and outputs will shed some light on the working of these systems.

Among inputs of a political system there are two basic kinds: demands and support. These inputs give a political system its dynamic character. They furnish it both with the raw material or information that the system is called upon to process and with the energy to keep it going.

The reason why a political system emerges in a society at all—that is, why men engage in political activity—is that demands are being made by persons or groups in the society that cannot all be fully satisfied. In all societies one fact dominates political life: scarcity prevails with regard to most of the valued things. Some of the claims for these relatively scarce things never find their way into the political system but are satisfied through the private negotiations of or settlements by the persons involved. Demands for prestige may find satisfaction through the status relations of society; claims for wealth are met in part through the economic system; aspirations for power find expression in educational, fraternal, labor, and similar private organizations. Only where wants require some special organized effort on the part of society to settle them authoritatively may we say that they have become inputs of the political system.

Systematic research would require us to address ourselves to several key questions with regard to these demands.

(1) How do demands arise and assume their particular character in a society? In answer to this question, we can point out that demands have their birth in two sectors of experience: either in the environment of a system or within the system itself. We shall call these the external and internal demands, respectively.

Let us look at the external demands first. I find it useful to see the environment not as an undifferentiated mass of events but rather as systems clearly distinguishable from one another and from the political system. In the environment we have such systems as the ecology, economy, culture, personality, social structure, and demography. Each of these constitutes a major set of variables in the setting that helps to shape the kind of demands entering a political system. For purposes of illustrating what I mean, I shall say a few words about culture.

The members of every society act within the framework of an ongoing culture that shapes their general goals, specific objectives, and the procedures that the members feel ought to be used. Every culture derives part of its unique quality from the fact that it emphasizes one or more special aspects of behavior and this strategic emphasis serves to differentiate it from other cultures with respect to the demands that it generates. As far as the mass of the people is concerned, some cultures, such as or own, are weighted heavily on the side of economic wants, success, privacy, leisure activity, and rational efficiency. Others, such as that of the Fox Indians, strive toward the maintenance of harmony, even if in the process the goals of efficiency and rationality may be sacrificed. Still others, such as the Kachins of highland Burma, stress the pursuit of power and prestige. The culture embodies the standards of value in a society and thereby marks out areas of potential conflict, if the valued things are in short supply relative to demand. The typical demands that will find their way into the political process will concern the matters in conflict that are labeled important by the culture. For this reason we cannot hope to understand the nature of the demands presenting themselves for political settlement unless we are ready to explore systematically and intensively their connection with the culture. And what I have said about culture applies, with suitable modifications, to other parts of the setting of a political system.

But not all demands originate or have their major locus in the environment. Important types stem from situations occurring within a political system itself. Typically, in every on-going system, demands may emerge for alterations in the political relationships of the members themselves, as the result of dissatisfaction stemming from these relationships. For example, in a political system based upon representation, in which equal representation is an important political norm, demands may arise for equalizing representation between urban and rural voting districts. Similarly, demands for changes in the process of recruitment of formal political leaders, for modifications of the way in which constitutions are amended, and the like may all be internally inspired demands.

I find it useful and necessary to distinguish these from external demands because they are, strictly speaking, not inputs of the system but something that we can call "withinputs," if we can tolerate a cumbersome neologism, and because their consequences for the character of a political system are more direct than in the case of external demands. Furthermore, if we were not aware of this difference in classes of demands, we might search in vain for an explanation of the emergence of a given set of internal demands if we turned only to the environment.

(2) How are demands transformed into issues? What determines whether a demand becomes a matter for serious political discussion or remains some-

thing to be resolved privately among the members of society? The occurrence of a demand, whether internal or external, does not thereby automatically convert it into a political *issue*. Many demands die at birth or linger on with the support of an insignificant fraction of the society and are never raised to the level of possible political decision. Others become issues, an issue being a demand that the members of a political system are prepared to deal with as a significant item for discussion through the recognized channels in the system.

The distinction between demands and issues raises a number of questions about which we need data if we are to understand the processes through which claims typically become transformed into issues. For example, we would need to know something about the relationship between a demand and the location of its initiators or supporters in the power structures of the society, the importance of secrecy as compared with publicity in presenting demands, the matter of timing of demands, the possession of political skills or know-how, access to channels of communication, the attitudes and states of mind of possible publics, and the images held by the initiators of demands with regard to the way in which things get done in the particular political system. Answers to matters such as these would possibly yield a conversion index reflecting the probability of a set of demands being converted into live political issues.

If we assume that political science is primarily concerned with the way in which authoritative decisions are made for a society, demands require special attention as a major type of input of political systems. I have suggested that demands influence the behavior of a system in a number of ways. They constitute a significant part of the material upon which the system operates. They are also one of the sources of change in political systems, since as the environment fluctuates it generates new types of demand-inputs for the system. Accordingly, without this attention to the origin and determinants of demands we would be at a loss to be able to treat rigorously not only the operation of a system at a moment of time but also its change over a specified interval. Both the statics and historical dynamics of a political system depend upon a detailed understanding of demands, particularly of the impact of the setting on them.

III. INPUTS: SUPPORT

Inputs of demands alone are not enough to keep a political system operating. They are only the raw material out of which finished products called decisions are manufactured. Energy in the form of actions or orientations promoting and resisting a political system, the demands arising in it, and the decisions issuing from it must also be put into the system to keep it running. This input I shall call support. Without support, demands could not be satisfied or conflicts in goals composed. If demands are to be acted upon, the members of a system undertaking to pilot the demands through to their transformation into binding decisions and those who seek to influence the relevant processes in any way must be able to count on support from others in the system. Just how much support, from how many and which members of a political system, are separate and important questions that I shall touch on shortly.

What do we mean by support? We can say that A supports B either when A acts on behalf of or when he orients himself favorably toward B's goals, interests, and actions. Supportive behavior may thus be of two kinds. It may consist of actions promoting the goals, interests, and actions of another person. We may vote for a political candidate, or defend a decision by the highest court of the land. In these cases, support manifests itself through overt action.

On the other hand, supportive behavior may involve not external observable acts, but those internal forms of behavior we call orientations or states of mind. As I use the phrase, a supportive state of mind is a deep-seated set of attitudes or predispositions, or a readiness to act on behalf of some other person. It exists when we say that a man is loyal to his part, attached to democracy, or infused with patriotism. What such phrases as these have in common is the fact that they refer to a state of feelings on the part of a person. No overt action is involved at this level of description, although the implication is that the individual will pursue a course of action consistent with his attitudes. Where the anticipated action does not flow from our perception of the state of mind, we assume that we have not penetrated deeply enough into the true feelings of the person but have merely skimmed off his surface attitudes.

Supportive states of mind are vital inputs for the operation and maintenance of a political system. For example, it is often said that the struggle in the international sphere concerns mastery over men's minds. To a certain extent this is true. If the members of a political system are deeply attached to a system or its ideals, the likelihood of their participating in either domestic or foreign politics in such a way as to undermine the system is reduced by a large factor. Presumably, even in the face of considerable provocation, ingrained supportive feelings of loyalty may be expected to prevail.

We shall need to identify the typical mechanisms through which supportive attitudes are inculcated and continuously reinforced within a political system. But our prior task is to specify and examine the political objects in relation to which support is extended.

(1) *The Domain of Support*. Support is fed into the political system in relation to three objects: the community, the regime, and the government. There must be convergence of attitude and opinion as well as some willingness to act with regard to each of those objects. Let us examine each in turn.

(a) The political community. No political system can continue to operate unless its members are willing to support the existence of a group that seeks to settle differences or promote decisions through peaceful action in common. The point is so obvious—being dealt with usually under the heading of the growth of national unity—that it may well be overlooked; and yet it is a premise upon which the continuation of any political system depends. To refer to this phenomenon we can speak of the political community. At this level of support we are not concerned with whether a government exists or whether there is loyalty to a constitutional order. For the moment we only ask whether the members of the group that we are examining are sufficiently oriented toward each other to want to contribute their collective energies toward pacific settlement of their varying demands.

The American Civil War is a concrete illustration of the cessation of input of support for the political community. The war itself was definitive evidence that the members of the American political system could no longer contribute to the existence of a state of affairs in which peaceful solution of conflicting demands was the rule. Matters had come to the point where it was no longer a question of whether the South would support one or another alternative government, or whether it could envision its demands being satisfied through the normal constitutional procedures. The issue turned on whether there was sufficient mutual identification among the members of the system for them to be able to work together as a political community. Thus in any political system, to the extent that there is an in-group or we-group feeling and to the extent that the members of the system identify one another as part of this unit and exclude others according to some commonly accepted criteria, such as territoriality, kinship, or citizenship, we shall say that they are putting in support for the political community.

(b) The regime. Support for a second major part of a political system helps to supply the energy to keep the system running. This aspect of the system I shall call the regime. It consists of all those arrangements that regulate the way in which the demands put into the system are settled and the way in which decisions are put into effect. They are the so-called rules of the game, in the light of which actions by members of the system are legitimated and accepted by the bulk of the members as authoritative. Unless there is a minimum convergence of attitudes in support of these fundamental rules—the constitutional principles, as we call them in Western society—there would be insufficient harmony in the actions of the members of a system to meet the problems generated by their support of a political community. The fact of trying to settle demands in common means that there must be known principles governing the way in which resolutions of differences of claims are to take place.

(c) The government. If a political system is going to be able to handle the conflicting demands put into it, not only must the members of the system be prepared to support the settlement of these conflicts in common and possess some consensus with regard to the rules governing the mode of settlement; they must also be ready to support a government as it undertakes the concrete tasks involved in negotiating such settlements. When we come to the outputs of a system, we shall see the rewards that are available to a government for mobilizing support. At this point, I just wish to draw attention to this need on the part of a government for support if it is going to be able to make decisions with regard to demands. Of course, a government may elicit support in many ways: through persuasion, consent, or manipulation. It may also impose unsupported settlements of demands through threats of force. But it is a familiar axiom of political science that a government based upon force alone is not long for this world; it must buttress its position by inducing a favorable state of mind in its subjects through fair or foul means.

The fact that support directed to a political system can be broken down conceptually into three elements—support for the community, regime, and government—does not mean, of course, that in the concrete case support for each of these three objects is independent. In fact we might and normally do find all three kinds of support very closely intertwined, so that the presence of one is a function of the presence of one or both of the other types.

For example, withdrawal of support from the government of Louis XVI in effect also meant that members of the French monarchical system were challenging at least the regime; as it turned out in the ensuing revolution and civil war, there was even doubt whether the members of the system would continue to support a unified political community. In this case, what was initially opposition to the ruling sovereign—that is, to the government—quickly turned out to signify a lack of sufficient support for the regime and ultimately, to some extent, for the political community. But this is not always so and fortunately, from the point of view of social order, it is not typically the case. We are accustomed to calling for a change of government without thereby suggesting dissatisfaction with the regime or community. And at times, although this is less frequently true, the community shows sufficient intention to continue as a cooperating group to be able to accept a challenge to the regime. From 1832 to the 1880's England underwent a serious modification in its regime, introducing the basic elements of a system of popular democracy, without serious diminution of input of support at the community level. It is always a matter for empirical enquiry to discover the degree to which support at any one level is dependent upon support at the others.

This very brief discussion of support points up one major fact. If a system is to absorb a variety of demands and negotiate some sort of settlement among them, it is not enough for the members of the system to support only their own demands and the particular government that will undertake to promote these demands. For the demands to be processed into outputs it is equally essential that the members of the system stand ready to support the existence of a political community and some stable rules of common action that we call the regime.

(2) *Quantity and Scope of Support.* How much support needs to be put into a system and how many of its members need to contribute such support if the system is to be able to do the job of converting demands to decisions? No ready answer can be offered. The actual situation in each case would determine the amount and scope required. We can, however, visualize a number of situations that will be helpful in directing our attention to possible generalizations.

Under certain circumstances very few members need to support a system at any level. The members might be dull and apathetic, indifferent to the general operations of the system, its progress or decisions. In a loosely connected system such as India has had, this might well be the state of mind of by far the largest segment of the membership. Either in fact they have not been affected by national decisions or they have not perceived that they were so affected. They may have little sense of identification with the present regime and government and yet, with regard to the input of demands, the system may be able to act on the basis of the support offered by the known 3 percent of the Western-oriented politicians and intellectuals who are politically active. In other words, we can have a small minority putting in quantitatively sufficient supportive energy to keep the system going. However, we can venture the hypothesis that where members of a system are putting in numerous demands, there is a strong probability that they will actively offer support or hostility at one of the three levels of the system, depending upon the degree to which these demands are being met through appropriate decisions.

Alternatively, we may find that all the members of a system are putting in support, but the amount may be so low as to place one or all aspects of the system in jeopardy. Modern France is perhaps a classic illustration. The input of support at the level of the political community is probably adequate for the maintenance of France as a national political unit. But for a variety of historical and contemporary reasons, there is considerable doubt as to whether the members of the French political system are putting in anything but a low order of support to the regime or any particular government. This low amount of support, even though spread over a relatively large segment of the population, leaves the French political system on somewhat less secure foundations than is the case with India. There support is less widespread but more active —that is, quantitatively greater—on the part of a minority. As this illustration indicates, the amount of support is not necessarily proportional to its scope.

It may seem from the above discussion as though the members of a political system either put in support or withhold it—that is, demonstrate hostility or apathy. In fact, members may and normally do simultaneously engage in supportive and hostile behavior. What we must be interested in is the net balance of support.

IV. MECHANISMS OF SUPPORT

To this point I have suggested that no political system can yield the important outputs we call authoritative decisions unless, in addition to demands, support finds its way into the system. I have discussed the possible object to which support may be directed, and some problems with regard to the domain, quantity, and scope of support. We are now ready to turn to the main question raised by our attention to support as a crucial input: how do systems typically manage to maintain a steady flow of support? Without it a system will not absorb sufficient energy from its members to be able to convert demands to decisions.

In theory, there might be an infinite variety of means through which members could be induced to support a system; in practice, certain well-established classes of mechanisms are used. Research in this area needs to be directed to exploring the precise way in which a particular system utilizes these mechanisms and to refining our understanding of the way in which they contribute to the making of authoritative policy.

A society generates support for a political system in two ways: through outputs that meet the demands of the members of society; and through the processes of politicization. Let us look at outputs first.

(1) *Outputs as a Mechanism of Support.* An output of a political system, it will be recalled, is a political decision or policy. One of the major ways of strengthening the ties of the members to their system is through providing decisions that tend to satisfy the day-to-day demands of these members. Fundamentally this is the truth that lies in the aphorism that one can fool some of the people some of the time but not all of them all of the time. Without some minimal satisfaction of demands, the ardor of all but the most fanatical patriot is sure to cool. The outputs, consisting of political decisions, constitute a body of specific inducements for the members of a system to support that system.

Inducements of this kind may be positive or negative. Where negative, they threaten the members of the system with various kinds of sanctions ranging from a small monetary fine to physical detention, ostracism, or loss of life, as in our own system with regard to the case of legally defined treason. In every system support stems in part from fear of sanctions or compulsion; in autocratic systems the proportion of coerced support is at a maximum. For want of space I shall confine myself to those cases where positive incentives loom largest.

Since the specific outputs of a system are policy decisions, it is upon the government that the final responsibility falls for matching or balancing outputs of decisions against input of demand. But it is clear that to obtain the support of the members of a system through positive incentives, a government need not meet all the demands of even its most influential and ardent supporters. Most governments, or groups such as political parties that seek to control governments, succeed in building up a reserve of support. This reserve will carry the government along even though it offends its followers, so long as over the extended short run these followers perceive the particular government as one that is in general favorable to their interests. One form that this reserve support takes in Western society is that of party loyalty, since the party is the typical instrument in a mass industrialized society for mobilizing and maintaining support for a government. However, continuous lack of specific rewards through policy decisions ultimately leads to the danger that even the deepest party loyalty may be shaken.

For example, labor has continued to support the Democratic Party even though much of the legislation promoted by members of that party has not served to meet labor's demands. In some measure, large sections of labor may continue to vote and campaign vigorously on behalf of the Democratic Party because they have no realistic alternative other than to support this party; but in addition the Democrats have built up in recent years, especially during the Roosevelt era, a considerable body of good will. It would take repeated neglect of labor's demands on the part of the Democratic Party to undermine the strong urban working-class support directed toward it and the government that the party dominates from time to time.

Thus a system need not meet *all the demands* of its members so long as it has stored up a reserve of support over the years. Nor need it satisfy even *some of the demands of all its members.* Just whose demands a system must seek to meet, how much of their demands, at what time, and under what conditions are questions for special research. We can say in advance that at least the demands of the most influential members require satisfaction. But this tells us little unless we know how to discover the influentials in a political system and how new sets of members rise to positions of influence.

The critical significance of the decisions of governments for the support of the other two aspects of a system—namely, the political community and the regime—is clear from what I have said above. Not all withdrawal of support from a government has consequences for the success or failure of a regime or community. But persistent inability of a government to produce satisfactory outputs for the members of a system may well lead to demands for changing of the regime or for dissolution of the political community. It is for this reason that the input-output balance is a vital mechanism in the life of a political system.

(2) *Politicization as a Mechanism of Support.* It would be wrong to consider that the level of support available to a system is a function exclusively of the outputs in the form of either sanctions or rewards. If we did so conclude, we could scarcely account for the maintenance of numerous political systems in which satisfaction of demands has been manifestly low, in which public coercion is limited, and yet which have endured for epochs. Alternately, it might be difficult to explain how political systems could endure and yet manage to flout or thwart urgent demands, failing thereby to render sufficient *quid pro quo* for the input of support. The fact is that whatever reserve of support has been accumulated through past decisions is increased and reinforced by a complicated method for steadily manufacturing support through what I shall call the process of politicization. It is an awkward term, but nevertheless an appropriately descriptive one.

As each person grows up in a society, through a network of rewards and punishments the other members of society communicate to and instill in him the various institutionalized goals and norms of that society. This is well known in social research as the process of socialization. Through its operation a person learns to play his various social roles. Part of these goals and norms relate to what the society considers desirable in political life. The ways in which these political patterns are learned by the members of society constitute what I call the process of politicization. Through it a person learns to play his political roles, which include the absorption of the proper political attitudes.

Let us examine a little more closely something of what happens during the process of politicization. As members of a society mature, they must absorb the various orientations toward political matters that one is expected to have in that society. If the expectations of the members of society with regard to the way each should behave in specific political situations diverged beyond a certain range, it would be impossible to get common action with regard to the making of binding decisions. It is essential for the viability of an orderly political system that the members of the system have some common basic expectations with regard to the standards that are to be used in making political evaluations, to the way people will feel about various political matters, and to the way members of the system will perceive and interpret political phenomena.

The mechanism through which this learning takes place is of considerable significance in understanding how a political system generates and accumulates a strong reserve of support. Although we cannot pursue the details, we can mention a few of the relevant dimensions. In the first place, of course, the learning or politicization process does not stop at any particular period for the individual; it starts with the child and, in the light of our knowledge of learning, may have its deepest impact through the teen age. The study of the political experiences of and the influences operating on the child and the adolescent emerges as an important and neglected area of research.

In the second place, the actual process of politicization at its most general level brings into operation a complex network of rewards and punishments. For adopting the correct political attitudes and performing the right political acts, for conforming to the generally accepted interpretations of political goals, and for undertaking the institutionalized obligations of a member of the given system, we are variously rewarded or punished. For conforming we are made to feel worthy, wanted, and respected and often obtain material advantages such as wealth, influence, improved opportunities. For deviating beyond the permissible range, we are made to feel unworthy, rejected, dishonored, and often suffer material losses.

This does not mean that the pattern of rewards and punishments is by any means always effective; if it were, we would never have changed from the Stone Age. A measure of non-conformity may at certain stages in the life history of a political system itself become a respected norm. Even where this is not the case, the most seductive rewards and the severest punishments will never succeed in preventing some of the members of a system from pursuing what they consider to be their inextinguishable interests and from seeking, with varying degrees of success, to change the goals and norms of the system. This is one of the important sources of political change closely associated with changes in the inputs of demands that are due to a changing environment. But we cannot pursue this crucial matter of the nature of political change, as it would lead us off in a new direction.

In the third place, the means used for communicating the goals and norms to others tend to be repetitive in all societies. The various political myths, doctrines, and philosophies transmit to each generation a particular interpretation of the goals and norms. The decisive links in this chain of transmission are parents, siblings, peers, teachers, organizations, and social leaders, as well as physical symbols such as flags or totems, ceremonies, and rituals freighted with political meaning.

These processes through which attachments to a political system become built into the maturing member of a society I have lumped together under the rubric of politicization. They illustrate the way in which members of a system learn what is expected of them in political life and how they ought to do what is expected of them. In this way they acquire knowledge about their political roles and a desire to perform them. In stable systems the support that accrues through these means adds to the reservoir of support being accumulated on a day-to-day basis through the outputs of decisions. The support obtained through politicization tends to be relatively—although, as we have seen, not wholly—independent of the vagaries of day-to-day outputs.

When the basic political attachments become deeply rooted or institutionalized, we say that the system has become accepted as legitimate. Politicization therefore effectively sums up the way in which legitimacy is created and transmitted in a political system. And it is an empirical observation that in those instances where political systems have survived the longest, support has been nourished by an ingrained belief in the legitimacy of the relevant governments and regimes.

What I am suggesting here is that support resting on a sense of the legitimacy of a government and regime provides a necessary reserve if the system is to weather those frequent storms when the more obvious outputs of the system seem to impose greater hardships than rewards. Answers to questions concerning the formation, maintenance, transmission, and change of standards of legitimacy will contribute generously to an understanding of the way in which support is sufficiently institutionalized so that a system may regularly and without excessive expenditure of effort transform inputs of demand into outputs of decisions.

That there is a need for general theory in the study of political life is apparent. The only question is how best to proceed. There is no one royal road that can be said to be either the correct one or the best. It is only a matter of what appears at the given level of available knowledge to be the most useful. At this stage it appears that system theory, with its sensitivity to the input-output exchange between a system and its setting offers a fruitful approach. It is an economical way of organizing presently disconnected political data and promises interesting dividends.

One of the most central interests of American sociologists specializing in government and politics is voting behavior. Ever since the national elections of 1948, they have conducted many sociological studies, employing the survey technique, in order to determine what social factors are at work in the community decision-making process that we identify as "voting." Sociologists are also curious to know the extent to which social variables such as age, sex, education, occupation, and religion are related to the way people vote.

In the spring of 1961, voters in the Michigan community of Kalamazoo rejected an ordinance which had been adopted earlier that year and which provided for the establishment of a housing commission in order to serve the city's housing needs. To provide some sociological answers to the questions of how and why people vote the way they do, Professor Donald H. Bouma of Western Michigan University conducted a survey, and in the pages that follow, he reports and analyzes the methodology and findings of the study.

35. WHY KALAMAZOO VOTED NO *

DONALD H. BOUMA
Western Michigan University

INTRODUCTION

After one of the most heated controversies the city had ever seen, voters in Kalamazoo, on April 3, 1961 rejected, by an 8,656 to 5,962 vote, a proposal to retain a city housing commission which had been established six weeks earlier by the Kalamazoo City Commission to deal with the housing problem of low-income families.

The 15,412 votes cast in the balloting, which also included state offices to be filled, was the largest by far ever recorded in a spring election and the largest for any nonpresidential election. Previous spring election totals had ranged from around 6,000 votes to a high of 8,824 in 1955 when an annexation issue aroused special interest.

The most striking feature of the election, however, was not the heat of the controversy nor the size of the vote. Rather, it was the fact that practically every organization in the city—with one notable exception—was on record in favor of the housing proposal, and most of them quite vocally so. The notable exception was the Kalamazoo Board of Realtors which almost singlehandedly

* Published by the W. E. Upjohn Institute for Employment Research, Kalamazoo, Michigan, June, 1962, pp. 1–32.

led the campaign for defeat—a campaign so successful that the housing issue was voted down in 36 of the 44 precincts in the city.

How was it possible for one community organization to win its way against the aroused combination of practically all of the other community organizations and power groups? Why did 59 percent of the voters choose to take its advice? What considerations influenced the voters as they made up their minds on the issue? These and similar questions are the concern of this study.

The housing controversy was one of those rapidly developing community issues. It had its beginning in November, 1960, when a report compiled by city building and health officials was presented to the seven-member city commission. The report outlined housing needs, termed the situation critical, and asked for authorization to gather information relative to formation of a local housing authority.[1]

Approval was given, and a second report recommended a housing ordinance and housing commission as the most practical method of dealing with what were described as the basic problems: (1) Those persons living in bad housing; (2) Those living on a low income, or financially indigent; (3) Those who need guidance to elevate their living patterns. The ordinance establishing a five-member housing commission was adopted on February 20, 1961, by a 6–1 vote of the city commission. It required the housing commission to investigate all possibilities of privately financed housing before seeking federal help.

Realtors Lead Referendum Drive

The ordinance reached the ballot by referendum, called by virtue of petitions gathered in a drive spearheaded by the Board of Realtors. Over 3,000 signatures were obtained on the petitions, although only 1,001 were needed.

During the campaign, the Board of Realtors was joined in the opposition fight by the Retail Lumber Dealers Credit Association, Home Builders Association, Kalamazoo Chapter of the Society of Residential Appraisers, Taxpayers Committee, and Citizens Committee for Good Government. The Kalamazoo County Young Republicans Club was also listed with those against the ordinance until the day of the election when it publicly switched and came out for the issue.

Taking official stands in favor of the issue was a large array of business, political, civic, and social organizations, cutting across all sectors of the community. Included in the list were the following: Kalamazoo County Council of Churches, as well as many individual congregations; League of Women Voters; American Association of University Women; Committee on Aging; YWCA Board of Directors; NAACP; Kalamazoo County Council of Social

[1] According to the 1960 Census of Housing, out of a total of about 25,500 dwelling units in the City of Kalamazoo, approximately 21,100 were in sound condition, 3,300 were deteriorating, and 1,100 were dilapidated. Thus, 17 percent of all housing units in the city were in an unsound condition.

Agencies; Downtown Kalamazoo Association (an association of businessmen); Business and Professional Women's Club; Community Improvement Association; Kalamazoo Labor Council AFL-CIO; Kalamazoo Council on Human Relations; Kalamazoo Nursing Council; county Republican party; county Democratic party; and others.

Both Sides See Housing Problem

During the campaign both sides agreed that there was a problem in providing adequate housing for Kalamazoo's low-income families, but differed over the solution. Proponents argued that the housing commission provided the best means of meeting the problem and that public housing would be used only if private financing could not do the job. They said that public housing would not affect local taxes. They cited examples of public housing projects which provided more to local government income through payments in lieu of taxes to the city, schools, and county than the run-down area previously did in tax returns. They claimed that public housing is no more socialistic than other government programs, such as highways and airports, which are an accepted part of daily living.

Those against the ordinance argued that public housing would inevitably follow upon its adoption and this would result in a rise in federal taxes and also in local taxes since the projects would remove land from the assessment roll but would still require city and school services. Public housing was called socialistic and it was claimed that it would compete with private landlords. Opponents claimed that it was not fair to deprive some homeowners of property through public condemnation, and not fair to ask those who worked to own their homes to pay the rent for a "new privileged class."

A spokesman for the realtors admitted that 4,000 Kalamazoo homes were in substandard condition, but insisted that the blighted areas could be eliminated through enforcement of the building codes. The proponents answered that if the houses were condemned, the people would have no place to live that they could afford. The realtors suggested that a nonprofit organization be formed to secure local funds to solve the housing problem. Proponents agreed that this idea might have merit, but that a housing commission would be the agency to look into this possibility.

The realtors said the solution lay in fixing up older homes and in the last few days of the campaign dramatically displayed a house which they purchased and renovated for $7,600 and offered to sell for the same price to a low-income family.

PURPOSE AND METHODOLOGY OF STUDY

Because of the unusual factors present in the election, including the alignment and degree of involvement of community power groups, a study was designed to attempt to ascertain and assess some of the significant elements in this community decision-making process. A grant from the W. E. Upjohn Institute for Employment Research to the Center for Sociological Research at Western Michigan University financed the study.

The director of the study had previously analyzed the basis for and legitimizing of the dominant social power position of a real estate board in the neighboring city of Grand Rapids. In that city, also, the realtors had been successful in influencing community decisions even though opposed by a cross-sectional constellation of official and unofficial organizations.

It was decided to focus the present study not on the real estate board and its power position in influencing community decisions, but rather on the citizens of Kalamazoo, in an attempt to determine why they reacted as they did in the housing election. The purpose was to assess the effectiveness of various techniques used to help the voter make up his mind, and to determine to what extent variables such as education, income, occupation, age, sex, length of residence, religion, home ownership, and others, were related to the way people voted on the housing issue.

The project was designed as a case study of the dynamics of the community decision-making process, focusing in particular on factors influencing voter preference. It was intended to develop a better understanding of the values which characterize the community and the factors influencing them. Of major importance was the citizens' perception of the interplay of community organizations and the relative effectiveness of various groups seeking to be influential in the making of an important community decision.

The study was concerned with whether the citizens accepted the definitions of the situation projected by the opposing power groups, and why the Board of Realtors was more successful than the array of 30 community groups in convincing the voters of its value system.

Which, if any, of the socioeconomic subgroups of the community were most responsible for the defeat of the housing proposal? Did members of organizations tend to vote in accord with the public stand of their group? That is, did union members vote as their union advised, church members as their churches advised, Republicans as their party advised, etc? Was it just a free-floating anxiety or confusion which caused people to vote no, or did they have rather fixed reasons? What reasons did people give for the defeat? Would the nonvoters have changed the results of the election? These concerns focused the inquiry.

The research methodology involved an interview study of 250 households representative of Kalamazoo citizens. Dwelling units were drawn from the Kalamazoo Standard Sample which was devised by the Survey Research Center at the University of Michigan. The interviewers used a 5-page schedule containing 61 items. Some of the questions had structured responses; others were open-end and called for free response. Field interviewing was done within two weeks after the election so the effects of the campaign could be assessed without too much memory strain. A total of 244 usable interviews was obtained.

THE VOTE AND THE VOTERS

The issue as stated on the ballot was: Shall the ordinance passed by the City Commission of the City of Kalamazoo on the 20th day of February, 1961, providing for the creation of a Housing Commission, go into effect?

Almost half of the respondents (46 percent) said that they had voted on the issue. As may be noted in Table 1, this compares with 40 percent of the 37,000 registered voters of the city who actually voted on the issue.

TABLE 1. Comparison of Election Results with Study Group Sample

		Voters on Issue		*Voted Yes*		*Voted No*	
Elector Group	*Number of Electors*	*Number*	*Percent of Electors*	*Number*	*Percent of Voters*	*Number*	*Percent of Voters*
City	37,000 [a]	14,618	40	5,962	41	8,656	59
Study sample	244	113 [b]	46	42	39	67	61

[a] Registered as of April 3, 1961.

[b] Of whom four respondents did not know how they voted. Percentage of yes or no votes in this table and others which follow is based upon a total of 109 respondents who knew how they voted.

Of those who did vote, 39 percent voted in favor of the housing issue, while 61 percent voted against it. This is an almost exact parallel of the actual voting in the city which found 5,962 (41 percent) voting for, and 8,656 (59 percent) voting against. This is one indication of the representativeness of the sample used in this study.

When those who did not vote were asked the reason, over half of them (53 percent) said they did not know, while 18 percent said they had no interest in the election, 16 percent said they could not get to the polls, and the remaining 12 percent said they were confused by the issue.

The nonvoters were asked how they would have voted if they had, and 40 percent said they did not know while 34 percent said they would have voted in favor and 26 percent against. Therefore the nonvoters who had a preference favored the housing program and would have given it a 56 percent yes vote. Had they voted, however, they would not have changed the results of the election. When voters are combined with nonvoters who took a stand the negative vote drops from 61 percent to 54 percent. When those with no opinion are allocated according to the same percentage as the yes and no stands of the other nonvoters, the percentage of no votes drops to 52 percent.

Personal Characteristics of the Sample

Table 2 shows the composition of the sample, and of those in the sample who voted, in terms of their sex, race, political affiliation, and membership in a union. Of the respondents, 40 percent were women. It was found that a higher percentage of women than of men voted (49 percent and 43 percent, respectively), and that a higher percentage of women voting voted yes (41 percent to 34 percent).

TABLE 2. Distribution of All Respondents and of Respondents Voting Affirmatively on Housing Issue, by Sex, Race, Political Party, and Union Membership of Chief Wage Earner

	All Respondents		*Voted on Issue*		*Voted Yes*	
Item	*Number*	*Percent of Total*	*Number*	*Percent of R's* [a]	*Number*	*Percent of R's Voting* [b]
Sex						
Men	97	40	42	43	14	34
Women	147	60	71	49	28	41
Race						
White	229	94	107	47	37	36
Nonwhite	15	6	6	40	5	83
Negro	13	5	6	46	5	83
Political Party						
Republican	97	40	57	59	22	41
Democratic	61	25	24	39	12	50
Independent	50	20	26	52	8	32
Not given	36	15	6	17	0	0
Union Membership						
Member	70	29	29	42	9	32
Nonmember	170	70	84	50	33	41
Did not know	4	2	0	0	0	0

[a] Percents in this column reflect number voting as percent of total number in each group as given on same line under "All Respondents."

[b] Percents shown in this column reflect number voting yes as percent of number in each group who voted, as given on same line under "Voted on Issue." Out of 113 who voted on the issue, four did not know (or were unwilling to admit) whether they voted affirmatively or negatively. The percents reflect the deletion of these four from the "Voted on Issue" column. "R's" refers to respondents.

Negroes constituted 5 percent, and other nonwhites 1 percent, of all respondents. The percentage of Negroes voting was 46, practically the same as for the study total. In contrast with the whites, however, it will be seen from Table 2 that almost all of the voting Negroes gave the proposal an affirmative vote.

Asked about party preference, 40 percent of the respondents said they generally voted as Republicans, 25 percent as Democrats, 20 percent as independents, and 14 percent said they did not know. The Republicans had the best voting turnout with 59 percent of them balloting on the housing issue, compared with 52 percent of the independents, and 40 percent of the Democrats. However, the Democrats recorded the largest percentage (50) of yes votes, followed by the Republicans and independents (41 percent and 32 percent, respectively). Voters of neither party, then, gave the housing issue a favorable nod even though both the county Democratic party and the county Republican party had given it public endorsement.

About 30 percent of the respondents were members of families where the chief wage earner was a union member. In one of the surprise findings of the study it was revealed that the negative vote among union members was higher than for nonunion members, 68 percent negative for union members, compared with 59 percent for those not union affiliated. This was true in spite of the fact that public endorsement had been given the housing issue by the Kalamazoo Labor Council AFL-CIO.

Length of Residence and Ownership of Homes

Respondents were asked how long they had lived in the city of Kalamazoo and whether they were home owners or renters. As may be noted from Table 3 there were almost twice as many respondents who had resided in Kalamazoo for more than ten years as there were who had lived in the city for ten years or less; and twice as many owners as there were renters.[2]

TABLE 3. Distribution of All Respondents and of Respondents Voting Affirmatively on Housing Issue, by Length of Residence in Area and by Home Ownership

	All Respondents		*Voted on Issue*		*Voted Yes*	
Item	*Number*	*Percent of Total*	*Number*	*Percent of R's*	*Number*	*Percent of R's Voting*
Length of Residence						
10 years or less: Total	*91*	*37*	*36*	*40*	*15*	*40*
Less than 1 year	15	6	3	20	2	67
1 to 5 years	33	14	11	33	2	17
5 to 10 years	43	18	22	52	11	50
Over 10 years: Total	*153*	*63*	*77*	*50*	*27*	*38*
Home Ownership						
Renters	80	33	23	29	11	48
Owners	164	67	90	55	31	36

[2] The percent of home owners among our respondents (67) is another indication of the representativeness of the sample. Based upon the 1960 Census of Housing, 64 percent of the occupied dwelling units were owner-occupied.

The percentage of respondents who voted on the issue increased with length of residence; and of those voting, a slightly higher percentage of the longer residents (over 10 years) voted against the issue. Proportionately, about twice as many owners as renters voted on the issue. Among home owners there were almost twice as many against the proposal as there were in favor of it. Among renters the vote was almost equally divided between those for and those against the proposal.

Occupation and Family Income

The only occupational group to favor the housing issue was the business and professional with a 54 percent yes vote (Table 4). The percentage of yes votes for other groups was as follows: unskilled and white-collar groups each had 29 percent; the skilled labor group, 33 percent; and the unemployed-retired group, 43 percent.

As regards the relationship between total family income and the way people voted in the housing election, the income data as shown in Table 4 indicate that high- and low-income groups generally were in favor of the housing proposal while middle-income groups were strongly negative. Yes votes were 57 percent in the under-$2,000 group, dropped at each income division to a low of 22 percent in the $6,000-$8,000 group, then rose to 60 percent in the

TABLE 4. Distribution of All Respondents and of Affirmative Votes, by Occupational Grouping and by Family Income

	All Respondents		*Voted Yes*	
Item	*Number*	*Percent of Total*	*Number*	*Percent of R's Voting*
Occupational Group				
Business and professional	45	18	15	54
Sales and white-collar	44	18	7	29
Skilled labor	31	13	4	33
Unskilled labor	71	29	7	29
Unemployed and retired	36	15	6	43
Other	17	7	3	50
Annual Family Income				
Under $2,000	30	12	4	57
$2,000–$3,999	35	14	4	40
$4,000–$5,999	65	27	11	31
$6,000–$7,999	48	20	5	22
$8,000 and over	31	13	12	60
No answer	35	14	6	43

Note: See footnotes to Table 2 for explanation of calculation of percentages voting yes.

over-$8,000 group. When the Negro vote was eliminated from the under-$2,000 group, the affirmative vote dropped to 50 percent.

Age Distribution and Education

Those 40 years of age and over compiled a better voting record and registered more yes votes than the under-40 group, although no age group gave the housing issue its approval. As indicated in Table 5 the respondents were a balanced representation of various age groups. Forty percent of those under 40 years of age voted, while 51 percent of those 40 and over voted. Although only 32 percent of those under 40 favored the housing issue, 43 percent of those 40 and over did.

It was found that the percentage of respondents voting went up in direct proportion to the amount of their education, ranging from 23 percent for those with less than eight years of schooling, to 66 percent for those who completed college. As with income, the percentage of yes votes was highest among those with the most and those with the least education, 64 percent for the college-completed group and 80 percent for the less-than-eighth-grade group.

When the respondents were divided into one group which had completed high school or more, and another group which had not completed high school, marked differences appeared. While 59 percent of the high school group voted, only 30 percent of the less-than-high-school group did. Yes votes represented 42 percent of the high school group and only 30 percent of the others. Again, it should be noted that approval for the housing ordinance was given by neither group.

Denominational Membership

Did religious affiliation, if any, have any relationship to the way the people voted on the housing issue? Respondents were asked of what religious denomination, if any, they were a member. The results were as follows: Methodist, 24 percent; Baptist, 14 percent; Catholic, 12 percent; Reformed and Christian Reformed, 10 percent; Episcopal, 3 percent; Congregational, 2 percent; Jewish, Moslem, Russian Orthodox, 2 percent; other Protestant (Presbyterian, Lutheran, etc.), 15 percent; no religious affiliation, 18 percent.

There was no important difference between Catholic and Protestant voters in the housing election. Catholic voters showed a 40 percent favorable vote (which was par for both the study sample and the actual vote in the community), while Protestants showed a 42 percent favorable vote. It may be noted that no Catholic group took a public stand one way or the other during the campaign, while the Kalamazoo Ministerial Alliance, comprising most Protestant groups, as well as individual Protestant organizations did publicly endorse the housing ordinance.

A very high negative vote was tallied by those listing no denominational affiliation, with 87 percent stating they voted no. There was only one Jewish voter in the sample.

TABLE 5. Distribution of all Respondents and of Respondents Voting Affirmatively on Housing Issue, by Age Group and by Educational Attainment

	All Respondents		*Voted on Issue*		*Voted Yes*	
Item	*Number*	*Percent of Total*	*Number*	*Percent of R's*	*Number*	*Percent of R's Voting*
Age Group						
All under 40 years	*104*	*43*	*42*	*40*	*13*	*32*
20 to 29	55	23	17	31	5	29
30 to 39	49	20	25	51	8	33
All 40 and over	*140*	*57*	*71*	*51*	*29*	*43*
40 to 49	49	20	29	59	13	45
50 to 59	39	16	16	41	6	38
60 and over	52	21	26	50	10	44
Education						
Did not complete high school	*101*	*41*	*30*	*30*	*9*	*30*
Less than eighth grade	22	9	5	23	4	80
Completed eighth grade	29	12	8	28	4	50
Some high school	50	20	17	34	1	6
High school completed and beyond	*143*	*59*	*83*	*58*	*33*	*42*
Completed high school	62	25	33	53	10	32
Some college	43	18	25	58	7	30
Completed college	38	16	25	66	16	64

Differences between Protestant denominations were very great, but because some denominations had comparatively few persons, these differences are not necessarily significant. Thus, for example, Congregationalists gave a negative vote unanimously, but since there were only four cases this finding has little meaning. As noted above, the Reformed-Christian Reformed group was larger. This group gave only a 9 percent affirmative vote. The largest denomination, Methodists, gave a 43 percent affirmative vote. The next largest denomination was the Baptist, and this denomination gave the largest percentage of affirmative votes, 63 percent. It should be noted regarding the Baptists that most Negroes in the study were Baptists, and the findings for this denomination reflects the highly favorable vote among Negroes. When the Negroes are removed from the Baptist group, the affirmative vote drops to 54 percent. Two Episcopalian voters in the sample split their votes. All "other Protestants" combined gave a 53 percent favorable vote.

The relationship to voting decision of the eleven variables which were analyzed may be summarized as follows:

SEX—Housing proposal was rejected by both men and women, but women had a higher favorable vote.

RACE—Rejected by whites, strongly approved by nonwhites.

PARTY PREFERENCE—Democratic voters had a higher percentage of yes votes than either Republican or independents, but it was approved by none of the three groups.

LENGTH OF RESIDENCE—Rejected by both long- and short-term residents, but the latter had a slightly higher percentage voting yes.

HOME OWNERSHIP—Rejected by both owners and renters, but renters had a higher yes vote.

UNION MEMBERSHIP—Rejected by both union and nonunion members, but the yes vote of union members was smaller.

OCCUPATION—Rejected by all occupational groups except the business and professional, which gave it a slim margin.

AGE—Rejected by both those 40 years of age and over and those under 40, although the 40-and-over group had a higher yes vote.

RELIGION—Rejected by both Catholic and Protestant voters, but the highest rejection rate was by the unchurched.

INCOME—Rejected strongly by middle-income groups, but high- and low-income groups generally were in favor.

EDUCATION—Rejected by both those who had not completed high school and those who had, but favored by smaller groups at each extreme: those with less than eight years of schooling and college graduates.

Pronounced support for the housing proposal, then, came only from nonwhites, the college graduates, those with under 8 years of schooling, and the extreme income groups.

WHY THEY VOTED AS THEY DID

Those who voted in favor of the housing proposal were asked their reasons in an open-end question. Answers were grouped into categories as shown in Table 6. One-third of those who voted affirmatively gave as their first reason the need of some people for better places to live at low rent, and another one-third said it was good for the city. About 12 percent said they wanted to help people or that it was because of their Christian conscience, and 9 percent said there was need for a study of the housing problem. The other 13 percent gave random reasons, including one person who voted yes because of the "antics of the real estate board." Less than one-third of the respondents gave a second reason, and most of these cited the need for low-rent housing.

It may be noted that the reasons given were focused on the needs that were emphasized by the proponents of the measure. No one said they voted yes to back the city commission or because prestige people or groups were for it.

TABLE 6. *Reasons for Voting Yes*

Reasons	*Number*	*Percent*
Need for better places to live at low rent	14	33
Good for city	14	33
Help people; Christian conscience	5	12
Needed study of housing	4	9
Other reasons	5	12
Total	42	99 [a]

[a] Percentages do not add to 100 because of rounding.

Those who voted no were also asked their reasons in an open-end question. Here the reasons were quite diffused, in contrast with the strongly focused reasons of the yes voters. As shown in Table 7, the most often cited reason for a no vote, by 24 percent, was that people should help themselves. This was often expressed as, "It won't help me and why should I help them. They should help themselves." Increase in taxes was the reason given by 16 percent, and 12 percent said it was not good for the city and a better plan could be devised. Only 10 percent said they were opposed because it was socialistic or would be involved in politics, and another 10 percent said the housing would "just become run down again." It was called unnecessary by 9 percent, and too controversial or confusing by 9 percent. Another 9 percent could give no reason.

Only 25 percent could give a second reason, and these were widely scattered. That no one gave as an explanation for a no vote the fact that the realtors were against it indicates that the values cited by the realtors in the campaign had become well internalized—or that the realtor values simply reflected dominant values in the community.

TABLE 7. *Reasons for Voting No*

Reasons	*Number*	*Percent*
People should help themselves; it wouldn't help me	16	24
Taxes would go up	11	16
Not good for city; find another plan	8	12
Would become run-down again	7	10
Socialistic; politics	7	10
Was not necessary	6	9
Confused; too controversial	6	9
Dont' know	6	9
Total	67	99 [a]

[a] Percentages do not add to 100 because of rounding.

It is interesting to note that the most important reason given—that people should help themselves—was not a theme given considerable prominence in the campaign. However, this reason, as well as the "just become run-down again" reason, does reflect one of the dramatic episodes of the campaign. The *Kalamazoo Gazette* reported a city official as saying at a meeting: "Crowded conditions are not brought about by a lack of housing, but because they (the people involved) like to live like rats."

The value of self-help was also approached in a separate question. When the respondents were asked whether they thought most people who live in poor housing could get better housing if they wanted it, 38 percent said yes, 44 percent said no, and 18 percent did not know.

Higher taxes, the theme most widely used by the realtors during the campaign, was second in importance, while socialistic trend, also widely cited during the campaign, was a poor third.

TABLE 8. *Opinions As to Effect Passage of Housing Proposal Would Have on Local and Federal Taxes*

	Local Tax		*Federal Tax*	
Effect	*Number*	*Percent of Total*	*Number*	*Percent of Total*
Would result in increase	122	50	84	35
Would result in no increase	74	30	93	38
Don't know	48	20	67	27
Total	244	100	244	100

When questioned directly on whether they thought local taxes would go up if the housing issue passed, 50 percent of the respondents said yes, 30 percent said no, and 20 percent did not know. If the increase in local taxes as the result of passage of the housing measure actually was a debatable issue, the 50-30 acceptance of the realtors' position would be called a success for the campaign of the realtors. However, since as a matter of fact higher taxes would not have followed passage of the proposal (not even if public housing actually were built), which fact was emphasized by the proponents, the success of the realtors in selling their theme to the citizenry is even more remarkable. There is probably nothing in the analysis of the election which more clearly demonstrates the effectiveness of the realtors' campaign.

The realtors also claimed that federal income taxes would rise if the housing issue passed. The proponents, in a series of advertisements, conceded this point by saying, "Your income tax *might* go up one-tenth of one penny per year." (This concession was a strange one. A fixed amount is budgeted each year for federally assisted housing developments and a yes vote in Kalamazoo would have had no effect on the federal budget.)

Strangely enough, when the respondents were asked whether they felt their federal income tax would go up if the housing issue passed (a point both groups conceded) only 35 percent said yes, 38 percent said no, and 27 percent did not know.

The campaign of the realtors also stressed the threat of socialism. When the respondents were asked whether they felt that public housing is socialistic, 35 percent said yes, 41 percent said no, and 23 percent did not know.

The fear-of-socialism value was approached in one additional way. Immediately after adoption of the housing ordinance, the city manager, with 6–1 approval of the city commission, appointed the five-member housing commission. The members were well-known and representative of the community. At no time was there any criticism of the individuals appointed. The respondents were asked if they thought the persons appointed to the housing commission were the kind that might go for a "socialistic" project. Only 14 percent said yes, while 35 percent said no, 2 percent said some of them, and 49 percent said they did not know.

All of the respondents, both voters and nonvoters, were asked in an open-end or free-response type question why they thought most people voted against housing. This provided a measure of the conceptions people had of other's motives. The answers are shown in Table 9.

TABLE 9. *Why Respondents Thought Most People Voted Against Housing*

Reasons	*Number*	*Percent of Total*
Taxes	105	59
Confusion, apathy	17	9
People should help themselves	15	8
Socialistic	14	8
Realtors' influence	9	5
Bad for city, not necessary	8	5
Other reasons	11	6
Total	179	100

About six out of every ten gave taxes as the reason. The three next most frequently cited reasons were confusion and apathy on the part of voters, the feeling that voters felt that people should help themselves, and that voters regarded the proposal as socialistic. These three reasons combined account for 25 percent of the reasons why respondents thought most people voted against housing. Realtor influence was given as the reason by 5 percent, and another 5 percent said because it was not necessary or it was bad for the city. Upon being probed, only 13 percent could give a second reason and most of these said taxes.

Only one percent listed race prejudice as the reason, although a number of observers of city politics surmised that it played a larger role. A blight-elimination program would affect a high percentage of the nonwhite community. A specific question was addressed to this problem. When the respondents were asked whether they thought that race was a factor in the defeat of the housing proposal, 30 percent said yes, 48 percent said no, and 22 percent said they did not know.

The "Dutch" vote was also mentioned by some observers as a reason for the defeat, although none of the respondents gave this as a reason. Some support for this is found in the high negative vote (91 percent) of Reformed and Christian Reformed church members, denominations made up primarily of Dutch-Americans. However, this group constituted only 10 percent of the total in the study. To determine the conception people had, respondents were asked what they thought was the percentage of Kalamazoo people who were of Dutch descent. Excluding those who did not know, 43 percent thought that 50 percent or more of the residents of Kalamazoo were of Dutch descent, 16 percent thought about 40 percent, 24 percent said 30 percent, 11 percent said 20 percent, and 7 percent said 10 percent or under were of Dutch descent.

A survey just completed by the author, using the name-analysis method, indicates that Dutch-Americans constitute about 20 percent of the local population. That almost 60 percent of the respondents guessed twice as high or higher demonstrates the tendency, discovered in many other studies, for people to overestimate the size of a minority, no matter what the minority is.

When asked whether most of the people they talked with were in favor of or against the housing measure, 41 percent said against, 20 percent in favor, and 39 percent did not know.

WHAT HELPED THEM DECIDE HOW TO VOTE?

The study was concerned not only with how and why people voted in the housing election but also with the factors which helped them come to a decision on how to vote. When asked what most helped them decide, the largest number of those with an opinion (44 percent) said that it was their own opinion or a matter of religious conviction to them. Talking with their spouses or other people helped 14 percent make up their minds. Radio and TV was given the credit by 11 percent, and 10 percent said the newspaper (and the letters-to-the-editor column) was most influential. Other factors which received scattered mention were: personal experience with poor housing, letters from churches, meetings, study of issues.

Almost half of those queried, however, did not know what most helped them to decide how to vote. Of the small number who could state a second factor the largest number indicated the newspaper.

Analysis of the role of the mass media in the community decision-making processes, especially that of the newspaper, is complicated by the fact that there is typically a combination of advertising on the issue, straight news reporting, editorializing, and with the newspaper, letters-to-the-editor columns. Ordinarily, only one of these, the editorials, would reflect the position of the newspaper itself. However, in an earlier study by the author in another community (Grand Rapids), it was found that people had a tendency to impute the official position of the newspaper on a controversial issue from the predominant message of the advertising, rather than from the editorials.

TABLE 10. *Major Factor in Decision of Respondents on How to Vote*

Major Factor in Decision	*Number*	*Percent*
Own opinion or religion	55	44
Talking with spouse or other people	18	14
Radio and TV	14	11
Newspaper	13	10
Study of issues	13	10
Personal experience with poor housing	5	4
Other (realtors, letter from churches, meetings)	8	7
Total	126	100

Role of the Newspaper

The city's daily newspaper clearly indicated in several editorials that it was in favor of the proposal. However, when the respondents were asked if they thought the *Kalamazoo Gazette* favored the issue, only 36 percent said yes, while 17 percent said no, and 47 percent said they did not know. When almost half of the people do not even know the stand, and when for every two who do know (to say nothing about being convinced by it) there is one who gets it wrong, one is presented with a rather dim view of the significance of an editorial position on a controversial issue which so caught the community interest.

Further analysis of the data provided additional support for the conclusion that the editorial position of the newspaper had little or no effect on the outcome of the election. In fact, those who thought the *Gazette* favored the housing proposal had a smaller percentage of yes votes (36 percent) than those who thought the stand was negative (40 percent) or than those who did not know (40 percent).

The effect of newspaper advertising was analyzed separately, as shown in Table 11. When the respondents were asked if most of the newspaper ads seemed to be in favor or against, 25 percent said in favor, 9 percent said against, 30 percent said about even, and 37 percent did not remember the ads. Only one in five said that the newspaper ads helped them make up their minds in voting, with two-thirds claiming that the ads did not help them. The remaining 14 percent did not know.

TABLE 11. *Opinion of Respondents Regarding Position of Most Newspaper Ads and the Influence of Ads on Their Decisions*

Item	*Number*	*Percent of Total*
A. Did ads help you decide how to vote?		
Yes	48	20
No	163	66
Don't know	33	14
B. Were most ads in favor or against?		
In favor	60	25
Against	22	9
About even	72	30
Don't know	90	37

Influence of Radio and TV

The influence of radio and TV was also investigated in a separate set of questions, with results much like those for the newspaper. It has been noted earlier that the three media (newspaper, radio, and TV) were given about equal credit as factors helping people make up their minds as to how to vote. When asked specifically if radio and TV ads helped them make up their minds on how to vote, 24 percent said yes (20 percent for newspapers), 61 percent said no (66 percent for newspapers), and 16 percent said they did not know (14 percent for newspapers). What slight difference there is is in favor of radio and TV, in spite of the fact that these media did no "editorializing" on the issue.

TABLE 12. *Effect of Radio and TV Programs on Voter Choice*

Item	*Number*	*Percent of Total*
A. Did radio-TV programs help you decide?		
Yes	58	24
No	148	61
Don't know	38	16
B. Were most programs in favor or against?		
In favor	50	20
Against	15	6
About even	90	37
Don't recall programs	89	36

When asked whether most of the radio and TV programs seemed to be in favor of or against the housing proposal, 20 percent said in favor of, 6 percent against, 37 percent about even, and 36 percent did not recall any programs.

The results are remarkably similar to the newspaper results cited above: about the same percentage could recall nothing about the programs or ads; about the same percentage thought the material was evenly divided, pro and con; and about the same percentage that did see an emphasis thought it was on the side in favor of the housing proposal.

The fact that so few stated that the mass media helped them decide how to vote does not necessarily mean that the mass media in Kalamazoo are unimportant in determining important community decisions. The influence may be of a subtle nature that people do not recognize when asked to identify decision-making determinants. Further, they may play their most important role in reinforcing opinions already held, that is, not so much in helping people make up their minds, but rather in keeping them from changing their minds.

Direct Mail

Direct mailing of informational material was used to a considerable extent by both sides in the campaign. As in the case of the mass media, more of the respondents thought that more of this mail was in favor of (25 percent) than against (12 percent) the housing proposal. About 23 percent thought the pros and cons were evenly balanced, while 40 percent did not remember receiving any mail.

TABLE 13. *Effect of Direct Mail on Voter Choice*

Item	*Number*	*Percent of Total*
A. Did mailed material help you decide?		
Yes	21	9
No	182	75
Don't know	41	17
B. Was most mail in favor of or against?		
In favor of	61	25
Against	30	12
About even	56	23
Don't remember any mail	97	40

Very few people (9 percent) said that the mail received at their homes helped them make up their minds in voting, while 75 percent said it did not, and 17 percent did not know.

Other Factors

Confusion in the minds of the citizenry is often the consequence of a heated campaign characterized by charge and countercharge, by assertion and denial. Confusion is often thought to lead to nonvoting and to negative voting. "If confused, vote no," is an old political saw, and thus one can at times successfully defeat an issue simply by creating enough confusion.

Of all respondents, 41 percent admitted that they felt somewhat confused during the campaign, while 34 percent said they knew clearly how they should vote, and 25 percent did not want to say. It was found that a smaller percentage (53 percent) of those who were somewhat confused voted than those who experienced no confusion (69 percent). However, there was no greater tendency for the confused who did vote to vote no than for those who knew clearly. In fact, there was a slightly higher percentage (63 percent) of no votes among the "knew clearly's" than among the "somewhat confused's" (60 percent). This information is summarized in the following table.

TABLE 14. *Effect on Vote of Confusion About Issue*

	Respondents		*Voted on Housing*		*Voted Yes*	
Understanding of Issue	*Number*	*Percent of Total*	*Number*	*Percent of R's*	*Number*	*Percent of R's Voting*
Somewhat confused	100	41	52	52	20	40
Knew clearly how to vote	84	34	58	69	21	37
Did not answer	60	25	3	5	1	50
Total	244	100	113	46	42	39

Note: See footnotes to Table 2 for explanation of calculation of percentages voting and percentages voting yes.

When asked the free-response question "What most helped you decide how to vote?" only one person mentioned the remodeled older house which the realtors displayed just prior to the election as an alternative method of blight elimination. However, when asked directly if the remodeled house helped them make up their minds in voting, 14 percent said yes, 53 percent said no, 12 percent said they did not know, and 20 percent said they had never heard of it.

What may be concluded, then, about what most helped people decide how to vote? Almost six out of every ten said that their decision was mostly a matter of their own opinion, their religion, or the result of discussion with their spouses or other people. Analysis of the various techniques used by the opposing groups in the campaign to influence the decision-making process seems to bear this out. Relatively small percentages of people credited these factors with helping them make up their minds. Further, most of these factors were seen as favoring the housing proposal and, of course, the vote turned out to be a negative one.

We have the interesting situation, then, where most of the organized groups of the community were on public record in favor of the housing proposal, and where most of the people felt that most of the opinion-shaping influences during the campaign were also in favor of the proposal—despite which most of the people voted no. In other words, the situation was not that the larger number of groups in favor were ineffective in getting their message to most of the people. Nor was it a case of the organized minority versus the unorganized majority, as is sometimes the situation. No, most people got the affirmative message, but they were not buying it. All of this makes the role of the real estate board most intriguing. Somehow the realtors were effective in tuning in on the basic value system of the community.

VESTED INTERESTS IN THE ELECTION

During the campaign there were recurrent charges that one group or another had a selfish interest in the outcome of the referendum. A surprisingly large percentage of people believed this to be true. When asked if they thought any group had something to gain for itself by the outcome of the vote, 44 percent of them said yes; 30 percent, no; and 26 percent said they did not know.

TABLE 15. *Beliefs Regarding Stake of Realtors and Downtown Businessmen in Outcome of Election*

	All Respondents		*Voted Yes*	
Stake in Outcome	*Number*	*Percent of Total*	*Number*	*Percent of Voters*
A. Did realtors have anything to gain by a no vote?				
Yes	116	48	24	44 [a]
No	62	25	6	19
Don't know	66	27	12	52
B. Did downtown businessmen have anything to gain by a no vote?				
Yes	39	16	6	35
No	107	44	25	52
Don't know	98	40	11	25

[a] Table should be read as follows: Of those respondents who thought that realtors had something to gain by a no vote, 44 percent of the number voting (55) voted affirmatively.

And there was no doubt as to which group they had in mind. By far the largest percentage (55 percent) said it was the real estate group. (The question was asked in the form of free-response, with no suggestions given as to possible responses.) Other groups received only scattered mention as follows: apartment owners and property holders, 7 percent; poor people, 7 percent; construction companies, 6 percent; Downtown Kalamazoo Association, 5 percent; the mayor or other city commissioners, 3 percent; all others, 3 percent; would not say, 15 percent. Even upon probing, only 7 percent would give a second choice.

In a question directed specifically to this point and asked of all respondents whether or not they thought some group had something to gain, 48 percent said they thought the realtors had something to gain for themselves by a no vote; 25 percent said they did not think so; and 27 percent did not know.

Even those who thought the realtors had a selfish interest in the outcome produced a majority (56 percent) of negative votes on the housing proposal. However, those who thought the realtors had nothing to gain produced an even higher (81 percent) negative vote. This indicates the measure of identification of the voters with the value system of the realtors. The voters did not choose between two vested interest positions but, rather, clearly recognized the self-interest position of the realtors and accepted it, or recognized it as their own.

Because the role of the realtors was so important in the election, an additional open-end question was used. When asked, "Why do you think the realtors opposed the housing issue?" 60 percent said because it would hurt the realtors' business or because of self-interest. Other than the 31 percent who said they did not know, there was only scattered mention of other items. Again, there was not only a recognition of the self-interest position of the realtors but an identification with it, as 58 percent of those who said the realtors opposed the issue for business reasons voted against the proposal.

TABLE 16. *Beliefs as to Why Realtors Opposed Housing Proposal*

Beliefs	*Number*	*Percent*
Lose business, self interest	147	60
Socialistic	8	3
Not necessary, another way better	6	2
Other (taxes, people help selves)	8	3
Don't know	75	31
Total	244	99

All of this indicates that the people did not perceive the realtors as fighting the battle to preserve important community values, but rather as fighting for their own best interests—and they approved of it.

Frequently during the campaign it was charged that the downtown businessmen had a selfish interest in seeking a yes vote in the election. As mentioned above, in answer to an open-end question, only 5 percent of the respondents thought downtown businessmen had something to gain from the election. When all respondents were specifically asked if they thought downtown businessmen had anything to gain for themselves by a yes vote, only 16 percent said yes, 44 percent said no, and 40 percent said they did not know.

Further, those who perceived a downtown self-interest produced a higher percentage of no votes (65 percent) than those who saw no self-interest (48 percent). The "don't know's" produced the highest negative vote (77 percent). In other words, there was a rejection of downtown business values as perceived, as contrasted with the acceptance of realtor values previously discussed.

In a free-response type question respondents were asked why they thought the city commission voted for a housing commission. Almost half could give no answer, while 35 percent said that it was for the good of the city and the commissioners knew the need. Another 6 percent said it was for selfish reasons; 5 percent said because there was need for a study of housing conditions; and the remainder of responses was scattered.

TABLE 17. *Beliefs as to Why City Commission Adopted Housing Ordinance*

Beliefs	*Number*	*Percent*
Good for city, knew the need	86	35
Selfish reasons	14	6
To study conditions	13	5
Other (politics, federal funds)	14	6
Don't know	117	48
Total	244	100

DID VOTERS IDENTIFY OPPOSING FORCES?

Although more than 30 groups were publicly on record as favoring the housing proposal, people were hard pressed to identify any of them. Likely this was because most of the publicity in favor was not identified with any established group. Most advertisements urging a yes vote bore only the name, in very small print, "Action Committee for Kalamazoo Housing," an *ad hoc* group organized just for the campaign.

When asked which groups they could remember as being in favor of the housing proposal, 57 percent said that they could not recall any. Most frequently mentioned as being in favor, by 19 percent of the respondents, was the city commission. The mass media were scarcely mentioned in spite of the editorial position of the *Kalamazoo Gazette.* Educational groups received scant mention even though faculty members of two colleges in the city were actively involved in the campaign for a yes vote. The Downtown Kalamazoo Association, charged by opponents with having a selfish interest in the election, was mentioned by only 2 percent. Surprisingly, the League of Women Voters was mentioned as a first or second choice by about 6 percent.

Only 8 percent remembered church groups as being in favor of the proposition in spite of a full-page ad in the newspaper on Easter Sunday, the day before the election, in which church groups strongly urged a yes vote. The influence of the churches of the city on this important issue was minimal. This is all the more significant when it is remembered that the election came at a time of the year when religious interest is probably at its highest point.

When asked directly what stand the Kalamazoo Ministerial Alliance (an organization representing most Protestant ministers) took on the housing proposal, 44 percent said that it was in favor, 1 percent said it was against, but 55 percent said they did not know.

Only about one-third of the respondents had an answer when asked why they thought the ministerial alliance took the stand it did. Of these, 66 percent said it was for humanitarian reasons (to get better housing for the poor); 14 percent said that church doctrines demanded it; 9 percent, because it was for the good of the city; and 10 percent listed negative reasons, including "perhaps bribed," "influenced by subversive groups," "more collection money," and "to gain converts."

When asked which groups they remembered as being opposed to the housing proposal, 61 percent singled out the real estate board. Only 36 percent said they did not know, contrasting with the 57 percent who could not identify any group in favor of the issue. The remaining 2 percent said the Kalamazoo Home Owners Association, small home owners, or "the common class." Only 10 percent of the respondents could name a second choice for a group that was opposed.

WHICH GROUPS ARE CONSIDERED INFLUENTIAL?

How did people evaluate the effectiveness of the various groups in presenting their positions? A free-response question concerning this revealed that over half had no firm opinion. Of those who did, 70 percent selected the real estate board, 13 percent picked the city commission, 6 percent said the churches, and another 6 percent simply said "those in favor." The other 5 percent were scattered with less than 1 percent selecting the newspaper.

The housing issue, with the interesting alignment of community groups, provides a case study of influential factors in the decision-making process. This is more than an academic exercise since the outcome of an election is proof of the pudding. One may contemplate and debate which are the truly influential groups in a community, but an election involving the representative organizations of the city is the moment of truth.

To get at the conceptions people had of the relative influence of various groups on the making of a community-wide decision—not just the housing issue—a specific question was asked with a list of possible choices. People were asked which, of all the organizations in Kalamazoo, has the most influence on public issues. Leading the list (27 percent) was the newspaper, followed closely by radio and TV (25 percent). The Downtown Kalamazoo Association was picked by 14 percent and ministers and the churches by 11 percent. The Republican party was named by 7 percent (1 percent picked the Democratic party), another 7 percent said the real estate board, and 5 percent said unions.

TABLE 18. *Beliefs About Which Organization in Kalamazoo Has the Most Influence on Public Issues First and Second Choices*

	First Choice		*Second Choice*	
Organization	*Number*	*Percent of Total*	*Number*	*Percent of Total*
Newspaper	58	27	50	27
Radio and TV	54	25	55	29
Downtown Kalamazoo Association	30	14	19	10
Ministers and churches	24	11	24	13
Board of Realtors	16	7	14	7
Republican party	14	7	7	4
Unions	11	5	12	6
Democratic party	2	1	2	1
Others	5	2	4	2
Total	214	99	187	99

For the second most influential organization, the mass media again headed the list with radio and TV named by 29 percent and the newspaper by 27 percent. Others were: churches, 13 percent; Downtown Kalamazoo Association, 10 percent; realtors, 7 percent; unions, 6 percent; Republican party, 4 percent; Democratic party, 1 percent; others, 2 percent.

Even though the realtors had just won a very important battle in an instance of community decision making, defeating the combined forces of almost all other community groups, only 7 percent of the people chose the real estate board as having the most influence, and another 7 percent picked it as the second most influential. One can only surmise what the percentage would have been if the question had been asked prior to the housing campaign and election.

It was noted that 70 percent had thought the real estate board to be most effective in presenting its position in the election, but only a small percentage saw the board as being generally effective as an influential group. On the other hand, the mass media and the businessmen's group were not said to be very influential in the concrete case of the housing election, but considerable credit was given them for influence in the abstract. There is no research evidence on the role played by the realtors in the making of the broad range of decisions in this community. It may be that typically the realtors do not effectively enter the decision-making processes. Or it may be that they do, but do so in such a way that they are not recognized as a power group, or at least are not resented as such. It may be that people traditionally think of the mass media and business groups as being influential in the decision-making process, whether they actually are or not.

In the Grand Rapids study cited earlier it was found that the real estate board had been very effective in influencing a large number of significant community decisions, both in the arena of elections and in the arena of governmental decisions of boards and commissions. However, this position of power was recognized by only a small percentage of community leaders questioned in the study, and, in fact, by only a small percentage of realtors themselves. This "sleeper effect" may also be involved in the decision-making process in Kalamazoo.

DOES KALAMAZOO HAVE A HOUSING PROBLEM?

Both sides during the campaign acknowledged that the city had a housing problem. The proponents, buttressed by the study report to the city commission by city building and health officials, called the housing problem a critical one requiring new modes of attack. The realtors claimed that the problem was not serious and could be handled with tools already available.

What did the people of the community think about the housing situation? When asked whether they thought Kalamazoo had a housing problem, 66 percent said yes, 20 percent said no, and only 14 percent did not know. There was, then, marked agreement that the community faced a problem.

TABLE 19. *Beliefs About Existence of a Housing Problem in Kalamazoo Related to How Respondents Voted*

	All Respondents		*Voted on Issue*		*Voted Yes*	
Does City Have a Housing Problem?	*Number*	*Percent of Total*	*Number*	*Percent of R's*	*Number*	*Percent of R's Voting*
Yes	162	66	81	50	35	45
No	49	20	19	40	5	26
Don't know	33	14	13	39	2	17
Total	244	100	113	46	42	39

Note: See footnotes to Table 2 for explanation of calculation of percentages voting and percentages voting yes.

Those who thought there was a housing problem were asked, in a free-response type question, what kind of a housing problem it was. The vast majority (70 percent) mentioned either that the rents were too high for low-income people, that there was a shortage of units for low-income people, or that housing was in poor condition and crowded. Shortage of housing in general was named by 9 percent and racial discrimination by 4 percent. Almost 10 percent said they did not know. The remaining percentage was scattered among such items as "landlords won't keep up property," "people won't care for property," "zoning," and "too many houses."

Those who thought there was a housing problem had a higher percentage voting in the election, and a higher percentage of them voted yes. While 50 percent of those who thought there was a problem voted, 40 percent of the no-problem group did, and 39 percent of the don't know's. Just over 45 percent of those who saw a problem voted yes, while only 26 percent and 17 percent of the other groups voted yes.

When asked specifically whether they thought the city had a low-rent housing problem, 59 percent of the respondents said it did; 22 percent said it did not; and the remaining 19 percent said they did not know.

Those respondents who thought the city had a low-rent housing problem (144) were then asked which of the various alternative solutions presented to them they favored. As may be noted from Table 20, public housing was given as a solution with the greatest frequency, followed by some "other" way, and then by remodeling of older homes. However, there were about as many respondents who did not know how the low-rent housing problem ought to be solved as there were who thought the solution lay in public housing.

TABLE 20. *Solutions to Low-Rent Housing Problem Indicated by Respondents Who Thought There Was Such a Problem in Kalamazoo*

Solution	*Number*	*Percent*
Public housing	43	30
Remodeling older houses	27	19
Some "other" way	30	21
Don't know	44	31
Total	144	101

All respondents were asked whether they were familiar with public housing projects in other cities (Kalamazoo has no public housing). Only 69, or 28 percent, of the total number of respondents said they were. Those who were familiar with public housing were then asked to give their impressions of such projects. This information is presented in Table 21.

TABLE 21. *Impression of Public Housing Projects by Respondents Who Said They Were Familiar with Such Projects in Other Cities*

Impression	*Number*	*Percent*
Favorable	29	42
Unfavorable	28	41
Definitely unfavorable	9	13
Don't know	3	4
Total	69	100

It may be concluded that there was no strongly negative public image of public housing. Almost three-fourths of the people had no familiarity with public housing, and the unfavorable impressions were only slightly greater than the favorable ones among those who said they were familiar with projects. Of all 244 respondents, only 37 (or 15 percent) had an unfavorable impression.

Which groups did people think were most affected by housing conditions in the city? The largest number (44 percent) said poor people, while 23 percent said Negroes, 13 percent said old people, another 13 percent did not know, and 7 percent said "others." Although some observers "explained" the negative vote in terms of Negroes being the primary beneficiaries of any contemplated housing project, it is interesting to note that people did not consider them to be the primary beneficiaries. It is true, of course, that the categories above are not mutually exclusive, and if a respondent had in mind the economically disprivileged Negro he could have selected as a response either "poor people" or "Negroes."

It may be remembered that earlier in this study it was noted that while only 1 percent of the respondents listed race prejudice as the reason why most people voted against the housing proposal, a specific question addressed to this factor showed that race was considered an element in the defeat by 30 percent of the people.

Which group affected by the housing situation were people most ready to help through the proposal at issue? From an analysis of yes votes it seems that people were most ready to help the poor (41 percent, yes), then Negroes (38 percent, yes), then the aged (33 percent, yes). In other words, 41 percent of those who thought poor people were affected most by the problem voted yes, etc. The differences are not great and in no case was there a majority of yes votes.

In conclusion, the study showed that there was a general citizen awareness of a housing problem in the community, specifically a shortage of adequate units for low-income people. There was general awareness of the fact that many organizations in the city were advocating a yes vote, and that the realtors opposed a housing ordinance aimed at the problem. It was quite apparent that members failed to follow the lead of organizations which had endorsed and worked for the proposal.

The Board of Realtors was outstandingly effective in giving people reasons to vote no. People clearly felt the realtors had a selfish interest in the election, but this did not disturb them. People voted as the realtors advised, and gave the reasons the realtors did.

Church groups, active in the campaign, were especially ineffective in spite of the fact that the election came at a high point of the church year. Defeat of the proposal can hardly be pinned on any segment of the population because opposition was quite general.

There is general awareness of a housing problem and this is always the first step in alleviating any undesirable condition. In the twelve months which have elapsed since defeat of the housing proposal no significant changes have occurred. The problem remains.

SUMMARY OF FINDINGS

1. The percentage of those in the study who voted against the housing proposal (61 percent) was practically the same as in the actual election (59 percent).

2. Nonvoters were in favor of the proposal, but their votes would not have changed the results of the election.

3. A higher percentage of women than of men voted and relatively more of the women voted yes.

4. A much higher percentage of nonwhites than whites voted in favor. The percentage of Negroes voting was the same as the percentage of whites.

5. More Democrats than either Republicans or independents voted favorably, but voters of neither major party gave the proposal a favorable margin. Of the respondents who were Republicans 59 percent voted on the issue, while the corresponding percentage of Democrats was 39 percent.

6. Union members had a higher negative vote than nonunion members.

7. The percentage of respondents who voted on the issue increased with length of residence in the city. Of all those voting, respondents who were residents for more than ten years had a slightly higher percentage voting no than the respondents who lived in the city for ten years or less.

8. Property owners constituted two-thirds of the respondents. Their voting record was almost twice as high as for renters, and their negative vote was higher.

9. The only occupational group to favor the proposal—by a slight majority—was the business and professional.

10. High- and low-income groups generally were in favor of, while middle-income groups were strongly opposed to having the housing ordinance.

11. By age, those 40 and over compiled a better voting record and registered more yes votes than those under 40, although neither gave its approval.

12. The percentage of respondents voting went up in direct proportion to the amount of education. The percentage of yes votes was highest among those with the most and those with the least education.

13. Catholic and Protestant voters both rejected the proposal and by about the same margin, although a very high negative vote (87 percent) was registered by those listing no denominational affiliation. Differences within the Protestant group were great, ranging from a 63 percent yes vote in one denomination to a 91 percent negative vote in another. Although church groups actively campaigned for the proposal, it cannot be said that they played an influential role in the election.

14. Pronounced support for the proposal came only from nonwhites, col-

lege graduates, those with less than eight grades of schooling, and the extreme income groups.

15. Most of those who voted yes gave as their reason for doing so, first, the need for some people in the city to have a better place to live at low rent; and second, that it would be good for the city. Reasons for negative votes were quite diffused, but most often cited was that people should help themselves.

16. Half of the respondents believed the realtors' assertion that local taxes would go up if the housing measure passed. Of the many facets of the study which indicate the significantly effective role played by the real estate board in determining this decision, this is one of the most important.

17. The majority of those who had an opinion did not feel that public housing was socialistic, although 35 percent did.

18. Most people thought the outstanding reason for rejection of the housing proposal was fear of tax increase. While only 1 percent listed race prejudice, a direct probe revealed that 30 percent thought race was a factor in the defeat.

19. The majority said that the decision as to how they voted was a matter of their own opinion or religion or a result of talking with their spouses or other people.

20. The mass media—newspaper, radio, and TV—played a minor role in influencing people's decisions as to how to vote. The editorial position of the newspaper had little or no effect.

21. Very few people thought the mail received at their homes helped them make up their minds.

22. The remodeled older house of the realtors had practically no effect on the election.

23. Most of the people thought that most of the propaganda during the campaign was in favor of the proposal—but they were not letting it influence them.

24. The realtors were the only group clearly recognized by the people as having a selfish interest in the election outcome, but this did not prevent people from voting with the realtors. There was an important identification with the value system of the real estate board. On the other hand, although comparatively few voters thought that the downtown businessmen had a selfish interest, most of these voters rejected the proposal.

25. Although more than 30 groups were publicly on record as favoring the housing proposal, people were hard pressed to identify any of them. Most often mentioned was the city commission. However, most people remembered the real estate board when asked which group was opposed.

26. Most people thought that of all the groups involved in the housing campaign the realtors were most effective in presenting their position.

27. When asked to pick from a check list the organization which has the most influence on public issues (in general, not just housing), the majority

selected the mass media with 27 percent choosing the newspaper and 25 percent, radio and TV. Only 7 percent said the real estate board.

28. Two-thirds of the respondents thought the city had a housing problem, and the vast majority said the problem involved a shortage of adequate units for low-income people. There was no pronounced opinion as to what solution or approach should be used, although public housing gathered the most support.

29. There was no strongly negative image of public housing. The vast majority had no familiarity with public housing, and the unfavorable impressions were only slightly greater than the favorable ones among those who had familiarity.

30. Poor people were considered to be most affected by housing conditions in the city, with Negroes ranking next.

APPENDIX

A summary of some of the findings of the study which are not included in the tables in the body of the report is presented here. Unless otherwise shown, the number of cases upon which percentages are based is 244. Because of rounding, percentages do not always add up to exactly 100.

Question	*Response*	*Number*	*Percent*
1. Do you think the mall has been a good thing for the city?	Yes	127	52
	No	60	25
	Don't know	57	23
2. Did you feel that public housing is socialistic?	Yes	86	35
	No	101	41
	Don't know	57	23
3. Do you think any group had something to gain for itself by the outcome of the election?	Yes	108	44
	No	72	30
	Don't know	64	26
4. If yes, which group or groups did you feel had something to gain?	Real estate	59	55
	Property holders (to sell), apartment owners	8	7
	Poor people	8	7
	Construction companies	6	6
	Downtown merchants association	5	5
	Mayor or city commission	3	3
	Others	3	3
	Won't say	16	15
	Total	108	101
5. Do you think the *Kalamazoo Gazette* favored the housing issue?	Yes	88	36
	No	41	17
	Don't know	115	47

Question	Response	Number	Per-cent
6. Did you feel that the remodeled house of the realtors helped you make up your mind in voting?	Yes	35	14
	No	130	53
	Don't know	30	12
	Never heard of it	49	20
7. Which community group was most effective in presenting its position on the housing issue?	Real estate board	72	30
	City commission	14	6
	Those in favor	7	3
	Churches	6	2
	Other	7	3
	Don't know	138	57
8. What stand did the Kalamazoo Ministerial Alliance take on the housing issue?	In favor	108	44
	Against	3	1
	Don't know	133	55
9. What kind of housing problem does Kalamazoo have, if there is a problem?	Poor houses, crowded	59	36
	Too expensive, high rents, shortage of low income units	55	34
	Shortage of housing	14	9
	Racial	7	4
	Landlords won't take care of property or take kids	3	2
	Too many houses	3	2
	People won't care for property	3	2
	Tax problem or zoning	1	1
	Don't know	17	10
	Total	162	100
10. Which group do you think is affected most by housing conditions in Kalamazoo?	Poor people	108	44
	Negroes	56	23
	Old people	32	13
	Others	16	7
	Don't know	32	13
11. Were most of the people you talked with in favor of or against the housing issue?	In favor	49	20
	Against	99	41
	Don't know	96	39
12. Do you think the men appointed to the housing commission were the kind that might go for a "socialistic" project?	Yes	34	14
	No	86	35
	Some of them	4	2
	Don't know	120	49
13. Do you think race was a factor in the defeat of housing?	Yes	74	30
	No	117	48
	Don't know	53	22

Question	*Response*	*Number*	*Per-cent*
14. What percentage of the people of Kalamazoo are of Dutch descent, do you think?	About 5%	4	2
	About 10%	10	4
	About 20%	24	10
	About 30%	50	20
	About 40%	33	14
	50% or over	91	37
	Don't know	32	13
15. Do you think most people who live in poor housing could get better housing if they wanted it?	Yes	93	38
	No	108	44
	Don't know	43	18

DYSFUNCTION

In most societies, individuals perform in several roles corresponding to several institutions, but their rewards for quality of performance may be given them on different bases in the different situations. For example, rewards in the economic institution may be in money, whereas within the family the rewards may be in affection.

However, in some societies such as American society, one type of role and the associated institution may become so important that their values intrude on other roles and institutions. As a result, the evaluations of performances in the dominant institutions tend to condition people's performances in others. The consequences may be strains on individuals and on the over-all goal achievements of the society.

In the concluding article of Part III, Melvin M. Tumin applies this approach to the impact of the economic on the family institution. After specifying nine distinguishing elements in the American economic structure and nine parallel elements in American family life, he observes an increasing tendency for certain economic norms and values to invade the family sphere. The major consequence of this concentration of rewards within one institution is what Professor Tumin calls a social imbalance.

36. SOME DYSFUNCTIONS OF INSTITUTIONAL IMBALANCES *

MELVIN M. TUMIN
Princeton University

In most if not all human societies one of the several institutions essential for social viability is given special emphasis. There is also a corollary attention to the means by which the functions of this institution are achieved and upon

* *Behavioral Science,* Vol. 1, No. 3, July, 1956, pp. 218–223.

the values inherent in the means-ends sequence. Sometimes religious devotion is stressed; some societies are highly political in ultimate orientation; others emphasize primarily the facts and fictions of kinship; and in still others, the production of goods and services assumes the highest importance. Which institutional-complex is emphasized can vary over time within any single society.

Any set of institutions can coexist such that, as the human actors perform the tasks called for, by the means prescribed, within the limits of the values affirmed, they may find themselves impeded in their pursuit by contradictions within the separate institutions; or they may find that their activities in each institution are mutually facilitated; or what they do under one institutional aegis may have few consequences for the achievement of other institutional ends.

Emphasis on one institution may produce certain strains and stresses which affect behavior in other institutional areas. The amount of stress and strain will vary with the character of the emphasis. For instance, if most available social goods and services are distributed as rewards for performance of roles in the emphasized institution, other institutions will suffer from absence of rewards required to motivate performance of necessary roles.

Considerations like these indicate the effects of alternative types of institutional emphases. One may probably account for varying intensities of stratification in a society in terms of the relative emphases given to various institutions. This paper focuses upon one particular emphasis, that given to economic institutions in modern United States. How does the economic structure—especially job-recruitment, placement, performance, and reward—compare with the structure of kinship-role-playing, and how do these structures interact? Among the distinguishing elements of the economic structure are the following:

1. There are formal mechanisms for identifying, recruiting, training, and allocating talent to its most appropriate niches.

2. There is a specialized division of labor, organized in terms of a hierarchy of skills.

3. There are formal measures of role efficiency, formally stated and publicly known norms of performance, and formal mechanisms to control deviation from these expected norms.

4. There is a system of rewards by which different positions in the skill hierarchy are differently rewarded.

5. The rewards are measured in units which can be compared.

6. They consist primarily of scarce and desired goods and services.

7. The importance to the society of a given occupation is measured by its location in the skill hierarchy.

8. Prestige is allocated to a position proportionate to its place on the ladder, and, as a corollary, different positions are considered to have different moral worth.

9. Rewards and opportunities not immediately associated with prestige are also distributed according to place in the hierarchy.

By contrast, the familial institution has the following elements:

1. There are few if any formal mechanisms for location, recruitment, and placement of differential talents, and indeed the matter of talent is virtually not raised.

2. The division of labor is rudimentary. Sex and age criteria are employed in role differentiation, but without any formal or implied hierarchy of skills.

3. There is relatively loose definition of what constitutes efficient role playing, though there are norms which prescribe the range of acceptable performance. At the lower end, there are legal definitions of such things as neglect and desertion; at the upper end there are only informal community restraints against overperformance.

4. There is no formal system of rewards.

5. Such rewards as are present are not formulable in measurable units and hence cannot easily be compared from one position to another.

6. The rewards primarily consist of the gratifications inherent in the role-playing itself and such community approbation as one can command, and, at least in theory, these rewards are abundant rather than scarce.

7. All the role players who stay within the accepted normative range are considered equally important to the society. No hierarchical ladder of greater and lesser functional value can systematically be constructed.

8. There being no hierarchical ladder of importance, it is not possible to assign differential prestige for differential position. If there are any role-evaluations, they are made on the basis of the conscientiousness with which one fulfills his expectations, given his resources.

9. There are no distinctive rewards or opportunities arising from differences in role-performance.

When we juxtapose the foregoing two sets of features, it becomes apparent that there are genuine differences between the economic and kinship institutions, and that at least some aspects are mutually exclusive.

Traditionally we have viewed the operative economic rules as deviations from highest principles of conduct, but have also tended to assume that much of this deviation is unavoidable. Similarly, we tend to look upon familial role-playing as embodying a set of principles which are more in harmony with our highest values, but which are capable of being followed only within the family province. In short, the ends desired from economic and familial effort and the means required by those ends are considered to be different enough to warrant disparate organizations and norms.

Forms of Invasion of Family Life

In actual fact, we note an increasing tendency for certain economic rules of conduct to invade the family sphere, coloring the quality of family life.

The invasion assumes a variety of forms. These include:

a. Competition among parents for invidious distinction as parents in terms of the goods and services with which children are supplied.

b. Judgment by the wife of the adequacy of the husband in terms of the economic level of his "breadwinning" and the prestige of his occupation.

c. Awarding of affection to children on the basis of achievement.

d. Emulation by families of a style of life whose worth is measured by economic resources.

e. Judgment by children of the adequacy of their parents in terms of the economic level maintained.

f. Segregation of clusters of families from each other, residentially, socially, and educationally, on the basis of economic-class attributes.

These tendencies may be identified as imports from the economic sphere, insofar as they derive from the occupational structure, and the ways in which prestige-allocation is tied to income and occupation.

Consequences of Invasion

The entrance into family life of economic norms and values has consequences not only within family structure, but also, resonantly, in economic and general social structure, as well. For example:

1. *Production of dissensus through class differentiation.* If consensus in the society on major values is important and if the family is the chief agency for developing such values, then, consensus is hampered relatively to the extent to which family units are set apart from each other, and placed in different relationships to the norms, by virtue of differentiated economic position.

2. *Reinforcement of psychic strain.* If psychic stability is valued; and if the job situation, by virtue of its competitive and impersonal atmosphere, generates psychic stresses; and if personalized and individuated acceptance and affection in the home helps restore equilibrium; then it follows that altering this home atmosphere in the direction of a market-place orientation will maintain and reinforce rather than diminish the psychic strain generated at the job.

3. *Threats to social cohesion.* The cohesiveness of any society significantly depends on the extent to which its members sense their value to their society, and in turn value their membership. The economic structure operates so that differentiated rewards in power and property also yield different amounts of prestige or units of social worth. By contrast, the structure of family life is such that any parent is considered equally worthy with all other parents if he plays his parental role equally conscientiously. Those who rate highly on the economic index of social worth will tend to generalize this rating to an overall social position. And comparably those who rate less well economically, but who can esteem themselves for their conscientious fulfilment of parental duties, will tend to generalize their self-images derived from their parental roles to a more general social image of themselves. In short, favorable self-definitions achieved through conscientious parenthood help to balance unfavorable self-images acquired in devalued economic roles. Conversely, though perhaps questionably and in fewer cases, economic success may counterbalance failures in family relationships. So, multiple institutional affiliations provide oppor-

tunities for larger numbers to develop a sense of worthwhileness than would otherwise be possible, and this results in their feeling more valuable to society and so prizing more highly their membership in it. Therefore, any influx into family life of invidious distinctions based on economic criteria is likely to diminish social cohesiveness.

4. *Impact on personality development in children.* A major motif in family life, which is claimed to be systematically important for adequate personality development, is that no discriminations be made with regard to the amount of affection given to various children by their parents. Such a non-discriminating system is possible only where all children are considered to have equal rights to this affection by virtue of their being children of the same parents. One observable effect of the invasion of economic norms is the tendency to introduce "achievement" as a criterion by which to judge the amount of affection a child is to receive, and, in accordance, to award different amounts of affection in proportion to differential achievement. If the original premise regarding the need for equal affection as a basis for sound personality development is valid, it follows that the introduction of "differentiated achievement" may impair the family's role in personality development.

5. *Dangers for job productivity.* Productivity on the job varies relatively to the extent to which the producer feels his productive role is valued. The differentiated reward structure of economic activity distributes this sense of valued-role unequally. If such distinctions enter into other institutions like the family, they may make for more generalized discontent which can ultimately lower productivity in the economic sphere as well as impair the functions of the family.

6. *Impact upon family stability.* Since the modern family has lost many functions it once had, the affectional tie is now the principal binder among the members. If, as a result of the introduction of economic norms, spouse relations are made to vary with the adequacy of the "breadwinning" of the male, then varying economic fortunes over time and differences between breadwinners at any one time provide two major sources of instability in spouse relations. The tendency to judge the adequacy of a husband by the income he is able to provide may help account for the now-evident greater instability of marriages in lower socioeconomic levels.

Here, then, are six ways in which the entrance into family life of certain economic norms and values may affect achievement of economic, familial, and more general social goals and values.

The Consequences of Concentration and Unequal Distribution of Rewards

What are the causes for the spread of normative principles across institutional lines? To what extent does the system of distribution of rewards set the process in motion?

The line of events can be spelled out as follows. Let us assume, to start, that any society has to offer, by way of rewards, three items: property, power, and prestige. These can be distributed equally or unequally, and they can be distributed primarily within one institutional framework (e.g., as job rewards alone, or religious rewards alone), or they can be spread through various institutions (e.g., property rewards for the job, prestige rewards for religious purity.)

Four major types of distribution-systems are thus made possible by the variations inherent in the possible combinations: (1) equal-concentrated; (2) unequal-concentrated; (3) equal-diffused; (4) unequal-diffused.

1. The equal-concentrated system is one in which major social rewards are distributed primarily for role performance in a limited number of institutions, in which the tendency is toward equality of reward because "conscientiousness at role" is the criterion of merit.

2. The unequal-concentrated system is one in which, as above, the rewards are distributed in only a few situational frameworks, but here the tendency is toward maximum inequality, because "differential talent" or "differential birth" are criteria of merit.

3. The equal-diffused system is one in which various desired scarce goods and services are allocated to reward performances in a range of institutions, and in which the tendency is toward equality of reward as noted in (1) above.

4. The unequal-diffused system is one in which as in (3) above, rewards are spread through various institutions, and in which the tendency is toward inequality as noted in (2) above.

If we take "adequate role performance" as our end, and if we assume that such performance requires sufficient reward as motivation, then two hypotheses are suggested:

(1) The fewer the institutions within which such rewards are adequate, the lower is the level of role performance likely to be within those institutions which have inadequate rewards. Conversely, the more institutions there are with adequate rewards, the higher is the over-all average of role-performance likely to be, though, in any given institution, the performance may be below that which it would be if it had a disproportionate share of the rewards.

(2) The more equal the chance for everyone to gain an equal amount of the available rewards, the higher is the over-all average of motivation likely to be in any given institution, and throughout all institutions, though the motivation of some individuals may be lessened because there are no distinctions between themselves and their colleagues. Conversely, the less equal the chances for equal reward, the lower is the over-all average of motivation likely to be, even though the motivation of some individuals may be higher.

If these hypotheses prove valid, then it follows that the unequal-concentrated system of rewards is likely to yield the lowest over-all average motivation for adequate role performance, and the equal-diffused system would likely yield the highest over-all average.

It is further suggested here that probably the equal-concentrated system would be more generally productive than the unequal-diffused system. The premise here is that the importance of concentration of rewards is diminished by the fact of equality more than is the importance of inequality diminished by the fact of diffusion.

The institutional arrangement in modern United States resembles most closely the unequal-concentrated type. While it is not possible empirically to demonstrate that alternative arrangements would yield a higher average motivation to conscientious role performance, we can suggest ways in which the fact of concentration and inequality of distribution of rewards operate to produce the effects previously cited. Alternative arrangements can then be compared in terms of their likely effects.

Two major effects of the American institutional arrangement are evident. The first is that as a result of the great emphasis placed upon job-achievement and its correlates, it becomes difficult to give enough socially-rewarding meaning to the values of other institutions to enable them to compete successfully on their own terms. There is relatively inadequate reward for conscientious role performance in other institutions. As a result, values from the economic institution invade other institutions and we get the consequences which we have already briefly outlined. This invasion is dysfunctional to the extent that the entering values are inappropriate to the roles to which they become attached.

A second effect is the strain created by the presence of publicly-symbolized inequality in fundamental conditions of life in a society which places a central value upon the equality of worth of all men. In a caste-society, where acceptance of birth-inequalities is the rule, these differences are not likely to be of great significance. There is no presumption of equal opportunity, and hence no implied moral condemnation for relative failure. But in modern American society, the notion that equal opportunity is available is built into the core of economic ideology. Hence such differences as appear are taken to indicate greater or lesser adequacy, importance, and ultimately, moral worth. On the assumption that all men strive to maximize the number of favorable definitions of themselves in their effective environment, we ought to expect that men will react strongly to the implications of unequal worth embodied in the unequal distributions of the symbols of worth, namely, property, power, and prestige. By and large these reactions ought to take the form of behavior designed in some way to reduce the inequalities, to diminish comparisons with others, or to deny the appropriateness of the criteria of evaluation.

The scope of these problems varies with the range of statuses to which one is urged to refer himself for comparison.

In a caste society the problems generated by inequality are likely to be confined within castes since relative self-evaluation tends to be intra-caste. In an open class society, however, the problems are likely to assume society-wide proportions since relative self-evaluation tends to be inter-class. In short, inequality is likely to create problems wherever it occurs, but its scope will vary with the system of stratification.

Reactions to Symbolized Inequality

It is not possible at this point to outline systematically what sorts of compensatory reactions are pursued by individuals of various personality types. We do not yet know enough about the differential incidence of these reactions to construct adequate typologies. But it is evident that reactions directed toward compensation for publicly symbolized inferiority are widespread. A number of them may be listed here:

1. Spending disproportionate amounts of one's resources on status symbols which help confuse the status picture and give an appearance of higher standing than the individual in fact enjoys.
2. Rejection of the values of this world and immersion of self in a belief system which defines earthly inequalities as temporal and insignificant and other-worldly equalities as eternal and prime.
3. Compulsive denial of the significance of the publicly accepted criteria of worth, and insistence upon the equality of all men as measured by criteria which cannot be publicly symbolized. Often associated with this orientation is spontaneous and aggressive reaction to any suggestion of inequality, resulting sometimes in belligerent public conduct to prove to oneself and to others that "no one can push me around."
4. Excessive reliance upon sentimentality and warmth, as criteria of the worthiness of others: the cult of friendship; the constant search for public affirmation that one is loved.
5. Exaggerated authoritarian behavior in those situations where power can be exercised, such as in the home.
6. Denial of the importance of distinction for one's self, together with investment of one's hopes and aspirations in one's children, as a means to become elevated, by ascription, to a status one could not reach by personal achievement.
7. Rejection of existing criteria of worth as immoral, and participating in political movements whose aims are nominally to establish a society in which more valid criteria of human worth are dominant.
8. Confining oneself as much as possible to interaction only with one's peers, thus reducing the effectiveness of symbolic reminders of inequality.

It must be asserted immediately that not every incidence of these tendencies is to be interpreted as compensatory behavior. We recognize the *sui generis* legitimacy of many of these tendencies. And it must also be admitted that all these reactions can occur within the range of socially accepted norms. But we also recognize that each of these reaction types is capable, without much extension, of developing into a normatively disapproved, if not psychiatrically pathological, mode of conduct.

If, then, we can safely identify these as among the common ways in which persons react to a sense of their inadequacies in property, power, and prestige; and if, in turn, we can identify these inadequacies as resulting from the fact that the major rewards of the society are distributed unequally, then, it would seem efficient, in order to maximize goal-achievement, to make it more possible for larger numbers to achieve more nearly equal rewards. This assumes of course that we desire to continue achieving not only our economic goals but also those results from family life which we can realize only if it is not impinged on by inappropriate values from the economic sphere.

We have provisionally identified the concentration of rewards within one institution as a major source of social imbalance. The natural suggestion is, of course, to bring about greater diffusion. But this involves complex problems regarding the dominance and subordinacy of various institutions within a society. Though every society emphasizes certain roles as more important than others, the identifiable problems arising from *great* concentration would suggest that every society has a vested interest in being cautious in permitting any one institution to become preponderant.

Sources of Institutional Dominance

In this regard, a number of ways in which institutions may become and be dominant can be cited:

1. Through monopolization of the scarce and desired rewards.
2. Through excessive demands upon time and energy.
3. Through generalized social emphasis upon the products of the institution.
4. By virtue of the strategic character of the products or services, as when no activity can be undertaken without ritual by specialists.
5. By virtue of ignorance of alternative possibilities.

This is a partial check list of the kinds of imbalances of which any society must ever remain wary if it is to prevent consequences which hamper attainment of a wide range of desired goals.

SELECTED SUPPLEMENTARY READINGS FOR PART III

Benson, Purnell Handy, *Religion in Contemporary Culture* (New York: Harper & Bros., 1960).

Chinoy, Ely, *Automobile Workers and the American Dream* (Garden City, N.Y., Doubleday & Co., 1955).

Gross, Edward, *Work and Society* (New York: Thomas Y. Crowell Co., 1958).

Hoult, Thomas Ford, *The Sociology of Religion* (New York: The Dryden Press, 1958).

Lipset, Seymour Martin, *Political Man: The Social Bases of Politics* (Garden City, N.Y.: Anchor Books, Doubleday & Co., 1961).

MacIver, Robert, *The Web of Government* (New York: The Macmillan Co., 1947).

Martinson, Floyd M., *Marriage and the American Ideal* (New York: Dodd, Mead & Co., 1960).

Sussman, Marvin B., *Sourcebook in Marriage and the Family* (Boston: Houghton Mifflin Co., 2nd ed., 1963).

Waller, Willard, and Hill, Reuben, *The Family: A Dynamic Interpretation* (New York: The Dryden Press, rev. ed., 1951).

Yinger, J. Milton, *Religion, Society, and the Individual* (New York: The Macmillan Co., 1957).

PART FOUR

Social Stratification

INTRODUCTION

Except possibly in the simplest tribal groups, it is normal for any society not only to be organized structurally and functionally in social institutions, but also to have a hierarchy of status systems that evolve from the process of self-and-other differentiation and ranking. The superordinate strata of statuses are often labeled as "upper," "elite," "majority," or "dominant"; the subordinate strata are frequently characterized as "lower" or "minority." Both sets of strata are founded on the unequal social distribution of four instruments: prestige and authority on the one hand, and power and wealth on the other. The first two attributes are subjective aspects of social status; the latter two are the objective instruments.

In a socially stratified population, each stratum—whether it be a class, caste, or ethnic group—is regarded by itself and others as being differentiated in prestige, authority, power, wealth, contacts, activities, and value orientations. The status each stratum enjoys is the degree of esteem accorded its members while they occupy a given position vis-à-vis other strata in the population.

CLASS

What are the alleged functions of social stratification? It serves, first of all, to define what the membership of a given stratum may expect and even demand from others in privileges and rights. It also spells out distinctive roles that people are expected to perform. Not the least important function of social stratification, according to some sociologists, is to provide a style of life or subculture more precise than that which is shared with all members of the society in the general culture. In one of the previous readings on socialization, for example, Davis and Havighurst offered important research findings on the imprint of one kind of social stratification, social class, on child rearing and personality development.

Some kinds of social stratification are segmental in that they prevail within a given community but not in others. Segmental stratification is also found in a given institution, differentiating and ranking the statuses and roles in the family, the factory, the church, or the government according to the unequal amounts of prestige, authority, power, and wealth they may claim. We know, for instance, that a patriarch, a president, a manager, and a bishop are among the highest in status in their respective institutional structures.

The sociologist is quite understandably more attentive to those comprehensive and integrated systems of social stratification that cut across institutions and, in some instances, even across communities to differentiate and rank virtually all members of an entire society. While such strata are generally less precise than those found within the institution or the community, a person's positions in them are nevertheless to a considerable degree the inductive product of the various segmental statuses to which he belongs. We refer here especially to caste and class stratification. Ethnic stratification is less cumulative of segmental statuses than are caste and class, but it also pervades sufficiently beyond specific institutions and communities to warrant consideration as societal in scope. In addition, ethnic stratification is actually functionally enmeshed with caste and class in American society.

Caste and class systems of stratification have much in common. Both are rank order arrangements in which the instruments of power, wealth, prestige, and authority are unequally distributed between the upper and lower strata. But caste stratification is an entirely ascriptive system, for the membership in the two or more castes have no socially acceptable opportunity to rise or fall into each other's stratum. Nor is marriage between castes tolerated. Class stratification, on the other hand, is partly ascribed and partly achieved; a person at birth is ascribed the class of his or her parents but may achieve another class status later in life. Interclass marriages do take place. While caste and class stratification can and do coexist in some societies, a caste system is more likely to flourish in relatively static, rural, and agricultural societies. A class system is more prevalent in a dynamic, urban, and industrial society.

It is proper to begin the readings on social stratification with what is regarded as the leading systematic orientation to principles of stratification in contemporary sociology. Kingsley Davis and Wilbert E. Moore, in the following article, stress the functional necessity of stratification, seeking to show the relationship between stratification and the remainder of the social structure of a society.

37. SOME PRINCIPLES OF STRATIFICATION *

KINGSLEY DAVIS AND WILBERT E. MOORE

University of California, Berkeley, and Princeton University

In a previous paper some concepts for handling the phenomena of social inequality were presented. In the present paper a further step in stratification theory is undertaken—an attempt to show the relationship between stratifica-

* *American Sociological Review,* Vol. 10, No. 2, April, 1945, pp. 242–249.

tion and the rest of the social order. Starting from the proposition that no society is "classless," or unstratified, an effort is made to explain, in functional terms, the universal necessity which calls forth stratification in any social system. Next, an attempt is made to explain the roughly uniform distribution of prestige as between the major types of positions in every society. Since, however, there occur between one society and another great differences in the degree and kind of stratification, some attention is also given to the varieties of social inequality and the variable factors that give rise to them.

Clearly, the present task requires two different lines of analysis—one to understand the universal, the other to understand the variable features of stratification. Naturally each line of inquiry aids the other and is indispensable, and in the treatment that follows the two will be interwoven, although, because of space limitations, the emphasis will be on the universals.

Throughout, it will be necessary to keep in mind one thing—namely, that the discussion relates to the system of positions, not to the individuals occupying those positions. It is one thing to ask why different positions carry different degrees of prestige, and quite another to ask how certain individuals get into those positions. Although, as the argument will try to show, both questions are related, it is essential to keep them separate in our thinking. Most of the literature on stratification has tried to answer the second question (particularly with regard to the ease or difficulty of mobility between strata) without tackling the first. The first question, however, is logically prior and, in the case of any particular individual or group, factually prior.

THE FUNCTIONAL NECESSITY OF STRATIFICATION

Curiously, however, the main functional necessity explaining the universal presence of stratification is precisely the requirement faced by any society of placing and motivating individuals in the social structure. As a functioning mechanism a society must somehow distribute its members in social positions and induce them to perform the duties of these positions. It must thus concern itself with motivation at two different levels: to instill in the proper individuals the desire to fill certain positions, and, once in these positions, the desire to perform the duties attached to them. Even though the social order may be relatively static in form, there is a continuous process of metabolism as new individuals are born into it, shift with age, and die off. Their absorption into the positional system must somehow be arranged and motivated. This is true whether the system is competitive or non-competitive. A competitive system gives greater importance to the motivation to achieve positions, whereas a non-competitive system gives perhaps greater importance to the motivation to perform the duties of the positions; but in any system both types of motivation are required.

If the duties associated with the various positions were all equally pleasant to the human organism, all equally important to societal survival, and all equally in need of the same ability or talent, it would make no difference who got into which positions, and the problem of social placement would be greatly reduced. But actually it does make a great deal of difference who gets into which positions, not only because some positions are inherently more agreeable than others, but also because some require special talents or training and some are functionally more important than others. Also, it is essential that the duties of the positions be performed with the diligence that their importance requires. Inevitably, then, a society must have, first, some kind of rewards that it can use as inducements, and, second, some way of distributing these rewards differentially according to positions. The rewards and their distribution become a part of the social order, and thus give rise to stratification.

One may ask what kind of rewards a society has at its disposal in distributing its personnel and securing essential services. It has, first of all, the things that contribute to sustenance and comfort. It has, second, the things that contribute to humor and diversion. And it has, finally, the things that contribute to self respect and ego expansion. The last, because of the peculiarly social character of the self, is largely a function of the opinion of others, but it nonetheless ranks in importance with the first two. In any social system all three kinds of rewards must be dispensed differentially according to positions.

In a sense the rewards are "built into" the position. They consist in the the "rights" associated with the position, plus what may be called its accompaniments or perquisites. Often the rights, and sometimes the accompaniments, are functionally related to the duties of the position. (Rights as viewed by the incumbent are usually duties as viewed by other members of the community.) However, there may be a host of subsidiary rights and perquisites that are not essential to the function of the position and have only an indirect and symbolic connection with its duties, but which still may be of considerable importance in inducing people to seek the positions and fulfil the essential duties.

If the rights and perquisites of different positions in a society must be unequal, then the society must be stratified, because that is precisely what stratification means. Social inequality is thus an unconsciously evolved device by which societies insure that the most important positions are conscientiously filled by the most qualified persons. Hence every society, no matter how simple or complex, must differentiate persons in terms of both prestige and esteem, and must therefore possess a certain amount of institutionalized inequality.

It does not follow that the amount or type of inequality need be the same in all societies. This is largely a function of factors that will be discussed presently.

THE TWO DETERMINANTS OF POSITIONAL RANK

Granting the general function that inequality subserves, one can specify the two factors that determine the relative rank of different positions. In general those positions convey the best reward, and hence have the highest rank, which (a) have the greatest importance for the society and (b) require the greatest training or talent. The first factor concerns function and is a matter of relative significance; the second concerns means and is a matter of scarcity.

Differential Functional Importance. Actually a society does not need to reward positions in proportion to their functional importance. It merely needs to give sufficient reward to them to insure that they will be filled competently. In other words, it must see that less essential positions do not compete successfully with more essential ones. If a position is easily filled, it need not be heavily rewarded, even though important. On the other hand, if it is important but hard to fill, the reward must be high enough to get it filled anyway. Functional importance is therefore a necessary but not a sufficient cause of high rank being assigned to a position.

Differential Scarcity of Personnel. Practically all positions, no matter how acquired, require some form of skill or capacity for performance. This is implicit in the very notion of position, which implies that the incumbent must, by virtue of his incumbency, accomplish certain things.

There are, ultimately, only two ways in which a person's qualifications come about: through inherent capacity or through training. Obviously, in concrete activities both are always necessary, but from a practical standpoint the scarcity may lie primarily in one or the other, as well as in both. Some positions require innate talents of such high degree that the persons who fill them are bound to be rare. In many cases, however, talent is fairly abundant in the population but the training process is so long, costly, and elaborate that relatively few can qualify. Modern medicine, for example, is within the mental capacity of most individuals, but a medical education is so burdensome and expensive that virtually none would undertake it if the position of the M.D. did not carry a reward commensurate with the sacrifice.

If the talents required for a position are abundant and the training easy, the method of acquiring the position may have little to do with its duties. There may be, in fact, a virtually accidental relationship. But if the skills required are scarce by reason of the rarity of talent or the costliness of training, the position, if functionally important, must have an attractive power that will draw the necessary skills in competition with other positions. This means, in effect, that the position must be high in the social scale—must command great prestige, high salary, ample leisure, and the like.

How Variations Are to Be Understood. In so far as there is a difference between one system of stratification and another, it is attributable to whatever factors affect the two determinants of differential reward—namely, functional importance and scarcity of personnel. Positions important in one society may not be important in another, because the conditions faced by the societies, or their degree of internal development, may be different. The same conditions, in turn, may affect the question of scarcity; for in some societies the stage of development, or the external situation, may wholly obviate the necessity of certain kinds of skill or talent. Any particular system of stratification, then, can be understood as a product of the special conditions affecting the two aforementioned grounds of differential reward.

MAJOR SOCIETAL FUNCTIONS AND STRATIFICATION

Religion. The reason why religion is necessary is apparently to be found in the fact that human society achieves its unity primarily through the possession by its members of certain ultimate values and ends in common. Although these values and ends are subjective, they influence behavior, and their integration enables the society to operate as a system. Derived neither from inherited nor from external nature, they have evolved as a part of culture by communication and moral pressure. They must, however, appear to the members of the society to have some reality, and it is the role of religious belief and ritual to supply and reinforce this appearance of reality. Through belief and ritual the common ends and values are connected with an imaginary world symbolized by concrete sacred objects, which world in turn is related in a meaningful way to the facts and trials of the individual's life. Through the worship of the sacred objects and the beings they symbolize, and the acceptance of supernatural prescriptions that are at the same time codes of behavior, a powerful control over human conduct is exercised, guiding it along lines sustaining the institutional structure and conforming to the ultimate ends and values.

If this conception of the role of religion is true, one can understand why in every known society the religious activities tend to be under the charge of particular persons, who tend thereby to enjoy greater rewards than the ordinary societal member. Certain of the rewards and special privileges may attach to only the highest religious functionaries, but others usually apply, if such exists, to the entire sacerdotal class.

Moreover, there is a peculiar relation between the duties of the religious official and the special privileges he enjoys. If the supernatural world governs the destinies of men more ultimately than does the real world, its earthly representative, the person through whom one may communicate with the supernatural, must be a powerful individual. He is a keeper of sacred tradition, a skilled performer of the ritual, and an interpreter of lore and myth. He is in such close contact with the gods that he is viewed as possessing some of their characteristics. He is, in short, a bit sacred, and hence free from some of the more vulgar necessities and controls.

It is no accident, therefore, that religious functionaries have been associated with the very highest positions of power, as in theocratic regimes. Indeed, looking at it from this point of view, one may wonder why it is that they do not get *entire* control over their societies. The factors that prevent this are worthy of note.

In the first place, the amount of technical competence necessary for the performance of religious duties is small. Scientific or artistic capacity is not required. Anyone can set himself up as enjoying an intimate relation with deities, and nobody can successfully dispute him. Therefore, the factor of scarcity of personnel does not operate in the technical sense.

One may assert, on the other hand, that religious ritual is often elaborate and religious lore abstruse, and that priestly ministrations require tact, if not intelligence. This is true, but the technical requirements of the profession are for the most part adventitious, not related to the end in the same way that science is related to air travel. The priest can never be free from competition, since the criteria of whether or not one has genuine contact with the supernatural are never strictly clear. It is this competition that debases the priestly position below what might be expected at first glance. That is why priestly prestige is highest in those societies where membership in the profession is rigidly controlled by the priestly guild itself. That is why in part at least, elaborate devices are utilized to stress the identification of the person with his office—spectacular costume, abnormal conduct, special diet, segregated residence, celibacy, conspicuous leisure, and the like. In fact, the priest is always in danger of becoming somewhat discredited—as happens in a secularized society—because in a world of stubborn fact, ritual and sacred knowledge alone will not grow crops or build houses. Furthermore, unless he is protected by a professional guild, the priest's identification with the supernatural tends to preclude his acquisition of abundant worldly goods.

As between one society and another it seems that the highest general position awarded the priest occurs in the medieval type of social order. Here there is enough economic production to afford a surplus, which can be used to support a numerous and highly organized priesthood; and yet the populace is unlettered and therefore credulous to a high degree. Perhaps the most extreme example is to be found in the Buddhism of Tibet, but others are encountered in the Catholicism of feudal Europe, the Inca regime of Peru, the Brahminism of India, and the Mayan priesthood of Yucatan. On the other hand, if the society is so crude as to have no surplus and little differentiation, so that every priest must be also a cultivator or hunter, the separation of the priestly status from the others has hardly gone far enough for priestly prestige to mean much. When the priest actually has high prestige under these circumstances, it is because he also performs other important functions (usually political and medical).

In an extremely advanced society built on scientific technology, the priesthood tends to lose status, because sacred tradition and supernaturalism drop into the background. The ultimate values and common ends of the society tend to be expressed in less anthropomorphic ways, by officials who occupy fundamentally political, economic, or educational rather than religious positions. Nevertheless, it is easily possible for intellectuals to exaggerate the degree to which the priesthood in a presumably secular milieu has lost prestige. When the matter is closely examined the urban proletariat, as well as the rural citizenry, proves to be surprisingly god-fearing and priest-ridden. No society has become so completely secularized as to liquidate entirely the belief in transcendental ends and supernatural entities. Even in a secularized society some system must exist for the integration of ultimate values, for their ritualistic expression, and for the emotional adjustments required by disappointment, death, and disaster.

Government. Like religion, government plays a unique and indispensable part in society. But in contrast to religion, which provides integration in terms of sentiments, beliefs, and rituals, it organizes the society in terms of law and authority. Furthermore, it orients the society to the actual rather than the unseen world.

The main functions of government are, internally, the ultimate enforcement of norms, the final arbitration of conflicting interests, and the overall planning and direction of society; and externally, the handling of war and diplomacy. To carry out these functions it acts as the agent of the entire people, enjoys a monopoly of force, and controls all individuals within its territory.

Political action, by definition, implies authority. An official can command because he has authority, and the citizen must obey because he is subject to that authority. For this reason stratification is inherent in the nature of political relationships.

So clear is the power embodied in political position that political inequality is sometimes thought to comprise all inequality. But it can be shown that there are other bases of stratification, that the following controls operate in practice to keep political power from becoming complete: (a) The fact that the actual holders of political office, and especially those determining top policy must necessarily be few in number compared to the total population. (b) The fact that the rulers represent the interest of the group rather than of themselves, and are therefore restricted in their behavior by rules and mores designed to enforce this limitation of interest. (c) The fact that the holder of political office has his authority by virtue of his office and nothing else, and therefore any special knowledge, talent, or capacity he may claim is purely incidental, so that he often has to depend upon others for technical assistance.

In view of these limiting factors, it is not strange that the rulers often have less power and prestige than a literal enumeration of their formal rights would lead one to expect.

Wealth, Property, and Labor. Every position that secures for its incumbent a livelihood is, by definition, economically rewarded. For this reason there is an economic aspect to those positions (e.g., political and religious) the main function of which is not economic. It therefore becomes convenient for the society to use unequal economic returns as a principal means of controlling the entrance of persons into positions and stimulating the performance of their duties. The amount of the economic return therefore becomes one of the main indices of social status.

It should be stressed, however, that a position does not bring power and prestige *because* it draws a high income. Rather, it draws a high income because it is functionally important and the available personnel is for one reason or another scarce. It is therefore superficial and erroneous to regard high income as the cause of a man's power and prestige, just as it is erroneous to think that a man's fever is the cause of his disease.

The economic source of power and prestige is not income primarily, but the ownership of capital goods (including patents, good will, and professional reputation). Such ownership should be distinguished from the possession of consumers' goods, which is an index rather than a cause of social standing. In other words, the ownership of producers' goods is, properly speaking, a source of income like other positions, the income itself remaining an index. Even in situations where social values are widely commercialized and earnings are the readiest method of judging social position, income does not confer prestige on a position so much as it induces people to compete for the position. It is true that a man who has a high income as a result of one position may find this money helpful in climbing into another position as well, but this again reflects the effect of his initial, economically advantageous status, which exercises its influence through the medium of money.

In a system of private property in productive enterprise, an income above what an individual spends can give rise to possession of capital wealth. Presumably such possession is a reward for the proper management of one's finances originally and of the productive enterprise later. But as social differentiation becomes highly advanced and yet the institution of inheritance persists, the phenomenon of pure ownership, and reward for pure ownership, emerges. In such a case it is difficult to prove that the position is functionally important or that the scarcity involved is anything other than extrinsic and accidental. It is for this reason, doubtless, that the institution of private property in productive goods becomes more subject to criticism as social development proceeds toward industrialization. It is only this pure, that is, strictly legal and functionless ownership, however, that is open to attack; for some form of active ownership, whether private or public, is indispensable.

One kind of ownership of production goods consists in rights over the labor of others. The most extremely concentrated and exclusive of such rights are found in slavery, but the essential principle remains in serfdom, peonage, encomienda, and indenture. Naturally this kind of ownership has the greatest significance for stratification, because it necessarily entails an unequal relationship.

But property in capital goods inevitably introduces a compulsive element even into the nominally free contractual relationship. Indeed, in some respects the authority of the contractual employer is greater than that of the feudal landlord, inasmuch as the latter is more limited by traditional reciprocities. Even the classical economics recognized that competitors would fare unequally, but it did not pursue this fact to its necessary conclusion that, however it might be acquired, unequal control of goods and services must give unequal advantage to the parties to a contract.

Technical Knowledge. The function of finding means to single goals, without any concern with the choice between goals, is the exclusively technical sphere. The explanation of why positions requiring great technical skill receive fairly high rewards is easy to see, for it is the simplest case of the rewards being so distributed as to draw talent and motivate training. Why they seldom if ever receive the highest rewards is also clear: the importance of technical knowledge from a societal point of view is never so great as the integration of goals, which takes place on the religious, political, and economic levels. Since the technological level is concerned solely with means, a purely technical position must ultimately be subordinate to other positions that are religious, political, or economic in character.

Nevertheless, the distinction between expert and layman in any social order is fundamental, and cannot be entirely reduced to other terms. Methods of recruitment, as well as of reward, sometimes lead to the erroneous interpretation that technical positions are economically determined. Actually, however, the acquisition of knowledge and skill cannot be accomplished by purchase, although the opportunity to learn may be. The control of the avenues of training may inhere as a sort of property right in certain families or classes, giving them power and prestige in consequence. Such a situation adds an artificial scarcity to the natural scarcity of skills and talents. On the other hand, it is possible for an opposite situation to arise. The rewards of technical position may be so great that a condition of excess supply is created, leading to at least temporary devaluation of the rewards. Thus "unemployment in the learned professions" may result in a debasement of the prestige of those positions. Such adjustments and readjustments are constantly occurring in changing societies; and it is always well to bear in mind that the efficiency of a stratified structure may be affected by the modes of recruitment for positions. The social order itself, however, sets limits to the inflation or deflation of the prestige of experts: an over-supply tends to debase the rewards and discourage recruitment or produce revolution, whereas an under-supply tends to increase the rewards or weaken the society in competition with other societies.

Particular systems of stratification show a wide range with respect to the exact position of technically competent persons. This range is perhaps most evident in the degree of specialization. Extreme division of labor tends to create many specialists without high prestige since the training is short and the required native capacity relatively small. On the other hand it also tends to accentuate the high position of the true experts—scientists, engineers, and administrators—by increasing their authority relative to other functionally important positions. But the idea of a technocratic social order or a government or priesthood of engineers or social scientists neglects the limitations of knowledge and skills as a basis for performing social functions. To the extent that the social structure is truly specialized the prestige of the technical person must also be circumscribed.

VARIATION IN STRATIFIED SYSTEMS

The generalized principles of stratification here suggested form a necessary preliminary to a consideration of types of stratified systems, because it is in terms of these principles that the types must be described. This can be seen by trying to delineate types according to certain modes of variation. For instance, some of the most important modes (together with the polar types in terms of them) seem to be as follows:

(a) *The Degree of Specialization.* The degree of specialization affects the fineness and multiplicity of the gradations in power and prestige. It also influences the extent to which particular functions may be emphasized in the invidious system, since a given function cannot receive much emphasis in the hierarchy until it has achieved structural separation from the other functions. Finally, the amount of specialization influences the bases of selection. Polar types: *Specialized, Unspecialized.*

(b) *The Nature of the Functional Emphasis.* In general when emphasis is put on sacred matters, a rigidity is introduced that tends to limit specialization and hence the development of technology. In addition, a brake is placed on social mobility, and on the development of bureaucracy. When the preoccupation with the sacred is withdrawn, leaving greater scope for purely secular preoccupations, a great development, and rise in status, of economic and technological positions seemingly takes place. Curiously, a concomitant rise in political position is not likely, because it has usually been allied with the religious and stands to gain little by the decline of the latter. It is also possible for a society to emphasize family functions—as in relatively undifferentiated societies where high mortality requires high fertility and kinship forms the main basis of social organization. Main types: *Familistic, Authoritarian* (*Theocratic* or sacred, and *Totalitarian* or secular), *Capitalistic.*

(c) *The Magnitude of Invidious Differences.* What may be called the amount of social distance between positions, taking into account the entire scale, is something that should lend itself to quantitative measurement. Considerable differences apparently exist between different societies in this regard, and also between parts of the same society. Polar types: *Equalitarian, Inequalitarian.*

(d) *The Degree of Opportunity.* The familiar question of the amount of mobility is different from the question of the comparative equality or inequality of rewards posed above, because the two criteria may vary independently up to a point. For instance, the tremendous divergences in monetary income in the United States are far greater than those found in primitive societies, yet the equality of opportunity to move from one rung to the other in the social scale may also be greater in the United States than in a hereditary tribal kingdom. Polar types: *Mobile* (open), *Immobile* (closed).

(e) *The Degree of Stratum Solidarity.* Again, the degree of "class solidarity" (or the presence of specific organizations to promote class interests) may vary to some extent independently of the other criteria, and hence is an important principle in classifying systems of stratification. Polar types: *Class organized, Class unorganized.*

EXTERNAL CONDITIONS

What state any particular system of stratification is in with reference to each of these modes of variation depends on two things: (1) its state with reference to the other ranges of variation, and (2) the conditions outside the system of stratification which nevertheless influence that system. Among the latter are the following:

(a) *The Stage of Cultural Development.* As the cultural heritage grows, increased specialization becomes necessary, which in turn contributes to the enhancement of mobility, a decline of stratum solidarity, and a change of functional emphasis.

(b) *Situation with Respect to Other Societies.* The presence or absence of open conflict with other societies, of free trade relations or cultural diffusion, all influence the class structure to some extent. A chronic state of warfare tends to place emphasis upon the military functions, especially when the opponents are more or less equal. Free trade, on the other hand, strengthens the hand of the trader at the expense of the warrior and priest. Free movement of ideas generally has an equalitarian effect. Migration and conquest create special circumstances.

(c) *Size of the Society.* A small society limits the degree to which functional specialization can go, the degree of segregation of different strata, and the magnitude of inequality.

COMPOSITE TYPES

Much of the literature on stratification has attempted to classify concrete systems into a certain number of types. This task is deceptively simple, however, and should come at the end of an analysis of elements and principles, rather than at the beginning. If the preceding discussion has any validity, it indicates that there are a number of modes of variation between different systems, and that any one system is a composite of the society's status with reference to all these modes of variation. The danger of trying to classify whole societies under such rubrics as *caste, feudal,* or *open class* is that one or two criteria are selected and others ignored, the result being an unsatisfactory solution to the problem posed. The present discussion has been offered as a possible approach to the more systematic classification of composite types.

Professors Davis' and Moore's article on stratification has been widely recognized as the most influential analysis of its kind in contemporary sociology. However, as was to be expected, it was not received without dissent and much criticism.

Fellow sociologists in the years following its publication expressed considerable doubt that social inequality is purely positive and functional. They disagreed with Davis' and Moore's allegation that stratification guarantees that the most important societal tasks will be performed by the most competent persons. Some even claimed that stratification, on the contrary, is dysfunctional, for it discourages the development of considerable talent in a society. Access to motivation, recruitment, and training is unequal. They argued that Davis' and Moore's analysis appeared to justify any system of social stratification that existed as "natural," "right," and "inevitable," and therefore it could and would be used to rationalize the *status quo*.

One of the most penetrating critiques of Davis' and Moore's work was made by their colleague at Princeton, Melvin M. Tumin. In the next article, he raises several questions about the inevitability and positive functionality of stratification. Furthermore, Professor Tumin proposes eight negative functions or dysfunctions of stratified systems and thereby seriously weakens Davis' and Moore's basic thesis.

38. SOME PRINCIPLES OF STRATIFICATION: A CRITICAL ANALYSIS *

MELVIN M. TUMIN

Princeton University

The fact of social inequality in human society is marked by its ubiquity and its antiquity. Every known society, past and present, distributes its scarce and demanded goods and services unequally. And there are attached to the positions which command unequal amounts of such goods and services certain highly morally-toned evaluations of their importance for the society.

The ubiquity and the antiquity of such inequality has given rise to the assumption that there must be something both inevitable and positively functional about such social arrangements.

Clearly, the truth or falsity of such an assumption is a strategic question for any general theory of social organization. It is therefore most curious that the basic premises and implications of the assumption have only been most casually explored by American sociologists.

The most systematic treatment is to be found in the well-known article by Kingsley Davis and Wilbert Moore, entitled "Some Principles of Stratification." More than twelve years have passed since its publication, and though it is one of the very few treatments of stratification on a high level of generalization, it is difficult to locate a single systematic analysis of its reasoning. It will be the principal concern of this paper to present the beginnings of such an analysis.

* *American Sociological Review*, Vol. 18, No. 4, August, 1953, pp. 387–394.

The central argument advanced by Davis and Moore can be stated in a number of sequential propositions, as follows:

(1) Certain positions in any society are functionally more important than others, and require special skills for their performance.

(2) Only a limited number of individuals in any society have the talents which can be trained into the skills appropriate to these positions.

(3) The conversion of talents into skills involves a training period during which sacrifices of one kind or another are made by those undergoing the training.

(4) In order to induce the talented persons to undergo these sacrifices and acquire the training, their future positions must carry an inducement value in the form of differential, i.e., privileged and disproportionate access to the scarce and desired rewards which the society has to offer.

(5) These scarce and desired goods consist of the rights and perquisites attached to, or built into, the positions, and can be classified into those things which contribute to (a) sustenance and comfort, (b) humor and diversion, (c) self-respect and ego expansion.

(6) This differential access to the basic rewards of the society has as a consequence the differentiation of the prestige and esteem which various strata acquire. This may be said, along with the rights and perquisites, to constitute institutionalized social inequality, i.e., stratification.

(7) Therefore, social inequality among different strata in the amounts of scarce and desired goods, and the amounts of prestige and esteem which they receive, is both positively functional and inevitable in any society.

Let us take these propositions and examine them *seriatim*.

(1) Certain positions in any society are more functionally important than others and require special skills for their performance.

The key term here is "functionally important." The functionalist theory of social organization is by no means clear and explicit about this term. The minimum common referent is to something known as the "survival value" of a social structure. This concept immediately involves a number of perplexing questions. Among these are: (a) the issue of minimum vs. maximum survival, and the possible empirical referents which can be given to those terms; (b) whether such a proposition is a useless tautology since any *status quo* at any given moment is nothing more and nothing less than everything present in the *status quo*. In these terms, all acts and structures must be judged positively functional in that they constitute essential portions of the *status quo;* (c) what kind of calculus of functionality exists which will enable us, at this point in our development, to add and subtract long and short range consequences, with their mixed qualities, and arrive at some summative judgment regarding the rating an act or structure should receive on a scale of greater or lesser functionality? At best, we tend to make primarily intuitive judgments. Often enough, these judgments involve the use of value-laden criteria, or, at least, criteria which are chosen in preference to others not for any sociologically systematic reasons but by reason of certain implicit value preferences.

Thus, to judge that the engineers in a factory are functionally more important to the factory than the unskilled workmen involves a notion regarding the dispensability of the unskilled workmen, or their replaceability, relative to that of the engineers. But this is not a process of choice with infinite time dimensions. For at some point along the line one must face the problem of adequate motivation for *all* workers at all levels of skill in the factory. In the long run, *some* labor force of unskilled workmen is as important and as indispensable to the factory as *some* labor force of engineers. Often enough, the labor force situation is such that this fact is brought home sharply to the entrepreneur in the short run rather than in the long run.

Moreover, the judgment as to the relative indispensability and replaceability of a particular segment of skills in the population involves a prior judgment about the bargaining-power of that segment. But this power is itself a culturally shaped *consequence* of the existing system of rating, rather than something inevitable in the nature of social organization. At least the contrary of this has never been demonstrated, but only assumed.

A generalized theory of social stratification must recognize that the prevailing system of inducements and rewards is only one of many variants in the whole range of possible systems of motivation which, at least theoretically, are capable of working in human society. It is quite conceivable, of course, that a system of norms could be institutionalized in which the idea of threatened withdrawal of services, except under the most extreme circumstances, would be considered as absolute moral anathema. In such a case, the whole notion of relative functionality, as advanced by Davis and Moore, would have to be radically revised.

(2) Only a limited number of individuals in any society have the talents which can be trained into the skills appropriate to these positions (i.e., the more functionally important positions).

The truth of this proposition depends at least in part on the truth of proposition 1 above. It is, therefore, subject to all the limitations indicated above. But for the moment, let us assume the validity of the first proposition and concentrate on the question of the rarity of appropriate talent.

If all that is meant is that in every society there is a *range* of talent, and that some members of any society are by nature more talented than others, no sensible contradiction can be offered, but a question must be raised here regarding the amount of sound knowledge present in any society concerning the presence of talent in the population.

For, in every society there is some demonstrable ignorance regarding the amount of talent present in the population. *And the more rigidly stratified a society is, the less chance does that society have of discovering any new facts about the talents of its members.* Smoothly working and stable systems of stratification, wherever found, tend to build-in obstacles to the further exploration of the range of available talent. This is especially true in those societies where the opportunity to discover talent in any one generation varies with the differential resources of the parent generation. Where, for instance, access to education depends upon the wealth of one's parents, and where wealth is differentially distributed, large segments of the population are likely to be deprived of the chance even to *discover* what are their talents.

Whether or not differential rewards and opportunities are functional in any one generation, it is clear that if those differentials are allowed to be socially inherited by the next generation, then, the stratification system is specifically dysfunctional for the discovery of talents in the next generation. In this fashion, systems of social stratification tend to limit the chances available to maximize the efficiency of discovery, recruitment and training of "functionally important talent."

Additionally, the unequal distribution of rewards in one generation tends to result in the unequal distribution of motivation in the succeeding generation. Since motivation to succeed is clearly an important element in the entire process of education, the unequal distribution of motivation tends to set limits on the possible extensions of the educational system, and hence, upon the efficient recruitment and training of the widest body of skills available in the population.

Lastly, in this context, it may be asserted that there is some noticeable tendency for elites to restrict further access to their privileged positions, once they have sufficient power to enforce such restrictions. This is especially true in a culture where it is possible for an elite to contrive a high demand and a proportionately higher reward for its work by restricting the numbers of the elite available to do the work. The recruitment and training of doctors in modern United States is at least partly a case in point.

Here, then, are three ways, among others which could be cited, in which stratification systems, once operative, tend to reduce the survival value of a society by limiting the search, recruitment and training of functionally important personnel far more sharply than the facts of available talent would appear to justify. It is only when there is genuinely equal access to recruitment and training for all potentially talented persons that differential rewards can conceivably be justified as functional. And stratification systems are apparently *inherently antagonistic* to the development of such full equality of opportunity.

(3) The conversion of talents into skills involves a training period during which sacrifices of one kind or another are made by those undergoing the training.

Davis and Moore introduce here a concept, "sacrifice" which comes closer than any of the rest of their vocabulary of analysis to being a direct reflection of the rationalizations, offered by the more fortunate members of a society, of the rightness of their occupancy of privileged positions. It is the least critically thought-out concept in the repertoire, and can also be shown to be least supported by the actual facts.

In our present society, for example, what are the sacrifices which talented persons undergo in the training period? The possibly serious losses involve the surrender of earning power and the cost of the training. The latter is generally borne by the parents of the talented youth undergoing training, and not by the trainees themselves. But this cost tends to be paid out of income which the parents were able to earn generally by virtue of *their* privileged positions in the hierarchy of stratification. That is to say, the parents' ability to pay for the training of their children is part of the differential *reward* they, the parents, received for their privileged positions in the society. And to charge this sum up against sacrifices made by the youth is falsely to perpetrate a bill or a debt already paid by the society to the parents.

So far as the sacrifice of earning power by the trainees themselves is concerned, the loss may be measured relative to what they might have earned had they gone into the labor market instead of into advanced training for the "important" skills. There are several ways to judge this. One way is to take all the average earnings of age peers who did go into the labor market for a period equal to the average length of the training period. The total income, so calculated, roughly equals an amount which the elite can, on the average, earn back in the first decade of professional work, over and above the earnings of his age peers who are not trained. Ten years is probably the maximum amount needed to equalize the differential. There remains, on the average, twenty years of work during each of which the skilled person then goes on to earn far more than his unskilled age peers. And, what is often forgotten, there is then still another ten or fifteen year period during which the skilled person continues to work and earn when his unskilled age peer is either totally or partially out of the labor market by virtue of the attrition of his strength and capabilities.

One might say that the first ten years of differential pay is perhaps justified, in order to regain for the trained person what he lost during his training period. But it is difficult to imagine what would justify continuing such differential rewards beyond that period.

Another and probably sounder way to measure how much is lost during the training period is to compare the per capita income available to the trainee with the per capita income of the age peer on the untrained labor market during the so-called sacrificial period. If one takes into account the earlier marriage of untrained persons, and the earlier acquisition of family dependents, it is highly dubious that the per capita income of the wage worker is significantly larger than that of the trainee. Even assuming, for the moment, that there is a difference, the amount is by no means sufficient to justify a lifetime of continuing differentials.

What tends to be completely overlooked, in addition, are the psychic and spiritual rewards which are available to the elite trainees by comparison with their age peers in the labor force. There is, first, the much higher prestige enjoyed by the college student and the professional-school student as compared with persons in shops and offices. There is, second, the extremely highly valued privilege of having greater opportunity for self-development. There is, third, all the psychic gain involved in being allowed to delay the assumption of adult responsibilities such as earning a living and supporting a family. There is, fourth, the access to leisure and freedom of a kind not likely to be experienced by the persons already at work.

If these are never taken into account as rewards of the training period it is not because they are not concretely present, but because the emphasis in American concepts of reward is almost exclusively placed on the material returns of positions. The emphases on enjoyment, entertainment, ego enhancement, prestige and esteem are introduced only when the differentials in these which accrue to the skilled positions need to be justified. If these other rewards were taken into account, it would be much more difficult to demonstrate that the training period, as presently operative, is really sacrificial. Indeed, it might turn out to be the case that even at this point in their careers, the elite trainees were being differentially rewarded relative to their age peers in the labor force.

All of the foregoing concerns the quality of the training period under our present system of motivation and rewards. Whatever may turn out to be the factual case about the present system—and the factual case is moot—the more important theoretical question concerns the assumption that the training period under *any* system must be sacrificial.

There seem to be no good theoretical grounds for insisting on this assumption. For, while under any system certain costs will be involved in training persons for skilled positions, these costs could easily be assumed by the society-at-large. Under these circumstances, there would be no need to compensate anyone in terms of differential rewards once the skilled positions were staffed. In short, there would be no need or justification for stratifying social positions on *these* grounds.

(4) In order to induce the talented persons to undergo these sacrifices and acquire the training, their future positions must carry an inducement value in the form of differential, i.e., privileged and disproportionate access to the scarce and desired rewards which the society has to offer.

Let us assume, for the purposes of the discussion, that the training period is sacrificial and the talent is rare in every conceivable human society. There is still the basic problem as to whether the allocation of differential rewards in scarce and desired goods and services is the only or the most efficient way of recruiting the appropriate talent to these positions.

For there are a number of alternative motivational schemes whose efficiency and adequacy ought at least to be considered in this context. What can be said, for instance, on behalf of the motivation which De Man called "joy in work," Veblen termed "instinct for workmanship" and which we latterly have come to identify as "intrinsic work satisfaction?" Or, to what extent could the motivation of "social duty" be institutionalized in such a fashion that self interest and social interest come closely to coincide? Or, how much prospective confidence can be placed in the possibilities of institutionalizing "social service" as a widespread motivation for seeking one's appropriate position and fulfilling it conscientiously?

Are not these types of motivations, we may ask, likely to prove most appropriate for precisely the "most functionally important positions?" Especially in a mass industrial society, where the vast majority of positions become standardized and routinized, it is the skilled jobs which are likely to retain most of the quality of "intrinsic job satisfaction" and be most readily identifiable as socially serviceable. Is it indeed impossible then to build these motivations into the socialization pattern to which we expose our talented youth?

To deny that such motivations could be institutionalized would be to overclaim our present knowledge. In part, also, such a claim would seem to derive from an assumption that what has not been institutionalized yet in human affairs is incapable of institutionalization. Admittedly, historical experience affords us evidence we cannot afford to ignore. But such evidence cannot legitimately be used to deny absolutely the possibility of heretofore untried alternatives. Social innovation is as important a feature of human societies as social stability.

On the basis of these observations, it seems that Davis and Moore have stated the case much too strongly when they insist that a "functionally important position" which requires skills that are scarce, "must command great prestige, high salary, ample leisure, and the like," if the appropriate talents are to be attracted to the position. Here, clearly, the authors are postulating the unavoidability of very specific types of rewards and, by implication, denying the possibility of others.

(5) These scarce and desired goods consist of rights and perquisites attached to, or built into, the positions and can be classified into those things which contribute to (a) sustenance and comfort; (b) humor and diversion; (c) self respect and ego expansion.

(6) This differential access to the basic rewards of the society has as a consequence the differentiation of the prestige and esteem which various strata acquire. This may be said, along with the rights and perquisites, to constitute institutionalized social inequality, i.e., stratification.

With the classification of the rewards offered by Davis and Moore there need be little argument. Some question must be raised, however, as to whether any reward system, built into a general stratification system, must allocate equal amounts of all three types of reward in order to function effectively, or whether one type of reward may be emphasized to the virtual neglect of others. This raises the further question regarding which type of emphasis is likely to prove most effective as a differential inducer. Nothing in the known facts about human motivation impels us to favor one type of reward over the other, or to insist that all three types of reward must be built into the positions in comparable amounts if the position is to have an inducement value.

It is well known, of course, that societies differ considerably in the kinds of rewards they emphasize in their efforts to maintain a reasonable balance between responsibility and reward. There are, for instance, numerous societies in which the conspicuous display of differential economic advantage is considered extremely bad taste. In short, our present knowledge commends to us the possibility of considerable plasticity in the way in which different types of rewards can be structured into a functioning society. This is to say, it cannot yet be demonstrated that it is *unavoidable* that differential prestige and esteem shall accrue to positions which command differential rewards in power and property.

What does seem to be unavoidable is that differential prestige shall be given to those in any society who conform to the normative order as against those who deviate from that order in a way judged immoral and detrimental. On the assumption that the continuity of a society depends on the continuity and stability of its normative order, some such distinction between conformists and deviants seems inescapable.

It also seems to be unavoidable that in any society, no matter how literate its tradition, the older, wiser and more experienced individuals who are charged with the enculturation and socialization of the young must have more power than the young, on the assumption that the task of effective socialization demands such differential power.

But this differentiation in prestige between the conformist and the deviant is by no means the same distinction as that between strata of individuals each of which operates *within* the normative order, and is composed of adults. The *latter* distinction, in the form of differentiated rewards and prestige between social strata is what Davis and Moore, and most sociologists, consider the structure of a stratification system. The *former* distinctions have nothing necessarily to do with the workings of such a system nor with the efficiency of motivation and recruitment of functionally important personnel.

Nor does the differentiation of power between young and old necessarily create differentially valued strata. For no society rates its young as less morally worthy than its older persons, no matter how much differential power the older ones may temporarily enjoy.

(7) Therefore, social inequality among different strata in the amounts of scarce and desired goods, and the amounts of prestige and esteem which they receive, is both positively functional and inevitable in any society.

If the objections which have heretofore been raised are taken as reasonable, then it may be stated that the only items which any society *must* distribute unequally are the power and property necessary for the performance of different tasks. If such differential power and property are viewed by all as commensurate with the differential responsibilities, and if they are culturally defined as *resources* and not as rewards, then, no differentials in prestige and esteem need follow.

Historically, the evidence seems to be that every time power and property are distributed unequally, no matter what the cultural definition, prestige and esteem differentiations have tended to result as well. Historically, however, no systematic effort has ever been made, under propitious circumstances, to develop the tradition that each man is as socially worthy as all other men so long as he performs his appropriate tasks conscientiously. While such a tradition seems utterly utopian, no known facts in psychological or social science have yet demonstrated its impossibility or its dysfunctionality for the continuity of a society. The achievement of a full institutionalization of such a tradition seems far too remote to contemplate. Some successive approximations at such a tradition, however, are not out of the range of prospective social innovation.

What, then, of the "positive functionality" of social stratification? Are there other, negative functions of institutionalized social inequality which can be identified, if only tentatively? Some such dysfunctions of stratification have already been suggested in the body of this paper. Along with others they may now be stated, in the form of provisional assertions, as follows:

(1) Social stratification systems function to limit the possibility of discovery of the full range of talent available in a society. This results from the fact of unequal access to appropriate motivation, channels of recruitment and centers of training.

(2) In foreshortening the range of available talent, social stratification systems function to set limits upon the possibilty of expanding the productive resources of the society, at least relative to what might be the case under conditions of greater equality of opportunity.

(3) Social stratification systems function to provide the elite with the political power necessary to procure acceptance and dominance of an ideology which rationalizes the *status quo,* whatever it may be, as "logical," "natural" and "morally right." In this manner, social stratification systems function as essentially conservative influences in the societies in which they are found.

(4) Social stratification systems function to distribute favorable self-images unequally throughout a population. To the extent that such favorable self-images are requisite to the development of the creative potential inherent in men, to that extent stratification systems function to limit the development of this creative potential.

(5) To the extent that inequalities in social rewards cannot be made fully acceptable to the less privileged in a society, social stratification systems function to encourage hostility, suspicion and distrust among the various segments of a society and thus to limit the possibilities of extensive social integration.

(6) To the extent that the sense of significant membership in a society depends on one's place on the prestige ladder of the society, social stratification systems function to distribute unequally the sense of significant membership in the population.

(7) To the extent that loyalty to a society depends on a sense of significant membership in the society, social stratification systems function to distribute loyalty unequally in the population.

(8) To the extent that participation and apathy depend upon the sense of significant membership in the society, social stratification systems function to distribute the motivation to participate unequally in a population.

Each of the eight foregoing propositions contains implicit hypotheses regarding the consequences of unequal distribution of rewards in a society in accordance with some notion of the functional importance of various positions. These are empirical hypotheses, subject to test. They are offered here only as exemplary of the kinds of consequences of social stratification which are not often taken into account in dealing with the problem. They should also serve to reinforce the doubt that social inequality is a device which is uniformly functional for the role of guaranteeing that the most important tasks in a society will be performed conscientiously by the most competent persons.

The obviously mixed character of the functions of social inequality should come as no surprise to anyone. If sociology is sophisticated in any sense, it is certainly with regard to its awareness of the mixed nature of any social arrangement, when the observer takes into account long as well as short range consequences and latent as well as manifest dimensions.

SUMMARY

In this paper, an effort has been made to raise questions regarding the inevitability and positive functionality of stratification, or institutionalized social inequality in rewards, allocated in accordance with some notion of the greater and lesser functional importance of various positions. The possible alternative meanings of the concept "functional importance" has been shown to be one difficulty. The question of the scarcity or abundance of available talent has been indicated as a principal source of possible variation. The extent to which the period of training for skilled positions may reasonably be viewed as sacrificial has been called into question. The possibility has been suggested that very different types of motivational schemes might conceivably be made to function. The separability of differentials in power and property considered as resources appropriate to a task from such differentials considered as rewards for the performance of a task has also been suggested. It has also been maintained that differentials in prestige and esteem do not necessarily follow upon differentials in power and property when the latter are considered as appropriate resources rather than rewards. Finally, some negative functions, or dysfunctions, of institutionalized social inequality have been tentatively identified, revealing the mixed character of the outcome of social stratification, and casting doubt on Davis and Moore's contention that

> Social inequality is thus an unconsciously evolved device by which societies insure that the most important positions are conscientiously filled by the most qualified persons.

Of all the forms of social stratification that may develop in a society, none has captivated the attention of sociologists more than social class. Not the least intriguing aspect of class stratification in American society is the persistent classless ideology that carries over from preurban and preindustrial life. It compels many Americans to insist stubbornly, even to this day, that "social class is a foreign, un-American concept." The facts now—especially the facts of urban, industrial life—are very much in conflict with the old ideology. Accordingly, contemporary sociology has had to face the reality of this form of social stratification on the American scene.

Income, for example, is one of the important criteria by which modern society is stratified into classes. In every economy, as Sumner put it, "there are dinners without appetites at one end of the table, and appetites without dinners at the other"; and American society is no exception. Behind the glittering facade of the "affluent society" and the highest average per-capita income in the world, it has been estimated that up to one-fourth of the American people are in poverty or otherwise suffer as economically deprived. Handicapped by lack of school and skills, they do not benefit by automation and other industrial changes. Not only do they fail to share in the fruits of the higher productivity improved technology affords, but they find themselves at disadvantage by the obsolescence of the unskilled and semiskilled work on which they once relied. Furthermore, there is a culture of poverty that makes the poor different from the rich in ways that transcend money. Almost everything about them, from the condition of their teeth to the way they make love, is permeated by the fact of their poverty.

At the other end of the income spectrum in American society, salaried executives now outnumber self-employed professionals and businessmen. In 1963, the Bureau of the Census reported that the families of managers and salaried professionals then accounted for approximately half of those in the highest 5 per cent of American incomes, whereas the self-employed accounted for only one-fourth—an almost exact reversal of the situation in 1950. To be in the highest 5 percent in 1950 required at least an income of $9,000; by 1963 it required more than $14,385. This turnabout in the patterns of American income was largely the result of the postwar growth of large corporations. However, although the salaried person has improved his financial status, he still has little chance of entering the ranks of the *very* rich in the American economy. Of the 398 Americans who had incomes of more than $1 million in 1961, virtually all were either completely self-employed or drew very little of their income from salaries.

Despite the rapid development of social class analysis in American sociology, there is still no complete consensus on the meaning of the term as a research tool. In the following article, Milton M. Gordon proposes a series of analytical questions to aid in the discovery of common ground. His questions, first of all, revolve around definition, which may be in terms of economic power, status ascription, group life, cultural attributes, political power, or their combination. Professor Gordon also raises pertinent questions about class placement, class differences, class mobility, and the relationship between class and ethnic stratification.

39. SOCIAL CLASS IN AMERICAN SOCIOLOGY *

MILTON M. GORDON
University of Massachusetts

The term "social class"—often shortened to "class"—is used by sociologists to refer to the horizontal stratification of a population. Within this general delimitation the concept of class has no precise, agreed-upon meaning but is

* *The American Journal of Sociology,* Vol. LV, No. 3, November, 1949, pp. 262–268.

used either as an omnibus term, to designate differences based on wealth, income, occupation, status, group identification, level of consumption, and family background, or by some particular researcher or theorist as resting specifically on some one of these enumerated factors. There is substantial agreement, however, that the stratifications of class are not by definition those of race, religion, and ethnic origin—although the two systems of stratification may be related—and that the concept implies the possibility of at least a minimum amount of movement from one class to another, in other words, of some vertical social mobility.

Two circumstances have inspired this writer to undertake a survey and critique of the use of the "class" framework in modern American sociology. One is the lack of precision or consensus in the use of the term itself in sociological theory and research, and the other is the rapid proliferation of professional monographs and articles using the concept. This combination of circumstances, while making for the possibility of an interesting variety of approaches to social-class phenomena, is obviously not calculated to produce the most fruitful type of complementary and comparable research, or even the greatest amount of insight into the phenomena themselves. It is time, then, to take stock—to see just where we have arrived in class theory and research and to analyze the component parts of our problem and posit their possible combinations in the hope of achieving a cohesive theoretical framework for the use of "social class" as a tool of sociological analysis and research.

Charles H. Page has surveyed the treatment and use of the concept of class in early American sociology. In this monograph, he has presented and analyzed class materials in the writings of Lester F. Ward, William Graham Sumner, Albion W. Small, Franklin H. Giddings, Charles Horton Cooley, and E. A. Ross, the "Fathers" of American sociology, as he calls them. The period of the Fathers was, of course, dominated by large-scale theorizing and analysis rather than by specific empirical research; Page notes the considerable attention paid to the concept and role of class in their work. In general, these early sociologists offered, with varying degrees of emphasis, two concepts of class: one a Marxian framework based on economic factors, the other concerned more with the subjective element of status feelings and class consciousness or identification. Page summarizes as follows:

> Throughout their [Ward, Sumner, *et al.*] writings, appear, though not always clearly expressed, two quite distinct approaches. All of them, at one time or another, used "class" in the generally accepted sense as a group demarcated by economic factors; by income, economic function, or relation to a system of production. This conception pushes to a category of secondary importance questions of group cohesion, "consciousness of kind," or class consciousness. These latter phenomena, however, are of primary interest to sociologists, especially to those like Giddings and Cooley, who found in the attitudinal relationships of society the very essence of their sociological material. And so a second conception of social class emerged, one based upon the "subjective elements of group consciousness." Cooley epito-

mized this conception in declaring that "the relation between the employing and hand-laboring classes is *first of all* a matter of personal attitudes. . . ." Cooley's elaboration of closed class and "caste sentiment" is an analysis based upon the "subjective" approach. Variously expressed and with different marks of stress, the same can be said of Ward's extensive plea for the educational upward levelling of the social strata of Sumner's treatment of the declining middle class and the cohering "proletariat," of Small's criticism of the rigid Marxian distinction and his description of "middle class consciousness," of Giddings' emphasis upon consciousness of kind as both a requirement of social class and a factor hindering class formation, and of Ross's stress of *status* as the criterion of class and his Cooley-like distinction between "open" and "closed" classes.[1]

Page does not devote a chapter to the work of the pioneer socioeconomist, Thorstein Veblen, because of the necessary limitations of his study, and the extensive treatment of Veblen in other monographs and surveys. He does, however, deal with Veblen's influence on the Fathers and in the case of Ward points out a reciprocal influence. We would observe that Veblen's distinction between the "predatory" or business class, engaged primarily in manipulating pecuniary symbols (in Veblen's analysis an enterprise essentially hostile to production), and the "industrious" or "working" class, which is the genuine producer of goods, falls within the economic category of class definition. The "institutional" analysis of economic processes with which he virtually devastated the premises of classical economics called into play a cross-cultural view of societal life which he used to great advantage in analyzing behavior attributes of class in his famous book *The Theory of the Leisure Class.* In this latter work, in which Veblen characterized major motivations of upper-class behavior as "conspicuous waste," "conspicuous leisure," and "conspicuous consumption," he undoubtedly laid the groundwork for a cultural analysis of class behavior. However, there are signs, at least in the eyes of the present writer, of a peculiar psychological interpretation which attributes a greater awareness of the behavior process in the participating individuals than a strictly cultural approach would dictate or validate.

The writings of the Fathers and Veblen on class, although they made their way into the textbooks and general treatises in sociology, did not lead directly to the founding of major schools of class research or theory. American sociology entered its second generation in the middle 1920's with class established as a necessary concept for the analysis of economic stratification and its possible psychological correlates, but with little class research in progress, a minimum of theoretical consideration of the precise meaning of the term, and practically no recognition of the class framework as a major area of investigation within the discipline.

This lull in attention to class in American sociology offers in itself an interesting problem of interpretation. We may note with Page probable ex-

[1] Charles H. Page, *Class and American Sociology: From Ward to Ross* (New York: Dial Press, 1940), pp. 252–53.

planations in the existing American ideology that class distinctions, by and large, did not exist in America, in the belief in the existence of virtually unlimited social mobility, and in the distrust of the term itself because of its close association with Marxian and other revolutionary "foreign" doctrines. Also, as a variable not present in an earlier day, there was the inflated economic prosperity of this period, with its consequent visible rise in the standards of living of large masses of the population. American social scientists were apparently not unaffected by these ideological and behavioral phenomena in the general population, the cumulative effect of which was calculated to diminish their interest in class.

The revival of interest in class phenomena in American sociology took place in almost incidental, and certainly sporadic, fashion in occasional monographs or portions of monographs of the ecological school—then burgeoning forth from its intellectual center, the University of Chicago—and in a compendium work on social mobility by the transplanted European scholar, Sorokin. In 1929, however, the Lynds published their *Middletown,* a frankly defined socioanthropological study of a midwestern American community, with a definite class focus; and in the early 1930's the anthropologist W. Lloyd Warner, with a corps of assistants, was already at work gathering the data for a completely class-oriented analysis of a New England community. One may, then, possibly surmise that the growing influence and penetration of the discipline of cultural anthropology, which was being felt at this time in other areas of sociological investigation as well, created the stimulus needed to revive social-class research and theory. Undoubtedly the reflections and experiences occasioned by the long and devastating economic depression of the thirties, with its repercussions in governmental remedies and the rise of industrial unionism, constituted another major stimulation.

Throughout the 1930's a growing number of monographs and articles appeared dealing with social-class materials, either explicitly using the term or focused on such components as "socioeconomic status," occupation, educational level, income, amount of rent, etc. Problems of differential fertility by income or occupation, the measurement of socioeconomic status, the relation of father's occupation to educational opportunities of the child, and other such problems were explored. Articles analyzing the possible meanings of the term "class" indicated growing attention to the subject, as did also considerations of class divisions within the Negro group. In 1937 the Lynds published their second Middletown study, which contained extensive class materials, and the late thirties saw also the publication of separate studies of a southern community by Dollard and Powdermaker which had a class focus. In the early 1940's the long-heralded "Yankee City" volumes by Warner and associates began to make their appearance.

The first four-fifths of the decade of the 1940's have witnessed a continuation of the upward trend in the quantity of research and theory with a class orientation—with a continuation, also, of the variety of definitions and approaches and the lack of consensus on the meaning of the term. It is at this point that we begin a retrospective survey and analysis of social-class materials in American sociology, dealing with the second major period of the discipline's existence, dating roughly from the middle 1920's to 1949.

This study covers the works of this period which explicitly use the class concept or which deal with stratification using component items generally admitted to fall within the field of class analysis—as, for instance, income, occupation, or educational attainment. A classification of material has been made, based wherever possible on major schools of class research and otherwise on the scope and subject matter of the writing. The divisions are as follows:

1. Class in the middle 1920's
   a) The ecological school
   b) Sorokin's *Social Mobility*
2. The Lynds—The Middletown studies
3. The Warner studies (including works by Davis and the Gardners, Drake and Cayton, and others)
4. Other community studies: Dollard, Powdermaker, West, Anderson, Mills, Hollingshead, Kaufman, *et al.*
5. Class theorists: MacIver, Parsons, Merton, Davis, Simpson, Speier, Cox, North, Bossard, *et al.*
6. Socioeconomic status and occupational rating scales as techniques used in other class studies.

The following set of questions is proposed for a full-scale analysis of any given class study, although the necessary limitations in scope of this work will preclude using the entire framework for the analysis of each division.

1. DEFINITION

What is the definition of class used? This question must obviously constitute the heart of our inquiry, since its answer defines both the subject matter and the necessary techniques of investigation. Words and definitions are essentially only arbitrary ways of referring to realities, but until there is agreement on what those realities are and what terms will consistently be used to refer to them, our work falls short of the goals of science. There is no general agreement among sociologists at the present time as to what factor or combination of factors delineates a social class. All concur that the concept of class deals with the horizontal stratification of a population, but whether it is based on economic power, occupation, status feelings, cultural differences, or their combination, and to what extent separate group life is indicated by the term, are questions on which there is no substantial agreement. And, indeed, in many cases there is little explicit recognition of the range of alternative factors and their possible relationships and combinations. Class is being used increasingly as a research tool but too often in a grab-bag fashion: the researcher knows that there is something in the bag, and when he pulls it out he then labels it, with some correctness but little precision, as class. Urgently needed is a delineation of the theoretically separable factors which operate to stratify the American population and of the nature and degree of their possible relationships and combinations.

Here is another way of stating the problem. The population of a given community may be stratified more or less objectively on the basis of one factor, as, for instance, income. If the investigator obtains such data, and then arbitrarily assigns the term "class" to divisions of this continuum of incomes, he is, at least so far, consistent. His additional tasks are (*a*) to show whether his points of divisions have any particular significance in terms of indicating group rather than individual difference; (*b*) to demonstrate how income is correlated with other single factors such as occupation, status, educational attainment, etc.; (*c*) to reveal to what extent social relationships are determined and demarcated by these income divisions; and (*d*) possibly to write learned articles castigating his colleagues for using the term "class" to refer to something other than income divisions.

Another investigator may study the same community, using a definition of class based on status ascription. Again, assuming that his status stratification of the population has been accurately made, he must justify his selection of points of division of the status continuum to form classes; show how status is related to income, occupation, education, etc.; and indicate what effect status has on social relationships. As before, there has been an arbitrary assignment of the term "class" to one factor and an analysis of its relationship to the other factors which stratify a population. The point is the need for the consideration of the existence of alternative factors of stratification and the relationship of all these factors to one another.

The more challenging possibility will inevitably occur to the theorist or investigator that possibly the term "class," instead of being applied to one factor as the constant with the other factors being considered as variables, may be applied to a particular combination of them. The danger here is in the too easy and inviting opportunity to construct patterns and indices which appear logically consistent but which only partially fit the realities of the social situation. To put together such factors as income, education, occupation, and status into a conceptual whole and apply the term "class" to this artifact should mean that the artifact has social reality. If it does, then it will reveal itself empirically in the actual social divisions of the community. If it does not, then the construct is an artificial one. It would be of greater value to search for the social divisions in the first place. Indices, and combinations of factors put together in the researcher's mind, might then be presumed to have predictive value rather than to stand for the social reality itself.

Accordingly, we have set up a list of theoretically discrete alternative factors with which a population's social structure may be analyzed within the concept of class. These factors and their subdivisions are as follows:

1. ECONOMIC POWER

a) Income (or a combination of income and wealth).
b) Occupation—relationship to the means of production.

2. STATUS ASCRIPTION

a) Corporate class-consciousness: A definite feeling of common-class membership and interests, with unhesitating ascription of superior and inferior status to clearly demarcated classes above and below; usually associated with attitudes of implicit or explicit protest on the part of the lower classes.

b) Generalized class awareness: Generalized, diffuse, and often obliquely phrased feelings of the existence of status differentials by groups, and one's own participation in one of these status levels.

c) Competitive class feeling: Individualized status ascription and competitive feeling with little or no sense of group participation or identification.

d) Felt or latent status: The problem of status analysis is complicated by the fact that status relationships may not, in a given situation, be reciprocally phrased or felt. Accordingly, we must make a distinction between *felt status* and *latent status.* In a status relationship between A and B, felt status refers to the situation where the superior status felt by A is explicitly or implicitly acknowledged by B. Latent status refers to a situation in which the superior status felt by A is objectively buttressed by the realities of the power structure of the society but is not felt or acknowledged by B. To put it in another way, latent status refers to status dynamics which would be called into play in operative situations regardless of whether the situations have actually taken place or are, at any given time, imagined by the person whose sense of status is for some reason blunted.

For instance, B, an individual of modest means and no family connections of superior status, studying at a large, well-established eastern university, may be oblivious to the social distinctions which have caused him to be ignored for membership by the fashionable fraternity; but if he should attempt to form clique relationships with members of this fraternity or to appear at one of its house parties, he would in all probability be snubbed. Furthermore, if he were to apply for a position in a Wall Street bond or brokerage house, the fact that he could not show high-status fraternity connections or display the attendant cultural behavior might well prevent him from obtaining the position. The fact that he does not envisage or attempt these things prevents the status dynamics from being called into play, and he may remain unaware of them. Nevertheless, were he to test the power structure, they would become operative. In other words, the latent status is present. Whether it becomes also felt status for the particular ego is an additional circumstance.

3. GROUP LIFE

An important question is to what degree the factors of class stratification singly or in combination produce stratification of group life. In other words, is a class, however defined, an effective social system within which the class member has most or all of his intimate and meaningful social contacts and whose other members have relatively equal access to him and his family members in clique, associational, and institutional relationships? As we have implied, if this proves consistently to be the case, it is even possible to use this criterion as the basic framework of class and to investigate the other factors as variables of this constant. From this point of view, classes would constitute a stratified set of empirically operative social systems, however reluctantly and obliquely recognized and admitted by its participants. The possibility of the existence of an ecological residential base for this hierarchy of social systems should also be investigated.

4. CULTURAL ATTRIBUTES

Do the various classes, however defined, display consistently different patterns of behavior and attitudes which may be attributed to their participation in different cultural subgroups within the national culture? Patterns of consumption, dress, speech, and participation in community life, attitudes, and patterns relating to focal points of interest in the culture, such as sex, morality, religion, the family, patriotism, making a living, forms of employment, education, the arts, sports, etc., offer possible points of cultural differentiation by class. The interesting and difficult question arises also as to what extent these differences, in so far as they exist, become internalized psychological elements of the personality pattern of the respective class members.

5. POLITICAL POWER

A fifth possible dimension of class stratification is political power. Sociologists have, thus far, done very little investigating of this factor in community structure, but its existence as a variable of stratification must be recognized. The relationship of political power either in the local community or on the national scene to economic power or to status position is a legitimate and challenging problem of class research.

The factors or dimensions listed above are major problems in the definition of class. We turn now to the remaining questions of class analysis.

II. ASCERTAINMENT

Proceeding from a given definition, how are the classes actually "determined" in the research situation? How is it decided whether ego belongs to one class rather than another? Once the definition of class is decided upon, the researcher has the problem of applying it operationally in his community or universe to separate the members of the respective classes. If the definition is primarily an economic one, he must secure data on incomes, property-ownership, and savings. If it is in terms of status, his interviews must actually reveal the status awareness of the respondents and how it is phrased. If he implies the existence of integrated group life by class levels, he must show how this actually operates in clique, associational, and family membership. If he posits cultural differences in behavior and attitudes as part of his definition, he must enumerate these differences as obtained by observation and interviews.

III. DIFFERENCES

The presence of class differences in behavioral or attitudinal patterns may be implicit in the definition of class used, or the differences may be variables discovered after the delineation of classes has been made. They may be observable in income; wealth; type of occupation; place and type of residence; rates of vital phenomena, such as births, deaths, and sickness; type of association belonged to; attitudes; clothes; speech patterns; personality patterns; and many other areas. At some point in the analysis we must ask what class differences are implied or revealed by the theorist or researcher of class.

IV. SOCIAL MOBILITY

The concept of class indicates the existence of some vertical social mobility. Otherwise, we would be dealing with a caste system. How much vertical social mobility, upward or downward, is indicated by the various writers on class, and what are the techniques by which such mobility is effected? Which factors make mobility difficult, and which facilitate it?

V. ETHNIC STRATIFICATION

Sociologists are generally agreed that two major systems of social stratification cut across American society. One is a system of stratification which may be labeled "social class"; the other is based on differences of race, religion, or nationality background—or, to use a convenient summary term, "ethnic group." A very interesting and crucial question is how these two systems are related. Do social-class similarities tend to obliterate the divisions along ethnic lines? Do the varying ethnic groups contain degrees of social-class differentiation? Are the standards of class differentiation the same for all ethnic groups? Do the differing social classes within the ethnic group still tend to remain *within* the ethnic group as far as effective social systems are concerned? These are some of the questions which the sociologist of class must deal with in this area, and they are complicated by the obvious possibility that the answers may differ for each ethnic group considered.

The foregoing five sets of questions and their subdivisions will be used as the major tools for the subsequent analysis of class materials in modern American sociology. Such an analysis should clarify the conceptual and research problems surrounding the term "social class" and aid in the reaching of a consensus on its meaning and operational usefulness in the observation of American social structure.

Regardless of their lack of unanimity in the definitions of social class they have employed in their research operations and literature, sociologists until quite recently generally assumed that social classes in American society during the past half-century had become more clearly distinguishable from each other and less fluid than earlier in American history. Today, however, there are many who are unable to be either affirmative or negative in answer to questions about American class rigidity. Their studies do not point conclusively in either direction. The evidence, they claim, is mixed, with some facts showing less rigidity at the same time that other facts support more rigidity. This finding of ambivalence in social forces is not unusual in the sociological analysis of a complex society.

In the following article, for instance, Ely Chinoy examines the inferential, historical material on the rate of social mobility. He observes that the channels for mobility have changed and so have the prerequisites for advancement. The rate of upward mobility in each channel has, in all probability, changed, too. But until there are more studies focused directly upon the experience of groups of individuals, Professor Chinoy emphasizes, we cannot determine whether the accelerating factors in social mobility have sufficient strength to offset those factors that are inhibiting.

40. SOCIAL MOBILITY TRENDS IN THE UNITED STATES *

ELY CHINOY

Smith College

The view that the rate of upward mobility in American society has declined seems to be widely held among social scientists. W. Lloyd Warner has commented, for example: "There is strong proof now that the American worker, as well as others, can no longer expect to achieve success with anything like the same probability as did his father and grandfather." Discussions of the Horatio Alger tradition of "rags to riches" and "strive and succeed" often refer to it as a myth once applicable to American society but now only an ideological prop to things as they are. Even introductory textbooks in sociology frequently assert that there has been a definite decline in the rate of upward movement in the social structure.

The recent appearance of several substantial studies which suggest that the rate of mobility may not have declined and the growing awareness among sociologists of the inadequacy of the available data call for an appraisal of our knowledge concerning possible changes in the rate of upward movement in American society. Only by assembling and collating the facts which are

* *American Sociological Review,* Vol. 20, No. 2, April, 1955, pp. 180–186.

available can we test the prevalent assertions about vertical mobility, see the gaps in our knowledge, and define the direction in which research should be channelled.

Students of social mobility have usually focused their attention upon movement in the occupational hierarchy. Despite difficulties inherent in the use of occupational data, no other type of information is as readily available or as amenable to systematic analysis. More important, however, are the theoretical and empirical reasons for using occupational mobility as equivalent to, or an index of, social mobility. Occupational data are relevant to all theories of stratification utilized by contemporary sociologists. For those who define class structure as a prestige hierarchy or as a member of "class-conscious" groups, occupation is both an index and a determinant of class position. For Marxists, occupational mobility is roughly the same as social mobility if occupations are classified on the basis of their relations to the means of production. For those whose categories of stratification follow Max Weber, occupation is of obvious utility because of its role in determining life chances in the marketplace.

The mass of available evidence demonstrates clearly the existence of a high correlation between occupation and the various criteria of class: prestige, income, wealth, style of life, and power. Although there is some disagreement on the relative importance of each of these variables within the total system, there seems ample warrant for concluding that in American society, at least, occupation is probably the most significant, that is, it is more likely to influence other variables than to be influenced by them.

The analysis of occupational mobility has taken two forms, inferential and direct. Inferential analysis focuses attention upon changes in American society which may affect the rate of mobility. Conclusions about trends are inferred from the facts of institutional, structural, and demographic change.

The second form of mobility analysis seeks to compare directly the social origins and career patterns of members of each class at different times in order to establish the frequency or rate of mobility and to discover any changes or trends. There are serious unresolved problems in this form of analysis. No adequate, clearly defined measure of the rate of mobility exists. Even if an adequate measure were available, there are few data concerning the origins and careers of representative groups of individuals in past generations with which to make comparisons with the present. The first steps toward filling gaps in our historical knowledge have been taken, but it is quite possible that we shall not be able to uncover more than scattered pieces of information.

These two modes of analysis are not unrelated lines of inquiry. The study of mobility among groups of individuals should be guided by hypotheses derived from the main features of historical development and must take into account changes in the class structure itself. Conversely, hypotheses drawn from the study of social change can only be tested by systematic investigation of the experience of groups of individuals.

The major changes in American society from which scholars have inferred that the rate of vertical mobility has declined have been the closing of the frontier, the cessation of mass immigration, the growth of giant corporations, and diminishing differences in the birth rates of various occupational groups. The principal stimulus to vertical mobility, in the judgment of most scholars, has been the occupational redistribution of the working population.

Let us examine each of these inferences.

For many years it has been almost a commonplace of American history that the closing of the frontier meant that dissatisfied and frustrated urban workers could no longer easily acquire land in the west. The investigations of Fred A. Shannon, Carter Goodrich and Sol Davidson have shown clearly, however, that after the Civil War urban workers did not take advantage in substantial numbers of land available on the frontier. The closing of the frontier, therefore, could not have caused any substantial decline in the rate of mobility of urban workers.

In the cities, the mass immigration which ended only with the First World War generated strong pressure for upward mobility among those who had come earlier. Since most immigrants entered the economy as unskilled laborers, earlier arrivals were able to work their way upwards in business and industry. Jobs at the bottom of the industrial heap now must be filled by native Americans instead of by recent immigrants. If other things were equal, therefore, only greater competition for desirable positions and an increased rate of downward mobility could compensate for the cessation of mass immigration.

The immigrants' contribution to vertical circulation was possible, however, only because of the rapid growth of the economy. Both immigration and the settling of the west contributed directly to that growth. When economic expansion came to a virtual halt during the thirties, many observers, convinced that the economy was "mature," concluded that the rich opportunities for individual advancement which had accompanied the nation's economic development could no longer exist. The expansion of the economy during and since the war has clearly disposed of the view that there was no longer room for economic growth. Yet in itself economic growth offers no assurance of continued or increasing mobility. Even in our highly productive, expanding economy, the possibility of a persisting volume of mass unemployment which might inhibit advancement for millions of individuals still exists. In addition, opportunity and mobility in a society dominated by giant corporations and big government differ in many ways from what they were in the past.

Since the end of the Civil War large corporations have increasingly dominated the economy. The effects of this trend upon the rate of mobility, however, are not clear. The size and scope of big business tend to obscure the fact that the relative size of the small business population has not decreased in the past century; nor has the rate of failure of small business increased substantially. It is still possible for men to go into business, as large numbers do each year, although the social and economic position of small businessmen has been significantly altered. They are confined largely to the fields of distribution and service in which the rate of failure is particularly high and the chances of growing from a small to a large business are limited. They have lost many of their entrepreneurial functions to the corporations whose products they usually sell or service, and their income and prestige may be less than that of many manual workers and clerical employees, and their style of life less rewarding.

Within giant corporations, increasing organizational complexity and extensive mechanization have changed the form and perhaps the frequency of mobility. There is considerable evidence that movement from the ranks of manual labor into management has diminished, although a declining rate of ascent from the bottom may be counterbalanced by increased mobility within white-collar ranks.

The development of giant bureaucracies in business and industry, and in government and mass organizations, together with the expansion of tertiary industries—service, distribution, communication—has, however, generated occupational shifts which have probably led to a substantial volume of upward mobility. There has been a marked increase in the proportion of the total working force engaged in white-collar, non-manual occupations, from twenty-one percent in 1910 to thirty-eight percent, in 1950. Most of this growth has been balanced by a sharp decrease in the farm population, from thirty-one percent in 1910 to only twelve percent in 1950.

The intensive mechanization of industry has also changed the composition of the working class, with possible consequences for the rate of mobility. Although the proportion of skilled workers has remained approximately the same, unskilled workers declined from fifteen percent to less than ten percent while semi-skilled workers increased from fifteen to twenty percent during the years from 1910 to 1950. These changes probably represent an upgrading of a large number of industrial workers.

Mobility generated by occupational changes was further stimulated for many years by differences in the birth rates of the major occupational groups. Professionals, businessmen, and clerical employees who were increasing their proportion in the total working force were not producing enough children to replace themselves, while manual workers and farmers were having more children than were necessary to maintain their numbers. The "social vacuum" created by the low birth rate of white-collar groups was filled by children of urban manual workers and farmers. Since a large number of migrants to the city seem to have come from the lower economic levels of agriculture, it is a plausible hypothesis that many of those who left the farm have become manual laborers, replacing workers—or their children—who in turn have moved into white-collar ranks.

The stimulus to mobility provided by differential birth rates has probably lessened in recent years with the increased fertility of white-collar workers, an increase which has seemingly narrowed the differences between manual and non-manual workers. The higher birth-rate among non-manual workers fills at least part of the "social vacuum" which existed in the past, while working class and farm families produce a smaller surplus population.

Upward mobility resulting from migration to the cities has been offset at least in part by a steady decline in the possibility of movement up the so-called agricultural ladder, whose steps went from hired hand to tenant to farm owner. The proportion of tenants among farmers increased steadily from 1880 to 1935, when forty-two percent of all farmers were tenants. Several studies after the First World War demonstrated clearly that farmers were taking longer to gain ownership of their land and suggested that many tenants were giving up their ambitions and moving to the city. Census data for the past fifty years verify this hypothesis, for the total number of farm owners has remained roughly the same from 1900 to 1950 while the number of tenants, which had increased slightly from 1900 to 1935, dropped by almost fifty percent from 1935 to 1950. The number of farm laborers has also diminished by one-third since 1930.

From this historical analysis no conclusive answer can be given to the question: What has been happening to the rate of upward mobility? The channels for mobility have changed, as have the prerequisites for advancement and, in all probability, the rate of upward movement within each channel. But we cannot yet determine, without more studies focused directly upon the experience of groups of individuals, whether the factors which have tended to maintain or increase the rate of vertical mobility have offset those circumstances which have inhibited ascent in the class structure.

What can we learn from those direct studies of mobility which are available? These studies fall into three categories: (1) research into the social origins and career patterns of specific occupational groups, usually those at the top of the occupational ladder; (2) investigations of mobility in samples drawn from specific localities; (3) a study by Richard Centers of a sample drawn from the total population. Most of these studies deal with intergenerational mobility, that is changes in occupation from father to son. Much less attention has been given to career advancement, that is movement from occupation to occupation during the lifetime of individuals.

A series of investigations which began with P. A. Sorokin's study of millionaires and F. W. Taussig and C. S. Joslyn's *American Business Leaders* provide considerable evidence that the proportion of top business owners and executives recruited from lower levels of American society has steadily declined. Although this fact possesses obvious sociological importance, it is not adequate evidence of an over-all decline in the rate of vertical mobility. Comparable data for other elite groups are not available, and increasing movement into other segments of the social structure may balance this decline in mobility into the upper ranks of business.

The direct studies of mobility which encompass all occupational groups found that "The general tendency is for more sons to be located on their fathers' levels than any other." Each of them also reported that a considerable proportion of its sample experienced some vertical mobility. Centers, for example, found that thirty-five percent of his sample were in positions which could be considered better than those of their fathers, while twenty-nine percent were in positions not as good as those of their fathers. Most of the mobility in all studies, however, was only to occupational levels adjacent to those of the fathers.

Comparison and collation of results of these direct studies in order to ascertain changes or trends in the rate of mobility are difficult for several reasons. First, there is considerable variation in the occupational categories which are used. The only classification which has been used consistently has been skilled workers. Some comparability can be achieved by combining categories, but only at the expense of precise analysis.

Second, no information is available about the specific localities in which studies have been done. One may legitimately ask whether the rate of mobility in any one area is typical of the entire society. Without data about these localities and their history, no answer to this question is possible. Nor are we able to judge which forces stimulating or inhibiting mobility are at work, and the findings therefore cannot be used to test precise hypotheses about variations in the rate of mobility.

Third, each of these investigations covered different periods of time. P. E. Davidson and H. D. Anderson secured their data in 1933–1934, Centers in 1945, R. Bendix, S. M. Lipset, and T. F. Malm in 1949–1950. The data used by Natalie Rogoff were from two periods, 1905–1912 and 1938–1941. It is quite possible that in each case short-run economic fluctuations might have affected the findings.

It is hardly, surprising, therefore, that the findings of these direct mobility studies have been variously interpreted. The studies by Davidson and Anderson and Richard Centers, for example, have been frequently taken as evidence of declining mobility. This conclusion rests, however, at least in part upon an image of the American past which may not correspond to the historical facts. But recently produced evidence that not as much mobility has existed in the past as Americans have long assumed has led to the conclusion, equally unwarranted by the available evidence, that there has been no decline in the rate of mobility.

Only the study by Natalie Rogoff seeks to deal systematically with the problem of changing rates of mobility. Her conclusion that no change has occurred has only limited value, however, because it is based upon a formula which excludes the effects of the changing occupational distribution and does not adequately balance the gains and losses in the rates of mobility of different occupational groups. Nor do we know enough as yet about the locality in which the research was done to enable us to draw wider conclusions. Fortunately other students will be able to examine and analyze in their own fashion the raw data collected by Miss Rogoff and included in her published report.

It seems clear, then, that neither inferential analysis based upon historical study nor direct analysis of mobility of groups of individuals can yet indicate whether there has been any change in the rate of vertical mobility in American society. The answer to that question must wait upon more detailed studies which not only build upon the research already done, but which also seek to test precise hypotheses concerning the impact of changing institutions, social organization, and demographic characteristics upon the rate of mobility. The balancing of the as yet unformulated mobility equation, which must take into account increased mobility through new channels of upward movement, decreased mobility through narrowing channels of advancement, changing frequencies of mobility in different groups, and trends in the nature of the class system itself, requires considerably more research energy and effort than sociologists have as yet devoted to the problem.

Despite the many difficulties inherent in the concept of social class, it has turned out to be one of the most useful "independent" (causal) variables applied by the sociologist in seeking to explain the influence of social structure and subculture on the thoughts, feelings, and actions of people. No study in applied sociology today can afford to overlook its possible use in accounting, at least in part, for the variation in value of the "dependent" (effect) variable under consideration.

The utility of social class as an independent variable in applied sociological research will be deeply appreciated if we turn to a study involving extremist political and religious behavior that is examined under cross-cultural scrutiny. Seymour M. Lipset's following article presents a variety of evidence from many societies strongly suggesting that lower-class status predisposes individuals to favor extremism in politics and religion. His evidence includes reports from surveys concerning differential class attitudes towards democratic values, psychological research on the personality traits of different strata, data on the composition and appeal of "chiliastic" religious sects, and materials bearing on the support of authoritarian movements.

According to Professor Lipset, the factors operating to support this predisposition are all those which make for a lack of sophistication, a complex view of causal relations, and heightened insecurity. He concludes that these findings suggest that the success of the Communist party among those of low status in poorer nations is positively related to its authoritarian character.

41. DEMOCRACY AND WORKING-CLASS AUTHORITARIANISM *

SEYMOUR M. LIPSET
University of California, Berkeley

Gradual realization that authoritarian predispositions and ethnic prejudice flow more naturally from the situation of the lower classes than from that of

* *American Sociological Review*, Vol. 24, No. 4, August, 1959, pp. 482–501.

the middle and upper classes in modern industrial society has posed a tragic dilemma for those intellectuals of the democratic left who once believed the proletariat necessarily to be a force for liberty, racial equality, and social progress. Ignazio Silone has asserted that "the myth of the liberating power of the proletariat has dissolved along with that other myth of progress. The recent examples of the Nazi labor unions, like those of Salazar and Peron . . . have at last convinced of this even those who were reluctant to admit it on the sole grounds of the totalitarian degeneration of Communism."

Dramatic demonstrations of this point have been given recently by the support of White Citizen's Councils and segregation by workers in the South, and by the active participation of many workers in the "race riots" in England. A "Short Talk with a Fascist Beast" (an 18 year old casual laborer who took part in the beating of Negroes in London), appearing in the left Socialist *New Statesman,* portrays graphically the ideological syndrome which sometimes culminates in such behavior:

> "That's why I'm with the Fascists," he says. "They're against the blacks. That Salmon, he's a Communist. The Labour Party is Communist too. Like the unions." His mother and father, he says, are strict Labour supporters. Is he against the Labour Party. "Nah, I'm for them. They're for y'know—us. I'm for the unions too." Even though they were dominated by Communists? "Sure," he says. "I like the Communist Party. It's powerful, like." How can he be for the Communists when the Fascists hate them?
>
> Len says, "Well, y'know, I'm for the Fascists when they're against the nigs. But the Fascists is really for the rich people y'know, like the Tories. All for the guv'nors, people like that. But the Communists are very powerful." I told him the Communist Party of Britain was quite small.
>
> "But," he says, "they got Russia behind them." His voice was full of marvel. "I admire Russia. Y'know, the people. They're peaceful. They're strong. When they say they'll do a thing, they do it. Not like us. Makes you think: they got a weapon over there can wipe us all out, with one wave of a general's arm. Destroy us completely and totally. Honest, those Russians. When they say they'll do a thing, they do it. Like in Hungary. I pity those people, the Hungarians. But did you see the Russians went in and stopped them. Tanks. Not like us in Cyprus. Our soldiers get shot in the back and what do we do? The Communists is for the small men." [1]

The demonstrations of working-class ethnic prejudice and support for totalitarian political movements which have upset many leftist stereotypes parallel findings in such different areas of social science research as public opinion, religion, family patterns, and personality structure. Many studies suggest that the lower-class way of life produces individuals with rigid and intolerant approaches to politics. These findings, discussed below, imply that one may anticipate wide-spread support by lower-class individuals and groups for extremist movements.

[1] Clancy Sigal, in the *New Statesman,* October 4, 1958, p. 440.

This assertion may seem to be contradicted by the facts of political history. Since their beginnings in the nineteenth century, workers' organizations and parties have been a major force in extending political democracy and in waging progressive political and economic struggles. Before 1914, the classic division between the working-class left parties and the right was not based solely upon stratification issues, such as redistribution of income, status, and educational opportunities, but also rested upon civil liberties and international policy issues. The workers, judged by the policies of their parties, were often the backbone of the fight for greater political democracy, religious freedom and minority rights, and international peace. The parties backed by the conservative middle and upper classes in much of Europe, on the other hand, tended to favor more extremist political forms, resist the extension of the suffrage, back the established church, and support jingoistic foreign policies.

Events since 1914 have gradually eroded these patterns. In some countries working-class groups have proved to be the most nationalistic and jingoistic sector of the population. In a number of nations, they have clearly been in the forefront of the struggle against equal rights for minority groups, and have sought to limit immigration or to impose racial standards in countries with open immigration. The conclusion of the anti-Facist era and the emergence of the cold war have shown that the struggle for freedom is not a simple variant of the economic class struggle. The threat to freedom posed by the Communist movement is as great as that once posed by Fascism and Nazism, and that movement, in all countries where it is strong, is based largely on the lower levels of the working-class or the rural population. No other party has been as thoroughly and completely based on the working-class and the poor. Socialist parties, past and present, have secured much more support from the middle classes than have the Communists.

Some socialists and liberals have suggested that the fact of working-class backing for Communism proves nothing about authoritarian tendencies in the working-class, since the Communist Party often masquerades as a party seeking to fulfill the classic western-democratic revolutionary values of liberty, equality and fraternity; they argue that most Communist supporters, particularly the less educated, are deceived into thinking that the Communists are simply more militant and more efficient socialists. I would suggest, however, the alternative hypothesis that, rather than being a source of strain, the intransigent, intolerant, and demonological aspects of Communist ideology attract members from the lower class of low income, low-status occupation, and little education. In modern industrial societies such persons have made up a very large part of the working class.

The social situation of the lower strata, particularly in poorer countries with low levels of education, predisposes them to view politics in simplistic and chiliastic terms of black and white, good and evil. Consequently, other things being equal, they should be more likely than other strata to prefer extremist movements which suggest easy and quick solutions to social problems and have a rigid outlook rather than those which view the problem of reform or change in complex and gradualist terms and which support rational values of tolerance.

The "authoritarianism" of any social stratum or class, of course, is highly relative, as well as modifiable by organizational commitments to democracy and by individual cross-pressures. Thus the lower class in any given country may be more authoritarian than the upper classes, but on an "absolute" scale all the classes in that country may be less authoritarian than any class in another country. In a country such as Britain, where norms of toleration are well-developed and widespread in every social stratum, even the lowest class may be less authoritarian, more "sophisticated" in the sense of having a longer time-perspective and a gradualist political outlook, than the most highly educated stratum in an underdeveloped country, where immediate problems and crises impinge on every class and short-term solutions may be sought by all groups.

Commitments to democratic procedures and ideals by the principal organizations to which low-status individuals belong may, however, influence their actual political behavior more than their underlying personal values, however authoritarian. A working class which has developed an early (prior to the Communists) loyalty to a democratic political or trade-union movement which has successfully fought for the social and economic rights of that class will not easily change its allegiance.

Commitments to other values or institutions by individuals may also override the most established authoritarian predispositions. Thus a Catholic worker who is strongly anti-capitalist may still vote for a relatively conservative party in France, Italy, or Germany because his ties to Catholicism are stronger determinants of his electoral choice than his resentments about his class status; a worker with a high authoritarian predisposition may defend democratic institutions against Fascist attack because his links to anti-Fascist working-class parties and unions affect his political behavior more than do his authoritarian values. Conversely, those who are not predisposed toward extremist political styles may back an extremist party because of certain aspects of its program and political role. Many persons supported the Communists in 1936 and 1943 as an anti-Fascist internationalist party.

The specific propensity of given social strata to support extremist or democratic political parties, then, cannot be derived or predicted from a knowledge of their psychological predispositions or from attitudes revealed by the survey data presented below. Both evidence and theory suggest, however, that the lower strata are relatively more authoritarian, that (again, other things being equal) they will be more attracted toward an extremist movement than toward a moderate and democratic one, and that, once recruited, they will not be alienated by its lack of democracy, while more educated or sophisticated supporters will tend to drop away.

TABLE 1. Responses of Different German Occupational Groups to Preferred Party System in Percentages (Males Only), 1953 *

Occupational Group	*Several Parties*	*One Party*	*No Party*	*No Opinion*	*N*
Civil Servants	88	6	3	3	111
Upper White-Collar	77	13	2	8	58
Free Professionals	69	13	8	10	38
Skilled Workers	65	22	5	8	277
Artisans	64	16	9	11	124
Lower White-Collar	62	19	7	12	221
Businessmen (Small)	60	15	12	13	156
Farmers	56	22	6	16	241
Semi-Skilled Workers	49	28	7	16	301
Unskilled Workers	40	27	11	22	172

* Computed from IBM cards supplied to author by the UNESCO Institute at Cologne from its 1953 survey of German opinion.

I shall first discuss basic lower-class attitudes toward civil liberties and non-economic liberalism in general and then examine certain parallels between religion and politics. After documenting some of the general patterns, I shall specify the elements in the general life-situation of lower class persons—the family patterns, typical educational experiences, characteristic tensions and insecurities, their isolated group existence and general lack of sophistication—which differentiate their life from that of the middle classes and make the poor receptive to authoritarian values and likely to support extremist movements.

DEMOCRATIC VALUES AND STRATIFICATION

The distinction between economic and non-economic liberalism helps to clarify the relationship between class position and political behavior. Economic liberalism refers to the conventional issues concerning redistribution of income, status, and power among the classes. The poorer everywhere are more liberal or leftist on such issues; they favor more welfare state measures, higher wages, graduated income taxes, support of trade-unions, and other measures opposed by those of higher class position. On the other hand, when liberalism is defined in non-economic terms—so as to support, for example, civil liberties for political dissidents, civil rights for ethnic and racial minorities, internationalist foreign policies, and liberal immigration legislation—the correlation is reversed.

Abundant data from almost every country in the world with competing political parties show that economic liberalism or leftism is inversely associated with socio-economic status. In Germany, for example, a study conducted by the UNESCO Institute at Cologne asked a systematic sample of 3,000 Germans: "Do you think that it would be better if there were one party, several parties, or no party?" The results analyzed according to occupational status indicate that the lower strata of the working class and the rural population were less likely to support a multi-party system (a reasonable index of democratic attitudes in westernized countries) than the middle and upper strata. (See Table 1.) Comparable results were obtained in 1958 when a similar question was asked of national or regional samples in Austria, Japan, Brazil, Canada, Mexico, West Germany, the Netherlands, Belgium, Italy, and France. Although the proportion favoring a multi-party system varied from country to country, within each nation low socio-economic status was associated with failure to support a multi-party system.

Somewhat similar findings were obtained in studies in Japan, Great Britain, and the United States in surveys designed to secure general reactions to problems of civil liberties or the rights of various minorities. In Japan, for example, the workers and the rural population tended to be more authoritarian and less concerned with civil liberties than the middle and upper classes.

In England, H. J. Eysenck found comparable differences between "tough-minded" and "tender-minded" people in their general social outlook. The first group tended to be intolerant of deviations from the standard moral or religious codes, anti-Negro, anti-Semitic, and xenophobic, while the "tender-minded" in general were tolerant of deviation, unprejudiced, and internationalist. In summing up his findings, based on attitude scales given to supporters of different British parties, Eysenck reports that "Middle-class Conservatives are more tender-minded than working-class Conservatives; middle-class Liberals are more tender-minded than working-class Liberals; middle-class Socialists are more tender-minded than working-class Socialists; and even middle-class Communists are more tender-minded than working-class Communists."

The evidence from various American studies dealing with attitudes toward civil liberties, as well as such other components of non-economic liberalism as ethnic prejudice, is also clear and consistent—the lower strata are the least tolerant. In the most systematic of these, based on a national sample of nearly 5,000 Americans, Stouffer divided his respondents into three categories, "less tolerant, in-between, and more tolerant," by using a scale based on responses to questions about the right of free speech for Communists, critics of religion, advocates of nationalization of industry, and the like. As the data presented in Table 2 demonstrate, tolerance increases with moves up the stratification ladder. Only 30 percent of those in manual occupations are in the "most tolerant" category, as contrasted with 66 percent of the professionals and 51 percent of the proprietors, managers, and officials. As in Germany and Japan, farmers are low in tolerance.

The findings of public opinion surveys in thirteen different countries that the lower strata are less committed to democratic norms than the middle classes are reaffirmed by the research of more psychologically oriented investigators, who have studied the social correlates of "authoritarian personality" structures as measured by the now famous "F scale." The most recent summary of the research findings of the many studies in this area shows a consistent association of authoritarianism with lower class and status. One survey of 460 Los Angeles adults reports that "the working class contains a higher proportion of authoritarians than either the middle or the upper class," and that among workers, those who explicitly identified themselves with "the working class" rather than "the middle class" were more authoritarian.

TABLE 2. Proportion of Male Respondents Who Are "More Tolerant" With Respect to Civil Liberties Issues *

Professional and Semi-Professional	66%	(159)
Proprietors, Managers and Officials	51	(223)
Clerical and Sales	49	(200)
Manual Workers	30	(685)
Farmers or Farm Workers	20	(202)

* Source: Samul A. Stouffer, *Communism, Conformity and Civil Liberties,* New York: Doubleday, 1955, p. 139. The figures for manual and farm workers were calculated from cards supplied by Professor Stouffer.

Recent research within lower status groups suggests the possibility of a *negative* correlation between authoritarianism and neuroticism. This would be congruent with the hypothesis that those who deviate from the standards of their group are more likely to be neurotic than those who conform. Hence, if we assume that authoritarian traits are conventional reactions of low status people, then the lower class anti-authoritarian should be more neurotic. As Anthony Davids and Charles W. Eriksen point out, where the "standard of reference on authoritarianism is quite high," people may be well adjusted *and* authoritarian. The absence of a relationship between authoritarian attitudes and neurotic traits among lower class groups reported by these authors is consistent with the hypothesis that authoritarian attitudes are "normal" and expected in such groups.

AUTHORITARIAN RELIGION AND STRATIFICATION

Many observers have called attention to a connection between low social status and fundamentalist or chiliastic religion. The liberal Protestant churches, on the other hand, almost invariably have been predominantly middle-class in membership. In the United States, this class division among the churches has created a dilemma for the clergy of the so-called liberal churches, who have tended to be liberal in their politics as well as in their religion and, hence, have often desired to spread their social and religious gospel among the lower strata. They have found, however, that the latter prefer ministers who preach of hell-fire and salvation, of a conflict between God and Satan, to those who advocate modern liberal Protestant theology.

Writing in the early period of the socialist movement, Friedrich Engels noted that early Christianity and the revolutionary workers' movement had "notable points of resemblance," particularly in their millennial appeals and lower-class base. Recently, Elmer Clark has shown that small sects in contemporary America, sects resembling early Christianity, "originate mainly among the religiously neglected poor." He writes:

[when] the revolts of the poor have been tinged with religion, which was nearly always the case until recent times, millennial ideas have appeared, and . . . these notions are prominent in most of the small sects which follow the evangelical tradition. Premillennarianism is essentially a defense mechanism of the disinherited; despairing of obtaining substantial blessings through social processes, they turn on the world which has withheld its benefits and look to its destruction in a cosmic cataclysm which will exalt them and cast down the rich and powerful.[2]

Troeltsch has characterized the psychological appeal of sectarian religion in a way that might as appropriately be applied to extremist politics:

It is the lower classes which do the really creative work, forming communities on a genuine religious basis. They alone unite imagination and simplicity of feeling with a nonreflective habit of mind, a primitive energy, and an urgent sense of need. On such a foundation alone is it possible to build up an unconditional authoritative faith in a Divine Revelation with simplicity of surrender and unshaken certainty. Only within a fellowship of this kind is there room for those who have a sense of spiritual need, and who have not acquired the habit of intellectual reasoning, which always regards everything from a relative point of view.[3]

Jehovah's Witnesses is an excellent example of a rapidly growing sect which "continues to attract, as in the past, the underprivileged strata." Their principal teaching is that the Kingdom of Heaven is at hand. "The end of the age is near. Armageddon is just around the corner, when the wicked will be destroyed, and the theocracy, or rule of God, will be set up upon the earth." And as in the case of Communist political millennialists, the organization of the Witnesses, whose membership in the United States is many hundreds of thousands, is "hierarchical and highly authoritarian. There is little democratic participation in the management or in the formation of policies of the movement as a whole."

Direct linkages between the social roots of political and of religious extremism have been observed in a number of countries. In Czarist Russia, the young Trotsky consciously recognized this relationship and successfully recruited the first working-class members of the South Russian Workers' Union (a revolutionary Marxist organization of the late 1890s) from adherents to religious sects. In Holland and Sweden, recent studies have shown that the Communists are strongest in regions which once were centers of fundamentalist religious revivalism.

[2] Elmer T. Clark, *The Small Sects in America,* New York: The Abingdon Press, 1949, pp. 16, 218–219.

[3] Ernst Troeltsch, *The Social Teaching of the Christian Churches,* London: George Allen and Unwin, 1930, Vol. 1, p. 44.

These findings do not imply that religious sects supported by lower-class elements become centers of political protest; in fact, the discontent and frustration otherwise flowing into channels of political extremism are often drained off by a transvaluational religion. The point here is that rigid fundamentalism and chiliastic dogmatism are linked to the same underlying characteristics, attitudes, and predispositions, which find another outlet in allegiance to authoritarian political movements.

In his excellent study of the sources of Swedish communism, Sven Rydenfelt demonstrates the competitive relationship between religious and political extremism. He analyzed the differences between two northern counties of Sweden, Vasterbotten and Norrbotten, in an attempt to explain the relatively low Communist vote in the former (two percent) and the much larger vote in the latter county (21 percent), although both have comparable social and economic conditions. The Liberal Party, which in Sweden gives much more support than any other to religious extremism, was very strong in Vasterbotten (30 percent) and correspondingly weak in Norrbotten (nine percent). Rydenfelt concludes that a general predisposition toward radicalism existed in both counties, containing some of the poorest, most socially isolated, and rootless groups in Sweden, but that the expression of radicalism differed, taking a religious form in one county, and a Communist in the other. "The Communists and the religious radicals, as for instance the Pentecostal sects, seem to be competing for the allegiance of the same groups."

THE TYPICAL SOCIAL SITUATION OF LOWER-CLASS PERSONS

A number of elements in the typical social situation of lower-class individuals may be singled out as contributing to authoritarian predispositions: low education, low participation in political organizations or in voluntary organizations of any type, little reading, isolated occupations, economic insecurity, and authoritarian family patterns. Although these elements are interrelated, they are by no means identical.

There is consistent evidence that degree of formal education, itself closely correlated with social and economic status, is also highly correlated with undemocratic attitudes. Data from Stouffer's study of attitudes toward civil liberties in America and from the UNESCO Research Institute's survey of German opinion bearing on a multi-party system presented in Tables 3 and 4 reveal this clearly.

These tables indicate that an increase in educational attainment has the effect of raising the proportion of democratic attitudes at each occupational level. Within each educational level, higher occupational status also seems to make for greater tolerance, but the increases associated with higher educational level are greater than those related to higher occupational level, when the other factor is held constant. It may be inferred that the quality of the educational experience is more highly associated with political tolerance than occupational experience *per se*. But both inferior education and low occupational position are highly intercorrelated, both are part of the complex making up low-status, and are associated with a lack of tolerance.

Low-status groups also participate less in formal organizations, read fewer magazines and books regularly, possess less information on public affairs, vote less, and, in general, are less interested in politics. The available evidence suggests that each of these attributes is related to democratic attitudes. Thus, an analysis of German data collected by the UNESCO Institute in 1953 found that at every occupational level those who belonged to voluntary associations

TABLE 3. The Relationship Between Occupation, Education, and Political Tolerance in the United States, 1955 *

	Percentage in the Two "Most Tolerant" Categories							
	Occupation							
Education	*Low Manual*		*High Manual*		*Low White Collar*		*High White Collar*	
Grade School	13	(228)	21	(178)	23	(47)	26	(100)
Some High School	32	(99)	33	(124)	29	(56)	46	(68)
High School Grad.	40	(64)	48	(127)	47	(102)	56	(108)
Some College	—	(14)	64	(36)	64	(80)	65	(37)
College Grad.	—	(3)	—	(11)	74	(147)	83	(21)

* Computed from IBM cards supplied by Samuel Stouffer from his study, *Communism, Conformity and Civil Liberties,* New York: Doubleday, 1955.

TABLE 4. The Relationship Between Occupation, Education, and Support of a Democratic Party System in Germany—1953 *

	Percent Favoring the Existence of Several Parties			
	Educational Level			
Occupation	*Elementary School*		*High School or Higher*	
Farm Laborers	29	(59)	—	
Manual Workers	43	(1439)	52	(29)
Farmers	43	(381)	67	(9)
Lower White Collar	50	(273)	68	(107)
Self-Employed Business	53	(365)	65	(75)
Upper White Collar	58	(86)	69	(58)
Officials (Govt.)	59	(158)	78	(99)
Professions	56	(18)	68	(38)

* Source: see Table 1.

were more likely to favor a multi-party than a one-party system. American findings also indicate that authoritarians join fewer "community groups" than non-authoritarians. A study of the determinants of economic and non-economic liberalism reports that on every occupational level the persons poorly informed on public questions are more likely to be both more radical on economic issues and less liberal on non-economic issues. Non-voters and those less interested in political matters are much more intolerant and xenophobic than those who vote and have political interests.

The authors of a study concerned with the "hard core" of "chronic know-nothings" suggest that such persons come disproportionately from the less-literate, lower socio-economic groups. These people are not only uninformed, but "harder to reach, no matter what the level or nature of the information." Here again is a hint at the complex character of the relations between education, liberalism, and status. Non-economic liberalism is not a simple matter of acquiring education and information; it must be considered at least in part a basic attitude which is actively discouraged by the social situation of lower-status persons. As Genevieve Knupfer has pointed out in her review of the literature bearing on the "underdog," "economic underprivilege is psychological underprivilege: habits of submission, little access to sources of information, lack of verbal facility. These things appear to produce a lack of self-confidence which increases the unwillingness of the low-status person to participate in many phases of our predominantly middle-class culture. . . ."

These characteristics also reflect the extent to which lower-class persons are *isolated* from the activities, controversies, and organizations of democratic society, an isolation which prevents them from securing that sophisticated and complex view of the political structure which makes understandable and necessary the norms of tolerance. It is instructive to examine in this connection those occupations which are most isolated, in every sense, from contact with the world outside their own occupational group. We should expect that persons in these occupations will support extremist movements and exhibit low political tolerance. Such in fact is the case. Manual workers in "isolated occupations" which require them to live among their workmates in one-industry towns or areas—for example, miners, maritime workers, loggers, fishermen, and sheep shearers—all exhibit high rates of Communist support in most countries.

Similarly, rural persons, both farmers and laborers, show high authoritarian predispositions. All public opinion surveys indicate that they oppose civil liberties and multi-party systems more than any other occupational group. Election surveys indicate farm owners to have been among the strongest supporters of Fascist parties, while farm workers and poor farmers and sharecroppers have given even stronger backing to the Communists in Italy, France, and India, for example, then have manual workers.

The same social conditions which are related to unsophistication and authoritarianism among workers are also associated with middle-class authoritarianism. The groups which have been most prone to support Fascist and other middle-class based extremist ideologies have been, in addition to farmers and peasants, the small businessmen of provincial communities. These groups are isolated from "cosmopolitan" culture and also rank far lower than any other non-manual occupational group in educational attainment.

If elements which contribute to a lack of sophistication and detachment from the general cultural values constitute an important factor associated with lower-class authoritarian proclivities, a second and no less important factor is a relative lack of economic and psychological security. Economic uncertainty, unemployment, and fluctuation in total income all increase with moves down the socio-economic ladder. White collar workers, even those who receive no more pay than skilled manual workers, are less likely to suffer the tensions created by fear of loss of income. Studies of marital instability indicate clearly that family tension is closely correlated with low income and financial insecurity. Economic insecurity clearly affects the political and attitudinal responses of groups. High states of tension encourage immediate alleviation through the venting of hostility against a scape-goat, the search for a short-term solution by support of extremist groups, or both. Considerable research indicates that the unemployed are less tolerant towards minorities, than the employed, are more likely to be Communists if they are workers, and to be Nazis if they are middle class. Those industries with many Communists among their employees are also characterized by a large amount of economic instability.

The insecurities and tensions which flow directly from economic instability are reinforced by the particular patterns of family life associated with the lower strata. There is more direct frustration and aggression in the day-to-day lives of members of the lower classes, both children and the adults. A comprehensive review of the many studies made in the past 25 years of child-rearing patterns in the United States reports that their "most consistent finding" is the "more frequent use of physical punishment by working-class parents. The middle-class, in contrast, resorts to reasoning, isolation, and . . . 'love-oriented' techniques of discipline. . . . Such parents are more likely to overlook offenses, and when they do punish they are less likely to ridicule or inflict physical pain." The link between such practices in lower-class families and adult hostility and authoritarianism is suggested by the findings of investigations in Boston and Detroit that physical punishments for aggression, characteristic of the working class, tend to increase rather than decrease aggressive behavior.

THE PERSPECTIVES OF LOWER-CLASS GROUPS

Acceptance of the norms of democracy requires a high level of sophistication and ego security. The less sophisticated and stable an individual, the more likely he is to favor a simplified and demonological view of politics, to fail to understand the rationale underlying the tolerance of those with whom he disagrees, and to find difficulty in grasping or tolerating a gradualist image of political change. Lack of sophistication and psychic insecurity, then, are basic "intervening variables" which clarify the empirical association between authoritarian attitudes and low status.

Several studies focusing on various aspects of working-class life and culture have emphasized different components of an unsophisticated perspective. Greater suggestibility, absence of a sense of past and future, inability to take a complex view, difficulty in abstracting from concrete experience, and lack of imagination each have been singled out as characteristic products of low status. All may be considered as interrelated indices of a more or less general lack of sophistication and ego stability, and also as part of the complex psychological basis of authoritarianism.

Suggestibility has been presented by one student of social movements as a major explanatory concept with which to account for participation in diverse extremist movements. The two conditions for suggestibility are both characteristic of low-status persons: *lack* of an adequate mental context, and a *fixed* mental context (a term of Hadley Cantril's, meaning "frame of reference" or "general perspective"). A poorly developed mental context reflects a limited education: a paucity of the rich associations which provide a basis for critical evaluation of experience. A fixed mental context—in a sense, the opposite side of the coin—reflects the tendency to elevate whatever general principles are learned to absolutes which are difficult to correct by experience.

Richard Hoggart, with reference to Britain, notes the same point. Low-status persons, he explains, without rich and flexible mental context are likely to lack a developed sense of the past *and* future:

> Their education is unlikely to have left them with any historical panorama or with any idea of a continuing tradition. . . . A great many people, though they may possess a considerable amount of disconnected information, have little idea of an historical or ideological pattern or process. . . . With little intellectual or cultural furniture, with little training in the testing of opposing views against reason and existing judgments, judgments are usually made according to the promptings of those group-apophthegms which come first to mind. . . . Similarly, there can be little real sense of the future. . . . Such a mind is, I think, particularly accessible to the temptation to live in a constant present.[4]

This concern with the present leads to a concentration on daily activities, without much inner reflection, imaginative planning of one's future, or abstract thinking. One of the few studies of lower-class children utilizing projective techniques reports:

> . . . these young people are making an adjustment which is orientated toward the outside world rather than one which rests on a developing acquaintance with their

[4] Richard Hoggart, *The Uses of Literacy,* London: Chatto and Windus, 1957, pp. 158–159.

own impulses and the handling of these impulses by fantasy and introspection. . . . They do not have a rich inner life, indeed their imaginative activity is meagre and limited. . . . When faced with a new situation, the subjects tend to react rapidly, and they do not alter their original impressions of the situation which is seen as a crude whole with little intellectual discrimination of components.[5]

Working-class life as a whole, and not merely the character of perception and imagination, has been seen as concrete and immediate. As Hoggart puts it, "if we want to capture something of the essence of working-class life . . . we must say that it is the 'dense and concrete' life, a life whose main stress is on the intimate, the sensory, the detailed and the personal. This would no doubt be true of working-class groups anywhere in the world." Hoggart sees the concreteness of the perceptions of working-class people as a main difference from those of middle-class people, who more easily meet abstract and general questions. He identifies the sharp British working-class distinction between "Us" and "Them" as:

. . . part of a more general characteristic of the outlook of most working-class people. To come to terms with the world of "Them" involves, in the end, all kinds of political and social questions, and leads eventually beyond politics and social philosophy to metaphysics. The question of how we face "Them" (whoever "They" are) is, at last, the question of how we stand in relation to anything not visibly and intimately part of our local universe. The working-class splitting of the world into "Us" and "Them" is on this side a symptom of their difficulty in meeting abstract or general questions.[6]

Hoggart is careful to emphasize that probably most persons in *any* social class are uninterested in general ideas, but still "training in the handling of ideas or in analysis" is far more characteristic of the demands of middle-class parents and occupations.

A recent discussion of variations in the conceptual apparatus of the different classes, which analyzes sources of variations in social mobility, also emphasizes the ways in which the different family patterns of the middle and working classes affect their authoritarianism. The author, B. Bernstein, points out that the middle-class parent stresses "an awareness of the importance between means and long-term ends, cognitively and affectually regarded . . . [and has] the ability to adopt appropriate measures to implement the attainment of distant ends by a purposeful means-end chain. . . . The child in the middle-classes and associated levels grows up in an environment which is finely and extensively controlled; the space, time and social relationships are explicitly regulated within and outside the family group." But while the middle-class child is led to understand the need to defer immediate gratifications

[5] B. M. Spinley, *The Deprived and the Privileged,* London: Routledge and Kegan Paul, 1953, pp. 115–116.

[6] Hoggart, *op. cit.,* p. 86.

for long-term advantages, the situation in the working-class family is quite different:

> The working-class family structure is less formally organized than the middle-class in relation to the development of the child. Although the authority within the family is explicit the values which it expresses do not give rise to the carefully ordered universe spatially and temporally of the middle-class child. The exercise of authority will not be related to a stable system of rewards and punishments but may often appear arbitrary. The specific character of long-term goals tends to be replaced by more general notions of the future, in which chance, a friend or a relative plays a greater part than the rigorous working out of connections. Thus present, or near-present activities, have greater value than the relation of the present activity to the attainment of a distant goal. The system of expectancies, or the time-span of anticipation, is shortened and this creates different sets of preferences, goals, and dissatisfactions. The environment limits the perception of the developing child of and in time. Present gratifications or present deprivations become absolute gratifications or absolute deprivations for there exists no developed time continuum upon which present activity can be ranged. Relative to the middle-classes, the postponement of present pleasure for future gratifications will be found difficult. By implication *a more volatile patterning of affectual and expressive behavior will be found in the working-classes.*[7]

This concern with the immediately perceivable, with the personal and concrete, is part and parcel of the short time-perspective and the inability to perceive the complex possibilities and consequences of actions which is referred to above as a lack of social sophistication. It is associated with some fundamental characteristics of low status, and often eventuates in a readiness to support extremist political and religious movements, and in a generally lower level of liberalism on non-economic questions.

Within extremist movements, these differences in the perceptions and perspectives of working-class persons affect their experiences, ease of recruitment, and reasons for defecting. Gabriel Almond's study of 221 ex-Communists in four countries provides some data on this point. He distinguishes between the "exoteric" (simple, for mass consumption) and "esoteric (complex, for the inner circle) doctrines of the party. "Relatively few working-class respondents had been exposed to the esoteric doctrine of the party before joining, and . . . they tended to remain unindoctrinated while in the party," in contrast with the middle-class members. Middle-class recruits who were potentially capable of absorbing a complex doctrine nevertheless "tended to come to the party with more complex value patterns and expectations which were more likely to obstruct assimilation into the party. . . . The working-class member, on the other hand, is relatively untroubled by doctrinal apparatus, less exposed

[7] B. Bernstein, "Some Sociological Determinants of Perception," *The British Journal of Sociology,* 9 (June, 1958), p. 168 (italics added).

to the media of communication, and his imagination and logical powers are relatively undeveloped."

One aspect of the lack of sophistication and education of lower-class persons is their anti-intellectualism (a phenomenon noted by Engels long ago as a problem faced by working-class movements). While the complex esoteric ideology of Communism may have been a principal feature drawing middle-class persons to it, the fundamental anti-intellectualism of extremist movements has been a source of strain for their "genuine" intellectuals, who find it difficult to view the world in black or white terms. In the Communist Party, these class differences are reflected in the fact that the working-class rank-and-file are least likely to become disturbed by ideological shifts, and least likely to defect. Their commitment, once established, cannot as easily be shaken by a sudden realization that the Party, after all, does not conform to liberal and humanistic values, as can the commitment of middle-class members, who usually joined for different reasons and values and maintain a more complex view both of their own lives and of politics.

Some evidence of the differential receptivity of leftist parties to middle- and working-class persons may be seen in the leadership composition of Socialist and Communist Parties. The former have been led by a higher proportion of intellectuals, in spite of an original ideological emphasis on maintaining a working-class orientation. The Communists, on the other hand, tend to alienate their intellectual leaders and to be led by those with preponderantly working-class occupations. Almond's study of the *Appeals of Communism* concludes:

> . . . while the party is open to all comers, working-class party members have better prospects of success in the party than middle-class recruits. This is probably due both to party policy, which has always manifested greater confidence in the reliability of working-class recruits, and to the difficulties of assimilation into the party generally experienced by middle-class party members.[8]

THE MAIN FINDINGS RESTATED

To sum up, the lower-class individual is more likely to have been exposed to punishment, lack of love, and a general atmosphere of tension and aggression since early childhood, experiences which often produce deep-rooted hostilities expressed by ethnic prejudice, political authoritarianism, and chiliastic transvaluational religion. His educational attainment is less than that of men with higher socio-economic status, and his association as a child with others of similar background not only fails to stimulate his intellectual interests but also creates an atmosphere which prevents his educational experience from increasing his general social sophistication and his understanding of different

[8] Gabriel Almond, *The Appeals of Communism*, Princeton: Princeton University Press, 1954, p. 190.

groups and ideas. Leaving school relatively early, he is surrounded on the job by others with a similar restricted cultural, educational, and family background. Little external influence impinges on his limited environment to increase his connections with the larger world and to heighten his sophistication. From early childhood, he has sought immediate gratifications in favor of activities which might have long-term rewards. The logic of both his adult employment and his family situation reinforces this limited time-perspective. As C. C. North has well put it, isolation from heterogeneous environments, characteristic of low-status, operates to "limit the source of information, to retard the development of efficiency in judgment and reasoning abilities, and to confine the attention to more trivial interests in life." All of these characteristics combine to produce a tendency to view politics, as well as personal relationships, in black-and-white terms, a desire for immediate action without critical reflection, impatience with talk and discussion, lack of interest in organizations which have a long-range gradualistic political perspective, and a readiness to follow leaders who offer a demonological interpretation of the presumably conspiratorial forces, either religious or political.

It is interesting to note that Lenin saw the character of the lower classes and the tasks of those who would lead them in terms similar to those presented in this paper. He specified as the chief task of the Communist parties the leadership of the broad masses, who are "slumbering, apathetic, hidebound, inert, and dormant"—a picture borne out by the data presented here. These masses, said Lenin, must be aligned for the "final and decisive battle" (a term reminiscent of Armageddon) by the Party which alone can present an unequivocal, uncompromising, unified view of the world, and an immediate program for drastic change. In contrast to "effective" Communist leadership, Lenin pointed to the democratic parties and their leadership as "vacillating, wavering, unstable" elements, a characterization that is probably valid for any political group lacking ultimate certainty in its program and willing to grant legitimacy to opposition groups.

The political outcome of these predispositions, however, as suggested above, is not determined by the multiplicity of factors bearing upon the development of authoritarian predispositions. Isolation, a punishing childhood, economic and occupational insecurities, and a lack of sophistication are conducive *both* to withdrawal, or even apathy, and to strong mobilization of hostile predispositions. The same underlying factors which predispose individuals toward support of extremist movements under certain conditions may result in withdrawal from political activity and concern under other conditions. Lack of information, social isolation, little participation in groups outside of one's immediate circle, a short-term time perspective, which generally characterize the lower strata, are associated both with low levels of political interest and involvement (while maintaining authoritarian attitudes) in "normal" non-crisis periods and with action in an extremist direction when those underlying predispositions are activated by a crisis and millennial appeals.

EXTREMISM AS A COMPLEX ALTERNATIVE: A TEST OF AN HYPOTHESIS

Thus far this paper has been concerned with the authoritarian proclivities of lower-status groups. One proposition which has been drawn from the analysis is that the lack of a complex and rich frame of reference, a tendency to view events from a concrete and short-term perspective, is the vital intervening variable between low status and a predisposition toward transvaluational extremist religion or politics. The proposition, however, does not simply suggest that the lower strata will be authoritarian; it implies that other things being equal, they will choose the least complex alternative. If we can find situations in which extremist politics represents the more complex rather than the less complex form of transvaluational politics, we should expect low status to be associated with *opposition* to such movements and parties.

A situation in which an extremist movement is the more complex alternative exists wherever the Communist Party is a small party competing against a large reformist party, as in England, the United States, Sweden, and Norway. Where the Party is small and weak, it can not hold out the promise of immediate changes in the situation of the most deprived. Rather, such small extremist parties usually present the fairly complex intellectual argument that tendencies inherent in the social and economic system will strengthen them in the long run. For the poorer worker, support of the Swedish Social-Democrats, the British Labor Party, or the American New Deal is a simpler and more easily understood way of securing redress of grievances or improvement of social conditions than supporting an electorally insignificant Communist Party.

The available evidence from countries such as Norway, Sweden, Canada, Brazil, and Great Britain suggests the validity of this interpretation. In these countries, where the Communist Party is small and a Labor or Socialist Party is much larger, the support of the Communists is stronger among the better-paid and more skilled workers than it is among the less skilled and poorer strata. In Italy, France, and Finland, where the Communists are the largest party on the left, the lower the income level of workers, the higher their Communist vote. A comparison of the differences in the relative income position of workers who vote Social-Democratic and those who back the Communists in two neighboring Scandinavian countries, Finland and Sweden, shows these alternative patterns clearly (see Table 5).

These assumptions concerning the relationship between Communist strength, differential time perspective involved in support of the party, and variations in the social base of its electoral appeal hold up for all countries for which data exist. Data from one other country, India, offer even better evidence for the hypothesis, however, because they permit a comparison of variations in electoral strength within a single country, and also because these data were located after the hypothesis was formulated and thus can be considered an independent replication.

TABLE 5. The Income Composition of the Working-Class Support of the Social-Democratic and Communist Parties in Finland and Sweden *

Finland—1956			*Sweden—1946*		
Income Class in Markkas	*Social Demo-crats*	*Com-munists*	*Income Class in Kronen*	*Social Demo-crats*	*Com-munists*
Under 100	8%	13%	Under 2,000	14%	8%
100–400	49	50	2,001–4,000	40	38
400–600	22	29	4,001–6,000	32	30
600 +	21	8	6,001 +	14	24
N	(173)	(119)		(5176)	(907)

* The Finnish data were secured from a special run made for this study by the Finnish Gallup Poll. The Swedish statistics were recomputed from data presented in Elis Hastad, *et al.*, editors, *"Gallup" och den Svenska Valjarkaren,* Uppsala: Hugo Gebers Forlag, 1950, pp. 175–176. Both studies include rural and urban workers.

TABLE 6. Communist and Socialist Preferences in India, by Class and Education *

	Communist Party Preferences in Kerala and Andhra	*Communist Party Preferences in Rest of India*	*Preferences for Socialist Parties in All-India*
Class			
Middle	7%	27%	23%
Lower Middle	19	30	36
Working	74	43	41
Education			
Illiterate	52%	43%	31%
Under-matric.	39	37	43
Matric. plus	9	20	26
N	(113)	(68)	(88)

* These figures have been computed from tables presented in the *Indian Institute of Public Opinion, Monthly Public Opinion Surveys,* Vol. 2, No. 4, 5, 6, 7 (Combined Issue), New Delhi, January-April, 1957, pp. 9–14. This was a pre-election poll, not a report of the actual voting results. The total sample consisted of 2,868 persons. The Socialist Party and the Praja-Socialist Party figures are combined here, since they share essentially the same moderate program. The support given to them in Andhra and Kerala was too small to be presented separately.

In India, the Communists are a major party, constituting the government or the major opposition (with 25 percent or more of the votes) in two states, Kerala and Andhra. While it has substantial strength in some other states, it is much weaker in the rest of India. If the proposition is valid that Communist appeal should be relatively greater among the lower and uneducated strata where the Party is powerful, and proportionately stronger among the higher and better educated ones where it is weak, the characteristics of Party voters should vary greatly in different parts of India. This is precisely what Table 6 shows. Where the Indian Communist Party is small, its support, like that of the two small moderate Socialist Parties, comes disproportionately from relatively well-to-do and better educated strata. The picture shifts sharply in Kerala and Andhra, where the Communists are strong. The middle class provides only seven percent of Communist support there, with the working class supplying 74 percent, showing the difference in the constituency of an extremist party when it becomes an effective political force. Educational differences among party supporters show a similar pattern.

HISTORICAL PATTERNS AND DEMOCRATIC ACTION

Complex historical factors explain why, in the face of profoundly antidemocratic tendencies in lower class groups, their political organizations and movements in the more industrialized democratic countries have supported *both* economic and political liberalism. Economic liberalism or leftism flows from their situation, producing demands for redistribution of the wealth, but their situation neither produces nor calls for non-economic liberalism, support of ethnic tolerance, and democratic norms. Of course, workers' organizations, trade unions, and political parties played a major role in extending political democracy in the nineteenth and early twentieth centuries. These struggles for political freedom by the workers, like those of the middle class before them, took place in the context of a fight for economic rights. Freedom of organization and of speech, as well as universal suffrage, were necessary means in the battle for a better standard of living, social security, shorter hours, and the like. The upper classes resisted the extension of political freedom as part of their defense of economic and social privilege.

Few groups in history have ever voluntarily espoused civil liberties and freedom for those who advocate measures they consider despicable or dangerous. Religious freedom emerged in the western world because the contending powers found themselves unable to destroy the other group without destroying the entire society, and because the very struggle led many men to lose faith and interest in religion, and consequently lose the desire to suppress dissent. Similarly, universal suffrage and freedom of organization and opposition developed in many countries either as concessions to the established strength of the lower classes or as means of controlling the lower classes, a tactic advocated and used by such sophisticated conservatives as Disraeli and Bismarck.

Once in existence and although originating in a conflict of interests, however, democratic norms, like others, become part of an institutional system. Thus, the western labor and socialist movement has incorporated these values into its general ideology. But the fact that the ideology of the movement is democratic does not mean that its supporters actually understand its implications. The evidence seems to indicate that understanding of and adherence to these norms are highest among leaders and lowest among followers. The general opinions or attitudinal predispositions of the rank and file are relatively unimportant in predicting behavior as long as the organizations to which they are loyal continue to act democratically. In spite of the workers' greater authoritarian propensity, their organizations which are anti-Communist still function as better defenders and carriers of democratic values than parties based on the middle class. In Germany, the United States, Great Britain, and Japan, individuals who support the democratic left party are more likely to support civil liberties and democratic values than people *within* each occupational stratum who back the conservative parties. That is, workers who back the democratic left are more likely to have tolerant or non-authoritarian attitudes than workers who support the conservative parties. Similarly, middle-class Social-Democrats are more prone to support civil liberties than middle-class conservatives. It is probable that organized social-democracy not only supports civil liberties but influences its supporters in the same direction.

Conservatism is especially vulnerable in a political democracy since there are more poor people than well-to-do and promises to redistribute wealth and to create a better life for the lower classes are difficult to rebut. Consequently, conservatives have traditionally feared a thorough-going political democracy and have endeavored in most countries—by restricting the franchise, or by manipulating the legislature through second chambers or overrepresentation of rural districts and small towns (traditional conservative strongholds)—to prevent a popular majority from controlling the government. The ideology of conservatism has often been based on élitist values which reject the idea that there is wisdom in the voice of the electorate. In addition, militarism and nationalism, often defended by conservatives, probably have an attraction for individuals with authoritarian predispositions.

It would be a mistake to conclude from the data presented in this paper that the authoritarian predispositions of the lower-classes necessarily constitute a threat to a democratic social system; nor should similar conclusions be drawn about the anti-democratic aspects of conservatism. Whether or not a given class supports restrictions on freedom depends on a wide constellation of factors of which those discussed here are only a part.

The instability of the democratic process in general and the strength of the Communists in particular are closely related to national levels of economic development, including degrees of educational attainment. The Communists represent a mass movement in the poorer countries of Europe and elsewhere, but are weak where economic development and educational attainment are high. The lower classes of the less developed countries are poorer, more insecure, less educated, and possess fewer status symbols than those of the more well-to-do nations. In the more developed stable democracies of western Europe, North America, and Australasia the lower classes are "in the society" as well as "of it": their cultural isolation is much less than the isolation of the poorer groups in other countries, who are cut off from participation by abysmally low incomes and very limited, if any, schooling. Thus the incorporation of the workers into the body politic in the industrialized western world has greatly reduced their authoritarian predispositions, although in the United States, for example, McCarthy demonstrated that an irresponsible demagogue who combines a nationalist and anti-élitist appeal can still secure considerable support from the less educated.

While the evidence as to the effects of rising standards of living and education permits us to maintain hopeful expectations concerning working-class political values and behavior in those countries in which extremism is weak, the available data suggest pessimistic conclusions with regard to the less economically developed, unstable democracies. Where an extremist party has secured the support of the lower classes, often by stressing equality and economic security at the expense of liberty, it is problematic whether this support can be taken away from it through use of democratic methods. The Communists, in particular, combine the two types of politics which have a basic appeal to these classes, economic radicalism and a chiliastic view of the world. Whether democratic working-class parties able to demonstrate convincingly their ability to defend economic and class interests can be built up in the less stable democracies is a moot question.

ETHNICITY

In the introduction to this part of the book on social stratification, we noted that there are two resemblances between class and ethnic stratification. In the first instance, both systems of stratification tend to cut across the entire society. Second, ethnic stratification is actually functionally enmeshed with class stratification, for the various ethnic groups contain degrees of social-class differentiation. Yet there is sufficient difference between ethnic dominant and minority groups on the one hand and upper and lower classes on the other to warrant separate analytical consideration.

The convergence, interaction, and stratification of ethnic groups in so-called intergroup relations refer primarily to races, religious groups, and nationalities that have either undergone subordination as minorities or are superordinate as dominant groups in relation to at least one minority counterpart. In their subordination, ethnic minorties are underprivileged in one or more ways, and they are the targets of prejudice and discrimination. Usually they are defensive and sensitive to group alignments and their low status. Like minorities, dominant groups do not necessarily depend on their numerical size in relation to other ethnic groups to account for their social status, for size is only one basis of power. Sociologically speaking, ethnic dominant groups are those races, religious groups, and nationalities that have social power—the ability to exploit the service or regulate the subservience of other ethnic groups. And this power may be derived not only from size but from superior weapons, property, finances, special knowledge, managerial and executive skills, and eminence derived from myths, legends, and history.

In the power relations between dominant and minority groups, there is persistent conflict that varies in intensity and explicitness. Whereas dominant groups tend to resist minority assertion and work to retain the existing distribution of power, minorities usually attempt either to gain autonomy or to achieve equality of status with the dominant groups. Relations between the two sets of groups become structured by reciprocal stimuli and responses. The social inferiority of the minority groups tends to provide justification for the dominant groups' discrimination against them; this, in turn, leads the minority groups to respond in ways that strengthen further the stereotypes held about them.

The following article by Morton B. King, Jr., was motivated by his dissatisfaction with the conceptual positions from which sociological analysis of dominant and minority group relations have usually proceeded. He proposes that the new and growing sociology of power would provide the best conceptual orientation for the study of this type of stratification.

42. THE MINORITY COURSE *

MORTON B. KING, JR.

Southern Methodist University

On my desk are twelve books, published since 1948. The publisher of each hopes I will adopt it as a text for a course called "Minority Groups." The titles, points of view, and contents vary widely. The most frequently-occurring word is "minority," yet the authors use it with different denotative and connotative meanings. There are also "race relations" and "inter-group relations" and "inter-cultural relations" and sometimes just "human relations"—although that seems a rather broad and ambitious topic for a single course. Some texts describe a long or short list of "groups" and may point out the contributions of each to "our American way of life." The main subject of others is prejudice or discrimination and their effects, often reflecting a neo-Freudian psychology. There are also studies of the Negro in the United States like those of E. Franklin Frazier and Maurice R. Davie. The typical recent text, however, contains larger or smaller amounts from each of several approaches.

The contents and approaches of these texts are disturbing to one who believes that sociology is concerned with the development of empirically-tested generalizations regarding human relationships. A course on "Minority Groups" should present, or attempt to develop, generalizations regarding "minorities." Yet, there is now no "sociology of minorities" in this sense. Nowhere in the "minority" literature can one find a systematic and comprehensive set of sociological generalizations. This lack is not so culpable, for such a set does not now exist. What surprises me is the fact that many authors do not seem to miss it. In the texts one finds many facts, most of them interesting and some of value. There are numerous hypotheses and frequent personal opinions, often stated as if they were conclusions. Preachments regarding what, or who, is

* *American Sociological Review*, Vol. 21, No. 1, February, 1956, pp. 80–83.

bad and proposals for reform are quite common. The few tested generalizations present are often hard to recognize and separate from less useful statements.

Anathema need not be pronounced on all, however. As early as 1932, Donald Young sought for generalizations within a sociological frame of reference not used again until Part II of George E. Simpson and J. Milton Yinger. Among other recent authors who have sought with varying success for some conceptual system are Brewton Berry, Charles F. Marden, Edward C. McDonagh and Eugene S. Richards, and Paul A. F. Walter. However, most of these texts, too, contain a little something for everybody: chapters on what prejudice is and what race isn't, sketches of selected minority groups, advice or proposals on how to solve "these problems." Berry and Marden, in very different ways, have been most successful perhaps in the search for sociological generalizations or uniformities of some kind.

Despite recent improvement, however, the teacher still seeks in vain for an objective, systematic, comprehensive, sustained, *sociological* analysis. A truly sociological approach to minority phenomena has been delayed, I believe, by two conditions. First, we have been preoccupied with "problems" and "what to do about them." Our zeal to change the way things now are (if only in the minds of our students) has led us to pass by the less interesting and more difficult tasks required for the slow building of research-sharpened concepts and empirically-tested generalizations. Yet just these tools are required for understanding and controlling behavior, whether or not it is "problem behavior." Secondly, sociological theory has lacked a conceptual position from which these phenomena can successfully be approached. It has been, and still is, difficult even to delimit a workable area for study.

If we would construct a "sociology of minorities," we must, therefore, do two things: approach our data with objectivity and develop a conceptual framework which is at once sociological and apt. The remainder of this paper gives my ideas on where to look and what to look for if we wish to perceive minority phenomena accurately and analyze them meaningfully. These ideas are not wholly original and are obviously hypotheses which require testing by use, both in research and in the classroom.

Prejudice and discrimination are not useful concepts for defining a sociology course, or field of research. Prejudice is a social psychological idea, which has tended to become psychiatric. Both prejudice and discrimination have value loadings which discourage objectivity. More important for our purpose, however, is the fact that persons are prejudiced against others, and discriminate against them, in many ways and for a variety of reasons which have nothing to do with "minorities."

To focus on groups of some kind certainly seems more sociological. It is deceptively simple, however, to define a minority group merely as one which is numerically smaller than another or to say that "It is certainly incontrovertible that two men can force one man to do what they want, and that ten men can do it even more easily. Given the same social organization, the larger number can always control the smaller . . ." One need only note that in Tunica County, Mississippi, Negroes compose 80 percent of the population, or that in any county the school board is smaller than the number of teachers it controls, to be reminded that in the real world of adult interaction "social organization" is rarely if ever "the same." The effect of size, including small size, on the interaction within and between groups is a valid and important sociological concern. It is not, however, what students of "minorities" have traditionally been interested in.

A group or category whose members differ from others of the same society in nationality, in culture, or in observable physical traits has been a favorite unit for study. The trouble is that the members of such groupings may or may not behave as or be treated as "minorities," depending upon the presence or absence of other factors. While the descriptive study of such groups has developed the useful and interesting sketches found in Francis J. Brown and Joseph S. Roucek and other texts, it has produced few if any tested generalizations regarding the relationships among members of different groups.

Relationships, not groups, should be the focus of attention. The concept "relationship" has some operational utility and represents the distinctively sociological level of analysis. Our task is, then, to define a particular kind of relationship, which may be called (with several reservations) the minority-dominant relationship.

Two characteristics of the relationship seem obvious: it is one between persons of unequal social power, who consequently have unequal access to the opportunities and rewards of the society. If social power is defined broadly as the ability to control the behaviors of others, then it is likely that there is some inequality of power in every relationship. In the minority-dominant relationship, however, the difference in social power is both marked and institutionalized, being rooted in fairly rigid social structures. However, the relationship between the President of the United States and any or all sociologists, or between the head football coach and his "scholarship boys," is also one of marked and institutionalized difference in social power.

The source of the difference in power provides another characteristic of the relationship. The difference arises because the individuals belong to categories between the members of which there is a certain culturally-determined pattern of reciprocal attitudes. The attitudes impute superiority to members of one category and inferiority to members of the other; and they assign roles which give members of the one more power and better access to the opportunities and rewards of the society than are available to members of the other.

But, you say, does not this describe class behavior also? And I answer that it does indeed.

It is my position that the new and growing "sociology of power" provides the general conceptual orientation for the study of minority phenomena. The power aspect of stratification is recognized, although prestige is commonly stressed. The two should be distinguished, and emphasis on the power aspect should prove fruitful for the study of the minority-dominant relationship. Stratification, viewed as structured or institutionalized power, is found in the relationships within all groups as well as in relationships between persons who belong to different categories and groups. Minority-dominant relations may be viewed as one kind of stratified relationship, a subhead under inter-class relationships.

Minority-dominant relationships may be distinguished from other inter-class relationships by two main criteria. First, the relationship springs from membership in the kind of categories called groups: "real" social groups whose members have a definite sense of belonging and well-developed "we-they" feelings. Secondly, the groups are distinguished by real or alleged differences in observable physical traits, in culture, or in both.

Physical and cultural differences do not, of themselves, create minority-dominant relationships. The differences are important as pegs upon which to hang culturally-entrenched stereotypes. The pattern of reciprocal attitudes which is a central feature of the minority-dominant relationship has four aspects: the attitudes of dominant members toward themselves and toward minority persons, and those of minority members toward themselves and toward dominant persons. The defining characteristic, without which the minority-dominant relationship does not exist, is the imputation by the majority of inherent superiority to themselves and of inherent inferiority to members of the minority group. Minority attitudes are subject to variation, at least four possibilities being readily observed. Minority persons may accept the dominant definition of the situation believing, "Yes, we are different and inferior." Some say, "Yes, we are different, but not inferior; one cannot judge such differences in this way." Perhaps the "official" and most common attitude of minority persons in the United States, is "No, we are not different; we are essentially alike in all important capacities." Finally, they may say, "We are indeed different, and superior."

To summarize, minority-dominant relationships are those which occur within a society between persons who belong to well-defined social groups whose members: (a) differ or are thought to differ in culture or observable physical characteristics; (b) respond to each other in terms of a pattern of culturally-defined reciprocal attitudes imputing inherent superiority to members of one group and inherent inferiority to members of another; and (c) have, because of membership in the groups, unequal access to the sources and instruments of institutionalized power and hence to the opportunities and rewards of the society.

Societies vary widely from each other in the nature and process of their ethnic relations. In some societies, the relative compatibility and harmony that mark racial, religious, and nationality relations stand in stark contrast to the sharp and overt conflict that characterizes others.

In the article that follows, Stanley Lieberson maintains that in order to understand these wide variations between one society and the next it is necessary to consider the conditions inherent in the intergroup contact. Assuming that ethnic groups differ in their social institutions, then contact between such groups involves the presence of different and, to an extent, incompatible social organizations. Furthermore, ethnic groups presumably differ in their capacity to impose their social order upon other ethnic groups.

On the basis of these assumptions, Professor Lieberson proposes as his major hypothesis that the intergroup cycle of phases or stages that follow from initial intergroup contacts will differ in societies where a migrant group imposes its structure on others from the cycle that develops in those societies where an indigenous group establishes its superordinance. He proceeds from this distinction to an examination of several dimensions of ethnic relations and stratification: political and economic control, multiple ethnic contacts, and conflict and assimilation.

43. A SOCIETAL THEORY OF RACE AND ETHNIC RELATIONS *

STANLEY LIEBERSON

University of Wisconsin

"In the relations of races there is a cycle of events which tends everywhere to repeat itself." Robert E. Park's assertion served as a prologue to the now classical cycle of competition, conflict, accommodation, and assimilation. A number of other attempts have been made to formulate phases or stages ensuing from the initial contacts between racial and ethnic groups. However, the sharp contrasts between relatively harmonious race relations in Brazil and Hawaii and the current racial turmoil in South Africa and Indonesia serve to illustrate the difficulty in stating—to say nothing of interpreting—an inevitable "natural history" of race and ethnic relations.

Many earlier race and ethnic cycles were, in fact, narrowly confined to a rather specific set of groups or contact situations. Emory S. Bogardus, for example, explicitly limited his synthesis to Mexican and Oriental immigrant groups on the west coast of the United States and suggested that this is but one of many different cycles of relations between immigrants and native Americans. Similarly, the Australian anthropologist A. Grenfell Price developed three phases that appear to account for the relationships between white English-speaking migrants and the aborigines of Australia, Maoris in New Zealand, and Indians of the United States and Canada.

This paper seeks to present a rudimentary theory of the development of race and ethnic relations that systematically accounts for differences between

* *American Sociological Review,* Vol. 26, No. 6, December, 1961, pp. 902–910.

societies in such divergent consequences of contact as racial nationalism and warfare, assimilation and fusion, and extinction. It postulates that the critical problem on a societal level in racial or ethnic contact is initially each population's maintenance and development of a social order compatible with its ways of life prior to contact. The crux of any cycle must, therefore, deal with political, social, and economic institutions. The emphasis given in earlier cycles to one group's dominance of another in these areas is therefore hardly surprising.

Although we accept this institutional approach, the thesis presented here is that knowledge of the nature of one group's domination over another in the political, social, and economic spheres is a necessary but insufficient prerequisite for predicting or interpreting the final and intermediate stages of racial and ethnic contact. Rather, institutional factors are considered in terms of a distinction between two major types of contact situations: contacts involving subordination of an indigenous population by a migrant group, for example, Negro-white relations in South Africa; and contacts involving subordination of a migrant population by an indigenous racial or ethnic group, for example, Japanese migrants to the United States.

After considering the societal issues inherent in racial and ethnic contact, the distinction developed between migrant and indigenous superordination will be utilized in examining each of the following dimensions of race relations: political and economic control, multiple ethnic contacts, conflict and assimilation. The terms "race" and "ethnic" are used interchangeably.

DIFFERENCES INHERENT IN CONTACT

Most situations of ethnic contact involve at least one indigenous group and at least one group migrating to the area. The only exception at the initial point in contact would be the settlement of an uninhabited area by two or more groups. By "indigenous" is meant not necessarily the aborigines, but rather a population sufficiently established in an area so as to possess the institutions and demographic capacity for maintaining some minimal form of social order through generations. Thus a given spatial area may have different indigenous groups through time. For example, the indigenous population of Australia is presently largely white and primarily of British origin, although the Tasmanoids and Australoids were once in possession of the area. A similar racial shift may be observed in the populations indigenous to the United States.

Restricting discussion to the simplest of contact situations, i.e., involving one migrant and one established population, we can generally observe sharp differences in their social organization at the time of contact. The indigenous population has an established and presumably stable organization prior to the arrival of migrants, i.e., government, economic activities adapted to the environment and the existing techniques of resource utilization, kinship, stratification, and religious systems. On the basis of a long series of migration studies, we may be reasonably certain that the social order of a migrant population's homeland is not wholly transferred to their new settlement. Migrants are required to make at least some institutional adaptations and innovations in view of the presence of an indigenous population, the demographic selectivity of migration, and differences in habitat.

For example, recent post-war migrations from Italy and the Netherlands indicate considerable selectivity in age and sex from the total populations of these countries. Nearly half of 30,000 males leaving the Netherlands in 1955 were between 20 and 39 years of age whereas only one quarter of the male population was of these ages. Similarly, over 40,000 males in this age range accounted for somewhat more than half of Italy's male emigrants in 1951, although they comprise roughly 30 percent of the male population of Italy. In both countries, male emigrants exceed females in absolute numbers as well as in comparison with the sex ratios of their nation. That these cases are far from extreme can be illustrated with Oriental migration data. In 1920, for example, there were 38,000 foreign born Chinese adult males in the United States, but only 2,000 females of the same group.

In addition to these demographic shifts, the new physical and biological conditions of existence require the revision and creation of social institutions if the social order known in the old country is to be approximated and if the migrants are to survive. The migration of eastern and southern European peasants around the turn of the century to urban industrial centers of the United States provides a well-documented case of radical changes in occupational pursuits as well as the creation of a number of institutions in response to the new conditions of urban life, e.g., mutual aid societies, national churches, and financial institutions.

In short, when two populations begin to occupy the same habitat but do not share a single order, each group endeavors to maintain the political and economic conditions that are at least compatible with the institutions existing before contact. These conditions for the maintenance of institutions cannot only differ for the two groups in contact, but are often conflicting. European contacts with the American Indian, for example, led to the decimation of the latter's sources of sustenance and disrupted religious and tribal forms of organization. With respect to a population's efforts to maintain its social institutions, we may therefore assume that the presence of another ethnic group is an important part of the environment. Further, if groups in contact differ in their capacity to impose changes on the other group, then we may expect to find one group "superordinate" and the other population "subordinate" in maintaining or developing a suitable environment.

It is here that efforts at a single cycle of race and ethnic relations must fail. For it is necessary to introduce a distinction in the nature or form of subordination before attempting to predict whether conflict or relatively harmonious assimilation will develop. As we shall shortly show, the race relations cycle in areas where the migrant group is superordinate and the indigenous group subordinate differs sharply from the stages in societies composed of a superordinate indigenous group and subordinate migrants.

POLITICAL AND ECONOMIC CONTROL

Emphasis is placed herein on economic and political dominance since it is assumed that control of these institutions will be instrumental in establishing a suitable milieu for at least the population's own social institutions, e.g., educational, religious, and kinship, as well as control of such major cultural artifacts as language.

Migrant Superordination. When the population migrating to a new contact situation is superior in technology (particularly weapons) and more tightly organized than the indigenous group, the necessary conditions for maintaining the migrants' political and economic institutions are usually imposed on the indigenous population. Warfare, under such circumstances, often occurs early in the contacts between the two groups as the migrants begin to interfere with the natives' established order. There is frequently conflict even if the initial contact was friendly. Price, for example, has observed the following consequences of white invasion and subordination of the indigenous populations of Australia, Canada, New Zealand, and the United States:

> During an opening period of pioneer invasion on moving frontiers the whites decimated the natives with their diseases; occupied their lands by seizure or by pseudo-purchase; slaughtered those who resisted; intensified tribal warfare by supplying white weapons; ridiculed and disrupted native religions, society and culture, and generally reduced the unhappy peoples to a state of despondency under which they neither desired to live, nor to have children to undergo similar conditions.[1]

The numerical decline of indigenous populations after their initial subordination to a migrant group, whether caused by warfare, introduction of venereal and other diseases, or disruption of sustenance activities, has been documented for a number of contact situations in addition to those discussed by Price.

In addition to bringing about these demographic and economic upheavals, the superordinate migrants frequently create political entities that are not at all coterminous with the boundaries existing during the indigenous populations' supremacy prior to contact. For example, the British and Boers in southern Africa carved out political states that included areas previously under the control of separate and often warring groups. Indeed, European alliances with feuding tribes were often used as a fulcrum for the territorial expansion of whites into southern Africa. The bifurcation of tribes into two nations and the migrations of groups across newly created national boundaries are both consequences of the somewhat arbitrary nature of the political entities created in

[1] A. Grenfell Price, *White Settlers and Native Peoples,* Melbourne: Georgian House, 1950, p. 1.

regions of migrant superordination. This incorporation of diverse indigenous populations into a single territorial unit under the dominance of a migrant group has considerable importance for later developments in this type of racial and ethnic contact.

Indigenous Superordination. When a population migrates to a subordinate position considerably less conflict occurs in the early stages. The movements of many European and Oriental populations to political, economic, and social subordination in the United States were not converted into warfare, nationalism, or long-term conflict. Clearly, the occasional labor and racial strife marking the history of immigration of the United States is not on the same level as the efforts to expel or revolutionize the social order. American Negroes, one of the most persistently subordinated migrant groups in the country, never responded in significant numbers to the encouragement of migration to Liberia. The single important large-scale nationalistic effort, Marcus Garvey's Universal Negro Improvement Association, never actually led to mass emigration of Negroes. By contrast, the indigenous American Indians fought long and hard to preserve control over their habitat.

In interpreting differences in the effects of migrant and indigenous subordination, the migrants must be considered in the context of the options available to the group. Irish migrants to the United States in the 1840's, for example, although clearly subordinate to native whites of other origins, fared better economically than if they had remained in their mother country. Further, the option of returning to the homeland often exists for populations migrating to subordinate situations. Harry Jerome reports that net migration to the United States between the midyears of 1907 and 1923 equalled roughly 65 percent of gross immigration. This indicates that immigrant dissatisfaction with subordination or other conditions of contact can often be resolved by withdrawal from the area. Recently subordinated indigenous groups, by contrast, are perhaps less apt to leave their habitat so readily.

Finally, when contacts between racial and ethnic groups are under the control of the indigenous population, threats of demographic and institutional imbalance are reduced since the superordinate populations can limit the numbers and groups entering. For example, when Oriental migration to the United States threatened whites, sharp cuts were executed in the quotas. Similar events may be noted with respect to the decline of immigration from the so-called "new" sources of eastern and southern Europe. Whether a group exercises its control over immigration far before it is actually under threat is, of course, not germane to the point that immigrant restriction provides a mechanism whereby potential conflict is prevented.

In summary, groups differ in the conditions necessary for maintaining their respective social orders. In areas where the migrant group is dominant, frequently the indigenous population suffers sharp numerical declines and their economic and political institutions are seriously undermined. Conflict often accompanies the establishment of migrant superordination. Subordinate indigenous populations generally have no alternative location and do not control the numbers of new ethnic populations admitted into their area. By contrast, when the indigenous population dominates the political and economic conditions, the migrant group is introduced into the economy of the indigenous population. Although subordinate in their new habitat, the migrants may fare better than if they remained in their homeland. Hence their subordination occurs without great conflict. In addition, the migrants usually have the option of returning to their homeland and the indigenous population controls the number of new immigrants in the area.

MULTIPLE ETHNIC CONTACTS

Although the introduction of a third major ethnic or racial group frequently occurs in both types of societies distinguished here, there are significant differences between conditions in habitats under indigenous domination and areas where a migrant population is superordinate. Chinese and Indian migrants, for example, were often welcomed by whites in areas where large indigenous populations were suppressed, but these migrants were restricted in the white mother country. Consideration of the causes and consequences of multi-ethnic contacts is therefore made in terms of the two types of racial and ethnic contact.

Migrant Superordination. In societies where the migrant population is superordinate, it is often necessary to introduce new immigrant groups to fill the niches created in the revised economy of the area. The subordinate indigenous population frequently fails, at first, to participate in the new economic and political order introduced by migrants. For example, because of the numerical decline of Fijians after contact with whites and their unsatisfactory work habits, approximately 60,000 persons migrated from India to the sugar plantations of Fiji under the indenture system between 1879 and 1916. For similar reasons, as well as the demise of slavery, large numbers of Indians were also introduced to such areas of indigenous subordination as Mauritius, British Guiana, Trinidad, and Natal. The descendents of these migrants comprise the largest single ethnic group in several of these areas.

McKenzie, after observing the negligible participation of the subordinated indigenous populations of Alaska, Hawaii, and Malaya in contrast to the large numbers of Chinese, Indian, and other Oriental immigrants, offers the following interpretation:

> The indigenous peoples of many of the frontier zones of modern industrialism are surrounded by their own web of culture and their own economic structure. Consequently they are slow to take part in the new economy especially as unskilled laborers. It is the individual who is widely removed from his native habitat that is most adaptable to the conditions imposed by capitalism in frontier regions. Im-

ported labor cannot so easily escape to its home village when conditions are distasteful as can the local population.[2]

Similarly, the Indians of the United States played a minor role in the new economic activities introduced by white settlers and, further, were not used successfully as slaves. E. Franklin Frazier reports that Negro slaves were utilized in the West Indies and Brazil after unsuccessful efforts to enslave the indigenous Indian populations. Large numbers of Asiastic Indians were brought to South Africa as indentured laborers to work in the railways, mines, and plantations introduced by whites.

This migration of workers into areas where the indigenous population was either unable or insufficient to work in the newly created economic activities was also marked by a considerable flow back to the home country. For example, nearly 3.5 million Indians left the Madras Presidency for overseas between 1903 and 1912, but close to 3 million returned during this same period. However, as we observed earlier, large numbers remained overseas and formed major ethnic populations in a number of countries. Current difficulties of the ten million Chinese in Southeast Asia are in large part due to their settlement in societies where the indigenous populations were subordinate.

Indigenous Superordination. We have observed that in situations of indigenous superordination the call for new immigrants from other ethnic and racial populations is limited in a manner that prevents the indigenous group's loss of political and economic control. Under such conditions, no single different ethnic or racial population is sufficiently large in number or strength to challenge the supremacy of the indigenous population.

After whites attained dominance in Hawaii, that land provided a classic case of the substitution of one ethnic group after another during a period when large numbers of immigrants were needed for the newly created and expanding plantation economy. According to Andrew W. Lind, the shifts from Chinese to Japanese and Portuguese immigrants and the later shifts to Puerto Rican, Korean, Spanish, Russian, and Philippine sources for the plantation laborers were due to conscious efforts to prevent any single group from obtaining too much power. Similarly, the exclusion of Chinese from the United States mainland stimulated the migration of the Japanese and, in turn, the later exclusion of Japanese led to increased migration from Mexico.

In brief, groups migrating to situations of multiple ethnic contact are thus subordinate in both types of contact situations. However, in societies where whites are superordinate but do not settle as an indigenous population, other racial and ethnic groups are admitted in large numbers and largely in accordance with economic needs of the revised economy of the habitat. By contrast, when a dominant migrant group later becomes indigenous, in the sense that the area becomes one of permanent settlement through generations for the

[2] R. D. McKenzie, "Cultural and Racial Differences as Bases of Human Symbiosis" in Kimball Young, editor, *Social Attitudes,* New York: Henry Holt, 1931, p. 157.

group, migrant populations from new racial and ethnic stocks are restricted in number and source.

CONFLICT AND ASSIMILATION

From a comparison of the surge of racial nationalism and open warfare in parts of Africa and Asia or the retreat of superordinate migrants from the former Dutch East Indies and French Indo-China, on the one hand, with the fusion of populations in many nations of western Europe or the "cultural pluralism" of the United States and Switzerland, on the other, one must conclude that neither conflict nor assimilation is an inevitable outcome of racial and ethnic contact. Our distinction, however, between two classes of race and ethnic relations is directly relevant to consideration of which of these alternatives different populations in contact will take. In societies where the indigenous population at the initial contact is subordinate, warfare and nationalism often —although not always—develops later in the cycle of relations. By contrast, relations between migrants and indigenous populations that are subordinate and superordinate, respectively, are generally without long-term conflict.

Migrant Superordination. Through time, the subordinated indigenous population begins to participate in the economy introduced by the migrant group and, frequently, a concomitant disruption of previous forms of social and economic organization takes place. This, in turn, has significant implications for the development of both nationalism and a greater sense of racial unity. In many African states, where Negroes were subdivided into ethnic groups prior to contact with whites, the racial unity of the African was created by the occupation of their habitat by white invaders. The categorical subordination of Africans by whites as well as the dissolution and decay of previous tribal and ethnic forms of organization are responsible for the creation of racial consciousness among the indigenous populations. As the indigenous group becomes increasingly incorporated within the larger system, both the saliency of their subordinate position and its significance increase. No alternative exists for the bulk of the native population other than the destruction or revision of the institutions of political, economic, and social subordination.

Further, it appears that considerable conflict occurs in those areas where the migrants are not simply superordinate, but where they themselves have also become, in a sense, indigenous by maintaining an established population through generations. In Table 1, for example, one can observe how sharply the white populations of Algeria and the Union of South Africa differ from those in nine other African countries with respect to the percent born in the country of settlement. Thus, two among the eleven African countries for which such data were available are outstanding with respect to both racial turmoil and the high proportion of whites born in the country. To be sure, other factors operate to influence the nature of racial and ethnic relations. However these data strongly support our suggestions with respect to the significance of differences between indigenous and migrant forms of contact. Thus where the migrant population becomes established in the new area, it is all the more difficult for the indigenous subordinate group to change the social order.

Additionally, where the formerly subordinate indigenous population has become dominant through the expulsion of the superordinate group, the situation faced by nationalities introduced to the area under earlier conditions of migrant superordination changes radically. For example, as we noted earlier, Chinese were welcomed in many parts of Southeast Asia where the newly subordinated indigenous populations were unable or unwilling to fill the economic niches created by the white invaders. However, after whites were expelled and

TABLE 1. Nativity of the White Populations of Selected African Countries, Circa 1950

Country	*Percent of Whites Born in Country*
Algeria	79.8
Basutoland	37.4
Bechuanaland	39.5
Morocco [a]	37.1 [c]
Northern Rhodesia	17.7
Southern Rhodesia	31.5
South West Africa [b]	45.1
Swaziland	41.2
Tanganyika	47.6
Uganda	43.8
Union of South Africa	89.7

Source: United Nations, *Demographic Yearbook,* 1956, Table 5.
[a] Former French zone.
[b] Excluding Walvis Bay.
[c] Persons born in former Spanish zone or in Tangier are included as native.
Note: Other non-indigenous groups included when necessary breakdown by race is not given.

the indigenous populations obtained political mastery, the gates to further Chinese immigration were fairly well closed and there has been increasing interference with the Chinese already present. In Indonesia, where Chinese immigration had been encouraged under Dutch domain, the newly created indigenous government allows only token immigration and has formulated a series of laws and measures designed to interfere with and reduce Chinese commercial activities. Thompson and Adloff observe that,

> Since the war, the Chinese have been subjected to increasingly restrictive measures throughout Southeast Asia, but the severity and effectiveness of these has varied with the degree to which the native nationalists are in control of their countries and feel their national existence threatened by the Chinese.[3]

[3] Virginia Thompson and Richard Adloff, *Minority Problems in Southeast Asia,* Stanford, California: Stanford University Press, 1955, p. 3.

Indigenous Superordination. By contrast, difficulties between subordinate migrants and an already dominant indigenous population occur within the context of a consensual form of government, economy, and social institutions. However confused and uncertain may be the concept of assimilation and its application in operational terms, it is important to note that assimilation is essentially a very different phenomenon in the two types of societies distinguished here.

Where populations migrate to situations of subordination, the issue has generally been with respect to the migrants' capacity and willingness to become an integral part of the on-going social order. For example, this has largely been the case in the United States where the issue of "new" vs. "old" immigrant groups hinged on the alleged inferiorities of the former. The occasional flurries of violence under this form of contact have been generally initiated by the dominant indigenous group and with respect to such threats against the social order as the cheap labor competition of Orientals in the west coast, the nativist fears of Irish Catholic political domination of Boston in the nineteenth century, or the desecration of sacred principles by Mexican "zoot-suiters" in Los Angeles.

The conditions faced by subordinate migrants in Australia and Canada after the creation of indigenous white societies in these areas are similar to that of the United States; that is, limited and sporadic conflict, and great emphasis on the assimilation of migrants. Striking and significant contrasts to the general pattern of subordinate immigrant assimilation in these societies, however, are provided by the differences between the assimilation of Italian and German immigrants in Australia as well as the position of French Canadians in eastern Canada.

French Canadians have maintained their language and other major cultural and social attributes whereas nineteenth and twentieth century immigrants are in process of merging into the predominantly English-speaking Canadian society. Although broader problems of territorial segregation are involved, the critical difference between French Canadians and later groups is that the former had an established society in the new habitat prior to the British conquest of Canada and were thus largely able to maintain their social and cultural unity without significant additional migration from France.

Similarly, in finding twentieth century Italian immigrants in Australia more prone to cultural assimilation than were German migrants to that nation in the 1800's, Borrie emphasized the fact that Italian migration occurred after Australia had become an independent nation-state. By contrast, Germans settled in what was a pioneer colony without an established general social order and institutions. Thus, for example, Italian children were required to attend Australian schools and learn English, whereas the German immigrants were forced to establish their own educational program.

Thus the consequences of racial and ethnic contact may also be examined in terms of the two types of superordinate-subordinate contact situations considered. For the most part, subordinate migrants appear to be more rapidly assimilated than are subordinate indigenous populations. Further, the subordinate migrant group is generally under greater pressure to assimilate, at least in the gross sense of "assimilation" such as language, than are subordinate indigenous populations. In addition, warfare or racial nationalism—when it does occur—tends to be in societies where the indigenous population is subordinate. If the indigenous movement succeeds, the economic and political position of racial and ethnic populations introduced to the area under migrant dominance may become tenuous.

A FINAL NOTE

It is suggested that interest be revived in the conditions accounting for societal variations in the process of relations between racial and ethnic groups. A societal theory of race relations, based on the migrant-indigenous and superordinate-subordinate distinctions developed above, has been found to offer an orderly interpretation of differences in the nature of race and ethnic relations in the contact situations considered. Since, however, systematic empirical investigation provides a far more rigorous test of the theory's merits and limitations, comparative cross-societal studies are needed.

Throughout the earliest years of sociological study of ethnic group relations and stratification, the key concepts—prejudice and discrimination—were assumed to refer to completely congruous and interdependent processes. Prejudice was thought to be the attitudinal aspect of intergroup hostility, comprised of an emotional component (feelings) and a cognitive component (stereotyped beliefs). Discrimination was defined as the behavioral aspect of intergroup hostility that is consequential to prejudice. Discrimination, in other words, was generally assumed to be practiced by prejudiced persons and could not be eliminated until prejudice first was removed.

More recent theory and research indicate that between privately held attitude (prejudice) and public action (discrimination), intervening factors—the situation —can influence the extent to which feeling and belief will be translated into matching action or even be repressed. Law and informal community restraints are the types of factors that can be interposed and create incongruities between attitude and behavior. It has also been pointed out that in ethnic intergroup relations, behavior typically shapes and alters attitudes contrary to the generally assumed sequence of attitude preceding and predisposing behavior. Some scholars and researchers have gone so far as to add that social situations do not intervene between behavior and attitude; rather they are the fountainhead of discrimination which in turn produces prejudiced attitudes. In the next and last article on ethnic stratification, Arnold M. Rose goes even further, suggesting that behavior and attitudes can vary independently of each other in separate and distinct processes.

44. INTERGROUP RELATIONS vs. PREJUDICE *

ARNOLD M. ROSE
University of Minnesota

The usual difference between sociologists and social psychologists in the study of race relations has been that the sociologist studies typical behavior patterns—often those of "discrimination" or "accommodation"— whereas the social psychologist studies attitudes and opinions called "prejudice" and "stereotyping," although, of course, there has never been a sharp division of labor. In recent years, there has been a tendency for these two interests to come together; both groups have come to assume that prejudice underlies discriminations, in the sense of the former being a cause of the latter. On the other hand certain authors—Robert K. Merton and George E. Simpson and J. M. Yinger, for example—have pointed out that under certain conditions prejudice and discrimination can vary independently. We shall go further and state that it may be desirable to assume that patterns of intergroup relations (including mainly discrimination and segregation) are quite distinct from attitudes of prejudice in that each has a separate and distinct history, cause, and process of change. In other words, from a heuristic standpoint it may be desirable to assume that patterns of intergroup relations, on the one hand, and attitudes of prejudice and stereotyping, on the other hand, are fairly unrelated phenomena although they have reciprocal influences on each other, as they also have in relation to seemingly extraneous phenomena, such as anxiety levels or class. Perhaps we should have been aware all along that attitudes and behaviors have an independent existence in the same individuals: there is the challenging study by Richard T. La Piere in 1934, confirmed more rigorously by Gerhart Saenger and E. Gilbert in 1950. Now there are several public opinion polls showing overwhelming proportions of various local populations against desegregation, and yet in many of the communities sampled, desegregation has proceeded apace without incident.

Let us first define terms. Race relations have to do with behavior patterns that occur in social systems—such as the caste system—which have their own historical development in the culture of a given society. Stereotyping is a universal mental tendency to subsume a large and complex category of phenomena in terms of a relatively few observations generalized to the whole category. Prejudice is a negative or positive attitude, often irrational and emotional in character, toward the stereotyped perception of a category of phenomena. Prejudice seems to take an especially virulent form when its object is an ethnic

* *Social Problems,* Vol. 4, No. 2, October, 1956, pp. 173–176.

category of people, but it has a more general frame of reference in that anything may become an object of prejudice.

Like all social systems, those affecting race relations are traditional culture patterns which are learned and adopted by new members of the society while they are becoming socialized in it. They define behavior and give it direction. They seem very stable and entirely "natural," but of course they have an origin, are subject to continual change as a result of deliberate or impersonal social forces, and are capable of disappearing entirely. Prejudice can be a mere rationalization of these social systems, but in a more significant psychological sense—the sense in which psychologists have studied the phenomenon—it is a product of individual experience and development. A whole gamut of studies have established that prejudice is an individual reaction to certain childhood and adult experiences, especially frustrations and restrictions, that are usually unrelated to people of other races. These unpleasant experiences produce a certain kind of personality, which tends to react toward its environment in a certain way, usually a combination of outward conformity and inward hostility. The outward conformity may tend to support with special vigor the established system of race relations, and the inward hostility may provide a special sharpness to a system that requires harsh interpersonal relations between members of two different ethnic groups. But this personality type—the "authoritarian personality," as the California group of psychologists calls it—has to manifest itself in this way whether there is another ethnic group around or not. Hence, it can be especially conformist toward traditional styles of housing and especially antagonistic toward modern styles of housing just as well as it can be "race prejudiced." Joseph Adelson and Patrick L. Sullivan have shown that persons scoring highest on the California prejudice scale were also found to score the highest on a misanthropy scale. It seems that the "authoritarian personality" hates not only Negroes, Jews, Orientals, and so on, but tends to hate everyone. This suggests that the California researchers have not been primarily concerned with the question that concerns sociologists working in the area of race relations: how does it come about that certain categories of people in a society—in American society these are particularly racial and cultural groups—are singled out as objects of significant discrimination?

There are, of course, alternative theories of prejudice, but they all have reference to individual psychological mechanisms. Because of this feature, I have come gradually to the opinion that race prejudice, as it has been conceptualized and studied by contemporary social psychologists, has little to do with patterns of intergroup relations in our society. The typical Southern system of intergroup relations—although it has some regional variations—is that which sociologists call "caste," or "no social equality." The typical Northern system—again with variations—is that of avoiding and ignoring the existence of Negroes. There is no evidence that the "authoritarian personality" or frustration-aggression or scapegoating, or any known source of "prejudice" in the psychological sense, is any more prevalent in the South than in the North. Yet there is a world of difference in intergroup relations as far as Negroes and whites are concerned.

Since 1940 intergroup relations in the United States have drastically changed. The key values of the systems underlying them have greatly weakened. Many white Southerners are willing to treat Negroes as equals under certain circumstances and many white Northerners have become aware of Negroes in their midst (and find it neither possible nor desirable to exclude them from their group activities). If present trends continue, the two typical systems of Negro-white relationships will disappear within a generation or two (although some of the slower moving effects will remain for centuries, such as tending to marry within the groups, weak traditions of Negroes in business, etc.). But there is little in the American way of life to diminish, at a corresponding rate, frustration and the "authoritarian personality." Prejudice will remain at approximately its present level of virulence, although it seems likely to have to find other objects.

Certain attitudes accompany a given system of intergroup relations, of course, but they are not central in the psychological study of prejudice. Among the typical white person's attitudes associated with the caste system of the South have been: (a) a belief that the Negro is biologically inferior to the white man and therefore incapable of having the white man's culture and emotional refinement; (b) a belief that the Negro is "all right in his place"—that is, Negroes are socially moral and decent if they are willing to accept a socially inferior position; (c) a belief that Negroes have special capacities for humor, fun, and sex; (d) a belief that Negroes are unreliable, shiftless, and untrustworthy; and so on. It is to be noted that not all of these attitudes or beliefs are negative; some of them are as positive as corresponding attitudes are toward dogs or children. They of course include stereotypes, but—as we have already noted—all human beliefs and attitudes are stereotyped except those based on intimate knowledge (such as a scientist has for his science or as family members have for each other). These attitudes seem to have developed in the United States around the beginning of the 19th century to justify and rationalize a revitalized economy based on slavery; while slavery had long been in existence at this time, these particular attitudes did not develop until slavery became very important for the economy and politics of the South and until there was a strong world-wide movement to abolish slavery. The use of these attitudes accompanied a change in the social structure and a change in ideology; they did not accompany a change in white children's experience with their family members or with other frustrations.

The conditions which led to the development of the caste system in the 19th century are no longer with us. The prosperity and political power of the South are no longer based on a large mass of cheap, unskilled labor engaged in the extremely unpleasant task of cotton growing. New forces have arisen which make the caste system increasingly less desirable and useful to the dominant white group in the South or any other section of the country: these include industrialization and automation, the leadership of the United States in the affairs of the free Western world, rising educational levels among both whites and Negroes, changed patterns of roles between the sexes among whites, and so on. These changes—both negative and positive—have made a mere hollow shell of tradition. The leaders of our nation—in the judicial, the executive, and even the legislative branches of the government, as well as in big business, big labor, and big publicity—have become at least vaguely aware of these changes, and have contributed to the dismantling of the elaborate caste system. Prejudice, stereotyping, and other attitudes arising from an authoritarian upbringing, frustration, free-floating anxiety, and so on, are undoubtedly tending to buttress the shell of caste that remains. But the latter attitudes are seemingly not declining as the walls come tumbling down; rather, they are being transferred to new objects and they have new manifestations. Some people, especially in the Deep South, are keeping their authoritarian attitudes and fears focused on changes in race relations, but these seem to be a minority even within the South. In a border city like Kansas City, Martin Loeb tells us, "when the law, either economic or constitutional, is firmly laid down they go along with it almost gratefully." It is important to know what changes of attitudes and other psychological adjustments are accompanying desegregation. This is useful so that anxieties can be reduced, and satisfaction increased. But it does not seem to be important for understanding the broad process of social change, or for engaging in social action to effect change. No study of prejudice, using any definition or any theory, helps us much in understanding or predicting what is going on in the desegregation process today. The explanation is apparently to be looked for in terms of legal, economic, political, and social structural forces.

Thus, prejudice has little to do with intergroup relations. They have to fit into each other at a given period of history, because some of the same people carry them both. But the laws of change—of origin, development and decay—which govern one are independent of those governing the other. One is sociogenic and the other psychogenic, and while they may both inhabit the same individual at a given time, they also may not. The study of their interrelationships is interesting, but the study of each one separately is much more important for the understanding and prediction of human behavior. Both are worthy of study in their own right.

It is frequently valuable for individuals from two or more disciplines to work together on common problems; this is true in the area of race relations. But theories and lines of research should not be determined by the fact that the investigators are being interdisciplinary. The development of theory should be guided by the nature of the research problem. If it happens that one given research problem calls for theory associated with one discipline, this should not be a cause for alarm to another discipline, for the latter will be in a better position to develop theories for other research problems of common interest. There are undoubted advantages to interdisciplinary, cooperative research, but there are sometimes also advantages to division of labor, to the cultivation of one's own specialized garden. For the scientist, the problem must remain paramount, and any aspect of method or the social relations of the scientists must be subordinated to the problem.

POWER

Throughout these readings on social stratification in Part IV, we have studied the pervasive influence of power relations, whether it be the upper caste or class in their relationships with lower castes and classes or the dominant ethnic group in its interaction with racial, religious, or nationality minorities.

In the last reading of this section, quite appropriately, we have one of the first modern attempts to take this important but not entirely clear concept of social power and subject it to incisive sociological analysis. Robert Bierstedt poses the five following strategic propositions: (1) power is a social phenomenon to a greater degree than it is political or economic; (2) it is distinguishable from prestige, influence, dominance, rights, force, and authority; (3) it is most closely related to force and authority; (4) it expresses itself differently in formal organization than it does in informal organization and the unorganized community; and finally, (5) the necessary components of power reside in a combination of numbers, social organization, and resources.

45. AN ANALYSIS OF SOCIAL POWER *

ROBERT BIERSTEDT
New York University

Few problems in sociology are more perplexing than the problem of social power. In the entire lexicon of sociological concepts none is more troublesome than the concept of power. We may say about it in general only what St. Augustine said about time, that we all know perfectly well what it is—until someone asks us. Indeed, Robert M. MacIver has recently been induced to remark that "There is no reasonably adequate study of the nature of social power." The present paper cannot, of course, pretend to be a "reasonably adequate study." It aims at reasonableness rather than adequacy and attempts to articulate the problem as one of central sociological concern, to clarify the meaning of the concept, and to discover the locus and seek the sources of social power itself.

The power structure of society is not an insignificant problem. In any realistic sense it is both a sociological (*i.e.*, a scientific) and a social (*i.e.*, a

* *American Sociological Review,* Vol. 15, No. 6, December, 1950, pp. 730–738.

moral) problem. It has traditionally been a problem in political philosophy. But, like so many other problems of a political character, it has roots which lie deeper than the *polis* and reach into the community itself. It has ramifications which can be discerned only in a more generalized kind of inquiry than is offered by political theory and which can ultimately be approached only by sociology. Its primitive basis and ultimate locus, as MacIver has emphasized in several of his distinguished books, are to be sought in community and in society, not in government or in the state. It is apparent, furthermore, that not all power is political power and that political power—like economic, financial, industrial, and military power—is only one of several and various kinds of social power. Society itself is shot through with power relations—the power a father exercises over his minor child, a master over his slave, a teacher over his pupils, the victor over the vanquished, the blackmailer over his victim, the warden over his prisoners, the attorney over his own and opposing witnesses, an employer over his employee, a general over his lieutenants, a captain over his crew, a creditor over a debtor, and so on through most of the status relationships of society. Power, in short, is a universal phenomenon in human societies and in all social relationships. It is never wholly absent from social interaction, except perhaps in the primary group where "personal identification" (Hiller) is complete and in those relations of "polite acquaintance" (Simmel) which are "social" in the narrowest sense. All other social relations contain components of power. What, then, is this phenomenon?

Social power has variously been identified with prestige, with influence, with eminence, with competence or ability, with knowledge (Bacon), with dominance, with rights, with force, and with authority. Since the intension of a term varies, if at all, inversely with its extension—*i.e.,* since the more things a term can be applied to the less precise its meaning—it would seem to be desirable to distinguish power from some at least of these other concepts. Let us first distinguish power from prestige.

The closest association between power and prestige has perhaps been made by E. A. Ross in his classic work on social control. "The immediate cause of the location of power," says Ross, "is prestige." And further, "The class that has the most prestige will have the most power." Now prestige may certainly be construed as one of the sources of social power and as one of the most significant of all the factors which separate man from man and group from group. It is a factor which has as one of its consequences the complex stratification of modern societies, to say nothing of the partial stratification of non-literate societies where the chief and the priest and the medicine-man occupy prestigious positions. But prestige should not be identified with power. They are independent variables. Prestige is frequently unaccompanied by power and when the two occur together power is usually the basis and ground of prestige rather than the reverse. Prestige would seem to be a consequence of power rather than a determinant of it or a necessary component of it. In any event, it is not difficult to illustrate the fact that power and prestige are independent variables, that power can occur without prestige, and prestige without power. Albert Einstein, for example, has prestige but no power in any significant sociological sense of the word. A policeman has power, but little prestige. Similarly, on the group level, the Phi Beta Kappa Society has considerable prestige—more outside academic circles than inside, to be sure —but no power. The Communist Party in the United States has a modicum of power, if not the amount so extravagantly attributed to it by certain Senators, but no prestige. The Society of Friends again has prestige but little power.

Similar observations may be made about the relations of knowledge, skill, competence, ability, and eminence to power. They are all components of, sources of, or synonyms of prestige, but they may be quite unaccompanied by power. When power does accompany them the association is incidental rather than necessary. For these reasons it seems desirable to maintain a distinction between prestige and power.

When we turn to the relationship between influence and power we find a still more intimate connection but, for reasons which possess considerable cogency, it seems desirable also to maintain a distinction between influence and power. The most important reason, perhaps, is that influence is persuasive while power is coercive. We submit voluntarily to influence while power requires submission. The mistress of a king may influence the destiny of a nation, but only because her paramour permits himself to be swayed by her designs. In any ultimate reckoning her influence may be more important than his power, but it is inefficacious unless it is transformed into power. The power a teacher exercises over his pupils stems not from his superior knowledge (this is competence rather than power) and not from his opinions (this is influence rather than power), but from his ability to apply the sanction of failure, *i.e.,* to withhold academic credit, to the student who does not fulfill his requirements and meet his standards. The competence may be unappreciated and the influence may be ineffective, but the power may not be gainsaid.

Furthermore, influence and power can occur in relative isolation from each other and so also are relatively independent variables. We should say, for example, that Karl Marx has exerted an incalculable influence upon the twentieth century, but this poverty-stricken exile who spent so many of his hours immured in the British Museum was hardly a man of power. Even the assertion that he was a man of influence is an ellipsis. It is the ideas which are influential, not the man. Stalin, on the other hand, is a man of influence only because he is first a man of power. Influence does not require power, and power may dispense with influence. Influence may convert a friend, but power coerces friend and foe alike. Influence attaches to an idea, a doctrine, or a creed, and has its locus in the ideological sphere. Power attaches to a person, a group, or an association, and has its locus in the sociological sphere. Plato, Aristotle, St. Thomas, Shakespeare, Galileo, Newton, and Kant were men of influence, although all of them were quite devoid of power. Napoleon Bonaparte and Abraham Lincoln were men of both power and influence. Genghis Khan and Adolf Hitler were men of power. Archimedes was a man of influence, but the soldier who slew him at the storming of Syracuse had no power. It is this distinction which gives point to Spengler's otherwise absurd contention that this nameless soldier had a greater impact upon the course of history than the great classical physicist.

When we speak, therefore, of the power of an idea or when we are tempted to say that ideas are weapons or when we assert, with the above-mentioned Bonaparte, that the pen is mightier than the sword, we are using figurative language, speaking truly as it were, but metaphorically and with synecdoche. Ideas are influential, they may alter the process of history, but for the sake of logical and sociological clarity it is preferable to deny to them the attribute of power. Influence in this sense, of course, presents quite as serious and as complex a problem as power, but it is not the problem whose analysis we are here pursuing.

It is relatively easy to distinguish power from dominance. Power is a sociological, dominance a psychological concept. The locus of power is in groups and it expresses itself in inter-group relations; the locus of dominance is in the individual and it expresses itself in inter-personal relations. Power appears in the statuses which people occupy in formal organization; dominance in the roles they play in informal organization. Power is a function of the organization of associations, of the arrangement and juxtaposition of groups, and of the structure of society itself. Dominance, on the other hand, is a function of personality or of temperament; it is a personal trait. Dominant individuals play roles in powerless groups; submissive individuals in powerful ones. Some groups acquire an inordinate power, especially in the political sense, because there are so many submissive individuals who are easily persuaded to join them and who meekly conform to the norms which membership imposes. As an example, one need mention only the growth of the National Socialist Party in Germany. Dominance, therefore, is a problem in social psychology; power a problem in sociology.

It is a little more difficult to distinguish power from "rights" only because the latter term is itself so ambiguous. It appears indeed in two senses which are exactly contradictory—as those privileges and only those which are secured by the state and as those which the state may not invade even to secure. We do not need to pursue the distinctions between various kinds of rights, including "natural rights," which are elaborated in the history of jurisprudence and the sociology of law to recognize that a right always requires some support in the social structure, although not always in the laws, and that rights in general, like privileges, duties, obligations, responsibilities, perquisites, and prerogatives, are attached to statuses both in society itself and in the separate associations of society. One may have a right without the power to exercise it, but in most cases power of some kind supports whatever rights are claimed. Rights are more closely associated with privileges and with authority than they are with power. A "right," like a privilege, is one of the perquisites of power and not power itself.

We have now distinguished power from prestige, from influence, from dominance, and from rights, and have left the two concepts of force and authority. And here we may have a solution to our problem. Power is not force and power is not authority, but it is intimately related to both and may be defined in terms of them. We want therefore to propose three definitions and then to examine their implications: (1) power is latent force; (2) force is manifest power; and (3) authority is institutionalized power. The first two of these propositions may be considered together. They look, of course, like circular definitions and, as a matter of fact, they are. If an independent meaning can be found for one of these concepts, however, the other may be defined in terms of it and the circularity will disappear. We may therefore suggest an independent definition of the concept of force. Force, in any significant sociological sense of the word, means the application of sanctions. Force, again in the sociological sense, means the reduction or limitation or closure or even total elimination of alternatives to the social action of one person or group by another person or group. "Your money or your life" symbolizes a situation of naked force, the reduction of alternatives to two. The execution of a sentence to hang represents the total elimination of alternatives. One army progressively limits the social action of another until only two alternatives remain for the unsuccessful contender—to surrender or die. Dismissal or demotion of personnel in an association similarly, if much less drastically, represents a closure of alternatives. Now all these are situations of force, or manifest power. Power itself is the predisposition or prior capacity which makes the application of force possible. Only groups which have power can threaten to use force and the threat itself is power. Power is the ability to employ force, not its actual employment, the ability to apply sanctions, not their actual application. Power is the ability to introduce force into a social situation; it is the presentation of force. Unlike force, incidentally, power is always successful; when it is not successful it is not, or ceases to be, power. Power symbolizes the force which *may* be applied in any social situation and supports the authority which *is* applied. Power is thus neither force nor authority but, in a sense, their synthesis.

The implications of these propositions will become clearer if we now discuss the locus of power in society. We may discover it in three areas, (1) in formal organization, (2) in informal organization, and (3) in the unorganized community. The first of these presents a fairly simple problem for analysis. It is in the formal organization of associations that social power is transformed into authority. When social action and interaction proceed wholly in conformity to the norms of the formal organization, power is dissolved without residue into authority. The right to use force is then attached to certain statuses within the association, and this right is what we ordinarily mean by authority. It is thus authority in virtue of which persons in an association exercise command or control over other persons in the same association. It is authority which enables a bishop to transfer a priest from his parish, a priest with his "power of the keys" to absolve a sinner, a commanding officer to assign a post of duty to a subordinate officer, a vice-president to dictate a letter to his secretary, the manager of a baseball team to change his pitcher in the middle of an inning, a factory superintendent to demand that a certain job be completed at a specified time, a policeman to arrest a citizen who has violated a law, and so on through endless examples. Power in these cases is attached to statuses, not to persons, and is wholly institutionalized as authority.

In rigidly organized groups this authority is clearly specified and formally articulated by the norms (rules, statutes, laws) of the association. In less rigidly organized groups penumbral areas appear in which authority is less clearly specified and articulated. Sometimes authority clearly vested in an associational status may not be exercised because it conflicts with a moral norm to which both members and non-members of the association adhere in the surrounding community. Sometimes an official may remove a subordinate from office without formal cause and without formal authority because such action, now involving power, finds support in public opinion. Sometimes, on the contrary, he may have the authority to discharge a subordinate, but not the power, because the position of the latter is supported informally and "extra-associationally" by the opinion of the community. An extreme case of this situation is exemplified by the inability of the general manager, Ed Barrow, or even the owner, Colonel Jacob Ruppert, to "fire" Babe Ruth from the New York Yankees or even, when the Babe was at the height of his fame, to trade him.

Sometimes these power relations become quite complicated. In a university organization, for example, it may not be clear whether a dean has the authority to apply the sanction of dismissal to a professor, or, more subtly, whether he has the authority to abstain from offering an increase in salary to a professor in order indirectly to encourage him to leave, or, still more subtly, whether, when he clearly has this authority of abstention, he will be accused of maladministration if he exercises it. It is similarly unclear whether a Bishop of the Episcopal Church has the authority to remove a rector from his parish when the latter apparently has the support of his parishioners. In other words, it sometimes comes to be a matter of unwise policy for an official to exercise the authority which is specifically vested in his position, and it is in these cases that we can clearly see power leaking into the joints of associational structure and invading the formal organization.

It may be observed that the power implied in the exercise of authority does not necessarily convey a connotation of personal superiority. Leo Durocher is not a better pitcher than the player he removes nor, in turn, is he inferior to the umpire who banishes him from the game. A professor may be a "better" scholar and teacher than the dean who dismisses him, a lawyer more learned in the law than the judge who cites him for contempt, a worker a more competent electrician than the foreman who assigns his duties, and so on through thousands of examples. As MacIver has written, "The man who commands may be no wiser, no abler, may be in no sense better than the average of his fellows; sometimes, by any intrinsic standard he is inferior to them. Here is the magic of government." Here indeed is the magic of all social organization.

Social action, as is well known, does not proceed in precise or in absolute conformity to the norms of formal organization. Power spills over the vessels of status which only imperfectly contain it as authority. We arrive, therefore, at a short consideration of informal organization, in which the prestige of statuses gives way to the esteem for persons and in which the social interaction of the members proceeds not only in terms of the explicit norms of the association but also in terms of implicit extra-associational norms whose locus is in the community and which may or may not conflict, at strategic points, with the associational norms. Our previous examples have helped us to anticipate what we have to say about the incidence and practice of power in informal organization. No association is wholly formal, not even the most rigidly organized. Social organization makes possible the orderly social intercourse of people who do not know each other—the crew of a ship and their new captain, the faculty of a university department and a new chairman, the manager of a baseball team and his new recruit, the citizen and the tax collector, the housewife and the plumber, the customer and the clerk. But in any association the members do become acquainted with each other and begin to interact not only "extrinsically" and "categorically," in terms of the statuses they occupy, but also "intrinsically" and "personally," in terms of the roles they play and the personalities they exhibit. Sub-groups arise and begin to exert subtle pressures upon the organization itself, upon the norms which may be breached in the observance thereof, and upon the authority which, however firmly institutionalized, is yet subject to change. These sub-groups may, as cliques and factions, remain within the association or, as sects and splinter groups, break away from it. In any event, no formal organization can remain wholly formal under the exigencies of time and circumstance. Power is seldom completely institutionalized as authority, and then no more than momentarily. If power sustains the structure, opposing power threatens it, and every association is always at the mercy of a majority of its own members. In all associations the power of people acting in concert is so great that the prohibition against "combinations" appears in the statutes of all military organizations and the right of collective petition is denied to all military personnel.

Power appears, then, in associations in two forms, institutionalized as authority in the formal organization and uninstitutionalized as power itself in the informal organization. But this does not exhaust the incidence of power with respect to the associations of society. It must be evident that power is required to inaugurate an association in the first place, to guarantee its continuance, and to enforce its norms. Power supports the fundamental order of society and the social organization within it, wherever there is order. Power stands behind every association and sustains its structure. Without power there is no organization and without power there is no order. The intrusion of the time dimension and the exigencies of circumstance require continual re-adjustments of the structure of every association, not excepting the most inelastically organized, and it is power which sustains it through these transitions. If power provides the initial impetus behind the organization of every association, it also supplies the stability which it maintains throughout its history. Authority itself cannot exist without the immediate support of power and the ultimate sanction of force.

As important as power is, however, as a factor in both the formal and informal organization of associations, it is even more important where it reigns, uninstitutionalized, in the interstices between associations and has its locus in the community itself. Here we find the principal social issues of contemporary society—labor vs. capital, Protestant vs. Catholic, CIO vs. AFL, AMA vs. FSA, Hiss vs. Chambers (for this was not a conflict between individuals), Republican vs. Democrat, the regents of the University of California vs. the faculty, Russia vs. the United States, and countless others throughout the entire fabric of society. It is not the task of our present analysis to examine these conflicts in detail but rather to investigate the role of power wherever it appears. And here we have two logical possibilities—power in the relations of like groups and power in the relations of unlike groups. Examples of the former are commercial companies competing for the same market, fraternal organizations of the same kind competing for members, religious associations competing for adherents, newspapers competing for readers, construction companies bidding for the same contracts, political parties competing for votes, and so on through all the competitive situations of society. Examples of the latter are conflicts between organized labor and organized management, between the legislative and executive branches of government, between different sub-divisions of the same bureaucracy (*e.g.,* Army vs. Navy), between university boards of trustees and an association of university professors, and so on through an equally large number of instances. Power thus appears both in competition and in conflict and has no incidence in groups which neither compete nor conflict, *i.e.,* between groups which do not share a similar social matrix and have no social relations, as for example the American Council of Learned Societies and the American Federation of Labor. Power thus arises only in social opposition of some kind.

It is no accident that the noun "power" has been hypostatized from the adjective "potential." It may seem redundant to say so, but power is always potential; that is, when it is used it becomes something else, either force or authority. This is the respect which gives meaning, for example, to the concept of a "fleet in being" in naval strategy. A fleet in being represents power, even though it is never used. When it goes into action, of course, it is no longer power, but force. It is for this reason that the Allies were willing to destroy the battleship *Richelieu,* berthed at Dakar, after the fall of France, at the price of courting the disfavor of the French. Indeed, the young officer attending his introductory lectures on naval strategy, is sometimes surprised to hear what he may consider an excessive and possibly even a perverse emphasis upon the phrase, "Protect the battleships." Why should the battleship, the mightiest engine of destruction afloat, require such care in assuring its protection with sufficient crusier, destroyer, and air support? The answer is that a battleship is even more effective as a symbol of power than it is as an instrument of force.

If power is one of the imperatives of society it may also be partly a pretense and succeed only because it is inaccurately estimated, or unchallenged. This, of course, is a familiar stratagem in war. But it occurs in the majority of power relationships in society. The threat of a strike may succeed when the strike will not. Blackmail may have consequences more dire than the exposure of the secret. The threat of a minority to withdraw from an association may affect it more than an actual withdrawal. The threat of a boycott may achieve the result desired when the boycott itself would fail. As an example of this last, movie exhibitors sometimes discover that if they ignore a ban imposed upon a picture by a religious censor, the ban not only does not diminish the attendance figures but increases them. In poker parlance—and indeed it is precisely the same phenomenon—a "bluff" is powerful, but the power vanishes when the bluff is called.

We may, in a comparatively brief conclusion, attempt to locate the sources of power. Power would seem to stem from three sources: (1) numbers of people, (2) social organization, and (3) resources. In a previous paper we have discussed in some detail the role of majorities in both unorganized and organized social groups, and in both the formal and informal aspects of the latter, and arrived at the conclusion, among others, that majorities constitute a residual locus of social power. It is neither necessary nor desirable to review this proposition here, beyond reiterating an emphasis upon the power which resides in numbers. Given the same social organization and the same resources, the larger number can always control the smaller and secure its compliance. If majorities, particularly economic and political majorities, have frequently and for long historical periods suffered oppression, it is because they have not been organized or have lacked resources. The power which resides in numbers is clearly seen in elections of all kinds, where the majority is conceded the right to institutionalize its power as authority—a right which is conceded because it can be taken. This power appears in all associations, even the most autocratic. It is the power of a majority, even in the most formally and inflexibly organized associations, which either threatens or sustains the stability of the associational structure.

As important as numbers are as the primary source of social power, they do not in themselves suffice. As suggested above, majorities may suffer oppression for long historical periods, they may, in short, be powerless or possess only the residual power of inertia. We arrive therefore at the second source of social power—social organization. A well organized and disciplined body of marines or of police can control a much larger number of unorganized individuals.

An organized minority can control an unorganized majority. But even here majorities possess so much residual power that there are limits beyond which this kind of control cannot be exercised. These limits appear with the recognition that the majority may organize and thus reverse the control. And an organized majority, as suggested in the paper previously referred to, is the most potent social force on earth.

Of two groups, however, equal or nearly equal in numbers and comparable in organization, the one with access to the greater resources will have the superior power. And so resources constitute the third source of social power. Resources may be of many kinds—money, property, prestige, knowledge, competence, deceit, fraud, secrecy, and, of course, all of the things usually included under the term "natural resources." There are also supernatural resources in the case of religious associations which, as agencies of a celestial government, apply supernatural sanctions as instruments of control. In other words, most of the things we have previously differentiated from power itself may now be re-introduced as among the sources of power. It is easily apparent that, in any power conflict, they can tip the balance when the other sources of power are relatively equal and comparable. But they are not themselves power. Unless utilized by people who are in organized association with one another they are quite devoid of sociological significance.

As a matter of fact, no one of these sources in itself constitutes power, nor does any one of them in combination with either of the others. Power appears only in the combination of all three—numbers, organization, and resources.

It may finally be of more than incidental interest to note that there is one, and only one, kind of social situation in which the power of opposing groups is completely balanced. The numbers on each "side" are equal, their social organization is identical, and their resources are as nearly the same as possible. This situation reveals itself in games and contests in which power components are cancelled out and the victory goes to the superior skill. Whether the game be baseball or bridge there is insistence, inherent in the structure of the game itself, upon an equalization of power and this is the universal characteristic of all sports and the basis of the conception "fair play." It would be foolish, of course, to assert that resources are always equal. The New York Yankees, for example, have financial resources which are not available to the St. Louis Browns and one bridge partnership may have better cards than its opponent. But such inequalities excite disapproval because they deny the nature of sport. The franchise of the Browns may be transferred from St. Louis for this reason, and tournament bridge is duplicate bridge so that all teams will play the same hands. When resources cannot be equalized, the situation ceases to be a game and sentiment supports the "underdog." We thus have here a most familiar but nevertheless peculiar power situation, one in which power is so balanced as to be irrelevant. Sport may be a moral equivalent for war, as William James wanted to believe, but it can never be a sociological equivalent. The two situations are only superficially similar. The difference between a conflict and a contest is that the former is a power phenomenon and the latter is not.

In this paper we have taken a somewhat vague and ambiguous concept, the concept of social power, and have attempted to sharpen the edges of its meaning. Among the proposals offered, the following may serve as a summary: (1) power is a social phenomenon *par excellence,* and not merely a political or economic phenomenon; (2) it is useful to distinguish power from prestige, from influence, from dominance, from rights, from force, and from authority; (3) power is latent force, force is manifest power, and authority is institutionalized power; (4) power, which has its incidence only in social opposition of some kind, appears in different ways in formal organization, in informal organization, and in the unorganized community; and (5) the sources and necessary components of power reside in a combination of numbers (especially majorities), social organization, and resources. All of these are preliminary and even primitive propositions. All of them require additional analysis.

SELECTED SUPPLEMENTARY READINGS FOR PART IV

Barron, Milton L. (ed.), *American Minorities* (New York: Alfred A. Knopf, 1957).

Bendix, Reinhard, and Lipset, Seymour (eds.), *Class, Status, and Power* (Chicago: The Free Press, 1953).

Francis, E. K., "The Nature of the Ethnic Group," *The American Journal of Sociology,* Vol. LII, No. 5, March, 1947, pp. 393–400.

Hatt, Paul K., "Occupation and Social Stratification," *The American Journal of Sociology,* Vol. LV, No. 6, May, 1950, pp. 533–543.

Hunter, Floyd, *Community Power Structure* (Chapel Hill, N.C.: University of North Carolina Press, 1953).

Mills, C. Wright, *The Power Elite* (New York: Oxford University Press, 1956).

Myrdal, Gunnar, *An American Dilemma* (New York, Harper & Row, rev. ed., 1962).

Sjoberg, Gideon, "Are Social Classes in America Becoming More Rigid?" *American Sociological Review,* Vol. 16, No. 6, December, 1951, pp. 775–783.

Veblen, Thorstein, *The Theory of the Leisure Class* (New York: Modern Library, 1934).

Warner, W. Lloyd, Meeker, Marchia, and Eells, Kenneth, *Social Class in America* (Chicago: Science Research Associates, 1949).

PART FIVE

Methodology in Sociological Research

INTRODUCTION

Having explored the conceptual outline of sociology, we now turn to the ways and means by which the contemporary sociologist, curious about some aspect of social behavior, seeks to solve the problem and obtain a valid and reliable answer. Our concern is with methodology in sociological research. Man has used the following eight basic methods throughout history to satisfy his curiosity and obtain knowledge about phenomena, sociological or otherwise:

1. Appeal to the supernatural
2. Chance or accident
3. Intuition
4. Appeal to authority
5. Logic
6. Common sense
7. Trial and error
8. Science

Two observations can be made about this list of knowledge-seeking methods. First of all, they are not mutually exclusive. For instance, the biological scientist in his laboratory may use common sense, logic, accident, trial and error, and intuition as well as science in order to find his answers. Second, most of these methods may succeed, but the important point to keep in mind is that the only reliable one is the scientific method. It is for this reason that since the nineteenth century, and with heightened efforts since World War II, sociology has sought to develop and utilize research techniques that are more or less in conformity with the scientific method.

By the scientific method we do not mean the specific procedures of any particular bloc of science, such as the natural sciences. While it is true that the techniques of each science vary in accordance with the particular phenomena and the most feasible style of operation in exploring them, the method is fundamentally common to all.

The scientific method, to begin with, calls for a point of view: the systematic doubt of anything lacking proof, and suspicion of dogmatism. Science is dynamic because it is self-correcting. Niels Bohr, a physicist and one of the most reputable scientists of this century, frequently told his students: "Every sentence I utter must be understood not as an affirmation, but as a question. Truth is something that we can attempt to doubt, and then perhaps, after much exertion, discover that part of the doubt is not justified." One day when an experiment took a totally unexpected turn, he told a group: "How wonderful we have met this paradox! Now we have some hope of making progress."

The two distinguishing assumptions of research guided by the scientific method are:

1. The universe is an orderly cosmos in which there are no results without causes. Uniformities and regularities are discoverable in all phenomena; therefore, a natural explanation can be found for every observable phenomenon.

2. Uniformities can be learned through systematic observation, thought, and verification. Conclusions are invalid unless they are supported by the evidence of fact.

The scientific method demands the systematic description of observed events under controlled conditions in such a way that the procedure may be repeated by others. It calls for the observation of relations between classes of phenomena, generalizing whenever possible about these relationships, and testing these generalizations with the expectation that they may have to be rejected or revised. In short, the fundamental processes of the scientific method are observation, description, induction, and deduction.

One basic way the scientific method differs from the everyday process of observation and common-sense knowledge is in making the observations as trustworthy as possible with regard to objectivity and representativeness. The scientist publicizes the procedural steps by which he tests and arrives at generalizations. He records what he sees, not what he wants to see; and he writes it in such a form that other observers can verify his findings. Without verification, the scientific method would be nonexistent.

Science, it has often been stressed, goes with the method, not with the subject matter or the results. In that sense, sociology can be scientific. Emile Durkheim, the eminent French sociologist who is credited with much of the scientific orientation that contemporary sociology has taken, insisted that the social realm, no less than any other, is a "natural realm which differs from the others only by a greater complexity. Now it is impossible that nature should differ radically from itself in one case and the other in regard to which is most essential. The fundamental relations that exist between things cannot be essentially dissimilar in the different realms."

The zeal of sociologists in their subscription to the scientific method in recent years provoked one anonymous bystander to observe, not without a degree of skepticism and sarcasm, that a sociologist is a man who sends one of his sons to Sunday School every week and keeps the other son home as a control group.

Whatever else this humorous comment conveys, it tells us that at least some sociologists appreciate that in sociological research design, as in all scientific endeavor, the ideal model is that of a controlled experiment.

In the first reading on sociological methodology that follows, Samuel A. Stouffer deplores the fact that quick, plausible answers in sociology are rewarded, whereas the tedious, modest experimental design is not in demand. He suggests that since full experimental design is very expensive, and not always possible, problems should be selected whose answers are worth the cost. This requires both theory, which leads to operational deductions, and preliminary fumbling research whose intrinsic wastefulness can be reduced if the number of variables is kept down to manageable limits and if such variables are unidimensional.

46. SOME OBSERVATIONS ON STUDY DESIGN *

SAMUEL A. STOUFFER
Harvard University

As a youth I read a series of vigorous essays in the *Century Magazine* by its editor, the late Glenn Frank. His theme was that the natural sciences had remade the face of the earth; now had arrived the age of the social sciences. The same techniques which had worked their miracles in physics, chemistry, and biology should, in competent hands, achieve equally dazzling miracles in economics, political science, and sociology. That was a long time ago. The disconcerting fact is that people are writing essays just like that today. Of course, the last two decades have seen considerable progress in social science—in theory, in technique, and in the accumulation of data. It is true that the number of practitioners is pitifully few; only a few hundred research studies are reported annually in sociology, for example, as compared with more than twenty thousand studies summarized annually in *Biological Abstracts.* But the bright promise of the period when Frank was writing has not been fulfilled.

Two of the most common reasons alleged for slow progress are cogent, indeed.

The data of social science are awfully complex, it is said. And they involve values which sometimes put a strain on the objectivity of the investigator even when they do not incur resistance from the vested interests of our society. However, an important part of the trouble has very little to do with the subject matter of social science as such but, rather, is a product of our own bad work habits. That is why this paper on the subject of study design may be relevant. So much has been spoken and written on this topic that I make no pretense to originality. But in the course of a little experience, especially in an effort during the war to apply social psychology to military problems, and in

* *The American Journal of Sociology,* Vol. LV, No. 4, January, 1950, pp. 355–361.

an undertaking to nurture a new program of research in my university, I have encountered some frustrations which perhaps can be examined with profit.

A basic problem—perhaps *the* basic problem—lies deeply imbedded in the thoughtways of our culture. This is the implicit assumption that anybody with a little common sense and a few facts can come up at once with the correct answer on any subject. Thus the newspaper editor or columnist, faced with a column of empty space to fill with readable English in an hour, can speak with finality and authority on any social topic, however complex. He might not attempt to diagnose what is wrong with his sick cat; he would call a veterinarian. But he knows precisely what is wrong with any social institution and the remedies.

In a society which rewards quick and confident answers and does not worry about how the answers are arrived at, the social scientist is hardly to be blamed if he conforms to the norms. Hence, much social science is merely rather dull and obscure journalism; a few data and a lot of "interpretation." The fact that the so-called "interpretation" bears little or no relation to the data is often obscured by academic jargon. If the stuff is hard to read, it has a chance of being acclaimed as profound. The rewards are for the answers, however tediously expressed, and not for rigorously marshaled evidence.

In the army no one would think of adopting a new type of weapon without trying it out exhaustively on the firing range. But a new idea about handling personnel fared very differently. The last thing anybody ever thought about was trying out the idea experimentally. I recall several times when we had schemes for running an experimental tryout of an idea in the sociopsychological field. Usually one of two things would happen: the idea would be rejected as stupid without a tryout (it may have been stupid, too) or it would be seized on and applied generally and at once. When the provost marshal wanted us to look into the very low morale of the MP's, our attitude surveys suggested that there was room for very much better selectivity in job assignment. There were routine jobs like guarding prisoners which could be given to the duller MP's, and there were a good many jobs calling for intelligence, discretion, and skill in public relations. We thought that the smarter men might be assigned to these jobs and that the prestige of these jobs would be raised further if a sprinkling of returned veterans with plenty of ribbons and no current assignment could be included among them. We proposed a trial program of a reassignment system in a dozen MP outfits for the purpose of comparing the resulting morale with that in a dozen matched outfits which were left untouched. Did we get anywhere? No. Instead, several of our ideas were put into effect immediately throughout the army without any prior testing at all.

The army cannot be blamed for behavior like that. In social relations it is not the habit in our culture to demand evidence for an idea; plausibility is enough.

To alter the folkways, social science itself must take the initiative. We must be clear in our own minds what proof consists of, and we must, if possible, provide dramatic examples of the advantages of relying on something more than plausibility. And the heart of our problem lies in study design *in advance,* such that the evidence is not capable of a dozen alternative interpretations.

Basically, I think it is essential that we always keep in mind the model of a controlled experiment, even if in practice we may have to deviate from an ideal model. Take the simple accompanying diagram. The test of whether a difference d is attributable to what we think it is attributable to is whether d is significantly larger than d'.

	Before	After	After — Before
Experimental group	x_1	x_2	$d = x_2 - x_1$
Control group	x'_1	x'_2	$d' = x'_2 - x'_1$

We used this model over and over again during the war to measure the effectiveness of orientation films in changing soldiers' attitudes. These experiences are described in Volume III of our *Studies in Social Psychology in World War II.*

One of the troubles with using this careful design was that the effectiveness of a single film when thus measured turned out to be so slight. If, instead of using the complete experimental design, we simply took an unselected sample of men and compared the attitudes of those who said they had seen a film with those who said they had not, we got much more impressive differences. This was more rewarding to us, too, for the management wanted to believe the films were powerful medicine. The gimmick was the selective fallibility of memory. Men who correctly remembered seeing the films were likely to be those most sensitized to their message. Men who were bored or indifferent may have actually seen them but slept through them or just forgot.

Most of the time we are not able or not patient enough to design studies containing all four cells as in the diagram above. Sometimes we have only the top two cells, as in the accompanying diagram. In this situation we have two observations of the same individuals or groups taken at different times. This is often a very useful design. In the army, for example, we would take a group of recruits, ascertain their attitudes, and restudy the same men later. From this we could tell whose attitudes changed and in what direction (it was almost always for the worse, which did not endear us to the army!). But exactly what factors in the early training period were most responsible for deterioration of attitudes could only be inferred indirectly.

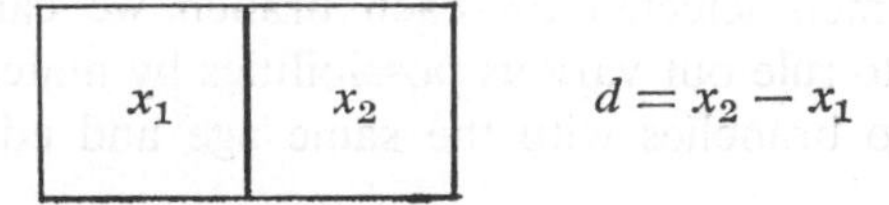

The panel study is usually more informative than a more frequent design, which might be pictured thus:

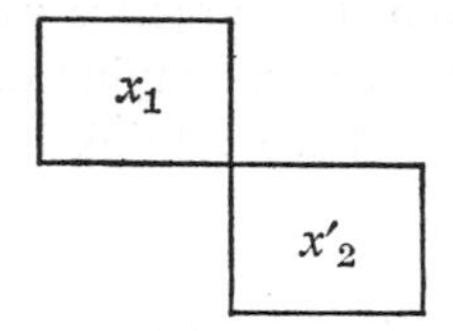

Here at one point in time we have one sample, and at a later point in time we have another sample. We observe that our measure, say, the mean, is greater for the recent sample than for the earlier one. But we are precluded from observing which men or what type of men shifted. Moreover, there is always the disturbing possibility that the populations in our two samples were initially different; hence the differences might not be attributable to conditions taking place in the time interval between the two observations. Thus we would study a group of soldiers in the United States and later ask the same questions of a group of soldiers overseas. Having matched the two groups of men carefully by branch of service, length of time in the army, rank, etc., we hoped that the results of the study would approximate what would be found if the same men could have been studied twice. But this could be no more than a hope. Some important factors could not be adequately controlled, for example, physical conditions. Men who went overseas were initially in better shape on the average than men who had been kept behind; but, if the follow-up study was in the tropics, there was a chance that unfavorable climate already had begun to take its toll. And so it went. How much men overseas changed called for a panel study as a minimum if we were to have much confidence in the findings.

A very common attempt to get the results of a controlled experiment without paying the price is with the design that might be as shown in the accompanying diagram. This is usually what we get with correlation analysis. We have two or more groups of men whom we study at the same point in time.

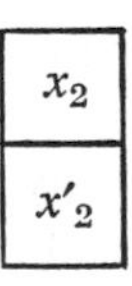

Thus we have men in the infantry and men in the air corps and compare their attitudes. How much of the difference between x'_2 and x_2 we can attribute to experience in a given branch of service and how much is a function of attributes of the men selected for each branch we cannot know assuredly. True, we can try to rule out various possibilities by matching; we can compare men from the two branches with the same age and education, for example.

But there is all too often a wide-open gate through which other uncontrolled variables can march.

Sometimes, believe it or not, we have only one cell:

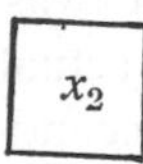

When this happens, we do not know much of anything. But we can still fill pages of social science journals with "brilliant analysis" if we use plausible conjecture in supplying missing cells from our imagination. Thus we may find that the adolescent today has wild ideas and conclude that society is going to the dogs. We fill in the dotted cell representing our own yesterdays with hypothetical data, where x_1 represents us and x_2 our offspring. The tragicomic part

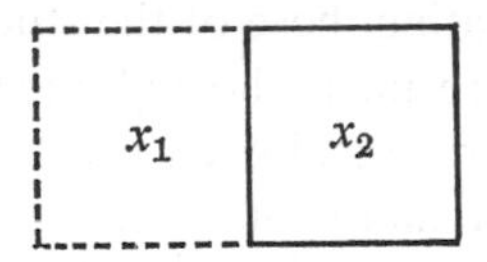

is that most of the public, including, I fear, many social scientists, are so acculturated that they ask for no better data.

I do not intend to disparage all research not conforming to the canons of the controlled experiment. I think that we will see more of full experimental design in sociology and social psychology in the future than in the past. But I am well aware of the practical difficulties of its execution, and I know that there are numberless important situations in which it is not feasible at all. What I am arguing for is awareness of the limitations of a design in which crucial cells are missing.

Sometimes by forethought and patchwork we can get approximations which are useful if we are careful to avoid overinterpretation. Let me cite an example:

In Europe during the war the army tested the idea of putting an entire platoon of Negro soldiers into a white infantry outfit. This was done in several companies. The Negroes fought beside white soldiers. After several months we were asked to find out what the white troops thought about the innovation. We found that only 7 percent of the white soldiers in companies with Negro platoons said that they disliked the idea very much, whereas 62 percent of the white soldiers in divisions without Negro troops said they would dislike the idea very much if it were tried in their outfits. We have:

	Before	After
Experimental		7%
Control		62%

Now, were these white soldiers who fought beside Negroes men who were naturally more favorable to Negroes than the cross-section of white infantrymen? We did not think so, since, for example, they contained about the same proportion of southerners. The point was of some importance, however, if we were to make the inference that actual experience with Negroes reduced hostility from 62 to 7 percent. As a second-best substitute, we asked the white soldiers in companies with Negro platoons if they could recall how they felt when the innovation was first proposed. It happens that 67 percent said they were initially opposed to the idea. Thus we could tentatively fill in a missing cell and conclude that, under the conditions obtaining, there probably had been a marked change in attitude.

Even if this had been a perfectly controlled experiment, there was still plenty of chance to draw erroneous inferences. The conclusions apply only to situations closely approximating those of the study. It happens, for example, that the Negroes involved were men who volunteered to leave rear-area jobs for combat duty. If other Negroes had been involved, the situation might have been different. Moreover, they had white officers. One army colonel who saw this study and whom I expected to ridicule it because he usually opposed innovations, surprised me by offering congratulations. "This proves," he said, "what I have been arguing in all my thirty years in the army—that niggers will do all right if you give 'em white officers!" Moreover, the study applied only to combat experience. Other studies would be needed to justify extending the findings to noncombat or garrison duty. In other words, one lone study, however well designed, can be a very dangerous thing if it is exploited beyond its immediate implications.

Now experiments take time and money, and there is no use denying that we in social science cannot be as prodigal with the replications as the biologist who can run a hundred experiments simultaneously by growing plants in all kinds of soils and conditions. The relative ease of experimentation in much—not all—of natural science goes far to account for the difference in quality of proof demanded by physical and biological sciences, on the one hand, and social scientists, on the other.

Though we cannot always design neat experiments when we want to, we can at least keep the experimental model in front of our eyes and behave cautiously when we fill in missing cells with dotted lines. But there is a further and even more important operation we can perform in the interest of economy. That lies in our choice of the initial problem.

Professor W. F. Ogburn always told his students to apply to a reported research conclusion the test, "How do you know it?" To this wise advice I should like to add a further question: "What of it?" I suspect that if before designing a study we asked ourselves, more conscientiously than we do, whether or not the study really is important, we would economize our energies for the few studies which are worth the expense and trouble of the kind of design I have been discussing.

Can anything be said about guides for selecting problems? I certainly think so. That is where theory comes in and where we social scientists have gone woefully astray.

Theory has not often been designed with research operations in mind. Theory as we have it in social science serves indispensably as a very broad frame of reference or general orientation. Thus modern theories of culture tell us that it is usually more profitable to focus on the learning process and the content of what is learned rather than on innate or hereditary traits. But they do not provide us with sets of interrelated propositions which can be put in the form: If x_1, given x_2 and x_3, then there is strong probability that we get x_4. Most of our propositions of that form, sometimes called "theory," are likely to be *ad hoc* common-sense observations which are not deducible from more general considerations and which are of the same quality as the observation, "If you stick your hand in a fire and hold it there, you will get burned."

Now in view of the tremendous cost in time and money of the ideal kind of strict empirical research operations, it is obvious that we cannot afford the luxury of conducting them as isolated fact-finding enterprises. Each should seek to be some sort of *experimentum crucis,* and, with rare exceptions, that will only happen if we see its place *beforehand* in a more general scheme of things. Especially, we need to look for situations where two equally plausible hypotheses deducible from more general theory lead to the expectation of different consequences. Then, if our evidence supports one and knocks out the other, we have accomplished something.

The best work of this sort in our field is probably being done today in laboratory studies of learning and of perception. I do not know of very good sociological examples. Yet in sociology experiments are possible. One of the most exciting, for example, was that initiated long before the war by Shaw and McKay to see whether co-operative effort by adult role models within a delinquent neighborhood would reduce juvenile delinquency. So many variables are involved in a single study like that that it is not easy to determine which were crucial. But there was theory behind the study, and the experimental design provided for controlling at least some variables.

It may be that in sociology we will need much more thinking and many more descriptive studies involving random ratlike movements on the part of the researcher before we can even begin to state our problems so that they are in decent shape for fitting into an ideal design. However, I think that we can reduce to some extent the waste motion of the exploratory period if we try to act as if we have some a priori ideas and keep our eyes on the possible relevance of data to these ideas. This is easier said than done. So many interesting rabbit tracks are likely to be uncovered in the exploratory stages of research that one is tempted to chase rabbits all over the woods and forget what his initial quarry was.

Exploratory research is of necessity fumbling, but I think that the waste motion can be reduced by the self-denying ordinance of deliberately limiting ourselves to a few variables at a time. Recently two of my colleagues and myself have been doing a little exploratory work on a problem in the general area of social mobility. We started by tabulating some school records of fifty boys in the ninth grade of one junior high school and then having members of our seminar conduct three or four interviews with each boy and his parents. We had all the interviews written up in detail, and we had enough data to fill a book—with rather interesting reading, too. But it was a very wasteful process because there were just too many intriguing ideas. We took a couple of ideas which were deducible from current general theory and tried to make some simple fourfold tables. It was obvious that, with a dozen variables uncontrolled, such tables meant little or nothing. But that led us to a second step. Now we are trying to collect school records and a short questionnaire on two thousand boys. We will not interview all these boys and their parents in detail. But, with two thousand cases to start with, we hope to take a variable in which we are interested and find fifty boys who are plus on it and fifty who are minus, yet who are approximately alike on a lot of other things. A table based on such matched comparisons should be relatively unambiguous. We can take off from there and interview those selected cases intensively to push further our exploration of the nexus between theory and observation. This, we think, will be economical, though still exploratory. Experimental manipulation is far in the future in our problem, but we do hope we can conclude the first stage with a statement of some hypotheses susceptible to experimental verification.

I am not in the least deprecating exploratory work. But I do think that some orderliness is indicated even in the bright dawn of a youthful enterprise.

One reason why we are not more orderly in our exploratory work is that all too often what is missing is a sharp definition of a given variable, such that, if we wanted to take a number of cases and even throw them into a simple fourfold table, we could.

Suppose we are studying a problem in which one of the variables we are looking for is overprotection or overindulgence of a child by his mother. We have a number of case histories or questionnaires. Now how do we know whether we are sorting them according to this variable or not? The first step, it would seem, is to have some way of knowing whether we are sorting them along any single continuum, applying the same criteria to each case. But to know this we need to have built into the study the ingredients of a scale. Unless we have some such ingredients in our data, we are defeated from the start. This is why I think the new interest social scientists are taking in scaling techniques is so crucially important to progress. In particular, the latent-structure theory developed by Paul F. Lazarsfeld, which derives Louis Guttman's scale as an important special case, is likely to be exceedingly useful, for it offers criteria by which we can make a small amount of information go a long way in telling us the logical structure of a supposed variable we are eager to identify. The details of Guttman's and Lazarsfeld's work are likely to promote a good deal of attack and controversy. Our hope is that this will stimulate others to think such problems out still better and thus make their work obsolete as rapidly as possible.

Trying to conduct a social science investigation without good criteria for knowing whether a particular variable may be treated as a single dimension is like trying to fly without a motor in the plane. Students of the history of invention point out that one reason why the airplane, whose properties had been pretty well thought out by Leonardo da Vinci, was so late in development was the unavailability of a lightweight power plant, which had to await the invention of the internal combustion motor. We are learning more and more how to make our light-weight motors in social science, and that augurs well for the future. But much work is ahead of us. In particular, we desperately need better projective techniques and better ways of getting respondents to reveal attitudes which are too emotionally charged to be accessible to direct questioning. Schemes like the latent-structure theory of Lazarsfeld should speed up the process of developing such tests.

I have tried to set forth the model of the controlled experiment as an ideal to keep in the forefront of our minds even when by necessity some cells are missing from our design. I have also tried to suggest that more economy and orderliness are made possible, even in designing the exploratory stages of a piece of research—by using theory in advance to help us decide whether a particular inquiry would be important if we made it; by narrowing down the number of variables; and by making sure that we can classify our data along a particular continuum, even if only provisionally. And a central, brooding hope is that we will have the modesty to recognize the difference between a promising idea and proof.

Oh, how we need that modesty! The public expects us to deal with great problems like international peace, full employment, maximization of industrial efficiency. As pundits we can pronounce on such matters; as citizens we have a duty to be concerned with them; but as social scientists our greatest achievement now will be to provide a few small dramatic examples that hypotheses in our field can be stated operationally and tested crucially. And we will not accomplish that by spending most of our time writing or reading papers like this one. We will accomplish it best by rolling up our sleeves and working at the intricacies of design of studies which, though scientifically strategic, seem to laymen trivial compared with the global concerns of the atomic age. Thereby, and only thereby, I believe, can we some day have the thrilling sense of having contributed to the structure of a social science which is cumulative.

Scientific research has been defined as systematic investigation, by experimentation and other techniques, having for its aim the revision of accepted knowledge in the light of newly discovered facts. To be most effective, research should be directed toward answering a specific question. But research is a technical operation, and not all questions can be answered in the form they are asked. For example, in sociology as in other disciplines there are many broad questions of great importance; but they must be broken down into simpler and more specific questions before they can be adequately attacked by research methods. As Professor Stouffer emphasized in the previous article, this formulation of questions and the design of adequately controlled procedures and observations are the essence of research.

In the first part of this book, Professor Bierstedt observed that it is unfortunately true that the greater the sociological significance of a question, the less likely it can be answered by tightly designed research techniques such as experimentation. We reiterate, however, that many of these broad and important questions can be fragmented into a series of more sharply focused questions, and in each instance one may formulate a hypothesis, an educated guess in answer to the question. The hypothesis may then be tested and verified by factual evidence.

A hypothesis whose purpose is to guide the research—that is, give direction to the empirical fact-gathering and the abstract theory-building—is a generalized statement about the relationship presumed to exist between two classes of facts or variables. Typically, a hypothesis states that "if A assumes this form, then B takes this shape," A and B being the variables or classes of facts believed to have a certain relationship to each other in answer to the researchable question. A is called the independent (causal) variable; B, the dependent (effect) variable. A sociological variable is any social trait, quality, or characteristic which can vary in value. When two variables are so related that if one takes on a set of definite values the corresponding values of the other are affected in a certain way, the former is called independent and the latter dependent. Modifying or test variables are those variables which may intervene between A and B, or antecede A prior to its impact on B, thus influencing their relationship. Wherever possible, research technique must "control" modifying variables in order to discern accurately the relationship between independent and dependent variables.

In the next article, Herbert Blumer notes the current tendency of variable analysis to become the standard procedure in sociological research. Recognizing its usefulness, he nevertheless finds it necessary to indicate its shortcomings and limitations.

47. SOCIOLOGICAL ANALYSIS AND THE "VARIABLE" *

HERBERT BLUMER

University of California, Berkeley

My aim in this paper is to examine critically the scheme of sociological analysis which seeks to reduce human group life to variables and their relations. I shall refer to this scheme, henceforth, as "variable analysis." This scheme is widespread and is growing in acceptance. It seems to be becoming the norm of

* Presidential address read at the annual meeting of the American Sociological Society, September, 1956; in *American Sociological Review,* Vol. 21, No. 6, December, 1956, pp. 683–690.

proper sociological analysis. Its sophisticated forms are becoming the model of correct research procedure. Because of the influence which it is exercising in our discipline, I think that it is desirable to note the more serious of its shortcomings in actual use and to consider certain limits to its effective application. The first part of my paper will deal with the current shortcomings that I have in mind and the second part with the more serious question of the limits to its adequacy.

SHORTCOMINGS IN CONTEMPORARY VARIABLE ANALYSIS

The first shortcoming I wish to note in current variable analysis in our field is the rather chaotic condition that prevails in the selection of variables. There seems to be little limit to what may be chosen or designated as a variable. One may select something as simple as a sex distribution or as complex as a depression; something as specific as a birth rate or as vague as social cohesion; something as evident as residential change or as imputed as a collective unconscious; something as generally recognized as hatred or as doctrinaire as the Oedipus complex; something as immediately given as a rate of newspaper circulation to something as elaborately fabricated as an index of anomie. Variables may be selected on the basis of a specious impression of what is important, on the basis of conventional usage, on the basis of what can be secured through a given instrument or technique, on the basis of the demands of some doctrine, or on the basis of an imaginative ingenuity in devising a new term.

Obviously the study of human group life calls for a wide range of variables. However, there is a conspicuous absence of rules, guides, limitations and prohibitions to govern the choice of variables. Relevant rules are not provided even in the thoughtful regulations that accompany sophisticated schemes of variable analysis. For example, the rule that variables should be quantitative does not help, because with ingenuity one can impart a quantitative dimension to almost any qualitative item. One can usually construct some kind of a measure or index of it or develop a rating scheme for judges. The proper insistence that a variable have a quantitative dimension does little to lessen the range or variety of items that may be set up as variables. In a comparable manner, the use of experimental design does not seemingly exercise much restriction on the number and kind of variables which may be brought within the framework of the design. Nor, finally, does careful work with variables, such as establishing tests of reliability, or inserting "test variables," exercise much restraint on what may be put into the pool of sociological variables.

In short, there is a great deal of laxity in choosing variables in our field. This laxity is due chiefly to a neglect of the careful reduction of problems that should properly precede the application of the techniques of variable analysis. This prior task requires thorough and careful reflection on the problem to make reasonably sure that one has identified its genuine parts. It requires intensive and extensive familiarity with the empirical area to which the problem refers. It requires a careful and thoughtful assessment of the theoretical schemes that might apply to the problem. Current variable analysis in our field is inclined to slight these requirements both in practice and in the training of students for that practice. The scheme of variable analysis has become for too many just a handy tool to be put to immediate use.

A second shortcoming in variable analysis in our field is the disconcerting absence of generic variables, that is, variables that stand for abstract categories. Generic variables are essential, of course, to an empirical science—they become the key points of its analytical structure. Without generic variables, variable analysis yields only separate and disconnected findings.

There are three kinds of variables in our discipline which are generally regarded as generic variables. None of them, in my judgment, is generic. The first kind is the typical and frequent variable which stands for a class of objects that is tied down to a given historical and cultural situation. Convenient examples are: attitudes toward the Supreme Court, intention to vote Republican, interest in the United Nations, a college education, army draftees and factory unemployment. Each of these variables, even though a class term, has substance only in a given historical context. The variables do not stand directly for items of abstract human group life; their application to human groups around the world, to human groups in the past, and to conceivable human groups in the future is definitely restricted. While their use may yield propositions that hold in given cultural settings, they do not yield the abstract knowledge that is the core of an empirical science.

The second apparent kind of generic variable in current use in our discipline is represented by unquestionably abstract sociological categories, such as "social cohesion," "social integration," "assimilation," "authority," and "group morale." In actual use these do not turn out to be the generic variables that their labels would suggest. The difficulty is that such terms, as I sought to point out in an earlier article on sensitizing concepts, have no fixed or uniform indicators. Instead, indicators are constructed to fit the particular problem on which one is working. Thus, certain features are chosen to represent the social integration of cities, but other features are used to represent the social integration of boys' gangs. The indicators chosen to represent morale in a small group of school children are very different from those used to stand for morale in a labor movement. The indicators used in studying attitudes of prejudice show a wide range of variation. It seems clear that indicators are tailored and used to meet the peculiar character of the local problem under study. In my judgment, the abstract categories used as variables in our work turn out with rare exception to be something other than generic categories. They are localized in terms of their content. Some measure of support is given to this assertion by the fact that the use of such abstract categories in variable research adds little to generic knowledge of them. The thousands of "variable" studies of attitudes, for instance, have not contributed to our knowledge of the abstract nature of an attitude; in a similar way the studies of "social cohesion," "social integration," "authority," or "group morale" have done nothing, so far as I can detect, to clarify or augment generic knowledge of these categories.

The third form of apparent generic variable in our work is represented by a special set of class terms like "sex," "age," "birth rate," and "time period." These would seem to be unquestionably generic. Each can be applied universally to human group life; each has the same clear and common meaning in its application. Yet, it appears that in their use in our field they do not function as generic variables. Each has a content that is given by its particular instance of application, e.g., the birth rate in Ceylon, or the sex distribution in the State of Nebraska, or the age distribution in the City of St. Louis. The kind of variable relations that result from their use will be found to be localized and non-generic.

These observations on these three specious kinds of generic variables point, of course, to the fact that variables in sociological research are predominantly disparate and localized in nature. Rarely do they refer satisfactorily to a dimension or property of abstract human group life. With little exception they are bound temporally, spatially, and culturally and are inadequately cast to serve as clear instances of generic sociological categories. Many would contend that this is because variable research and analysis are in a beginning state in our discipline. They believe that with the benefit of wider coverage, replication, and the co-ordination of separate studies disparate variable relations may be welded into generic relations. So far there has been little achievement along these lines. Although we already have appreciable accumulations of findings from variable studies, little has been done to convert the findings into generic relations. Such conversion is not an easy task. The difficulty should serve both as a challenge to the effort and an occasion to reflect on the use and limitations of variable analyses.

As a background for noting a third major shortcoming I wish to dwell on the fact that current variable analysis in our field is operating predominantly with disparate and not generic variables and yielding predominantly disparate and not generic relations. With little exception its data and its findings are "here and now," wherever the "here" be located and whenever the "now" be timed. Its analyses, accordingly, are of localized and concrete matters. Yet, as I think logicians would agree, to understand adequately a "here and now" relation it is necessary to understand the "here and now" context. This latter understanding is not provided by variable analysis. The variable relation is a single relation, necessarily stripped bare of the complex of things that sustain it in a "here and now" context. Accordingly, our understanding of it as a "here and now" matter suffers. Let me give one example. A variable relation states that reasonably staunch Erie County Republicans become confirmed in their attachment to their candidate as a result of listening to the campaign materials of the rival party. This bare and interesting finding gives us no picture of them as human beings in their particular world. We do not know the run of their experiences which induced an organization of their sentiments and views, nor do we know what this organization is; we do not know the social atmosphere or codes in their social circles; we do not know the reinforcements and rationalizations that come from their fellows; we do not know the defining process in their circles; we do not know the pressures, the incitants, and the models that came from their niches in the social structure; we do not know how their ethical sensitivities are organized and so what they would tolerate in the way of shocking behavior on the part of their candidate. In short, we do not have the picture to size up and understand what their confirmed attachment to a political candidate means in terms of their experience and their social context. This fuller picture of the "here and now" context is not given by variable relations. This, I believe, is a major shortcoming in variable analysis, insofar as variable analysis seeks to explain meaningfully the disparate and local situations with which it seems to be primarily concerned.

The three shortcomings which I have noted in current variable research in our field are serious but perhaps not crucial. With increasing experience and maturity they will probably be successfully overcome. They suggest, however, the advisability of inquiring more deeply into the interesting and important question of how well variable analysis is suited to the study of human group life in its fuller dimensions.

LIMITS OF VARIABLE ANALYSIS

In my judgment, the crucial limit to the successful application of variable analysis to human group life is set by the process of interpretation or definition that goes on in human groups. This process, which I believe to be the core of human action, gives a character to human group life that seems to be at variance with the logical premises of variable analysis. I wish to explain at some length what I have in mind.

All sociologists—unless I presume too much—recognize that human group activity is carried on, in the main, through a process of interpretation or definition. As human beings we act singly, collectively, and societally on the basis of the meanings which things have for us. Our world consists of innumerable objects—home, church, job, college education, a political election, a friend, an enemy nation, a tooth brush, or what not—each of which has a meaning on the basis of which we act toward it. In our activities we wend our way by recognizing an object to be such and such, by defining the situations with which we are presented, by attaching a meaning to this or that event, and where need be, by devising a new meaning to cover something new or different. This is done by the individual in his personal action, it is done by a group of individuals acting together in concert, it is done in each of the manifold activities which together constitute an institution in operation, and it is done in each of the diversified acts which fit into and make up the patterned activity of a social structure or a society. We can and, I think, must look upon human group life as chiefly a vast interpretative process in which people, singly and collectively, guide themselves by defining the objects, events, and situations which they encounter. Regularized activity inside this process results from the application of stabilized definitions. Thus, an institution carries on its complicated activity through an articulated complex of such stabilized meanings. In the face of new situations or new experiences individuals, groups, institutions and societies find it necessary to form new definitions. These new definitions may enter into the repertoire of stable meanings. This seems to be the characteristic way in which new activities, new relations, and new social structures are formed. The process of interpretation may be viewed as a vast digestive process through which the confrontations of experience are transformed into activity. While the process of interpretation does not embrace everything that leads to the formation of human group activity and structure, it is, I think, the chief means through which human group life goes on and takes shape.

Any scheme designed to analyze human group life in its general character has to fit this process of interpretation. This is the test that I propose to apply to variable analysis. The variables which designate matters which either directly or indirectly confront people and thus enter into human group life would have to operate through this process of interpretation. The variables which designate the results or effects of the happenings which play upon the experience of people would be the outcome of the process of interpretation. Present-day variable analysis in our field is dealing predominantly with such kinds of variables.

There can be no doubt that, when current variable analysis deals with matters or areas of human group life which involve the process of interpretation, it is markedly disposed to ignore the process. The conventional procedure is to identify something which is presumed to operate on group life and treat it as an independent variable, and then to select some form of group activity as the dependent variable. The independent variable is put at the beginning part of the process of interpretation and the dependent variable at the terminal part of the process. The intervening process is ignored or, what amounts to the same thing, taken for granted as something that need not be considered. Let me cite a few typical examples: the presentation of political programs on the radio and the resulting expression of intention to vote; the entrance of Negro residents into a white neighborhood and the resulting attitudes of the white inhabitants toward Negroes; the occurrence of a business depression and the resulting rate of divorce. In such instances—so common to variable analysis in our field—one's concern is with the two variables and not with what lies between them. If one has neutralized other factors which are regarded as possibly exercising influence on the dependent variable, one is content with the conclusion that the observed change in the dependent variable is the necessary result of the independent variable.

This idea that in such areas of group life the independent variable automatically exercises its influence on the dependent variable is, it seems to me, a basic fallacy. There is a process of definition intervening between the events of experience presupposed by the independent variable and the formed behavior represented by the dependent variable. The political programs on the radio are interpreted by the listeners; the Negro invasion into the white neighborhood must be defined by the whites to have any effect on their attitudes; the many events and happenings which together constitute the business depression must be interpreted at their many points by husbands and wives to have any influence on marital relations. This intervening interpretation is essential to the outcome. It gives the meaning to the presentation that sets the response. Because of the integral position of the defining process between the two variables, it becomes necessary, it seems to me, to incorporate the process in the account of the relationship. Little effort is made in variable analysis to do this. Usually the process is completely ignored. Where the process is recognized, its study is regarded as a problem that is independent of the relation between the variables.

The indifference of variable analysis to the process of interpretation is based apparently on the tacit assumption that the independent variable predetermines its interpretation. This assumption has no foundation. The interpretation is not predetermined by the variable as if the variable emanated its own meaning. If there is anything we do know, it is that an object, event or situation in human experience does not carry its own meaning; the meaning is conferred on it.

Now, it is true that in many instances the interpretation of the object, event or situation may be fixed, since the person or people may have an already constructed meaning which is immediately applied to the item. Where such stabilized interpretation occurs and recurs, variable analysis would have no need to consider the interpretation. One could merely say that as a matter of fact under given conditions the independent variable is followed by such and such a change in the dependent variable. The only necessary precaution would be not to assume that the stated relation between the variables was necessarily intrinsic and universal. Since anything that is defined may be redefined, the relation has no intrinsic fixity.

Alongside the instances where interpretation is made by merely applying stabilized meanings there are the many instances where the interpretation has to be constructed. These instances are obviously increasing in our changing society. It is imperative in the case of such instances for variable analysis to include the act of interpretation in its analytic scheme. As far as I can see, variable analysis shuns such inclusion.

Now the question arises, how can variable analysis include the process of interpretation? Presumably the answer would be to treat the act of interpretation as an "intervening variable." But, what does this mean? If it means that interpretation is merely an intervening neutral medium through which the independent variable exercises its influence, then, of course, this would be no answer. Interpretation is a formative or creative process in its own right. It constructs meanings which, as I have said, are not predetermined or determined by the independent variable.

If one accepts this fact and proposes to treat the act of interpretation as a formative process, then the question arises how one is to characterize it as a variable. What quality is one to assign to it, what property or set of properties? One cannot, with any sense, characterize this act of interpretation in terms of the interpretation which it constructs; one cannot take the product to stand for the process. Nor can one characterize the act of interpretation in terms of what enters into it—the objects perceived, the evaluations and assessments made of them, the cues that are suggested, the possible definitions proposed by oneself or by others. These vary from one instance of interpretation to another and, further, shift from point to point in the development of the act. This varying and shifting content offers no basis for making the act of interpretation into a variable.

Nor, it seems to me, is the problem met by proposing to reduce the act of interpretation into component parts and work with these parts as variables. These parts would presumably have to be processual parts—such as perception, cognition, analysis, evaluation, and decision-making in the individual; and discussion, definition of one another's responses and other forms of social interaction in the group. The same difficulty exists in making any of the processual parts into variables that exists in the case of the complete act of interpretation.

The question of how the act of interpretation can be given the qualitative constancy that is logically required in a variable has so far not been answered. While one can devise some kind of a "more or less" dimension for it, the need is to catch it as a variable, or set of variables, in a manner which reflects its functioning in transforming experience into activity. This is the problem, indeed dilemma, which confronts variable analysis in our field. I see no answer to it inside the logical framework of variable analysis. The process of interpretation is not inconsequential or pedantic. It operates too centrally in group and individual experience to be put aside as being of incidental interest.

In addition to the by-passing of the process of interpretation there is, in my judgment, another profound deficiency in variable analysis as a scheme for analyzing human group life. The deficiency stems from the inevitable tendency to work with truncated factors and, as a result, to conceal or misrepresent the actual operations in human group life. The deficiency stems from the logical need of variable analysis to work with discrete, clean-cut and unitary variables. Let me spell this out.

As a working procedure variable analysis seeks necessarily to achieve a clean identification of the relation between two variables. Irrespective of how one may subsequently combine a number of such identified relations—in an additive manner, a clustering, a chain-like arrangement, or a "feedback" scheme—the objective of variable research is initially to isolate a simple and fixed relation between two variables. For this to be done each of the two variables must be set up as a distinct item with a unitary qualitative make-up. This is accomplished first by giving each variable, where needed, a simple quality or dimension, and second by separating the variable from its connection with other variables through their exclusion or neutralization.

A difficulty with this scheme is that the empirical reference of a true sociological variable is not unitary or distinct. When caught in its actual social character, it turns out to be an intricate and inner-moving complex. To illustrate, let me take what seems ostensibly to be a fairly clean-cut variable relation, namely between a birth control program and the birth rate of a given people. Each of these two variables—the program of birth control and the birth rate—can be given a simple discrete and unitary character. For the program of birth control one may choose merely its time period, or select some reasonable measure such as the number of people visiting birth control clinics. For the birth rate, one merely takes it as it is. Apparently, these indications are sufficient to enable the investigator to ascertain the relations between the two variables.

Yet, a scrutiny of what the two variables stand for in the life of the group gives us a different picture. Thus, viewing the program of birth control in terms of *how it enters into the lives of the people,* we need to note many things such as the literacy of the people, the clarity of the printed information, the manner and extent of its distribution, the social position of the directors of the program and of the personnel, how the personnel act, the character of their instructional talks, the way in which people define attendance at birth control clinics, the expressed views of influential personages with reference to the program, how such personages are regarded, and the nature of the discussions among people with regard to the clinics. These are only a few of the matters which relate to how the birth control program might enter into the experience of the people. The number is sufficient, however, to show the complex and inner-moving character of what otherwise might seem to be a simple variable.

A similar picture is given in the case of the other variable—the birth rate. A birth rate of a people seems to be a very simple and unitary matter. Yet, in terms of what it expresses and stands for in group activity it is exceedingly complex and diversified. We need consider only the variety of social factors that impinge on and affect the sex act, even though the sex act is only one of the activities that set the birth rate. The self-conceptions held by men and by women, the conceptions of family life, the values placed on children, accessibility of men and women to each other, physical arrangements in the home, the sanctions given by established institutions, the code of manliness, the pressures from relatives and neighbors, and ideas of what is proper, convenient and tolerable in the sex act—these are a few of the operating factors in the experience of the group that play upon the sex act. They suffice to indicate something of the complex body of actual experience and practice that is represented in and expressed by the birth rate of a human group.

I think it will be found that, when converted into the actual group activity for which it stands, a sociological variable turns out to be an intricate and inner-moving complex. There are, of course, wide ranges of difference between sociological variables in terms of the extent of such complexity. Still, I believe one will generally find that the discrete and unitary character which the labeling of the variable suggests vanishes.

The failure to recognize this is a source of trouble. In variable analysis one is likely to accept the two variables as the simple and unitary items that they seem to be, and to believe that the relation found between them is a realistic analysis of the given area of group life. Actually, in group life the relation is far more likely to be between complex, diversified and moving bodies of activity. The operation of one of these complexes on the other, or the interaction between them, is both concealed and misrepresented by the statement of the relation between the two variables. The statement of the variable relation merely asserts a connection between abbreviated terms of reference. It leaves out the actual complexes of activity and the actual processes of interaction in which human group life has its being. We are here faced, it seems to me, by the fact that the very features which give variable analysis its high merit—the qualitative constancy of the variables, their clean-cut simplicity, their ease of manipulation as a sort of free counter, their ability to be brought into decisive relation—are the features that lead variable analysis to gloss over the character of the real operating factors in group life, and the real interaction and relations between such factors.

The two major difficulties faced by variable analysis point clearly to the need for a markedly different scheme of sociological analysis for the areas in which these difficulties arise. This is not the occasion to spell out the nature of this scheme. I shall merely mention a few of its rudiments to suggest how its character differs fundamentally from that of variable analysis. The scheme would be based on the premise that the chief means through which human group life operates and is formed is a vast, diversified process of definition. The scheme respects the empirical existence of this process. It devotes itself to the analysis of the operation and formation of human group life as these occur through this process. In doing so it seeks to trace the lines of defining experience through which ways of living, patterns of relations, and social forms are developed, rather than to relate these formations to a set of selected items. It views items of social life as articulated inside moving structures and believes that they have to be understood in terms of this articulation. Thus, it handles these items not as discrete things disengaged from their connections but, instead, as signs of a supporting context which gives them their social character. In its effort to ferret out lines of definition and networks of moving relation, it relies on a distinctive form of procedure. This procedure is to approach the study of group activity through the eyes and experience of the people who have developed the activity. Hence, it necessarily requires an intimate familiarity with this experience and with the scenes of its operation. It uses broad and interlacing observations and not narrow and disjunctive observations. And, may I add, that like variable analysis, it yields empirical findings and "here-and-now" propositions, although in a different form. Finally, it is no worse off than variable analysis in developing generic knowledge out of its findings and propositions.

In closing, I express a hope that my critical remarks about variable analysis are not misinterpreted to mean that variable analysis is useless or makes no contribution to sociological analysis. The contrary is true. Variable analysis is a fit procedure for those areas of social life and formation that are not mediated by an interpretative process. Such areas exist and are important. Further, in the area of interpretative life variable analysis can be an effective means of unearthing stabilized patterns of interpretation which are not likely to be detected through the direct study of the experience of people. Knowledge of such patterns, or rather of the relations between variables which reflect such patterns, is of great value for understanding group life in its "here-and-now" character and indeed may have significant practical value. All of these appropriate uses give variable analysis a worthy status in our field.

In view, however, of the current tendency of variable analysis to become the norm and model for sociological analysis, I believe it important to recognize its shortcomings and its limitations.

The sociological researcher can seldom collect data on all cases in his social universe. Instead he must sample his universe—that is, study only a segment of the total number of cases about which his hypothesis generalizes. According to the basic theory of sampling, this is justifiable if the cases selected for the sample are reliable, representative, and unbiased. They are reliable if they are actually specimens of the universe; they are representative if the cases studied do not differ systematically from those cases in the universe that are not studied; and they are unbiased if every case in the universe being sampled has an equal chance of being included in the sample.

In the following article, Frederick F. Stephan discusses the sampling problems that arise in sociological research in the development of techniques of observation and measurement and in the analysis and interpretation of data. Fundamentally, he observes, these problems stem from limitations on the number, accuracy, and scope of observations; and their solution consists of finding the most effective way of conducting research under these restrictions. There is no universally best method of sampling—the technique must be designed to fit the particular circumstances of each situation. Finally, Professor Stephan outlines the technical problems of sampling in terms of the initial specifications, design, costs and resources, accuracy, operation, and use.

48. SAMPLING *

FREDERICK F. STEPHAN
Princeton University

Sampling problems are becoming increasingly important in social research. This is fully as true for studies of public opinion and communication as it is for other fields. Sampling problems arise in the selection of subjects for laboratory experimentation and case study quite as much as in field surveys and mass interviewing. If they are disregarded or treated ineffectively, the risk of failure will be increased and sometimes the progress of research will be set back by fallacious results that are accepted as a dependable basis for further work or for practical action. In the early stages of scientific inquiry these dangers may not be very serious, since all results are regarded as crude approximations and are treated with due restraint. As the inquiry advances the risks increase, and one must give more than casual attention to sampling as well as other technical problems. A considerable body of theory and technical know-how is available for the solution of sampling problems, and new developments are being reported in the professional journals. While these techniques seem to add new complications to the complex problems of a researcher, they also offer opportunities to reduce the cost of the information he seeks and increase its value for his analytical purposes.

All sampling problems stem from the limitations that are imposed on observation. If one could observe directly all that one needs to know, there would be no occasion to make inferences about what has not been observed or to generalize one's knowledge. Science would merely be a systematic record of data, condensed, perhaps, by some convenient shorthand but never stretched over any void or extended into areas of ignorance. Of course, all the future, and most of the past and present is beyond the reach of direct observation. Generalization from limited observations is the rule, not the exception. Observation of a subject in a laboratory experiment and clinical examination of an individual are sampling operations in as fundamental a sense as are attitude testing or opinion surveying. When one studies a "unique case" or an organic system of interaction, the totality is perceived by the observer in terms of a set of partial and particular observations that fall short of complete knowledge and must be extended by processes of inference if they are to be more than historical facts. This phase of sampling has not been developed very far, but it is fully as important as the phases that are now receiving so much attention from research workers.

In studying a process of communication or some other complex system of

* *The American Journal of Sociology,* Vol. LV, No. 4, January, 1950, pp. 371–375.

human behavior and interaction, one is compelled to distribute one's efforts either evenly but thinly over the whole or more intensively over certain parts to the neglect of others. The most effective distribution will be different from one situation to another. The interrelationships that bind the parts into a system may likewise be observed through a selected set of parts or more superficially over the whole system. An anthropologist studies a culture, a language, or an institution through selected informants as well as by direct observation of some instances of behavior. A social psychologist can interview individuals or observe groups or do both. In any case, there is a sampling of individual and group expressions for the purpose of inferring the structure and functioning of the system.

Dispersed groups, such as publics, are difficult to observe, except by a succession of individual interviews and an analysis of the media of communication by which they interact. Their state at a particular time is measured by a survey or similar device, and changes from one time to another are measured by two or more surveys in the familiar "panel" procedure. It is these survey operations that have profited most by the development of sampling in recent years, largely because methods that were devised in other fields of research could be borrowed and adapted readily to opinion surveying.

The content of social communication is also difficult to observe. It may be studied intensively at selected points of time and in selected media or over selected periods. Some types of content may be studied more thoroughly than others. The methods that are used in inspecting industrial production processes may be helpful in this kind of sampling.

There is no "best" method of sampling that can be followed blindly in all instances. The most effective sampling methods are those that are designed specifically to fit the situation in which they are to be used. They are based on the general theory of sampling derived from mathematical statistics and economic theory, and they take advantage of what is known in advance about the population, system of interaction, or process that is to be sampled. They are designed to achieve the specific purposes of the study as effectively as is possible under the limitations set by the funds, personnel, time, and other resources that are available. In a word, they are tailored to fit the circumstances. In this respect they are like a manufacturing process that is engineered in terms of specifications set by the consumer and the technical equipment and cost relations of the plant. For simple jobs no elaborate planning is necessary; for some products thousands of dollars of preparatory work will be devoted to setting up the operation in order to produce the best results, taking into account many possibilities and considerations.

TWO RULES FOR THE AMATEUR SAMPLER

It would be a mistake to confine the discussion of sampling to the larger surveys, especially those nation-wide polls and canvasses that have done so much to stir up public interest in sampling and in which a careful job of sample design is feasible. For each such survey there may be scores of studies to be conducted on a smaller scale, geographically and financially. They may be more intensive and complicated in the variables they measure and the relationships they analyze. In the aggregate, and in some individual instances, they may turn out to be more important for research than some of the large-scale studies. So one may well ask, "Isn't there some simple dependable rule I can use to solve my sampling problem? I'm studying a limited group, not seeking a national average." Such a question deserves careful examination and a serious answer.

If it is put just this way, without any information about the population to be sampled and the resources that can be devoted to sampling, then one must necessarily sacrifice the advantages that come from fitting the sampling rule to the particular case. Hence, the answer could be, "Yes. You can have two choices."

Rule A is: Follow your common sense and select people by what seems to you to be a good way to get a group similar to the entire group in which you are interested. Test it with every convenient set of data you can obtain. Then be prudent in handling the results of your study, for you may be far off the beam without knowing it. As the airplane pilots say, you are "flying by the seat of your pants." With good luck you may not be too far off too often. If other phases of the study are correspondingly uncertain and not under full control, you are probably not adding a great deal to the total risks you are taking. If you are badly wrong, perhaps later experience, bitter though it may be, will set you right. If you are right, you have saved yourself a bit of trouble. This is the way you handle many other kinds of problems that you encounter, so perhaps you might as well do your sampling by the same rule-of-thumb method.

Rule B is for those who do not like to gamble or live dangerously. Such people may be less likely to make occasional brilliant discoveries or produce a flood of studies, but, like the tortoise, they may pass the hare before the race is finished. Rule B counsels: (1) Pin down very specifically the definition of the population you are studying and the variables you wish to measure. (This may be no more than the arduous task of making up your mind about just what you will attempt.) (2) Obtain a list of all the persons who make up that group or population or, lacking a list, divide the population into many small parts according to residence, place of work, or other suitable factors. Do this, however, in a way that tends to make each part a mixture of different kinds of people rather than a cluster of persons who are similar with regard to the variables you are studying. (This is where you may have to go contrary to your intuition.) (3) Select by some strictly random procedure enough of these parts to give you the number of persons you think you need after allowing for the loss of those you will not be able to study successfully. You may even make up sets of persons or parts, well balanced on the variables you know about beforehand, until you have every person in the population in the same number of sets. Then select strictly at random one such set as a sample. (4) Proceed to study the sample but keep a complete record of persons you miss and what information you can find out about them. Analyze this information and the variation shown within the sample by those you do get. From this arrive at the best estimate you can of the accuracy of the sample in representing the population on each variable. Do not lean too heavily on statistical theory unless you have followed very meticulously the procedure it assumes has been followed. (5) Use every opportunity to check the sample with other dependable data. Possibly add certain questions to the study for this purpose. (6) Record and report your methods and deviations adequately so that others can repeat them or form a somewhat independent appraisal of the sample.

So much for Rules A and B. Sometimes they will work quite well. At other times the results will not be satisfactory unless greater care is taken with the sampling. This can be done in several ways. First, one can learn something more about sampling from the reports of previous surveys, though most reports offer little in the way of useful tests of sampling methods, and from technical publications in statistics and related fields. Second, one can get help from advisers who have developed expertness in research methods. Finally, one may seek to develop new methods appropriate for his own situation by his own ingenuity and experimentation. How much time and effort one gives to sampling should be determined by the general strategy of his research plans, seeking the most effective use of his resources and the greatest yield of results. In many small or casual studies very little benefit may result from improvement of the sampling procedure, but in larger and more important studies there are great opportunities to attain a degree of accuracy with a well-designed and well-executed sample that cannot be attained by crude sampling, no matter how large the cruder sample may be. Hence, these amateur rules should only be followed when the circumstances do not warrant a more technical treatment of the sampling problems.

TECHNICAL PROBLEMS

The technical problems of a major sampling operation are too complex for detailed discussion in this paper. It is important that their general nature be widely known among those who produce or receive the results of research. Hence, a brief and simplified description of the principal kinds of technical problems is in order.

The first problem is that of the initial *specifications*. It is necessary to formulate rather specifically the purposes that are to be served by the sampling operation: the population of persons or other units of observation that are to be sampled; the variables that are to be observed; the accuracy of measurement that can be attained; the degree of accuracy required in the results; the resources that are available; and the other principal factors that will restrict the procedure and determine its suitability. If these conditions are vague, then there will be little basis for designing, or even for choosing, a particular sampling plan as better than other possible plans. If they are quite definite, they may establish automatically the general procedure or over-all plan for the sampling operation, leaving only the details to be determined.

A second problem is that of *design.* Within the limits set by the initial specifications one must shape up a general plan or a series of alternative plans to form a basis for organizing and solving the other technical problems. These plans will set forth the procedures by which the sample will be selected and the observations or interviews actually obtained for the sample. They may well proceed through to a trial run on the procedures that will be used to analyze the data and even to pretests, preliminary surveys, or preparatory runs of experiments. Concurrently or following this phase of designing, the more particular problems will be studied and solved, leading, finally, to the preparation of a complete plan of procedure with the necessary instructions and materials for its execution.

A third problem is that of *costs and resources.* In the simplest case the only cost is the research worker's time. In larger surveys the costs are those of a far-flung corps of interviewers with travel, training, supervision, office expenses, payments to respondents, recording and tabulating equipment, and many other categories of expense. Sampling affects these costs by determining the number, location, and type of persons who must be reached and by regulating other phases of the operation. Very little has been published on the actual costs of opinion surveys. Even less has been done in genuine cost analysis to determine how each of many possible modifications of design would increase or decrease costs. Hence, design may rest heavily on judgment in attempting to minimize the total cost of a survey.

It may be necessary to obtain certain equipment and materials and to train personnel. Lists of persons or dwellings or maps may be needed. Tests may be given and data assembled preliminary to the selection of subjects for laboratory or clinical study. These phases of the sampling procedure affect the design and the effectiveness of the entire operation.

A fourth problem is that of the analysis of *accuracy.* A dependable estimate of the accuracy of the results of the study is needed in advance to guide the planning and after the completion of the study to guide its use. Frequently, only the roughest guesses about accuracy are possible. There are several devices by which improved estimates of accuracy can be obtained if these devices are incorporated into the survey operation. The accuracy of the final results will be affected by many factors, and the estimate of accuracy may be built up from separate estimates of the effect of each or from over-all measurements such as those provided by previous surveys.

A fifth problem is that of *operation,* the actual execution of the procedures and plans that have been designed. This introduces many practical problems, some of which are rarely described or even mentioned in textbooks on research methods. One of the most important is that of controlling the loss of part of the sample as a consequence of various difficulties and accidents in completing the observations and carrying them through the analysis. Subjects may fall ill, respondents may refuse to answer questions, lists and maps may have inaccuracies, records may be damaged or lost, severe storms or disasters may make field work impossible, and many other influences may disturb the performance of the operation. The resulting deviations from plan will vary in their seriousness, but, unless they are checked and controlled, they may invalidate the results of the most thorough planning.

The last problem is that of *presentation and use.* The ultimate criterion for appraisal of sampling methods is how well their results satisfy the purposes for which the research was undertaken. It matters little how accurately the data were recorded somewhere along the line if, when the results of their analysis are put into practice, they have been misunderstood, distorted, inadequately defined, or ineffectively utilized. This is a point on which there is sure to be disagreement. The research worker may deny that he has any responsibility for what happens after he completes his report. However, he cannot escape taking some account of the use of his results, since otherwise he could just as well design his study as a game to be played for its own sake. When one starts seriously to design a procedure, all efforts are directed by the ultimate objective. They fail to the degree that it is not attained. Hence, errors of application and use must be considered in judging the appropriateness of a sample design or in comparing two or more methods. There is a great job to be done, and it is only barely started, of explaining sampling to the potential users of research results. It is very difficult to correct misconceptions and to instruct research workers in effective methods of interpreting and using the research product. An attitude of restrained confidence is not learned easily; investigators may err in the direction of blind faith or excessive caution. They should learn that the results of sampling are just as trustworthy as other information if one takes account in each instance of the degree of accuracy that has been attained.

These problems appear in various forms in each actual study or survey. Gradually, they are being introduced into textbooks, and increasingly they are appearing in the professional journals. More significant descriptions of sampling methods accompany survey reports, though there is still much to be desired in this direction. While experience is accumulating in this way, direct attacks should be made on these problems by special studies of sampling attached to regular surveys or by separately conducted studies. These studies should reveal some features of the geographic distribution of opinion by small areas and variations of opinion within the household that can be taken into account in designing samples. Studies of costs and of interviewer performance are needed. Tests of the accuracy and biases of measurement are very important, and calibration of all methods of observation is necessary. Ingenious devices are always welcomed. As the other phases of research operations become more accurate, the sampling phases should attain a comparable degree of accuracy. The more advanced the stage of research development, the more it can benefit from effective sampling procedures.

The survey is probably the most extensively employed technique in contemporary sociological and social psychological research. It operates on the principle that opinions and other reported responses about thoughts, feelings, and actions by a sample of persons similar in their characteristics to a "universe," or larger population, will approximate the responses of that universe. The chief tool used in the survey by interview is the schedule, the administration of which is conducted orally. When the survey utilizes written rather than oral stimuli, the instrument is called a questionnaire. Each procedure has advantages over the other, but the personal interview, despite its greater cost, is generally considered to be more desirable for most types of sociological surveys. Important tasks faced in personal interviews are the development of the schedule so that the answers secured will be a function of the intent of the questions, selection of the respondents by adequate sampling, and collection of the data in a manner that minimizes interviewer bias.

The following article by Herbert Hyman describes the findings of the National Opinion Research Center's project on the isolation, measurement, and control of interviewer effect on the quality of opinion-research data. He shows that variations in results derive from interviewer fallibility, unreliability of respondents, and, finally, interactional processes. Disparities in the group memberships of interviewer and respondent affect the results. Furthermore, beliefs the interviewer has about the respondent produce expectations which in turn also affect the results. Finally, Professor Hyman describes experiments on the role of situational factors in mediating interviewer effects and on the validity of interviewer data.

49. PROBLEMS IN THE COLLECTION OF OPINION-RESEARCH DATA *

HERBERT HYMAN

Columbia University

Opinion research has availed itself of many methods for the collection of data. The methods are as varied as the kinds of data which research workers have regarded as relevant, and there is almost no limit to what has been regarded as relevant. I did not invent the following examples of genius in devising circuitous methods of getting at sociopsychological phenomena; they can be documented: (1) the collection of historical records of behavior used as inferential measures of opinion, e.g., the use of statistics on the subscriptions

* *The American Journal of Sociology,* Vol. LV, No. 4, January, 1950, pp. 362–370.

to the *Nation* as a basis for conclusion about radicalism and its correlates; (2) the collection of behavioral data based on observation used as inferential measures of opinion, e.g., the use of statistics derived from listening to conversations as a basis for drawing conclusions about sex differences in values; (3) the collection of data derived from the content analysis of mediums, e.g., the characterization of unmarried women in recent novels used as a clue to attitudes toward the status of women; (4) even the collection of data based on measurements of psychophysical indices, e.g., reaction time, muscular steadiness, as correlates of a man's ideology or the measurement of the secretion of sweat as a clue to the reaction to advertisements. These examples—and many others that can be found in the literature—suggest that there apparently is no limit to the imagination of the social scientist in devising indirect approaches. Apart from the creative tendencies of the scientist, these indirect approaches reflect a distrust of the most obvious method in opinion research, the interview, since they all show a common aversion to asking a question in order to find out a man's opinions.

On the other hand, during the last two or three decades, the social psychologist, like the experimentalist and the clinician, has made increasing use of the direct approach wherein reliance is placed in substantial degree at least upon the subject's own verbal reports. The procedures have ranged from the application of quasi-clinical devices, such as thematic apperception tests or interpretations of slips of the tongue and those involving routine self-administered questionnaires to those involving the ordinary techniques of asking questions in the course of an interview. And the routine interviews vary from the single polling or intensive interview through such elaborate methods as a series of repeated interviews with the same individual to the genetic study of attitudes based on the reported entire life-history of the individual. Interviewing has also varied in technical respects from that of a group situation to a private interview and in terms of such details as method of recording, type of sponsorship, degree of anonymity, and the like.

This experience in the use of the direct approach has certainly revealed weaknesses, some of which are inherent in the method and some in the lack of discipline and insight in its application. There are always tough questions as to the reliability and validity of the data elicited by it. But before the method is discarded in favor of such indirect and inferential methods as those exemplified above, its demonstrated weaknesses should themselves be subjected to careful research to see whether they cannot be remedied. We have been engaged in this very type of methodological research at the National Opinion Research Center.

Therefore, I shall limit this discussion to some of the problems of collection of data by the methods of interviewing that prevail in most public opinion research. Against the vista of all possible methods for collecting data about opinions, this may seem narrow, but certainly the interview is the essential method in the field of opinion research. The interview is also central in the methods of clinical psychology, psychiatry, and ethnology, so that whatever *basic* knowledge we can gain about interviewing methods is applicable to many of the social sciences and is of general value. To the best of my knowledge, no evaluations have been made in ethnology of the effect that different interviewers have on the results they report as fact about a culture. And I know of only one isolated wartime study of the differences in diagnoses obtained by different psychiatrists. In the report of one of the most ambitious undertakings in the history of clinical psychology, the assessment of men for OSS duties, I can find only one tiny datum on the effect of different interviewers on the assessment ratings given to OSS candidates. In the light of these gaps in our knowledge, it would certainly seem that any evidence bearing on the quality of data collected by interviewing methods would be a notable contribution. Perhaps, merely by example, fields other than opinion research will be stimulated to inquire into the quality of their interview data.

The two-year study now in progress at the National Opinion Research Center is concerned with the isolation, measurement, and control of interviewer effects in *opinion* research, and we are indebted for financial support to the Rockefeller Foundation and for sponsorship to the Committee on Measurement of Opinion, Attitudes and Consumer Wants of the National Research Council and the Social Science Research Council. The findings represent the work of many colleagues in my own organization as well as the co-operation of individuals in many other research centers. There are many different ways to conceptualize our work. It is difficult to describe all the findings of these two years of work in a concise presentation, but I shall try to summarize some of our thinking and some of the findings.

Every day, throughout the United States, hundreds of people are asked questions by a public opinion interviewer, and thousands of these answers are put through an elaborate process of tabulation and analysis, and then elegant conclusions are drawn about the state of American public opinion. Would we have obtained a different set of results and a different picture of American public opinion if we had sent another corps of interviewers out to ask the same questions of the same people? And if the results would be different, how different? Obviously, in so far as different interviewers get different results, we know that our conclusions may be in error. We do know from past studies in this field, by S. A. Rice and by S. Shapiro and J. Eberhart, to cite only a few, that there are interviewer effects operating on our data. The magnitude of these effects is presumed to be small in most instances, but on occasion the tabulations based on the work of different interviewers assigned to equivalent samples have differed by as much as 50 percentage points. In our own work at NORC we have extended this body of data by a few studies in which we have been able to measure the magnitude of the differences in results obtained by interviewers assigned to equivalent respondents.

Presumably such studies should yield some empirical or historical basis for stating the margins of uncertainty that apply to future survey findings as a consequence of factors within the interview situation. Conceivably we can qualify our findings in future surveys in the light of such past knowledge about interviewer effects. However, in order to do this, we would need an archive of past estimates of interviewer effects under a wide variety of representative conditions. Only then might one know what appropriate allowance to make for error in any particular type of survey. This seems like an almost hopeless task when one considers the number of ways in which surveys can vary. The magnitude of these effects might be dependent on the types of respondents who are being sampled, the types of information being measured, the kinds of interviewers used, the mode of questioning, and the like. And for any given survey the combination of factors and conditions may be so peculiar that none of our past estimates of interviewer effects would apply. Or a given survey may be similar to past ones in certain respects and different in other respects. And if one does not know which particular factors are the *determinants* of interviewer effects, one has no basis for judging what the magnitude of interviewer effects might be in the new situation. It would only be by research that inquires not only into the magnitude but also into the determinants that one would know what are the essential factors to consider in deciding the susceptibility of a given survey to interviewer effects and in applying a past estimate.

Consequently, we have done only a limited number of such studies in which the mere magnitude of interviewer effects has been measured and have concentrated much more on understanding the sources of such effects.

What contributes to these effects? Classically, interviewer effects have been interpreted in terms of the interaction between interviewer and respondent. It was thought that the respondent is affected by the personality or characteristics of the interviewer and alters what he says in the light of the particular interviewer who speaks to him. In part, interviewer effects have nothing to do with the interaction that occurs between interviewer and respondent. These effects derive simply from the fact that interviewers are human beings, not machines, and they therefore do not all work identically nor are they infallible in performing difficult tasks. This is certainly suggested by what we might call "interviewer effects" in surveys involving sampling of physical materials. When field staffs are assigned the task of rating the quality of a sample of telephone poles, one cannot argue that the telephone pole reacts to the personality of the investigator. And the fact that different field workers may obtain different results in evaluating physical materials shows that some of the sources of error reside purely in the field worker and are not dependent on interaction in the immediate situation. And this is in line with a whole body of psychological theory ranging from classical research on testimony to the modern dynamic theory in the psychology of perception that individuals perceive the world in a way that is not dependent purely on their sensory acuity but on their wishes and personality structure and that there are large individual differences in judging, perceiving, and other functions.

In our own work specifically on interviewer effects, we have some experiments which show that the differences in results can be accounted for without any references to the interaction between interviewer and respondent. For example, in one experiment the mere changing of the method of recording that the interviewer is required to use in a regular survey changed the results. In another experiment in which the interviewer was required to listen to a dummy interview on a phonograph record and take down the answers, we found errors. The recording operation is purely in the hands of the interviewer, and consequently any effects operating cannot be attributed to the respondent's altering his behavior.

In part some of the interviewer effects observable in a survey derive purely from the respondents and really have nothing to do with the interviewer. They simply represent the unreliability of reports that respondents as human beings make. This is certainly suggested by classical studies of the unreliability of results from self-administered questionnaires, in which variations occur in the absence of any interviewer. It is also suggested by panel studies in which respondents are reinterviewed by the same interviewer after a lapse of time in which we find considerable change in the reporting of unchanged facts. In one minor experiment by the NORC, in which a small group of respondents in Mississippi was interviewed twice with the same questionnaire within a time interval of less than one hour by two competent interviewers, the results of the two interviews bear almost no resemblance to each other and seem to be nothing but answers at random, one thrown out at one moment in time and a different answer at another moment in time. This was, luckily, an extreme and unusual finding, but it certainly supports the notion that interviewer effects are to some extent merely unreliability of report.

Consequently, we may go too far at times in interpreting the variations in survey results as due to the sensitive reactions of respondents to the interviewer's characteristics, and we may err in thinking that the type of social situation common in public opinion research is one in which the respondent hangs on every word, gesture, and nuance of the interviewer's behavior and orients his own behavior accordingly. In one study we reinterviewed a small group of respondents within a few days after the regular survey interview and inquired about their feelings when they were interviewed originally. We found a few individuals who could not even recall what the interviewer looked like. I particularly remember the answer of the respondent who, upon being asked what he remembered most about the previous interviewer, was stumped for a while and then remarked after a few minutes of serious thought, "She was tall," and the answer of another respondent who, after being asked what he was most impressed by in the previous interview, said, "it was in one ear and out the other—it was the goddamnedest lot of bull." For such respondents whatever interaction there is with the interviewer must be at best minimal.

There are certain types of interviewer effects, however, that would best be accounted for by hypothesizing some interaction between interviewer and respondent. For example, a whole series of studies shows that survey results for specialized attitudes are affected by the disparities or similarities in the group membership of interviewer and respondent. For example, in two NORC surveys samples of Christian respondents in New York City were asked whether Jews in America had too much influence in the business world. Among those who were interviewed by Christian interviewers, 50 percent said the Jews had too much influence, but among those interviewed by Jewish interviewers, only 22 percent said so. In another survey in which respondents were asked whether they agreed with the statement "Prison is too good for sex criminals; they should be publicly whipped or worse," among women respondents who were interviewed by men interviewers 61 percent agreed with this statement; whereas when women were interviewed by women interviewers, only 49 percent agreed. It would seem either that women are less bloodthirsty when they are in the company of their own species or, put more precisely, that they feel more compelled to give the conventional and sanctioned attitude to a male interviewer. In another survey, in which one group of Negroes was interviewed by white interviewers and an equivalent group by Negro interviewers, similar effects were observed. For example, when asked whether the Army is unfair to Negroes, 35 percent of those interviewed by Negroes said "Yes," but only 11 percent of those interviewed by whites were willing to express this critical attitude. It is well documented that responses vary with the disparity between interviewer's and respondent's sex, class, color, religion, and other group-membership factors. And the systematic direction of these effects is such that one would not attribute them to mere unreliability but to the way in which the respondent alters his behavior in accordance with the kind of person who speaks to him.

A number of additional experiments suggest the mechanism by which such interactions or effects are mediated. A study by D. Robinson and S. Rohde showed that there was an orderly change in the anti-Semitic opinions expressed depending on the degree to which the interviewer looked Jewish and emphasized this fact by using a Jewish name. There is also evidence from secret-ballot surveys, in which the interviewer asks no questions, does no recording of answers, but merely hands the respondent a printed ballot on which the respondent registers his opinion, that the results vary with the type of interviewer who merely proffers the ballot to the respondent. This kind of evidence suggests not that the interviewer communicates his bias by a specific mechanism of intonation or probing or specific reactions to what is said but simply that respondents perceive something about the interviewer immediately from his mere appearance or behavior, interpret this for some reason in a certain way, and in turn alter their behavior. And the meaning they give to whatever they perceive may depend on a complex of cultural factors. For example, the study on the effect of the color of the interviewer on the opinions reported by Negroes was conducted in Memphis, and the change in results cited was 24 percentage points. When the identical question was asked in Harlem by Negro versus white interviewers, the change was only 7 percentage points—24 percentage points in Memphis, 7 in New York City. Clearly the respondents must have perceived the color of the interviewer in both cities, but the impact of color and the meaning given to this physical phenomenon was a product of the cultural patterns in the North as compared with those in the South, and the interviewer effects mirror these cultural forces.

One can use the findings of such experiments in building a better theoretical foundation in social psychology. We are now leaning away from our old notion that an attitude is a fixed thing that influences behavior and toward the idea that attitudes have situational components and may or may not come into play depending on a variety of environmental factors. We can fill in some of the concrete material for such a theory by interpreting the interview situation as a miniature of the larger social setting and seeing some of the interviewer effects as analogies to the influence of social factors on the expression of attitudes.

The way the *respondent* perceives the interviewer is only one side of the coin. Interviewer effects also derive from the way the *interviewer* perceives the respondent and subsequently alters his method of questioning, probing, recording, and the like. In the course of intensive interviews with interviewers designed to reveal their existential world, we noted that they had certain expectations about how their respondents would answer given questions. These expectations guide the interviewer at various choice-points throughout the interview and affect his decisions about probing and recording. As one interviewer put it, "Once they start talking, I can predict what they'll say." These expectations seem to be built on the basis of certain beliefs about the respondent. And these beliefs are of two main types. On the one hand, interviewers may entertain oversimplified stereotypes about the attitudes or behavior or roles that correspond to given status characteristics or group memberships. Merely on the basis of perceiving that the respondent is a man or woman, rich rather than poor, or Negro rather than white, they expect his answers to be of a certain nature, and this spuriously inflates the relation between group membership and certain attitudes. Such reactions by the interviewer to the group membership of the respondent and the corresponding reactions of respondents to the group membership of the interviewer, as mentioned earlier, provide incidental evidence of the pervasive influence of group membership on human behavior.

J. J. Feldman of the NORC's Chicago staff found differences in the results obtained by interviewers given equivalent samples on certain questions dealing with the extent to which the respondent and the spouse made purchases of given types of commodities. These differences seem to be explained best by the beliefs that different interviewers had as to the normal buying roles of men and women, e.g., whether a woman would normally have an automobile repaired or a man would normally buy house furnishings. A second type of belief that operates in the interviewer to produce expectations and therefore interviewer effects might be called "attitude structure expectations." Interviewers, like most human beings, seem to believe that other human beings have a logically consistent and integrated structure of attitudes. Consequently, on the basis of the early answers of respondents, they build up some belief as to what his further attitudes will be and anticipate that the later answers will fall in line. Such expectations presumably operate to produce spurious intercorrelations between attitudes. Harry Smith of the NORC's New York staff had interviewers listen to prepared phonograph records which simulated two normal interviews and record the answers they heard on a questionnaire. In both these records, lukewarm, equivocal answers were inserted which were identical in substance for both respondents. On one record the answers were imbedded in a context of previous answers that built up a picture of an isolationist respondent, and on the other the context of previous answers was that of an internationalist. One result will be vivid enough to demonstrate that attitude-structure expectations really influence the perception and recording of the answer. On a question whether the United States was spending too much on foreign aid, both respondents gave an answer which impartial judges, viewing the answer out of context, coded as "we're spending about the right amount." But among the 117 interviewers tabulated, only 20 percent classified the isolationist's answer as the "right amount" whereas 75 percent classified the internationalist's answer as the "right amount." This difference is accounted for essentially by the fact that 53 percent classified the isolationist as saying "we're spending too much."

The process by which such expectations are built up and can be maintained despite contradictory material can be illustrated by phenomenological data collected in the course of Smith's experiment. One of the interviewers was asked to report aloud his thinking as he participated in the experiment. No suggestion whatsoever was given to him that he describe the respondent or report on his expectations. Nevertheless, the following portions of his running account show the immediate formation of a picture of the respondent and the dynamics by which such expectations are maintained: After hearing the answer to Question 1: "I do have some impressions. The respondent seems very doubtful about giving his opinion—a little suspicious. I don't have too much respect for this particular respondent. My immediate impression is that he's one of those types of individuals who thinks in very personal terms." Following the answer to Question 2: "I was right. Immediately he's going off on tangents. He's not really interested in the survey. He's interested in getting rid of any personal feelings he has. I feel he's an old geezer." At Question 7 the first experimental answer was inserted which was a mild contradiction of the previous answers. However, instead of changing his beliefs, the interviewer rationalized the contradiction in such a way as to maintain his former impression. He remarked: "He's still wary about giving his *real* opinion. He started to backtrack."

Traditionally, it has been argued in discussions of interviewer bias that the interviewer is motivated to influence the results in the direction of his own attitude or ideology, and little attention has been given to the role of such cognitive factors as expectations. The relative importance of these two sources of bias can be illustrated, in a somewhat oversimplified fashion, by another finding from Smith's experiment.

In the finding already cited on the question of whether the United States was spending too much on foreign aid, it is seen that the influence of expectations built up by the context of previous answers was to cause 75 percent of the subjects to code the internationalist's answer as "the right amount" whereas only 20 percent coded the same answer in the isolationist context as "the right amount." Here we have the effect of expectations, in the aggregate, for interviewers holding *all* kinds of attitudes. Now, if we compare the results that interviewers who themselves are internationalist produced on the internationalist recording with the results that interviewers who themselves are isolationist produced on the isolationist recording, we should presumably enhance the difference between the two results, since we are compounding the two sources of bias—expectation *plus* interviewer's own attitude. We actually find for this comparison that 78 percent of the internationalist interviewers score the internationalist respondent as saying "the right amount" whereas only 19 percent of the isolationist interviewers classify the isolationist respondent as saying "the right amount." Adding the factor of interviewer attitude hardly increases the bias.

Such expectations must certainly operate in other fields of interviewing as sources of bias. In clinical work we tacitly recognize the existence of such expectations by talking of the "insightfulness" of the clinician. The difference is simply that we bar them as "biases" in public opinion research whereas we sanction them in clinical work.

As suggested earlier, interviewer effects may simply represent the fallibility of the human beings who are our interviewers and do not derive from any interaction between respondent and interviewer. Not all interviewers are identical in their structures, and their human failings appear when they are confronted with the difficult tasks we assign them. We have undertaken a few projects which start from the assumption that the situational features of the interview, the specific processes we require the interviewer to engage in, the pressures we put upon him in the interview, may either facilitate or reduce interviewer variations and interviewer errors. We must accept the inherent limitations of our human materials, and perhaps the next best thing is to examine our procedures and manipulate the interview process in such a way as to inhibit the *operation* of the human factors that would potentially create errors. Such an approach is eminently practical in that the survey process is flexible and within our control, and it would also seem to be more sophisticated theoretically. Instead of seeing bias as a fixed entity residing purely within the individual, we now see it as a product of the individual working within a certain type of environment, the interview.

In one such experiment Paul Sheatsley of the NORC's New York staff hypothesized that interviewers wish to avoid asking tedious, embarrassing, difficult questions. If we design our surveys so that such questions are supposed to be asked only if the respondent has given a certain answer previously, the interviewer might be prone to elicit or record the answer that permits him to avoid the difficult subquestions. Note that this point of view is not that the interviewer has some long-term desire to bias the answers and does it but that the bias is created by the temporary situational pressures upon the interviewer. This hypothesis was tested by having interviewers work with two equivalent ballots on two equivalent samples. In the one instance the ballot was so designed that a certain answer to an initial question called for the asking of four additional annoying subquestions; in the other instance, the opposing answer to the same question called for the four subquestions to be asked. If the pressure of the subquestions causes interviewers to distort results so as to avoid the additional work, the results on the initial question should be different in the two matched samples. In this instance, we found that there was no effect.

In another experiment of this same type we required interviewers, on the one hand, to classify the answers they received into pre-coded categories and in a matched control survey merely to record the answers verbatim. If the classification process releases the biasing tendencies of interviewers, we should find differences in the results. In brief we found that in the *aggregate* the classification process does not affect the data. However, among inexperienced members of the field staff the classification process does affect the results they obtain.

In line with our interest in the situational features of the interview, in the specific processes that mediate or create interviewer effects, we have naturally turned toward the idea of hidden observation of the total interview. In the two experiments just cited we have been able to *infer* the effects of given aspects of the process by special experimental designs. However, if we can bring the total interview situation into view, we can see what contribution each and every aspect of the total process makes to the final effects. We will be able to collect such information from a study being done by the American Jewish Committee to which we have contributed financial support and advice. In this study, stooge respondents are being interviewed by a crew of interviewers and a hidden wire recording of the entire interview is being made. From this study, which is still in progress, we will ultimately have information on errors in interviewer behavior in such separate aspects of the interview as the question-asking, the probing, and the recording. We will be able to state whether such errors change in magnitude progressively in time, whether the respondent's behavior in turn alters the interviewer's performance, whether errors are distributed among all questions or concentrated in certain types of question, whether there is a given type of interviewer who is prone to all kinds of error, or whether interviewing skills are discrete.

In many of the experiments cited thus far, we can demonstrate interviewer differences in the results and allocate these effects to certain characteristics of the interviewer or of the respondent or of the situation itself or of the interaction between interviewer and respondent. However, from a practical point of view, these experiments are not very helpful unless they establish what kinds of interviewers or procedures give us better or more valid results. Merely to reduce the variability in results might not improve their quality. Conceivably we might even screen our staff so as to get a homogeneous group of interviewers who would get identical results, all bad. Such thinking led us to undertake an experiment in Denver in which groups of interviewers are given equivalent assignments on a survey which includes questions on age, ownership of telephone, automobile ownership, charitable contributions, voting behavior in a series of elections, and a number of other characteristics. For each of these characteristics we have reliable information from official records about the actual status of *each individual* in the sample. Consequently, we will not only be able to state whether different interviewers obtain different results but, knowing which interviewers of given types obtain more valid results, we will be guided in the selection of personnel. These data are now being analyzed and will be published in the future by J. D. Cahalan, Helen Crossley, Hugh Parry, and others and, apart from their import for the problem of interviewer effects, will be a notable contribution to the almost untouched problem of validity.

In the nature of the case the emphasis in this paper has been upon defective work. But there are many surveys where one finds little variation in the results for different interviewers, and no one should contend that opinion research does not belong in the company of other sciences because of the unreliability of the interviewing methods. I am convinced that these types of error occur elsewhere and that opinion research is merely leading the way in subjecting its interviewing methods to critical examination. The problem of interviewer effects has now come into its own.

A generation ago, 95 percent of all sociologists were college and university teachers for the most part and individual researchers in their spare time. Today it is impossible to begin to fill the demand for sociologists as full-time "team" researchers, not only in universities but also in government, hospitals, prisons, large industry, and social welfare agencies. Increasingly, these researchers explore pragmatic social issues such as structural unemployment where joblessness has become chronic and seemingly permanent; the changing patterns of medical care with the disappearance of the family physician and the emergence of specialization, hospitalization, clinics, and group practice; and the problems created by the media of mass communication.

One of the strongest pressures on sociological researchers today is to develop techniques for gathering, interpreting, and utilizing the vast amount of data they are asked to accumulate. Traditionally, sociologists did their research individually with limited tools and resources on comparatively minuscule segments of the social landscape. Recently, however, the raw materials for this research have been enormously expanded through such developments as organized, large-scale sampling and the availability of highly sophisticated and efficient electronic computer systems.

This has raised several questions about the merits and demerits of individual versus organizational research. In the next article, Alfred McClung Lee discusses the processes in each type of research and urges that contemporary sociology retain a large niche for the individual researcher.

50. INDIVIDUAL AND ORGANIZATIONAL RESEARCH IN SOCIOLOGY *

ALFRED MCCLUNG LEE

Brooklyn College

Both "individual" and "organizational" research have grown with the sociological field. Both have made notable contributions.

What would contemporary sociology be without the findings of such significant "individual" researchers as William Graham Sumner, Ferdinand Tönnies, Émile Durkheim, Georg Simmel, William Isaac Thomas, Max Weber, and Charles Horton Cooley? Their work still has vitality that demands quotation and re-interpretation today both in introductory textbooks and in careful scientific monographs. The growing influence of so recently deceased a colleague as Willard Waller suggests that such independents can still make strikingly useful additions to our knowledge of human relationships.

What would contemporary sociology be without the contributions of organized investigators and so-called group researchers? The social bookkeeping reports of governmental units and the special surveys of civic bodies and business firms have a long and fruitful history. Their descriptions of artifacts, populations, and human behavior are part of the backdrop against which sociological knowledge has evolved since Auguste Comte and Herbert Spencer. Questions, suggestions, and occasionally plans and guidance from sociologists have helped such censuses and surveys to gain in accuracy and in social and scientific utility.

What is usually called group research rather than just organized investigation grew out of the work of individuals such as Frederic Le Play, Franklin Henry Giddings, Robert Ezra Park, Ernest W. Burgess, and F. Stuart Chapin as well as of the groups headed by such persons as Charles Booth, Paul U. Kellogg, A. L. Bowley, Robert S. and Helen M. Lynd, W. Lloyd Warner, Louis Wirth, Samuel A. Stouffer, and Paul F. Lazarsfeld. As part of this group research development, especially since the 1920s, came subsidies for group

* *American Sociological Review,* Vol. 16, No. 5, October, 1951, pp. 701–707.

projects by foundations and special interests and the establishment of research institutes and bureaus in connection with academic departments of sociology and anthropology as well as with the related departments of psychology, economics, and government.

Concomitant with this development, opinion and attitude studies have become a sizable element in industrial, distributive, and political planning in the United States and to an increasing extent in other Western countries. Industrialists have learned that "attitudes" have something to do with personnel morale, efficiency, and productivity and with the ways in which present and potential employees are likely to react in crisis situations. Consumer acceptance tests have helped distributors of items packaged and advertised for retail sale to select more effective labels, cartons, and advertisements. The relative accuracy of poll predictions of elections gave politicians and businessmen some respect for poll reports of all sorts prior to the failure of the commercial polls to predict correctly the November 2, 1948 Federal election results. But this set-back only temporarily placed commercial polling in a more accurate perspective. Public relations counselors, who once proved their worth to clients with bulging scrapbooks of press clippings, find a wide range of surveys and polls now available to them to attest to their accomplishments, all of course "scientifically" certified and some bearing the imprimaturs of renowned universities.

Before going further with what must in part be a comparison of "individual" and "organizational" research, let me offer further definitions of these terms.

By "individual" research, I refer to research carried on as nearly as possible as a personal venture on free time by (1) a teacher, (2) a person otherwise employed, or (3) a person with independent funds or so subsidized that he feels relatively free to pursue his own interests as he sees them. As R. S. Lynd has put it, "Upon those teachers who are on what is called, probably increasingly optimistically, 'permanent tenure,' there would appear to rest the special obligation to carry for their less-secure junior colleagues the main brunt of hard-hitting, constructive thought that spares no one, least of all themselves."

The "individual" researcher may or may not use clerical and mechanical aids. That depends upon his needs and resources. He may or may not relate his efforts to those of other researchers. If he is well trained and has the emotional and intellectual qualifications to be a scientist, he will be eager to accept, modify, or reject the findings of others and to relate his own work to theirs. He may base his conclusions and test and retest his theories primarily on his own first-hand observations, including his own experiments. For these purposes, his observations may be of few or many cases, and the cases may be a random choice or a carefully developed sample. Or the individual researcher may assess and use observations of others, such as census, ethnographic, court, legislative, administrative, sample-survey, and case-study reports. In order that he may have maximal flexibility and minimal embedment in institutional obligations, tensions, and other influences during his hours of research, the individual researcher needs to feel above all and as much as possible that his only criteria of achievement in research are those he associates with (1) his own drive to satisfy his own curiosity, (2) his own desire to extend or broaden human knowledge of society, and (3) his own conception of a scientist's personal integrity.

By "organizational" research, I refer to research that is carried on in an institutional setting and as an institutional function, in other words upon institutional rather than personal responsibility. This is something more ambitious than what is labeled above as organized investigation. Group research usually involves an effort to modify sociological theory. It is to group research rather than mere organized investigation that especial attention is to be given here. Allyn A. Young has described group research as "a common attack upon a particular problem or set of problems, by an organized body of investigators who apportion their work so as to get some of the advantages of the division of labor, and who may be able to turn over routine parts of their tasks to a corps of clerical assistants." To such a description, Donald Young adds this significant qualification: "It is assumed with good historical reason that basic innovations in social science may rarely be expected from large-scale projects; initiation of such projects has usually been stimulated by the findings of some previous innovator working on a modest scale. There seems to be no alternative to continued dependence on the individual worker for new ideas and pioneering studies."

Even in such a highly institutionalized type of research as that in the electron-tube industry, a researcher points to much the same situation when he notes, "The conception of an original idea, the finding of a basic principle, is essentially an individual effort." He reinforces this by asserting, "When the problem has been stated—always the most difficult step—and a sound approach to its solution is indicated, a group effort will bring the most rapid solution." In other words, he would allot only routine efforts to a "research task force."

What advantages to researchers and to scientific development does subsidized and institutionalized group research provide? Group-researchers contend that a research organization should be nothing more nor less than a medium through which capable researchers are freed from extraneous activities and responsibilities and given the essentials of modern research—specialized associates, technical and clerical assistants, and expensive machinery. The group brings together trained persons with diverse backgrounds and skills who benefit from interstimulation. Such association is especially productive, it is claimed, when the group specialists focus their efforts upon the solution of a common theoretical or practical problem or group of problems. Once a research organization designs a research project, the human and mechanical machine as a whole can start to function. The machine can carry out controlled observations on adequate samples of large populations. It can process these observations with precision and efficiency. Its top staff specialists can join not only in planning such a project but also in assuring adequate execution and thorough analyses, criticisms, and interpretations of results.

These are brief favorable descriptions of independent and institutionalized research. For the purposes of characterization, fairly extreme rather than intermediate types are selected. It might be argued, to illustrate, that certain work done by graduate students is of an independent sort, and this may be so. It depends upon the graduate student and the graduate department in which he is working. It might also be argued that a professor "has given heavy hostages to fortune: he has a family to rear, usually on a not too ample salary; his income depends upon the academic advancements he can win, and these in turn depend upon 'productive research.' . . . He lives in a world which, by and large, is not asking, 'Is Smith trying to get at the facts? Is he trying to be fair and constructive at the same time that he is unwilling to pull his punch?' but which asks, 'Are you for us, or against us?' " But there are now, as there have been for many generations in many countries, academic and other social scientists who, to be picturesque with V. L. Parrington, "decline to block the path to the Promised Land with retainer-fees."

Unfavorable descriptions of what are derisively called "lone wolf" research and "assembly-line" research need also be given.

A great many see the individual sociological researcher in the mid-twentieth-century world as a lone and primitively equipped David going forth to meet a vastly expanded and awesomely armored Goliath, modern society. The analogy is appealing to group-research partisans. Apologists for "assembly-line" research say that their teams outfitted with modern machinery and drilled to precision in techniques have become as essential to sociological research as are *Panzer* divisions to modern international relations.

A great many others would, significantly enough, reject both this statement and its analogy. They see group research as a profitable but bungling and overrated bureaucratic device which comes to end-products of greater political than scientific significance. If all the clashes of views, facts, and personalities within a group were published, the gain to science would be far greater than vague unified end-products are likely to yield. As in the U. S. Supreme Court, minority reports might stand the tests of subsequent experience and verification far more substantially than those of the majority. But minority statements and "minutes of proceedings" in which differences of view within the group are ironed out seldom appear in the publications of group research organizations.

More systematically, what are principal criticisms leveled against contemporary individual research? Here are two common ones of some weight. It is said that individual researchers are likely to be more intuitive impressionistic, and subject to the use of the *Verstehen* operation than group researchers. The necessarily individualistic individual researchers are also likely to be thought inpudent, imprudent, repugnant, confusing, or confused by the more socialized or bureaucratic group researchers: The individualists "do not fit in." They do not know "how to sell their ideas." They do not know "how to sell themselves." They are "lone wolves." They live in "ivory towers" or now, more probably, "white farmhouses." They "lack savvy." For any of many combinations of possible life-history factors, they are what Robert Ezra Park called "marginal men." At any rate, they are not, as it has been said of many group researchers in social science, "assimilated members of the American business community."

What are the principal criticisms made against contemporary group research? Here, as with individual research, a comprehensive list is not attempted. Of these criticisms, two contrast especially with those mentioned for individual research, and two are more peculiar to group operation. These criticisms have to do with (1) observation, (2) decision-making processes, (3) interests, and (4) organizational imperatives. Let us look at each of these briefly in turn.

1. *Observation.* Sociological group research typically underrates the importance of first-hand observation and relegates it to minor staff members. It exaggerates the importance of *a priori* constructions arrived at in committee: hypotheses, definitions, specifications of data to be sought, procedures, research or experiment designs. Relatively unskilled and underpaid workers carry out in a prescribed and routine manner what observations are made. It has frequently been said in opinion research that when an interviewer becomes competent he can make a great deal more doing something other than opinion interviewing. In scientific work generally, a great many would agree with W. H. Hudson that "an observer is a rarer thing than a genius" and would add that he is far more productive in contributions to science.

In order to explain away and to adjudge unscientific the first-hand observings and the careful weighings of data by a Sumner or a Cooley, their ability to make what Francis Bacon so long ago called "a fresh examination of particulars" must be labeled "intuitive," "impressionistic," or *"Verstehen,"* as is suggested above. It does not seem to occur to rationalists for the exclusive superiority of "assembly-line" methods that basic to all scientific research are sense impressions of phenomena. These are basic to and underlie whatever processing might later be given to reports of sense data. If observations are inferior, partial, or badly recorded, all else in the research effort is impaired. If observation turns up one verified and verifiable fact at odds with existing theory, the whole project gains more therefrom than from any amount of statistical manipulation, except to the extent that the latter might *help to reveal novelty in observation.* As Irving Langmuir notes, scientists "have to be prepared for the unexpected, for things that don't make sense according to our old ideas," and he adds, "the more you try to dominate scientists the less they can deal with unforeseen."

2. *Decision-making processes.* In group research, the prestige, aggressiveness, and plausibility of the advocate of an idea frequently give that idea

weight out of all proportion to its scientific significance. One thus has in group decision-making processes the phenomena associated with "committee thinking." These phenomena are quite useful in democratic decision-making for political or business purposes, but they have little relevance or pertinence to scientifically useful assessments, analyses, and generalizations of systematic sense impressions.

The prestige factor in decision-making gains much from a person's ability to bring funds into the group. Here as elsewhere not only he who pays the piper but also he who takes the money from the paymaster to the piper—the go-between—both exert direct and indirect influences upon the selection of both piper and tune.

It is of course a commonplace in polite discussion to ignore many consequences of the go-between's entrepreneurial role. Members of a group ordinarily maintain an oral ritual in which the go-between's preëminence in the group is attributed to his alleged fruitfulness as a source of ideas or of administrative wisdom rather than to the overshadowing fact that he is the principal channel of power and hence the dominant instrument of control. He may also, it should be admitted, be a stimulating theorist and a wise administrator.

A great many foundations create and build entrepreneurism in research by preferring to make sizable grants to institutions for group research rather than to individuals. Notable exceptions are, as examples, the Wenner-Gren Foundation and, in part, the Social Science Research Council.

3. *Interests.* As a result of skilled leadership in "committee thinking" and of the need to offer commercially understandable services to potential clients and foundations, groups develop a lack of flexibility rather quickly. They acquire vested interests in personnel, in one or several personalities, in methods, and in theories. This problem afflicts individual researchers more acutely than groups, but the greater power and persistence of groups makes such inflexible vested interests the more serious in the cases of groups. Individuals rise and fall with their methods and theories. The brief span of a person's professional career delimits the period during which prestige and control can maintain useless theories. But groups can give methods and theories a sanction, a dignity, a following, an authority long after they are seen by outsiders to have little or no scientific merit.

4. *Organizational imperatives.* To keep group research going, constant attention must be given by one or more of the group to the cultivation of sources of income. These are the go-betweens mentioned above. In all cases that have come to my attention and about which I have been able to gain fairly adequate data, including a great many group researches in social, biological, and physical fields for a range of sponsors, this ever-present necessity pervades much of the thinking of the whole staff whether they like it or not and whether their income source is private industry, a government agency, a foundation, a university committee, or a combination of several such. This

consciousness of payroll problems is not as conducive to detached and objective research as group research is usually claimed to be.

The operational imperatives of both independents and group researchers tend, as A. H. Maslow indicates, to place premiums upon means-centering in investigations rather than upon scientific-problem-centering. By means-centering, he refers "to the tendency to consider that the essence of science lies in its instruments, techniques, procedures, apparatus and its methods rather than in its problems, questions, functions or goals." This especially "tends to push into a commanding position in [what is called] science the technicians and the 'apparatus men,' rather than the 'question-askers' and the problem-solvers." It is easier to gain institutional support for a technology that stresses, as Maslow observes, "elegance, polish, 'technique,' and apparatus" rather than for the irritating questionings and novel observations of scientists.

If the foregoing were the only problems associated with individual and organizational research, few would be greatly concerned. In competition, individual research would continue to outpace the organizational in the ways indicated in my quotation above from Donald Young, an advocate of group research. But the primary problem is this: Group research has now so absorbed the interests, aspirations, and resources of graduate departments of sociology that the training of individual well-rounded journeymen in sociological research is being eclipsed. The situation has thus now arisen that it is becoming fairly difficult to locate young staff members for a college or university who are trained to be liberal arts college and graduate school professors and to carry on the independent research that needs to go therewith.

This situation is not unique to sociology. It arrived much earlier in the physical and biological sciences, Writing in *Chemical and Engineering News,* Harry A. Toulmin, Jr., states in part as follows:

> Freedom of the scientist—as of any individual—means his right to hold his own social, political, and economic opinions. . . .
> Freedom of the scientist should also mean the right to select the things in which he wishes to do his research and the privilege, subject only to considerations of national security, to publish such scientific information as he wishes.
> I do not go along with the present trend in some universities toward regimenting scientific and engineering personnel by preventing them from doing research work unless it is controlled by a government, a foundation, or by rigid corporate policies. I do not go along with arbitrary control of patent rights of university personnel as the result of their own work. I do not go along with the contention of some universities that their research foundations can properly participate in studies leading to Ph.D. degrees, accept compensation from commercial sponsors who seek this cheaper form of doing their research, and agree to suppress the publication of the resulting theses until the convenience of the commercial sponsor is served. That is not freedom of science—that is not a true university.[1]

[1] Harry A. Toulmin, Jr., "The Freedom of Science—Its Opportunities and Responsibilities," *Chemical and Engineering News,* 27 (1949), p. 980.

Toulmin is speaking primarily of chemistry. He might just as well, as it is becoming increasingly apparent, have been speaking of abuses now rapidly mushrooming in sociology.

We sociologists are presumably students of scientific methodology and of the stultifying as well as the useful influences of bureaucracy and institutionalism. We are also presumably committed primarily to scientific rather than commercial or manipulative goals, or we would have found an easier and more direct route to financial rewards. Why, therefore, are we sociologists—of all specialists—now permitting our graduate training programs to be distorted by the same anti-scientific tendencies against which Toulmin inveighs in chemistry?

There is certainly a need for the training of social engineers, social technicians for employment by business management, government, trade unions, and others. These include both skilled organizational investigators and analyst-counselors. But there is an even greater need for the scientist-professor, for professors who are sociological scientists and for scientists who can conduct their independent researches as concomitants of their instructional work with students. There is also, it should be emphasized, a need for the training of group researchers as well as—but not to the exclusion of—well-rounded journeymen of the individualistic and independent sort.

To cut my discussion short, I shall point merely to a few factors against which even we students of human relationships apparently cannot maintain very effective defenses. As Gerald Wendt observes in a recent book review, and many other writers on science have discerned the same thing, "American culture . . . is essentially unscientific, although the products of science are everywhere." He would have been more accurate, in my estimation, if he had said, "Human cultures are unscientific." After all, when the scientist struggles to overcome the handicaps Francis Bacon characterized as the "idols and false notions which are now in possession of human understanding, and have taken deep root therein," he is fighting especially the preconceptions in any given culture which look upon innovations, innovators, and questioners as annoying and even subversive.

Overriding all else in mass society—East and West—is preoccupation with the control and manipulation of social power by elite groups and by their hired technical specialists. The unsettling consequences of scientific observation are far more difficult to sell to power-seekers than dependable techniques, dependable research teams, and dependable and supposedly scientific ammunition for political, legal, and industrial competition and conflict. Thus, to a very large extent, professionals in our society find it expedient to become peddlers not of knowledge and wisdom but of techniques. They develop and merchandise managerial techniques to entrepreneurs of large social power, techniques that at least appear to be useful tools and weapons.

That is the "big time" aspect of technique peddling. Related to this is what Jessie Bernard refers to as "an almost insatiable demand for techniques today."

This is the mass aspect of the same general development. As Bernard notes, "Scarcely a single issue of any popular journal appears without rules for something or other: how to stay young and beautiful; how to win friends and influence people; how to stop worrying and live; how to secure peace of mind; how to achieve salvation; how to find God."

No inference should be drawn from what is said that I am arguing in any sense against an appropriate use of the very best techniques available to scientists. As A. H. Maslow puts it, "The working scientist must, of course, be concerned with his techniques, but only because they can help him achieve his proper ends. Once he forgets this, he becomes like the man spoken of by Freud who spent all his time polishing his glasses instead of putting them on and seeing with them."

Sociological research is necessarily a marginal, extra-moral, and extra-class-mores calling. Scientific sociologists somehow succeed in resisting the overwhelming societal and class compulsions to forego curiosity and to manufacture salable weapons of power-conflict and plausible sedatives for tension-worn humanity. In my estimation, those who succeed in contributing to the science of sociology will be the ones who continue to resist those influences today as they have been such persons in the past. In this work, however, more aid is needed from graduate departments in the development of journeymen sociologists rather than merely of compatible and clever group researchers. This would facilitate the achievement of more substantial gains in sociology.

Only through more keen and precise observations of human relations, only through the devoted work of more and more keen and curious observers can sociology as a science increase its potentialities for service to humanity.

As a consequence of the large-scale development of empirical research in the discipline since World War II, sociologists have moved into two diametrically opposed, often embittered camps: the theorists "pure and simple" versus the technique-minded, fact-gathering empiricists. The former have stressed what is significant about social structure and cultural behavior, apart from its truth; the latter, what can be proven or validated, aside from whether it is significant.

One of the reasons why Robert K. Merton's position in contemporary sociology, as we saw in the first reading in this book, is strategic and pre-eminent is that he does not accept any logical basis for theory and empirical research to be opposed to each other. He has constantly stressed that generalizations can be tempered at least with disciplined observation. At the same time, close and detailed observation need not be rendered trivial by avoidance of its theoretical pertinence and implications. In the last article of this part on methodology in sociological research, Professor Merton takes up four impacts of empirical sociological research on the development of social theory: the initiation, reformulation, refocusing, and clarification of theory.

51. THE BEARING OF EMPIRICAL RESEARCH UPON THE DEVELOPMENT OF SOCIAL THEORY *

ROBERT K. MERTON
Columbia University

History has a certain gift for outmoding stereotypes. This can be seen, for example, in the historical development of sociology. The stereotype of the social theorist high in the empyrean of pure ideas uncontaminated by mundane facts is fast becoming no less outmoded than the stereotype of the social researcher equipped with questionnaire and pencil and hot on the chase of the isolated and meaningless statistic. For in building the mansion of sociology during the last decades, theorist and empiricist have learned to work together. What is more, they have learned to talk to one another in the process. At times, this means only that a sociologist has learned to talk to himself since increasingly the same man has taken up both theory and research. Specialization and integration have developed hand in hand. All this has led not only to the realization that theory and empirical research *should* interact but to the result that they *do* interact.

As a consequence, there is decreasing need for accounts of the relations between theory and research to be wholly programmatic in character. A growing body of theoretically oriented research makes it progressively possible to discuss with profit the actual relations between the two. And, as we all know, there has been no scarcity of such discussions. Journals abound with them. They generally center on the role of theory in research, setting forth, often with admirable lucidity, the functions of theory in the initiation, design and prosecution of empirical inquiry. But since this is not a one-way relationship, since the two *inter*act, it may be useful to examine the other direction of the relationship: the role of empirical research in the development of social theory. That is the purpose of this paper.

THE THEORETIC FUNCTIONS OF RESEARCH

With a few conspicuous exceptions, recent sociological discussions have assigned but one major function to empirical research: "testing" or "verification" of hypotheses. The model for the proper way of performing this function is as familiar as it is clear. The investigator begins with a hunch or hypothesis, from this he draws various inferences and these, in turn, are subjected to

* *American Sociological Review,* Vol. 13, No. 5, October, 1948, pp. 505–515.

empirical test which confirms or refutes the hypothesis. But this is a logical model, and so fails, of course, to describe much of what actually occurs in fruitful investigation. It presents a set of logical norms, not a description of the research experience. And, as logicians are well aware, in purifying the experience, the logical model may also distort it. Like other such models, it abstracts from the temporal sequence of events. It exaggerates the creative role of explicit theory just as it minimizes the creative role of observation. For research is not merely logic tempered with observation. It has its psychological as well as its logical dimensions, although one would scarcely suspect this from the logically rigorous sequence in which research is usually reported. It is both the psychological and logical pressures of research upon social theory which we seek to trace.

It is my central thesis that empirical research goes far beyond the passive role of verifying and testing theory: it does more than confirm or refute hypotheses. Research plays an active role: it performs at least four major functions which help shape the development of theory. It *initiates,* it *reformulates,* it *deflects* and *clarifies* theory.

1. *The Serendipity Pattern*

(The unanticipated, anomalous and strategic datum exerts a pressure for initiating theory.)

Under certain conditions, a research finding gives rise to social theory. In a previous paper, this was all too briefly expressed as follows: "Fruitful empirical research not only tests theoretically derived hypotheses; it also originates new hypotheses. This might be termed the 'serendipity' component of research, *i.e.,* the discovery, by chance or sagacity, of valid results which were not sought for."

The serendipity pattern refers to the fairly common experience of observing an *unanticipated, anomalous and strategic* datum which becomes the occasion for developing a new theory or for extending an existing theory. Each of these elements of the pattern can be readily described. The datum is, first of all, unanticipated. A research directed toward the test of one hypothesis yields a fortuitous by-product, an unexpected observation which bears upon theories not in question when the research was begun.

Secondly, the observation is anomalous, surprising, either because it seems inconsistent with prevailing theory or with other established facts. In either case, the seeming inconsistency provokes curiosity; it stimulates the investigator to "make sense of the datum," to fit it into a broader frame of knowledge. He explores further. He makes fresh observations. He draws inferences from the observations, inferences depending largely, of course, upon his general theoretic orientation. The more he is steeped in the data, the greater the likelihood that he will hit upon a fruitful direction of inquiry. In the fortunate circumstance that his new hunch proves justified, the anomalous datum leads ultimately to a new or extended theory. The curiosity stimulated by the anomalous datum is temporarily appeased.

And thirdly, in noting that the unexpected fact must be "strategic," *i.e.*, that it must permit of implications which bear upon generalized theory, we are, of course, referring rather to what the observer brings to the datum than to the datum itself. For it obviously requires a theoretically sensitized observer to detect the universal in the particular. After all, men had for centuries noticed such "trivial" occurrences as slips of the tongue, slips of the pen, typographical errors, and lapses of memory, but it required the theoretic sensitivity of a Freud to see these as strategic data through which he could extend his theory of repression and symptomatic acts.

The serendipity pattern, then, involves the unanticipated, anomalous and strategic datum which exerts pressure upon the investigator for a new direction of inquiry which extends theory. Instances of serendipity have occurred in many disciplines, but I should like to draw upon a current sociological research for illustration. In the course of our research into the social organization of Craftown, a suburban housing community of some 700 families, largely of working class status, we observed that a large proportion of residents were affiliated with more civic, political and other voluntary organizations than had been the case in their previous places of residence. Quite incidentally, we noted further that this increase in group participation had occurred also among the parents of infants and young children. This finding was rather inconsistent with commonsense knowledge. For it is well known that, particularly on the lower economic levels, youngsters usually tie parents down and preclude their taking active part in organized group life outside the home. But Craftown parents themselves readily explained their behavior. "Oh, there's no real problem about getting out in the evenings," said one mother who belonged to several organizations. "It's easy to find teen-agers around here to take care of the kids. There are so many more teen-agers around here than where I used to live."

The explanation appears adequate enough and would have quieted the investigator's curiosity, had it not been for one disturbing datum: like most new housing communities, Craftown actually has a very small proportion of adolescents—only 3.7%, for example, in the 15–19 year age group. What is more, the majority of the adults, 63%, are under 34 years of age, so that their children include an exceptionally large proportion of infants and youngsters. Thus, far from there being many adolescents to look after the younger children in Craftown, quite the contrary is true: the ratio of adolescents to children under ten years of age is 1:10, whereas in the communities of origin, the ratio hovers about 1:1.5.

We were at once confronted, then, by an anomalous fact which was certainly no part of our original program of observation. This should be emphasized. We manifestly did not enter and indeed could not have entered upon the field research in Craftown with a hypothesis bearing an illusory belief in the abundance of teen-age supervisors of children. Here was an observation both unanticipated and anomalous. Was it also strategic? We did not prejudge its "intrinsic" importance. It seemed no more and no less trivial than Freud's observation during the last war (in which he had two sons at the front) that he had mis-read a newspaper headline, "Die *Feinde* vor Görz" (The *Enemy* before Görz), as "Der *Friede* von Görz" (The *Peace* of Görz). Freud took a trivial incident and converted it into a strategic fact. Unless the observed discrepancy between the subjective impressions of Craftown residents and the objective facts could undergo a somewhat similar transformation it had best be ignored, for it plainly had little "social significance."

What first made this illusion a peculiarly intriguing instance of a general theoretic problem was the difficulty of explaining it as merely the calculated handiwork of vested-interests engaged in spreading a contrary-to-fact belief. Generally, when the sociologist with a conceptual scheme stemming from utilitarian theory observes a patently untrue social belief, he will look for special groups in whose interest it is to invent and spread this belief. The cry of "propaganda!" is often mistaken for a theoretically sound analysis. But this is clearly out of the question in the present instance: there are plainly no special-interest groups seeking to misrepresent the age-distribution of Craftown. What, then, was the source of this social illusion?

Various other theories suggested points of departure. There was Marx's postulate that it is men's "social existence which determines their consciousness." There was Durkheim's theorem that social images ("collective representations") in some fashion reflect a social reality although "it does not follow that the reality which is its foundation conforms objectively to the idea which believers have of it." There was Sherif's thesis that "social factors" provide a framework for selective perceptions and judgments in relatively unstructured situations. There was the prevailing view in the sociology of knowledge that social location determines the perspectives entering into perception, beliefs and ideas. But suggestive as these general orientations were, they did not directly suggest *which* features of "social existence," *which* aspects of the "social reality," *which* "social factors," *which* "social location" may have determined this seemingly fallacious belief.

The clue was inadvertently provided by further interviews with residents. In the words of an active participant in Craftown affairs, herself the mother of two children under six years of age:

> "My husband and I get out together much more. You see, there are more people around to mind the children. *You feel more confident about having some thirteen-or-fourteen-year-old in here when you know most of the people. If you're in a big city, you don't feel so easy about having someone who's almost a stranger come in.*"

This clearly suggests that the sociological roots of the "illusion" are to be found in the structure of community relations in which Craftown residents are enmeshed. The belief is an unwitting reflection, not of the statistical reality, but of the community cohesion. It is not that there are objectively more adolescents in Craftown, but more who are *intimately known* and who, therefore, *exist socially* for parents seeking aid in child supervision. Most Craftown residents having lately come from an urban setting now find themselves in a community in which proximity has developed into reciprocal intimacies. The illusion expresses the perspective of people for whom adolescents as potential child-care aides "exist" only if they are well-known and therefore merit confidence. In short, perception was a function of confidence and confidence, in turn, was a function of social cohesion.

From the sociological viewpoint, then, this unanticipated finding fits into and extends the theory that "social perception" is the product of a social framework. It develops further the "psychology of social norms," for it is not merely an instance of individuals assimilating particular norms, judgments, and standards from other members of the community. The social perception is, rather, a by-product, a derivative, of the structure of human relations.

This is perhaps sufficient to illustrate the operation of the serendipity pattern: an unexpected and anomalous finding elicited the investigator's curiosity, and conducted him along an unpremeditated by-path which led to a fresh hypothesis.

2. *The Recasting of Theory*

(New data exert pressure for the elaboration of a conceptual scheme.)

But it is not only through the anomalous fact that empirical research invites the extension of theory. It does so also through the repeated observation of hitherto neglected facts. When an existing conceptual scheme commonly applied to a given subject-matter does not adequately take these facts into account, research presses insistently for its reformulation. It leads to the introduction of variables which have not been systematically included in the scheme of analysis. Here, be it noted, it is not that the data are anomalous or unexpected or incompatible with existing theory; it is merely that they have not been considered pertinent. Whereas the serendipity pattern centers in an apparent inconsistency which presses for resolution, the reformulation pattern centers in the hitherto neglected but relevant fact which presses for an extension of the conceptual scheme.

Examples of this in the history of social science are far from limited. Thus it was a series of fresh empirical facts which led Malinowski to incorporate new elements into a theory of magic. It was his Trobrianders, of course, who gave him the clue to the distinctive feature of his theory. When these islanders fished in the inner lagoon by the reliable method of poisoning, an abundant catch was assured and danger was absent. Neither uncertainty nor uncontrollable hazards were involved. And here, Malinowski noted, magic was not practiced. But in the open-sea fishing, with the uncertain yield and its often grave dangers, the rituals of magic flourished. Stemming from these pregnant observations was his theory that magical belief arises to bridge the uncertainties in man's practical pursuits, to fortify confidence, to reduce anxieties, to open up avenues of escape from the seeming impasse. Magic was construed as a supplementary technique for reaching practical objectives. It was these empirical facts which suggested the incorporation of new dimensions into earlier theories of magic—particularly the relations of magic to the fortuitous, the dangerous and the uncontrollable. It was not that these facts were *inconsistent* with previous theories; it was simply that these conceptual schemes had not taken them adequately into account. Nor was Malinowski testing a preconceived hypothesis—he was developing an enlarged and improved theory on the basis of suggestive empirical data.

For another example of this pressure of empirical data for the recasting of a specific theory we turn closer home. The investigation dealt with a single dramatic instance of mass persuasion: broadcasting at repeated intervals over a span of eighteen hours, Kate Smith, a radio star, sold large quantities of war-bonds in the course of the day. It is not my intention to report fully on the dynamics of this case of mass persuasion; for present purposes, we are concerned only with the implications of two facts which emerged from the study.

First of all, in the course of intensive interviews many of our informants—New Yorkers who had pledged a bond to Smith—expressed a thorough disenchantment with the world of advertising, commercials and propaganda. They felt themselves the object of manipulation—and resented it. They objected to being the target for advertising which cajoles, insists and terrorizes. They objected to being engulfed in waves of propaganda proposing opinions and actions not in their own best interests. They expressed dismay over what is in effect a pattern of *pseudo-Gemeinschaft*—subtle methods of salesmanship in which there is the feigning of personal concern with the client in order to manipulate him the better. As one small businessman phrased it, "In my own business, I can see how a lot of people in their business deals will make some kind of gesture of friendliness, sincerity and so forth, most of which is phony." Drawn from a highly competitive, segmented metropolitan society, our informants were describing a climate of reciprocal distrust, of *anomie,* in which common values have been submerged in the welter of private interests. Society was experienced as an arena for rival frauds. There was small belief in the disinterestedness of conduct.

In contrast to all this was the second fact: we found that the persuasiveness of the Smith bond-drive among these same informants largely rested upon their firm belief in the integrity and sincerity of Smith. And much the same was found to be true in a polling interview with a larger cross-section sample of almost a thousand New Yorkers. Fully 80% asserted that in her all-day marathon drives, Smith was *exclusively* concerned with promoting the sale of war bonds, whereas only 17% felt that she was *also* interested in publicity for herself, and a negligible 3% believed she was *primarily* concerned with the resulting publicity.

This emphasis on her sincerity is all the more striking as a problem for research in the molding of reputations because she herself appeared on at least six commercially sponsored radio programs each week. But although she is engaged in apparently the same promotional activities as others, she was viewed by the majority of our informants as the direct antithesis of all that these other announcers and stars represent. In the words of one devotee, "She's sincere and *she really means anything* she ever says. It isn't just sittin' up there and talkin' and gettin' paid for it. She's different from what other people are."

Why this overwhelming belief in Smith's sincerity? To be sure, the same society which produces a sense of alienation and estrangement generates in many a craving for reassurance, an acute will to believe, a flight into faith. But why does Smith become the object of this faith for so many otherwise distrustful people? Why is she seen as genuine by those who seek redemption from the spurious? Why are her motives believed to rise above avarice, and ambition and pride of class? What are the social-psychological sources of this image of Smith as sincerity incarnate?

Among the several sources, we wish to examine here the one which bears most directly upon a theory of mass persuasion. The clue is provided by the fact that a larger proportion of those who heard the Smith marathon war-bond drive are convinced of her disinterested patriotism than of those who did not. This appears to indicate that the marathon bond-drive enhanced public belief in her sincerity. But we must recognize the possibility that her devoted fans, for whom her sincerity was unquestioned, would be more likely to have heard the marathon broadcasts. Therefore, to determine whether the marathon did in fact extend this belief, we must compare regular listeners to her programs with those who are not her fans. Within each group, a significantly larger proportion of people who heard the marathon are convinced of Smith's exclusive concern with patriotic purpose. This is as true for her devoted fans as for those who did not listen to her regular programs at all. In other words, we have caught for a moment, as with a candid camera, a snapshot of Smith's reputation of sincerity in the process of being even further enhanced. We have frozen in mid-course the process of building a reputation.

But if the marathon increased the belief in Smith's sincerity, how did this come about? It is at this point that our intensive interviews, with their often ingenuous and revealing details, permit us to interpret the statistical results of the poll. The marathon had all the atmosphere of determined, resolute endeavor under tremendous difficulties. Some could detect signs of strain—and courageous persistence. "Her voice was not quite so strong later, but she stuck it out like a good soldier," says a discerning housewife. Others projected themselves into the vividly imagined situation of fatigue and brave exertion. Solicitous reports by her coadjutor, Ted Collins, reinforced the emphatic concern for the strain to which Smith was subjecting herself. "I felt, I can't stand this any longer," recalls one informant. "Mr. Collins' statement about her being exhausted affected me so much that I just couldn't bear it." The marathon took on the attributes of a sacrificial ritual.

In short, it was not so much what Smith *said* as what she *did* which served to validate her sincerity. It was the presumed stress and strain of an eighteen-hour series of broadcasts, it was the deed not the word which furnished the indubitable proof. Listeners might question whether she were not unduly dramatizing herself, but they could not escape the incontrovertible evidence that she was devoting the entire day to the task. Appraising the direct testimony of Smith's behavior, another informant explains that "she was on all day and the others weren't. So it seemed that she was sacrificing more and was more sincere." Viewed as a process of persuasion, the marathon converted initial feelings of scepticism and distrust among listeners into at first a reluctant, and later, a full-fledged acceptance of Smith's integrity. The successive broadcasts served as a fulfillment in action of a promise in words. The words were reinforced by things she has actually done. The currency of talk was accepted because it is backed by the gold of conduct. The gold reserve, moreover, need not even approximate the amount of currency it can support.

This empirical study suggests that propaganda-of-the-deed may be effective among the very people who are distrustful of propaganda-of-the-word. Where there is social disorganization, *anomie,* conflicting values, we find propaganditis reaching epidemic proportions. Any statement of value is likely to be discounted as "mere propaganda." Exhortations are suspect. But the propaganda of the deed elicits more confidence. Members of the audience are largely permitted to draw their conclusions from the action—they are less likely to feel manipulated. When the propagandist's deed and his words symbolically coincide, it stimulates belief in his sincerity. Further research must determine whether this propaganda pattern is significantly more effective in societies suffering from *anomie* than in those which are more fully integrated. But not unlike the Malinowski case-in-point, this may illustrate the role of research in suggesting new variables to be incorporated into a specific theory.

3. *The Re-Focusing of Theoretic Interest*

(New methods of empirical research exert pressure
for new foci of theoretic interest.)

To this point we have considered the impact of research upon the development of particular theories. But empirical research also affects more general trends in the development of theory. This occurs chiefly through the invention of research procedures which tend to shift the foci of theoretic interest to the growing points of research.

The reasons for this are on the whole evident. After all, sound theory thrives only on a rich diet of pertinent facts and newly invented procedures help provide the ingredients of this diet. The new, and often previously unavailable, data stimulate fresh hypotheses. Moreover, theorists find that their hypotheses can be put to immediate test in those spheres where appropriate research techniques have been designed. It is no longer necessary for them to wait upon data as they happen to turn up—researches directed to the verification of hypotheses can be instituted at once. The flow of relevant data thus increases the tempo of advance in certain spheres of theory whereas in others, theory stagnates for want of adequate observations. Attention shifts accordingly.

In noting that new centers of theoretic interest have followed upon the invention of research procedures, we do not imply that these alone played a decisive role. The growing interest in the theory of propaganda as an instrument of social control, for example, is in large part a response to the changing historical situation, with its conflict of major ideological systems; new technologies of mass communication which have opened up new avenues for propaganda; and the rich research treasuries provided by business and government interested in this new weapon of war, both declared and undeclared. But this shift is also a by-product of accumulated facts made available through such newly developed, and confessedly crude, procedures as content-analysis, the panel technique and the focused interview.

Examples of this impact in the recent history of social theory are numerous but we have time to mention only a few. Thus, the increasing concern with the theory of character and personality formation in relation to social structure became marked after the introduction of new projective methods; the Rorschach test, the thematic apperception test, play techniques and story completions being among the most familiar. So, too, the sociometric techniques of Moreno and others, and fresh advances in the technique of the "passive interview" have revived interest in the theory of interpersonal relations. Stemming from such techniques as well is the trend toward what might be called the "rediscovery of the primary group," particularly in the shape of theoretic concern with informal social structures as mediating between the individual and large formal organizations. This interest has found expression in an entire literature on the role and structure of the informal group, for example, in factory social systems, bureaucracy and political organizations. Similarly, we may anticipate that the recent introduction of the panel technique—the repeated interviewing of the same group of informants—will in due course more sharply focus the attention of social psychologists upon the theory of attitude formation, decisions among alternative choices, factors in political participation and determinants of behavior in cases of conflicting role demands, to mention a few types of problems to which this technique is especially adapted.

Perhaps the most direct impact of research procedures upon theory has resulted from the *creation* of sociological statistics organized in terms of theoretically pertinent categories. Talcott Parsons has observed that numerical data are scientifically important only when they can be fitted into analytical categories and that "a great deal of current research is producing facts in a form which cannot be utilized by any current generalized analytical scheme." These well-deserved strictures of a scant decade ago are proving progressively less applicable. In the past, the sociologist has largely had to deal with *precollected series* of statistics usually assembled for nonsociological purposes and, therefore, not set forth in categories directly pertinent to any given theoretical system. As a result, at least so far as quantitative facts are concerned, the theorist was compelled to work with makeshift data bearing only a tangential relevance to his problems. This not only left a wide margin for error—consider the crude indexes of social cohesion upon which Durkheim had to rely—but it also meant that theory had to wait upon the incidental and, at times, almost accidental availability of relevant data. It could not march rapidly ahead. This picture has now begun to change.

No longer does the theorist depend almost exclusively upon the consensus of administrative boards or social welfare agencies for his quantitative data. Gabriel Tarde's programmatic sketch a half century ago of the need for statistics in social psychology, particularly those dealing with attitudes, opinions and sentiments, has become a half-fulfilled promise. So, too, investigators of community organization are creating statistics on class structure, associational behavior, and clique formations, and this has left its mark on theoretic interests. Ethnic studies are beginning to provide quantitative data which are re-orienting the theorist. It is safe to suppose that the enormous accumulation of sociological materials during the war—notably by the Research Branch of the Information and Education Division of the War Department—materials which are in part the result of new research techniques, will intensify interest in the theory of group morale, propaganda and leadership. But it is perhaps needless to multiply examples.

What we have said does not mean that the piling up of statistics of itself advances theory; it does mean that theoretic interest tends to shift to those areas in which there is an abundance of *pertinent* statistical data. Moreover, we are merely calling attention to this shift of focus, not evaluating it. It may very well be that it sometimes deflects attention to problems which, in a theoretic or humanistic sense, are "unimportant"; it may divert attention from problems with larger implications onto those for which there is the promise of immediate solutions. Failing a detailed study, it is difficult to come to any overall assessment of this point. But the pattern itself seems clear enough in sociology as in other disciplines: as new and previously unobtainable data become available through the use of new techniques, theorists turn their analytical eye upon the implications of these data and bring about new directions of inquiry.

4. *The Clarification of Concepts*

(Empirical research exerts pressure for clear concepts.)

A good part of the work called "theorizing" is taken up with the clarification of concepts—and rightly so. It is in this matter of clearly defined concepts that social science research is not infrequently defective. Research activated by a major interest in methodology may be centered on the *design* of establishing causal relations without due regard for analyzing the variables involved in the inquiry. This methodological empiricism, as the design of inquiry without correlative concern with the clarification of substantive variables may be called, characterizes a large part of current research. Thus, in a series of effectively designed experiments, F. S. Chapin finds that "the rehousing of slum families in a public housing project results in improvements of the living conditions and the social life of these families." Or through controlled experiments, psychologists search out the effects of foster home placement upon children's performances in intelligence tests. Or, again through experimental inquiry, researchers seek to determine whether a propaganda film has achieved its purpose of improving attitudes toward the British. These several cases, and they are representative of a large amount of research which has advanced social science method, have in common the fact that the empirical variables are not analyzed in terms of their conceptual elements. As Rebecca West, with her characteristic lucidity, put this general problem of methodological empiricism, one might "know that A and B and C were linked by certain causal connexions, but he would never apprehend with any exactitude the nature of A or B or C." In consequences, these researches further the procedures of inquiry, but their findings do not enter into the repository of cumulative social science theory.

But in general, the clarification of concepts, commonly considered a province peculiar to the theorist, is a frequent result of empirical research. Research sensitive to its own needs cannot avoid this pressure for conceptual clarification. *For a basic requirement of research is that the concepts, the variables, be defined with sufficient clarity to enable the research to proceed,* a requirement easily and unwittingly not met in the kind of discursive exposition which is often miscalled "sociological theory."

The clarification of concepts ordinarily enters into empirical research in the shape of establishing *indices* of the variables under consideration. In non-research speculations, it is possible to talk loosely about "morale" or "social cohesion" without any clear conceptions of what is entailed by these terms, but they *must* be clarified if the researcher is to go about his business of systematically observing instances of low and high morale, of social cohesion or cleavage. If he is not to be blocked at the outset, he must devise indices which are observable, fairly precise and meticulously clear. The entire movement of thought which was christened "operationalism" is only one conspicuous case of the researcher demanding that concepts be defined clearly enough for him to go to work.

This has been typically recognized by those sociologists who combine a theoretic orientation with systematic empirical research. Durkheim, for example, despite the fact that his terminology and indices now appear crude and debatable, clearly perceived the need for devising indices of his concepts. Repeatedly, he asserted that "it is necessary . . . to substitute for the internal fact which escapes us an external fact that symbolizes it and to study the former through the latter." The index, or sign of the conceptualized item, stands ideally in a one-to-one correlation with what it signifies (and the difficulty of establishing this relation is of course one of the critical problems of research). Since the index and its object are so related, one may ask for the grounds on which one is taken as the index and the other as the indexed variable. As Durkheim implied and as Suzanne Langer has indicated anew, the index is that one of the correlated pair which is perceptible and the other, harder or impossible to perceive, is theoretically relevant. Thus, attitude scales make available indices of otherwise not discriminable attitudes, just as ecological statistics represent indices of diverse social structures in a given area.

What often appears as a tendency in research for quantification (through the development of scales) can thus be seen as a special case of attempting to clarify concepts sufficiently to permit the conduct of empirical investigation. The development of valid and observable indices becomes central to the use of concepts in the prosecution of research. A final illustration will indicate how research presses for the clarification of ancient sociological concepts which, on the plane of discursive exposition, have remained ill-defined and unclarified.

A conception basic to sociology holds that individuals have multiple social roles and tend to organize their behavior in terms of the structurally defined expectations assigned to each role. Further, it is said, the less integrated the society, the more often will individuals be subject to the strain of incompatible social roles. Type-cases are numerous and familiar: the Catholic Communist subjected to conflicting pressures from party and church, the marginal man suffering the pulls of conflicting societies, the professional woman torn between the demands of family and career. Every sociological textbook abounds with illustrations of incompatible demands made of the multiselved person.

Perhaps because it has been largely confined to discursive interpretations and has seldom been made the focus of systematic research, this central problem of conflicting roles has yet to be materially clarified and advanced beyond the point reached decades ago. W. I. Thomas and F. Znaniecki long since indicated that conflicts between social roles *can* be reduced by conventionalization and by role-segmentation (by assigning each set of role-demands to different situations). And others have noted that frequent conflict between roles is dysfunctional for the society as well as for the individual. But all this leaves many salient problems untouched: on which grounds does one predict the behavior of persons subject to conflicting roles? And when a decision must be made, which role (or which group solidarity) takes precedence? Under which conditions does one or another prove controlling? On the plane of discursive thought, it has been suggested that the role with which the individual identifies most fully will prove dominant, thus banishing the problem through a tautological pseudo-solution. Or, the problem of seeking to predict behavior consequent to incompatibility of roles, a research problem requiring operational clarification of the concepts of solidarity, conflict, role-demands and situation, has been evaded by observing that conflicts of roles typically ensue in frustration.

More recently, empirical research has pressed for clarification of the key concepts involved in this problem. Indices of conflicting group pressures have been devised and the resultant behavior observed in specified situations. Thus, as a beginning in this direction, it has been shown that in a concrete decision-situation, such as voting, individuals subject to these cross-pressures respond by delaying their vote-decision. And, under conditions yet to be determined, they seek to reduce the conflict by escaping from the field of conflict: they "lose interest" in the political campaign. Finally, there is the intimation in these data that in cases of cross-pressures upon the voter, it is socio-economic position which is typically controlling.

However this may be, the essential point is that, in this instance as in others, the very requirements of empirical research have been instrumental in clarifying received concepts. The process of empirical inquiry raises conceptual issues which may long go undetected in theoretic inquiry.

There remain, then, a few concluding remarks. My discussion has been devoted exclusively to four impacts of research upon the development of social theory: the initiation, reformulation, refocusing and clarification of theory. Doubtless there are others. Doubtless, too, the emphasis of this paper lends itself to misunderstanding. It may be inferred that some invidious distinction has been drawn at the expense of theory and the theorist. That has not been my intention. I have suggested only that an explicitly formulated theory does not invariably precede empirical inquiry, that as a matter of plain fact the theorist is not inevitably the lamp lighting the way to new observations. The sequence is often reversed. Nor it is enough to say that research and theory must be married if sociology is to bear legitimate fruit. They must not only exchange solemn vows—they must know how to carry on from there. Their reciprocal roles must be clearly defined. This paper is a brief essay toward that definition.

SELECTED SUPPLEMENTARY READINGS FOR PART V

Bennis, Warren G., "Some Barriers to Teamwork in Social Research," *Social Problems,* Vol. 3, No. 4, April, 1956, pp. 223–235.

Cohen, Morris R., and Nagel, Ernest, *An Introduction to Logic and Scientific Method* (New York: Harcourt, Brace & Co., 1934).

Dornbusch, Sanford M., and Schmid, Calvin F., *A Primer of Social Statistics* (New York: McGraw-Hill Book Co., 1955).

Durkheim, Emile, *The Rules of Sociological Method,* translated by George E. G. Catlin (Chicago: The Free Press, 1950).

Goode, William J., and Hatt, Paul K., *Methods in Social Research* (New York: McGraw-Hill Book Co., 1952).

Greenwood, Ernest, *Experimental Sociology* (New York: King's Crown Press, 1945).

Guttman, Louis, "A Basis for Scaling Qualitative Data," *American Sociological Review,* Vol. 9, No. 2, April, 1944, pp. 139–150.

Mayer, Martin, "Sampling the Samplers," *Esquire,* November, 1960, pp. 186, 188, 190–192, 195–197.

Riley, Matilda White, *Sociological Research: A Case Approach* (New York: Harcourt, Brace & World, 1963).

Stouffer, Samuel A., "Measurement in Sociology," *American Sociological Review,* Vol. 18, No. 6, December, 1953, pp. 591–597.

PART SIX

Sociological Theory

INTRODUCTION

Whether it is individually or organizationally conducted, the ultimate aim of all sociological research is to build sound theory about the nature of social reality and its impact on human thoughts, feelings, and actions. Theory, which is merely another name for abstract knowledge or generalizations, is sound only if it satisfactorily describes and integrates the facts about which it generalizes. How does theory-building proceed in sociology? There are several paths it may properly take.

First of all, one may proceed from the starting point of a hypothesis, an unsupported and generalized statement or a working supposition about the relationship presumed to exist between two variables. A few empirical studies may verify this hypothesis, but the verification has not extended beyond that to all conceivable studies. In such a case one may say the hypothesis is partially verified and has become a theory. Should further studies, more representative of the universe in which the research question was provoked, continue to verify the theory, one may refer to the generalization as a scientific law. That is, the generalization has acquired such a high degree of probable truth that for practical purposes it can be considered completely true. In short, hypothesis, theory, and scientific law, in the order given, represent a scalar system of "theoretical" soundness, ranging from no verification, to partial verification, to sufficient verification.

Another way to view a theory in comparison with a hypothesis is that the former is more abstract and complex than the latter. Some sociologists, are reluctant to pursue the verification of one isolated, researchable hypothesis at a time. In their eagerness to generalize about as much social reality as possible, they formulate an all-inclusive theoretical system, a logically interrelated complex of hypotheses that permits an overview of the social forest, parts of which may be torn from their context and empirically tested. Between these polar positions stands theory-building of the "middle range" represented by Robert K. Merton. Theories in this sense are intermediate in scope, applicable only to limited ranges of social phenomena, such as social class and bureaucracy. They are neither as minute as the isolated, although verifiable and routine hypothesis on the one hand, nor as grandiose and pretentious as the theoretical system-building on the other.

Still another type of theory-building is by inference and derivation. In testing one or more hypotheses, we may also indirectly verify logically related hypotheses that cannot be directly tested. For example, if hypothesis A is not researchable because it is too comprehensive, it may nevertheless be deduced that if hypothesis A is true, derivative and researchable hypotheses B and C must also be true. If we test B and C and they are verified, our confidence in hypothesis A is enhanced. Sometimes, too, a number of verified hypotheses, by recombination, provide a new hypothesis to be used in answering a question close to but different from the original question.

To illustrate, the early sociological studies of voting behavior verified hypotheses about the effect of religion, community type, and social class on choice of political party in elections. Catholics, urbanites, and lower-class people were found to show marked preference for Democratic candidates, whereas Protestant, rural folk, and the middle classes showed preference for Republicans. But why do some people, prior to elections, manifest no clear-cut commitment to either party whereas others do? The three primary hypotheses mentioned above suggested the new hypothesis that people who are subject to cross-pressures by virtue of membership in groups with conflicting political tendences delay their final vote decision significantly more than do those who are subject to consistent pressures from their group affiliations.

GENERAL THEORY

There are several criteria of what constitutes "good" theory. First, it should account for all the important and observable facts in the problem. Second, it should do so with a minimum number of qualifications, for a theory that has fewer complexities is preferable to a more complicated one. Third, it should be predictive. Last, it should suggest further areas of knowledge to be investigated.

Whenever possible, sociological theory should interact with empirical facts throughout the whole process of theory-building. Hypotheses are required in order to delineate the kind of facts that are to be observed, but scientifically observed facts in turn may lead to verification or modification of the hypothesis under scrutiny. This circularity between theory and fact is no less important in sociology than in the other scientific disciplines.

In the first reading on sociological theory that follows, Dennis H. Wrong notes that sociological theory originates in the asking of general questions about man and society. The answers lose their meaning, he claims, if they are elaborated without reference to the questions, as has been the case in much contemporary theory. An example is the Hobbesian question of how men become tractable to social controls. The twofold answer of contemporary sociological theory is that man internalizes social norms and seeks a favorable self-image by conforming to the expectations of others. Such a model of man, according to Professor Wrong, denies the very possibility of his being anything but a thoroughly socialized being and thus denies the reality of the Hobbesian question. The Freudian view of man, on the other hand, which sociologists have misrepresented, sees man as a social though never a fully socialized creature. Sociologists, concludes Professor Wrong, need to develop a more complex, dialectical conception of human nature instead of relying on an implicit conception that is tailor-made for special sociological problems.

52. THE OVERSOCIALIZED CONCEPTION OF MAN IN MODERN SOCIOLOGY *

DENNIS H. WRONG
New York University

Gertrude Stein, bed-ridden with a fatal illness, is reported to have suddenly muttered, "What, then, is the answer?" Pausing, she raised her head, murmured, "But what is the question?" and died. Miss Stein presumably was pondering the ultimate meaning of human life, but her brief final soliloquy has a broader and humbler relevance. Its point is that answers are meaningless apart from questions. If we forget the questions, even while remembering the answers, our knowledge of them will subtly deteriorate, becoming rigid, formal, and catechistic as the sense of indeterminacy, of rival possibilities, implied by the very putting of a question is lost.

Social theory must be seen primarily as a set of answers to questions we ask of social reality. If the initiating questions are forgotten, we readily misconstrue the task of theory and the answers previous thinkers have given become narrowly confining conceptual prisons, degenerating into little more than a special, professional vocabulary applied to situations and events that can be described with equal or greater precision in ordinary language. Forgetfulness of the questions that are the starting points of inquiry leads us to ignore the substantive assumptions "buried" in our concepts and commits us to a one-sided view of reality.

Perhaps this is simply an elaborate way of saying that sociological theory can never afford to lose what is usually called a "sense of significance;" or, as it is sometimes put, that sociological theory must be "problem-conscious." I choose instead to speak of theory as a set of answers to questions because reference to "problems" may seem to suggest too close a linkage with social criticism or reform. My primary reason for insisting on the necessity of holding constantly in mind the questions that our concepts and theories are designed to answer is to preclude defining the goal of sociological theory as the creation of a formal body of knowledge satisfying the logical criteria of scientific theory set up by philosophers and methodologists of natural science. Needless to say, this is the way theory is often defined by contemporary sociologists.

* *American Sociological Review*, Vol. 26, No. 2, April, 1961, pp. 183–193.

Yet to speak of theory as interrogatory may suggest too self-sufficiently intellectual an enterprise. Cannot questions be satisfactorily answered and then forgotten, the answers becoming the assumptions from which we start in framing new questions? It may convey my view of theory more adequately to say that sociological theory concerns itself with questions arising out of problems that are inherent in the very existence of human societies and that cannot therefore be finally "solved" in the way that particular social problems perhaps can be. The "problems" theory concerns itself with are problems *for* human societies which, because of their universality, become intellectually problematic for sociological theorists.

Essentially, the historicist conception of sociological knowledge that is central to the thought of Max Weber and has recently been ably restated by Barrington Moore, Jr. and C. Wright Mills is a sound one. The most fruitful questions for sociology are always questions referring to the realities of a particular historical situation. Yet both of these writers, especially Mills, have a tendency to underemphasize the degree to which we genuinely wish and seek answers to trans-historical and universal questions about the nature of man and society. I do not, let it be clear, have in mind the formalistic quest for social "laws" or "universal propositions," nor the even more formalistic effort to construct all-encompassing "conceptual schemes." Moore and Mills are rightly critical of such efforts. I am thinking of such questions as, "How are men capable of uniting to form enduring societies in the first place?"; "Why and to what degree is change inherent in human societies and what are the sources of change?"; "How is man's animal nature domesticated by society?"

Such questions—and they are existential as well as intellectual questions—are the *raison d'être* of social theory. They were asked by men long before the rise of sociology. Sociology itself is an effort, under new and unprecedented historical conditions, to find novel answers to them. They are not questions which lend themselves to successively more precise answers as a result of cumulative empirical research, for they remain eternally problematic. Social theory is necessarily an interminable dialogue. "True understanding," Hannah Arendt has written, "does not tire of interminable dialogue and 'vicious circles' because it trusts that imagination will eventually catch at least a glimpse of the always frightening light of truth."

I wish briefly to review the answers modern sociological theory offers to one such question, or rather to one aspect of one question. The question may be variously phrased as, "What are the sources of social cohesion?"; or, "How is social order possible?"; or, stated in social-psychological terms, "How is it that man becomes tractable to social discipline?" I shall call this question in its social-psychological aspect the "Hobbesian question" and in its more strictly sociological aspect the "Marxist question." The Hobbesian question asks how men are capable of the guidance by social norms and goals that makes possible an enduring society, while the Marxist question asks how, assuming this capability, complex societies manage to regulate and restrain destructive conflicts between groups. Much of our current theory offers an oversocialized view of man in answering the Hobbesian question and an over-integrated view of society in answering the Marxist question.

A number of writers have recently challenged the overintegrated view of society in contemporary theory. In addition to Moore and Mills, the names of Reinhard Bendix, Lewis A. Coser, Ralf Dahrendorf, and David Lockwood come to mind. My intention, therefore, is to concentrate on the answers to the Hobbesian question in an effort to disclose the oversocialized view of man which they seem to imply.

Since my view of theory is obviously very different from that of Talcott Parsons and has, in fact, been developed in opposition to his, let me pay tribute to his recognition of the importance of the Hobbesian question—the "problem of order," as he calls it—at the very beginning of his first book, *The Structure of Social Action.* Parsons correctly credits Hobbes with being the first thinker to see the necessity of explaining why human society is not a "war of all against all;" why, if man is simply a gifted animal, men refrain from unlimited resort to fraud and violence in pursuit of their ends and maintain a stable society at all. There is even a sense in which, as Coser and Mills have both noted, Parsons' entire work represents an effort to solve the Hobbesian problem of order. His solution, however, has tended to become precisely the kind of elaboration of a set of answers in abstraction from questions that is characteristic of contemporary sociological theory.

We need not be greatly concerned with Hobbes' own solution to the problem of order he saw with such unsurpassed clarity. Whatever interest his famous theory of the origin of the state may still hold for political scientists, it is clearly inadequate as an explanation of the origin of society. Yet the pattern as opposed to the details of Hobbes' thought bears closer examination.

The polar terms in Hobbes' theory are the state of nature, where the war of all against all prevails, and the authority of Leviathan, created by social contract. But the war of all against all is not simply effaced with the creation of political authority: it remains an ever-present potentiality in human society, at times quiescent, at times erupting into open violence. Whether Hobbes believed that the state of nature and the social contract were ever historical realities—and there is evidence that he was not that simple-minded and un-sociological, even in the seventeenth century—is unimportant; the whole tenor of his thought is to see the war of all against all and Leviathan dialectically, as coexisting and interacting opposites. As R. G. Collingwood has observed, "According to Hobbes . . . *a body politic is a dialectical thing,* a Heraclitean world in which at any given time there is a negative element." The first secular social theorist in the history of Western thought, and one of the first clearly to discern and define the problem of order in human society long before Darwinism made awareness of it a commonplace, Hobbes was a dialectical thinker who refused to separate answers from questions, solutions to society's enduring problems from the conditions creating the problems.

What is the answer of contemporary sociological theory to the Hobbesian question? There are two main answers, each of which has come to be understood in a way that denies the reality and meaningfulness of the question. Together they constitute a model of human nature, sometimes clearly stated, more often implicit in accepted concepts, that pervades modern sociology. The first answer is summed up in the notion of the "internalization of social norms." The second, more commonly employed or assumed in empirical research, is the view that man is essentially motivated by the desire to achieve a positive image of self by winning acceptance or status in the eyes of others.

The following statement represents, briefly and broadly, what is probably the most influential contemporary sociological conception—and dismissal—of the Hobbesian problem: "To a modern sociologist imbued with the conception that action follows institutionalized patterns, opposition of individual and common interests has only a very limited relevance or is thoroughly unsound." From this writer's perspective, the problem is an unreal one: human conduct is totally shaped by common norms or "institutionalized patterns." Sheer ignorance must have led people who were unfortunate enough not to be modern sociologists to ask, "How is order possible?" A thoughtful bee or ant would never inquire, "How is the social order of the hive or ant-hill possible?" for the opposite of that order is unimaginable when the instinctive endowment of the insects ensures its stability and built-in harmony between "individual and common interests." Human society, we are assured, is not essentially different, although conformity and stability are there maintained by non-instinctive processes. Modern sociologists believe that they have understood these processes and that they have not merely answered but disposed of the Hobbesian question, showing that, far from expressing a valid intimation of the tensions and possibilities of social life, it can only be asked out of ignorance.

It would be hard to find a better illustration of what Collingwood, following Plato, calls *eristical* as opposed to dialectical thinking: the answer destroys the question, or rather destroys the awareness of rival possibilities suggested by the question which accounts for its having been asked in the first place. A reversal of perspective now takes place and we are moved to ask the opposite question: "How is it that violence, conflict, revolution, and the individual's sense of coercion by society manage to exist at all, if this view is correct?" Whenever a one-sided answer to a question compels us to raise the opposite question, we are caught up in a dialectic of concepts which reflects a dialectic in things. But let us examine the particular processes sociologists appeal to in order to account for the elimination from human society of the war of all against all.

THE CHANGING MEANING OF INTERNALIZATION

A well-known section of *The Structure of Social Action,* devoted to the interpretation of Durkheim's thought, is entitled "The Changing Meaning of Constraint." Parsons argues that Durkheim originally conceived of society as controlling the individual from the outside by imposing constraints on him through sanctions, best illustrated by codes of law. But in Durkheim's later work he began to see that social rules do not "merely regulate 'externally' . . . they enter directly into the constitution of the actors' ends themselves." Constraint, therefore, is more than an environmental obstacle which the actor must take into account in pursuit of his goals in the same way that he takes into account physical laws: it becomes internal, psychological, and self-imposed as well. Parsons developed this view that social norms are constitutive rather than merely regulative of human nature before he was influenced by psychoanalytic theory, but Freud's theory of the superego has become the source and model for the conception of the internalization of social norms that today plays so important a part in sociological thinking. The use some sociologists have made of Freud's idea, however, might well inspire an essay entitled, "The Changing Meaning of Internalization," although, in contrast to the shift in Durkheim's view of constraint, this change has been a change for the worse.

What has happened is that internalization has imperceptibly been equated with "learning," or even with "habit-formation" in the simplest sense. Thus when a norm is said to have been "internalized" by an individual, what is frequently meant is that he habitually both affirms it and conforms to it in his conduct. The whole stress on inner conflict, on the tension between powerful impulses and superego controls the behavioral outcome of which cannot be prejudged, drops out of the picture. And it is this that is central to Freud's view, for in psychoanalytic terms to say that a norm has been internalized, or introjected to become part of the superego, is to say no more than that a person will suffer guilt-feelings if he fails to live up to it, not that he will in fact live up to it in his behavior.

The relation between internalization and conformity assumed by most sociologists is suggested by the following passage from a recent, highly-praised advanced textbook: "Conformity to institutionalized norms is, of course, 'normal.' The actor, having internalized the norms, feels something like a need to conform. His conscience would bother him if he did not." What is overlooked here is that the person who conforms may be even more "bothered," that is, subject to guilt and neurosis, than the person who violates what are not only society's norms but his own as well. To Freud, it is precisely the man with the strictest superego, he who has most thoroughly internalized and conformed to the norms of his society, who is most wracked with guilt and anxiety.

Paul Kecskemeti, to whose discussion I owe initial recognition of the erroneous view of internalization held by sociologists, argues that the relations between social norms, the individual's selection from them, his conduct, and his feelings about his conduct are far from self-evident. "It is by no means true," he writes, "to say that acting counter to one's own norms always or almost always leads to neurosis. One might assume that neurosis develops even more easily in persons who *never* violate the moral code they recognize as valid but repress and frustrate some strong instinctual motive. A person who 'succumbs to temptation,' feels guilt, and then 'purges himself' of his guilt in some reliable way (e.g., by confession) may achieve in this way a better balance, and be less neurotic, than a person who never violates his 'norms' and never feels conscious guilt." [1]

Recent discussions of "deviant behavior" have been compelled to recognize these distinctions between social demands, personal attitudes towards them, and actual conduct, although they have done so in a laboriously taxonomic fashion. They represent, however, largely the rediscovery of what was always central to the Freudian concept of the superego. The main explanatory function of the concept is to show how people repress themselves, imposing checks on their own desires and thus turning the inner life into a battlefield of conflicting motives, no matter which side "wins," by successfully dictating overt action. So far as behavior is concerned, the psychoanalytic view of man is less deterministic than the sociological. For psychoanalysis is primarily concerned with the inner life, not with overt behavior, and its most fundamental insight is that the wish, the emotion, and the fantasy are as important as the act in man's experience.

Sociologists have appropriated the superego concept, but have separated it from any equivalent of the Freudian id. So long as most individuals are "socialized," that is, internalize the norms and conform to them in conduct, the Hobbesian problem is not even perceived as a latent reality. Deviant behavior is accounted for by special circumstances: ambiguous norms, anomie, role conflict, or greater cultural stress on valued goals than on the approved means for attaining them. Tendencies to deviant behavior are not seen as dialectically related to conformity. The presence in man of motivational forces bucking against the hold social discipline has over him is denied.

Nor does the assumption that internalization of norms and roles is the essence of socialization allow for a sufficient range of motives underlying conformity. It fails to allow for variable "tonicity of the superego," in Abram Kardiner's phrase. The degree to which conformity is frequently the result of coercion rather than conviction is minimized. Either someone has internalized the norms, or he is "unsocialized," a feral or socially isolated child, or a psychopath. Yet Freud recognized that many people, conceivably a majority, fail to acquire superegos. "Such people," he wrote, "habitually permit themselves to do any bad deed that procures them something they want, if only they are sure that no authority will discover it or make them suffer for it; their anxiety relates only to the possibility of detection. Present-day society has to take into account the prevalence of this state of mind." The last sentence suggests that Freud was aware of the decline of "inner-direction," of the Protestant conscience, about which we have heard so much lately. So let us turn to the other elements of human nature that sociologists appeal to in order to explain, or rather explain away, the Hobbesian problem.

[1] Paul Kecskemeti, *Meaning, Communication, and Value,* Chicago: University of Chicago Press, 1952, pp. 244–245.

MAN THE ACCEPTANCE-SEEKER

The superego concept is too inflexible, too bound to the past and to individual biography, to be of service in relating conduct to the pressures of the immediate situation in which it takes place. Sociologists rely more heavily therefore on an alternative notion, here stated—or, to be fair, overstated—in its baldest form: "People are so profoundly sensitive to the expectations of others that all action is inevitably guided by these expectations."

Parsons' model of the "complementarity of expectations," the view that in social interaction men mutually seek approval from one another by conforming to shared norms, is a formalized version of what has tended to become a distinctive sociological perspective on human motivation. Ralph Linton states it in explicit psychological terms: "The need for eliciting favorable responses from others is an almost constant component of [personality]. Indeed, it is not too much to say that there is very little organized human behavior which is not directed toward its satisfaction in at least some degree." The insistence of sociologists on the importance of "social factors" easily leads them to stress the priority of such socialized or socializing motives in human behavior. It is frequently the task of the sociologist to call attention to the intensity with which men desire and strive for the good opinion of their immediate associates in a variety of situations, particularly those where received theories or ideologies have unduly emphasized other motives such as financial gain, commitment to ideals, or the effects on energies and aspirations of arduous physical conditions. Thus sociologists have shown that factory workers are more sensitive to the attitudes of their fellow-workers than to purely economic incentives; that voters are more influenced by the preferences of their relatives and friends than by campaign debates on the "issues;" that soldiers, whatever their ideological commitment to their nation's cause, fight more bravely when their platoons are intact and they stand side by side with their "buddies."

It is certainly not my intention to criticize the findings of such studies. My objection is that their particular selective emphasis is generalized—explicitly or, more often, implicitly—to provide apparent empirical support for an extremely one-sided view of human nature. Although sociologists have criticized past efforts to single out one fundamental motive in human conduct, the desire to achieve a favorable self-image by winning approval from others frequently occupies such a position in their own thinking. The following "theorem" has been, in fact, openly put forward by Hans Zetterberg as "a strong contender for the position as the major Motivational Theorem in sociology":

> An actor's actions have a tendency to become dispositions that are related to the occurence [*sic*] of favored uniform evaluations of the actor and-or his actions in his action system.[2]

[2] Hans L. Zetterberg, "Compliant Actions," *Acta Sociologica,* 2 (1957) p. 188.

Now Zetterberg is not necessarily maintaining that this theorem is an accurate factual statement of the basic psychological roots of social behavior. He is, characteristically, far too self-conscious about the logic of theorizing and "concept formation" for that. He goes on to remark that "the maximization of favorable attitudes from others would thus be the counterpart in sociological theory to the maximization of profit in economic theory." If by this it is meant that the theorem is to be understood as a heuristic rather than an empirical assumption, that sociology has a selective point of view which is just as abstract and partial as that of economics and the other social sciences, and if his view of theory as a set of logically connected formal propositions is granted provisional acceptance, I am in agreement. (Actually, the view of theory suggested at the beginning of this paper is a quite different one.)

But there is a further point to be made. Ralf Dahrendorf has observed that structural-functional theorists do not "claim that order *is based on* a general consensus of values, but that it *can be conceived of in terms of* such consensus and that, if it is conceived of in these terms, certain propositions follow which are subject to the test of specific observations." The same may be said of the assumption that people seek to maximize favorable evaluations by others, indeed this assumption has already fathered such additional concepts as "reference group" and "circle of significant others." Yet the question must be raised as to whether we really wish to, in effect, define sociology by such partial perspectives. The assumption of the maximization of approval from others is the psychological complement to the sociological assumption of a general value consensus. And the former is as selective and one-sided a way of looking at motivation as Dahrendorf and others have argued the latter to be when it determines our way of looking at social structure. The oversocialized view of man of the one is a counterpart to the over-integrated view of society of the other.

Modern sociology, after all, originated as a protest against the partial views of man contained in such doctrines as utilitarianism, classical economics, social Darwinism, and vulgar Marxism. All of the great nineteenth and early twentieth century sociologists saw it as one of their major tasks to expose the unreality of such abstractions as economic man, the gain-seeker of the classical economists; political man, the power-seeker of the Machiavellian tradition in political science; self-preserving man, the security-seeker of Hobbes and Darwin; sexual or libidinal man, the pleasure-seeker of doctrinaire Freudianism; and even religious man, the God-seeker of the theologians. It would be ironical if it should turn out that they have merely contributed to the creation of yet another reified abstraction in socialized man, the status-seeker of our contemporary sociologists.

Of course, such an image of man is, like all the others mentioned, valuable for limited purposes so long as it is not taken for the whole truth. What are some of its deficiencies? To begin with, it neglects the other half of the model of human nature presupposed by current theory: moral man, guided by his built-in superego and beckoning ego-ideal. In recent years sociologists have been less interested than they once were in culture and national character as backgrounds to conduct, partly because stress on the concept of "role" as the crucial link between the individual and the social structure has directed their attention to the immediate situation in which social interaction takes place. Man is increasingly seen as a "role-playing" creature, responding eagerly or anxiously to the expectations of other role-players in the multiple group settings in which he finds himself. Such an approach, while valuable in helping us grasp the complexity of a highly differentiated social structure such as our own, is far too often generalized to serve as a kind of *ad hoc* social psychology, easily adaptable to particular sociological purposes.

But it is not enough to concede that men often pursue "internalized values" remaining indifferent to what others think of them, particularly when, as I have previously argued, the idea of internalization has been "hollowed out" to make it more useful as an explanation of conformity. What of desire for material and sensual satisfactions? Can we really dispense with the venerable notion of material "interests" and invariably replace it with the blander, more integrative "social values"? And what of striving for power, not necessarily for its own sake—that may be rare and pathological—but as a means by which men are able to *impose* a normative definition of reality on others? That material interests, sexual drives, and the quest for power have often been over-estimated as human motives is no reason to deny their reality. To do so is to suppress one term of the dialectic between conformity and rebellion, social norms and their violation, man and social order, as completely as the other term is suppressed by those who deny the reality of man's "normative orientation" or reduce it to the effect of coercion, rational calculation, or mechanical conditioning.

The view that man is invariably pushed by internalized norms or pulled by the lure of self-validation by others ignores—to speak archaically for a moment—both the highest and the lowest, both beast and angel, in his nature. Durkheim, from whom so much of the modern sociological point of view derives, recognized that the very existence of a social norm implies and even creates the possibility of its violation. This is the meaning of his famous dictum that crime is a "normal phenomenon." He maintained that "for the originality of the idealist whose dreams transcend his century to find expression, it is necessary that the originality of the criminal, who is below the level of his time, shall also be possible. One does not occur without the other." Yet Durkheim lacked an adequate psychology and formulated his insight in terms of the actor's cognitive awareness rather than in motivational terms. We do not have Durkheim's excuse for falling back on what George C. Homans has called a "social mold theory" of human nature.

SOCIAL BUT NOT ENTIRELY SOCIALIZED

I have referred to forces in man that are resistant to socialization. It is not my purpose to explore the nature of these forces or to suggest how we ought best conceive of them as sociologists—that would be a most ambitious undertaking. A few remarks will have to suffice. I think we must start with the recognition that *in the beginning there is the body*. As soon as the body is mentioned the specter of "biological determinism" raises its head and sociologists draw back in fright. And certainly their view of man is sufficiently disembodied and non-materialistic to satisfy Bishop Berkeley, as well as being de-sexualized enough to please Mrs. Grundy.

Am I, then, urging us to return to the older view of a human nature divided between a "social man" and a "natural man" who is either benevolent, Rousseau's Noble Savage, or sinister and destructive, as Hobbes regarded him? Freud is usually represented, or misrepresented, as the chief modern proponent of this dualistic conception which assigns to the social order the purely negative role of blocking and re-directing man's "imperious biological drives." I say "misrepresented" because, although Freud often said things supporting such an interpretation, other and more fundamental strains in his thinking suggest a different conclusion. John Dollard, certainly not a writer who is oblivious to social and cultural "factors," saw this twenty-five years ago: "It is quite clear," he wrote, ". . . that he (Freud) does not regard the instincts as having a fixed social goal; rather, indeed, in the case of the sexual instinct he has stressed the vague but powerful and impulsive nature of the drive and has emphasized that its proper social object is not picked out in advance. His seems to be a drive concept which is not at variance with our knowledge from comparative cultural studies, since his theory does not demand that the 'instinct' work itself out with mechanical certainty alike in every varying culture." [3]

So much for Freud's "imperious biological drives!" When Freud defined psychoanalysis as the study of the "vicissitudes of the instincts," he was confirming, not denying, the "plasticity" of human nature insisted on by social scientists. The drives or "instincts" of psychoanalysis, far from being fixed dispositions to behave in a particular way, are utterly subject to social channelling and transformation and could not even reveal themselves in behavior without social molding any more than our vocal chords can produce articulate speech if we have not learned a language. To psychoanalysis man is indeed a social animal; his social nature is profoundly reflected in his bodily structure.

But there is a difference between the Freudian view on the one hand and both sociological and neo-Freudian conceptions of man on the other. To Freud man is a *social* animal without being entirely a *socialized* animal. His very social nature is the source of conflicts and antagonisms that create re-

[3] John Dollard, *Criteria for the Life History,* New Haven: Yale University Press, 1935, p. 120.

sistance to socialization by the norms of any of the societies which have existed in the course of human history. "Socialization" may mean two quite distinct things; when they are confused an oversocialized view of man is the result. On the one hand socialization means the "transmission of the culture," the particular culture of the society an individual enters at birth; on the other hand the term is used to mean the "process of becoming human," of acquiring uniquely human attributes from interaction with others. All men are socialized in the latter sense, but this does not mean that they have been completely molded by the particular norms and values of their culture. All cultures, as Freud contended, do violence to man's socialized bodily drives, but this in no sense means that men could possibly exist without culture or independently of society. From such a standpoint, man may properly be called as Norman Brown has called him, the "neurotic" or the "discontented" animal and repression may be seen as the main characteristic of human nature as we have known it in history.

But isn't this psychology and haven't sociologists been taught to foreswear psychology, to look with suspicion on what are called "psychological variables" in contradistinction to the institutional and historical forces with which they are properly concerned? There is, indeed, as recent critics have complained, too much "psychologism" in contemporary sociology, largely, I think, because of the bias inherent in our favored research techniques. But I do not see how, at the level of theory, sociologists can fail to make assumptions about human nature. If our assumptions are left implicit, we will inevitably presuppose of a view of man that is tailor-made to our special needs; when our sociological theory over-stresses the stability and integration of society we will end up imagining that man is the disembodied, conscience-driven, status-seeking phantom of current theory. We must do better if we really wish to win credit outside of our ranks for special understanding of man, that plausible creature whose wagging tongue so often hides the despair and darkness in his heart.

American sociology has always been distinguishable from its European counterpart by a greater emphasis on fact-gathering and a lesser emphasis on theoretical system-building. Since World War II, however, there has been a renewed and vigorous interest in theory-building among American sociologists. Realizing that the data they have collected do not speak for themselves and that sound theory is essential, they have turned for guidance to the European system-builders, notably Pareto, Durkheim, Simmel, Mannheim, and Weber. Weber's influence has been predominant, and his leading American exponent is Talcott Parsons of Harvard.

To Weber and Parsons, human behavior is essentially social action—that is, it involves two or more actors who have a set of mutually oriented, subjectively intended expectations. The individual actor's action is guided by an awareness of other persons whose behavior is regarded by the actor as influencing the attainment of his own goals. When these stable and regulated interactions of two or more actors are oriented not only toward each other but also toward a collective goal so that they comprise an organized system, we may speak of them as a social action system. The basic components of a social action system are means, ends, conditions, and institutional norms.

Although social action theory is now the leading theoretical perspective in American sociology, not all American sociologists accept it uncritically. In the following article, G. E. Swanson examines the theory as it has been developed by Professors Parsons and Shils and concludes that it is inadequate for the purposes originally assigned to it.

53. THE APPROACH TO A GENERAL THEORY OF ACTION BY PARSONS AND SHILS *

G. E. SWANSON

University of Michigan

For more than ten years, Talcott Parsons has spoken about the uses of, and the need for, general theory in sociology. Having been promised that general theory would provide sociology with all the benefits that it has supplied other disciplines—such benefits as universality, necessity, and accuracy of proof—it was natural that sociologists awaited the publication of Parsons' and Edward A. Shils' book *Toward a General Theory of Action* with keen anticipation.

The published discussions and reviews of this effort of Parsons, and of Parsons and Shils, to develop an approach to a general theory of action and of social systems have included much talk about style of writing, vagueness of concepts, and unjustified psychologizing, with little attention to the assumptions that underlie their work and to the insights it may contain. Since these assumptions are the residue that is likely to have the greatest effect on the development of general sociological theory, it seems appropriate to make them explicit and to explore their implications.

At the beginning of their work the authors tell us something of what we may expect. Their theory is of "the categorial type," which means that it

> . . . involves a system of classes which is formed to fit the subject matter, so that there are intrinsic relations among the classes, and these are in accord with the relations among the items of the subject matter. Thus, in these systems, the principles of classification, themselves, include statements of certain relationships among classes. The elements are so defined as to constitute an interdependent system. . . . A categorial system in this sense is always logically prior to the laws which state further relations between its elements. The laws state generalized relationships of interdependence between variables in the system. The laws pre-

* *American Sociological Review,* Vol. 18, No. 2, April, 1953, pp. 125–134.

suppose the definitions of the variables, and they presuppose those relations which are logically implied by the definitions and by the kind of system in question. Insofar as specific laws can be formulated and verified, a categorial system evolves into a theoretical system.[1]

Or, again,

The present monograph is a straightforward exposition of a conceptual scheme.[2]

At no point do they claim to present a theoretical system. What they do say is that they want to try out the usefulness of certain assumptions about the bases from which a general theory of "action" could be built. Their initial effort seems to be a matter of formulating some assumptions about theory building in general, and about theory-building in disciplines concerned with "action" in particular, of presenting some primitive categories for analyzing "action," and, finally, of showing how these primitive categories, in various combinations and permutations, can be used to encompass all of the phenomena now designated in existing concepts describing action. In this way, for example, Parsons tries to show how Nazi ideology may be thought of as a product of the combination of the second-order concepts of ascription and universalism or how the professional relation to a client is one special case of the second-order concepts of universalism, affective neutrality, specificity, collective focus, and achievement.

By so "deriving" higher level concepts from more primitive elements, Parsons and Shils hope to give one kind of evidence for the fruitfulness of the primitive concepts they propose for later use in deductive systems (i.e., adequate primitive concepts should be capable of representing the differentiations in the phenomena under study), and, in a preliminary way, to show the conceptual interconnections among these variables.

The kinds of evaluation we may make of their work are limited by these intentions. It is not germane to say that they predict nothing, because no predictions are attempted or intended. But we may ask such a question as the following: How adequate are the primitive concepts proposed by Parsons and Shils for redefining and ordering the major concepts now used by sociologists? It is this problem that the present paper examines.

In one sense, the primitive concepts of Parsons and Shils are stated in the following quotation, "*The frame of reference of action* involves actors, a situation of action, and the orientation of the actor to that situation." Action is behavior "oriented to the attainment of ends in situations, by means of the normatively regulated expenditure of energy."

. . . There are four points to be noted in this conceptualization of behavior: (1) Behavior is oriented to the attainment of ends or goals or other anticipated

[1] Talcott Parsons and Edward A. Shils (eds.), *Toward a General Theory of Action*, Cambridge: Harvard University Press, 1951, p. 50.

[2] *Ibid.*, p. 51.

states of affairs. (2) It takes place in situations. (3) It is normatively regulated. (4) It involves the expenditure of energy or effort or "motivation" (which may be more or less organized independently of its involvement in action). Thus, for example, *a man driving his automobile to a lake to go fishing* might be the behavior analyzed. In this case, (1) to be fishing is the "end" toward which our man's behavior is oriented; (2) his situation is the road and the car and the place where he is; (3) his energy expenditures are normatively regulated—for example, this driving behavior is an *intelligent* means of getting to the lake; (4) but he does spend energy to get there; he holds the wheel, presses the accelerator, pays attention, and adapts his action to changing road and traffic conditions. When behavior can be and is so analyzed, it is called action.[3]

Presumably, then, any behavior that involves some awareness of a goal, and that is organized to choose means for reaching such a goal which have previously been learned to be more effective rather than less effective, will be action. This is to be contrasted with behaviors without goals (if such exist) or those cases in which a goal is known, but the means to the goal are completely unknown. Since few behaviors of interest to sociologists fall into these last two classifications, except as matters of degree, the distinction is probably of little moment for their work.

At any rate, it is the properties of actors, situations, and the orientations of actors to situations that will be manipulated by these authors to define the conceptual battery of sociology and, we may suppose, at some later date, to predict the phenomena of social systems. These properties, then, represent the primitive concepts that will actually be used in future theory building and they are the center of our concern here.

(1) *Properties of Actors.* We are told very little about the properties of actors, as such, other than that they may be individuals or collectivities. The actions produced are processes of "change of state in such empirical systems of action." At other points, we are told that the actor behaves toward his world in terms of its "significance for direct gratification or deprivation of impulse-needs." Finally, the actor must be capable of having, and of acting on, the kinds of orientation to situations that appear below.

(2) *Properties of Situations.* There is a little more information about the situation encountered by the actor. He may find that situation consisting of "a class of social objects (individuals and collectivities) and a class of non-social (physical and cultural) objects." Social objects may be sub-classified in two ways. The actor-subject may see these objects "solely in terms of what [an actor-object] *is* and irrespective of what that actor [-object] *does.*" In the former case he is concerned with the actor-object as a complex of qualities; in the latter, as a complex of performances. The actor-subject may, secondly, see social objects as having "such a broad and undefined significance for [him] that he feels obliged to grant them any demand they make of him," or he may

[3] *Ibid.*, p. 53.

see social objects as having "such a narrow and clearly defined significance for [him] that [he] does not feel obliged to grant them anything that is not clearly called for in the definition of the relationship which obtains between them." The first of these situations is called diffuse; the second, specific.

Nonsocial objects ("any objects which are not actors") are called "physical" if they do not interact with "the actor-subject as other actors do; and . . . constitute only objects, not subjects, of cognitive, cathectic and evaluative orientation." When nonsocial objects have the additional property of being produced through interaction they are called "cultural." Laws, ideas, and recipes would be examples of cultural objects.

(3) *Varieties of Orientations of Actors to Situations.* Like the properties of situations, the orientations of actors to situations are of two major varieties. One of these is called "motivational orientation," the other, "value-orientation." Motivational orientation

refers to those aspects of the actor's orientation to his situation which are related to actual or potential gratification or deprivation of the actor's need-dispositions. We will speak of three *modes* of motivational orientation.

i. The *cognitive* mode involves the various processes by which an actor *sees* an object in relation to his system of need-dispositions. Thus it would include the "location" of an object in the actor's total object-world, the determination of its properties and actual and potential functions, its differentiations from other objects, and its relations to certain general classes.

ii. The *cathectic* mode involves the various processes by which an actor invests an object with affective significance. Thus it would include the positive or negative cathexes implanted upon objects by their gratificational or deprivational significance with respect to the actor's need-dispositions or drives.

iii. The *evaluative* mode involves the various processes by which an actor allocates his energy among the various actions with respect to various cathected objects in an attempt to optimize gratification. Thus it would include the processes by which an actor organizes his cognitive and cathectic orientations into intelligent plans. . . . Evaluation is functionally necessary for the resolution of conflicts among interests and among cognitive interpretations which are not resolved automatically; and which thus necessitate *choice,* or at least specific selective mechanisms.

Value orientation refers to those aspects of the actor's orientation which commit him to the observance of certain norms, standards, criteria of selection, whenever he is in a contingent situation which allows (and requires) him to make a choice. . . . On a cultural level we view the organized set of rules or standards as such, abstracted, so to speak, from the actor who is committed to them by his own value-orientations and in whom they exist as need-dispositions to observe these rules. Thus a culture includes a set of *standards.* An individual's value orientation is his commitment to these standards. . . .

We shall speak of three modes of value-orientation, which parallel the modes of motivational orientation.

i. The *cognitive* mode of value-orientation involves the various commitments to standards by which the validity of cognitive judgments is established . . . [Among these would be the standards setting the validity of observations, the relevance of data, and the importance of problems.]

ii. The *appreciative* mode of value-orientation involves the various commitments to standards by which the appropriateness or consistency of the cathexis of an object or class of objects is assessed . . . these standards purport to give us rules for judging whether or not a given object, sequence, or pattern will have immediate gratificatory significance.

iii. The *moral* mode of value-orientation involves the various commitments to standards by which certain consequences of particular actions and types of action may be assessed with respect to their effects upon systems of action. . . . Specifically, they guide the actor's choices with a view to how the consequences of these choices will affect (*a*) the integration of his own personality system and (*b*) the integration of the social systems in which he is a participant.[4]

The examination of the properties of actors, situations, and actors' orientations to situations seems to reveal that there are not three categories of properties here, but one—the orientations of actors to situations. Inspection of the properties of situations shows that each of them is defined by the way actors may experience it. The actor's properties are his potential for having such experiences as gratification, deprivation, or the modes of orientation. The modes of orientation, themselves, are simply additional potentialities for relating to objects. They are varieties of the more fundamental capacity for experiencing gratification and deprivation.

Some interesting implications follow from this conclusion. The present paper will discuss three of them: (1) The nature of the variables that will be used in prediction if this kind of primitive category is employed, (2) the method of prediction implied, and (3) the suitability of these particular categories for such prediction.

(1) *The Nature of the Variables for Use in Prediction.* It will be helpful to phrase this problem as one of stating the dependent variable *to* which one might predict from these categories of actors' orientations and the independent variable *from* which the predictions will be derived. The dependent variable is action and its varieties. The independent variable will be a predisposition of the actor to take one kind of action as against another.

(2) *The Method of Prediction Implied.* If we accept the common approach of saying that predispositions to behave are a part of any total act, then what we do in predicting action is to forecast the later phases of acts from their predispositional stages. Parsons and Shils provide no formal method to enable prediction to the predispositions themselves. The major problems of prediction that might be handled by their concepts will be those that tell us (a) the conditions under which predispositions will result in one form of action rather than another and, with the formal nature of the resulting action held constant, what will be (b) the substantive nature of the manifestations of

[4] *Ibid.*, pp. 58–60.

combinations of predispositions of a particular nature (e.g., Nazi ideology being a product of ascription and universalism). It is instructive that the formal "derivations" appearing in this book are precisely of the latter type.

All current behavior theories seem to be of this kind. All of them predict in the style: Given an organism of type X with predispositions A and B, the following behavior will result; or: If one adds predisposition C to A and B, the organism's behavior will be different in *c* ways from what it would otherwise have been.

An example may be taken from a recent experiment by Leon Festinger and John Thibaut. These investigators brought small populations into the laboratory and put them to work on a task that could only be solved through the reaching of some consensus among the people involved. The situation was arranged to insure that there would be considerable diversity of opinion among the participants and that these differences of opinion would be such that the participants would perceive them as falling on a single continuum. The prediction was that these conditions would force participants to communicate more frequently to those of their number holding the opinions most extremely different from those held by most group members.

If the prediction in this experiment were restated in terms of one variety of reinforcement theory, it might read like this: *General theory:* When humans are faced with a series of barriers to a desired goal, they will try to remove those barriers. *Operational definitions:* For college students at the University of Michigan, reaching a solution to the experimental problem is a goal. Persons holding divergent ideas from those of the rest of the group will prevent the achievement of consensus. Therefore they will be manipulated to remove their differences. *Epistemic correlations:* From the general knowledge of the experimenters through experience in our culture, these operations are valid replications of the nature and relations among the concepts of the general theory. Therefore they will provide a valid test of that theory.

What we have done here is to state that, to the extent that the theoretical and conceptual materials are validly replicated, the prediction will hold. We have placed the *theoretically* necessary and sufficient conditions for our prediction within the already existing behavior predispositions of the organism, and said that organisms having such predispositions will behave overtly in predictable ways.

Sociologists will remember that such writers as Herbert Spencer and Ellsworth Huntington took certain objective conditions external to the organism, assumed they would all be experienced in the same ways by all organisms, and that, as we have assumed, overt behaviors would follow from these induced predispositions. It was in large part to take account of the fact that there often was no one-to-one correspondence between the "objective" nature of the environment and the way the organism dealt with it that led psychologists as well as sociologists to build theories that predicted behavior from the environment conceptualized in the terms in which it was experienced.

(3) *The Suitability of These Categories for the Prediction of Action.* The predispositions to behave that are specifically listed in the statement of Parsons' and Shils' "Frame of Reference" included three sub-types of the predisposition to be gratified and deprived: the cognitive, cathectic, and evaluative modes. Another kind of predisposition, the value orientations, are really derivations from the motivational modes of orientation. All that is added to the natural propensities of the organism to experience his situation through cognizing, cathecting, and evaluating is the learning of specific standards that give focus to these aspects of behavior. The two sub-classes of social objects seem to be of a different order and cannot be discussed in detail in this paper. It is the three motivational modes, then, that give us most of the basic sub-types of the experiencing of gratification and deprivation, and they may be a center for our attention, since, presumably, their combinations will someday be used among the principal independent variables in predictions.

Parsons' and Shils' present use of these three aspects of behavior takes the form of arranging them into some relatively informal combinations as a basis for defining further orientations to the situation. They are "informal" in the sense that the properties of these orientations are not specified with rigor nor are the rules for their combination stated in clean, precise ways.

It is striking that these three major analytic categories are the very ones that were central to the faculty psychologies of the eighteenth and nineteenth centuries, typically expressed as in Immanuel Kant's "ultimate modes of psychical functioning"—modes of knowing, feeling and willing. It is certain that Parsons and Shils are far too sophisticated to resurrect the sterilities of the older faculty psychology, but it is impressive that the difficulties one finds in using their categories for prediction include those usually mentioned in *post mortems* on faculty psychology.

The experience of psychologists with these three aspects of behavior may help us to test the probable usefulness of Parsons' and Shils' scheme. As long as cognizing, cathecting, and evaluating were considered to be "ultimate and distinct functions" present in all behavior, no differential predictions could be made from them and the result was sterility. When as Gardner Murphy suggests, they were treated as "labels for complex activities which [required] further study," the possibility of hypothesis construction opened again. When psychologists abandoned using them as explanatory variables and turned to still more primitive variables, and to variables permitting a more detailed description of events—to concepts such as reward-deprivation, or to other properties of the perceptual field—the possibility of building systematic learning and personality theories appeared.

A second difficulty that psychologists found in working with this trichotomy was its arbitrary division of behavior into three parts. Since they wanted to predict the whole acts of organisms, they sought for some concepts that could be assigned dynamic properties for that task. Such notions as those connected with reinforcement were among those finally chosen. Using these ideas, it was possible to predict, for example, that all of behavior, including knowing, thinking, and deciding, would take certain forms.

The doubts of still other psychologists about the fruitfulness of thinking in terms of such distinctions as these come from empirical observation that each unit of observed behavior (a) involves perception-need-feeling-belief-emotion-etc., and that (b) these do not vary at random with reference to each other. Consequently, there is a growing emphasis on the evolving of laws of behavior that will involve "all the parameters of [behavior] simultaneously." As Krech has phrased it:

> . . . Experimentally this means that we cannot talk about "varying the stimulus conditions and holding motivation constant," or "varying motivation and holding knowledge constant." Varying the stimulus conditions will vary the [organization of behavior] and therefore *all* of its attributes.[5]

A fourth difficulty involves the operational problems of the system. As many experimenters have made explicit, it is possible to control the things that are available for people to cognize, but it is impossible to vary such materials and hold reward constant. Hence, the recent wave of studies of the effects of social experience on perception hold the objective visual field constant while varying the reward-deprivation properties of the phenomena. Or, in learning experiments, there is a growing tendency to say that it is impossible, at least at present, to rule out the possibility of reinforcement and, hence, to judge whether learning can occur in its absence.

We may expect extensions of Parsons' and Shils' scheme to be confronted by these four issues, but the problem that seems most critical in working with this trichotomy lies in its inability to lend itself to use as part of dynamic theories as contrasted with static descriptions. The key to this property lies, I think, in what we have already seen to be the nature of current behavior theories—that is, their prediction from predispositions present in the organism to subsequent behavior. These theories are essentially equilibrium theories, although, generally, theories of a moving or "quasi-stationary" equilibrium. This means that they conceive that the organism, if allowed to function over time in an unchanging environment, will develop a habitual, repetitive behavior pattern. The organism's behavior changes because the environment changes. And there lies the problem. As we have seen, to get around the fact that many environmental changes had no one-to-one relationship with particular organismic responses, psychologists invented a terminology that said in effect: let us bring environmental changes into our system by classifying them in terms of the properties through which these organisms experience them, and in terms of which the response of the organism is determined. Thus a hungry rat runs faster as he approaches food, not because there is anything in the

[5] David Krech, "Notes Toward a Psychological Theory," *Journal of Personality*, 18 (September, 1949), p. 80.

food that draws him to it, but because food corresponds to an available gratification in a behavioral field in which a force or motive or need for this gratification exists. The food, and the hunger sensations induced by artificial starvation, are simply operational equivalents of the concepts of the system. The theory postulates that the environment that determines responses is the environment as experienced, and the concepts of the theory are geared to permit the description of the environment as experienced. Terms of various systems illustrative of this include: drive, goal, valence, barrier, motive, attitude, path, sign-gestalt, reinforcement, and reward.

The point to be made is that these terms, and the theories of which they are a part, lend themselves to dynamic formulations because they unite the nature of the organism with the nature of the environment as a source of change in the organism. By contrast, cognition, cathection, and evaluation are almost exclusively intra-organismic terms. As such, they are capable of describing some events occurring within the organism, but not of relating those occurrences to the events that set them in motion and determine their direction. This means, contrary to Parsons and Shils, that the road from these categories to a theoretical system is not simply a matter of hooking their categories to a motivational scheme, but that it will require a comprehensive redefinition of all second, third, and *n*-order categories in terms of some set of primitive concepts more suitable for the expression of laws of behavior. In the course of such a redefinition, it may be possible to derive by definition categories additional to those they have already defined.

One test of the fruitfulness of using the three motivational modes as part of a battery of primitive concepts of the organism's predispositions, from which we can derive other concepts that we need, is to see what Parsons and Shils have done with them. (Let us keep in mind, again, that "derive" is here used to mean "combine to produce by definition"; not "to predict from the logical interrelationships among postulates.") Their answer is to be found in the definition of the "pattern variables" that play so crucial a part in their analyses of empirical data.

First, let us establish that these pattern variables are derived in the manner stated above. In their introduction of the material, Parsons and Shils say:

> . . . There are further important conceptual entities and classificatory systems to be defined, but these, in a sense, derive from the basic terms that have already been defined. The point is that the further entities can be defined largely in terms of the entities and relationships already defined, with the introduction of a minimum of additional material.
>
> . . . If one were to look back over the sections of this chapter devoted to the objects of the situation and to the orientation of the actor to the situation . . . , he would see that an actor in a situation is confronted by a series of major dilemmas of orientation, a series of choices that the actor must make before the situation has a determinate meaning for him. The objects of the situation do not interact with the cognizing and cathecting organism in such a fashion as to determine auto-

matically the meaning of the situation. Rather, the actor must make a series of choices before the situation will have a determinate meaning. Specifically, we maintain, the actor must make five specific dichotomous choices before any situation will have a determinate meaning. The five dichotomies which formulate these choice alternatives are called the *pattern variables* because any specific orientation (and consequently any action) is characterized by a pattern of the five choices. Three of the pattern variables derive from the absence of any biologically given hierarchy of primacies among the various modes of orientation. In the first place, the actor must choose whether to accept gratification from the immediately cognized and cathected object or to evaluate such gratification in terms of its consequences for other aspects of the action system. (That is, one must decide whether or not the evaluative mode is to be operative at all in a situation.) In the second place, if the actor decided to evaluate, he must choose whether or not to give primacy to the moral standards of the social system or subsystem. In the third place, whether or not he decides to grant primacy to such moral standards, he must choose whether cognitive or appreciative standards are to be dominant, the one set with relation to the other. . . .

The other pattern variables emerge from indeterminacies intrinsic to the object situation: social objects as relevant to a given choice situation are either quality complexes, depending on how the actor chooses to see them; social objects are either functionally diffuse (so that the actor grants them every feasible demand) or functionally specific (so that the actor grants them only specifically defined demands), depending on how the actor chooses to see them or how he is culturally expected to see them.[6]

The present objective is to reflect on certain properties of those pattern variables derived from the orientations of the actor-subject. In this case, the following remarks will often apply to those derived from alternatives within the class of social objects as well.

Parsons and Shils argue that these five derived choices are exhaustive. This claim is especially crucial, since it is said that these five choices are the most general statements of the behaviors that define all possible situations for actors. If this is true, and if our earlier statement is correct that newer behavior theories predict from the predispositions of the actor to subsequent behavior, then these choices represent the second-order categories for stating the independent variables for truly predictive theorizing.

Parsons and Shils say that there are three assumptions underlying their "contention that the five pattern-variable dilemmas are an exhaustive set."

. . . These assumptions are: (1) acceptance of the basic frame of reference as we have defined it; (2) acceptance of the level of generality on which we are proceeding, which is the *first* level of derivation from the basic frame of reference; (3) acceptance of our method of derivation through the establishment of primacies among types of interest and the resolution of ambiguities intrinsic to the world of social objects.[7]

[6] Parsons and Shils, *op. cit.*, pp. 76–77.
[7] *Ibid.*, p. 91.

In the absence of any clear criteria for knowing whether we are working on the "*first* level of derivation from the basic frame of reference" it is uncertain whether any seeming exceptions to their rule of exhaustiveness are valid, but some things come to mind that seem to be possible bases for doubting the rule. We notice, for example, that a whole set of concepts referring to organizational forms are never derived by Parsons or by Parsons and Shils from these pattern variable dilemmas or from the pattern variables. Among them are such ideas as: crowd, social class, bureaucracy, social movement, mass action, community, or nation. Nor is there a derivation by definition of the interpersonal relationships subsumed under the "social processes" of three or four decades ago: cooperation, competition, conflict, assimilation, and accommodation, to say nothing of such sub-types of each as those elaborated by Georg Simmel. Nor do we find derivations by definition of the more genotypic concepts used to describe interpersonal influence, for example, authority, legitimacy, power, coordination, communication, leader, follower, prestige, or of the highly general categories for describing social systems such as integration, division of labor, mobility, or stratification. Finally, there is no derivation of a whole range of concepts such as the rate, frequency, duration, and intensity of the contacts among individuals. (In fact it is hard from this scheme to tell what it is that is in process in social life. Is it the physical movements of actors, their ideas, the modifications they make in each other's behavior, or what?)

Parsons and Parsons and Shils do use concepts such as the underived examples mentioned above. They are critical to their extension of the scheme. But, and this is the important point, these ideas appear neither in the initial concepts of the frame of reference nor are they given even an informal derivation from the orientational modes of the actor that form the prospective independent variables of a future theoretical scheme. They are brought in because they are necessary, but they are not formally related to the rest of the system.

It may be, of course, that they could be formally related, that Parsons and Shils were not interested in doing that job, or that they just did not get around to it. What seems likely is that such formal relating is difficult, if not impossible, using their present concepts.

In view of the intra-organismic nature of the basic categories of Parsons and of Parsons and Shils, it is not surprising that such use as their categories have is largely in the area of describing intra-organic events—in this case, primarily the treatment of the ideologies of populations as they presently exist in the functioning of those populations, and, further, that this treatment is a kind of Benedictean "patterns of culture" approach in which the connections between the details of those ideologies and their master themes are shown largely by shrewd intuition and a kind of *Verstehen* rather than by formal derivation.

It seems to me that the ranges of conventional sociological concepts that they fail to derive are the very ones that tend to require some uniting of organisms with the environing conditions set by other organisms. They are the concepts that correspond to the properties of social systems *as systems.* There is not space here to state personal preferences for the primitive concepts from which system properties might be derived, but it can be pointed out that concepts stating the environment as experienced have been used for the description, and for the *prediction,* of such phenomena.

The absence of derivations of terms describing the system-properties of social systems may be a function of Parsons' choice of the dependent variable for sociological theory. He states:

> Sociological theory . . . is for us that aspect of the theory of social systems which is concerned with the phenomena of the institutionalization of patterns of value-orientation in the social system, with the conditions of that institutionalization, and of changes in the patterns, with conditions of conformity with and deviance from a set of such patterns and with motivational processes in so far as they are involved in all of these. . . .[8]

And "institutionalization" of a social practice or standard occurs to the extent that:

> . . . from the point of view of any given actor in the system, it is both a mode of the fulfillment of his own need-dispositions and a condition of "optimizing" the reactions of other significant actors. . . .[9]

While it is doubtful that the Parsons-Shils frame of reference has the categories needed to predict to this order of dependent variable, such a variable is consistent with the lack of derivation of system properties from that frame of reference, for this dependent variable describes the conditions under which an actor will come to view a given behavior as gratifying to himself and others. Thus one might be interested in the degree of integration or stratification or mobility in a population insofar as these conditions would affect its members' acquiring such a conception of the reward-deprivation qualities of a given behavior, but, presumably, one would not be interested in the prediction of these conditions for their own sake.

Parsons, and Parsons and Shils, have performed a major service in clearing away many old controversies, in showing the reasonableness of a behavioral foundation for general theory in social science as a whole and in sociology in particular, in clarifying the interrelations among many concepts, and in the insightful interpretation of particular pieces of data. However, the behavioral scheme they propose is inadequate for deriving the events they hope some time to order.

[8] Talcott Parsons, *The Social System,* Glencoe, Illinois: The Free Press, 1951, p. 552.
[9] *Ibid.,* p. 38.

Confronted with this criticism by Professor Swanson and by others, Professor Parsons chose to respond by clarifying his general theory of social action and placing his work in the perspective of the work of other social scientists, past and present, rather than to attempt answering the criticisms in detail.

In the following article, he attempts to make three major points about his theory as a frame of reference for sociology. He stresses, first of all, that it is not a brand new innovation, but rather a development continuing the threads of theory construction in both Europe and America. Second, he maintains that it is not a static scheme of ideas; it is a dynamic body of thought, unevenly developed, that will require further work and refinement in the years ahead. Last, Professor Parsons claims that his theory is not sheer speculation, divorced from the fact-gathering processes of sociology as a science. Rather, it is useful in new empirical research on a number of different fronts.

54. SOME COMMENTS ON THE STATE OF THE GENERAL THEORY OF ACTION *

TALCOTT PARSONS
Harvard University

In view of the fact that two books [1] in which I have had an important hand which were published about two years ago, have led to considerable comment both in this *Review* and elsewhere, the Editor of the Review has kindly invited me to "have my say in the matter." In considering how this opportunity could be used most effectively it has seemed best to focus attention on two things, namely clarification, and the placing of the work in perspective, rather than attempting to answer criticisms in detail. Reference will be made to a number of these criticisms, but I feel that the problem of communication and understanding should in an important sense take precedence. Furthermore, considerable additional work has been done since the two books in question were written; a brief report on some aspects of this work may help to clarify some of the points of difficulty.

The first important point I would like to make is that, while I, and I think several of my colleagues, felt that the two books in question documented what was in certain respects a considerable advance in the differentiation and integration of the conceptual scheme we have been calling the theory of action, they were in no sense meant to suggest any fundamental break in the con-

* *American Sociological Review,* Vol. 18, No. 6, December, 1953, pp. 618–631.

[1] *Toward a General Theory of Action,* Edited by Talcott Parsons and Edward A. Shils, Harvard University Press, 1951, and *The Social System,* by Talcott Parsons, The Free Press, 1951.

tinuity of theoretical development in the field as a whole; we feel that they stand in the most intimate relation to a great deal of work done before, and going on concurrently in other circles. This of course includes both sociology and the neighboring fields of psychology and anthropology.

With respect to my personal orientation as a sociologist, I am of course aware of the fact that through the double circumstances of having come into the field through economics, and having received my graduate training in Europe, certain European sociologists have exercised the most conspicuous and direct influence on my theoretical thinking. A main reason for my early interest in the work of Max Weber, and later that of Pareto, lay in the fact that these men dealt constructively, in my opinion, with the problems concerning the relation between economic and sociological theory which underlay the "institutionalist" controversy of the time in American Economics. In my opinion the then dominant "Veblenian" group among the American institutionalists failed conspicuously to solve these problems while others, like Wesley Mitchell, seemed to me to be sheer empiricists who essentially abandoned the attempt at theoretical analysis in favor of description of statistical trends. Furthermore, it was only after I became fully aware that Durkheim, in his study of the division of labor, was dealing with essentially the same problems, that I really felt I could adequately understand and evaluate Durkheim's work.

This economic and European background has undoubtedly given a certain "slant" to my work, and habits of using terminology, which has perhaps made communication with some of the older traditions of American sociology more difficult than it would have been had I had a regular American graduate training. But I have been increasingly aware of the extent to which many of these American writers were dealing with cognate problems, though often in such different terms that translation was not easy. In the background I found Sumner important. Of the American writers of the last generation, however, I think I have profited most by the work of W. I. Thomas and G. H. Mead, the latter particularly in connection with recent phases of my own work. Both have been most important in helping to build what for me are the critically important bridges between sociology and psychology. In a *theoretical* sense I have found both Cooley and Park highly suggestive, but not providing the same order of *specific* conceptual developments with which to work constructively. Simmel's importance as a bridge between European and American theory is of course very great. It is quite frankly my opinion, however, that the American tradition of that generation did not produce a constructive *theorist* in the strictly technical sense who had the stature of either Max Weber or Durkheim.

If I made one contribution, in my own earlier work, beyond those made by these European writers themselves (including of course Pareto and Simmel) it was the demonstration that all of these men, and certain others who were called economists, e.g., Sombart, had been converging on a *single* theoretical scheme. This was of course not known at the time—for me it was an emergent finding which became clear only late in this period of my work. It was not to be found in the secondary literature, which I canvassed thoroughly. The predominant tendency was to allocate these writers to various different "schools." I am quite sure that a careful critical study of the principal American theorists of the time, which to my knowledge has even now not been made in the requisite terms, would reveal that they could all be placed, with relative ease, in terms of the same general scheme.

It goes without saying that anthropological and psychological influences have also been prominent in my own background but I will not take space to detail them here.

One more major theoretical influence should be briefly mentioned. Though the concept of system has come into the social sciences through several channels, in my own case first through economics, this influence was greatly reinforced by contact with its use in biological science, notably physiology. Building on knowledge of biology gained in an undergraduate major, contact with the late L. J. Henderson, both as an interpreter of Pareto and in other ways, stamped the importance of the concept of system as a theoretical tool indelibly on my mind. This was again reinforced by interest in the work of W. B. Cannon, especially his book, *The Wisdom of the Body*.

I have taken the space to sketch this series of theoretical interests and contacts, in order to recall to the reader the way in which the theoretical work under immediate discussion fits into the background of the relevant intellectual currents of our time. To me, in surveying this background again, the overwhelming impression is that of the unity and coherence of the main movement. It is true that certain groups of writers on the borderlines of sociology have taken positions which, whatever their *relative* justification in the polemical situations of the time, have proved either to be untenable in themselves, or so remote from the interests of sociological theory as not to be positively useful to the task of the sociological theorist. I should be inclined to put in this category first, certain aspects of the "institutionalist" position in economics, second, the extreme at least of "instinctivism" in psychology, including some interpretations current in the psychoanalytic camp, third, radical behaviorism in psychology, including both the Watsonian repudiation of the "subjective" and the attempts, some still current, to generalize strict "S-R" theory into a theory of *all* social and cultural behavior; finally, fourth, some of the versions of "culturology" of which different variants are exemplified by the work of Ruth Benedict and of Leslie White. This does not mean at all that there are not components in any and all of these movements which are positively useful to sociology, but their *general* structures as theoretical positions are from my point of view no more admissible and usable as schemes in terms of which to unify a theory of action or behavior, which *includes sociology,* than was the utilitarian scheme which was dominant in the later nineteenth century. Very broadly these, to me "deviant," attempts to synthesize, represent on the one side "positivistic" schemes, on the other side "idealistic" ones. With these qualifications, however, it seems to me that the general movement of theoretical development has clearly been in line with the scheme which I and my colleagues have called the "theory of action" as an emerging and as yet of course, very incomplete, single body of theory comprising the whole range of the sciences of action, or to use the Ford Foundation's term, the "behavior sciences."

For some purposes of exposition and some types of analysis it is convenient, even sometimes necessary, to separate out the problems of conceptual structure from those of empirical reference in a body of scientific thought. It has, however, been my contention from the beginning, that the theoretical development itself simply could not be understood apart from the continual process of interaction between theoretical reasoning and empirical observation. Sometimes the empirical problems have concerned the interpretation of broad features of the structure of large-scale societies, such as the problems of "capitalism" and of "contractual relations" as they concerned Weber and Durkheim, or of the "circulation of elites" as it concerned Pareto. Sometimes, as in the case of Durkheim's famous study of suicide rates, it concerns statistical data in relation to more specific aspects of these very broad problems. Sometimes it has concerned anthropological studies of the structure of kinship relations or of magical and religious practices in non-literate communities, as in the work of Malinowski, Firth, Kluckhohn. The program of community studies has of course carried this type of empirical work into our own society, sometimes under directly anthropological auspices. Empirical research also may take the form of study by direct observation and interview of selected crucial institutionalized situations in a society, as in the case of my own work on medical practice. There has of course been an immense amount of clinical observation of individual personalities, in therapeutic and other kinds of situations, and a rapidly developing study of attitudes from carefully sampled populations.

These are only a few of the many types of empirical work which concurrently, and in interaction with theoretical development, have been going on continually. It is most important to recognize the diversity of different types of study, their places on a macro-scopic-microscopic range of levels, their varying degrees of technical sophistication, etc. I would like particularly to emphasize that studies such as Weber's comparative work in the field of the sociology of religion and Durkheim's analysis of the data about Australian totemism, both of which simply made the most of available published sources, were *empirical* studies in the strictest and highest sense. The very rapid development of techniques of empirical research in our own generation has not constituted the *beginning* of empirical work, but has immensely widened the the field and accelerated the pace of empirical discovery by putting far more powerful tools in the hands of the researcher than he possessed before.

I hope I have successfully made clear that, in my opinion, the current levels of the general theory of action rest on solid foundations in the development in our fields, foundations both of theoretical thinking and of empirical research in the closest interdependence with each other. Now let us turn to direct consideration of the present state of our theory, both as documented in the two books under discussion and as having developed farther since their publication.

Perhaps the best way to introduce this discussion is explicitly to raise the question, what may legitimately be considered to be *new* in this level of theoretical work? Since I have just been stressing its continuity with previous work this becomes a particularly important question. Professor Ellsworth Faris in his review of *The Social System* seems to interpret me and my colleagues as resting a claim to originality mainly on "the discovery of the combination of interdependence and independence of personality, culture and system (organization)." In the sense in which he imputes the claim to us, of course he is right in repudiating its newness. But I think he misunderstands the sense in which we feel we have achieved something new. Of course, in the history of theory which I have just reviewed, certain highly significant levels of insight into these connections have been commonplaces throughout the period which is directly relevant, and many of them go much farther back. Certainly Cooley, Thomas, Mead and Park, like Pareto, Durkheim and Weber, had what we may call the "broad" insight, and in different ways contributed important specifications and developments at many points.

As in so many other cases in the history of science, the important point is not a matter of the broad insight in this sense, but of the level on which this insight has become incorporated into a differentiated and integrated conceptual scheme, which both does justice to known fact—as an instrument of codification—and makes possible a higher level of generality of formulation and analytical reasoning than before, including the revelation of areas of ignorance and the formulation of relatively specific hypotheses. It is then quite true that in our opinion the focus of the theoretical contribution lies in the interrelations of these three foci of the organization of action, but it is not the fact that we understand that they are in general closely related, but the detailed *way* in which we analyze those interrelationships that we consider our contribution to lie.

This contribution may be considered to lie on two main levels. The first is that documented in the *General Statement* which opened our collaborative volume, *Toward a General Theory of Action.* This statement was explicitly the result of an attempt among nine men, with rather widely different backgrounds and views on various subjects, to find the greatest possible measure of *common ground.* It was then completely understood that there would be further areas with reference to which we would part company on the basis of differences of interests, of presuppositions, of emphasis or, in a few cases, of direct and explicit substantive disagreement. In the circumstances it would be expected that the agreement would be on a rather high level of generality.

In retrospect I should consider the following four points to constitute the most important aspects of that agreement: The first is making the existence of a common frame of reference of which the keynote is the *relational* focus on actor *and* situation, quite explicit. This essentially eliminates, in one major respect, the old "behaviorist" controversy, so far as we are concerned. Put as sharply as possible, whatever differences of emphasis and interest there may be between a Sears, with his background in Hullian S-R psychology, a Tolman with his animal psychology interests, a Murray with his modified psychoanalytic background and primary interest in personality, a Kluckhohn with his "configurational" interest in culture, and Shils' and my own social-system emphasis, is explicitly held *not* to involve the kinds of differences of basic frame of reference which mean that discussion which gets below the surface must focus mainly on justification of one's frame of reference without ever getting to common substantive empirical and theoretical questions.

The second important point is building certain of the broad fundamentals of "behavior psychology," in a sense broad enough to include both Tolman and Hull, into this frame of reference. Then many of the old controversies as to whether or not such a category as "purpose" has any place in "scientific psychology" or whether for the anthropologist or sociologist utilizing any of psychology at this level may not lead him into fatal basic fallacies, can, for our purposes, be considered to be obsolete and need no longer worry us in their *general* form.

The third, and for present purposes exceedingly crucial area of agreement, is that with respect to the concept of social *interaction* and its critical significance for *all* the disciplines concerned. Though a psychology relatively independent of the concept of interaction can be worked out up to a point, we agreed that this category, with its peculiar emergent phenomena of the complimentarity of expectations and "double contingency," is essential to the analysis of *all* the higher forms of organization of action alike, in their social system, personality and cultural aspects. In certain respects, of course, this insight has been the stock in trade of the sociologists and the social psychologists in the Cooley-Mead tradition, but it has *not* been common to the "behavior sciences" as a whole. It seems to me that its significance, on the relatively elementary levels included in the General Statement, lies primarily in bringing into relation with this more "sociological" tradition, above all the psychologists in the "experimental" tradition, and to a lesser extent, in the psychoanalytic tradition. But even some anthropologists have tended to "by-pass" the phenomena of interaction.

Finally, fourth, we feel that the statement related these levels of theoretical consideration to the primary fields of interest of sociologists and anthropologists in social systems and culture, by indicating, in a general way of course, how both cultures and social systems could be shown to develop and change in the processes of goal-oriented behavior *in social interaction*. The fact that cultural patterns are to be conceived both as institutionalized in social systems and as internalized in personality systems is the keynote of this point of view.

It is almost obviously true that *none* of the components which has gone into this extremely general synthesis is new. But to bring all of them together in explicit and orderly relations to each other and in such a way as to be subscribed to with only two dissents by leading proponents of all the main disciplinary traditions involved, is something new. Of course no such document can be considered in any way as "definitive." But it is our hope that this can help substantially to prevent reversion to the old levels of sterile controversy. In short, we conceived this as a contribution to the elimination of the "war of schools" as a dominant feature of the contemporary social science scene.

In *Toward a General Theory of Action* we attempted to make a clear distinction between the area of common agreement included in the General Statement, and an order of theoretical construction which was to be treated as exposition of the more individual views on their own responsibility of the particular authors. Shils' and my monograph "Values, Motives and Systems of Action" belongs in this latter category, as does of course my own *Social System* and a variety of subsequent writings, notably my contributions to *Working Papers in the Theory of Action.*

Let me repeat: all of what we treated in the General Statement as common ground is assumed as underlying this more special and technical development. This includes the goal-orientatedness of action interpreted as constituting a system of *relations* between actor(s) and situation, the fact that this involves processes which have cognitive, "cathectic" and evaluative aspects, the fundamental importance and the essential characteristics of social interaction and, finally, the fundamental importance of culture to both personalities and social systems, including the conception of its internalization and institutionalization.

If these fundamentals are treated as assumed, then it is correct, as several reviewers have noted, that the "core" of the more personal theoretical contribution which Shils and I have made is to be found, in our opinion, in what we have called the "pattern variables." These, it will be remembered, are five dichotomous "dilemmas of choice" which, we have contended, define *alternative directions* in which the orientation of action can go. These are, in a different order from that in which they were originally presented, (1) Specificity—Diffuseness; (2) Affectivity—Affective Neutrality; (3) Universalism—Particularism; (4) Quality—Performance (earlier formulated as Ascription—Achievement), and (5) Self-Orientation—Collectivity-Orientation. We contended that, on the requisite level of abstraction this constituted an exhaustive list. We further contended that the variables did not constitute only a "list" but were grouped to form a scheme which had the property of "symmetrical asymmetry," namely 1 and 2 form a pair, 3 and 4 form a pair, and the fifth is unpaired.

Dr. M. Brewster Smith in his review of *Toward a General Theory* has formulated four questions about the pattern variables which are most pertinent and can serve as a basis for organizing the present discussion. These are: (1)

Are the pattern variables in fact an exhaustive list? (2) Are they appropriately regarded as dichotomous? (3) Do the systems of classification which they generate "fit" the needs of personality, social and cultural theory? and (4) Do the pattern variables contribute to a satisfactory general theory of social behavior?

In order to approach the first two of Dr. Smith's questions it is necessary to distinguish clearly between these two, the "general frame of reference" level and the pattern variable level of conceptualization. How can the distinction between and relations of these two "levels" be stated? I think the best way of putting it is to say that the "general frame of reference" concerns the basic characteristics of "action" as a category of phenomena, without special reference to the nature and problems of the *systems* in which the relations of units of action to each other are organized. The pattern variable level on the other hand *makes explicit the problems of relationship of action units in systems.*

On the more general frame of reference level, we have said three main things which are relevant to the concept of system. The first is that any system of action is *relational* relative to the "components" conceived to make it up, namely "actors" and "objects." The second is that these may be conceived to "interact" which is, I think, in the most general form to say that *the same* concrete unit may be conceived as *both* actor and object in different perspectives. The third thing said is that the relevant systems are "boundary-maintaining," in this respect being more like organisms than like the systems of classical mechanics. They maintain a difference between states "internal" to a given system and those in the situation or environment of the system. They have the property of "integration," interpreted as involving the control both of internal states and of boundary-processes in such a way as to maintain this internal-external differential.

As I see it now, the pattern variables are a way of making explicit and formulating in a technical and orderly way, the basic frame of reference in terms of which these properties of action at the level of complexity where their organization in system is involved, "make sense." They formulate the "directions of movement," i.e., the basic *modes* of "change of state" of a unit in its relations to others in a system and to the state of the system in relation to the situation external to it. These directions must be taken into account, precisely by discriminating them from each other and ordering them, if the process of action is to be analyzed as process in systems in the classical scientific sense. Alternatively stated, the pattern variables constitute categories for the orderly description and comparative analysis of the "structure" of systems of action as systems.

It is in this context that I wish to discuss Dr. Smith's first question, "are the pattern-variables in fact an exhaustive list?" and also his second "are they properly regarded as dichotomous?"

There is a sense in which we may treat all of the pattern variables as ways of formulating the consequences of the fact that human social action is not a state of Nirvana in the Buddhist sense. It is subject to certain fundamental restrictions, which is almost another way of saying that it is process occurring in systems. These restrictions are of two most fundamental orders. The first derives from the finitude of the temporal existence of man, and therefore the necessity of some process of selection or "decision" about time-allocation, about when to seek direct gratification, when to impose discipline in the interest of future states. The second set of restrictions concerns the implications of the coexistence of many different organized entities of action which may be treated as units or systems according to the perspective. Any given unit of a system, an "actor," is subject to the exigencies of coexisting in at least one system with other units and, in turn, this system is subject to the exigencies of coexisting with other systems which constitute a "situation" to it.

The dichotomous character of the pattern variables derives from the fact that both of these sets of restrictions constitute basic *dilemmas*. With respect to either pair, namely the alternative to "take it now" vs. to give priority to continuity and stability over time, and the alternative to protect the solidarity of the interactive system vs. optimizing relations with the situation external to the system, it is not possible for a process to "go in both directions at once." We conceive these relations logically to be comparable to those of pairs of rectilinear coordinates of a space. The essential point is a very familiar one. Given the x and y coordinates in the usual sense, it is possible to increase or decrease the values of both variables at once only by changing the distance of a point from the point of origin. But this distance is not a function of the relation between x and y but of other variables. So far as the relation between x and y is concerned, the value of x can only be increased by decreasing the value of y and vice versa. This is the sense in which the pattern variables state "dilemmas," that is, are dichotomous. It can be seen that this sense of dichotomous mutual exclusiveness is in no way incompatible with the idea of continuity of variation with respect to such a variable.

If this is correct, then the fact that there is one basic dilemma having to do with time-allocation, and one with "space," i.e., the coexistence of units and systems, makes sense if we mean by it that these two "problems of organization" of units in systems *are not reducible* to each other. Given a particular unit of organization of action, an actor, no level of "optimization" of the distribution of gratifications over time, however high, will by itself solve the problems of his relations to other units. Similarly, no solution of the problem of integration with other units in a system, or adaptation to objects outside the system will by itself solve his time-allocation problem. This is the sense in which we conceive the two basic dilemmas to be independent of each other.

What, then, can we say of the significance of the three different groupings of the pattern-variables?, namely to constitute the "object-categorization pair" (universalism-particularism and quality-performance), the "attitudinal pair" (specificity-diffuseness and affectivity-neutrality) and finally the as yet unpaired self-collectivity orientation?

Put very schematically, we are saying that we can and must view *any* system of action from three different perspectives. The most familiar of these to American common sense is that action "consists" of human personalities, interacting with each other. The second, somewhat less familiar, one is that it is or involves one or more social systems, i.e., systems *constituted by interactive relationships* (not personalities) and the third, that in both respects any action system is a process which is "normatively" regulated, its common culture is *in one respect* a system of norms.

Seen in these terms the question of the exhaustiveness of the pattern variable list reduces to two others. The first is whether the basic "functional problems" of systems of action can be reduced to four, while the second is whether there is any fundamental significance in the classification of the three "aspects" of the organization of action which we have called social system, personality and culture. If this is the logic of the problem, then it should follow that the list should contain a sixth dilemma to pair with that of self-collectivity. I have recently come to the conclusion that this should be the case.

The four basic functional problems of systems of action we have formulated are (1) "adaptation," i.e., to objects in the situation outside the system, (2) "goal-attainment," i.e., establishment of "consummatory" relations to situational objects—by "instrumental" processes, (3) "integrative," the maintenance of a state of internal "harmony" or absence of "conflict" among the units of the system and (4) "latent pattern-maintenance and tension-management," the maintenance *both* of the structure of the internalized-institutionalized normative or cultural patterns, *and* motivation to conformity with their requirements.

It seems clear that this is an irreducible list, judged by the needs of the frame of reference of action. It has worked sufficiently well, so that I think it is legitimate to place the burden of proof on him who would reduce it farther or expand it.

We now conceive the two pairs of "attitudinal" and "object-categorization" pattern variables, as *each* formulating these four system-problems or *dimensions* as we have called them (*Working Papers,* Ch. III). Each does so from one of the two "sides" or aspects of the relational system which we conceive action to be. This arrangement is shown in Figure 1.

If this interpretation is correct, then, within the same specific system reference, we have not formulated eight independent variables, but only four, which is a great gain from the point of view of manageability. But the two different formulations are none the less significant, because they call attention to the fundamental fact that, except in limiting cases, we are *always* dealing with the interpenetration of *at least two systems.* Every social system, that is to say, involves in some degrees and senses, the "participation" of a plurality of personalities. The "attitudinal" version of the variables formulates the primary involvement of the personalities regarded as systems, which always transcends any particular role. The "object-categorization" version, on the other hand, formulates the fact that members of a collectivity are objects to each other in the sense that *their relative locations in a system* always transcend the involvement of any particular personality in that system. He is "oriented to" all of them as objects, but he, *in his role,* is only one of these objects and is always differentiated from others in the system. Furthermore, what we have called the "symmetrical asymmetry" of the pattern variable system shows that the organization of these dual system-references relative to each other *cannot* be random, but must involve systematically determinate relations. Further basic significances of the difference of "aspects" are to be found in the distinction, in processes of interaction, between performances and sanctions, and closely related to this, between facilities and rewards.

FIGURE 1. System Problems and Pattern Variables.

System Problem	Attitudinal Aspect	Object-Categorization Aspect
Adaptation	Specificity	Universalism
Goal-Attainment	Affectivity	Performance (Achievement)
System-Integration	Diffuseness	Particularism
Pattern-Maintenance and Tension-Management	Affective Neutrality	Quality (Ascription)

What now of the fifth pattern-variable, self-orientation vs. collectivity-orientation and its relation to the normative or cultural aspect of systems of action? It has become increasingly clear for some time that this concerned the relations of a given system of reference to other systems. We are aware that a "society" and a total "personality" are limiting cases of the concept system of action. They must in turn be treated as composed of complex networks of subsystems, which are organized in a "hierarchical" order of greater and lesser inclusiveness. Collectivity-orientation then formulates the respects in which membership in a superordinate system is a directly governing consideration for action in or as a member of any given subsystem. Self-orientation on the other hand formulates the area within which the norms or interests of the superordinate system are not directly governing, that is where they may be treated only as "regulative" rather than "constitutive" of the relationship in question. In familiar social system terms, in ordinary economic transactions in his capacity as "consumer" in our society an individual is free, within the regulative limits of "fair dealing," to use his income in the manner he conceives to be most advantageous *to him*. The same individual, however, in his capacity as an administrative officer in an organization (e.g,, chairman of a university department) in making up a department budget is positively obligated to give first consideration to the interests of the department as a collectivity, that is as a social system, not to his individual wishes.

All roles in social systems—to use this type for illustration—are governed by the norms of its institutionalized culture. What this pattern variable does is, in the relations of systems to each other as distinguished from their internal affairs, to distinguish between two modes of normative control to which action is subject, those positively defining obligations of membership in superordinate collectivities, and those merely setting the limits of permissible action relative to the superordinate collectivity. If the reference is *only* internal, the cognate category is the integration of the system itself. The inference is that the *cultural* level always involves a reference *beyond* the system which is the focus of analysis.

Within the available limitations of space this is the best answer I can give at present to the first two of Dr. Smith's questions. The terms used differ substantially from those of the original exposition, but I hope they will be clearer. A great deal of analytical work has gone on in the meantime which has clarified a number of questions which were obscure in the earlier stages of development of the scheme.

I may now turn to the third and fourth questions, whether the pattern variables "fit the needs" of theory in the relevant fields and whether they contribute to a "satisfactory general theory of social behavior." Following the leads of Dr. Smith's exposition under these headings I shall interpret question three to concern the "fit" with current theoretical categories in the respective fields, and question four to concern the empirical usefulness of the scheme. The two questions of course cannot be completely separated, but these two emphases will form convenient points of reference for organizing the rest of the material.

Let us start with the theory of the social system, that is sociology. The first beginnings of the pattern variable scheme came from the attempt to discriminate types of social structure, taking the lead first from Toennies' distinction of *Gemeinschaft* and *Gesellschaft,* and then from some of Max Weber's refinements of this. To me its first great utility was that it made it possible to formulate the precise sense in which the professional role was differentiated both from that of the businessman, and from that for example of the father of a family, thus in Toennies' terms belonged to *neither* of his two main categories, but had properties Toennies ascribed to both.

For many years I have been greatly concerned with the development of categories for the systematic classification of social structures, because of my conviction that without them systematic comparative analysis would not be possible and the levels of generalization accessible to sociology would remain exceedingly low. We would lack, that is to say, the kind of framework which the classification of species and comparative anatomy have given to the biological sciences.

Since the breakdown of the older evolutionary theories we simply have not had such a scheme, indeed some of us have tried to make a virtue out of necessity and act as though the "richness" of the variety of social structures in principle defied analysis, and this was "a good thing." By far the most important attempt was that of Max Weber in the *Theory of Social and Economic Organization.* But this, for reasons which cannot be gone into here, left a great many problems unsolved.

The new level of development of the scheme of pattern variables which came with *Toward a General Theory of Action* and *The Social System* have, in my opinion, made it possible to make a substantial advance toward such a classification of social structures, one which for the first time goes beyond the level reached by Max Weber. This analysis culminates in Chapter IV of *The Social System.* There is no space to discuss it in detail here. It did, however, seem to me that it had proved possible to derive, step by step from the general frame of reference, and from the conception of organization of action in social systems, all of the main types of social structure with which sociologists have regularly been working. I am sure that this could be much more adequately and elegantly done now than it was at that time, and when the time for revision of this book (*The Social System*) arrives, I expect to undertake the job. Hence all I wish to assert now is that this attempt constitutes a substantial advance over what has previously been available in the literature. This, and recognition of the importance of the task for sociology, are the two points I wish to emphasize.

There is, however, one further general point. In my own earlier work I considered the pattern variables to be categories of social structure as such. It was one of the most important insights of the new work under review that they were in fact categories of systems of action in general. Hence their use in order to derive categories of social structure necessarily involves a logical step in derivation which makes the transition from the most general level to that of social interaction. Thus for example affective neutrality could, if referred only to an individual actor, mean simply inhibition, in the immediately current situation, of an impulse to direct gratification. But as a category of the institutional organization of a social system it must mean more than this, it must refer to a generalized obligation, for those in a certain type of role in the social system, to refrain from gratifying impulses which would interfere with a given *type* of performance or relationship in the social system. Put in personality terms, mechanisms other than simple inhibition, namely those involving "superego" controls, seem to be essential for this function.

One general remark may be made about the problem of "fitness" in the sense of derivation of concepts in common use from more general sources.

This concerns the apparent assumption that it is a valid criterion of the significance of the pattern variables that more concrete concepts should be derivable from them *alone* without reference to the other aspects of the frame of reference and general theory. This is like requiring—and I think the analogy is relevant—that the orbit of a planet should be derivable from the three dimensions of Euclidean space without reference to the categories of mass or velocity. We have *never* contended that the pattern variables as such exhausted the "primitive" concepts of the theory of action. Only on such an assumption is the capacity to derive the kinds of concepts we have been discussing from the pattern variables *alone* a test of the validity or usefulness of these concepts.

A few words may be said about the "fitness" of our categories to personality and cultural theory. It was a primary insight of the work now being reviewed that the pattern variables were *not* confined in their relevance to the level of social systems, but were categories of the *general* theory of action. Has this been borne out in the fields of personality and cultural theory? Since I am a sociologist and neither a psychologist nor an anthropologist, I have not devoted as much attention to these fields as I have to the analysis of social systems as such. However, particularly on the basis of as yet unpublished work, both of others and my own, I do not hesitate to say that it has now been amply borne out.

The first attempts in Shils' and my chapter on Personality and in Tolman's monograph to give psychological meanings to the pattern variables were necessarily crude. A great advance became possible when we understood the relations of the pattern variables to the system-problems as these have been outlined above. On this basis it has, for example, proved possible to show that the main organization of the personality at the completion of the oedipal transition can be characterized as a system of four basic need-disposition units which correspond to the four basic attitude types as derived from the combinations of the attitudinal pattern variables. It is further possible to show that more refined discriminations in orientation to the social object-world, e.g., in peer group and school, are analyzable in terms of the object-categorization types.

It has, furthermore, proved possible to show that this classification of the basic orientations of need-disposition types corresponds directly with Freud's famous structural analysis of the personality into Id, Ego and Superego, if one assumption be allowed, namely that the Ego has two importantly differentiated aspects which we call Adaptive and Integrative, respectively. This distinction is, I think, itself actually made by Freud, e.g., in discriminating "reality-testing" from the "ego-ideal."

There is no space to carry this analysis further here. I must rest content with stating that if these contentions can be validated, and they will soon be available for general examination, they will fully bear out the contention that the pattern variables are indeed relevant to personality theory.

The case of "culture theory" is from the present point of view much more difficult than that of either sociological or psychological theory. This, apparently, is a function of the fact that the culturally oriented anthropologists have devoted substantially less attention to categorization and classification than have either sociologists or psychologists. There can in the first place be no doubt that our theoretical scheme is in accord with the broad "cultural point of view," if one point of interpretation is granted. This is that such a point of view does not basically challenge the independent significance of the social system as a mode or level of the organization of action. There is a tendency in some anthropological circles to do this, but it is far from universal. If, on the other hand, the primary emphasis is on the "social heritage" which is learned by the individual, there is as such no difficulty. Furthermore, the pattern variables can be shown to formulate modes of organization of symbolic meanings in patterns and in this connection I am sure that they can make important independent contributions to the theory of culture. The latter, however, has not put forward classifications which are directly comparable with that of the pattern variables.

In this all-too-brief review of Dr. Smith's third question I have necessarily overlapped somewhat with his fourth, "Do the pattern variables contribute to a satisfactory general theory of social behavior?" As noted above I interpret this question mainly in terms of empirical adequacy. I should like to divide my answer into two parts. The first concerns the codification of already available empirical generalizations, the second its use as an instrument for the finding and validation of new empirical generalization.

With regard to the first aspect, I regard recent developments in this conceptual scheme as extensions of the work of codification which I undertook in the *Structure of Social Action*. There the principal empirical generalizations present in the work of Marshall, Pareto, Durkheim and Max Weber were carefully reviewed and where they were not, as for example in certain respects was true of Marshall's view of social evolution, shown to be untenable, they were shown to be subsumable under a common conceptual scheme. This was true for example of Weber's and Durkheim's very different generalizations about the "institutional" factors in an "individualistic" system of market relations, and of some of their generalizations about the relations between religion and social structure, derived directly in the one case from the study of Australian totemism, in the other from the comparative study of the more "advanced" religious systems.

More generally, I see no serious difficulties in codifying the available body of empirical generalization in the field of comparative analysis of the larger-scale social systems in these terms; various attempts in this direction have already been made in my own work.

Another very important work of codification has been made possible by demonstrating the precise relationships between the pattern variables and Bales' categories of the interaction process. This makes it possible to bring into the same general scheme analysis of social systems both on the large-scale and on the small group level. We are so optimistic about the possibilities of this that we are working directly now on a study of stratification in small groups which is conceptualized in exactly the same terms as have been used in analyzing the stratification of the large-scale society; namely pattern-variable terms.

Closely related to this is the field of the relations between social structure and personality. In a forthcoming publication it has proved possible to analyze the process of socialization as a process of social interaction precisely in these terms and through that analysis to carry the use of the pattern variables in the formulation of the structure of personality as a system very much farther than was done before. This is also true of the classification of the mechanisms of personality process which have there been arranged in terms of their relations to the pattern variables. In the process it has been possible to relate this analysis quite explicitly and in detail to several current bodies of empirical generalization, notably Freud's scheme of the stages of psycho-sexual development, and Piaget's conceptions of the development from "moral realism" to "cooperation" and also of the development of logical thinking in the child.

Closely related to this is the contact of this scheme with "reference group" theory. Thus the distinction made by Merton and Kitt between what they call the individual's "attitudes" and his "self-image and self-appraisal" can be shown to involve exactly the same distinction which has been made between the "attitudinal" aspect of the pattern variable system and the "object-categorization" aspect. I think it is not too much to say that the reference group scheme and that of the pattern variables are coming rapidly to be capable of direct mutual translation.

These examples will have to suffice to indicate that on the level of codification the general scheme of the theory of action, including its pattern variable level, is proving to be a powerful instrument of the unification and generalization of the empirical knowledge we already possess. It is not too much to say that this process of codification has only begun and the prospect is that as more work is done the generality of the scheme in empirical fields will be more and more extensively demonstrated.

Finally, it is possible to say only a word about the scheme as a direct instrument of new empirical research. Here I shall cite only three examples from my own experience. In the first place the first beginnings of the pattern variable scheme were worked out in connection with a study of the institutional pattern of modern medical practice and its relation to the mechanisms of social control. For this study, which I think it fair to say achieved results well beyond common sense, the theoretical scheme was an indispensable guide from the stage of formulating the problems on.

Second, in a study of social mobility currently going on in collaboration with Samuel A. Stouffer and Florence Kluckhohn, a long-range systematic attempt is being made to use and develop this type of theory in predicting from the characteristics of families, peer groups and schools, and the place of a boy in them, what place in the occupational system he will come to occupy. In this connection the adult occupational system is being treated as a system of reference groups toward which a boy may be thought of as coming to be selectively oriented. The socialization process in all three of the "socializing agencies" mentioned above is being analyzed as a process of social interaction. The basic point of reference for the family aspect of the analysis, for instance, is the attempt to define the conditions in the family as a system under which a boy will tend to "identify" with his father in the sense of tending to realize the father's values (not necessarily actual status) in his own occupational future. From these reference points then we are attempting to formulate hypotheses as to the effects of certain selected variations from these conditions.

The third case is the study of stratification in small groups mentioned above. Here we are attempting to study the differences in the stratification of the group and its perception by the members which will be made by conditions which put a premium on instrumental performance functions in the group on the one hand, of integrative functions on the other.

We have taken as our major point of reference the theoretical formulation made for the large-scale society, that the rank order of valuation of performance types (functions in the system) and that of the distribution among units of facilities and rewards will tend to coincide. This coincidence, we hypothesize, is common to all stable social systems, large or small. What will be the *content* of the valued performances, facilities and rewards will, however, vary as a function both of the value-system of the group and of situational and personality factors. Our attempt is to take the value system as the independent variable and study the changes in these categories which result from changes in it. The central hypothesis then is that in so far as instrumental values are successfully inculcated in a group the instrumental leadership functions will have highest prestige and the greatest facilities will be placed at the disposal of instrumental leaders, and similarly with integrative leadership when the values are integrative. Of course we also expect various other features of the stratification system to vary, such as the degree of fluidity or rigidity, and the type of symbolization of prestige. There is no space to develop this farther here. These three examples have been introduced only to make clear that the use of this type of theory in going empirical research is much more than merely programmatic. A good many other examples could also be cited.

In conclusion I would like to leave the reader, I think, with three major impressions about the general theory of action as a conceptual scheme. The first is that it is not something which has been invented "out of the blue" and thrust into our social science scene, but is very much a development out of the lines of theoretical thinking which have deep roots in both European and American tradition. Appreciation of just how the lines of influence operate cannot, however, be arrived at by superficial comparison of concepts and their definitions, but requires careful critical analysis. When this is carried out I am entirely confident that the continuity with our past will be amply evident.

The second major point is that it is not a static scheme which has been put before the profession to "take or leave" but is a rapidly and dynamically developing body of ideas on a variety of different levels. This of course means that it is unevenly developed in different parts. At the time the two books with which this discussion has been primarily concerned were written, their authors took special pains to emphasize that they expected further developments to take place. The event has amply borne out this expectation. This rapid development is of course a source of difficulty and sometimes confusion because it makes it so difficult to maintain consistency of terminology. But that it is definite *development,* not aimless wandering, I am fully satisfied.

Finally, the claim that this conceptual scheme is part of empirical science and not just "speculative" is meant with the utmost seriousness. Any reader who takes the trouble to analyze carefully the scope of codification which already has been carried out in its terms should, I think, find little difficulty in convincing himself of this. But further, I have emphasized that it is being used most seriously in new empirical research on a number of fronts. In this respect as in that of theoretical formulation as such, it is to be thought of as a developing conceptual scheme.

In the relationship between sociological theory-building and the research operation, three interdependent concepts play a central role: model, methodology, and measurement. One cannot be understood without the others because each influences the others.

A model in sociology is an abstract statement about the properties or characteristics of data. It is a set of assumptions or postulates not being tested directly. The construction of models, or "ideal types" as they are frequently called, depends on methodology, the strategy of research. The reason for this dependence is that the model undergoes systematic changes during research, first as a result of the methods employed in the data collection, and then as a consequence of the methods utilized in the analysis of the data. Measurement, which is the process of assessing the properties of data, is, in turn, dependent on the model. This is because the fitting or measuring of models in relation to the data can be no better than the quality of the process of abstraction—that is, the model construct—in the first place.

In the next article, James M. Beshers considers these interrelationships in detail. He also explores two contrasting approaches to theory construction that assign quite different roles to models. The simplicity criterion approach relies heavily on convenience in selecting models, whereas the interdependence postulate approach relies on plausibility.

55. MODELS AND THEORY CONSTRUCTION *

JAMES M. BESHERS
Johns Hopkins University

The concepts of model, methodology, and measurement have assumed importance in the behavioral sciences concurrently with the refinement of research technique, the adaptation of statistics, and the increase of rigor and precision in the statement of theoretical schemes. These three concepts may be used to examine the emerging research process. They may clarify the relationships among the elements and activities of current research. In particular, they may shed light upon the interdependence among theoretical assumptions, methods of data collection, methods of data analysis, and types of data, thereby facilitating the construction of research design.

C. H. Coombs and others have attacked these problems using mathematical models and non-metric measurement theory to deal with psychological data. In one discussion they have brought out some of the general relationships between model building and research. Recently, Coombs has analyzed the relationships among types of data, theoretical assumptions, methods of data collection, and methods of data analysis.

The point of view in this paper is similar to that of Coombs, but directed more to the attention of the general sociologist. Therefore less emphasis is placed on mathematical models *per se* and on psychological data. It is hoped that gains in readability will offset the loss of specificity that this approach implies.

RELATIONSHIP OF THEORY AND RESEARCH

The emerging relationship of theory and research in sociology has been discussed by Robert K. Merton and Hans L. Zetterberg. Merton regards research as a process with broader implications for theory than mere hypothesis testing. Any research project, considered in its entirety, may clarify theory, reformulate theory, initiate new theory, or deflect theory entirely, as well as verify theory. These consequences may follow from all parts of the research process—the design phase, the exploratory, pretesting phase, the data collection phase, and the analysis. The exploratory, flexible nature of the research process is stressed throughout Merton's discussion. Zetterberg, in contrast, approaches theory construction by conceiving of research as a verificational process. Theory is evaluated largely in terms of its utility for verification. Therefore Zetterberg stresses such properties of theory as formal deductive

* *American Sociological Review,* Vol. 22, No. 1, February, 1957, pp. 32–38.

relationships between postulates and theorems, parsimonious and unambiguous statement of theorems, and the ease with which hypotheses may be empirically tested. These considerations lead Zetterberg to recommend the use of axiomatic theory in sociological theory construction.

The positions of Merton and Zetterberg are complementary. The former emphasizes the implications of a realistic appraisal of the research process for theory, but does not elaborate on the specific nature of theory. The latter develops highly specific principles of theory construction, but maintains a fairly narrow conception of the research process. An eventual synthesis would include the thought of both men, but would modify each position in light of its neglected aspects.

MODELS

Mathematical models are constructed by abstracting the properties of some data by measurement, and by expressing these properties in a set of symbolic statements that include the logical relationships that hold for the entire set of statements. Any mathematical statement may be regarded as a model by identifying the symbols of the mathematical statement with some data. However, it is convenient to restrict the designation "mathematical model" to the body of statements that constitute the axioms of a mathematical system, however small. Thus, in applying a mathematical system to a set of data, one usually notes the congruence of the assumptions, or axioms, of the mathematical system with the data.

In sociology the concept corresponding to model is the construct, or ideal-type, e.g., the Protestant ethic. The construct is an abstract statement of properties of data, but it is not expressed in symbolic form, nor is the process of abstraction as explicit as measurement. Constructs can usually be found independent of developed theories, but those constructs contained within a general theoretical system are analogous to mathematical models (as discussed above). Perhaps the set of assumptions, or axioms, of a sociological theory could be referred to as a model in the same sense as a mathematical model, e.g., system model—system theory.

A model in this sense might be confused with several other kinds of statements used in sociology, especially the concept of hypothesis. Within a particular theoretical framework the hypotheses are subject to tests; statements in the model are not directly subject to test. The same statements, which may be part of the model in one theory, may under some circumstances be hypotheses in another theory. This view is similar to Zetterberg's statement that the distinction between postulates and theorems is arbitrary, so long as logical requirements are fulfilled. For him, however, all statements are equally testable.

Two exceptions to Zetterberg's statement may be made. First, one may argue that certain statements are inherently untestable, but that important testable hypotheses may be derived from these statements. The untestable statements in the theoretical model could have heuristic value. Freud assumes the existence of an unconscious mind, or part of the mind. His statement, although untestable, seems reasonable in light of data from dreams and psychoanalytic therapy. Many hypotheses have been derived from the Freudian assumptions and tested.

Second, one may argue that certain statements that may be testable in some circumstances, depending upon the theoretical formulation and the development of research methods, may be more appropriately treated as assumptions rather than hypotheses in most circumstances. In particular, statements analogous to the measurement assumptions in mathematical models are of this kind. Such statements specify those properties of the data which determine the nature of statements of relationship of units and variables in the data. For example, one can test for linearity of data relationships, for the existence of continua in the data, or for normality of the data. Frequently such properties are assumed in order to facilitate model construction.

Models to this point have been discussed in relation to axiomatic theories and verificational research like Zetterberg's analysis of theory. This view should be modified by considering the realities of the research process as conceived of by Merton. As expressed by Katona,

> There exists an alternative to developing an axiomatic system into a full-fledged theoretical model in advance of testing the theory through observations. Controlled observations should be based on hypotheses, and the formulation of an integrated theory need not be delayed until all observations are completed. Yet theory construction is part of the process of hypothesis-observation-revised hypothesis and prediction-observation, and systematization should rely on some empirical research.[1]

In any research project a model is the set of assumptions, or postulates, not being directly tested. Some efforts may be made to test the model during the research project, but the main objective of the research is to test hypotheses that have been developed from the model. For example, the assumption of the normal curve is frequently part of a statistical model, and this assumption is frequently tested in a preliminary phase of a statistical investigation. The model of one research project may become hypotheses in another project.

Within a specific research project, a model initially may be a loose verbal statement but in the end may be refined into a precise mathematical statement. Similarly, as a new area for research is opened up, models are generated by a series of exploratory research projects that (1) identify important factors, (2) assess the relative importance of these factors, and (3) state the relationships among these factors. These models would be made up of the assumptions of the research project, loosely phrased as they might be.

This discussion has identified models as the assumptions of an axiomatic

[1] George Katona, "Rational Behavior and Economic Behavior," *Psychological Review*, 60 (September, 1953), p. 317.

theory and as the assumptions of a research project. This identification may seem optimistic in that few research projects have been built around theoretical schemata meeting the criteria Zetterberg imposes. But there are analogues in many projects: basic concepts are introduced, general assumptions are made, and hypotheses are derived (not necessarily deduced) from these considerations.

If a project has a systematic discussion of concepts, assumptions, and hypotheses, then the set of assumptions may be regarded as a model, although perhaps a rudimentary one. Similarly, models may be identified with theoretical formulations lacking the formal properties of axiomatic theory.

In general, models are constructed with two criteria in mind. First, they should be convenient: they should facilitate the processes of research design, hypothesis formation, and data analysis. Second, they should be plausible: they should be congruent with the data they are supposed to represent. For example, many economists assume as part of their model that the motivation of the entrepreneur is to maximize profits. This is a very convenient assumption, is consistent with other assumptions commonly found in the same model, and it may be used to generate mathematical models that possess some predictive value. Yet this assumption is challenged by other economists for lack of plausibility. Observation of the motivation of specific entrepreneurs suggests that aspects of this problem have been neglected.

METHODOLOGY

Model construction is in part dependent upon methodology. In each research project a strategy of research is developed. Theory, data, data collection, and data analysis must be congruent; the research design should bring them together in an appropriate fashion. As a sequence of research projects is carried out on related problems, the accumulated experience of each research design becomes systematized. This systematized body of knowledge is methodology. Thus methodology includes balancing theoretical considerations with research considerations, as well as attaining a consistency of research tools.

The relationship of methodology to model construction is evident in the research process. In a particular project, certain assumptions must be made at the outset. Certain relationships are to be investigated, either at an exploratory or a verificational level; these relationships must be stated explicitly. Initially, these relationships are phrased in a manner that is significant for theory and has some meaning in terms of the data. As data collection proceeds, the problems of data analysis such as coding become more apparent, and the statement of the model becomes more specific. Finally, the method of analysis chosen should be pertinent to the model and should imply a more specific statement of the model. Thus the model undergoes systematic changes, first as a consequence of the methods of data collection, and later as a consequence of the methods of analysis.

MEASUREMENT

Measurement is the process of assessing the properties of data. Frequently measurement is regarded as part of verification procedures—the experimenter measures the data to test hypotheses—but measurement may also refer to the classification procedures of exploratory research, as well as to the abstraction of general properties of the data in model building.

The functions of measurement in model building have been generally neglected, but the plausibility of models is in large part dependent upon the adequacy of measurement in this sense. Models are an abstraction of the properties of the data, and the "fit" of models to the data is dependent upon the quality of the process of abstraction.

MEASUREMENT AND MODELS

The relationship of measurement and models frequently comes up as a problem of choice between two general types of mathematical model—the causal model and the statistical model. Hans Reichenbach discusses the problem in the social sciences. A causal model states the lawful relationship between events. A statistical model states the relative frequency of occurrence of certain events based on the modern theory of probability. A statistical model will be preferred if the data are complex or of a special nature, if the laws are complex or unknown, or if the experimental procedure requires randomization. The first condition may be assessed by measurement procedures as defined in this paper; the second condition seems to depend upon the first, for the complexity of a law depends upon properties of the data; and the third condition depends upon the particular methodology chosen.

In addition, however, a choice between these two types of models depends upon the type of theoretical question under investigation. Both models predict, but the kinds of prediction are quite different. The causal model permits the classical statement of science, the law, and therefore seems more useful for theoretical purposes. But the statistical model not only describes the distribution of a phenomenon, but also permits the application of statistical decision theory. In many cases a solution from a statistical model, although not providing precisely the same information as a causal one, may provide sufficient information for the question at hand. Of course, the measurement problems of sociology restrict model construction of the type familiar in natural science, but models will be chosen in sociology in the same general manner as they are in the natural sciences.

TYPOLOGIES

The measurement problems of sociology frequently give rise to a type of model called a typology. A typology is a statement of gross differences between social units or social phenomena that are similar in certain other respects. Thus "Gemeinschaft" and "Gesellschaft" characterize gross differences between similar social units—societies, communities, families, or even behavior. The gross differences may be assumed to vary along a continuum, or they may be assumed to be discrete. Frequently the gross differences can be identified as many factors that run along dimensions, with the polar types indicated in the typology. However, not all typologies are explicit on this point, and some assume dichotomies rather than continuous dimensions. The typologies that consist of specific dimensions are a special case of Paul F. Lazarsfeld's general theory of property-space. The problems of constructing typologies are best described by Lazarsfeld.

Typologies have been most useful in social research when used in conjunction with comparative analysis. For example, several societies that are similar in some respects may exhibit gross differences in their economic systems; a typology may be constructed to reflect these differences. A second typology may then be constructed from the gross differences between the value systems in the several societies. The two typologies may then be used to study the relationships between the economic systems and the values in these societies. This is, in brief, the methodology of Weber's *Protestant Ethic.*

SIMPLICITY AND INTERDEPENDENCE

Two contrasting approaches to theory construction can be identified currently in the behavioral sciences. These two may be characterized as the "simplicity" criterion approach and the interdependence postulate approach. In psychology, for example, learning theorists lean toward the simplicity approach, while Gestalt theorists contend that the interdependence postulate is the primary element in theory construction. These two approaches take radically different views of the role of models in theory construction and research.

The simplicity approach is widespread among research minded scholars and is in part an expression of the view that theory is a system of testable propositions stated parsimoniously. There are four characteristics to the simplicity approach: first, the primitive concepts are chosen from simple words in ordinary language, e.g., drive, cue, response; second, the primitive and derived concepts stand for elementary phenomena in behavior, e.g., a response; third, the primitive and derived concepts are readily associated with operations and measurements, that is, easy to define operationally, e.g., an amount of reward is an amount of food; and fourth, the simplest relationships are assumed to exist, e.g., learning is seen as a negative, or positive growth function—a logarithmic function.

The interdependence postulate approach places the processes of model building and measurement in the central position in theory construction. Interdependence adherents argue that the true relationships may be determined by measurement, and that these relationships constitute parts of models that must be included in all theories dealing with these data. Thus the Gestalt perception experiments were designed to demonstrate that all perceptual phenomena must be explained in Gestalt terms.

The contrast between the two positions is a consequence of different criteria. The simplicity criterion approach leans heavily towards convenience in its selection of models, while the interdependence approach leans towards plausibility in its selection of models.

The spokesmen for the interdependence approach have failed to spell out the meaning of interdependence. Criteria have not been developed for determining the existence of interdependence in a particular set of data and the measurement procedures needed for reaching a decision on interdependence have not been systematically discussed. This lack may be overcome by (1) an extension of Ludwig von Bertalanffy's conception of logical homologies of system theory to behavioral science data, and (2) the adoption of a statistical criterion for the existence of interdependence in a set of data, probably a criterion derived from the statistical concept of interaction in analysis of variance.

Not only are the models quite different in these two approaches to theory construction, but the methodologies implied by them tend to vary. The methodology commonly used with the simplicity approach consists of measurements on a set of discrete elements, e.g., unit acts, traits. These measurements are then "summed up" in the analysis, and conclusions from research are reported in this manner. The methodology appropriate for the interdependence approach consists of measurement in reference to inferred properties of organization, or complex interrelationships. These measurements are then analyzed in relation to the organizational properties, i.e., holistically.

The contrast between the simplicity criterion approach and the interdependence postulate approach is represented in sociology by the small-group theorists and the system, or structure-function, theorists. Whereas psychologists disagree on the applicability of a model based on rat behavior to the study of human behavior, sociologists disagree on the applicability of theory and research in a laboratory setting to the problems of the field setting.

This contrast may seem surprising, since small-group theory and research received its impetus from Kurt Lewin's field theory, a Gestalt derivative. Nevertheless, small-group theory construction is governed by criteria that implement experimentation. Simple concepts are cast in simple statements of relationship.

In contrast, the system theory approach is holistic, emphasizing the interdependent relations of parts within the total system. First, sociological system analysis must identify system boundaries. The criterion used to identify boundaries will be based on the data, either a social interaction criterion or otherwise. Second, the structure-functional analysis of interdependence will also be determined by the interdependence properties of the data, e.g., Malinowski's treatment of institutions was holistic because the activities of the Trobrianders were so intertwined. Both the analysis of functional prerequisites and of equilibrium are based upon considerations of the total system.

What is the implication of this discussion for theory construction and methodology? First of all, both approaches are valid. The simplicity criterion approach contains elements necessary for all research. Further, it is the most efficient approach in circumstances that do not justify the use of elaborate models.

The interdependence postulate approach is most efficient when the data demand holistic analysis. Further, the models used by this approach have more plausibility in general than those employed by the simplicity approach. Finally, holistic methodology provides answers to questions that cannot be posed by the simplicity approach, e.g., equilibrium analysis.

There are, however, several intermediate positions. One is to use the simplicity criterion supplemented by an interdependence model. Thus a laboratory experiment, utilizing the results of field research on interdependence to construct a research model, may reach conclusions of some significance for field researchers. Such a relationship is discussed by Leon Festinger and Daniel Katz. However, these authors conceive of field research as exploratory; the culmination of the ideal research project is in the laboratory. This view neglects the possibility that certain social phenomena may not be replicable in the laboratory, and that some field research may be entirely contained within a holistic methodology, as is the case with functional anthropology and most studies of the community.

Another approach is to recognize the applicability of holistic methods but to use the simplicity criterion on a heuristic basis. That is, assume that relationships amenable to the simplicity approach are so strong that the main characteristics of a set of data may be explained without reference to interdependence. Thus the simplicity criterion would be used to gain a first approximation, leaving to subsequent research the problem of gaining a fuller understanding with an interdependence model.

These intermediate methodological approaches are important. A set of data may be characterized as having high interdependence, some interdependence, or negligible interdependence. Now consider a research project covering several sets of data; in all likelihood these sets of data can be classified at least two ways in interdependence. Therefore the methodology of the research project will have to be sufficiently flexible to handle these sets of data together.

Intermediate methodological approaches may also be instrumental in the process of translating research results from the two approaches into a common theoretical statement. Probably any general theory would include an interdependence postulate, with lack of interdependence a special case. But the use of the interdependence model in simplicity criterion research should facilitate such translation of research findings.

In contemporary sociology there still is no unified and comprehensive theoretical system that could serve as a vehicle for the co-ordination and integration of existing sociological knowledge. Instead, we find a variety of theories and theoretical approaches concerning the nature of society and its impact on man's thoughts, feelings, and actions.

For the purpose of bringing at least some external order into this situation, Helmut R. Wagner, the author of the following article, suggests a classificatory system that distinguishes three major categories of sociological theory on the basis of general methodological criteria. These are positive or natural-science theories, interpretative theories treating sociology as a science "sui generis," and nonscientific or evaluative social theories.

56. TYPES OF SOCIOLOGICAL THEORY: TOWARD A SYSTEM OF CLASSIFICATION *

HELMUT R. WAGNER
Hobart and William Smith Colleges

A sociologist studying the "state of general theory" in his discipline is likely to find a perplexing multivariety of basic orientations. At least, I could not convince myself that the writings of modern theorists constitute one coherent body of systematic theory. At present, no unified theory exists which could serve effectively as an instrument for the coordination and integration of all or even most of the existing sociological knowledge.

Sociology may be considered a science suspended between research and application, or a Liberal-Arts discipline aiming at "knowledge for the sake of knowing," or a "movement" centering in the development of a new intellectual stance toward the social universe. Yet, whatever position we prefer, it is not a foregone conclusion that the discipline tends toward the establishment of a "unified body of (empirical and theoretical) knowledge." Sociologists may desire that their discipline *should* become such a unified body in which all special fields are logically integrated, systematically interlinked, and united under the comprehensive umbrella of a general theory. Up to now, however, the actual developments in American sociology have conspicuously deviated from such expectations.

THE PROBLEM OF CLASSIFICATION

Whether sociology moves toward theoretical unification is not decided by assertion; neither does it depend on statements of methodological "necessity."

* *American Sociological Review,* Vol. 28, No. 5, October, 1963, pp. 735–742.

It is a matter of factual investigation. The preparation of such an investigation entails taking stock of the theories in existence. The successful execution of this task, in turn, hinges on the use of a suitable classificatory system. It is my purpose to suggest such a scheme.

Prior attempts to classify sociological theories reflect the bewildering multiplicity of the discipline. There is neither agreement as to the number of classes nor accord as to their labels. Indeed there is no consensus with regard to the criteria on which the classification of theories should rest.

It cannot be claimed that any classificatory system, as such, is more "logical" and more "systematic" than another. The decisive question is whether it is heuristically more useful. Three criteria may be used for ascertaining this usefulness: (1) is the scheme internally consistent; (2) does it make distinctions where there are significant differences; and (3) does it cover the whole range of existing theories.

The first point presupposes the use of one type of criteria: substantive or methodological—and preferably of a single criterion. The second point involves interpretation. A decision as to what constitute "significant differences" may depend on the general conception of sociology the classifier holds and prefers. The third point, by contrast, can be settled by agreement on the following principle: As long as the American Sociological Association, by majority decision, has not set down the criteria for orthodox sociological theory, and has not agreed on formal procedures against heterodox theorists, any theory advanced by any of its members in his professional capacity is to be considered sociological theory. If operationism has any place in sociology, it is here: as long as we run our discipline as we do now, sociology is and remains "what sociologists do." Sociological theory is what sociological theorists construct and consider as such.

Having found that none of the existing schemes satisfy all three of these criteria equally well, I developed another classificatory system, based on a broad methodological rationale: sociological theories shall be distinguished according to their authors' conceptions of the general character and the basic purposes of sociology as a realm of intellectual inquiry.

On the basis of this rationale, I propose a division of sociological theories into the following main categories:

1. *Positive Sociological Theories, whose authors consider, or actually treat, sociology as a natural science.*
2. *Interpretative Sociologies, whose authors consider, or actually treat, sociology as a social science in contradistinction to the natural sciences.*
3. *Non-scientific or Evaluative Social Theories, whose authors neither consider nor actually treat sociology as a positive or interpretative science.*

What follows is a condensed representation of the classificatory system developed with the help of the three main categories formulated above. (See also Table 1.)

TABLE 1. Modern American Sociological Theories

A Classificatory Scheme *

A. Positive Sociological Theories	
1. *Neo-Positivism*	
Physicalistic Neo-Positivism	Positive Historical Sociology
Mathematical Model Theory	Cultural-Lag Theory
	Theory of Manipulated Change
2. *Human Ecology*	
Chicago Tradition	
Systematic Ecological Theory	Geo-Biological Theory of Change
3. *Structure-Functionalism*	
Theory and Methodology	
Biologistic Functionalism	Organicistic-Cyclical Theory
Cultural Functionalism	
Sociological Functionalism	Functional Theory of Change
Micro-Functionalism	
Holistic Culture Theory	
Rural-Community System	
Organization Theory	
Urban Functionalism	
Regional Functionalism	
Societal Functionalism	
Social-System Theory	
Universal Structure-Functionalism	
4. *Social Behaviorism* (Positive Action Theory)	
Physicalistic Behaviorism	
Bio-Psychological Behaviorism	
Normativistic Behaviorism	
5. *Bio-Psychological Theory of Culture*	
Instinct and Social Forces	
Freudian Anthropology	Anthropological Neo-Evolutionism
Freudian Social-Psychology	
Neo-Freudian Cult-Pers. Th.	
Neo-Freudian Culture Theory	
Neo-Freudian Sociology	Sociological Neo-Evolutionism
Generalized Freudian Theory	
B. Interpretative Sociology	
6. *Theory of Cultural Understanding*	
Theory of Culture-Ethos	Historistic Tradition
Cultural Linguistics	
National-Type Theory	
Culture Configuration	
Mass-Society Ethos	

* The left-hand column contains analytical theories in general; the right-hand column names the corresponding theories of social change.

TABLE 1—*Continued*

B. Interpretative Sociology (*cont.*)	
7. *Interpretative Sociology of Action and Interaction*	
The Weberian Tradition	Historical Typology
Interaction Theory	Culture-Change Theory
	Universal Theory of History
8. *Interpretative Social Psychology*	
Meadian Tradition	
Social Psychology of Manipulation	
Symbolic-Interaction Theory	
9. *Social Phenomenology*	
Phenomenological Sociology	
Phenomenological Social Psychology	
Theory of Religious Experience	
C. Non-Scientific or Evaluative Social Theories	
10. *Social-Philosophical Theory*	
Sociology of Knowledge	
Philosophy of Society	Philosophy of History
11. *Ideological Social Theory*	
Lynd's Manifesto	
Conflict Theory	Neo-Marxian Trend
12. *Humanitarian Reform Theory*	
Anthropological Approach	
Sociological Approach	Social-Reform Theory of Change

POSITIVE SOCIOLOGICAL THEORIES

Positive sociological theories are based on the assumption that sociology is, or should operate as if it were, a natural science. Their authors propagate or practice "objective" procedures, regardless of whether they utilize mechanical, field-theoretical, or biological models, foster behaviorist reductionism, or consider sociology a positive social-behaviorist science. We may distinguish five subcategories of this kind.

Neo-positivism, as established and popularized in the thirties, purports to operate on the basis of a physical model. It largely identifies scientific procedure with quantification and measuring, and conceives of sociology as an applied science of social engineering. Many proponents of applied quantitative research operate without resorting to large-scale theory; the goal of the theoretical mathematization of sociological knowledge, however, is pursued independently. Advanced forms of neo-positivist theory are based on systems of interlinked causal (instead of functional) propositions which are expected to lend themselves to an eventual mathematical restatement of the theory.

Modern human ecology is a second form of general positive theory. It is based on what may be called the social-biological approach of plant and animal ecologists. Broadened and systematized by Amos Hawley in 1950, it has been converted, from a specialty within the fields of urban or regional sociology, into a systematic theory transgressing its traditional boundaries. Conspicuously, it aims now at a general treatment of social organization, the term taken in the broad sense of a theory of social structures.

Structure-functionalism constitutes the third variation of positive theories. It consists of a number of subtypes of anthropological and sociological prominence. Essentially, these theories are built to conform to a morphological-physiological model of the organism. While differing considerably from each other, they fall into a pattern of growing scope and complexity in about the following order: micro-functionalism of small-group theory; holistic theory of the cultural community; theory of rural social systems; organization theory; urban functionalism; etc. On a larger scale, the functional approach has been applied to the construction of theories of society as a whole. Most comprehensive among them are those dealing with "the social system"; and especially those universal theories that consider the social system, again, as but one system among a larger set of analytical-general system-structures.

Social behaviorism, a fourth type of positive theory, comprises non-subjective, non-voluntaristic theories of action and interaction, or of social behavior in general. They may be erected according to mechanistic or field-theoretical conceptions, operate in terms of a modernized stimulus-response psychology, or postulate the behavioral determinism of cultural norms. It seems to be characteristic of these theories that they usually occur in combination with other variations of sociological positivism.

Bio-psychological theory of culture is introduced as a final type of positive theory. It is rooted in the psycho-dynamic concepts of modern instinct-psychology. In sociology proper, theories of this type play a minor although not negligible role; in anthropology, they seem to be more frequent. Mostly, they represent applications or adaptations of Freudian psychoanalysis to culture-personality theory and related topics; but occasional versions aim at the construction of a theory of culture as a whole.

INTERPRETATIVE SOCIOLOGY

The second main category of our classification system is that of interpretative sociology. It comprises theories whose authors, while insisting on adherence to the general methodological rules of science, do not consider sociology a natural science. Adhering to Max Weber's conception of a "value-free" sociology, they claim that sociology is a realm of social inquiry that is methodologically *sui generis*. They justify this position in terms of the particularities, and uniqueness, of the human subject matter of the discipline. Their theories, consequently, pay attention to the "subjective" and "voluntaristic" aspects of social behavior. Their methodology is based on the combination of the "outside view" of the sociological or anthropological observer with the "inside view" of the participants in the observed events and processes. Four main variations of interpretative sociology may be distinguished, two of them closely interrelated.

The first type of interpretative sociology may be called *theory of cultural understanding*. Theories of this kind deal with the "ethos" or "feeling tone" of cultural communities. They issue from attempts to capture and represent the "spirit" of social collectivities, and translate it into the language of the sociological discipline as well as that of our culture. Anthropologists have made this approach familiar to American sociologists, but some sociologists utilize it in their dealings with the "ethos" of modern societies, or larger segments thereof.

A second type of interpretative sociological theory will be labeled *interpretative theory of action and interaction*. It can be traced to Max Weber's theory of action and subjective understanding. It starts micro-sociologically with simple action-constellations of persons who intentionally address themselves to others and enter into a subjectively meaningful exchange with them. The sociologist, on his part, arrives at a correct interpretation of the course of such an interaction when he ascertains its meaning for the participants. Thereby, he "understands" it in its subjective aspects. To gain a workable sociological basis, however, the interpretative sociologist proceeds from individual case studies to the construction of a theory of subjective action and interaction which is based on *typical* expectations. As a rule, a proponent of this approach places his micro-sociological action theory into the framework of larger theoretical and possibly historical structures. This macro-sociological framework may be, but is not always, consistent with the starting point of subjective action theory.

A third variation of interpretative sociology is *symbolic-interaction theory*. Theories of this subcategory remain on the micro-sociological level; they constitute one type of modern social psychology. Heavily relying on the philosophical behaviorism of George H. Mead, they are concerned with processes of symbolic (verbal) interaction on the inter-subjective level: main topics are the genesis and operation of social cognition in interactive processes.

Some of the "symbolic interactionists" also pay attention to the cognitive processes through which the individual perceives and constructs the social world around him. This reversal of symbolic-interactionist procedure constitutes a fourth variety of interpretative sociology. It shall be called *social phenomenology*. This approach is concerned with the seemingly universal mental forms and processes of consciously experiencing, perceiving, and accepting those aspects of man's social universe which constitute not only his "knowledge" of inter-personal relations but also the "meaning" of his social experience. Central to social phenomenology is the experience of inter-subjectivity: men do not only interact with one another, they "understand" each other.

EVALUATIVE SOCIAL THEORIES

The third main category of general sociological theory covers non-scientific or evaluative social theories. They are propagated by writers who neither call sociology a science nor consider it subject to scientific rules of procedure. As a rule, they reject not only the principle of positive "objectivity," a basic maxim of the "natural-science" approach; they also oppose the principle of "value-neutrality," a fundamental tenet of the "social science" orientation of interpretative sociology. Instead, they proceed on the basis of their philosophical premises, their ideological convictions, and their value systems. Thus, systematic philosophical expositions, coherent ideological orientations, sets of social ideals, or systems of moral principles become the basis of such theories. In every case, the value premises are built directly into the theoretical system. Many sociologists object to this procedure, and some are inclined to banish evaluative theories from the discipline, but they have not been successful. In fact, we recognize the existence of three types of these anti-positivistic, non-scientific, and value-partial theories.

Social-philosophical theory constitutes the first kind of its category. In this group fall the grand-scale philosophies of society or of history, insofar as they are written with a sociological bent. Next come philosophical theories sailing under the flag of the sociology of knowledge. One of the most recent contributions to philosophical sociology operates with Hegelian conceptions, although it rejects the historicistic implications of Hegelianism.

A second type may be called *ideological social theory*. The authors of such theories are committed to a more or less elaborate social-critical ideology, sometimes a mellow version of a Marxist orientation. They may link their sociology to a call for concerted action toward a more or less drastic change of their society.

A third sub-category of evaluative social theory issues from moral and social-ethical convictions rather than philosophical-ideological orientations. This *humanitarian reform theory* is involved in social criticism; but it focuses on discrete "social problems" rather than the social order as a whole. Authors of this orientation call for melioration of selected social conditions and for piecemeal reforms. Recent literature of this type comes from both the anthropological and the sociological camps.

THEORIES OF SOCIAL CHANGE

There is no methodological reason for separating "theory of social change" from the bulk of sociological theories. In principle, any of the so-called theories of change can be subsumed under one of the categories embodied in my classificatory scheme. But modern American sociology is characterized by the almost complete separation of historical considerations from the main body of theory and investigation. For this purely external reason, I divided the scheme into two parallel sections. One is devoted to analytical theories in general, that is, theories in which the problems of social change do not play a conspicuous part. The second one comprises theories of social change, that is, theories mainly directed to problems of basic social change, broad cultural developments, or historical processes.

Positive theories of social change comprise the older "historical sociology," cultural-lag theory, organicistic-cyclical theory, and neo-evolutionary orientations. *Interpretative sociology of change* either operates in the historicistic tradition, or leans on historical-typological theories. *Evaluative theories of change* may spring from the traditions of the older philosophy of history, follow neo-Marxian trends, or inhere in certain theories of social reform.

CONCLUSION

This scheme for classifying general sociological theories embraces all contemporary large-scale theory. It brings some external order into a field which seems to be no less chaotic than many other areas of sociological investigation. A scheme like this serves its purpose when it helps to bring the house of sociological theory in order. At best, a basis may be gained for subsequent systematic comparison.

Doubtlessly, agreements exist in certain areas among some theories; these could be reinforced by a standardization of terminology. Partial overlap may exist even among theories which I would classify under different categories. Yet, even a highly selective systematic survey of modern theories, like that of Charles and Zona Loomis, demonstrates the precariousness of agreement among theories considered related to each other. If one directs attention to the whole scope of present-day sociological theories, he has difficulty escaping the impression that non-coherence, disagreement and contradictions prevail over integrative tendencies. I cannot convince myself of the existence of any definite trend toward an eventual unification of presently disjunctive theories, or toward the gradual elimination of all but one of today's non-compatible types. General theories, in modern American sociology, represent a multiverse, and are likely to continue to do so in the foreseeable future.

This, however, need not be interpreted as the failure of sociology as a scholarly endeavor. It is a characteristic phenomenon, and in an essential sense an indigenous product, of a pluralistic society with its array of intellectual climates of opinions and its non-coherent value-systems. Since it functions within this society, it faces an ever changing and continuously self-complicating subject matter which, for all practical purposes, appears to be boundless. On both counts it allows for and invites a variety of approaches, all of which may produce comprehensive theories that are satisfactory for their purposes—up to a point—but which fail to answer crucial questions posed in terms of different points of departure. More likely than not, Max Weber was right when he spoke of the "absurdity of the idea . . . that it could be the goal of the cultural sciences . . . to construct a closed system of concepts in which reality is subsumed under a final system." Possibly sociology will remain an area of social inquiry and reflection which, on the power of the multivariety of possible approaches to a seemingly inexhaustible subject matter, will continue to exist as a pluralistic discipline.

SOCIAL CHANGE

Sociologists and anthropologists have constantly been confronted with the need to develop theories of social and cultural change, for there is an insatiable curiosity about the dynamics of society and its patterns of behavior. So far, their greatest success has been in the identification and description of the sources and processes of change. Their greatest frustration has been in seeking out the pattern and direction of change.

It is clear, for example, that discovery and invention (the co-ordination of previously separate traits) are the basic processes of all social and cultural change, and that existing social structure and culture—not necessity—are the mothers of invention. It is also clear that the accumulation of social and cultural phenomena tends to accelerate the rate of change. At one time, anthropologists disagreed among themselves vehemently about the prevalence of parallelism (independent and duplicated discovery and invention) versus diffusion (unique discovery and invention and borrowing by other people from the discoverer and inventor). Now, however, the battle is over; it is firmly established that diffusion is more prevalent, for it is easier to borrow social and cultural traits than to discover and invent them.

But what are the patterns and directions of change? In the article that follows, Wilbert E. Moore asserts that the apologetic attitude of sociologists on the subject is unwarranted, for both empirical generalizations and theoretical derivations are available. A pure theory of change, independent of the patterns undergoing transformation, would be uninteresting. On the other hand, social change can be integrated with standard theory around the very structural topics already in use.

57. A RECONSIDERATION OF THEORIES OF SOCIAL CHANGE *

WILBERT E. MOORE

Princeton University

The mention of "theory of social change" will make most social scientists appear defensive, furtive, guilt-ridden, or frightened. Yet the source of this unease may be in part an unduly awe-stricken regard for the explicitly singular and implicitly capitalized word "Theory." The several social scientific disciplines, and notably economics and sociology, do provide some fairly high-level,

* *American Sociological Review,* Vol. 25, No. 6, December, 1960, pp. 810–818.

empirically-based, and interdependent propositions concerning social change.

The present paper presents some suggested conceptual organization of the problem, and some illustrations of interrelated propositions. The exposition is taxonomic and programmatic rather than discursive. Many of the alleged propositions are hypothetical, but any resemblance between them and real data, living or dead, would be comforting.

THE POSSIBILITY AND SCOPE OF THEORIES

The current anxious pessimism concerning the topic of social change can be readily traced to several related sources. One such source is clearly the downfall or slight acceptability of global, simplifying theories. Sweeping evolutionary or cyclical doctrines have provided a relatively poor fit to data. Even where generalization may have been "justified," the loss of information in the process of abstraction has resulted in relevance to only minute segments of observed changes, or, in other words, in low predictive power.

Against this background of critical examination and rejection of general theories, the major and rather successful positive effort of social scientists over recent decades has been directed to static, cross-sectional, or "structural-functional" analysis. Now structures and functions, paraphrased as "patterns" and "consequences," are not inherently static. However, the theorists who have been most explicit about their concepts, assumptions, and specific theoretical problems have provided little guidance to the orderly transformation of social systems. Wherever an implicit "equilibrium" model is used, changes in patterns of action and their relationships tend to be viewed as deriving from "external" sources, and thus in some sense accidental. The system is viewed as reacting to change either by returning to the *status quo ante* or, more probably, by establishing a new equilibrium. Thus *given* a specifiable change in any component of the system, both the processes and results of social transformation may be traced. But this frame of reference provides little guidance to the occurrence of the initial change, save in the concept of "dysfunction" as a challenge to the notion of perfect integration.

The abandonment of "the quest for origins" in functional analysis—following the dictum that each item of culture or social action is to be explained by the rest of the system—has also meant, commonly, an abandonment of concern for sequences and transformations. It is noteworthy that historical relativism, although nominally rejected by sociologists as unnecessary defeatism, is closely akin to extreme cultural relativism, which implies a rejection of *both* static and dynamic laws of any substantial generality.

The pessimism about laws of social change is scarcely warranted. Scholars and textbook writers (not elsewhere classified) would do well to re-read the works of those theorists who exhibit a more than casual concern for the past and the future as well as for the current state of affairs. Among contemporary theorists, Pitirim A. Sorokin and Robert M. MacIver stand out as scholars who show a major and insistent concern for change as a part of the very nature of social existence, rather than as a regrettable disturbance in the normally placid interdependence of self-equilibrating systems.

Between the global theories, which explain too little because they attempt too much, and the relativistic position that views all change as unique, there is a large middle territory. Within that spacious terrain one may note the standardized internal dynamics of groups of various types, and identify the sources, forms, directions, and rates of change in types and segments of social systems. If the resulting theory is not exactly simple, neither is it wholly simple-minded.

THE SOURCES OF CHANGE

Perhaps the most outstanding progress in the theory of social change has been made in the identification and analysis of the sources of change. In very general terms, this progress has resulted from the abandonment of causes primarily external to social systems and of single-factor explanations, with the correlative acceptance of "immanent" change as the prime mover in social dynamics.

Various Determinisms.—The long search for a singular cause of social change is understandable if regrettable. Simplicity is always an aim in theoretical work. If a single factor external to the social system could be identified as the source of change, simplicity would be further aided by avoidance of any confusion or uncertainty about the direction of the causal influence. That comfortable position had to be abandoned, however, in view of several basic difficulties:

(1) Climatic trends, physiographic features, and biological characteristics change very slowly relatively to the social dynamics for which causes are sought. A constant cannot explain a variable in any system of logic.

(2) The purity of the causal direction is spurious. Human activity alters climate, topography, and human biology. "Natural selection" in the human species is always "social selection." Population changes are by no means independent of social structures.

(3) The relevance of human heredity and the non-human environment is always conditional and relative to the technology, social organization, and cultural values of human societies.

The abandonment of "external" causes in favor of causes of change within the system gains little if the theorist clings to a single "determinism." Among the many difficulties, extensively analyzed by Sorokin, the principal ones include, first, the conceptual confusion in identifying the leading variable, so that, for example, technology is equated with "material culture" rather than with a set of applicable scientific principles, or the "economic factor" subsumes such normative elements as property codes; second, the failure to avoid interdependence of variables in functional systems and, therefore, third, a complete failure to find empirical confirmation of alleged principles.

Adaptation to External Events.—Some of the literature on social change essentially avoids questions of primacy of sources, and attends rather to the consequences of external events. Thus shifts and crises deriving from climatic change or physiographic events leave the sources of change largely unpredicted and uncontrolled, but still influential on social systems. Detection of standardized consequences, or a typology of them, however, may still be possible without prediction of the initial events. Even if such external sources of change are beyond the reach of sociological theory, they may still be left within the analytical system if the consequences have sufficient pattern to warrant generalization.

The theoretical situation is not essentially different if the "external" source of change is another "society" or "culture." The literature on acculturation, or contact and diffusion, generally does not predict the occurrence of contact, but rather classifies types of contact and types of consequences. Here, however, the sources of change are not beyond the theoretical limits of sociological inquiry, but rather beyond the actual limits of reliable research.

Two generalizations appear justified with reference to adaptation to "external" events or influences. Both are of a long-term and largely unidirectional or cumulative character. With reference to "natural" influences, accumulated knowledge of methods of prediction and control, together with an increased independence of social systems from the non-human environment, serves more and more to cushion (but not to eliminate) the impact of shifts and crises. With reference to inter-system contacts, on the other hand, the multiplication of agencies of communication serves to reduce the isolation and thus the autonomy of societies, to increase the proportion and rate of changes from external sources, and thereby to increase "cultural" interdependence and even homogeneity.

Resolution of Human Problems.—If the search for sources of change turns inward to social systems themselves, it becomes apparent that there are persistent problems of the "human condition" that seem to be universal potential sources of positive human effort. Assuming that there are common "functional requisites of any society," these may be viewed as providing minimal rather than ideal or stable conditions for the survival of systems. Although the translation of functions into values has been strongly criticized by Sorokin and others, it does appear empirically that at least a partial translation is tenable. For example, it is doubtful that health, longevity, and improved material conditions of life have ever been neglected or rejected by any substantial number of the population in any historical or contemporary culture. The virtually universal contemporary acceptance of the "gospel of economic development," despite the documented diversity of cultural values, can scarcely be understood otherwise. Incidentally, this illustration does not imply a baldly "materialistic interpretation": there are many other problems of the human condition, such as normative conformity and the search for "meaning" in a super-empirical sense, that also provide the basis for recurrent social innovation.

On a less general level, and consistent with diversity of cultural values, one may still find prevalent inconsistencies between ideal values and patterned social behavior, inconsistencies that provide a potential, and probable, basis for efforts at closer approximation.

Sorokin is undoubtedly correct in insisting upon the uneven attention given to empirical science and rational technology through time and space. Yet, he is also correct in noting the long-term linear "growth of human knowledge and inventions." The explanation of the cumulative trend seems clear. In the attempt to solve human problems, empirically verifiable knowledge and techniques of rational intervention in the natural or social order do not suffer long-term defeats in the face of competing systems of explanation and control. This interpretation argues that persistent problems provide challenges to social innovation, and the secular growth of science and technology implies that rational, secular solutions have a higher probability of acceptance and retention than any alternatives. It may be suggested, in fact, that a rational, technical orientation to the natural or social order is an essentially irreversible intellectual revolution.

Flexibilities in the System.—A number of characteristics of human societies assure the probability of change, but without substantial guidance as to form, direction, or rate. Two principal systemic flexibilities are especially noteworthy: uncertainties in socialization, and role ranges and deviations.

To say that children are born into a society or culture is elliptical. They are normally born into a family unit, which in turn can be expected to be only partially representatives of a generalized and uniform set of values and normative and cognitive orientations. The universality of social differentiation structurally precludes exact uniformity in family position. Even when they occupy similar positions in the social structure, it is extremely unlikely that families will follow exactly uniform patterns of child care and rearing, or indeed that the same family will exhibit uniform behavior in the intimate interaction with successive offspring. Thus biological individual differences interact with diverse personality and structural factors to provide a rather wide range of possible variation. On a strictly actuarial view of socialization, uniformities are somewhat more remarkable than variations.

The uncertainties of socialization are given added point by the virtual impossibility of absolute role specification, even in a "tightly integrated" social system. Granting the probability of ranges of tolerable conduct within recurrent patterns of social relations, the opportunity if not the certainty of innovation exists.

Strains Inherent in the System.—The conception of an "integrated" social system, which informs much of the writing in contemporary sociology—often implicitly—is a model useful for many purposes, but is clearly contrary to fact. The use of some such model provides a first approximation to the systematic tracing of consequences of given changes, but does not account for change itself. For the latter, a somewhat different analytical model is appropriate, namely, one that permits identification of internal or immanent sources of change, including inherent strains.

Several types of inherent strains in ongoing societies are identifiable. Three may be noted as especially significant: demographic imbalances, universal scarcity situations, and the "dialectic" conflict between normative alternatives.

Although the conception of population changes as being essentially "biological" variables, external to social systems, is untenable, it remains true that demographic behavior is extremely unlikely to provide a precise total and differential control of fertility and mortality. In other words, precise stability of population size through time is unlikely, as is, *a fortiori,* precise maintenance of existing numerical distributions among social categories.

Over the short run for most areas of the world and for most periods of history, demographic imbalances probably have resulted in "fluctuations" and adjustments. Over the long run it appears clear that human populations have grown, although most rapidly in the modern era. The modern era has been characterized by a fairly standard sequence, probably unique for any given population, but repeated through space: the "demographic transition" from high fertility and mortality to low vital rates, with rapid intervening growth owing to mortality decline prior to fertility decline. As fertility is brought under deliberate and relatively effective control, its short-run fluctuations closely approximate various changes in levels of economic activity. The negative correlation between the number of children and the family's capacity to support them tends to be reduced or to disappear entirely. Still, no population reproduces its contemporary social differentials precisely. Moreover, the future consequences of current fertility behavior may exhibit, for example, substantial lack of "phasing" of labor supplies and labor demand.

The conception of universal scarcities is in effect a necessary extension of an assumption underlying much of economics. Not only are goods and services, or their monetary representation, likely to be scarce relative to human "wants," but so are time and loyalty (or "affective energy"). These three scarcities are often interrelated, so that allocations of loyalty may be indicated by allocation of time or treasure or both. However, they are analytically distinct. Any viable social system requires norms that determine allocation of these scarcities, but the latter remain omnipresent sources of potential strain in individual behavior and in the relations between and among various groups and social categories.

It is *not* suggested that the strains owing to scarcities form the basis for, say, the empirically untenable Marxian theory of "class struggle." But such strains would appear to be a pregnant source of competition within and among social groupings, and accordingly of normative innovation in the attempt to maintain order *and equity*. The equity of any system of differential allocation of scarce values is subject to challenge as to both principles and results. The same is true of any attempt at equalization. To assume that a system of undifferentiated equality in claims and rewards would be more stable (or equitable) than a differential system is pure prejudice.

A final immanent source of change may be suggested. The literature of sociology abounds with dichotomous classifications, ranging from culture-types through forms of social cohesion or relationship, to paired normative alternatives. Although such modes of classification are "primitive" in the sense that they attempt analysis in terms of attributes rather than variables, they are not useless. It is the beginning of wisdom to identify the dichotomies as polar extremes on a range of variation, and the pursuit of wisdom to note that "pure" types do not concretely exist. A very considerable gain in wisdom results, however, from recognizing the paired alternatives as conflicting principles of social organization and regulation, both of which are persistent in the system. Predominant institutionalization of one alternative does not dispel or dismiss its counterpart.

A few illustrations of this essentially "dialectical" view of social systems may serve to indicate its possible value in resolving some theoretical difficulties that stem from the alternative notions of stable "integration." Sociologists have noted, for example, that "achieved status" systems retain elements of "ascription," and conversely. Although not so commonly noted, it is doubtful that predominant attention to common descent as the strongest bond in the "consanguine" kinship system entirely dispells the probable affective bonds arising in the "conjugal" relation, and conversely. The persistence of various reciprocities among adult siblings and between adult generations despite various inequalities in the mobility of the nuclear family is by this view not anachronistic. The more probable prediction is that of continued persistence if not actual increase in such phenomena, with all the strains that are thus entailed.

Similarly, Talcott Parsons' list of "pattern variables" (for example, universalism-particularism, diffuseness-specificity) seem more useful as identifications of conflicting principles actually and always present than simply as concepts available to the observer to remind him that other situations are different.

This view of social dynamics is consistent with Sorokin's position with reference to "immanent change" and the "principle of limit," but is not repetitive of his position. When Sorokin discusses alternative forms of social relationship (familistic, contractual, compulsory) or forms of government (authoritarian, democratic) he describes them as forms that "fluctuate" in their predominance through time. It appears more useful, and more consistent with the data, to account for such "fluctuations" by the continued presence of competing principles.

What the dialectic principle and other sources of change permit is a theoretical point of view that voids the inhibitions of a static equilibrium model, as well as a partial "accounting" for observed changes. The identification of common sources of change does not, however, uniformly aid in generalization about the direction and rate of change. The notion of successive approximations in the solution of human problems does invite a suggested relation with the apparently cumulative character of knowledge, as noted above. And the dialectic principle of normative alternatives does invite speculation about possible repetitive cycles (of the pendulum-swing variety). But the latter speculation has scant empirical basis and would require careful methodological formulation for reliable testing.

THE FORM AND DIRECTION OF CHANGE

A "pure" theory of social change might be viewed as concerned with any alterations in social phenomena (however defined) through time, with sole concern for such questions as form, sequence, direction, and rate. Such a mode of abstraction is analogous to the "pure" theory of "formal" sociology, which attends to the forms or types of social relations or interaction, in abstraction from the functional or meaningful content of such relations.

Some basis for such a "pure" theory exists, crudely in the common distinction between "evolutionary" and "cyclical" theories, more elaborately in detailed distinctions among forms of change. It may be useful in the present context to note some of the possible formal models of the direction of social change, for such models can be employed for purposes of identification and classification even when the starting point is substantive rather than formal.

Sorokin identifies three principal "patterns of direction" of change: linear —subdivided as unilinear, oscillating, spiral, and branching; cyclical; and variably or creatively recurrent direction, which may be approximately paraphrased as "cycles with trend."

Several methodological points now may be appropriately noted. First, the form and direction of change clearly are in part a function of the time periods and observational units. Second, the shape of a curve fitted to trend data accordingly depends in part on the detail demanded—for example, a curvilinear trend may be made rectilinear by greater generalization (and consequent loss of information or "goodness of fit"). Third, wherever reliable quantities are available, the available mathematical alternatives in curve-fitting are much more numerous than Sorokin's or similar alternatives. Fourth, the possible formal models are further multiplied if "interaction in process" or other complicating features are introduced.

In addition, it should be remembered that not all changes are necessarily directional in any significant sense, or perhaps even consequential for the social analyst. For some changes Sorokin's neutral term "fluctuations" seems to be appropriate. Others may be regarded as "variations on themes." Persons, including scholarly persons, living through large and obvious changes in the conditions of life may have the impression that all is flux, if not chaos. Yet some generalities and some particulars remain remarkably constant. It is presumably unnecessary here to enter an extended discussion of the theory of social structure, but a few reminders may be in order. First, fair agreement obtains among analysts concerning the functions essential for the survival of any society. These functions do not *determine* appropriate structures, but they obviously *limit* them. Thus many changes involve ranges of *structural substitutability* for constant ends and functions. Second, the specification of a number of characteristics of the particular type of society or the special characteristics of one system radically limits the range of potential substitution, but does not eliminate variation that, within these limits, may be "random."

These methodological points are of some consequence in view of the probability that increased attention to the phenomena of change will be accompanied by increased emphasis on "measurement." They do not insure "good" theory, since that is first of all a matter of asking the right questions, but they do warn of some analytical options and hazards.

In view of the great diversity of social phenomena, it would probably be possible to illustrate each of the principal directional forms. Such illustration is not attempted here. Rather, two varieties of change are added to the previous list, each of some consequence in the analysis of major contemporary social transformations.

Some sequences (not "cycles") are apparently unique in given systems, but are partially repeated in space, through time. The "demographic transition" is noted above; at an even more general level, "economic modernization" or "industrialization" is another illustration. History of course does not precisely repeat itself either in time or "laterally" in space, but sufficient common elements appear to warrant generalization.

A more complex form of change involves "interaction in process." This may be identified by the rather cumbersome designation, "cumulative, retroactive evolution." The essentials of the pattern are segmental changes that cannot continue until later "stages" react back on the initial ones. The simplest illustrations are the first and second "agricultural revolutions" separated in time by intervening industrialization, each step being essential. Similarly, it appears probable that "automation" requires not only its technological foundations as such, but the intervening and interactive development of manifold managerial and professional services, made possible in turn by earlier gains in technical productivity.

UNEQUAL PROBABILITY AND RATE

Theoretically, innovation may occur at any point in the social structure; functional theory and various "equilibrium" models do not tell us where or when it is most likely. And although functional theory, or "systems" analysis, starts from the assumption that any change has repercussions throughout the system, we do not in fact know either this assumption to be true in detail or the path, rate, and degree of dependent change. The rejection of uniform "determinisms" does not necessarily imply the alternative of "equal probability." A more systematic inquiry into the principal sources of change, whether at the general level used here or with reference to more particular social systems, would seem to be the proper course of future inquiry with respect to "lead" and "lags." The grain of truth in technological determinism, for example, appears to be the likelihood that innovation occurs with disproportionate frequency in the means for accomplishing seemingly standard ends, with frequently unanticipated repercussions. This sequence may give rise to the sequential alternation of innovation and accommodation. The possibility of rapid spread and acceptance of new cultural values and ideologies, however, provides a suitably chastening warning against simplification.

THE POSSIBILITIES OF "INTEGRATED" THEORY

Although a "pure" theory of social change can be contemplated, this is not viewed as the preferable path of progress. Even if change is the first criterion of selection for such a theory, nothing of empirical consequence can be said without specification of what is changing. The "structural-functionalists" are thus technically correct in maintaining that statics must *precede* dynamics. But it is equally true that quite unrealistic static propositions may be produced unless statics *is followed by* dynamics.

The conventional organization of general sociological treatises relegates the topic of social change to the final chapter(s). Surely there is an alternative approach. This would be to adopt some modest variant of the standard sociological or anthropological ways of identifying and ordering the principal segments of social systems. Most social science of whatever discipline consists of structural-functional analysis—asking what are the patterns, what are their interrelations? To these would be added several insistent questions: (1) What are the intrinsic dynamics of this segment? Examples might include the tendency of bureaucracies to proliferate offices, or the complex sequence in competitive structures of instrumental innovation, conservative reaction, and additional regulation. (2) What changes are the orderly consequences of intersegment functional interaction? Here, the interpenetration of occupational interest groups like unions, and complex work organizations like corporations afford illustrations. (3) What are the predictable leads, lags, tensions—such as the lead of deliberate change and the lag of adversely affected interests? (4) What are the reliable consequences for whole societies of these trends and interplays? An example is the pushing of common values to higher, indeed rarefied, levels of generalization while primary-group values may be intensified and particularized. (5) What can be painted with a broad brush on large canvases about inter-society relations and the trend of human kind generally? An important example is provided by the creation of common material standards of life without effective agreement on an equitable rationale for actual inequalities or even on the more ultimate values of human existence.

In sum, an "integrated" theory of social change will be as singular or plural as sociological theory as a whole, and will include about the same subdivisions and topics. It is not only later than we think, as always, but we are also nearer home.

SOCIAL PROBLEMS

American sociology has always found a close association between social change and social problems. When the first sociologists appeared in a few universities shortly after the Civil War, the setting was one of turbulent social and cultural change. Urbanization, industrialization, and immigration, the triple foci of dynamism in late nineteenth-century America, profoundly shook a society theretofore permeated by the traditional patterns and values of rural, Anglo-Saxon, and Puritanical Protestant ways of life. In retrospect, it should not surprise us that the first major emphasis in American sociology was the search for the causes and solutions of the new social problems that stemmed from the growing cities, factories, and immigrants. Slums, immigrant maladjustment, family conflict, poverty, dependency, and crime were among the leading preoccupations of the pioneers in sociology.

American sociology has changed course, but it has never abandoned this original preoccupation. Whereas some of the early work tended to view each social problem as discrete and discontinuous in relation to other social problems, many of today's theorists and researchers have assumed a functional approach, one which looks on specific problems (as well as social institutions) as parts of an interrelated and functional whole.

In the next article, Marshall B. Clinard, addressing a British audience, shows how the study of social problems and deviant behavior in the United States calls for the use of concepts and theory such as norms, subcultures and social groups, class structure, role theory and self-conceptions, and typological classifications and urbanism.

58. CONTRIBUTIONS OF SOCIOLOGY TO UNDERSTANDING DEVIANT BEHAVIOUR *

MARSHALL B. CLINARD
University of Wisconsin

Many sociologists are attempting to apply sociology to the solution of numerous problem areas. Today one finds applied sociologists doing extensive research on such deviant behaviour as criminality, juvenile delinquency, mental illness, alcoholism, suicide, marriage and family maladjustments, and racial and ethnic discrimination. An increasing number of sociologists, for example, are even on the research staffs of correctional institutions, psychiatric departments, mental hospitals, and alcoholic treatment centres in the United States. Out of this applied and other sociological research come a number of sociological theories and concepts which appear useful. These

* *The British Journal of Criminology,* October, 1962, pp. 110–129.

concepts include the relation of deviant behaviour to social norms, subcultures and social groups, class structure, role theory and self-conceptions, typological classifications and urbanism.

SOCIAL NORMS

A major interest of sociologists is the definition of the norms involved and the differences in society's tolerance of various types of norm violations. All deviations from social norms are by no means always disapproved. Inventions, for example, represent violations of norms which may be strongly approved. Other violations may be tolerated, and still others may be mildly disapproved.

Deviant behaviour consists of those violations of norms which are of a sufficient degree to exceed the general tolerance limit of a society. This means, of course, that the norms which constitute deviant behaviour are not necessarily the same in various cultures, nor are they the same in a given culture over a period of time. Homosexual behaviour, prostitution, or drunkenness do not constitute deviant behaviour in some societies today. Some Scandinavian countries, for example, have such different interpretations of sexual norms that many delinquent and criminal acts in American society would not be regarded as such there. Changed attitudes in the United States over the past fifty years toward tobacco smoking by juveniles and young adults are an indication of how deviant behaviour can be redefined in time. Formerly there was great preoccupation with smoking among younger groups, laws were passed forbidding it, and often they were strictly enforced. Smoking was thought to be related to a variety of other social problems.

In studying deviant behaviour the sociologist is interested in having the norms involved stated fairly explicitly. On this basis, certainly, one cannot assume that there is a "non-conformist personality type," for such would depend upon the assumption that all norms were violated regardless of their nature. For that reason most sociologists are also sceptical of loose terms like "socially maladjusted," "anti-social," "emotionally disturbed," "abnormal," "mentally ill," "sexually deviant," and even an omnibus category like "delinquency." For example, an operational definition of delinquent norms appears to be more useful than the inclusion of undefined areas of behaviour. The definition of excessive drinking and alcoholism involves a deviation from the norms of drinking behaviour within a culture and dependence on alcohol in the life organisation of the individual. Such a definition includes the amount of alcohol consumed, the purpose and meaning of the drinking, the social handicap to the individual, and the degree of inability to refrain from excessive drinking. Even the norms involved in mental disorder need to be so stated that we can determine with some precision who is mentally ill and who is not, whom we are to treat and whom not to treat. Even here an operational definition may turn out to be more satisfactory than the usual vague, unprecise and value-laden definition of "mental health."

Sociological studies on a broad front of strongly disapproved norm violations have shown marked differences between the official visibility and the actual extent of norm violations. Social visibility varies according to the type of deviant behaviour, as well as the sex, age, or social class to which a person belongs. Some deviations, like kidnapping or murder, may become highly visible. Others, like homosexuality, pre-marital sexual relations, or drunkenness which is not public may be only slightly visible. White collar crime, *i.e.,* among higher status groups committed in connection with their occupations, has a very low social visibility. Sociological studies using broader samples have revealed extensive violations of many norms among groups which had been thought not to have many deviants. Such studies have also shown that only a small part of most deviant behaviour becomes officially recognised, and that it often may represent biased samples of delinquents, sex deviants, criminals, alcoholics or mental patients.

SUB-CULTURES AND SOCIAL GROUPS

The sociologist is particularly concerned with the effect of the culture, sub-cultures, and group relationships on deviant behaviour. The term culture refers to normative standards of behaviour, and the sociologist is interested in how the conflicting norms and values of the general culture and sub-cultures are related to deviant behaviour. Society or social groups refer to the interaction and relationships among human beings, and the sociologist is interested in the effect of all types of such group relationships.

The family, while important, is only one of many groups which may be related to deviant behaviour either in terms of norms or social relationships. Among others are neighbourhoods, schools, gangs, cliques, occupations, and religious groups. Alcoholism, for example, represents far more than simply a product of anxieties or personality traits left over from early family interaction or other childhood experiences. Alcoholism implies changes in the nature of interpersonal relationships with others, in attitudes toward drinking, in social roles and in conception of self. This process may take as long as fifteen or twenty years. Some interesting sociological findings support the conclusion that the groups to which a person belongs are related to his excessive drinking, and that alcoholism may be largely a product of the difficulties arising from the excessive drinking itself. Group drinking and cultural factors play an important part in determining who becomes an excessive drinker. In modern society there seem to be pronounced differences in excessive drinking according to the drinking habits of one's companions as shown by differences in the incidence of alcoholism by sex, social class, occupation, religious and ethnic affiliation. Jews and Italians, for example, have a low rate of alcoholism.

Large modern societies consist of a variety of sub-cultures and social groups, each often with its own set of norms and values not only as to what constitutes proper conduct but also even as to the goals of life itself. Sub-cultures, like cultures, tell a person what he must do, ought to do, should do, may do, and must not do. A. K. Cohen has suggested that sub-cultures emerge in a highly differentiated society when, in effective interaction with one another, a number of persons have similar problems. Sociological research has shown the existence of pronounced differences in normative structures of sub-cultures involving persons of different age groups, social classes, occupations, racial, religious and ethnic groups, neighbourhoods and regions. In addition, there are some even more limited sub-cultures such as those among teenage gangs, prostitutes, alcoholics, drug addicts, homosexuals, professional and organised criminals. Even institutions for the treatment of deviants, such as prisons, are actually sub-cultures with their own social systems. In fact, so diverse are the norms of most large societies that there are probably only a few norms which are accepted as binding on all persons.

This means three things: (1) that within a modern society there may be almost as pronounced differences among various groups about the norms of accepted behaviour as there are between large cultures; (2) that to explain logically how members of certain deviant groups in a society come to act the way they do can be explained in the same way, for example, that an Eskimo learns culturally to become an Eskimo; and (3) that when we speak of the norms of a given family we are likely to be referring actually to the social class, occupational, or other sub-cultural group to which the family belongs.

Some, of course, will raise the question, and correctly so, that intimate contact with deviant sub-cultures does not affect all persons in the same manner. Sociological research has suggested that the explanation for this lies in the fact that, first, no deviant sub-culture exists as a closed system for all its members, for even in a high delinquency area they are exposed to other norms. Second, the self-conception of the individual may serve as an insulator against participation in deviant norms. Recent sociological studies of delinquency, for example, indicate that the conception of self as a "good boy" is one of the chief insulators in areas of high delinquency. Such a self-conception is not only acquired in the family, but also through the school and neighbourhood.

Another useful concept for explaining differential behaviour is whether group membership constitutes a reference group to the person. Membership in a group has little meaning for deviant behaviour unless the individual comes to identify with it.

Recognition of sub-cultures in a society seems to have further implications. Rather than seeing a society, neighbourhood, or family as "disorganised" we come to see that the issue is one of conflicting norms. The presence of gambling, the wide use of alcohol, patronage of pubs or taverns, or greater freedom in sexual relations do not necessarily mean that these conditions are naturally "bad" or "disorganised." The slum sex code may be as highly organised and normative regarding pre-marital relations in one direction as the middle-class sex code is in the other.

Another criticism of the loose use of the term "disorganisation" is that actually modern society consists of competing systems of organised sub-cultures. Many sub-cultures of deviant behaviour such as delinquent gangs, homosexuality, organised crime, prostitution, and white collar crime including political corruption, may be highly organised. The norms and values of the slums are highly organised, as W. F. Whyte has shown in his *Street Corner Society*. Finally, as several sociologists have suggested, it is possible that a variety of sub-cultures may contribute, through their diversity, to the unity or integration of a society rather than weaken it.

CLASS STRUCTURE

Modern societies are socially differentiated in many ways; probably no differentiation is greater than the variations in behaviour among the social classes based on occupation, income, residence and way of life. Studies of class structure have shown how value orientation, patterns of family life, and behaviour in general not only represent but serve actually to integrate class ways of life. So different are the social norms and other behaviour of, for example, various American social classes, that the differences in behaviour are probably actually greater than between the accepted conduct of members of the same social class but, say, from some other Western European or even Asiatic societies. Kinsey and others, for example, have shown the existence of great class differences in sex behaviour and even the nature of the sex relation itself. Studies by A. W. Green, K. Davis, and others have shown that even family-rearing patterns of the lower and middle classes are greatly different. The use of physical punishment is an acceptable form of disciplining children in lower-class families. The middle-class boy is more likely to be whipped if he fights; the lower-class boy if he does not, or if he loses. Studies have shown great differences in the norms, behaviour, and family structure of teen-age youth by social class.

Much of this research has directly or indirectly contributed to the understanding of deviant behaviour. There are great differences in the incidence and nature of different types of deviant behaviour by social class. R. K. Merton has proposed a modification of Durkheim's "anomie" to explain all deviant behaviour in terms of class structure, namely, that all forms of deviant behaviour result from differentials in the access to success goals by legitimate means. The great incidence of juvenile delinquency among the lower class has been shown in many sociological studies. To R. A. Cloward and L. E. Ohlin delinquency arises from the disparity between what lower-class youths are led to want and what is actually available to them. Desiring such conventional goals as economic and educational success, they are faced with limitations on legitimate avenues of access to these goals. Being unable to revise their goals downward, they experience frustration and turn to delinquency if the norms are available to them. Cohen has suggested that delinquent gang behaviour is a product of group solutions to the status problems, needs and frustrations of the American lower-class boy in a world of predominantly middle-class values and virtues, expressed through middle-class teachers, social workers, judges and others. Miller has gone even further with his theory that gang delinquency is a product of the subcultural norms of the lower class. Other sociological investigations have found that auto theft is more likely to be a middle-class juvenile offence. Many of the sex offences of juveniles appear to be related to social class.

The rates for crime in general are higher in lower-class areas. Nearly all crimes of violence such as murder are committed by lower-class adults, and the nature of lower-class sub-culture and family life seems to offer an explanation of the origin of most murders.

Sociological studies have shown the existence of wide-scale violations of law by persons in the upper and middle classes, politicians, government officials, businessmen, labour union leaders, doctors and lawyers. These findings indicate that general theories of the relation of crime to poverty, bad housing or low intelligence have little validity. Moreover, sociological research suggests that it is hard to see how psychiatric or psychoanalytic theory can explain most crime in the face of evidence of widespread violations of law among all classes and the existence generally of a low order of business, political and labour ethics in many societies.

Probably in no area has social class shown more pronounced differences than in mental disorder. R. E. Faris and H. W. Dunham showed this years ago in their Chicago study of the residences of public and private mental patients. More recently, A. B. Hollingshead, a sociologist, and F. Redlich, a psychiatrist, have shown great differences in the relative incidence and nature of neuroses and psychoses by social class. Schizophrenia was nine times more prevalent among those of the lowest social class. There were even class differences in the type of the neuroses.

The incidence of suicide is related to occupation and social class. This has been established by many studies including P. Sainsbury's study of London suicides.

Studies of class differences in deviant behaviour demonstrate the need for awareness by psychiatrists, clinical psychologists and social workers of class differences so that they, as middle- and upper-class persons, can share the perspective of the lower-class person. The lower-class person, for example, is more likely to regard mental disorder as a sin, or biological in origin; is more afraid to be thought mentally ill and more likely to be rejected by his family. In theory, professional persons have greater difficulty communicating with lower-class persons and lower-class persons in communicating with them.

In the treatment of delinquency and crime there is also need for the professional person to share the perspectives of the various social classes. This may be so difficult that in New Jersey they are now using experimentally citizen conference committees from the same class, consisting of neighbours, relatives and friends, in supervising juvenile probationers in place of, or as a supplement to, professional persons.

ROLE THEORY AND SELF-CONCEPTION

Deviant behaviour, like all human behaviour, develops out of a process of social interaction and communication with other persons. The study of social roles, organised systems of behaviour expectations and attitudes, and particularly the concepts of role playing and role taking are especially important theoretical tools in the study of deviant behaviour. In the course of the day the activities of a human being are the performance of a series of roles, the behaviour for which he has largely learned from the groups to which he belongs. The diversity of social roles, provided by the variety of sub-cultures and urbanism, is an important factor in the extent of certain types of social deviation in a society. Much of delinquent and criminal behaviour represents the acting out of roles. Moreover, because of the diversity of roles in modern urban society and their lack of co-ordination, the responses of persons to certain situations may often fail to conform to what is expected. A person's evaluation of his role and the evaluation of others may not always be the same. Such role conflicts become important in the analysis of mental disorder and the problems of older persons. Even minority discrimination is a problem of role conflict.

Self-conception is an important corollary in the sociological and social psychological analysis of roles. Self-conception is the image in our minds of the "self" (ourselves) that we try to enhance or defend. It is when individuals have their behaviour socially defined and identify with this definition that they take on behaviour patterns and attitudes characteristic of a definite deviant type. When deviant behaviour is consciously incorporated into the self-image this identification itself is a motive for further behaviour. Societal reaction may reinforce the deviant's self-image.

Whether of deviants or non-deviants, self-conception does not appear to be a static entity fixed as the result of family experience. It can be modified throughout life. The self-conception of a mentally ill person, alcoholic, or suicide is the product not only of the reactions of the father and mother, but of wife and husband, employer, neighbours, other relatives and friends. The self-conception of some types of deviants is the product of the sub-cultures to which they belong. The identification and label, for example, of "delinquent," "criminal," "neurotic," "psychotic," "alcoholic," or "drug addict" may later result in serious consequences on self-conception. Certainly minor deviations, such as certain acts of delinquency, may become intensified through this labelling process.

On the basis of sociological research, social workers can show that improper handling of self-attitudes, by other staff personnel, whether in courts, prisons, or mental hospitals, can make the efforts of social workers extremely difficult. If courts and penal institutions work in a punitive way as dispensers of justice, or if treatment centres for the mentally ill or alcoholics are simply places of custody, social workers who try to take a therapeutic view may find their work largely negated as far as self-feelings of the deviant go.

TYPES OF DEVIANT BEHAVIOUR

Sociologists interested in the study of deviant behaviour have attempted to develop more precise classifications than are denoted by such omnibus categories as delinquents, criminals, the mentally ill, suicides, alcoholics or drug addicts. Typing of deviants is generally the result of the study of behaviour syndromes. Thus criminal types have been worked out on the basis of social roles, self-conception, association with criminal norms, progression in crime, and the role of personality traits. Two main types may be distinguished, individual and career, and more specifically such types as the criminal insane, extreme sex deviates, occasional criminal offenders, habitual petty offenders, white collar criminals, ordinary criminal careers, organised criminals and professional criminals.

Although little has been done as yet, it is also necessary to delimit various types of delinquents and patterned types of offences in which delinquents engage. A delinquent who commits a sex offence is likely to be a very different type from most delinquents who steal autos or commit vandalism. A. J. Reiss, a sociologist, using 736 psychiatric records and combining them with social correlates has, for example, classified youthful offenders into three types.

A classification in terms of behaviour systems is a far cry from psychiatric and other categories based on the nature of personality traits or personal adjustment, since the latter actually fail to distinguish the sophisticated from the unsophisticated offender, or usually the offender from the non-offender. Certainly no set of personality traits characterise all deviants or for that matter all delinquents or criminals.

Sociologists working with those from other disciplines have also been interested in classifying types of alcoholic drinkers, drug addicts, suicides and more recently types of role conflicts in mental disorders and in old age. Research on drug addiction likewise has shown the necessity for considering types of addicts. Sociological study of opiate addicts, for example, has shown a social psychologically different process from the addiction process among non-opiate users. Likewise marihuana use, which is of course not addictive in the strict sense, seems to result from still another and different social psychological process. Working with psychiatrists, a classification of mental disorders in terms of types of interpersonal relations and role behaviour may eventually be developed. Suicide has been classified by sociologists into various types. The extensive research work by sociologists in the adjustment of older persons may enable us to classify the role and status problems of old age, particularly as they relate to mental disorders, into several types. The retired professional person, for example, certainly seems to encounter different problems from that of the worker.

The practical implications of typology of deviants for social work is great. Social workers, or in fact any practitioner, can in this way approach the deviant not with a general frame of reference applicable to all but with different therapies based on given typology. In this way the social worker, psychiatrist or clinical psychologist can work out diagnostic and treatment typologies to each one of which presumably different therapeutic procedures might be applied. For example, there are certainly delinquents and criminals whose personality traits and personal organisation are seriously disturbed emotionally and who exhibit unique personality traits. For them therapy must deal with this type of personality organisation, presumably using psychiatric theories. Nearly all delinquents and criminals, however, appear to be normal psychologically and not "emotionally sick," and the problem basically with them is one of changing their attitudes. This requires great skill on the part of social workers and other practitioners to devise procedures and situations which will accomplish this.

URBANISM

Deviant behaviour is largely a product of social and cultural forces of the wider society. These forces include, particularly, urbanism and the values of the general culture. A recent report on the relation of social welfare to the urbanised society has stated:

> The massive changes wrought by industrialisation in the Western world are now spreading at an accelerated pace to the most isolated parts of the world. . . . Urban-industrial society is the central stage for more and more of the human drama. American social work is part and product of the larger social and cultural setting in which it lives. While it helps to shape the larger society, social work reflects more than it determines the nature of the whole. It cannot be understood apart from its social context. And the more we understand its links to society and culture, the better we will see opportunities to influence the development of welfare services and the profession of social work.[1]

The rapid spread of urbanism, or the "mass society," has contributed a great deal to the increase in deviant behaviour in the contemporary world. By urbanism is meant a way of life accompanied by characteristics such as individualism, rapid cultural change, emphasis on materialism, culture conflict, and, above all, a decline in intimate communication and informal social control. These characteristics have generally accompanied urbanisation, which refers to population concentration, and which, in turn, is largely but not exclusively a product of industrialisation. Urbanism is not always associated with urbanisation, however, for rural areas are increasingly displaying these characteristics. Conversely, one may have enclaves within large cities which display

[1] Wilensky, H., and Ledeaux, C. N. *Industrial Society and Social Welfare.* New York: Russell Sage Foundation, 1958, p. 13.

little of the characteristics of urbanism, and cities themselves may vary in the degree to which they have urban characteristics.

The process is transforming social relations all over the world. Two out of three Americans and four out of five persons in Great Britain now live in urban areas, some of them of immense size. In the Russell Sage Foundation volume, *Industrial Society and Social Welfare,* it was recognised that industrial-urban society is the central stage for an increasing amount of the social problems of mankind and that "These massive changes in American society are the major determinants of the social problems which create the demand for social welfare services."

Urban women have become more self-sufficient, more demanding of equality, and less satisfied with traditional family roles. There is evidence that this situation has not only changed the nature of family life but also has affected our high urban divorce rates. Under conditions of urbanism the aged often have been left stranded. Many sociological studies have shown that there has been a loss of status and of satisfying roles, and that personal dissatisfactions have arisen from the conflict between the role expectations of the older persons and their role achievements. This appears to be reflected in some of the mental problems of the aged.

Most of all, urban life has fractured much of the conventional family system and has, instead, brought new groupings mainly on the basis of age, occupation and the like. Urbanism has made possible the growth of teenage subcultures which are often at variance with family, school and adult norms. This conflict, as yet, has not been as great in the middle class but appears to be on the increase. To these effects of urbanism can be traced a great deal of the explanation for contemporary delinquency among youths. Much teenage delinquency in an urban society probably represents a definition of excitement and a means of gaining status among the peer group.

The problem of an urban society such as ours can be illustrated by studies of the extent and effect of contemporary mobility on deviant behaviour. According to estimates based on contemporary trends, a worker in his lifetime today in America is likely to change his residence eight times and two or three of them would involve an entirely different community. Such mobility, even within a community, often means a loss of relatives and neighbors. Children and adults are faced with new norms and social roles, as well as the reconciliation of old norms and roles with new ones. Personal reputation comes to mean less to the mobile person as the influence of personal social controls declines. Controls become more secondary, the urban family comes to be, as Reuben Hill has termed it, "the lonely family."

Mobile persons appear to encounter considerable difficulties. In a New York State study of first admissions to mental hospitals, migrants were found to have considerably higher rates than non-migrants. The differentials between these two groups were frequently more than 100 percent and sometimes as high as 200 to 300 percent. The rates were greater for all psychoses, and for schizophrenia and the manic-depressive disorders. A recent large scale study by a sociologist of the epidemiology of mental disorders in Texas has shown a much higher rate for rural migrants to cities.

Studies of many kinds of deviant behaviour have shown the pronounced effects of urbanisation and urbanism. Rates for delinquency and most crimes, for example, vary directly with the degree of urbanisation of the community. With few exceptions the same is true for rates of alcoholism, suicide and many other forms of deviant behaviour.

CONCLUSIONS

Sociologists are still for the most part not practitioners for nearly all sociologists are teachers and research workers. This does not mean, however, that many sociologists have not entered and are not entering areas of applied work. Sociologists, as a group, offer little competition to those in applied areas such as social work, psychiatry, or clinical psychology. Their role, today, is one of offering their research findings to those who are in a position to use them. In a rapidly expanding era of knowledge about human behaviour, practitioners must continually change and adapt their practical programme as new knowledge becomes available. They cannot have a frozen frame of reference. The wider application of sociological knowledge by social workers, psychiatrists and clinical psychologists could conceivably result in entirely new approaches to deviant behaviour. Such new approaches could be tested against conventional procedures to determine which is the more effective. One writer has distinguished between the social scientist and the practitioner as follows:

> Unlike the scientist, the practitioner does not produce knowledge by contributing to scientific theory. His success depends on how skilfully he uses what is already known . . . the typical practitioner is not a producer, but a consumer, of scientific knowledge . . . when the practitioner does contribute to scientific theory, he is really in the role of the scientist.[2]

So far there is little indication that either the frame of reference or the findings derived from sociology or the sociological study of deviant behaviour are being used extensively by either social workers, clinical psychologists, or psychiatrists. Social work and psychiatric journals have only a scattering of references to sociology; nearly all references are to psychiatric, psychoanalytic, or social work books and studies. While this statement would, of course, be much more applicable to social workers in case and group work than community organisation, one must agree with A. J. Kahn, a social worker, who has stated that "Although the social work knowledge now in use does include a good deal of borrowed psychiatry and psychological concepts (there has

[2] Greenwood, E. "Social Science and Social Work: A Theory of Their Relationship." *Soc. Sci. Rev.* 29, 1955, p. 27.

been) much less borrowing from sociology, social anthropology and related disciplines."

On the other hand, most psychiatric studies upon which social work depends either indicate a woeful ignorance of sociological writing and research or choose to ignore it, for any mention of its existence is striking. With few exceptions, psychiatrists rarely test their theories using scientific methods, including representative samples and control groups, but assume the validity of a preconceived theory. Even the Gluecks, who appear to be much respected by some social workers and psychiatrists, in their so-called multi-discipline research teams have apparently not had a professional sociologist on their staffs nor do they make more than passing reference in their research studies to the related and contradictory findings by sociologists. W. C. Reckless, for example, has re-examined the findings of their *Unraveling Juvenile Delinquency* in which they assume that the companionship factor is not important in delinquency. Having or not having delinquent gang companions was the ninth highest statistical association in a list of over 100 items.

In fact, most of the contemporary psychiatric and psychoanalytic literature on deviant behaviour, which is also utilised by many social workers, purports to show that the etiology of deviant behaviour can be traced in the final analysis to family interaction, particularly the effect of early family experiences. Events occurring at forty years of age, for example, may be explained by some occurrences at age four. The theory of predetermination of adult behaviour on the basis of heredity has largely disappeared; in its place is predetermination based on early family interaction. For the most part, the sociological approach to deviant behaviour, while certainly recognising the importance of the family, does not agree with this theory in even paramount or exclusive emphasis on the family or on parental models as the determinants of either deviant or non-deviant behaviour.

Whether family predetermination is a valid theory of deviant behaviour actually has not been rigorously tested. Sociologists, because of their wider orientation and training, could contribute a great deal to the solution of this crucial theoretical issue if they were to make more studies specifically directed at the relation of extra-family experiences and social interaction in adult life to deviant behaviour. This would include additional research on the relation of peer groups, school, neighbourhoods, occupations, marriage and other extra-family areas of social interaction in relation to delinquency and crime as well as mental disorders, alcoholism, drug addiction, discrimination, and other types of deviant behaviour.

The wider use of role theory in the studies of adult life may result in a demonstration that early life situations, particularly those in the family, have less importance in the etiology of deviant behaviour than is often presumed at the present time. Sutherland's classic study of *The Professional Thief* clearly demonstrated that criminal roles could be developed out of experience in later life.[3]

[3] Clinard, M. B. "Areas for Research in Deviant Behavior." *Sociology and Social Research,* 42, No. 6, 1958, pp. 416–417.

It is true, as some claim, that sociological findings may not in themselves suggest any direct practical application for psychiatric or social work, and there is often even disdain for any suggestion of practical use. The social worker or psychiatrist who deals with individuals and clients often finds it difficult to use sociological data. Sometimes it consists of undigested empiric facts with little relation from one study to another. This can be a frustrating experience for someone who may have had no previous sociological training whatsoever or, if he had, it was almost entirely limited to undergraduate courses in sociology.

Still, the use to which sociological research on deviant behaviour may be applied is primarily the problem of the practitioner and not the sociologist. The situation is no different from that of the application to medicine of the research findings of those scientists who discovered in their laboratories the existence of certain chemical processes which became the basis of the modern "miracle drugs" of medical practice.

Moreover, the fact that psychiatric or psychoanalytic findings about deviant behaviour are more frequently derived from therapy rather than from basic research and, therefore, by their very nature have more immediate application, may account for their more ready acceptance by psychiatric and social workers. Neither ease of application nor the fact that a theory was developed out of practical work are evidence of the validity of a theory.

There is evidence that the estrangement of sociology from psychiatry, clinical psychology and social work is diminishing. Sociologists are increasingly being drawn into areas of applied science. Their assistance in psychiatric and social work problems is being more frequently sought. Many sociologists are now associated with departments of psychiatry in America. Sociological materials are being extensively employed in some recent social work books. In America, the Russell Sage Foundation has been particularly useful in bringing social workers and sociologists closer together. Programmes involving professional training in both social work and sociology are beginning in several American universities. It is hoped that in the future sociology, psychiatry, clinical psychology and social work may have closer associations to the mutual advantage of all.

Of all the sociological research projects conducted on specific social problems, it is doubtful whether any one ever made a more revolutionary contribution to theory than Edwin H. Sutherland's study of white collar crime. Until his research landmark, sociologists in general and criminologists in particular were inclined to overlook antitrust violations, false advertisements, employee coercion, and infringements against patents, copyrights, and trademarks as criminal behavior and social problems. Professor Sutherland's study of 547 court decisions involving 74 corporations definitely revealed that these white-collar violations met the two abstract criteria of crime: legal description of an act as social injuries and legal provision of a penalty for the act.

Yet white collar crimes are often subject to differential implementation, such as civil court action, thus minimizing the stigma and consequences of crime. The reasons for this differential treatment are the high prestige and status of the businessman (with whom the judge and, indeed, the criminologist of the past have readily identified), the penological trend away from punishment, and the relatively unorganized resentment of the public against white collar criminals.

In one of his articles on white-collar crime that follows, the implication of Professor Sutherland's analysis is that traditional theories of crime causation are grossly inadequate. If white-collar crime really is crime, then poverty, sibling displacement, and culture conflict obviously do not suffice as explanations of criminal behavior.

59. IS "WHITE COLLAR CRIME" CRIME? *

EDWIN H. SUTHERLAND

Indiana University

The argument has been made that business and professional men commit crimes which should be brought within the scope of the theories of criminal behavior. In order to secure evidence as to the prevalence of such white collar crimes an analysis was made of the decisions by courts and commissions against the seventy largest industrial and mercantile corporations in the United States under four types of laws, namely, antitrust, false advertising, National Labor Relations, and infringement of patents, copyrights, and trademarks. This resulted in the finding that 547 such adverse decisions had been made, with an average of 7.8 decisions per corporation and with each corporation having at least 1. Although all of these were decisions that the behavior was unlawful, only 49 or 9 percent of the total were made by criminal courts and were *ipso facto* decisions that the behavior was criminal. Since not all unlawful behavior is criminal behavior, these decisions can be used as a measure of criminal behavior only if the other 498 decisions can be shown to be decisions that the behavior of the corporations was criminal.

This is a problem in the legal definition of crime and involves two types of questions: May the word "crime" be applied to the behavior regarding which these decisions were made? If so, why is it not generally applied and why have not the criminologists regarded white collar crime as cognate with other crime? The first question involves semantics, the second interpretation or explanation.

A combination of two abstract criteria is generally regarded by legal scholars as necessary to define crime, namely: legal description of an act as socially injurious, and legal provision of a penalty for the act.

* *American Sociological Review,* Vol. 10, No. 2, April, 1945, pp. 132–139.

When the criterion of legally defined social injury is applied to these 547 decisions the conclusion is reached that all of the classes of behaviors regarding which the decisions were made are legally defined as socially injurious. This can be readily determined by the words in the statutes—"crime" or "misdemeanor" in some, and "unfair," "discrimination," or "infringement" in all the others. The persons injured may be divided into two groups: first, a relatively small number of persons engaged in the same occupation as the offenders or in related occupations, and, second, the general public either as consumers or as constituents of the general social institutions which are affected by the violations of the laws. The antitrust laws are designed to protect competitors and also to protect the institution of free competition as the regulator of the economic system and thereby to protect consumers against arbitrary prices, and to protect the institution of democracy against the dangers of great concentration of wealth in the hands of monopolies. Laws against false advertising are designed to protect competitors against unfair competition and also to protect consumers against fraud. The National Labor Relations Law is designed to protect employees against coercion by employers and also to protect the general public against interferences with commerce due to strikes and lockouts. The laws against infringements are designed to protect the owners of patents, copyrights, and trademarks against deprivation of their property and against unfair competition, and also to protect the institution of patents and copyrights which was established in order to "promote the progress of science and the useful arts." Violations of these laws are legally defined as injuries to the parties specified.

Each of these laws has a logical basis in the common law and is an adaptation of the common law to modern social organization. False advertising is related to common law fraud, and infringement to larceny. The National Labor Relations Law, as an attempt to prevent coercion, is related to the common law prohibition of restrictions on freedom in the form of assault, false imprisonment, and extortion. For at least two centuries prior to the enactment of the modern antitrust laws the common law was moving against restraint of trade, monopoly, and unfair competition.

Each of the four laws provides a penal sanction and thus meets the second criterion in the definition of crime, and each of the adverse decisions under these four laws, except certain decisions under the infringement laws to be discussed later, is a decision that a crime was committed. This conclusion will be made more specific by analysis of the penal sanctions provided in the four laws.

The Sherman antitrust law states explicitly that a violation of the law is a misdemeanor. Three methods of enforcement of this law are provided, each of them involving procedures regarding misdemeanors. First, it may be enforced by the usual criminal prosecution, resulting in the imposition of fine or imprisonment. Second, the attorney general of the United States and the several district attorneys are given the "duty" of "repressing and preventing" violations of the law by petitions for injunctions, and violations of the injunctions are punishable as contempt of court. This method of enforcing a criminal law was an invention and, as will be described later, is the key to the interpretation of the differential implementation of the criminal law as applied to white collar criminals. Third, parties who are injured by violations of the law are authorized to sue for damages, with a mandatory provision that the damages awarded be three times the damages suffered. These damages in excess of reparation are penalties for violation of the law. They are payable to the injured party in order to induce him to take the initiative in the enforcement of the criminal law and in this respect are similar to the earlier methods of private prosecutions under the criminal law. All three of these methods of enforcement are based on decisions that a criminal law was violated and therefore that a crime was committed; the decisions of a civil court or a court of equity as to these violations are as good evidence of criminal behavior as is the decision of a criminal court.

The Sherman antitrust law has been amended by the Federal Trade Commission Law, the Clayton Law, and several other laws. Some of these amendments define violations as crimes and provide the conventional penalties, but most of the amendments do not make the criminality explicit. A large proportion of the cases which are dealt with under these amendments could be dealt with, instead, under the original Sherman Law, which is explicitly a criminal law. In practice, the amendments are under the jurisdiction of the Federal Trade Commission, which has authority to make official decisions as to violations. The Commission has two principal sanctions under its control, namely: the stipulation and the cease and desist order. The Commission may, after the violation of the law has been proved, accept a stipulation from the corporation that it will not violate the law in the future. Such stipulations are customarily restricted to the minor or technical violations. If a stipulation is violated or if no stipulation is accepted, the Commission may issue a cease and desist order; this is equivalent to a court's injunction except that violation is not punishable as contempt. If the Commissions' desist order is violated, the Commission may apply to the court for an injunction, the violation of which is punishable as contempt. By an amendment to the Federal Trade Commission Law in the Wheeler-Lea Act of 1938 an order of the Commission becomes "final" if not officially questioned within a specified time and thereafter its violation is punishable by a civil fine. Thus, although certain interim procedures may be used in the enforcement of the amendments to the antitrust law, fines or imprisonment for contempt are available if the interim procedures fail. In this respect the interim procedures are similar to probation in ordinary criminal cases. An unlawful act is not defined as criminal by the fact that it is punished, but by the fact that it is punishable. Larceny is as truly a crime when the thief is placed on probation as when he is committed to prison. The argument may be made that punishment for contempt of court is not punishment for violation of the original law and that, therefore, the original law does not contain a penal sanction. This reasoning is specious since the original law provides the injunction with its penalty as a part of the procedure for enforcement. Consequently all of the decisions made under the amendments to the antitrust law are decisions that the corporations committed crimes.

The laws regarding false advertising, as included in the decisions under consideration, are of two types. First, false advertising in the form of false labels is defined in the Pure Food and Drug Law as a misdemeanor and is punishable by a fine. Second, false advertising generally is defined in the Federal Trade Commission Act as unfair competition. Cases of the second type are under the jurisdiction of the Federal Trade Commission, which uses the same procedures as in antitrust cases. Penal sanctions are available in antitrust cases, as previously described, and are similarly available in these cases of false advertising. Thus, all of the decisions in false advertising cases are decisions that the corporations committed crimes.

The National Labor Relations Law of 1935 defines a violation as "unfair labor practice." The National Labor Relations Board is authorized to make official decisions as to violations of the law and, in case of violation, to issue desist orders and also to make certain remedial orders, such as reimbursement of employees who had been dismissed or demoted because of activities in collective bargaining. If an order is violated, the Board may apply to the court for enforcement and a violation of the order of the court is punishable as contempt. Thus, all of the decisions under this law, which is enforceable by penal sanctions, are decisions that crimes were committed.

The methods for the repression of infringements vary. Infringements of a copyright or a patented design are defined as misdemeanors, punishable by fines. No case of this type has been discovered against the seventy corporations. Other infringements are not explicitly defined in the statutes on patents, copyrights, and trademarks as crimes and agents of the state are not authorized by these statutes to initiate actions against violators of the law. Nevertheless, infringements may be punished in either of two ways: First, agents of the State may initiate action against infringers under the Federal Trade Commission Law as unfair competition and they do so, especially against infringers of copyrights and trademarks; these infringements are then punishable in the same sense as violations of the amendments to the antitrust laws. Second, the patent, copyright, and trade mark statutes provide that the damages awarded to injured owners of those rights may be greater than (in one statute as much as threefold) the damages actually suffered. These additional damages are not mandatory, as in the Sherman antitrust law, but on the other hand they are not explicitly limited to wanton and malicious infringements. Three decisions against the seventy corporations under the patent law and one under the copyright law included awards of such additional damages and on that account were classified in the tabulation of decisions as evidence of criminal behavior of the corporations. The other decisions, 74 in number, in regard to infringements were classified as not conclusive evidence of criminal behavior and were discarded. However, in 20 of these 74 cases the decisions of the court contain evidence which would be sufficient to make a *prima facie* case in a criminal prosecution; evidence outside these decisions which may be found in the general descriptions of practices regarding patents, copyrights, and trademarks, justifies a belief that a very large proportion of the 74 cases did, in fact, involve wilful infringement of property rights and might well have resulted in the imposition of a penalty if the injured party and the court had approached the behavior from the point of view of crime.

In the preceding discussion the penalties which are definitive of crime have been limited to fine, imprisonment, and punitive damages. In addition, the stipulation, the desist order, and the injunction, with reference to punishment for contempt, have the attributes of punishment. This is evident both in that they result in some suffering on the part of the corporation against which they are issued and also in that they are designed by legislators and administrators to produce suffering. The suffering is in the form of public shame, as illustrated in more extreme form in the colonial penalty of sewing the letter "T" on the clothing of the thief. The design is shown in the sequence of sanctions used by the Federal Trade Commission. The stipulation involves the least publicity and the least discomfort, and it is used for minor and technical violations. The desist order is used if the stipulation is violated and also if the violation of the law is appraised by the Commission as wilful and major. This involves more public shame; this shame is somewhat mitigated by the statements made by corporations, in exculpation, that such orders are merely the acts of bureaucrats. Still more shameful to the corporation is an injunction issued by a court. The shame resulting from this order is sometimes mitigated and the corporation's face saved by taking a consent decree. The corporation may insist that the consent decree is not an admission that it violated the law. For instance, the meat packers took a consent decree in an antitrust case in 1921, with the explanation that they had not knowingly violated any law and were consenting to the decree without attempting to defend themselves because they wished to co-operate with the government in every possible way. This patriotic motivation appeared questionable, however, after the packers fought during almost all of the next ten years for a modification of the decree. Although the sequence of stipulation, desist order, and injunction indicates that the variations in public shame are designed, these orders have other functions, as well, especially a remedial function and the clarification of the law in a particular complex situation.

The conclusion in this semantic portion of the discussion is that 473 of the 547 decisions are decisions that crimes were committed.

This conclusion may be questioned on the ground that the rules of proof and evidence used in reaching these decisions are not the same as those used in decisions regarding other crimes, especially that some of the agencies which rendered the decisions did not require proof of criminal intent and did not presume the accused to be innocent. These rules of criminal intent and presumption of innocence, however, are not required in all prosecutions under the regular penal code and the number of exceptions is increasing. In many states a person may be committed to prison without protection of one or both of these rules on charges of statutory rape, bigamy, adultery, passing bad checks, selling mortgaged property, defrauding a hotel keeper, and other offenses. Consequently the criteria which have been used in defining white collar crimes are not categorically different from the criteria used in defining other crimes, for these rules are abrogated both in regard to white collar crimes and other crimes, including some felonies. The proportion of decisions rendered against corporations without the protection of these rules is probably greater than the proportion rendered against other criminals, but a difference in proportions does not make the violations of law by corporations categorically different from the violations of laws by other criminals. Moreover, the difference in proportion, as the procedures actually operate, is not great. On the one side, many of the defendants in usual criminal cases, being in relative poverty, do not get good defense and consequently secure little benefit from these rules; on the other hand, the Commissions come close to observing these rules of proof and evidence although they are not required to do so. This is illustrated by the procedure of the Federal Trade Commission in regard to advertisements. Each year it examines several hundred thousand advertisements and appraises about 50,000 of them as probably false. From the 50,000 it selects about 1,500 as patently false. For instance, an advertisement of gum-wood furniture as "mahogany" would seldom be an accidental error and would generally result from a state of mind which deviated from honesty by more than the natural tendency of human beings to feel proud of their handiwork.

The preceding discussion has shown that the seventy corporations committed crimes according to 473 adverse decisions, and also has shown that the criminality of their behavior was not made obvious by the conventional procedures of the criminal law but was blurred and concealed by special procedures. This differential implementation of the law as applied to the crimes of corporations eliminates or at least minimizes the stigma of crime. This differential implementation of the law began with the Sherman antitrust law of 1890. As previously described, this law is explicitly a criminal law and a violation of the law is a misdemeanor no matter what procedure is used. The customary policy would have been to rely entirely on criminal prosecution as the method of enforcement. But a clever invention was made in the provision of an injunction to enforce a criminal law; this was not only an invention but was a direct reversal of previous case law. Also, private parties were encouraged by treble damages to enforce a criminal law by suits in civil courts. In either case, the defendant did not appear in the criminal court and the fact that he had committed a crime did not appear in the face of the proceedings.

The Sherman antitrust law, in this respect, became the model in practically all the subsequent procedures authorized to deal with the crimes of corporations. When the Federal Trade Commission bill and the Clayton bill were introduced in Congress, they contained the conventional criminal procedures; these were eliminated in committee discussions, and other procedures which did not carry the external symbols of criminal process were substituted. The violations of these laws are crimes, as has been shown above, but they are treated as though they were not crimes, with the effect and probably the intention of eliminating the stigma of crime.

This policy of eliminating the stigma of crime is illustrated in the following statement by Wendell Berge, at the time assistant to the head of the antitrust division of the Department of Justice, in a plea for abandonment of the criminal prosecution under the Sherman antitrust law and the authorization of civil procedures with civil fines as a substitute.

> While civil penalties may be as severe in their financial effects as criminal penalties, yet they do not involve the stigma that attends indictment and conviction. Most of the defendants in antitrust cases are not criminals in the usual sense. There is no inherent reason why antitrust enforcement requires branding them as such.[1]

If a civil fine were substituted for a criminal fine, a violation of the antitrust law would be as truly a crime as it is now. The thing which would be eliminated would be the stigma of crime. Consequently, the stigma of crime has become a penalty in itself, which may be imposed in connection with other penalties or withheld, just as it is possible to combine imprisonment with a fine or have a fine without imprisonment. A civil fine is a financial penalty without the additional penalty of stigma, while a criminal fine is a financial penalty with the additional penalty of stigma.

When the stigma of crime is imposed as a penalty it places the defendant in the category of criminals and he becomes a criminal according to the popular stereotype of "the criminal." In primitive society "the criminal" was substantially the same as "the stranger," while in modern society "the criminal" is a person of less esteemed cultural attainments. Seventy-five percent of the persons committed to state prisons are probably not, aside from their unesteemed cultural attainments, "criminals in the usual sense of the word." It may be excellent policy to eliminate the stigma of crime in a large proportion of cases, but the question at hand is why the law has a different implementation for white collar criminals than for others.

Three factors assist in explaining this differential implementation of the law, namely, the status of the business man, the trend away from punishment, and the relatively unorganized resentment of the public against white collar criminals. Each of these will be described.

First, the methods used in the enforcement of any law are an adaption to

[1] Wendell Berge, "Remedies Available to the Government under the Sherman Act," *Law and Contemporary Problems*. 7:111. January, 1940.

the characteristics of the prospective violators of the law, as appraised by the legislators and the judicial and administrative personnel. The appraisals regarding business men, who are the prospective violators of the four laws under consideration, include a combination of fear and admiration. Those who are responsible for the system of criminal justice are afraid to antagonize business men; among other consequences, such antagonism may result in a reduction in contributions to the campaign funds needed to win the next election. Probably much more important is the cultural homogeneity of legislators, judges, and administrators with business men. Legislators admire and respect business men and cannot conceive of them as criminals, that is, business men do not conform to the popular stereotype of "the criminal." The legislators are confident that these business men will conform as a result of very mild pressures.

This interpretation meets with considerable opposition from persons who insist that this is an egalitarian society in which all men are equal in the eyes of the law. It is not possible to give a complete demonstration of the validity of this interpretation but four types of evidence are presented in the following paragraphs as partial demonstration.

The Department of Justice is authorized to use both criminal prosecutions and petitions in equity to enforce the Sherman antitrust law. The Department has selected the method of criminal prosecution in a larger proportion of cases against trade unions than of cases against corporations, although the law was enacted primarily because of fear of the corporations. From 1890 to 1929 the Department of Justice initiated 438 actions under this law with decisions favorable to the United States. Of the actions against business firms and associations of business firms, 27 percent were criminal prosecutions, while of the actions against trade unions 71 percent were criminal prosecutions. This shows that the Department of Justice has been comparatively reluctant to use a method against business firms which carries with it the stigma of crime.

The method of criminal prosecution in enforcement of the Sherman antitrust law has varied from one presidential administration to another. It has seldom been used in the administrations of the presidents who are popularly appraised as friendly toward business, namely, McKinley, Harding, Coolidge, and Hoover.

Business men suffered their greatest loss of prestige in the depression which began in 1929. It was precisely in this period of low status of business men that the most strenuous efforts were made to enforce the old laws and enact new laws for the regulation of business men. The appropriations for this purpose were multiplied several times and persons were selected for their vigor in administration of the laws. Of the 547 decisions against the seventy corporations during their life careers, which have averaged about forty years, 63 percent were rendered in the period 1935–1943, that is, during the period of the low status of business men.

The Federal Trade Commission Law states that a violation of the antitrust laws by a corporation shall be deemed to be, also, a violation by the officers and directors of the corporation. However, business men are practically never convicted as persons and several cases have been reported, like the six per-cent case against the automobile manufacturers, in which the corporation was convicted and the persons who direct the corporation were all acquitted.

A second factor in the explanation of the differential implementation of the law as applied to white collar criminals is the trend away from reliance on penal methods. This trend advanced more rapidly in the area of white collar crimes than of other crimes because this area, due to the recency of the statutes, is least bound by precedents and also because of the status of business men. This trend is seen in the almost complete abandonment of the most extreme penalties of death and physical torture; in the supplanting of conventional penal methods by non-penal methods such as probation and the case work methods which accompany probation; and in the supplementing of penal methods by non-penal methods, as in the development of case work and educational policies in prisons. These decreases in penal methods are explained by a series of social changes: the increased power of the lower socio-economic class upon which previously most of the penalties were inflicted; the inclusion within the scope of the penal laws of a large part of the upper socio-economic class as illustrated by traffic regulations; the increased social interaction among the classes, which has resulted in increased understanding and sympathy; the failure of penal methods to make substantial reductions in crime rates; and the weakening hold on the legal profession and others of the individualistic and hedonistic psychology which had placed great emphasis on pain in the control of behavior. To some extent overlapping those just mentioned is the fact that punishment, which was previously the chief reliance for control in the home, the school, and the church, has tended to disappear from those institutions, leaving the State without cultural support for its own penal methods.

White collar crime is similar to juvenile delinquency in respect to the differential implementation of the law. In both cases, the procedures of the criminal law are modified so that the stigma of crime will not attach to the offenders. The stigma of crime has been less completely eliminated from juvenile delinquents than from white collar criminals because the procedures for the former are a less complete departure from conventional criminal procedures, because most juvenile delinquents come from a class with low social status, and because the juveniles have not organized to protect their good names. Because the juveniles have not been successfully freed from the stigma of crime they have been generally held to be within the scope of the theories of criminology and in fact provide a large part of the data for criminology; because the external symbols have been more successfully eliminated from white collar crimes, white collar crimes have generally not been included within these theories.

A third factor in the differential implementation of the law is the difference in the relation between the law and the mores in the area of white collar crime.

The laws under consideration are recent and do not have a firm foundation in public ethics or business ethics; in fact certain rules of business ethics, such as the contempt for the "price chiseler," are generally in conflict with the law. These crimes are not obvious, as is assault and battery, and can be appreciated readily only by persons who are expert in the occupations in which they occur. A corporation often violates a law for a decade or longer before the administrative agency becomes aware of the violation, and in the meantime the violation may have become accepted practice in the industry. The effects of a white collar crime upon the public are diffused over a long period of time and perhaps over millions of people, with no person suffering much at a particular time. The public agencies of communication do not express and organize the moral sentiments of the community as to white collar crimes in part because the crimes are complicated and not easily presented as news, but probably in greater part because these agencies of communication are owned or controlled by the business men who violate the laws and because these agencies are themselves frequently charged with violations of the same laws. Public opinion in regard to picking pockets would not be well organized if most of the information regarding this crime came to the public directly from the pick-pockets themselves.

This third factor, if properly limited, is a valid part of the explanation of the differential implementation of the law. It tends to be exaggerated and become the complete explanation in the form of a denial that white collar crimes involve any moral culpability whatever. On that account it is desirable to state a few reasons why this factor is not the complete explanation.

The assertion is sometimes made that white collar crimes are merely technical violations and involve no moral culpability, i.e., violation of the mores, whatever. In fact, these white collar crimes, like other crimes, are distributed along a continuum in which the *mala in se* are at one extreme and the *mala prohibita* at the other. None of the white collar crimes is purely arbitrary, as is the regulation that one must drive on the right side of the street, which might equally well be that he must drive on the left side. The Sherman antitrust law, for instance, is regarded by many persons as an unwise law and it may well be that some other policy would be preferable. It is questioned principally by persons who believe in a more collectivistic economic system, namely, the communists and the leaders of big business, while its support comes largely from an emotional ideology in favor of free enterprise which is held by farmers, wage-earners, small business men, and professional men. Therefore, as appraised by the majority of the population it is necessary for the preservation of American institutions and its violation is a violation of strongly entrenched moral sentiments.

The sentimental reaction toward a particular white collar crime is certainly different from that toward some other crimes. This difference is often exaggerated, especially as the reaction occurs in urban society. The characteristic reaction of the average citizen in the modern city toward burglary is apathy unless he or his immediate friends are victims or unless the case is very spectacular. The average citizen, reading in his morning paper that the home of an unknown person has been burglarized by another unknown person, has no appreciable increase in blood pressure. Fear and resentment develop in modern society primarily as the result of the accumulation of crimes as depicted in crime rates or in general descriptions, and this develops both as to white collar crimes and other crimes.

Finally, although many laws have been enacted for the regulation of occupations other than business, such as agriculture or plumbing, the procedures used in the enforcement of those other laws are more nearly the same as the conventional criminal procedures, and law-violators in these other occupations are not so completely protected against the stigma of crime as are business men. The relation between the law and the mores tends to be circular. The mores are crystallized in the law and each act of enforcement of the laws tends to re-enforce the mores. The laws regarding white collar crime, which conceal the criminality of the behavior, have been less effective than other laws in re-enforcement of the mores.

APPLIED SOCIOLOGY

American sociology has always differed significantly from its European counterpart with regard to the emphasis on the development of pure versus applied science. Generally speaking, European sociology has evolved almost solely as a pure science, in keeping with the philosophical precursors of sociology, concerned with knowledge about man in society "for its own sake." This has not been the case in America. From the very beginning, and consistent with the strong reformist tendencies of early American sociology as well as the pragmatic culture of American society, some sociologists have constantly insisted that at least part of their discipline should be applied. It should be concerned with acquiring knowledge and techniques that will aid in the ultimate solution of social problems, the making of social policy, and the greater efficiency of the mechanisms of social control.

Since the early 1930's, for instance, there has been a growing sense that sociology and the related social sciences could contribute to policy and administration on both the local and national levels of government. During the economic depression of 1929–1939, sociologists were asked to furnish some of the criteria of welfare needs. During World War II, problems in social relations in the armed services and defense plants called for expert knowledge on the controllability and relative efficiency of different social variables in producing purposive change, such as a reduction of conflict and tension.

Sociologists worked with anthropologists, psychologists, and other behavioral specialists in organization and propaganda analysis, problems of morale, intelligence and counterintelligence, selection of personnel, area studies, and attitude and opinion surveys for the ultimate applied purpose of creating greater efficiency in both civilian and military operations. Since the war, advertising agencies have added sociologists to their staffs to ascertain what is socially significant about consumers that will facilitate a more receptive market for their commodities. Social work agencies are increasingly turning to sociological researchers to find out what social and cultural variables are important in inhibiting and promoting their respective case-work and group-work programs.

In the final article of this last part of the book, Alvin W. Gouldner identifies some of the theoretical and conceptual needs of applied sociology and the other applied social sciences, noting that some of these needs are still not met by the present development of pure theory.

60. THEORETICAL REQUIREMENTS OF THE APPLIED SOCIAL SCIENCES *

ALVIN W. GOULDNER
Washington University

It seems reasonable to assume that the applied social sciences develop more rapidly under some conditions than others. The aim of this paper is to take this simple assumption seriously, and to identify the theoretic and conceptual tools most conducive to the maturation of the applied social sciences. The ultimate objective is to codify these, so that they can constitute a paradigm useful for the systematic inspection of the different applied fields. Such a paradigm could provide a working model of what is "par" for the course. At the same time, it could also indicate those areas in pure social science where further work might bridge the gap between it and applied efforts.

Applied social science has distinctive intellectual requirements largely because it is exposed to special exigencies and tensions. Its theories and concepts not only have to pass inspection before the bar of science, but they must also prove serviceable in coping with this specific set of social tensions. It is not enough, therefore, to examine the intellectual tools of applied social science in terms of their manifest scientific functions as technical instruments. They must also be considered in the light of their latent social functions for the peculiar system of human relations in which they are implicated. In this way, it may be seen that certain of the devices of applied social science, which sometimes seem scientifically senseless, are at least sociologically sensible.

Attention is directed to two historically different planes of work in applied social science. One of these is the ongoing work in such areas as race relations, housing, industrial sociology, criminology, or mass communications research. The second plane involves inspection of the work of such classic contributors

* *American Sociological Review,* Vol. 22, No. 1, February, 1957, pp. 92–102.

to the applied social sciences as Karl Marx, Emile Durkheim, and Sigmund Freud.

THE MODEL OUTLINED

Unlike pure science, the applied social sciences are not oriented solely to values intrinsic to science—such as increased information, objectivity, prediction, parsimony, replication, and the like. Applied social science is characterized by an orientation to the values of laymen, as well as of scientists. These lay values, extrinsic to science as such, are regarded by the applied social scientist as legitimate points of orientation for his professional and scientific work.

There seem to be four such value-foci on which the work of applied social scientists centers:

1. The reduction of various forms of social deviancy, as exemplified in efforts to rehabilitate criminals or juvenile delinquents.
2. Improvement of the efficiency or effectiveness with which diverse lay goals are pursued, as exemplified in the work of some industrial sociologists or applied anthropologists.
3. The reduction of tensions or conflicts, such as the work of some race relations specialists.
4. The reduction of tensions that a group experiences in relation to its "environment," such as those found in personnel testing, market research, and public relations surveys.

Applied social scientists are more likely to use laymen as a reference group in organizing their professional work, and their work is more likely to occur in the context of, and be influenced by, their relationship with laymen. For these reasons the applied social scientist is constrained to include among his dependent variables certain lay "social problems." As part of his work the applied social scientist is ultimately concerned with identifying those independent variables which can not only account for, but which can remedy, these "social problems." Preliminary though the model is at this point, it may yet be sufficient to permit discussion of why Marx, Durkheim, and Freud have been characterized as applied social scientists.

FREUD, MARX, AND DURKHEIM

It is easy to accept Freud as an applied scientist, and, indeed he is widely regarded as the twentieth century's master clinician. However, in viewing Marx as an applied social scientist the stance needed is that of a Machiavellian operationalism. The objective is neither to bury nor to praise him. The assumption is simply that he is better understood for being understood as an applied sociologist. This is in part the clear implication of Marx's *Theses on Feurbach,* which culminate in the resounding 11th thesis: "The philosophers have only interpreted the world in different ways; the point, however, is to change it." This would seem to be the tacit creed of applied scientists everywhere.

Marx is no Faustian, concerned solely with understanding society, but a Promethean who sought to understand it well enough to influence and to change it. He was centrally concerned with the social problems of a lay group, the proletariat, and there can be little doubt that his work is motivated by an effort to reduce their suffering, as he saw it. His diagnosis was that their increasing misery and alienation engendered endemic class struggle; his prognosis claimed that this would culminate in revolution; his therapeutic prescription was class consciousness and active struggle.

Here, as in assessing Durkheim or Freud, the issue is not in whether this analysis is empirically correct or scientifically adequate. Furthermore, whether or not this formulation seems to eviscerate Marx's revolutionary core, as critics on the left may charge, or whether the formulation provides Marx with a new veneer of academic respectability, as critics on the right may allege, is entirely irrelevant from the present standpoint. Insofar as Marx's or any other social scientists' work conforms to a generalized model of applied social science, insofar as it is professionally oriented to the values and social problems of laymen in his society, he may be treated as an applied social scientist.

Despite Durkheim's intellectualistic proclivities and rationalistic pathos, he was too much the product of European turbulence to turn his back on the travail of his culture. "Why strive for knowledge of reality, if this knowledge cannot aid us in life," he asked. "Social science," he said, "can provide us with rules of action for the future." Durkheim, like Marx, conceived of science as an agency of social action, and like him was professionally oriented to the values and problems of laymen in his society. Unless one sees that Durkheim was in some part an applied social scientist, it is impossible to understand why he concludes his monumental study of *Suicide* with a chapter on "Practical Consequences," and why, in the *Division of Labor,* he proposes a specific remedy for anomie.

Durkheim is today widely regarded as a model of theoretic and methodologic sophistication, and is thus usually seen only in his capacity as a pure social scientist. Surely this is an incomplete view of the man who regarded the *practical* effectiveness of a science as its principal justification. To be more fully understood, Durkheim also needs to be seen as an applied sociologist. His interest in religious beliefs and organization, in crime and penology, in educational methods and organization, in suicide and anomie, are not casually chosen problem areas. Nor did he select them only because they provided occasions for the development of his theoretical orientation. These areas were in his time, as they are today, problems of indigenous interest to applied sociologists in Western society, precisely because of their practical significance.

Whatever their many differences, Marx, Durkheim, and Freud share the applied social scientist's concern with bringing social science to bear on the problems and values of laymen with a view to remedying their disturbances. In characterizing them as applied social scientists, reference is made to only one of many roles they played. An applied social scientist is a role, and the person playing this role can and does play others, and he may, therefore, also be a pure social scientist as well.

It is in such role-playing terms that these men are regarded as applied social scientists. It is to be expected that their work will bear the impress of the problems and needs of applied social science and may also contain some clues concerning the ways in which these needs can be variously satisfied, even by the applied social sciences today.

LAYMEN'S HYPOTHESES

In dealing with lay "social problems," the applied social scientist is confronting questions for which laymen often believe they have answers. Laymen usually have some explanation or favored hypotheses concerning the source of their problems. However inadequate the applied social scientist may judge these to be, he cannot blithely ignore them. He must take some of the laymen's favored hypotheses into account if he is to establish or maintain a relationship with them. Thus Marx had to consider whether "love" or Christian Ethics could be regarded as an adequate lever of social change. Durkheim had to consider whether economic poverty could account for suicide, and Freud had to examine whether the prevailing biologistic explanations of mental disturbance were adequate. All of these men had to consider lay hypotheses, even if only to discredit them.

All social scientists, pure or applied, are of course obliged to test competing hypotheses in analyzing a problem. Applied social science, however, necessarily draws some of its competing hypotheses from a distinctive source, namely laymen. The applied social scientist may systematically examine a hypothesis, even if he puts little credence in it, because the resultant research may cement his rapport with a lay group.

The Western Electric studies thus began with experiments testing the effects of improved illumination or rest periods on industrial productivity, for these involved hypotheses then favored by industrial personnel. Recent studies of jury behavior have sought to test hypotheses, favored by the legal profession, which had assumed that "hung juries" could be eliminated by relaxing the unanimity rule. The manifest function of testing independent variables favored by laymen is to provide compliances with lay expectations that strengthen the acceptance of social scientists. The latent function of such tests, however, is to document the inadequacy and breakdown of lay hypotheses, thus enlarging the area of intellectual discretion allowable to applied social scientists, and easing their introduction of independent variables that are novel to laymen.

PURE AND APPLIED SCIENCE

If the applied social scientist is to find the theories of pure social science useful to him, there need to be in the pure theory some conceptual elements that can be reconceptualized into lay concepts, or vice versa. Unfortunately, however, this is not always the case.

An example may be found in the kind of phenomenon disaster specialists have been studying. Some of the difficulties encountered in the development of disaster research may occur because present pure theory in sociology does not allow for ready reconceptualization of the layman's notion of disaster. What after all is the common meaning of disaster? Webster defines it as "an unforeseen and ruinous mischance or misadventure which happens, often suddenly, either through culpable lack of foresight or through adverse external agency." Among other things, it commonly involves a sudden destruction of the material props of human action—homes, means of transportation, stores, furniture, food supplies, clothing—often, though not always, by the intrusion of sudden changes in the natural environment, such as floods, fires, blizzards, tornadoes, hurricanes, etc.

There are at least three counts on which pure sociological theory today fails to aid in the analysis of this problem: (1) It has very little to say about, and does not systematically deal with, the role of material props. Even the concept of "culture," which at one time involved reference to material traits, is increasingly defined in terms of normative elements alone. The theoretical location of material props, therefore, becomes steadily obscured as it gets thrust into a residual limbo. (2) Present pure sociological theory has given little thought to the relationship between social or cultural systems, and the so-called natural environment. Anthropologists like Betty J. Meggers and Julian H. Steward continue to confront this problem, but sociologists apparently find little of interest in it. (3) A disaster involves not only a change, but usually a fairly sudden one. Pure sociological theory, however, has only begun to develop models adequate to cope with the analysis of change, and is even more removed from the analysis of change tempo involving questions of sudden transition. The problem of change tempo is important to almost all applied social scientists, as the controversy over "gradualistic" desegregation in the South presently dramatizes.

Unless applied social scientists can find existent pure theories containing concepts that can be reconceptualized into independent and dependent variables significant to laymen, they are under pressure to design their own formal theories, into which they can build the necessary bridging concepts. Perhaps the best example of this is Freud's work, which deliberately incorporated such lay concepts as "sexuality" in its formal theory, in a sense at least partially convergent with the manner in which it is used in everyday thinking.

The applied social scientist not only focuses on social problems perceivable to laymen but also requires knowledge to remedy them. Applied social science, therefore, is greatly concerned with facilitating the prediction and production of social and cultural change. Regardless of whether the applied social scientist wishes to make workers more efficient, or to transform alcoholics into mild-mannered tea-drinkers, or to reshape ethnic bigots into tolerant democratic citizens, he requires knowledge, theories, and concepts, which bear upon the processes of *change,* to help him analyze and facilitate it.

The applied sociologist seeks knowledge that will shed light upon the problems of men in his society and will facilitate their solution. Unlike the pure scientist, who delights in maximizing knowledge either for its own sake or to test hypotheses and extend theories, the applied social scientist will sometimes forego sources of knowledge, however rich in data they may be, if he fears their use will impede the intended change. For example, psychoanalysts might better verify and extend data derived from their patients by enlisting the aid of the patient's family and friends, but they ordinarily and voluntarily forego use of such channels. One finds a similar refusal to maximize sources of information in the work of the Tavistock group, the staff of which discourages respondents from communicating information in confidence. The impulse toward change dominates and may be at variance with the impulse to know.

CRITERIA FOR CONCEPT SELECTION

If it is to be useful for change purposes, the applied social scientist's knowledge must have certain characteristics, which distinguish it from that of the pure social scientist's. The latter, for example, aims at identifying variables with predictive power, and the more powerful and reliable the prediction, the better. The applied social scientist's criteria for assessing the adequacy of an independent variable include predictive potency but go beyond this, adding certain standards not relevant to the pure scientist. For one, the applied social scientist inspects his independent variables to determine the extent to which they are accessible to control. Since his ultimate objective involves the furtherance of some kind of change, not all independent variables are equally suitable for this purpose, nor is the one with the highest correlation coefficient always the best.

For example, no matter how high an inverse correlation is found between the rate of urbanization and the birth rate, the applied demographer can do little to reduce the birth rate by manipulating the degree of urbanization. Demographers can, however, focus on an item, namely contraceptive materials and information, which they can control, at least in greater measure. Even if urbanization and industrialization are much more highly correlated with the birth rate than is the degree of available contraceptive material and information, the latter assumes strategic significance because of its controllability. Thus the applied social scientist is concerned not merely with identifying predictively potent independent variables, but also with discovering some that are accessible to control.

There are a number of circumstances in which even a predictively potent independent variable will be of little use to the applied social scientist. One such is where there exists no technology by means of which it can be managed. Therefore, for instance, Huntington's sunspot theory of economic cycles had little appeal to New Deal statesmen. Contrariwise, because Keynesian theory identified a controllable element, the state, which could be used to restore economic equilibrium, it became the dominant economic theory of New Deal liberals. As one writer puts it:

> The system of economic thought which has become regnant in the last generation is the Keynesian. . . . Keynesian ideas have been accepted not because they explained more than others but because they provided a set of causal laws whose independent variables were accessible to action in the immediate present.[1]

For similar reasons, students of social disorganization have long been drawn to the hypothesis that there is a "causal linkage between 'bad' housing and social disorganization." This is so, not because they have regarded this hypothesis as possessing a shred of theoretical elegance, but rather because its independent variable was controllable and accessible. In this connection one might well inspect William C. Loring's recent research, which appears to have found a correlation between certain indices of social disorganization and the amount of space occupied by a family, or a density factor. Loring's paper convincingly demonstrates that there is no inherent incompatibility between theoretical sophistication and a concern for controllable variables.

Notice that the last two illustrations from demography and housing both invoke the forgotten man of sociological research, elements of so-called "material culture." It may be briefly indicated here that one meaning of Marx's materialism may be reappraised in this light. For while Marx was no crude materialist, there is a substantial sense in which he was impressed with the material props of human action, and stressed their importance. This, it may be guessed, was due as much to his commitment to an applied sociology as to his polemic against Hegel's idealism. For the material props of action are distinguished by their relative accessibility to control. Indeed, in one of its expressions "materialism" might almost be defined as an assertion, not of the ontological importance of "hard" matter, but of the strategic significance of any accessible variable, tangible or not. So-called material factors such as housing space, machines, or contraceptives are of interest to applied sociologists because they are open to control. It is likely that such concepts will continue to be required and highly regarded by applied sociologists.

In race relations research similar concerns with controllable variables are discernible. For reasons similar to those involved in Keynesian economics, the role of the state and of legal institutions continues to be given great stress

[1] Lewis S. Feuer, "Causality in the Social Sciences," *Journal of Philosophy,* 51 (November, 1954), pp. 683–684.

by those seeking to modify patterns of ethnic discrimination. This despite the fact that, since Sumner's time, pure sociological theory has given scant analysis to legal institutions. The initial emphasis on the role of "stereotypes" involved a focus on the cognitive aspects of the prejudiced person's orientation to an ethnic minority, in part because these were regarded as the most controllable elements in his orientation. It was assumed that the beliefs bigots held about minorities could be more readily managed than could their affective feeling states, by directing accurate information at those holding the stereotypes. Even an excellent and recent volume on prejudice opens its section on methods of opposing prejudice with a discussion of ways of "eliminating false beliefs." It is likely that the emergence of the concept of "stereotype," conceived of as a learned and not as a biologically given orientation to the minority group, and thus as relatively controllable, did much to foster modern race relations work.

There is a second circumstance in which even a predictively potent independent variable will provide little help to the applied social scientist. This involves situations in which, from the standpoint of the participating laymen, the instrumental management of a variable would violate their values. For example, even though contraceptives are technologically controllable, they are not instrumentally manageable from the value standpoint of a believing Catholic population. Similarly, even though changes in informal organization are technologically feasible, they may violate values that stress that human beings should not be treated as means to an end, thus giving rise to charges of "manipulation." One reason that legal institutions and material props have played such a large part in the work of applied social scientists is that, in a culture such as our own, they are both instrumentally manageable and technologically controllable.

A third circumstance which may limit the value of an independent variable to an applied social scientist is the question of its cost. Utilization of a variable as a change agent always depends, in some measure, on whether or not there is some other variable available that can accomplish the same results with less cost. There is always a question of just how much change one is securing for a given expenditure of scarce resources. These are the kinds of problems that students of mass communication media frequently have to assess. Earlier, they sought to appraise whether it was most economical to use either the newspapers or the radio to communicate a given message. Presently, they may seek to assess how many minutes of radio time are worth a minute of television time. In like manner, Dodd's "Project Revere" seeks to determine the effectiveness of given amounts of a single type of communication stimulus, particularly leaflets, attempting to determine the proportion of a community that will be reached by varying amounts of leaflets.

Finally, it might be added that much of the interest in leadership in the applied social sciences functions to identify presumably efficient loci of intervention for purposes of group or mass persuasion. In John P. Dean and Alex Rosen's cogent *Manuel of Intergroup Relations* for example, about a fourth of their 27 propositions, specifying ways and means of reducing discrimination, deal rather directly with the role of leadership.

SYSTEM ANALYSIS

The applied social scientist's concern with the controllability and relative efficiency of different variables in producing given changes also has implications for the larger kinds of theoretical models he requires and utilizes. These distinctive contingencies dispose the applied social scientist to use models of system analysis, for several reasons: (1) System models forewarn the applied social scientist of the possibility that a change in one part of the system may yield unforeseen and undesirable consequences in another part of the system, due to the interdependence of its elements. (2) System models indicate that changes may be secured in one element, not only by a frontal attack upon it but also by a circumspect and indirect manipulation of more distantly removed variables. These, because of system interdependence, may ultimately produce the desired changes in the target variable. (3) For this reason as well as others, system analysis therefore directs attention to the multiple possibilities of intervention with respect to a single problem.

Yet, insofar as such a model focuses only on the interdependence of elements within a system, it provides no clue, by itself, concerning preferential points of entry into that system. It fails to establish any generalized basis in terms of which the scarce resources available for change may be economically allocated among the diverse components of the system. It fails, in short, to satisfy the applied social scientist's interest in the comparative costs and efficiency of different variables.

Because the resources available for change-efforts are scarce, the applied social scientist requires some basis for assigning weights to different components in the systems with which he deals. He needs some basis for assessing their differential influence in determining various outcomes. If this need occurs in the absence of determinate methods of mathematical resolution, there is a tendency for the system model to break down in monistic, single-factor directions. Thus in both Marx and Freud's work there is, on the one hand, a focus on *systems* of social relations and personality, respectively. On the other hand, however, there is also a tendency monistically to focus on certain factors, such as economic or production relations in Marx's case, or on sexual etiology in Freud's. Such monistic tendencies may be regarded as efforts to adapt to the economic exigencies of applied social science, and not merely as absolute expressions of theoretical preference. Tendencies toward monistic breakdown in the models of applied social science probably also derive, in some measure, from the scientist's relationship with a lay group who may find single-factor analysis more intelligible than system models.

A monistic resolution of the economic exigencies of applied social science seems to be manifested even in the analyses of a resolute system theorist such as Talcott Parsons. In his effort to develop a strategy for changing conquered Germany after World War II, Parsons identifies the economic-occupational structures as "much the most promising as a lever of institutional change . . . [because] it is a highly strategic point in the total structure . . . [and] through its close structural interdependence with kinship and the class structure, change there would have major repercussions in these neighboring areas." Parson's stress here on the economic-occupational structure is surprisingly reminiscent of a Marxian analysis. If such a convergence between Parsons and Marx exists, it is certainly not because Parsons is a Marxist. Parsons converges with Marx because he confronts himself with a problem essentially similar to that to which Marx had persistently committed himself, namely, the introduction of planned change in a society. This necessarily involves questions of the economic allocation of scarce resources and thus requires the choice of efficient points of entry into a system of interdependent variables.

THE THEORY OF UNANTICIPATED CONSEQUENCES

Still another expression of the applied social scientist's interest in the identification of controllable variables is to be found in his persistent use of a theory of unanticipated consequences. It is noteworthy that Marx, Durkheim, and Freud, all developed some version of a theory of unanticipated consequences.

Marx noted that the events that occur in a society governed by market institutions, and with only casually integrated economic enterprises, could not be predicted on the basis of knowing the actors' individual motives. For the things that happen, said Marx, are often sought by no man. Entrepreneurs seek profit and orient their production to this anticipation, yet their very actions have the unanticipated consequence of generating market gluts and economic depressions.

Durkheim's most prominent use of the theory of unanticipated consequences is in his analysis of suicide. Here he showed that events, which were seemingly understandable as acts of deliberate intention, could be understood as the unforeseen consequences of adherence to certain values. The higher suicide rate of Protestants, for example, is not regarded by Durkheim as due to their deliberate conformity with any cultural prescription concerning suicide, but as the unanticipated consequence of conformity to other values that have no explicit implication for suicide.

Similarly, Freud was interested in the play of unanticipated consequences on a third level, the psychological. In his analysis of *The Psychopathology of Everyday Life,* he sought to show how language lapses and dreams derived from conflicts in individual motivation. Freud observed that human behavior was replete with unanticipated consequences because human personality contained unconscious motivations, which conflicted with the aims of which people were aware.

This convergence of Marx, Durkheim, and Freud in the identification and analysis of unanticipated consequences would seem to stem in part from their common participation in a system of applied social science, which exerts pressure to focus on the problematic concerns of laymen. The lay vocabulary is filled with terms indicating an interest in discriminating between foreseen and unforeseen occurrences. In the lay vocabulary, moreover, the unexpected is almost equivalent to the undesirable. Thus synonyms (in Roget's) for unexpected are: bolt from the blue, bewilderment, disappointment, disillusionment, miscalculation, to be caught unawares or off one's guard, stunned, staggered, and the like.

Unforeseen consequences are not, of course, always undesirable to the layman, as indicated by a term such as a "pleasant surprise." Nevertheless, other things equal, that is, given two identical events, one foreseen and the other unexpected, the former is usually preferential from the actor's standpoint. One may have had to prepare even for *desired* events, but could not do so if they occurred unexpectedly. It is probably for this reason that the antonyms of unexpected, in lay terminology (again according to Roget), include words such as: preparation, provision, precaution, rehearsal, manufacture, arrange, and so forth. If not to the scientist, then to the layman, *prévoir* literally means *pouvoir*. The applied social scientist's interest in unforeseen events is, in important part, a focus on events that laymen find threatening. Stated differently, it is an interest in events over which laymen have lost control and for which, therefore, their need for assistance in regaining it has become manifest. A concern with unanticipated consequences by the applied social scientist, therefore, locks onto the motivations and engages the profoundest interests of laymen.

The theory of unanticipated consequences has its closest links with the needs of both laymen and applied social scientists alike when it implicates the layman himself in the very difficulties of which he complains. Insofar as a theory of unanticipated consequences implies, as in Marx's case, that the layman's own profit-seeking activities produce economic depressions, that his adherence to certain values elicits suicide as in the Durkheimian case, or that his difficulties stem from his own unconscious motivations as in the Freudian analysis, then the problems have been defined as having more directly controllable roots. For if it is the layman's own behavior that produces his own problems, at least in part, then a change in his own behavior can aid in remedying the problem. Thus the theory of unanticipated consequences is particularly suitable to the needs of applied social science, because it identifies independent variables more directly accessible to control.

Philip Selznick's important contribution to the theory of unanticipated consequences is of interest precisely on this count, for it directly stresses the degree to which unanticipated consequences derive from the controllable actions of those who suffer from them. Selznick conceives of the actions from which unanticipated consequences stem as "commitments." In so doing he focuses on the ways in which these actions contain voluntaristic components of decision and therefore of choice.

By stressing that there are elements of decision and choice even in constraining situations, the notion of commitment identifies areas of intervention and control in them. The concept of commitment also indicates the ways in which present constraints are outcomes of earlier decisions and choices on the actors' part. This implies that the earlier choices were in some sense freer and possessed a greater variety of functional alternatives than did later ones. Different phases in the decision-making process are thus demarcated, distinguishing those phases having a greater area of controllability.

It is in part for these reasons that the work of present applied social scientists is replete with analyses of unanticipated consequences. In mass communications research, for example, an orientation to unanticipated consequences has been standardized in the notion of the "boomerang effect." This concept directs the researcher to ascertain whether a given message has produced an audience response in conformity with the sender's intention, or whether it has yielded unforeseen consequences directly contrary to those intended. It has thus been discovered by students of race relations that certain communications intended to reduce ethnic intolerance have, in some measure, strengthened it, or have led the audience to an unexpected identification with the prejudiced person rather than the victim of prejudice. In criminology students of juvenile delinquency have indicated that arresting and booking juvenile delinquents may have the unforeseen consequence of crystallizing a criminal self-image.

In these and many other examples that can be drawn from current efforts in applied sociology, the problems of which laymen complain are analyzed as the unanticipated consequences of their own policies, actions, and commitments. Thus a theory of unanticipated consequences systematically directs the attention of layman and applied social scientist alike to problem-generating forces most directly accessible to their control.

The theory of unanticipated consequences also has another, this time a rhetoric function, for the social system of applied social science. It systematically directs attention to factors most likely to be overlooked by laymen, that is, their own behavior and the ways in which it contributes to their own problems. This is not likely to be regarded as common-sensical by laymen. On the contrary, it is frequently an important source of sudden "insight" that contributes so powerfully to the layman's validation of the applied social scientist's status.

One of the needs of applied social science, therefore, is for the full development of a generalized theory of unanticipated consequences. Consistent though not identical with this, is a need for a diversity of concepts, varying with the field of application, which direct laymen's attention to patterns of behavior and belief of which he was unaware. In short, an applied social science greatly needs a multiplicity of middle range concepts of both latent functions and latent structures.

The modern era in industrial sociology, for example, hinges on the introduction of a concept of latent structure, namely, "informal organization," in the Western Electric studies. This concept identified new areas of social organization that were utilizable for the realization of organizational objectives. It has been used precisely in this way, not only in factories, but in schools and mental hospitals as well, where it has literally brought into focus hitherto neglected social resources.

In this connection it is instructive to recall Robert K. Merton's rationale for introducing the concept of latent functions. He observes that there is an unfortunate tendency for some social scientists to confine themselves to the study of manifest functions, thus allowing the focus of their studies to be set by the interests of practical men of affairs. Pressures in the direction noted by Merton arise most compellingly when a social scientist has implicated himself in the social system of applied science. In effect, then, it may be said that Merton sees the concept of latent functions serving as a corrective for the applied proclivities of social scientists, facilitating their pursuit of the theoretic issues of pure science. The point here, however, is that not even the needs of applied social science are well served by dealing solely with manifest functions. The concepts of latent function and latent structure are equally useful to the applied social sciences.

CONCLUSION

An effort has been made to indicate some of the theoretical and conceptual needs of applied social sciences. It should be clear that some of these needs are not well met by the present development of pure theory. There is no intention, however, to suggest that the program of pure or basic theory ought to be organized, either in whole or part, around the discernible needs of the applied fields. It is likely, however, that even the most inveterate of pure theorists will profit from examining the hiatuses between the needs of applied fields and the accomplishments of the basic ones. For it may be that these gaps signalize not only a handicap of the applied scientist, but also an unnecessary defect in pure theory itself.

If this paper has seemed to contain a curious juxtaposition of classical theorists and current empiricists, the implication is twofold. It is a mild suggestion to those presently involved in applied efforts that, even today, they may gain much from recognizing the continuity between their own efforts and those of the major and earlier sociologists. Current applied social scientists may see deeper significance in their work if they recognize that it is neither peripheral nor new foliage but that, on the contrary, it emerges from the deepest taproots of their disciplines and has the most venerable tradition. Finally, it is implied that the true office of the theorist is best performed when he exposes old theories to the current empirical tasks of his discipline.

SELECTED SUPPLEMENTARY READINGS FOR PART VI

Abel, Theodore, "The Present Status of Social Theory," *American Sociological Review,* Vol. 17, No. 2, April, 1952, pp. 156–164.

Bendix, Reinhard, *Max Weber: An Intellectual Portrait* (Garden City, N.Y., Anchor Books, Doubleday & Co., 1962).

Borgatta, Edgar F., and Meyer, Henry J. (eds.), *Sociological Theory* (New York: Alfred A. Knopf, 1956).

Coser, Lewis A., and Rosenberg, Bernard (eds.), *Sociological Theory* (New York: The Macmillan Co., 1957).

Gross, Llewellyn (ed.), *Symposium on Sociological Theory* (New York: Harper & Row, 1959).

Hartung, Frank E., "Problems of the Sociology of Knowledge," *Philosophy of Science,* Vol. 19, No. 1, January, 1952, pp. 17–32.

Merton, Robert K., *Social Theory and Social Structure* (Chicago: The Free Press, 1957).

Mills, C. Wright, *The Sociological Imagination* (New York: Oxford University Press, 1959).

Parsons, Talcott, *The Social System* (Chicago: The Free Press, 1951).

Rose, Arnold M., "Theory for the Study of Social Problems," *Social Problems,* Vol. 4, No. 3, January, 1957, pp. 189–199.

Index of Names

Index of Subjects